LIBRARY COPY
THALES RESEARCH LIMITED

2 2 MAY 2005

WORTON DRIVE
WORTON GRANGE
READING
RG2 0SB ENGLAND

SMART ENVIRONMENTS

WILEY SERIES ON PARALLEL AND DISTRIBUTED COMPUTING
SERIES EDITOR: Albert Y. Zomaya

Parallel & Distributed Simulation Systems / Richard Fujimoto

Surviving the Design of Microprocessor and Multimicroprocessor Systems: Lessons Learned / Veljko Milutinovic

Mobile Processing in Distributed and Open Environments / Peter Sapaty

Introduction to Parallel Algorithms / C. Xavier and S.S. Iyengar

Solutions to Parallel and Distributed Computing Problems: Lessons from Biological Sciences / Albert Y. Zomaya, Fikret Ercal, and Stephan Olariu (Editors)

New Parallel Algorithms for Direct Solution of Linear Equations / C. Siva Ram Murthy, K.N. Balasubramanya Murthy, and Srinivas Aluru

Practical PRAM Programming / Joerg Keller, Christoph Kessler, and Jesper Larsson Traeff

Computational Collective Intelligence / Tadeusz M. Szuba

Parallel & Distributed Computing: A Survey of Models, Paradigms, and Approaches / Claudia Leopold

Fundamentals of Distributed Object Systems: A CORBA Perspective / Zahir Tari and Omran Bukhres

Pipelined Processor Farms: Structured Design for Embedded Parallel Systems / Martin Fleury and Andrew Downton

Handbook of Wireless Networks and Mobile Computing / Ivan Stojmenoviic (Editor)

Internet-Based Workflow Management: Toward a Semantic Web / Dan C. Marinescu

Parallel Computing on Heterogeneous Networks / Alexey L. Lastovetsky

Tools and Environments for Parallel and Distributed Computing Tools / Salim Hariri and Manish Parashar

Distributed Computing: Fundamentals, Simulations, and Advanced Topics, Second Edition / Hagit Attiya and Jennifer Welch

Smart Environments: Technology, Protocols, and Applications / Diane J. Cook and Sajal K. Das (Editors)

SMART ENVIRONMENTS
TECHNOLOGIES, PROTOCOLS, AND APPLICATIONS

Diane J. Cook and Sajal K. Das

WILEY-INTERSCIENCE
A JOHN WILEY & SONS, INC., PUBLICATION

> A NOTE TO THE READER
> This book has been electronically reproduced from digital information stored at John Wiley & Sons, Inc. We are pleased that the use of this new technology will enable us to keep works of enduring scholarly value in print as long as there is a reasonable demand for them. The content of this book is identical to previous printings.

This book is printed on acid-free paper. ∞

Copyright © 2005 by John Wiley & Sons, Inc. All rights reserved.

Published by John Wiley & Sons, Inc., Hoboken, New Jersey.
Published simultaneously in Canada.

No part of this publication may be reproduced, stored in a retrieval system or transmitted in any form or by any means, electronic, mechanical, photocopying, recording, scanning or otherwise, except as permitted under Sections 107 or 108 of the 1976 United States Copyright Act, without either the prior written permission of the Publisher, or authorization through payment of the appropriate per-copy fee to the Copyright Clearance Center, 222 Rosewood Drive, Danvers, MA 01923, (978) 750-8400, fax (978) 750-4470. Requests to the Publisher for permission should be addressed to the Permissions Department, John Wiley & Sons, Inc., 111 River Street, Hoboken, NJ 07030, (201) 748-6011, fax (201) 748-6008, E-Mail: PERMREQ@WILEY.COM.

To order books or for customer service please, call 1(800)-CALL-WILEY (225-5945).

Limit of Liability/Disclaimer of Warranty: While the publisher and author have used their best efforts in preparing this book, they make no representations or warranties with respect to the accuracy or completeness of the contents of this book and specifically disclaim any implied warranties of merchantability or fitness for a particular purpose. No warranty may be created or extended by sales representatives or written sales materials. The advice and strategies contained herein may not be suitable for your situation. You should consult with a professional where appropriate. Neither the publisher nor author shall be liable for any loss of profit or any other commercial damages, including but not limited to special, incidental, consequential, or other damages.

For general information on our other products and services please contact our Customer Care Department within the U.S. at 877-762-2974, outside the U.S. at 317-572-3993 or fax 317-572-4002.

Wiley also publishes its books in a variety of electronic formats. Some content that appears in print, however, may not be available in electronic format.

Library of Congress Cataloging-in-Publication Data is available.

ISBN 0-471-54448-5

Printed in the United States of America

10 9 8 7 6 5 4 3 2 1

To my parents, Gilbert and Nancy Cook, for their love, support, and inspiration.
 —Diane

To my parents, Baidyanath and Bimala Das, for their love and passion for education.
 —Sajal

CONTENTS

Contributors — ix

Foreword — xi
Howard E. Shrobe

Acknowledgments — xvii

PART 1. INTRODUCTION — 1

1. **Overview** — 3
   Diane J. Cook and Sajal K. Das

PART 2. TECHNOLOGIES FOR SMART ENVIRONMENTS — 11

2. **Wireless Sensor Networks** — 13
   Frank L. Lewis

3. **Power Line Communication Technologies** — 47
   Haniph A. Latchman and Anuj V. Mundi

4. **Wireless Communications and Pervasive Technology** — 63
   Marco Conti

5. **Middleware** — 101
   G. Michael Youngblood

6. **Home Networking and Appliances** — 129
   Dave Marples and Stan Moyer

PART 3. ALGORITHMS AND PROTOCOLS FOR SMART ENVIRONMENTS — 151

7. **Designing for the Human Experience in Smart Environments** — 153
   Gregory D. Abowd and Elizabeth D. Mynatt

8. Prediction Algorithms for Smart Environments 175
Diane J. Cook

9. Location Estimation (Determination and Prediction) Techniques in Smart Environments 193
Archan Misra and Sajal K. Das

10. Automated Decision Making 229
Manfred Huber

11. Security, Privacy and Trust Issues in Smart Environments 249
P.A. Nixon, W. Wagealla, C. English, and S. Terzis

PART 4. APPLICATIONS 271

12. Lessons from an Adaptive Home 273
Michael C. Mozer

13. Smart Rooms 295
Alvin Chen, Richard Muntz, and Mani Srivastava

14. Smart Offices 323
Christophe Le Gal

15. Perceptual Environments 345
Alex Pentland

16. Assistive Environments for Individuals with Special Needs 361
Abdelsalam Helal, William C. Mann, and Choonhwa Lee

PART 5. CONCLUSIONS 385

17. Ongoing Challenges and Future Directions 387
Sajal K. Das and Diane J. Cook

Index 393

CONTRIBUTORS

Gregory D. Abowd College of Computing and GVU Center, Georgia Institute of Technology, 801 Atlantic Drive, Atlanta, GA 30332-0280

Alvin Chen Electrical Engineering Department, University of California at Los Angeles, 7702-B, Boelter Hall, Box 951594, Los Angeles, CA 90095-1594

Marco Conti National Research Council, Instituto di Informatica e Telematica, Room B.63, Via G. Moruzzi, 1, 56124 Pisa, Italy

Diane J. Cook Department of Computer Science and Engineering, The University of Texas at Arlington, Box 19015, Arlington, TX 76019

Sajal K. Das Crewman, Department of Computer Science and Engineering, The University of Texas at Arlington, Box 19015, Arlington, TX 76019

C. English Department of Computer and Information Sciences, The University of Strathclyde, Livingstone Tower, 26 Richmond Street, Glasgow G1 1XQ, Scotland

Abdelsalam Helal CISE Department, University of Florida, 448 Computer Science Engineering Building, Gainesville, FL 32611

Manfred Huber Department of Computer Science and Engineering, The University of Texas at Arlington, Box 19015, Arlington, TX 76019

Haniph A. Latchman Electrical and Computer Engineering Department, University of Florida, NEB 463—P.O. Box 116130, Gainesville, FL 32611-6130

Choonhwa Lee CISE Department, University of Florida, 448 Computer Science Engineering Building, Gainesville, FL 32611

Christophe Le Gal PRIMA Group, GRAVIR Lab, INRIA, Joanneum Research, Institute of Digital Image Processing, Wastiangasse 6, A-8010 Graz, Austria

Frank L. Lewis ARRI, The University of Texas at Arlington, Arlington, TX 76019

William C. Mann CISE Department, 448 Computer Science Engineering Building, University of Florida, Gainesville, FL 32611

Dave Marples Telcordia Technologies, Inc., RRC-1A361, One Telcordia Drive, Piscataway, NJ 08854

Archan Misra Pervasive Security and Networking Department, IBM T.J. Watson Research Center, 19 Skyline Drive, Hawthorne, NY 10532

Stan Moyer Telcordia Technologies, Inc., RRC-1A361, One Telcordia Drive, Piscataway, NJ 08854

Michael C. Mozer Department of Computer Science, University of Colorado, Regent Road and Colorado Avenue, Boulder, CO 80309-0430

Anuj V. Mundi Electrical and Computer Engineering Department, University of Florida, NEB 463—P.O. Box 116130, Gainesville, FL 32611-6130

Richard Muntz Electrical Engineering Department, University of California at Los Angeles, 7702-B, Boelter Hall, Box 951594, Los Angeles, CA 90095-1594

Elizabeth D. Mynatt Georgia Institute of Technology, College of Computing, 801 Atlantic Drive, Atlanta, GA 30332-0280

Paddy Nixon Department of Computer and Information Sciences, The University of Strathclyde, Livingstone Tower, 26 Richmond Street, Glasgow G1 1XQ, Scotland

Alex Pentland The Media Laboratory, Massachusetts Institute of Technology, Wiesner Building, 20 Ames Street, Cambridge, MA 02139-4307

Mani Srivastava Electrical Engineering Department, University of California at Los Angeles, 7702-B, Boelter Hall, Box 951594, Los Angeles, CA 90095-1594

Howard E. Shrobe Artificial Intelligence Laboratory, Massachusetts Institute of Technology, Cambridge, MA 02139

S. Terzis Department of Computer and Information Sciences, The University of Strathclyde, Livingstone Tower, 26 Richmond Street, Glasgow G1 1XQ, Scotland

W. Wagealla Department of Computer and Information Sciences, The University of Strathclyde, Livingstone Tower, 26 Richmond Street, Glasgow G1 1XQ, Scotland

G. Michael Youngblood Department of Computer Science and Engineering, The University of Texas at Arlington, Box 19015, Arlington, TX 76019

■ FOREWORD

HOWARD E. SHROBE

MIT Computer Science and Artificial Intelligence Laboratory

In 1991, Mark Weiser described his vision of an emerging world of pervasive, embedded computation. He predicted "a physical world that is richly and invisibly interwoven with sensors, actuators, displays, and computational elements, embedded seamlessly in the everyday objects of our lives and connected through a continuous network." This vision is becoming a reality: the ever-increasing availability of inexpensive computation and storage has introduced computers into nearly every facet of our everyday lives, while a revolution in communications has brought high-bandwidth communications into our homes and offices. Wireless communications also has exploded, making digital services available nearly everywhere.

But what is the nature of this revolution in technology? How will it impact our lives? And what new technical challenges will it present? The ubiquity of computation and communication is not the only manifestation of the revolution. Much of this emerging computation is embedded: the processors in your phones, cars, personal digital assistants (PDAs), and home appliances. Increasingly, these embedded computers are acting in concert with other computational elements as part of a larger ensemble. Thus, we have processors at one end of the spectrum providing megahertz cycle rates and a few kilobytes of memory, while at the other end we have machines providing gigahertz cycle rates, gigabytes of primary storage, and terabytes of persistent storage. Across every dimension of interest—processor power, primary memory, persistent storage, communications bandwidth, and display capabilities—we witness a variability of at least three orders of magnitude. This broad span of capabilities represents a new computational framework, particularly when we realize that the ubiquity of communications bandwidths often makes it possible to locate computational tasks at whatever point in this hierarchy makes the most sense. This represents a radically new framework for distributed and mobile computation.

A second striking new feature of the emerging ubiquitous computing environment is the mobility of the user. We are already beginning to see the convergence of a variety of technologies, all of which serve as personal computational accessories: Internet-capable smart cell phones, wireless-enabled PDAs, and music players, such as the Apple IPOD, that move with the user but in one way or another are tapped into the pervasive communications and computing environment. In the past, the fact that most people used only a single desktop computer led to a struggle over what would occupy that critical desktop position; now, the fact that most people are willing to carry at most one mobile device (e.g., a PDA, cell phone, music player) is leading to a struggle over what will occupy the critical "belt loop" position and over what networks that single device on the user's belt will link into the broader computational world. However this plays out, it is still the case that in most places where the user lives and works, far more abundant computational resources are built in. Thus, the mobility of the user raises many more questions about how we can dynamically link the limited computing power that travels with the user to the much vaster computational power that is present in the environment.

A third new feature is that these systems never stop. They are not used to "run a job" and then shut down; they are always on, always available. Our normal model of upgrading the software in a system consists of taking a system down, installing upgrades, and then rebooting, but this model ill fits the components of a ubiquitous computing environment. Instead, these systems need to evolve in place, with new software being installed while they are running. In general, ubiquitous computation will be far more dynamic and evolutionary. As we build systems that are intended to last for very long periods of time, it becomes necessary to recognize that we can't anticipate all future issues at design time, but will instead need to make many more decisions at run-time, to allow the systems to learn from their own experience and to adopt a philosophy of "delayed binding".

A fourth new feature is that the computational nodes we are considering are often equipped with sensors and effectors. They are embedded in the physical world with which they interact constantly. Previously, this type of embedded computing was the province of the specialized subfield of real-time controllers; indeed, many of our current embedded computing components have emerged from the world of control systems. But they are now being asked to perform a different role: sensing and acting on behalf of the user and performing more human-like tasks.

Finally, the ubiquitous computing revolution involves constant human-computer interaction. And it is this feature that is most crucial. The challenge we face is to make this revolution wear a human face, to focus on human-centered ubiquitous computing. Michael Dertouzos reflected on the emerging ubiquitous computing paradigm with a certain degree of horror. He observed that VCRs, cash registers, and ATMs all represent the computerization of common, everyday tasks, but that the way in which computers were deployed led to needless inflexibility, unintuitive interactions, the inability of even experts to do simple things, and general dehumanization. Computation is increasingly being used to eliminate certain kinds of jobs that were previously done by people with a certain degree of expertise (e.g., phone operators) and is making those tasks part of the everyday burden on the rest of us, who must now acquire some of that expertise (anyone who has tried to make a long-distance call from certain foreign countries will understand this perfectly); sometimes this makes life easier, but often it doesn't. If the new technology fails to meet us humans at least partway, then things get a great deal worse, as Dertouzos observed. What if ubiquitous computing were to bring us the ubiquitous need to interact with systems as unpleasant as early VCRs and phone menu systems?

Surely we can do better. It is worth observing that Moore's law (that computing doubles in capability roughly every 18 months) is fixing virtually everything but us humans; unfortunately, we don't scale with silicon densities. This means that increasingly the critical resources are human time, attention, and decision-making ability. We used to think of computational resources as scarce and shaped the interface to make the computer's life easier; now we must do the reverse. We have abundant computational resources; we need to shape the interface to make the human's jobs easier.

Research on smart environments is intended to address this issue. Smart environments combine perceptual and reasoning capabilities with the other elements of ubiquitous computing in an attempt to create a human-centered system that is embedded in physical spaces. Perceptual capabilities allow the system to situate itself within the world of human discourse. Reasoning capabilities allow the system to behave flexibly and adaptively as the context changes and as resources become more or less available.

We can identify an agenda of challenges to be met if we are to make such intelligent environments the norm:

- We must provide a comprehensive infrastructure and a firm computation foundation for the style of distributed computing that ubiquitous computing requires. This includes protocols for both wired and wireless communications media and middleware for distributed computing, agent systems, and the like.
- We must develop frameworks that allow systems to respond adaptively to user (and internal) requests. This would include the ability to dynamically discover new resources; the ability to choose from among a set of alternative plans for achieving a goal in light of the task context and the availability of critical resources; the ability to recognize, diagnose, and recover from failures; the ability to generate new plans; and the ability of the system to learn from its experiences and to improve its own performance.
- We must develop frameworks that allow us to integrate information from many perceptual sources, to make sense of these inputs, and to do so even in the presence of sensor failures and noise.
- We must provide the systems with extensive knowledge of the human world. In particular, these systems must be capable of reasoning about how we think of space (e.g., that floors in a building are a significant organizational construct or that a desk establishes a work zone separate from the space around it in an office), organizational structures, tasks, projects, etc. This is a huge challenge, which in its largest form constitutes teaching our systems all of commonsense knowledge. However, in practice, we can focus on particular domains of application, such as office environments, home environments, and cars, which are more bounded, although still enormously challenging.
- We must develop notions of context that help the system ground its reactions to the events going on around it. In practice, much of the research on context has focused on *location.* This research has been largely motivated by a concern for

the mobile user, for whom location is indeed a strong indicator of context. Many technologies have been developed to help a mobile computer know where it is (e.g., the Global Positioning System in the outside environment; badge readers, beacons, and the like for the inside environment), but there is still much to be done in this area. Within individual spaces, location is also a strong cue to context because where you are in a room is often a strong cue to what you're going to do. If I'm sitting at my desk, then I'm doing one type of activity, while if I'm stretched out on my couch, I'm likely to be doing another. Systems with cameras and machine vision have been developed that can track people's locations within an individual space and make such inferences about what they're doing. Finally, we note that context is a much broader notion than simply one's location. Task context, in particular, represents another important component of context that has been relatively little explored. To further complicate matters, most people are in more than one task context at any particular time. Much more needs to be done in this area. Context plays two critical roles. First, it helps to determine how the system should respond to an event; if a person walks into a dark room, then turning the lights on makes sense unless there is a group of people in the room watching a movie. Second, context establishes perceptual bias, helping to disambiguate perceptual signals. One would make very different sense of the phonemes in "recognize speech" if one were instead talking about environmental disasters that could "wreck a nice beach."

- We must develop techniques to restructure the human-computer interface along human-centered lines. In many cases, this will mean replacing conventional keyboard and pointer interfaces by speech recognition, machine vision, natural language understanding, sketch recognition, and other modes of communication that are natural to people. The best interface is often the one that you need not notice at all (as Weiser observed), so unnatural use of perceptual interfaces could be as bad as the thing they are meant to replace. I believe that perceptual interfaces are part of the answer, but the overall goal is to make the computers seem as natural to interact with as another person. Sometimes this means that the system should have no interface; it should just recognize what's going on and do the right thing. At other times, it means that the system should engage in a dialogue with a person. No single metaphor, such as the desktop as a metaphor for the personal computer, governs the range of interactions that are required. Rather, we want a system that is truly human-centered and natural to interact with; this requires not just perception but also a significant understanding of the semantics of the everyday world and the reasoning capabilities to use this understanding flexibly.

- Finally, we must develop techniques for providing guarantees of security and privacy. I mention this point last because it often occurs as an afterthought in any system design. But in the context of perceptually enabled, intelligent environments, security and privacy are make-or-break issues. We cannot deploy perceptually based systems broadly until we can realistically promise people that their privacy will be respected, that the information gathered will not be used to their detriment, and that the systems are secure against penetration. The issue, however, is quite complex. Generally speaking, technologies that protect security and privacy tend to work against convenience; even in conventional computing systems, most people don't take even basic precautions because the benefit doesn't seem worth the bother. In pervasive computing systems, the issues become even more complex because the range of interacting parties is both extremely broad and quite dynamic. We will need to develop techniques for structuring ubiquitous computing environments into domains or societies that represent individual entities in the real world (e.g., a person or a particular space) and for then clustering these into larger aggregations reflecting social and physical organization. It will be necessary to build access controls into the resource discovery protocols to reflect ownership and control. I shouldn't be able to discover that you have a projector in your office and then simply allocate it for my use (which would happen in many of our current resource discovery models). Instead, I should have to negotiate with you to obtain access. In addition, we need to recognize that most access control systems are too rigid and lack contextual sensitivity. For example, for reasons of privacy, I might have a rule that says I don't want my location to be divulged; however, if someone in my family were injured, my privacy would suddenly matter much less to me. So we will ultimately need to treat privacy and security with the same contextual sensitivity that we do almost all other decision making in intelligent environments.

These are significant challenges, and most of them will not be dealt with completely for many years. However, they are challenges that need to be taken up. Many of the chapters in this book address these issues and represent significant first steps on a march of many miles.

ACKNOWLEDGMENTS

Creating a book that describes a multidisciplinary area of rapid growth, such as smart environments, is a challenge. The result has been a collaborative effort of academia and industry researchers from around the world. The authors of this edited book have been exceptional at exchanging ideas and initiating collaborations as well as contributing chapters based on their own research efforts, and we thank them for their fine contributions. We also would like to thank Kirsten Rohstedt and Val Moliere of John Wiley for their assistance. We recognize the impact of the faculty and staff at the University of Texas at Arlington on this work and thank them for their support. We gratefully acknowledge the support of NSF ITR grants that made our research programs so exciting. Finally, we dedicate this book to our families, who increased in number during the creation of this book and gave generously of their time and encouragement.

Please visit our web site at http://www.cse.uta.edu/~cook/se/.

PART 1
INTRODUCTION

CHAPTER 1

Overview

DIANE J. COOK and SAJAL K. DAS
Department of Computer Science and Engineering
The University of Texas at Arlington

This book is about technologies and standards for smart environments. Smart environments link computers to everyday settings and commonplace tasks. The desire to create smart environments has existed for decades, and recent advances in such areas as pervasive computing, machine learning, and wireless and sensor networking now allow this dream to become a reality. In this book we introduce the necessary technologies, architectures, algorithms, and protocols to build a smart environment and describe a variety of existing smart environment applications.

A smart environment is a small world where all kinds of smart devices are continuously working to make inhabitants' lives more comfortable. A definition of *smart* or *intelligent* is the ability to autonomously acquire and apply knowledge, while *environment* refers to our surroundings. We therefore define a smart environment as one that is able to acquire and apply knowledge about an environment and also to adapt to its inhabitants in order to improve their experience in that environment. A schema of smart environments is presented in Figure 1.1.

The type of experience that individuals wish from their environment varies with the individual and the type of environment. They may wish the environment to ensure the safety of its inhabitants, they may want to reduce the cost of maintaining the environment, or they may want to automate tasks that are typically performed in the environment. The expectations of such environments have evolved with the history of the field.

1.1 FEATURES OF SMART ENVIRONMENTS

1.1.1 Remote Control of Devices

The most basic feature of smart environments is the ability to control devices remotely or automatically. Powerline control systems have been available for decades,

---

Smart Environments: Technologies, Protocols, and Applications, edited by D.J. Cook and S.K. Das
ISBN 0-471-54448-5 © 2005 John Wiley & Sons, Inc.

4   OVERVIEW

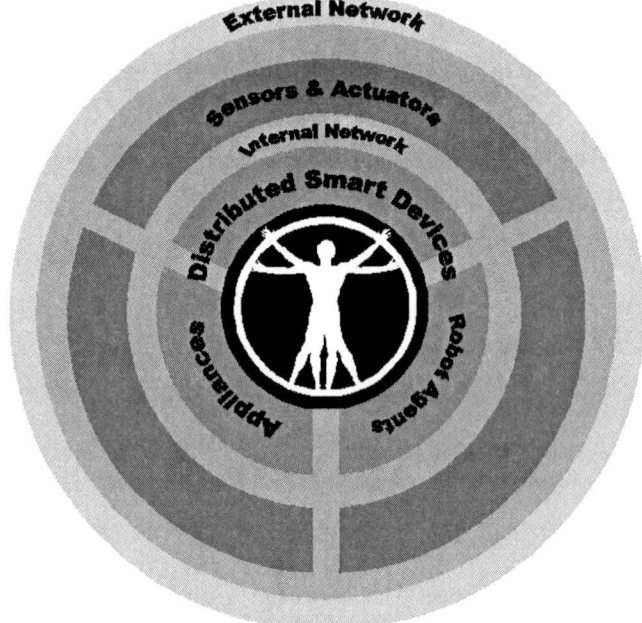

Figure 1.1   Schematic view of smart environments.

and basic controls offered by X10 can be easily purchased and installed. By plugging devices into such a controller, inhabitants of an environment can turn lights, coffee makers, and other appliances on or off in much the same way that couch potatoes switch television stations with a remote control (Figure 1.2). Computer software can additionally be employed to program sequences of device activities and to capture device events executed by the powerline controllers.

With this capability, inhabitants are freed from the requirement of physical access to devices. The individual with a disability can control devices from a distance, as can the person who realized when he got to work that he left the sprinklers on. Automated lighting sequences can give the impression that an environment is occupied while the inhabitants are gone, and basic routine procedures can be executed by the environment with minimal intervention.

1.1.2   Device Communication

With the maturing of wireless technology and communication middleware, smart environment designers and inhabitants have been able to raise their standards and expectations. In particular, devices use these technologies to communicate with each other, sharing data to build a more informed model of the state of the environment and the inhabitants, and retrieving information from outside sources over the Internet or wireless communication infrastructure to respond better to current state and needs.

1.1 FEATURES OF SMART ENVIRONMENTS

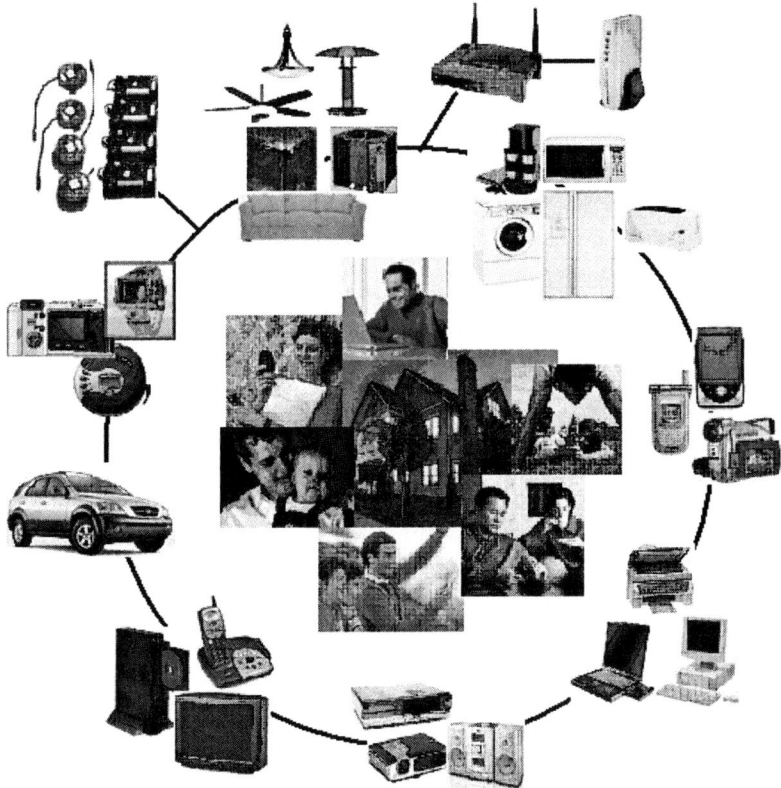

Figure 1.2 Device control in smart environments.

Such *connected environments* have become the focus of many industry-developed smart homes and offices. With these capabilities, for example, the environment can access the weather page of the newspaper to determine the forecast and query the moisture sensor in the lawn to determine how long the sprinklers should run. Devices can access information from the Internet such as menus, operational manuals, or software upgrades, and can post information such as a grocery store list generated from monitoring inventory in an intelligent refrigerator or a trash can.

Activation of one device can trigger other sequences so that the bedroom radio, kitchen coffee maker, and bathroom towel warmer are turned on when the alarm goes off. Inhabitants can benefit from interaction between devices so that the television sound is muted when the telephone or doorbell rings, and temperature as well as motion sensors can interact with other devices to ensure that the temperature is kept at a desired level wherever the inhabitants are located within the environment. Moreover, a smart environment will provide a neat service-forwarding capability with the help of individual smart devices that communicate with each other without human intervention. For example, a mobile phone call will be automatically forwarded to the land-wire phone when the inhabitant stays in a smart environment, and e-mail will be forwarded to the mobile phone through a smart environment instead of an outdoor cellular network.

1.1.3 Information Acquisition/Dissemination from Intelligent Sensor Networks

Tremendous advances have been made in the development of sensor technology and in the ability of sensors to share information and make low-level decisions. As a result, environments can provide constant small adjustments based on sensor readings and can better customize behaviors to the nuances of the inhabitants' surroundings. Using motion detectors or pressure sensors, the presence of individuals in the environment can be detected and lights, music, or climate control can be adjusted accordingly. Water and gas sensors can monitor potential leaks and force the valves to close when a danger arises. Low-level control of devices offers fine-tuning in response to changing conditions, such as adjusting window blinds as the amount of daylight coming into a room changes. Networks composed of these sensors can share data and offer information to the environment at speeds and levels of complexity not experienced in the earlier versions of smart environments. The Smart Sofa developed at Trinity College in Dublin, Ireland, can identify an individual based on his or her weight and, theoretically, can use this information to customize the settings of devices around the house correspondingly.

1.1.4 Enhanced Services by Intelligent Devices

Smart environments are frequently outfitted with individual smart devices. These devices provide varied and impressive capabilities. When networked together and tied to intelligent sensors and the outside world, the impact of these devices becomes even more powerful. Such devices are becoming the focus of a number of manufacturers, including Electrolux, Whirlpool, and a collection of startup companies.

For example, Frigidaire and Whirlpool offer intelligent refrigerators with features that include web cameras to monitor inventory, bar code scanners, and Internet-ready interactive screens. Through interactive cameras, inhabitants away from home can view the location of security or fire alerts, and remote caregivers can check on the status of their patients or family members. Merloni's Margherita 2000 washing machine is similarly Internet controlled and uses sensor information to determine appropriate cycle times. Other devices such as microwaves, coffee makers, and toasters are quickly joining the collection.

In addition, specialized machines have been designed in response to the growing interest in assistive environments. AT&T's Kids Communicator resembles a hamster exercise ball and is equipped with a wireless videophone and remote maneuverability to monitor the environment from any location. A large group of companies, including Friendly Robotics, Husqvarna, Technical Solutions, and the University of Florida's Lawn Nibbler, have developed robotic lawn mowers to ease the burden of this time-consuming task, and indoor robot vacuum cleaners, including Roomba and vacuums from Electrolux, Dyson, and Hitachi, are gaining in popularity and usability. Researchers at MIT's Media Lab are investigating new, specialized devices, such as an oven mitt that can tell if food has been thoroughly warmed. A breakthrough development from companies such as Philips is an interactive tablecloth that provides cable-free power to all chargeable objects placed on the table's surface. An environment that can combine the features of these devices with the information-gathering and remote-control power of previous research will realize many of the initial goals of smart environment designers.

1.1.5 Predictive and Decision-Making Capabilities

The features of a smart environment described up to this point provide the potential for fulfilling the goal of a smart environment: to improve the experience of inhabitants of the environment. However, control of these capabilities is mostly in the hands of the users. Only through explicit remote manipulation or careful programming can these devices, sensors, and controllers adjust the environment to fit the needs of the inhabitants. Full automation and adaptation rely on the software itself to learn or acquire information that allows the software itself to improve its performance with experience.

Specific features of recent smart environments that meet these criteria incorporate predictive and automatic decision-making capabilities into the control paradigm. Behaviors of inhabitants as well as of the environment can be predicted based on observed activities and known features. A model can be built of inhabitants' patterns that can be used to customize the environment for future interactions. For example, an intelligent car can collect information about the driver, including typical times and routes to work, theatres, and restaurants, as well as store preferences, and commonly used gas stations. Combining this information with data collected by the inhabitant's home and office, as well as Internet-gathered specifics on movie times, restaurant menus, and locations, plus sales at various stores, the car can make recommendations based on the learned model of activity patterns and preferences.

Similarly, building a model of device performance can allow the environment to optimize its behaviors. For example, a smart kitchen may learn that the coffee maker requires 10 minutes to brew a full pot of coffee, and will start it up 10 minutes before it expects the inhabitants to want their first cup. Smart light bulbs may warn when they are about to expire, letting the factory automatically deliver replacements before the need is critical.

As a complement to predictive capabilities, a smart environment will be able to make decisions on how to automate its own behaviors to meet the specified goals. Device settings and the timing of events are now under the control of the environment. Such a smart environment will also have to choose among alternative methods of achieving a goal, such as turning on lights in each room entered by an inhabitant or anticipating where the inhabitant is heading and illuminating just enough of the environment to direct the individual to that location.

8 OVERVIEW

1.1.6 Networking Standards and Regulations

A smart environment will be able to control and manage all of its various networked devices (see Figure 1.3), such as computers, sensors, cameras, and appliances, from anywhere and at any time through the Internet. For example, when the inhabitant is away, she can still be in contact with her different environments to monitor their status and/or access her personal database. From that perspective, all the hardware and software for enabling the smart environments should be based on standards and regulations. Moreover, they should be easy to install, configure, and operate in order to be user-friendly to nonprofessional inhabitants/consumers. IEEE 802.11, IEEE 802.15, and Bluetooth, using FHSS (Frequency Hopping Spread Spectrum), DSSS (Direct Sequence Spread Spectrum), or the OFDM (Orthogonal Frequency Division Multiplexing) modulation technique under 2.4 or 5 GHz unlicensed ISM (Industrial Science Medical) band, and Home RF (Radio Frequency) technology have been applied to wireless networking infrastructures for smart environments. Alongside these, Ethernet (IEEE 802.3), PNA (Phoneline Networking Alliance), and X10 powerline networking have emerged as smart environment wired networking technologies. These technologies have advantages and disadvantages. For example, X10 powerline networking has the widest availability; however, X10 currently has a much lower speed than other PNA and wireless standards. Performance comparison, coexistence capability, and interoperability of the above

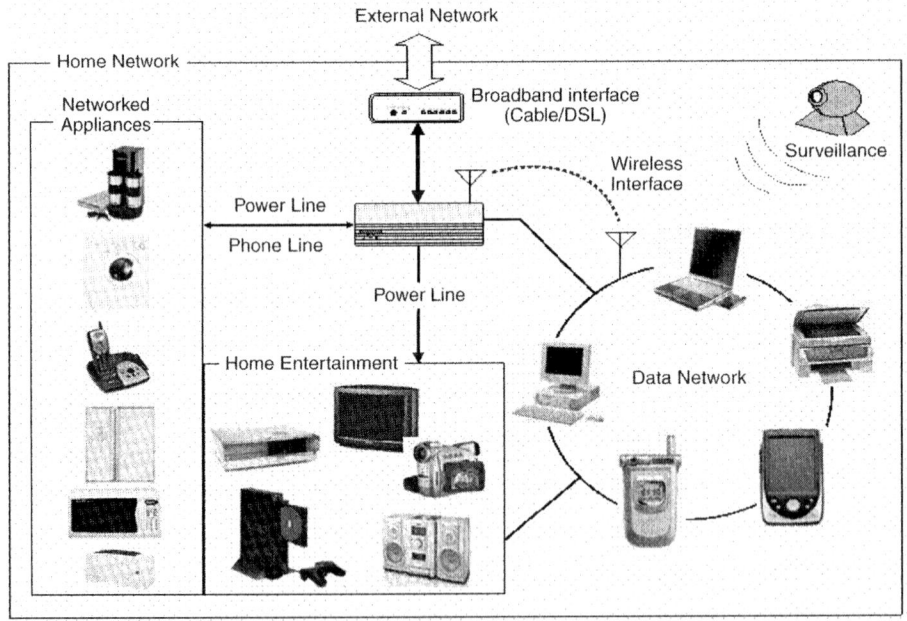

Figure 1.3 Networked devices in smart environments.

technologies have been preceded in the academic and industry research realms while implementing prototypes of smart environments using the above standards.

1.2 SMART ENVIRONMENTS PROJECTS

Although the dream of creating a smart environment has existed for decades, research on the topic has become increasingly intense in the past 10 years. Researchers have recently assembled related conferences and workshops, including the AAAI 1998 Spring Symposium on Intelligent Environments, the Workshop on Cooperative Buildings (CoBuild) in 1998 and 1999, the Conference on Managing Interactions in Smart Environments (MANSE) in 1999, and a special track on Intelligent Environments at the IEEE Conference on Pervasive Computing (PerCom) in 2003. Trade magazines including *Electronic House* and *Home Automation* have a large circulation, and the number of consumers purchasing X10 and related products is steadily increasing.

Reflecting the increased interest in smart environments, research labs in academia and industry are picking up the theme and creating environments with their own individual spin and market appeal. The Georgia Tech Aware Home, the Adaptive House at the University of Colorado at Boulder, INRIA, and the MavHome smart home at the University of Texas at Arlington are all described in this book. Other types of smart environments, including smart offices, classrooms, and cars, have been designed by MIT, Stanford, the University of California at San Diego, Ambiente, Nissan, and Intel. Connected homes with device communication capability have become the focus of companies such as Philips, Cisco, GTE, Sun, Ericsson, and Microsoft. Still other groups have focused on smart environments to assist individuals with health challenges. These projects include the Gloucester Smart Home, the Edinvar Assisted Interactive Dwelling House, and the Intel Proactive Health project.

1.3 OVERVIEW OF BOOK

Our intent is to provide a practical foundation for designing smart environments, including the underlying technologies, algorithms, architectures, and protocols, as well as describe successful smart environment projects developed in a variety of settings. The chapters in this book are written by leading researchers in the area of smart environments. Each contributor provides a survey of techniques applicable to the task of building smart environments and describes a particular approach applied in an existing project.

The remainder of this book is divided into four parts. The second part, consisting of five chapters, gives an overview of various technological components and networking elements of smart environments. The first chapter of this part relates to sensors and intelligent sensor networks for information acquisition and dissemination from the surroundings. The second chapter discusses powerline control methods and issues, currently the most common method of controlling devices in automated environments. Wireless communications and pervasive computing technology are fundamental capabilities of intelligent environments and are discussed in the next chapter, followed by a discussion of current middleware technology and standards that support smart environments. The second part concludes with a chapter on the promise and the challenges of home networking and appliances.

The third part of this book, consisting of five chapters, is devoted to the architectures, algorithms, and protocols for smart environments. The first chapter in this part explores the design and evaluation of the human's physical experience in smart environments. The second and third chapters deal with prediction algorithms and their roles in a smart environment, for tracking and anticipating mobility patterns as well as activity patterns of individuals in the environment. The following chapter concentrates on techniques that allow the environment to make decisions that will meet the goals specified by the designer and the environment's inhabitants. Finally, we discuss privacy and security issues raised by smart environments.

In the fourth part, consisting of five chapters, we highlight representative smart environment projects. These projects span a variety of applications. The first application looks at a successful smart home project, the second describes the design of smart rooms, the third provides an overview of a smart office project, and the fourth applies smart environment technology to a range of environments using perceptual intelligence. We conclude with a chapter describing a project for environments designed to support individuals with special needs.

The final part of the book summarizes the various chapters and discusses ongoing challenges and future research directions. The URLs of various smart environment projects are also given.

PART 2
TECHNOLOGIES FOR SMART ENVIRONMENTS

CHAPTER 2

Wireless Sensor Networks

FRANK L. LEWIS

Automation and Robotics Research Institute
The University of Texas at Arlington

2.1 INTRODUCTION

Smart environments represent the next step in building, utilities, industrial, home, shipboard, and transportation systems automation. Like any sentient organism, the smart environment relies first and foremost on sensory data from the real world. Sensory data come from multiple sensors of different modalities in distributed locations. The smart environment needs information about its surroundings as well as about its internal workings; this is captured in biological systems by the distinction between *exteroceptors* and *proprioceptors*.

The challenges in the hierarchy of detecting the relevant quantities, monitoring and collecting the data, assessing and evaluating the information, formulating meaningful user displays, and performing decision-making and alarm functions are enormous. The information needed by smart environments is provided by distributed wireless sensor networks, which are responsible for sensing as well as for the first stages of the processing hierarchy. The importance of sensor networks is highlighted by the number of recent funding initiatives, including the DARPA SENSIT program, military programs, and National Science Foundation program announcements.

Figure 2.1 shows the complexity of wireless sensor networks, which generally consist of a data acquisition network and a data distribution network, monitored and controlled by a management center. The plethora of available technologies makes even the selection of components difficult, let alone the design of a consistent, reliable, robust overall system.

The study of wireless sensor networks is challenging in that it requires an enormous breadth of knowledge from a wide variety of disciplines. In this chapter we outline communication networks, wireless sensor networks and smart sensors,

---

Smart Environments: Technologies, Protocols, and Applications, edited by D.J. Cook and S.K. Das
ISBN 0-471-54448-5 © 2005 John Wiley & Sons, Inc.

14   WIRELESS SENSOR NETWORKS

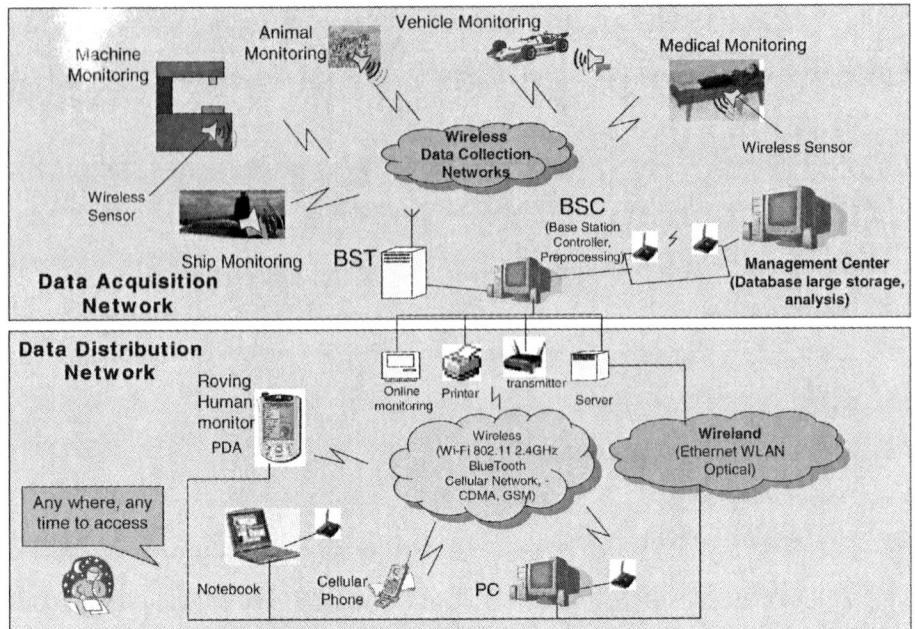

Figure 2.1 Wireless sensor networks.

physical transduction principles, commercially available wireless sensor systems, self-organization, signal processing and decision making, and, finally, some concepts for home automation.

2.2 COMMUNICATION NETWORKS

The study of communication networks can take several years at the college or university level. To understand and be able to implement sensor networks, however, several basic primary concepts are sufficient.

2.2.1 Network Topology

The basic issue in communication networks is the transmission of messages to achieve a prescribed message throughput (quantity of service) and quality of service (QoS). QoS can be specified in terms of message delay, message due dates, bit error rates, packet loss, economic cost of transmission, transmission power, etc. Depending on QoS, the installation environment, economic considerations, and the application, one of several basic network topologies may be used.

A communication network is composed of nodes, each of which has computing power and can transmit and receive messages over communication links, wireless sensors, or cable. The basic network topologies are shown in Figure 2.2 and include fully connected, mesh, star, ring, tree, and bus types. A single network may consist

2.2 COMMUNICATION NETWORKS

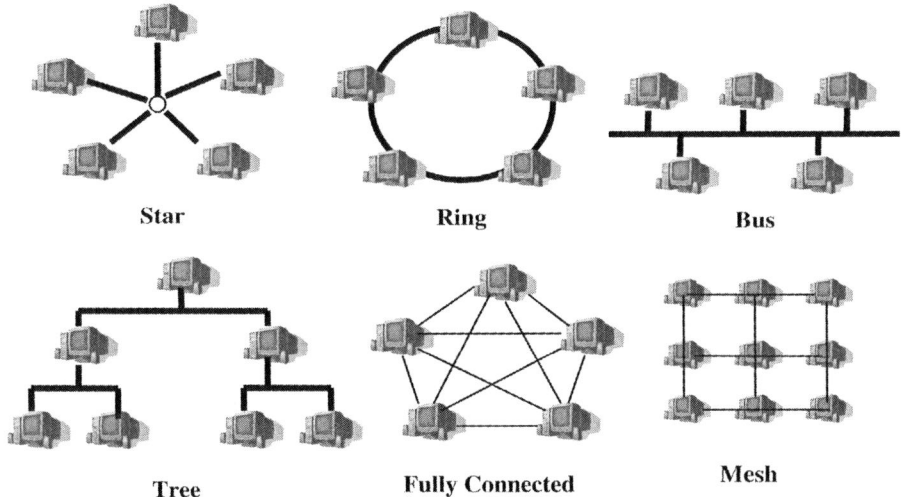

Figure 2.2 Basic network topologies.

of several interconnected subnets of different topologies. Networks are further classified as local area networks (LANs, e.g., inside one building) or wide area networks (WANs, e.g., between buildings).

Fully connected networks suffer from problems of (NP) complexity [Garey 1979]; as additional nodes are added, the number of links increases exponentially. Therefore, for large networks, the routing problem is computationally intractable even with the availability of large amounts of computing power.

Mesh networks are regularly distributed networks that generally allow transmission only to a node's nearest neighbors. The nodes in these networks are generally identical, so mesh nets are also referred to as *peer-to-peer nets* (see below). Mesh nets can be good models for large-scale networks of wireless sensors that are distributed over a geographic region, e.g., personnel or vehicle security surveillance systems. Note that the regular structure reflects the communications topology; the actual geographic distribution of the nodes need not be a regular mesh. Since there are generally multiple routing paths between nodes, these nets are robust to failure of individual nodes or links. An advantage of mesh nets is that, although all nodes may be identical and have the same computing and transmission capabilities, certain nodes can be designated as "group leaders" that take on additional functions. If a group leader is disabled, another node can then take over these duties.

All nodes of the *star topology* are connected to a single hub node. The hub requires greater message handling, routing, and decision-making capabilities than the other nodes. If a communication link is cut, it affects only one node. However, if the hub is incapacitated, the network is destroyed. In the *ring topology* all nodes perform the same function, and there is no leader node. Messages generally travel around the ring in a single direction. However, if the ring is cut, all communication

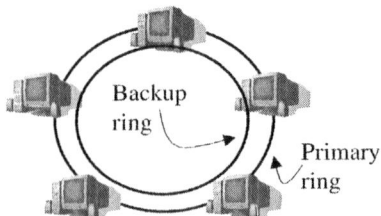

Figure 2.3 Self-healing ring.

is lost. The *self-healing ring network* (SHR) (Figure 2.3) shown has two rings and is more fault tolerant.

In the *bus topology*, messages are broadcast on the bus to all nodes. Each node checks the destination address in the message header, and processes the messages addressed to it. The bus topology is passive in that each node simply listens for messages and is not responsible for retransmitting any messages.

2.2.2 Communication Protocols and Routing

The topics of communication protocols and routing are complex and require much study. Some basic concepts useful for understanding sensor nets are presented here.

2.2.2.1 Headers Each message generally has a *header* identifying its source node, destination node, length of the data field, and other information (Figure 2.4). This is used by the nodes in proper routing of the message. In encoded messages, parity bits may be included. In *packet routing networks*, each message is broken into *packets* of fixed length. The packets are transmitted separately through the network and then reassembled at the destination. The fixed packet length makes for easier routing and satisfaction of QoS. Generally, voice communications use circuit switching, while data transmissions use packet routing.

In addition to the information content messages, in some protocols (e.g., FDDI; see below) the nodes transmit *special frames* to report and identify fault conditions. This allows network reconfiguration for fault recovery. Other special frames may include route discovery packets or *ferrets* that flow through the network, e.g., to identify the shortest paths, failed links, or transmission cost information. In some schemes, the ferret returns to the source and reports the best path for message transmission.

When a node desires to transmit a message, *handshaking protocols* with the destination node are used to improve reliability. The source and destination may

Preamble 8 bytes	Destination Address 6 bytes	Source Address 6 bytes	Length of Data field 2 bytes	Protocol header, Data, padding 0-1500 bytes

Figure 2.4 Ethernet message header.

transmit alternately as follows: request to send, ready to receive, send message, message received. Handshaking is used to guarantee QoS and to retransmit messages that were not properly received.

2.2.2.2 Switching Most computer networks use a *store-and-forward* switching technique to control the flow of information [Duato 1996]. Then, each time a packet reaches a node, it is completely buffered in local memory and transmitted as a whole. More sophisticated switching techniques include *wormhole*, which splits the message into smaller units known as *flow control units* or *flits*. The header flit determines the route. As the header is routed, the remaining flits follow it in pipeline fashion. This technique currently achieves the lowest message latency. Another popular switching scheme is *virtual-cut-through*. Here, when the header arrives at a node, it is routed without waiting for the rest of the packet. Packets are buffered either in software buffers in memory or in hardware buffers; various sorts of buffers are used including edge buffers, central buffers, etc.

2.2.2.3 Multiple Access Protocols When multiple nodes desire to transmit, protocols are needed to avoid collisions and lost data. In the ALOHA scheme, first used in the 1970s at the University of Hawaii, a node simply transmits a message when it desires. If it receives an acknowledgment, all is well. If not, the node waits for a random amount of time and retransmits the message.

In *Frequency Division Multiple Access* (FDMA), different nodes have different carrier frequencies. Since frequency resources are divided, this decreases the bandwidth available for each node. FDMA also requires additional hardware and intelligence at each node. In *Code Division Multiple Access* (CDMA), a unique code is used by each node to encode its messages. This increases the complexity of the transmitter and the receiver. In *Time Division Multiple Access* (TDMA), the radio frequency (RF) link is divided on a time axis, with each node being given a predetermined time slot it can use for communication. This decreases the sweep rate, but a major advantage is that TDMA can be implemented in software. All nodes require accurate, synchronized clocks for TDMA.

2.2.2.4 Open Systems Interconnection Reference Model (OSI/RM)
The International Standards Organization (ISO) OSI/RM architecture specifies the relation between messages transmitted in a communication network and applications programs run by the users. The development of this open standard has encouraged the adoption by different developers of standardized compatible systems interfaces. Figure 2.5 shows the seven layers of OSI/RM. Each layer is self-contained so that it can be modified without unduly affecting other layers. The Transport Layer provides error detection and correction. Routing and flow control are performed in the Network Layer. The Physical Layer represents the actual hardware communication link interconnections. The Applications Layer represents programs run by users.

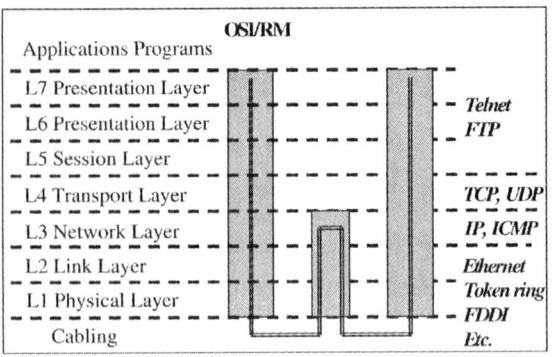

Figure 2.5 Open systems interconnection reference model.

2.2.2.5 Routing Since a distributed network has multiple nodes and services many messages, and since each node is a shared resource, many decisions must be made. There may be multiple paths from the source to the destination. Therefore, message routing is an important topic. The main performance measures affected by the routing scheme are throughput and average packet delay (QoS). Routing schemes should also avoid both deadlock and livelock (see below).

Routing methods can be fixed (i.e., preplanned), adaptive, centralized, distributed, broadcast, etc. Perhaps the simplest routing scheme is the *token ring* [Smythe 1999]. Here, a simple topology and a straightforward fixed protocol produce very good reliability and precomputable QoS. A token passes continuously around a ring topology. When a node desires to transmit, it captures the token and attaches the message. As the token passes, the destination reads the header and captures the message. In some schemes, it attaches a "message received" signal to the token, which is then received by the original source node. Then the token is released and can accept further messages. The token ring is a completely decentralized scheme that effectively uses TDMA. Though this scheme is very reliable, it results in a waste of network capacity. The token must pass once around the ring for each message. Therefore, there are various modifications of this scheme, including the use of several tokens.

Fixed routing schemes often use routing tables that dictate the next node to be routed to, given the current message location and the destination node. Routing tables can be very large for large networks and cannot take into account real-time effects such as failed links, nodes with backed-up queues, or congested links.

Adaptive routing schemes depend on the current network status and can take into account various performance measures, including the cost of transmission over a given link, congestion of a given link, reliability of a path, and time of transmission. They can also account for link or node failures.

Routing algorithms can be based on various network analysis and graph theoretic concepts in computer science (e.g., A-star tree search) or in operations research [Bronson 1997] including shortest-route, maximal flow, and minimum-span problems. Routing is closely associated with dynamic programming and the optimal control problem in feedback control theory [Lewis and Syrmos 1995]. Shortest path routing schemes find the shortest path from a given node to the destination node. If the cost, instead of the link length, is associated with each link, these algorithms can also compute minimum-cost routes. These algorithms can be centralized (find the shortest path from a given node to all other nodes) or decentralized (find the shortest path from all nodes to a given node). There are certain well-defined algorithms for shortest path routing, including the efficient Dijkstra algorithm [Kumar 2001], which has polynomial complexity. The Bellman-Ford algorithm finds the path with the smallest number of hops [Kumar 2001]. Routing schemes based on competitive game theoretic notions have also been developed [Altman et al. 2002].

2.2.2.6 Deadlock and Livelock Large-scale communication networks contain cycles (circular paths) of nodes. Moreover, each node is a shared resource that can handle multiple messages flowing along different paths. Therefore, communication nets are susceptible to *deadlock*, wherein all nodes in a specific cycle have full buffers and are waiting for each other. Then no node can transmit because no node can get free buffer space, so all transmission in that cycle comes to a halt. *Livelock*, on the other hand, is the condition wherein a message is continually transmitted around the network and never reaches its destination. Livelock is a deficiency of some routing schemes that route the message to alternate links when the desired links are congested without taking into account that the message should be routed closer to its final destination. Many routing schemes are available for routing with deadlock and livelock avoidance [e.g. Duato 1996].

2.2.2.7 Flow Control In queuing networks, each node has an associated queue or buffer that can stack messages. In such networks, flow control and resource assignment are important. The objectives of flow control are to protect the network from problems related to overload and speed mismatches and to maintain QoS, efficiency, fairness, and freedom from deadlock. If a given node A has high priority, its messages might be preferentially routed in every case, so that competing nodes are choked off as the traffic of A increases. Fair routing schemes avoid this problem. There are several techniques for flow control. In *buffer management*, certain portions of the buffer space are assigned for certain purposes. In *choke packet schemes*, any node sensing congestion sends choke packets to other nodes, telling them to reduce their transmissions. *Isarithmic schemes* have a fixed number of "permits" for the network. A message can be sent only if a permit is available. In *window* or *kanban* schemes, the receiver grants "credits" to the sender only if it has free buffer space. Upon receiving a credit, the sender can transmit a message. In *Transmission Control Protocol* (*TCP*) schemes (Tahoe and Reno), a source increases its transmission rate linearly as long as all its sent messages are acknowledged. When it detects a lost packet, it decreases its transmission rate exponentially. Since lost packets depend on congestion, TCP automatically decreases transmissions when congestion is detected.

2.2.3 Power Management

With the advent of ad hoc networks of geographically distributed sensors in remote site environments (e.g., sensors dropped from aircraft for personnel/vehicle surveillance), there is a focus on increasing the lifetimes of sensor nodes through power generation, power conservation, and power management. Current research is in designing small MEMS (microelectromechanical systems) RF components for transceivers, including capacitors, inductors, etc. The limiting factor now is in fabricating micro-sized inductors. Another area is the design of MEMS power generators using technologies including solar, vibration (electromagnetic and electrostatic), thermal, etc. (Figure 2.6).

RF-ID (RF identification) devices are transponder microcircuits having an L-C tank circuit that stores power from received interrogation signals and then uses that power to transmit a response. Passive tags have no onboard power source and limited onboard data storage, while active tags have a battery and up to 1 Mb of data storage (Figure 2.7). RF-ID operates in a low frequency range of 100 kHz–1.5 MHz or a high frequency range of 900 MHz–2.4 GHz, which has an operating range of up to 30 m. RF-ID tags are very inexpensive and are used in manufacturing and sales inventory control, container shipping control, etc. RF-ID tags are installed on water meters in some cities, allowing a metering vehicle to simply drive by and remotely read the current readings. They are also be used in automobiles for automatic toll collection.

Meanwhile, software power management techniques can greatly decrease the power consumed by RF sensor nodes. TDMA is especially useful for power conservation, since a node can power down or "sleep" between its assigned time slots, waking up in time to receive and transmit messages.

The required transmission power increases as the square of the distance between source and destination. Therefore, multiple short message transmission hops require less power than one long hop. In fact, if the distance between source and destination is R, the power required for single-hop transmission is proportional to R^2. If nodes between source and destination are taken advantage of to transmit n short hops instead, the power required by each node is proportional to R^2/n^2. This is a strong argument in favor of distributed networks with multiple nodes, i.e., nets of the mesh variety.

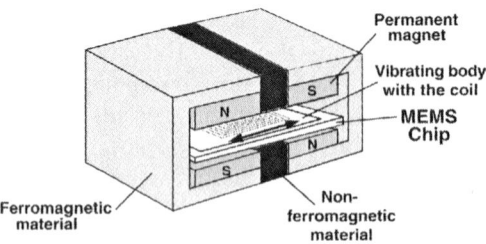

Figure 2.6 MEMS power generator using vibration and the electromagnetic method.

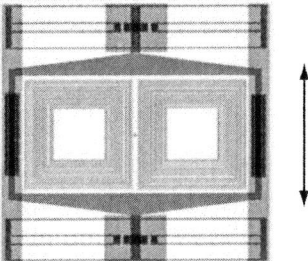

Figure 2.7 MEMS fabrication layout of a power generator dual vibrating coil showing folded beam suspension.

A current topic of research is *active power control*, whereby each node cooperates with all other nodes in selecting its individual transmission power level [Kumar 2001]. This is a decentralized feedback control problem. Congestion is increased if any node uses too much power, but each node must select a large enough transmission range so that the network remains connected. For n nodes randomly distributed in a disk, the network is asymptotically connected with probability 1 if the transmission range r of all nodes is selected using

$$r \geq \sqrt{\frac{\log n + \gamma(n)}{\pi n}}$$

where $\gamma(n)$ is a function that goes to infinity as n becomes large.

2.2.4 Network Structure and Hierarchical Networks

Routing tables for distributed networks increase exponentially as nodes are added. An $n \times m$ mesh network has nm links, and there are multiple paths from each source to each destination. *Hierarchical network structures* simplify routing and are amenable to distributed signal processing and decision making, since some processing can be done at each hierarchical layer.

It has been shown [Lewis et al. 1993] that a fully connected network has *NP*-hard complexity, while imposing routing protocols by restricting the allowed paths to obtain a *reentrant flow* topology results in polynomial complexity. Such streamlined protocols are natural for hierarchical networks.

Multicast Systems in mesh networks use a hierarchical leader-based scheme for message transmission [Chen et al. 2000]. Each group of nodes has a designated leader that is responsible for receiving messages from and transmitting to nodes outside the group. Part (a) of Figure 2.8 shows messages routed in a mesh net using standard peer-to-peer protocols. The link lengths of the transmission paths are shown. Parts (b) and (c) show the same two messages being routed using a multicast protocol. Note that the total transmission paths are significantly shorter. Multicast has been implemented using tree-based and path-based schemes.

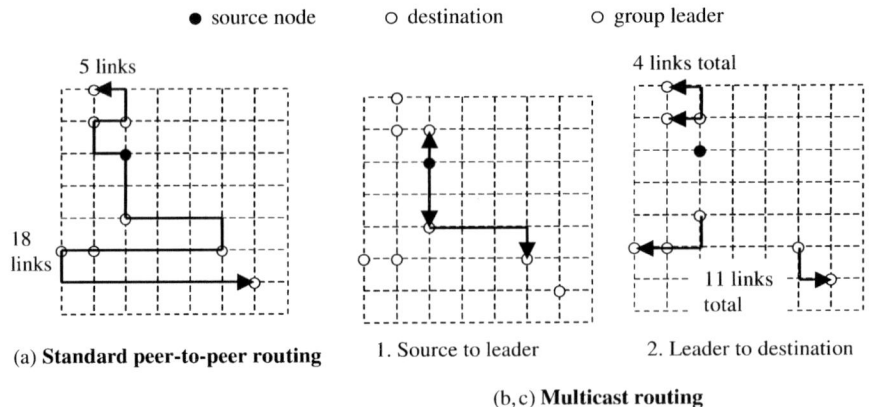

Figure 2.8 Multicast routing improves efficiency and reduces message path length. (From Chen et al. 2000.)

2.2.4.1 Hierarchical Networks

Much work has been done on formal hierarchical structures for distributed networks (Figure 2.9). Cao et al. [1999] study how to determine optimal configurations for hierarchical routing. Shi and Fonseka [1995] analyze hierarchical self-healing rings. Shah-Heydari and Yang [2001] show the importance of a consistent numbering scheme in hierarchical systems, which allows for a simplified tree-based routing scheme.

Figure 2.10 shows a basic four-element ring element consisting of four nodes and four links. It shows two ways of connecting these two rings, which results in two mesh networks of different structures. The first network consists of alternating one-way streets, while the second consists of alternating-direction vortices. It is interesting to analyze these two structures from the point of view of the notions of flow field divergence and curl.

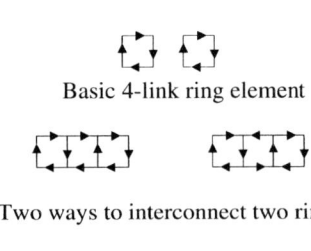

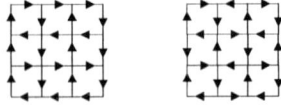

Figure 2.9 Constructing two mesh networks.

2.2 COMMUNICATION NETWORKS 23

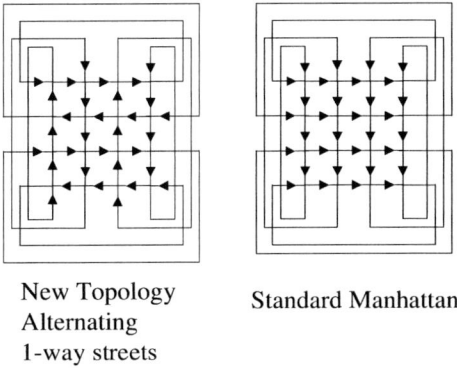

New Topology　　　　Standard Manhattan
Alternating
1-way streets

Figure 2.10 Interconnecting the edge links.

In any network, the phenomenon of *edge binding* means that much of the routing power of peripheral stations is wasted because peripheral links are unused. Thus, messages tend to reflect off the boundary into the interior or to move parallel to the periphery [Smith 1964]. To avoid this, the Manhattan geometry connects the nodes at one edge of the network to nodes at the opposite edge. Figure 2.12 shows the standard Manhattan geometry as well as a Manhattan net built from the alternating one-way street mesh just constructed.

As nodes are added, the number of links increases exponentially. This makes for NP-complexity problems in routing and failure recovery. To simplify network structure, we can use hierarchical clustering techniques. The hierarchical structure must be *consistent*, that is, it must have the same structure at each level. Figure 2.12 shows a 4 × 4 mesh net and a clustering into four groups. Note that the clustered structure has a dual ring SHR topology. To reduce the routing complexity, we can disable one of the rings and obtain a ring structure.

Figure 2.13 shows an 8 × 8 mesh net. Shown first are all the links, and then the hierarchical clustering with some links disabled to reduce complexity. We have chosen to keep the outer ring at each level. Note that the clockwise ring structure is the same at each level, resulting in a regular hierarchy.

Routing is very easy in this hierarchical network [Swamy 2003]. First, one selects a *consistent numbering scheme*. For example number the groups as 1, 2,

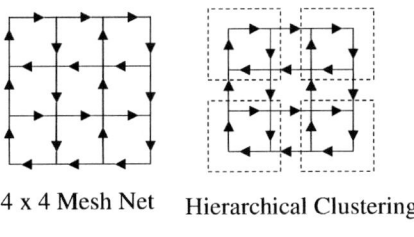

4 x 4 Mesh Net　　Hierarchical Clustering

Figure 2.11 Clustering the nodes.

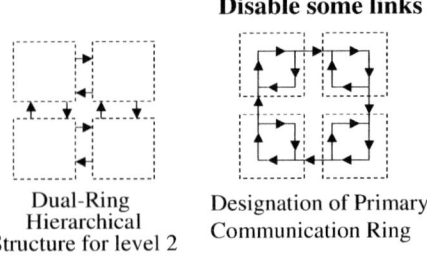

Figure 2.12 Reducing complexity.

3, 4, beginning at the top left and going clockwise. This is done at each level. Then, referring to the 8 × 8 mesh net in Figure 2.13, node 143, shown in the figure, is in the top left 4 × 4 group, within which it is in the fourth 2 × 2 group, within which it is the third node. Using this number scheme, one may construct a simple routing scheme wherein the same basic routing algorithm is repeated at each level of the hierarchy. This is not unlike quadtree routing in mobile robot path planning. Failure recovery is also straightforward. If a link fails, one may simply switch in one of the disabled links to take over. Code for this is very easy to write.

2.2.4.2 Distributed Routing, Decision Making, and Digital Signal Processing
It is natural in routing and failure recovery for these hierarchical networks to designate the entry node for each group as a *group leader*. This node must make additional decisions beyond those of the other nodes, including resource availability for deadlock avoidance, disabled link activation for failure recovery, and so on. This lays a very natural framework for distributed decision making and digital signal processing (DSP), wherein a group leader processes the data from the group prior to transmitting them. The group leader for communications should be the *entry node* of each group, while the group leader for DSP should be the *exit node* for each group.

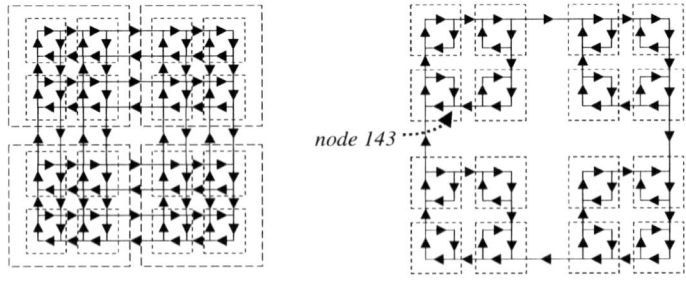

Figure 2.13 8×8 mesh net retaining links to form hierarchical ring structures.

2.2.5 Historical Development and Standards

Much of this information is taken from the PC Tech Guide [2003], which contains a thorough summary of communication network standards, topologies, and components. See also Jordan and Abdallah [2002].

2.2.5.1 Ethernet The Ethernet was developed in the mid-1970s by Xerox, DEC, and Intel and was standardized in 1979. The Institute of Electrical and Electronics Engineers (IEEE) released the official Ethernet standard IEEE 802.3 in 1983. The Fast Ethernet operates at 10 times the speed of the regular Ethernet and was officially adopted in 1995. It introduces new features such as full-duplex operation and auto-negotiation. Both of these standards use IEEE 802.3 variable-length frames having 64- to 1514-byte packets.

2.2.5.2 Token Ring In 1984 IBM introduced the 4 Mbit/s token ring network. The system was of high quality and robust, but its cost caused it to fall behind the Ethernet in popularity. IEEE standardized the token ring with the IEEE 802.5 specification. The Fiber Distributed Data Interface (FDDI) specifies a 100 Mbit/s token-passing, dual-ring LAN that uses fiberoptic cable. It was developed by the American National Standards Institute (ANSI) in the mid-1980s, and its speed far exceeded the current capabilities of both Ethernet and IEEE 802.5.

2.2.5.3 Gigabit Ethernet The Gigabit Ethernet Alliance was founded in 1996 and the Gigabit Ethernet standards were ratified in 1999, specifying a physical layer that uses a mixture of technologies from the original Ethernet and fiber optic cable technologies from FDDI.

Client-server networks became popular in the late 1980s with the replacement of large mainframe computers by networks of personal computers. Application programs for distributed computing environments are essentially divided into two parts: the client or front end and the server or back end. The user's PC is the client, and more powerful server machines interface to the network.

Peer-to-peer networking architectures have all machines with equivalent capabilities and responsibilities. There is no server and computers connect to each other, usually using a bus topology, to share files, printers, Internet access, and other resources.

Peer-to-peer (P2P) computing is a significant next evolutionary step over P2P networking. Here computing tasks are divided among multiple computers, the result being assembled for further consumption. P2P computing has sparked a revolution for the Internet age and has obtained considerable success in a very short time. The Napster MP3 music file-sharing application went live in September 1999 and attracted more than 20 million users by mid-2000.

2.2.5.4 802.11 Wireless Local Area Network (WLAN) IEEE ratified the IEEE 802.11 specification in 1997 as a standard for WLAN. Current versions of

802.11 (i.e., 802.11b) support transmission up to 11 Mbit/s. WiFi, as it is known, is useful for fast and easy networking of PCs, printers, and other devices in a local environment such as the home. Current PCs and laptops as purchased have the hardware to support WiFi. Purchasing and installing a WiFi router and receivers is within the budget and capability of home PC enthusiasts.

Bluetooth was initiated in 1998 and standardized by the IEEE as wireless personal area network (WPAN) specification IEEE 802.15. Bluetooth is a short-range RF technology aimed at facilitating communication of electronic devices with each other and with the Internet, allowing for data synchronization that is transparent to the user. Supported devices include PCs, laptops, printers, joysticks, keyboards, mice, cell phones, PDAs, and consumer products. Mobile devices are also supported. Discovery protocols allow new devices to be hooked up easily to the network. Bluetooth uses the unlicensed 2.4 GHz band and can transmit data of up to 1 Mbit/s, can penetrate solid nonmetal barriers, and has a nominal range of 10 m that can be extended to 100 m. A master station can service up to seven simultaneous slave links. Forming a network of these networks, e.g., a piconet, allows one master to service up to 200 slaves.

Currently, Bluetooth development kits can be purchased from a variety of suppliers, but the systems generally require a great deal of time, effort, and knowledge of programming and debugging. Forming piconets has not yet been streamlined and is unduly difficult.

Home RF was initiated in 1998 and has goals similar to those of Bluetooth for WPAN. Its goal is shared data/voice transmission. It interfaces with the Internet as well as with the Public Switched Telephone Network. It uses the 2.4 GHz band and has a range of 50 m, suitable for home and yard. A maximum of 127 nodes can be accommodated in a single network. *IrDA* is a WPAN technology that has a short-range, narrow-transmission-angle beam suitable for aiming and selective reception of signals.

2.3 WIRELESS SENSOR NETWORKS

Sensor networks are the key to gathering the information needed by smart environments, whether in buildings, utilities, industrial facilities, homes, ships, transportation systems automation, or elsewhere. Recent terrorist and guerrilla warfare countermeasures require distributed networks of sensors that can be deployed using aircraft, for example, and have self-organizing capabilities. In such applications, running wires or cabling is usually impractical. A sensor network is required that is fast and easy to install and maintain.

2.3.1 IEEE 1451 and Smart Sensors

Wireless sensor networks satisfy these requirements. Desirable functions for sensor nodes include ease of installation, self-identification, self-diagnosis, reliability, time awareness for coordination with other nodes, some software functions and DSP, and standard control protocols and network interfaces [IEEE 1451 Expo, 2001].

There are many sensor manufacturers and many networks on the market today. It is too costly for manufacturers to make special transducers for every network on the market. Different components made by different manufacturers should be compatible. Therefore, in 1993 the IEEE and the National Institute of Standards and Technology (NIST) began work on a standard for Smart Sensor Networks. IEEE 1451, the Standard for Smart Sensor Networks, was the result (Figure 2.14). The objective of this standard is to make it easier for different manufacturers to develop smart sensors and to interface those devices to networks.

2.3.1.1 Smart Sensor, Virtual Sensor

Figure 2.15 shows the basic architecture of IEEE 1451 [Conway and Hefferman 2003]. Major components include STIM, TEDS, TII, and NCAP, as detailed in the figure. A major outcome of IEEE 1451 studies is the formalized concept of a *smart sensor*. A smart sensor is a sensor that provides extra functions beyond those necessary for generating a correct representation of the sensed quantity [Frank 2000]. Included might be signal conditioning, signal processing, and decision-making/alarm functions. A general model of a smart sensor is shown in Figure 2.15. Objectives for smart sensors include moving the intelligence closer to the point of measurement; making it cost-effective to integrate and maintain distributed sensor systems; creating a confluence of transducers, control, computation, and communications toward a common goal; and seamlessly interfacing numerous sensors of different types. The concept of a *virtual sensor* is also depicted in Figure 2.15. A virtual sensor is the physical sensor/transducer, plus the associated signal conditioning and DSP required to obtain reliable estimates of the required sensory information. The virtual sensor is a component of the smart sensor.

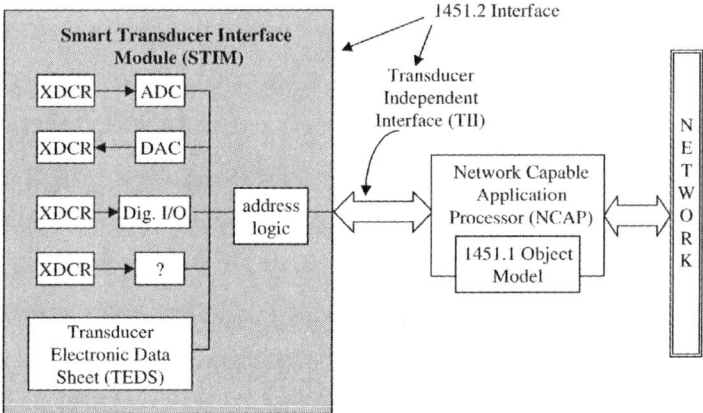

Figure 2.14 The IEEE 1451 standard for smart sensor networks.

28 WIRELESS SENSOR NETWORKS

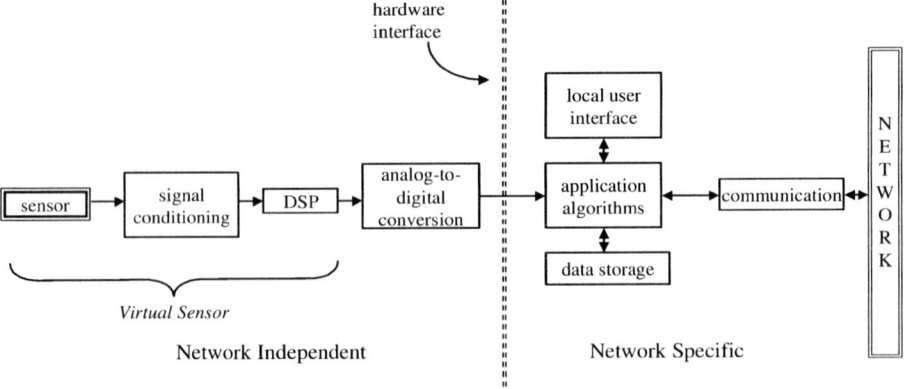

Figure 2.15 A general model of a smart sensor (IEEE 1451 Expo, October 2001).

2.3.2 Transducers and Physical Transduction Principles

A *transducer* is a device that converts energy from one domain to another. In Figure 2.16, it converts the quantity to be sensed into a useful signal that can be directly measured and processed. Since much signal conditioning (SC) and DSP are carried out by electronic circuits, the outputs of transducers that are useful for sensor networks are generally voltages or currents. Sensory transduction may be carried out using *physical principles*, some of which we review here. Microelectromechanical systems (MEMS) sensors are now very well developed and are available for most sensing applications in wireless networks. References for this section include Frank [2000], Kovacs [1998], Madou [1997], and de Silva [1999].

Mechanical sensors include those that rely on direct physical contact.

The piezoresistive effect converts an applied strain to a change in resistance that can be sensed using electronic circuits such as the Wheatstone bridge (discussed later). Discovered by Lord Kelvin in 1856, the relationship is $\Delta R/R = S\varepsilon$, with R being the resistance, ε the strain, and S the gauge factor, which depends on quantities such as the resistivity and the Poisson ratio of the material. There may be a quadratic term in ε for some materials. Metals and semiconductors exhibit piezoresistivity. The piezoresistive effect in silicon is enhanced by doping with boron (p-type silicon can have a gauge factor of up to 200). With semiconductor strain gauges, temperature compensation is important.

The piezoelectric effect, discovered by the Curies in 1880, converts an applied stress (force) to a charge separation or potential difference. Piezoelectric materials include barium titanate, (PZT), and single-crystal quartz. The relation between the change in force F and the change in voltage V is given by $\Delta V = k\Delta F$, where

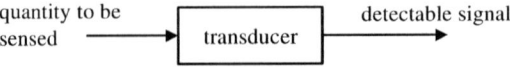

Figure 2.16 Sensory transducer.

k is proportional to the material charge sensitivity coefficients and the crystal thickness and inversely proportional to the crystal area and the material relative permittivity. The piezoelectric effect is reversible, so that a change in voltage also generates a force and a corresponding change in thickness. Thus, the same device can be *both a sensor and an actuator*. Combined sensor/actuators are an intriguing topic of current research.

Tunneling sensing depends on the exponential relationship between the tunneling current I and the tip/surface separation z given by $I = I_o e^{-kz}$, where k depends on the tunnel barrier height in electron volts. Tunneling is an extremely accurate method of sensing nanometer-scale displacements, but its highly nonlinear nature requires the use of feedback control to make it useful.

Capacitive sensors typically have one fixed plate and one movable plate. When a force is applied to the movable plate, the change in capacitance C is given as $\Delta C = \varepsilon A / \Delta d$, with Δd being the resulting displacement, A the area, and ε the dielectric constant. Changes in capacitance can be detected using a variety of electric circuits and converted to a voltage or current change for further processing. *Inductive sensors*, which convert displacement to a change in inductance, are also often useful.

Magnetic and electromagnetic sensors do not require direct physical contact and are useful for detecting proximity effects [Kovacs 1998].

The Hall effect, discovered by Edwin Hall in 1879, relies on the fact that the Lorentz force deflects flowing charge carriers in a direction perpendicular to both their direction of flow and an applied magnetic field (i.e., vector cross-product) (Figure 2.17). The Hall voltage induced in a plate of thickness T is given by $V_H = R I_x B_z / T$, with R being the Hall coefficient, I_x the current flow in direction x, and B_z the magnetic flux density in the z direction. R is four to five times larger in semiconductors than in most metals. The *magnetoresistive effect* is a related phenomenon depending on the fact that the conductivity varies as the square of the applied flux density.

Magnetic field sensors can be used to detect the remote presence of metallic objects. *Eddy-current sensors* use magnetic probe coils to detect defects in metallic structures such as pipes.

Thermal sensors are a family of sensors used to measure temperature or heat flux. Most biological organisms have developed sophisticated temperature-sensing systems [Kovacs 1998].

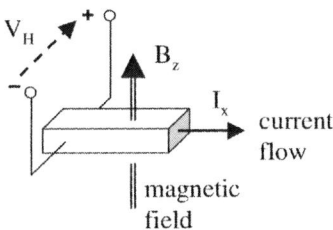

Figure 2.17 The Hall effect.

Thermomechanical transduction is used for temperature sensing and regulation in homes and automobiles. On changes in temperature T, all materials exhibit (linear) thermal expansion of the form $\Delta L/L = \alpha \Delta T$, with L being the length and α the coefficient of linear expansion. One can fabricate a strip of two joined materials with different thermal expansions. Then the radius of curvature of this thermal bimorph depends on the temperature change (Figure 2.18).

Thermoresistive effects are based on the fact that resistance R changes with temperature T. For moderate changes, the relation is approximately given by for many metals by $\Delta R/R = \alpha_R \Delta T$, with α_R being the temperature coefficient of resistance. The relationship for silicon is more complicated but is well understood. Hence, silicon is useful for detecting temperature changes.

Thermocouples are based on the thermoelectric *Seebeck effect*, whereby if a circuit consists of two different materials joined together at either end, with one junction hotter than the other, a current flows in the circuit. This generates a Seebeck voltage given approximately by $V \approx \alpha(T_1 - T_2) + \gamma(T_1^2 - T_2^2)$, with T_1 and T_2 being the temperatures at the two junctions. The coefficients depend on the properties of the two materials. Semiconductor thermocouples generally have higher sensitivities than do metal thermocouples. Thermocouples are inexpensive and reliable, and so are often used. Typical thermocouples have outputs on the order of 50 μV/°C, and some are effective for temperature ranges of -270°C to 2700°C.

Resonant temperature sensors rely on the fact that single-crystal SiO_2 exhibits a change in resonant frequency depending on the temperature change. Since this is a frequency effect, it is more accurate than amplitude-change effects, and has extreme sensitivity and accuracy for small temperature changes.

Optical transducers convert light to various quantities that can be detected [Kovacs 1998]. These transducers are based on one of several mechanisms. In the *photoelectric effect* (Einstein, Nobel Prize, 1921) one electron is emitted at the negative end of a pair of charged plates for each light photon of sufficient energy. This causes a current to flow. In *photoconductive sensors*, photons generate carriers that lower the resistance of the material. In *junction-based photosensors*, photons generate electron-hole pairs in a semiconductor junction that causes current flow. This is often misnamed the *photovoltaic effect*. These devices include photodiodes and phototransistors. *Thermopiles* use a thermocouple with one junction coated with a gold or bismuth black absorber, which generates heat on illumination.

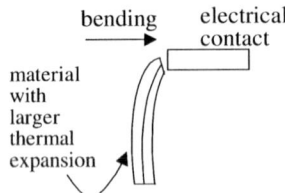

Figure 2.18 Thermal bimorph.

Solar cells are large photodiodes that generate voltage from light. *Bolometers* consist of two thermally sensitive resistors in a Wheatstone bridge configuration, one of which is shielded from the incident light. Optical transducers can be optimized for different frequencies of light, resulting in infrared detectors, ultraviolet detectors, etc.

Various devices, including accelerometers, are based on *optical fiber technology*, often using time-of-flight information.

Chemical and biological transducers [Kovacs 1998] include a very wide range of devices that interact with solids, liquids, and gases of all types. Potential applications include environmental monitoring, biochemical warfare monitoring, security area surveillance, medical diagnostics, implantable biosensors, and food monitoring. Effective use has been shown for NO_x (from pollution), organophosphorus pesticides, nerve gases (Sarin/gas, etc.), hydrogen cyanide, smallpox, anthrax, CO_x, SO_x, and others (Figure 2.19).

Chemiresistors have two interdigitated finger electrodes coated with specialized chemical coatings that change their resistance when they are exposed to certain chemical challenge agents. The electrodes may be connected directly to a Field Effect Transistor (FET), which amplifies the resulting signals *in situ* for good noise rejection. This device is known as an *interdigitated-gate electrode FET* (IGEFET). Arrays of chemiresistors, each device with a different chemically

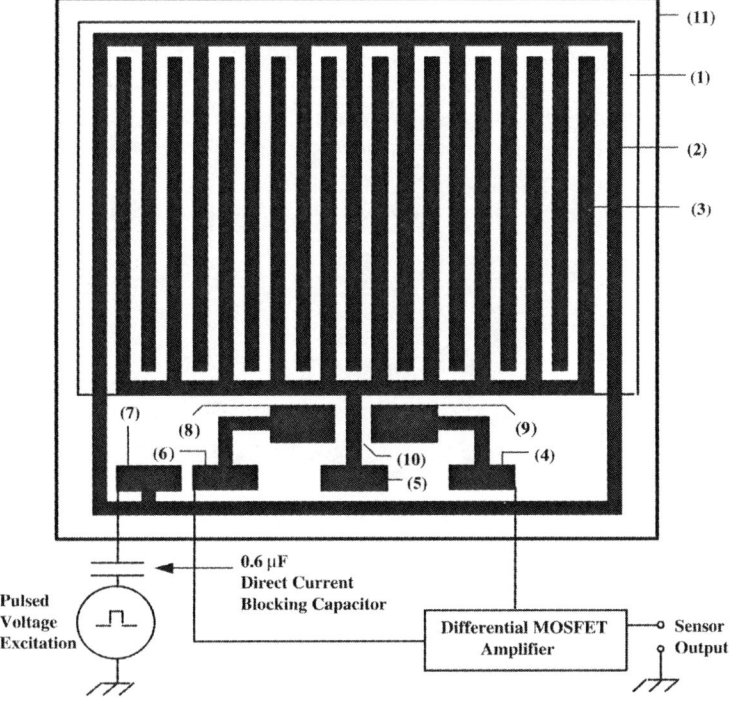

Figure 2.19 IGEFET structure (Kolesar et al. 1992).

active coating, can be used to increase specificity for specific challenge agents [Kolesar et al. 1992]. DSP, including neural network classification techniques, is important in correct identification of the agent.

Metal-oxide gas sensors rely on the fact that adsorption of gases onto certain semiconductors greatly changes their resistivities. In thin-film detectors, a catalyst such as platinum is deposited on the surface to speed the reactions and enhance the response. Useful as sensors are the oxides of tin, zinc, iron, zirconium, etc. Gases that can be detected include CO_2, CO, H_sS, NH_3, and ozone. Reactions are of the form $O_2 + 2e^- \rightarrow 2O^-$ so that adsorption produces an electron trap site, effectively depleting the surface of mobile carriers and increasing its resistance.

Electrochemical transducers rely on currents induced by oxidation or reduction of a chemical species at an electrode surface. These are among the simplest and most useful chemical sensors. An electron transfer reaction occurs that is described by $O + ze^- \Leftrightarrow R$, with O being the oxidized species, R the reduced species, and z the charge on the ion involved. The resulting current density is given in terms of z by the Butler-Volmer equation [Kovacs 1998].

Biosensors of various types depend on the high selectivity of many biomolecular reactions; for example, molecular binding sites of the detector may admit only certain species of analyte molecules (Figure 2.21). Unfortunately, such reactions are not usually reversible, so the sensor is not reusable. These devices have a biochemically active thin film deposited on a platform device that converts induced property changes (e.g., mass, resistance) into detectable electric or optical signals. Suitable conversion platforms include the IGEFET (above), ion-sensitive FET (ISFET), SAW (below), quartz crystal microbalance (QCM), microcantilevers, etc. To provide specificity to a prescribed analyte measurand, for the thin film one may use proteins (enzymes or antibodies), polysaccharide, nucleic acid, oligonucleotides [Choi et al. 2002], or an ionophore (which has selective responses to specific ion types). Arrays of sensors can be used, each having a different biochemically active film, to improve sensitivity. This has been used in the so-called electronic nose.

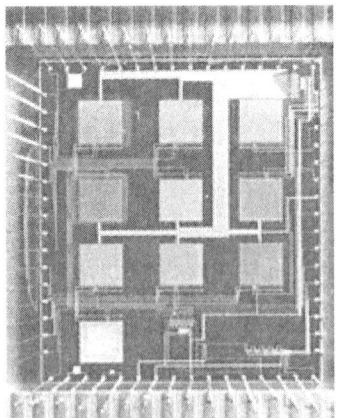

Figure 2.20 A 3×3 IGEFET sensor microarray.

the Butler-Volmer equation [Kovacs 1998].

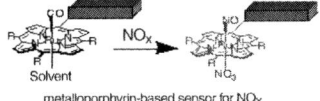

Figure 2.21 Biosensors based on molecular recognition (Rudkevich et al. 1996).

The electromagnetic spectrum can be used to fabricate various types of *remote sensors* (Figure 2.22). Generally the wavelength suitable for a particular application is based on the propagation distance, the level of detail and resolution required, the ability to penetrate solid materials or certain media, and the signal processing difficulty. Doppler techniques allow the measurement of velocities. Millimeter waves have been used for satellite remote monitoring. Infrared (IR) sensing is used for night vision and sensing heat. IR motion detectors are inexpensive and reliable. Electromagnetic waves can be used to determine distance using time-of-flight information; radar uses RF waves and lidar uses light (laser). The velocity of light is $c = 299.8 \times 10^6$ m/s. GPS uses RF for absolute position localization. Visible light imaging using cameras is used in a broad range of applications but generally requires sophisticated and computationally expensive DSP techniques, including edge detection, thresholding, segmentation, pattern recognition, motion analysis, etc.

Acoustic sensors include those that use sound as a sensing medium (Figure 2.23). Doppler techniques allow the measurement of velocities. Ultrasound often provides more information about mechanical machinery vibrations, fluid leakage, and

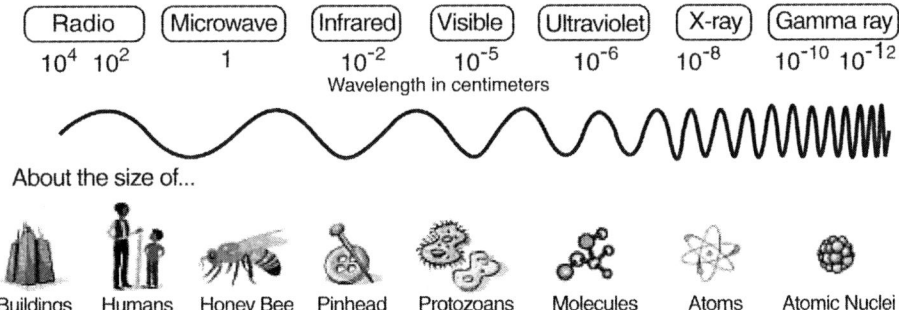

Figure 2.22 The electromagnetic spectrum. (Courtesy of http://imagers.gsfc.nasa.gov/ems/waves3.html)

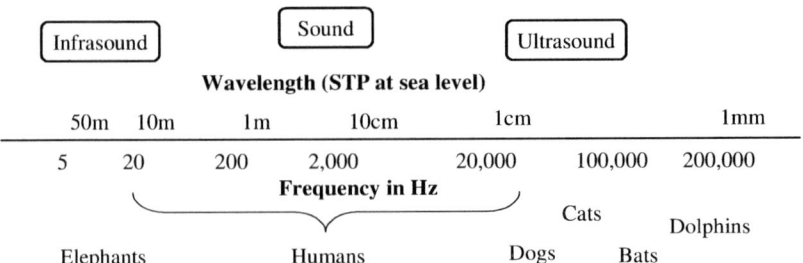

Figure 2.23 The acoustic spectrum.

impending equipment faults than do other techniques. Sonar uses sound to determine distance using time-of-flight information. It is effective in media other than air, including underwater. Caution is necessary because the propagation speed of acoustic signals depends on the medium. The speed of sound at sea level in a standard atmosphere is $c_s = 340.294$ m/s. Subterranean echoes from earthquakes and tremors can be used to glean information about the Earth's core as well as about the tremor event, but deconvolution techniques must be used to remove echo phenomena and to compensate for uncertain propagation speeds.

Acoustic wave sensors are useful for a broad range of sensing devices [Kovacs 1998]. These transducers can be classified as surface acoustic wave (SAW), thickness-shear mode (TSM), flexural plate wave (FPW), or acoustic plate mode (APM). The SAW, shown in Figure 2.24, consists of two sets of interdigitated fingers at either end of a membrane, one set for generating the SAW and one for detecting it. Like the IGEFET, these are useful platforms to convert property changes such as mass into detectable electrical signals. For instance, the surface of the device can be coated with a chemically or biologically active thin film. On presentation of the measurand to be sensed, adsorption might cause the mass m to change, resulting in a frequency shift given by the Sauerbrey equation $\Delta f = k f_0^2 \Delta m / A$, with f_0 being the membrane resonant frequency, constant k depending on the device, and A the membrane area.

2.3.3 Sensors for Smart Environments

Many vendors now produce commercially available sensors of many types that are suitable for wireless network applications. See, for instance, the websites of SUNX Sensors, Schaevitz, Keyence, Turck, Pepperl & Fuchs, National Instruments, UE

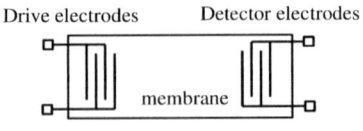

Figure 2.24 SAW sensor.

Systems (ultrasonic), Leake (IR), and CSI (vibration). Table 2.1 shows which physical principles may be used to measure various quantities. MEMS sensors are now available for most of these measurands.

2.3.4 Commercially Available Wireless Sensor Systems

Many commercially available wireless communications nodes are available, including Lynx Technologies, and various Bluetooth kits, including the Casira devices from Cambridge Silicon Radio, CSR.

Berkeley Crossbow Motes may be the most versatile wireless sensor network devices on the market for prototyping purposes (Figure 2.25). Crossbow (http://www.xbow.com/) makes three Mote processor radio module families—MICA (MPR300, first generation), MICA2 (MPR400), and MICA2-DOT (MPR500, second generation). Nodes come with five sensors installed—Temperature, Light, Acoustic (Microphone), Acceleration/Seismic, and Magnetic. These are especially suitable for surveillance networks for personnel and vehicles. Different sensors can

TABLE 2.1 Measurements for Wireless Sensor Networks

	Measurand	Transduction Principle
Physical Properties	Pressure	Piezoresistive, capacitive
	Temperature	Thermistor, thermomechanical, thermocouple
	Humidity	Resistive, capacitive
	Flow	Pressure change, thermistor
Motion Properties	Position	E-mag, GPS, contact sensor
	Velocity	Doppler, Hall effect, optoelectronic
	Angular velocity	Optical encoder
	Acceleration	Piezoresistive, piezoelectric, optical fiber
Contact Properties	Strain	Piezoresistive
	Force	Piezoelectric, piezoresistive
	Torque	Piezoresistive, optoelectronic
	Slip	Dual torque
	Vibration	Piezoresistive, piezoelectric, optical fiber, Sound, ultrasound
Presence	Tactile/contact	Contact switch, capacitive
	Proximity	Hall effect, capacitive, magnetic, seismic, acoustic, RF
	Distance/range	E-mag (sonar, radar, lidar), magnetic, tunneling
	Motion	E-mag, IR, acoustic, seismic (vibration)
Biochemical	Biochemical agents	Biochemical transduction
Identification	Personal features	Vision
	Personal ID	Fingerprints, retinal scan, voice, heat plume, vision motion analysis

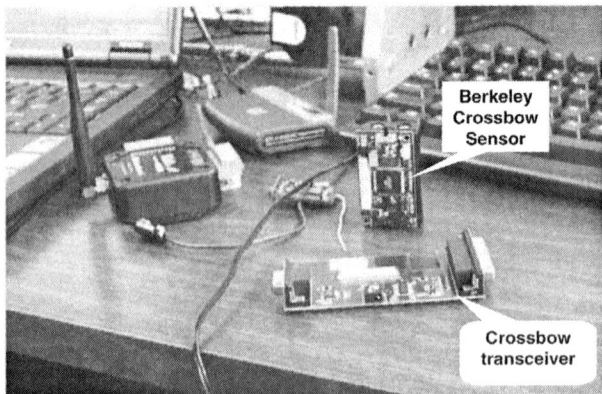

Figure 2.25 Berkeley Crossbow Motes.

be installed if desired. Their low power and small physical size enable placement virtually anywhere. Since all sensor nodes in a network can act as base stations, the network can configure itself and has multi-hop routing capabilities. The operating frequency is ISM band, either 916 or 433 MHz, with a data rate of 40 kbits/s and a range of 30 to 100 ft. Each node has a low-power microcontroller processor with a speed of 4 MHz, a flash memory with 128 kbytes, and (SRAM) and (EEPROM) of 4 kbytes each. The operating system is Tiny-OS, a tiny micro-threading distributed operating system developed by the University of California at Berkeley, with a NES-C (Nested C) source code language (similar to C). Installation of these devices requires a great deal of programming. A workshop is offered for training.

Microstrain's X-Link Measurement System (http://www.microstrain.com/) may be the easiest system to get up and running and to program (Figure 2.26). The frequency used is 916 MHz, which lies in the U.S. license-free ISM band. The sensor nodes are multichannel, with a maximum of eight sensors supported by a single wireless node. There are three types of sensor nodes—S-link (strain gauge),

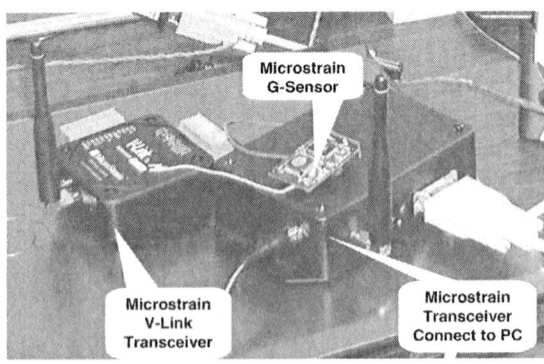

Figure 2.26 Microstrain wireless sensors.

G-link (accelerometer), and V-link (supports any sensors generating voltage differences). The sensor nodes have a preprogrammed (EPROM), so a great deal of programming by the user is not needed. Onboard data storage is 2 MB. Sensor nodes use a 3.6-V lithium ion internal battery (a 9 V rechargeable external battery is supported). A single receiver (Base Station) addresses multiple nodes. Each node has a unique 16-bit address, so a maximum of 2^{16} nodes can be addressed. The RF link between Base Station and nodes is bidirectional, and the sensor nodes have a programmable data logging sample rate. The RF link has a 30 m range with a 19200 baud rate. The baud rate on the serial RS-232 link between the Base Station and a terminal PC is 38400. The LabVIEW interface is supported.

2.3.5 Self-Organization and Localization

Ad hoc networks of nodes may be deployed using, e.g., aircraft or ships. Self-organization of ad hoc networks includes both *communications* self-organization and *positioning* self-organization. In the former, the nodes must wake up, detect each other, and form a communication network. Technologies for this are now standard, by and large developed within the mobile phone industry. Distributed surveillance sensor networks require information about the relative positions of the nodes for distributed signal processing, as well as absolute positioning information for reporting data related to detected targets.

2.3.5.1 Relative Layout Positioning—Localization Relative positioning or *localization* requires internode communications, and a TDMA message header frame that has both communications and localization fields is shown in Figure 2.27. There are various means for a node to measure the distance to its neighbors, mostly based on RF time-of-flight information. In air, the propagation speed is known, so time differences can be converted to distances. Given the relative distances between nodes, we want to organize the web into a grid specified in terms of relative positions.

An approach based on *robot kinematic transformations* provides a straightforward iterative technique for adding new nodes to a network. A homogeneous

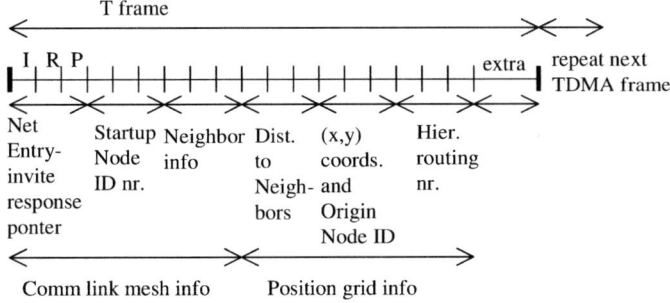

Figure 2.27 TDMA frame for communication protocols and localization.

transformation is a 4×4 matrix [Lewis et al. 1993]

$$A_i = \begin{bmatrix} R_i & p_i \\ 0 & 1 \end{bmatrix}$$

where R_i is a 3×3 rotation matrix and $p_i \in R^3$ is a translation vector. The T matrix defined by iterative rotations and translations as $T_{ij} = A_i A_{i+1} \ldots A_j$ allows one to express vectors in frame j in terms of the coordinates of frame i. If the network is a flat two-dimensional (2D) net, the z coordinates can be ignored, simplifying the problem.

Figure 2.28 shows how to start a self-organizing algorithm for relative positioning location. The first node to wake up is assigned the origin O. As nodes wake up, they are invited into the grid and distance is determined. The second node, a distance d_{12} from the first, defines the x and y axes. When the third node is discovered and two distances are measured, one computes its x and y coordinates as follows. Let A_{ij} denote the A matrix relating points i and j. Then, in standard fashion (c.f. the two-link robot arm) [Lewis et al. 1993], one computes A_{12}, A_{13}, A_{23} in terms of d_{12}, d_{13}, d_{23}. One can write the relative location in frame O of the new point 3 in two ways: $T_{13} = A_{13}$ and $T_{123} = A_{12}A_{23}$. The triangle shown in Figure 2.28 is a *closed kinematic chain* of the sort studied in [Liu et al. 1993]. The solution is obtained by requiring that the two maps T_{13} and T_{123} be *exact* at point 3. This means that the position vectors p_{13} and p_{123} (i.e., the third columns) of the two maps must be the same. This results in a nonlinear equation that can be solved for the distances.

Homogeneous transformations allow a *fast recursive procedure for integrating new nodes* into the grid. Suppose that a new node, number 4, enters the net. For unique positioning it must find distances to *three nodes* already in the grid. Then, based on relative distance information, one computes A matrices and T matrices to interrelate nodes 1, 2, 3, and 4. Then the x and y coordinates of node 4 relative to the origin are computed uniquely by forcing three maps to be exact at node 4. That is, $A_{14} = A_{12}A_{24} = A_{13}A_{34}$. Now the coordinates of the new node in terms of the base frame O for the subgrid can be computed.

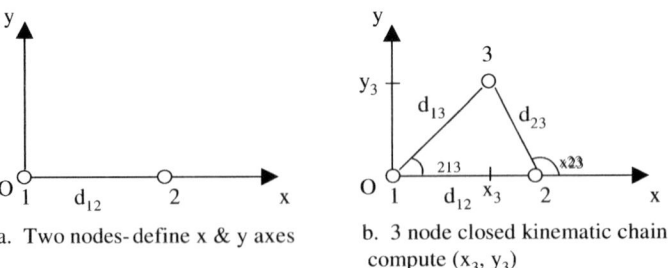

a. Two nodes- define x & y axes

b. 3 node closed kinematic chain- compute (x_3, y_3)

Figure 2.28 Integrating new nodes into a relative positioning grid.

2.3.5.2 Absolute Geographical Positioning

A network is said to be *relatively calibrated* if the relative positions of all nodes are known. Now it is necessary to determine the absolute geographic position of the network. The net is said to be (fully) *calibrated* if the absolute positions of all nodes are known. To determine the absolute node positions in a relatively calibrated flat 2D net, at least three nodes in the net must determine their absolute positions. There are many ways for a node to determine its absolute position, including Global Positioning System (GPS) and techniques based on stored maps, landmarks, or beacons [Bulusu et al. 2002].

2.3.5.3 Ultra Wideband (UWB) Radio

UWB is of great interest for communications in distributed sensor networks. This is because UWB is a short-range technology that can penetrate walls, it is suitable for multi-node transmissions, and it has built-in time-of-flight properties that make it very easy to measure ranges down to 1 cm with a range of 40 m. This means that the *same medium*, UWB, can be used for communications, localization, and target tracking in a distributed surveillance network. Moreover, UWB transceivers can be made very small and are amenable for MEMS technology; since pulse position modulation (PPM) is used, no carrier is needed, meaning that antennas are not inductive. Also, the receiver is based on a rake detector and correlator bank so that no IF stage is needed.

UWB uses signals like [Ray 2001]

$$s(t) = \sum_j w(t - jT_f - c_j T_c - \delta d_{\lfloor j/N_s \rfloor})$$

where $w(t)$ is the basic pulse with a duration of approximately 1 ns, often a wavelet or a Gaussian monocycle, and T_f is the frame or pulse repetition time. In a multinode environment, catastrophic collisions are avoided by using a pseudorandom sequence c_j to shift pulses within the frame to different compartments, and the compartment size is T_c s. One may have, for instance, $T_f = 1$ μs and $T_c = 5$ ns. Data are transmitted using digital PPM, where if the data bit is 0 the pulse is not shifted, and if the data bit is 1 the pulse is shifted by δ. The modulation shift is selected to make the correlation of $w(t)$ and $w(t - \delta)$ as negative as possible. The meaning of $d_{\lfloor j/N_s \rfloor}$ is that the same data bit is transmitted N_s times, allowing very reliable communications with a low probability of error.

2.4 SIGNAL PROCESSING AND DECISION MAKING

The figure showing the IEEE 1451 Smart Sensor includes basic blocks for signal conditioning (SC), DSP, and analog-to-digital (A/D) conversion. Let us briefly mention some of the issues here.

2.4.1 Signal Conditioning

Signals coming from MEMS sensors can be very noisy, of low amplitude, biased, and dependent on secondary parameters such as temperature. Moreover, one may not always be able to measure the quantity of interest, but only a related quantity. Therefore, SC is usually required. SC is performed using electronic circuitry, which may conveniently be built using standard VLSI fabrication techniques *in situ* with MEMS sensors. A reference for SC, A/D conversion, and filtering is [Lewis 1992].

A serious problem with MEMS sensors is undesired sensitivity to secondary quantities such as temperature. *Temperature compensation* can often be directly built into a MEMS sensor circuit. In Figure 2.29, showing a 3×3 array of (IGEFET) sensors, a 10th IGEFET is shown; this is for temperature compensation. Temperature compensation can also be added during the SC stage, as discussed below.

A basic technique for improving the signal-to-noise ratio (SNR) is *low-pass filtering*, since noise generally dominates the desirable signals at high frequencies. Shown in Figure 2.29 is an analog low-pass filter that also amplifies, constructed from an operational amplifier. Such devices are easily fabricated using VLSI semiconductor techniques. The time constant of this circuit is $\tau = R_2 C$. The transfer function of this filter is $H(s) = ka/(s+a)$ with a 3 dB cutoff frequency given by $a = 1/\tau$ rad and gain given by $k = R_2/R_1$. Here s is the Laplace transform variable. The cutoff frequency should be larger than the highest useful signal frequency of the sensor.

Alternatively, one may use a digital low-pass filter (LPF) implemented on a computer after sampling. A digital low-pass filter transfer function and the associated difference equation for implementation are given by

$$\text{Digital filter:} \quad \hat{s}_k = K \frac{z+1}{z-\alpha} s_k$$

$$\text{difference equation:} \quad \hat{s}_{k+1} = \alpha s_k + K(s_{k+1} + s_k)$$

Here, z is the z-transform variable treated as a unit delay in the time domain, s_k is the measured signal, and $\hat{s}_k$ is the *filtered* or *smoothed variable* with reduced noise content. The filter parameters are selected in terms of the desired cutoff frequency and the sampling period [Lewis 1992].

It is often the case that one can measure a variable s_k (e.g., position) but one needs to know its rate of change v_k (e.g., velocity). Due to the presence of noise, one cannot

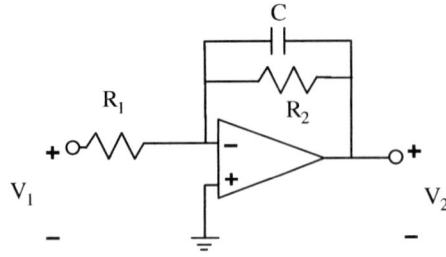

Figure 2.29 Analog low-pass filter.

2.4 SIGNAL PROCESSING AND DECISION MAKING

simply take the difference between successive values of s_k as the velocity. A filtered velocity estimate given by $v_{k+1} = \alpha v_k + K(s_{k+1} - s_k)$ both filters out noise and gives a smooth velocity estimate.

Often, changes in resistance must be converted to voltages for further processing. This may be accomplished by using a Wheatstone bridge (Figure 2.30) [de Silva 1989]. Suppose $R_1 = R$ in the figure is the resistance that changes, depending on the measurand (e.g., strain gauge), and the other three resistances are constant (quarter bridge configuration). Then the output voltage changes according to $\Delta V_0 = V_{ref} \Delta R / 4R$. We assume a balanced bridge so that $R_2 = R_1 = R$ and $R_3 = R_4$. Sensitivity can be improved by having two sensors *in situ*, such that the changes in each are opposite (e.g., two strain gauges on opposite sides of a flexing bar). This is known as a *half bridge*. If R_1 and R_2 are two such sensors and $\Delta R_1 = -\Delta R_2$, then the output voltage doubles. The Wheatstone bridge may also be used for differential measurements (e.g., for insensitivity to common changes of two sensors), to improve sensitivity, to remove zero offsets, for temperature compensation, and to perform other signal conditioning.

Specially designed operational amplifier circuits are useful for general signal conditioning [Frank 2000]. Instrumentation amplifiers provide differential input and common mode rejection, impedance matching between sensors and processing devices, calibration, etc. SLEEPMODE amplifiers (Semiconductor Components Ind., LLC) consume minimum power while asleep and activate automatically when the sensor signal exceeds a prescribed threshold.

2.4.2 Digital Signal Processing

Sensor fusion is important in a network of sensors of different modalities. A distributed vehicle/personnel surveillance network might include seismic, acoustic, IR motion, temperature, and magnetic sensors. The standard DSP tool for combining the information from many sensors is the *Kalman Filter* [Lewis 1986, 1992]. The Kalman Filter is used for communications, navigation, feedback control, and elsewhere and provides the accuracy that allowed man to navigate in space, eventually to reach the moon, and more recently to send probes to the limits of the solar system.

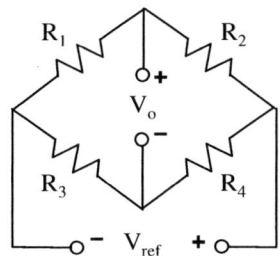

Figure 2.30 Wheatstone bridge.

A properly designed Kalman Filter allows one to observe only a few quantities, or *measured outputs*, and then reconstruct or estimate the full internal state of a system. It also provides low-pass filtering functions and amplification, and can be constructed to provide temperature compensation, common mode rejection, zero offset correction, etc. The *discrete-time Kalman Filter*, useful for DSP using microprocessors, is a dynamic filter given by

$$\hat{x}_{k+1} = A(I - KH)\hat{x}_k + Bu_k + AKz_k$$

where the sensed outputs are in a vector z_k, the control inputs to the system being observed are in vector u_k, and the estimates of the internal states are given by the vector $\hat{x}_k$. Note that the number of sensed outputs can be significantly less than the number of states one can estimate. In this filter, matrices A and B represent the known dynamics of the sensed system, and the sensed outputs are given as a linear combination of the states by $z_k = Hx_k$, where H is a known measurement matrix. The Kalman gain K is determined by solving a design equation known as the *Riccati Equation*. The Kalman Filter is the optimal linear estimator given the known system properties and prescribed corrupting noise statistics.

DSP is the most efficient means of computation in a network of distributed signal-processing nodes. The theory of *decentralized Kalman filtering* provides a formal mechanism for apportioning sensor filtering, reconstruction, and compensation tasks among a hierarchically organized group of nodes.

Other DSP tools include techniques used in spectrum analysis, speech processing, stock market analysis, etc. Statistical methods allow regression analysis, correlation analysis, principal component analysis, and clustering. Also available are a wide range of techniques based on neural network properties of classification, association, generalization, and clustering. Decision-making paradigms include fuzzy logic, Bayesian decision making, Dempster-Shafer, diagnostic/prescription-based schemes as used in the medical field, and so on. The MathWorks software MATLAB has extensive capabilities in all these areas, and specialized toolboxes provide powerful tools for DSP and decision making for distributed wireless sensor networks.

2.4.3 Decision Making and User Interface

Many software products are available to provide advanced DSP, intelligent user interfaces, decision assistance, and alarm functions. Among the most popular, powerful, and easy to use is National Instruments LabVIEW software. Available are toolkits for camera image processing, machinery signal processing and diagnostics, sensor equipment calibration and testing, feedback control, and more. Figure 2.31 shows a LabVIEW user interface for monitoring machinery conditions over the Internet for automated maintenance scheduling functions. Included are displays of sensor signals that can be selected and tailored by the user. The user can prescribe bands of normal operation, excursions outside of which generate alarms of various sorts and severity.

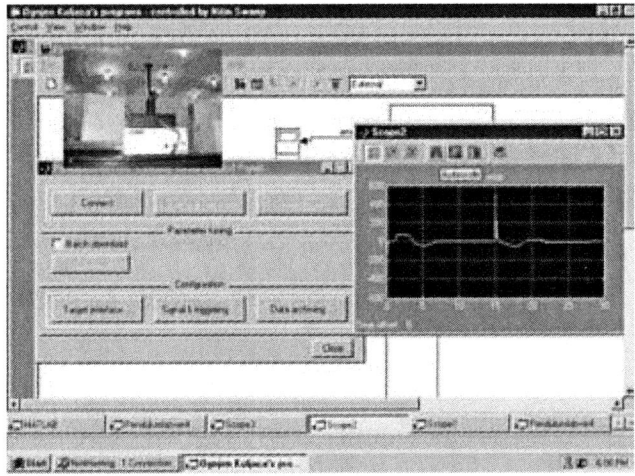

Figure 2.31 LabVIEW user interface for wireless Internet-based remote site monitoring.

2.5 BUILDING AND HOME AUTOMATION

Figure 2.32 shows how networks of various sorts might interact in the smart home environment. An excellent reference for this section is Frank [2000]. There are many available protocols for networking of the smart home, and it is not necessary to develop new protocols on one's own for commercially acceptable systems. The BACnet protocol has been developed by the building automation industry to provide a standard for interconnecting networks for building sensing and control. Networks that can be used include Ethernet, MS/TP, and LonWorks. Building energy management standards are being developed by the American Society of Heating, Refrigeration, and Air-Conditioning Engineers (ASHRAE). A major driver for the smart home is the power distribution industry, which could save

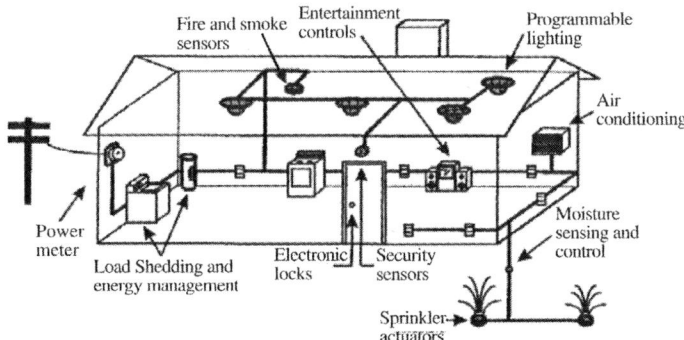

Figure 2.32 Smart home networks. (Reprinted with permission of Artech House, from R. Frank [2000].)

enormous sums with demand-side regulation and automated remote meter reading. The Intelligent Building Institute has been a force in developing appropriate standards.

The *X-10 protocol* is used for lamp and appliance controls. The more recently developed *Smart House Applications Language* (SHAL) includes over 100 message types for specific sensing and control functions. However, SHAL requires dedicated multiconductor wiring. The *Consumer Electronics bus* (CEBus), initiated by the Electronic Industries Association, provides both data and control channels and handles up to 10 Kbps. It is useful for the utility industry.

Several automotive protocols have been developed, some of which are also useful for building control. *CAN* is a serial communications protocol developed for automotive multiplex wiring systems. It has been adopted in industrial applications by manufacturers such as Allen-Bradley (in the DeviceNET system) and Honeywell (in SDS). CAN supports distributed real-time control with a high level of security, and is a multimaster protocol that allows any node in the network to communicate with any other node. Supported are user-defined message prioritization, multiple access/collision resolution, and error detection.

The *LonWorks protocol*, developed by Echelon Corporation (http://www.echelon.com/products/lonworks/default.htm), is very convenient for industrial and consumer applications. It supports all seven layers of the OSI/RM model, as well as fieldbus requirements, arbitration, and message coding. LonWorks operates on a peer-to-peer bus network basis. Devices in a LonWorks network communicate using LonTalk. This language provides a set of services that allow the application program in a device to send and receive messages from other devices over the network without needing to know the topology of the network or the names, addresses, or functions of other devices. The LonWorks protocol can also provide end-to-end acknowledgment of messages, authentication of messages, and priority delivery to provide bounded transaction times. Support for network management services allows remote network management tools to interact with devices over the network, including reconfiguration of network addresses and parameters, downloading of application programs, reporting of network problems, and start/stop/reset of device application programs. LonWorks networks can be implemented over basically any medium, including power lines, twisted pair, RF, IR, coaxial cable, and fiberoptics.

ACKNOWLEDGMENT

This research was supported by ARO Research Grant DAAD 19-02-1-0366 and NSF ITR grant IIS-0326505.

REFERENCES

E. Altman, T. Basar, T. Jimenez, and N. Shimkin, "Competitive routing in networks with polynomial costs," *IEEE Trans. Automat. Control*, vol. 47, no. 1, pp. 92–96, 2002.

REFERENCES

R. Bronson and G. Naadimuthu, *Operations Research*, 2nd ed., Schaum's Outlines, McGraw-Hill, New York, 1997.

N. Bulusu, J. Heidemann, D. Estrin, and T. Tran, "Self-configuring localization systems: design and experimental evaluation," pp. 1–31, *ACM TECS*, special issue on networked embedded computing, Aug. 2002.

J. Cao and F. Zhang, "Optimal configuration in hierarchical network routing," *Proc. Canadian Conf. Elect. and Comp. Eng.*, pp. 249–254, Canada, 1999.

T.-S. Chen, C.-Y. Chang, and J.-P. Sheu, "Efficient path-based multicast in wormhole-routed mesh networks," *J. Sys. Architecture*, vol. 46, pp. 919–930, 2000.

J. Choi, C. Conrad, C. Malakowsky, J. Talent, C.S. Yuan, and R.W. Gracy, "Flavones from *Scutellaria baicalensis* Georgi attenuate apoptosis and protein oxidation in neuronal cell lines," *Biochem. Biophys. Acta*, vol. 1571, pp. 201–210, 2002.

Conway and Heffernan, University of Limerick, 2003; http://wwww.ul.ie/~pei

C.W. de Silva, *Control Sensors and Actuators*, Prentice-Hall, Englewood Cliffs, NJ, 1989.

J. Duato, "A necessary and sufficient condition for deadlock-free routing in cut-through and store-and-forward networks," *IEEE Trans. Parallel and Distrib. Systems*, vol. 7, no. 8, pp. 841–854, Aug. 1996.

R. Frank, *Understanding Smart Sensors*, 2nd ed., Artech House, Inc., Norwood, MA, 2000; www.artechhouse.com

M.R. Garey and D.S. Johnson, *Computers and Intractability: A Guide to the Theory of NP-Completeness*. Freeman, San Francisco, 1979.

IEEE 1451, A Standard Smart Transducer Interface, Sensors Expo, Philadelphia, Oct. 2001; http://ieee1451.nist.gov/Workshop_04Oct01/1451_overview.pdf

R. Jordan and C.A. Abdallah, "Wireless communications and networking: an overview," Report, Electronics and Computer Engineering Department, University of New Mexico, 2002.

E.S. Kolesar, C.P. Brothers, C.P. Howe, et al., "Integrated circuit microsensor for selectively detecting nitrogen dioxide and diisopropyl methylphosphate," *Thin Solid Films*, vol. 220, pp. 30–37, 1992.

G.T.A. Kovacs, *Micromachined Transducers Sourcebook*, McGraw-Hill, Boston, 1998.

P.R. Kumar, "New technological vistas for systems and control: the example of wireless networks," *IEEE Control Systems Mag.*, pp. 24–37, Feb. 2001.

F.L. Lewis, *Optimal Estimation*, Wiley, New York, 1986.

F.L. Lewis, *Applied Optimal Control and Estimation*, Prentice-Hall, Englewood Cliffs, NJ, 1992.

F.L. Lewis, C.T. Abdallah, and D.M Dawson, *Control of Robot Manipulators*, Macmillan, New York, 1993.

F.L. Lewis and V.L. Syrmos, *Optimal Control*, 2nd ed., Wiley, New York, 1995.

K. Liu, M. Fitzgerald, and F.L. Lewis, "Kinematic analysis of a Stewart Platform manipulator," *IEEE Trans. Industrial Electronics*, vol. 40, no. 2, pp. 282–293, 1993.

S.H. Low, F. Paganini, and J.C. Doyle, "Internet congestion control," *IEEE Control Systems Mag.*, pp. 28–43, Feb. 2002.

M. Madou, *Fundamentals of Microfabrication*, CRC Press, Boca Raton, FL, 1997.

PC Tech Guide, 2003; http://pctechguide.com/29network.htm

S. Ray, "An introduction to ultra wide band (impulse) radio," Internal Report, Electronics and Computer Engineering Department, Boston University, Oct. 2001.

D.M. Rudkevich, J. Scheerder, and D.N. Reinhoudt, "Anion recognition by natural receptors," in *Molecular Design and Bioorganic Catalysis*, ed. C.S. Wilcox, pp. 137–162, Kluwer, Boston, 1996.

S. Shah-Heydari and O. Yang, "A tree-based algorithm for protection/restoration in optical mesh networks," *Proc. Canadian Conf. Elect. and Comp. Eng.*, vol. 2, pp. 1169–1174, 2001.

J. Shi and J.P. Fonseka, "Hierarchical self-healing rings," *IEEE/ACM Trans. Networking*, vol. 3, no. 6, pp. 690–697, Dec. 1995.

Smart Transducer Interface Standard, IEEE 1451, *Sensors Expo*, Philadelphia, Oct. 2001.

J.W. Smith, *On Distributed Communications*, Memorandum RM-3578-PR, Rand Corp., 1964; http://www.rand.org/publications/RM/RM3578

C. Smythe, "ISO 8802/5 token ring local area networks," *Elect. and Communic. Eng. J.*, vol. 11, no. 4, pp. 195–207, Aug. 1999.

N. Swamy, *Control Algorithms for Networked Control and Communication Systems*, PhD thesis, Department of Electronics Engineering, The University of Texas at Arlington, Texas, 2003.

CHAPTER 3

Power Line Communication Technologies

HANIPH A. LATCHMAN and ANUJ V. MUNDI
Electrical and Computer Engineering Department
University of Florida

3.1 INTRODUCTION

Internet access and in-house networking are becoming as vital as electricity for many establishment, including houses. Sixty percent of households in the United States connect to the Internet, only 10% of which are connected by broadband Internet services such as digital subscriber line (DSL) and cable [Galli03]. The large number of people still using slow dialup Internet access is largely due to the restricted availability and affordability of conventional broadband Internet services. The broadband Internet market calls for research on new techniques to provide broadband Internet services efficiently and affordably without compromising on the quality of services. Power line communication (PLC) is such an emerging technology that uses "no new wires" and provides networking services using the electrical wiring already deployed extensively throughout the world. This chapter discusses the key attributes of PLC technology and its development to support high data rates, that effectively transforms the power grid into an information highway. A description of the PLC channel characteristics and the modulation schemes used for mitigating noise are provided, and a brief description of various PLC protocols developed over the years is given. This is followed by a summary of the main features of the HomePlug 1.0 PLC home networking protocol, which has been adopted as the de facto in-home PLC standard that provides for internetworking. In addition, the chapter introduces current research on PLC networking to develop a high-speed PLC networking protocol (HomePlug AV) operating at 70–100 Mbps and aimed at supporting high-quality audio and video services in smart environments. This new technology will be well positioned to revolutionize in-home entertainment networking by providing a simple, reliable, and cost-effective solution for smart consumer

---

Smart Environments: Technologies, Protocols, and Applications, edited by D.J. Cook and S.K. Das
ISBN 0-471-54448-5   © 2005 John Wiley & Sons, Inc.

products such as personal video recorders, media centers, high-definition televisions (HDTV), and Internet home appliances [Latchman03]. Broadband Power Line (BPL) system implementation is also discussed as a PLC technology providing "last mile" broadband power line and wireless Internet access.

3.2 PRELIMINARIES ON PLC

PLC involves the use of a power supply grid for communication purposes. The power line network has an extensive infrastructure providing connection pathways to and within nearly every building or any other environment. For this reason, the use of this network for the transmission of information signals in addition to its traditional role as a power supply grid has a wide variety of applications. However, the power line wiring was designed for transmission of electrical power, nominally in the 50–60 Hz range and at most at about 400 Hz; thus, the use of this medium for data transmission at high frequencies presents some technically challenging problems. Furthermore, the power line is one of the most electrically contaminated environments, which makes reliable data communication via this medium extremely difficult. Moreover, the legal restrictions imposed on the use of various frequency bands in the power line spectrum limit the achievable data rates.

Power lines connect the power generation station to a variety of customers dispersed over a wide region. Power is transmitted using varying voltage levels and widely differing power line cables. Power line cable characteristics and the number of crossovers and interconnections play an important role in determining the kind of communication technology that may be used to create a viable communication system.

From a purely electrical power distribution perspective, the electrical current in the power line network is kept as low as possible, because the losses are directly proportional to the square of the current. As the losses in the grid are also proportional to distance, high voltages are used for long-distance transmission, medium voltages are used for intermediate distances, and low voltages are used for transmission over short distances and within the target building or environment. This creates a set of hierarchical voltage levels in the distribution grids. Based on the voltage levels at which they transfer power, power lines can be categorized as follows (see Figure 3.1):

1. High-voltage (HV) lines: These connect electricity generation stations to distribution stations. The voltage levels on these lines are typically on the order of 69 kV and above, and they run over distances of the order of tens of kilometers.
2. Medium-voltage (MV) lines: These connect the distribution stations to pole-mounted transformers. The voltage levels are 2.4 to 35 kV, and they run over distances of the order of a few kilometers.
3. Low-voltage (LV) lines: These connect pole-mounted transformers to individual households. The voltage levels on these lines are up to 600 V, and they run over distances of the order of a few hundred meters.

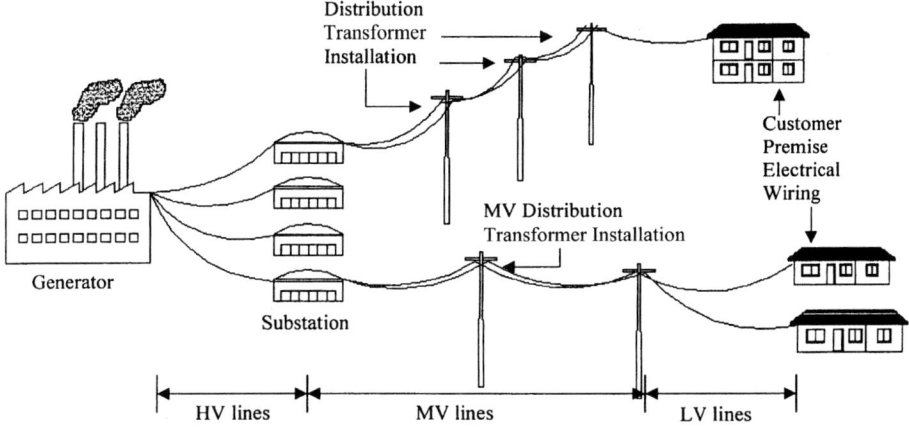

Figure 3.1 Power line distribution grid.

4. Customer premise electrical wires: These are connected to the low-voltage distribution transformer and run throughout the house to every electric outlet present. The voltage level on these wires is 110 or 220 V, and the customer premise may have single or multiple phase supply.

HV lines are excellent carriers for radio frequency (RF) communications signals, as they feature open wires with very few crossovers over quite long distances. An RF transmission power of about 10 watts is often sufficient to cover distances of more than 500 km. In 1922, the first carrier frequency system (CFS) communication system began to operate on high-tension lines in the frequency range of 15–1500 kHz. As in the past, the main purpose of such CFS communication systems was to maintain the operability of the power supply, providing monitoring and control functions.

MV and LV lines are characterized by a large number of cross-connections and different conductor types (e.g., open wire and cable). Long-distance RF signal propagation is extremely poor in such an environment, primarily due to the high attenuation and impedance mismatch. In the 1930's, ripple carrier signaling (RCS) began to be used to provide communication signals over MV and LV lines. RCS used the frequency range below 3 kHz down to 125 Hz with the amplitude shift keying (ASK) modulation technique to achieve a data rate of the order of a few bits per second. Load management and automatic reconfiguration of power distribution networks were among the most important tasks performed by RCS.

3.3 REGULATORY CONSTRAINTS FOR PLC

As mentioned above, in the past utility companies used PLC to maintain the power grid. The utility companies regarded the power distribution wiring as a natural medium for their relatively low data rate communication needs, however, high data rate communications over low-tension lines is now a reality. This development has been fueled by the explosive growth of the Internet, advances in digital signal processing, powerful error correction coding techniques, and very large scale integration (VLSI) of electronic hardware.

Frequencies used by these PLC devices are restricted by the limitations imposed by the regulatory agencies. The Federal Communications Commission (FCC) and the European Committee for Electrotechnical Standardization (CENELEC) govern regulatory rules in North America and Europe, respectively.

In North America, the frequency band from 0 to 500 kHz and a part of the 2 to 30 MHz unlicensed spectrum are used for PLC. However, the regulatory rules in Europe are more stringent. The spectrum is divided into the following five bands based on the regulations:

1. Frequency band from 3 to 9 kHz: The use of this frequency band is limited to energy providers; however, with approval, it may also be used by other parties inside their customers' premises.
2. Frequency band from 9 to 95 kHz: The use of this frequency band is limited to the energy providers and their concession holders. It is often referred as the *A-band*.
3. Frequency band from 95 to 125 kHz: The use of this frequency band is limited to the energy provider's customers; no access protocol is defined. This frequency band is often referred to as the *B-band*.
4. Frequency band from 125 to 140 kHz: The use of this frequency band is limited to the energy provider's customers; in order to make simultaneous operation of several systems within this frequency band possible, a carrier sense multiple access protocol using a center frequency of 132.5 kHz was defined. This frequency band is often referred to as the *C-band*.
5. Frequency band from 140 to 148.5 kHz: The use of this frequency band is limited to the energy provider's customers; no access protocol is defined. This frequency band is often referred to as the *D-band*.
6. Frequency band from 2 to 30 MHz: Efforts are being made in Europe, through CELNEC, to develop a new standard for electromagnetic compatibility for PLC systems in this frequency band. This spectrum is unlicensed by the FCC. HomePlug 1.0 protocol operates in this frequency band.

Apart from band allocation, regulatory bodies also impose limits on the radiation emitted by these devices. These consist of restrictions on the transmitted power in each of these frequency bands. Further information on regulatory constraints for PLC can be obtained in [Gebhardt03]

3.4 POWER LINE CHANNEL CHARACTERISTICS

Power lines were originally devised for transmission of power at 50–60 Hz. At high frequencies, the power line is very hostile to signal propagation. A brief overview of the PLC channel characteristics follows.

3.4.1 Attenuation in the PLC Channel

High-frequency signals can be injected into the power line by using an appropriately designed high-pass filter. Maximum signal power is received only when the impedance of the transmitter, power line, and receiver match. Dedicated communication channels like Ethernet have known impedance; thus, impedance matching is not a problem. However, power line networks usually consist of a variety of conductor types and cross sections joined randomly; therefore, a wide variety of characteristic impedances are encountered in the network. Further, network terminal impedance tends to vary both with communication signal frequencies and with time, depending upon the load pattern at the consumer's premises. This impedance mismatch results in a multipath effect characterized by deep notches associated with destructive interference at certain frequencies. In a typical home environment, the attenuation on a typical power line is 20 to 60 dB and depends heavily on the load. Figure 3.2 shows the attenuation characteristics of a sample PLC channel. Note the deep notches at 11, 13.5, and 15 MHz created by the multipath effect.

3.4.2 Noise in the PLC Channel

The major sources of noise in the PLC channel are electrical appliances that utilize the 60 Hz (North America) or 50 Hz (Europe) electric supply and generate noise components extending well into the high-frequency spectrum as harmonics of the line frequency. Apart from these, induced radio frequency signals from broadcast, commercial, military, citizen band, and amateur stations severely impair certain frequency bands on the PLC channel. Electrical appliances can be divided into three categories based on the nature of the noise they produce in the high-frequency bands. Impulsive noise is produced when electric switches are turned on or off. Periodic impulsive noise, the most common impulse noise, is generated by such sources as triac-controlled light dimmers. These devices introduce noise as they connect the lamp to the AC line partway through each AC cycle. These impulses occur at twice the AC line frequency, as this process is repeated every one-half AC cycle.

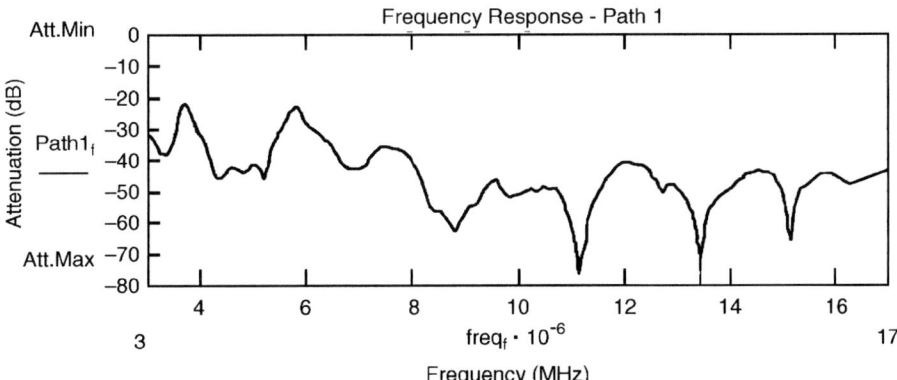

Figure 3.2 Attenuation in the PLC channel [Intellon03].

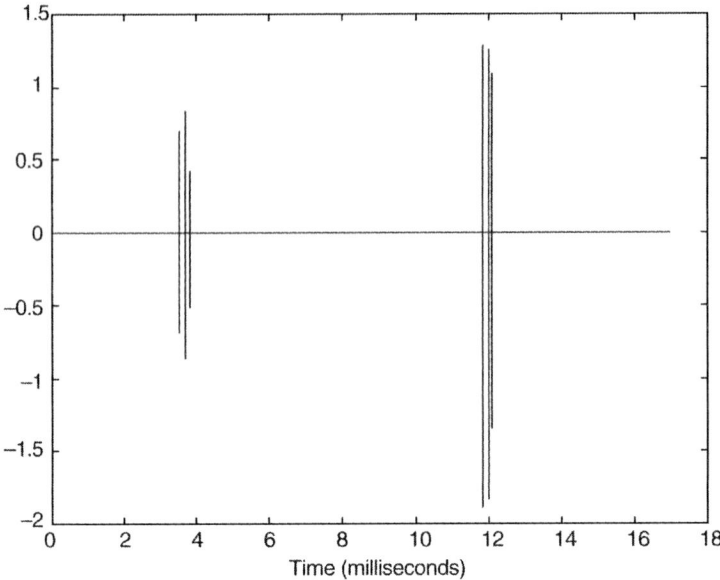

Figure 3.3 Sample of periodic impulsive noise produced by a dimmer [Intellon03].

Figure 3.3 shows the periodic impulsive noise caused by a dimmer on a PLC channel. Continuous impulsive noise is produced by a variety of series-wound AC motors. Such motors are found in electrical appliances like vacuum cleaners, drilling machines, electric shavers, and most of the common kitchen appliances. Commutator arching from these motors produces impulses at repetition rates in the range of several kilohertz. Continuous impulsive noise is the most severe of all the noise sources. Figure 3.4 shows the continuous impulsive noise created by a drill machine. High-bandwidth digital devices communicating on the power line need to use powerful error correction coding along with appropriate modulation techniques to cope with these impairments.

3.4.3 PLC Electromagnetic Compatibility

The use of power lines for communications involves transmission of information modulated on carrier frequencies in the 9 kHz to 30 MHz range. The skin depth effect at these frequencies causes the power lines to radiate high-frequency electromagnetic signals that make them leaky. The placement of any wireless service near PLC systems is bound to be subjected to interference. The interference is directly proportional to the transmission power and the distance between the installation and the power line. This calls for cautious design of filters to prevent the leakage of high-frequency signals. The solution that integrates the 802.11b wireless networking protocol (WiFi) with PLC is a typical case in which mitigating the

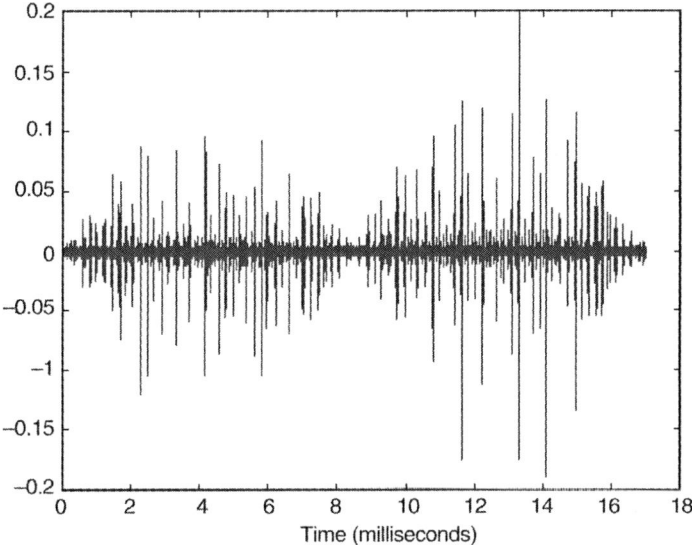

Figure 3.4 Sample of continuous impulsive noise created by an electric drill [Intellon03].

interference plays on important role before deploying the equipment. In the following section we look at the Orthogonal Frequency Division Modulation scheme and its application on the PLC channel.

3.5 OFDM MODULATION

The choice of modulation scheme depends on the nature of the physical medium in which it has to operate. A modulation scheme for use on a power line should have the following properties:

1. *Ability to overcome nonlinear channel characteristics:* The PLC channel has a very nonlinear channel characteristic that requires expensive, complex equalization schemes to attain data rates above 10 Mbps using single-carrier modulation. The modulation technique for use on the PLC channel should have the ability to overcome such nonlinearities without the need for highly involved channel equalization.
2. *Ability to cope with multipath spread:* Impedance mismatch on power lines results in an echo signal, causing a delay spread of the order of 1 ms. The modulation technique for use on the PLC channel should have the ability to handle such delay spreads.
3. *Ability to adjust dynamically:* Power line channel characteristics change dynamically as the load on the power supply varies. The modulation technique for use on the power line should have the ability to track such changes without involving a large overhead or complexity.

4. *Ability to mask certain frequencies:* PLC equipment uses the unlicensed frequency band. However, present and future regulatory rules limit radiation in some subbands or adjacent bands. This makes it highly desirable to have a modulation technique that can selectively mask certain frequency bands. This property would be helpful in the global compatibility and marketability of the PLC product.

A modulation scheme that has all these desirable properties is OFDM. OFDM is generally viewed as a collection of transmission techniques. It is currently used in European Digital Audio Broadcast (DAB) standards. Several DAB systems proposed for North America are based on OFDM. OFDM is also used in some variants of the 802.11x wireless networking protocol. Following are some of the advantages of OFDM [Lee03]:

- Very good at mitigating the effects of time dispersion
- Very good at mitigating the effect of in-band narrowband interference
- High bandwidth efficiency
- Scalable to high data rates
- Flexible and can be adaptive; different modulation schemes for subcarriers, bit loading, adaptable bandwidth/data rates possible
- Excellent (ICI) performance
- Channel equalization not required
- Phase lock of the local oscillators not required

For these reasons, successful PLC protocols such as the HomePlug 1.0 protocol use OFDM. One of the main aspects in the design of OFDM transmission schemes is the selection of the number of carriers and the cyclic prefix length, whose values play an essential role in performance achieved by the system. Their optimum values depend on the channel characteristics [Cañete03]. In the next section, we review some of the PLC protocols that have been proposed and developed. Then we describe the HomePlug 1.0 protocol.

3.6 PLC PROTOCOLS

Various protocols have been developed for low-bandwidth digital devices for communication on the power line. These protocols differ in the modulation technique, channel access mechanism, and frequency band used. Various products based on these protocols are available and are mainly used for home automation and home networking purposes. A brief overview of these protocols follows.

3.6.1 The X-10 Protocol

The X-10 technology is one of the oldest PLC protocols. It uses a form of ASK modulation technique. Although it was originally unidirectional (from controller to controlled modules), recently, some bidirectional products have also been implemented. X-10 controllers send their signals over the power line to simple receivers that are used mainly to control lighting and other appliances. Some controllers available today implement gateways between the power line and other medium such as RF, infrared, (USB), etc.

A 120 kHz amplitude-modulated carrier with a 0.5 watt signal is superimposed on the AC power line at zero crossings to minimize noise interference. Information is coded by bursts of high-frequency signals. To increase reliability, each bit of information is transmitted separately, thus limiting the transmission rate to 60 bits per second, assuming a 60 Hz line frequency. This represents poor bandwidth utilization, and the reliability of transmission is severely compromised in a noisy environment. These are the main reasons why this technology has limited applications.

3.6.2 The CEBus Protocol

The CEBus protocol uses a peer-to-peer communication model. To avoid collisions, a carrier sense multiple access with collision resolution and collision detection (CSMA/CRCD) protocol is used. The physical layer of the CEBus communication protocol is based on spread spectrum technology patented by Intellon Corporation. The CEBus power line carrier sweeps through a range of frequencies as opposed to the traditional spread spectrum techniques that use frequency hopping, time hopping, or direct sequence. A single sweep covers the frequency band from 100 to 400 kHz. This frequency sweep is called a *chirp*. Chirps are used for synchronization, collision resolution, and data transmission. Using this chirp technology, data rates of about 10 kb/s can be obtained. The frequency used by this technology restricts its use to the North American market.

3.6.3 The LonWorks Protocol

LonWorks is a technology developed by Echelon Corporation and provides a peer-to-peer communication protocol, implemented using a Carrier Sensed Multiple Access (CSMA) technique. Unlike CEBus, LonWorks is a narrowband spread spectrum modulation technique using the frequency band from 125 to 140 kHz. It uses a multibit correlator intended to preserve data in the presence of noise with a patented impulse noise cancellation technique. An advantage of narrowband signaling is that it can be used in both North American and European markets.

3.6.4 The HomePlug 1.0 Protocol Specifications

PLC can now be effectively used to achieve Ethernet class networking at the customer's premise over the existing electrical wiring. The electrical wiring is a very versatile networking backbone with an outlet in every room. The desire to use the existing wiring to establish an in-building network environment has led to the introduction of the HomePlug 1.0 protocol in the American market.

To achieve reliable data transmission at 10 mbps over the all-pervasive electrical wiring at the customer's premise requires the mitigation of extremely unpredictable noise. To achieve an acceptable bit error rate, powerful forward error correction (FEC) coding and decoding techniques and automatic repeat request (ARQ) techniques, along with OFDM and an appropriate Cyclic Prefix (CP), were adopted in the physical layer (PHY) and the Medium Access Control (MAC) of the HomePlug 1.0 protocol.

The OFDM with CP used in HomePlug 1.0 essentially splits the available bandwidth into many smaller subchannels. Unusable subcarriers are masked out intelligently, as mandated by the FCC (Part 15 Rules) and by channel conditions, and the best possible modulation and coding methods are applied on the rest of the participating subcarriers. OFDM in HomePlug 1.0 operates in a frequency band of 4.49–20.7 MHz. This band is divided into 128 evenly spaced subcarriers. Of these, 44 subcarriers are extremely noisy and hence are permanently masked. Besides these 44 subcarriers, 8 subcarriers that fall within the usable band are permanently masked to avoid interference with 40, 30, 20, and 17 m ham radio bands (Figure 3.5). This leaves a total of 76 tones to be used in the U.S. market. The applied tone masks are reconfigurable to mask any frequency subcarrier. This adaptive masking feature ensures compatibility in foreign markets. A more advanced technique called *bit loading* in OFDM with CP allows the use of a different modulation and coding scheme for each independent subcarrier, which can further improve the bit error rate. At any given time, the HomePlug 1.0 MAC PHY supports up to 139 distinct data rates, according to the number of usable carriers, modulation methods, and coding rates. The HomePlug 1.0 data rate can vary from 1 to 14 Mbps dynamically [Lin03]. This is possible because every HomePlug 1.0 node performs channel estimation every 5 seconds to adapt to the optimal data rate.

The HomePlug 1.0 MAC is a Carrier Sense Multiple Access/Collision Avoidance (CSMA/CA) protocol. In contrast Ethernet (802.3) has a Carrier Sense Multiple Access/Collision Detect (CSMA/CD) protocol in which all the nodes share the channel on a contention basis. Whenever a collision occurs due to simultaneous transmission of data by two or more nodes, it is detected by the

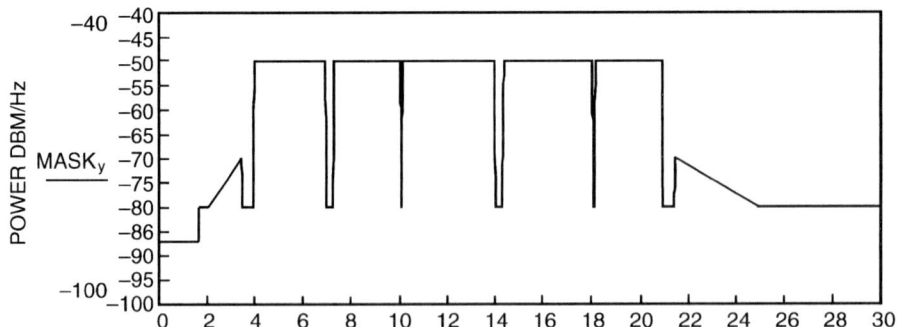

Figure 3.5 Tone map and masked subcarriers in HomePlug 1.0 [Intellon03].

individual node transceivers. Physical carrier sense (PCS) incorporated in the 802.3 PHY detects energy on the channel. A collision is declared upon sensing more energy on the channel than that transmitted by the individual nodes. Upon collision detection, each node uses a binary exponential backoff algorithm by waiting a random amount of time before subsequent transmission. CSMA/CD relies heavily on PCS for detecting collisions and resolving contention issues. This is possible because of the clean Ethernet channel. PCS alone is not reliable in the case of the HomePlug 1.0 MAC. The noisy PLC channel limits the transceiver's ability to differentiate the energy changes in the channel medium resulting from actual collisions as opposed to channel fluctuations and noise events. Hence, HomePlug 1.0 MAC incorporates the CSMA/CA protocol in which collisions are deliberately avoided rather than being detected after they occur. The HomePlug 1.0 PHY layer detects the preamble of the frame, and the MAC layer maintains a virtual carrier sense (VCS) timer. Each frame is preceded by a contention period of short time slots. If a station, using VCS, detects that no other node has started transmitting, it will start transmitting, hence the name *collision avoidance*.

HomePlug 1.0 MAC involves the use of a frame control and a preamble as a start of frame and end of frame delimiter. A tone map is included in the frame control, and this is used by the receiver to decode the following frame. Priority information used for contention resolution is included in the end of the frame delimiter (Figure 3.6).

The response interframe spacing (RIFS) delimiter facilitates the verification of the response to the currently transmitted frame. Compared to 802.11, no short interframe spacing (SIFS) is included in the HomePlug 1.0 MAC. A frame control bit indicates the node's desire to continue transmitting frames.

In order to support QoS, four priority classes are provided by the HomePlug 1.0 MAC: CA3, CA2, CA1, and CA0 in descending order of priority. Appropriate assertion of bits in the PR0 and PR1 slots allows prioritized channel access. If a higher-priority assertion is made by a frame, all lower-priority nodes defer transmission. At times when the same priority class is asserted by two contending frames, the resolution is continued in the contention window. CSMA/CA has a

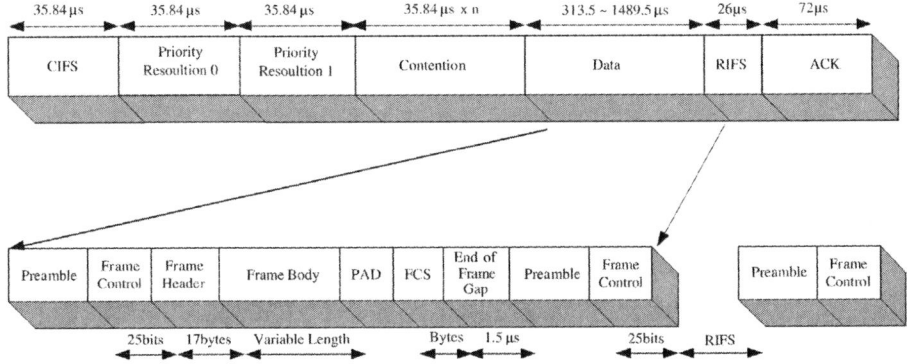

Figure 3.6 HomePlug 1.0 MAC frame structure [Lin03].

priority dependent backoff window size. The lower priority classes, i.e., CA0 and CA1, have a backoff schedule of 8-16-32-64 slots.

The higher-priority classes CA2 and CA3 have an 8-16-16-32 backoff schedule. Collision results in the incrementing of the range of contention slots over which a transmission is started. CIFS stands for *Contention-window Inter-Frame spacing.* In this window the nodes with the same priority assertion contend for the channel by decrementing a counter in the contention window time slots. Upon exhausting the counter, a node transmits a frame and resets its counter. Other contending nodes whose counter has not yet been exhausted continue decrementing the counter in the subsequent contention window. This process is continued until each node gets its slot to transmit. Higher-priority assertion suspends this process, and the frames with higher priorities are transmitted. The theoretical maximum MAC throughput supported by HomePlug 1.0 with a payload of 1500 bytes is 8.08 Mb/s. The standard boasts a PHY data rate of 14 Mb/s. A maximum practical MAC throughput of around 6 Mb/s was recorded during the extensive testing carried out in a home networking scenario by Yu-Ju Lin et al. [Lin03].

3.6.5 Current Research on the Power Line Networking Protocol (HomePlug AV)

A new protocol is currently being developed by the HomePlug alliance. The aim is to achieve data rates of about 100 Mb/s for in-home power line networking. Such a high data rate is desired to facilitate the distribution of data and multimedia including high-definition (HDTV) and stereophonic audio over the PLC network. Rigorous measurements and analysis of the PLC channel demonstrate its ability to support such high data rates. The HomePlug alliance has named this high-speed standard *HomePlug AV*, keeping in mind the audio and video applications associated with it. This new technology is at a stage where it poses a challenge to the conventional wired networking protocols of 100 Mbps Ethernet and creates space for new hybrid power line/wireless networks for future smart homes. In-home entertainment networking will be revolutionized altogether by this nascent technology, as well as by emerging solutions using wireless networks tuned for AV applications. HomePlug AV finds its strength in being simple, reliable, cost-effective, and "plug and play" in a literal and functional sense.

3.7 POWER LINE AND THE LAST MILE BROADBAND INTERNET ACCESS

PLC technology also has the potential to convert the most pervasive infrastructure, the power line distribution grids, into a backbone to offer broadband Internet service to every household and office (Figure 3.7). With over 18 million miles of power lines in the United States alone, the electrical grid is the most ubiquitous network. Offering broadband Internet access through the power line not only opens new business opportunities but also unveils a whole new view of the connected world.

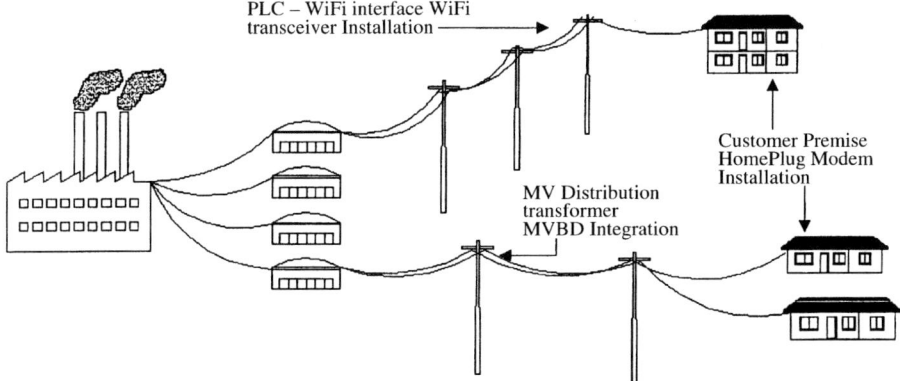

Figure 3.7 Broadband power line Internet access.

Developing countries that are deprived of the infrastructure to support current broadband Internet using technologies such as DSL and cable modems, can benefit from their existing power grid and can offer broadband Internet service even in the most remote locations. With recent advances in voice over Internet protocol (VoIP) services, voice as well as data services can be offered over PLC networks, thus simultaneously providing telephone and Internet access in areas where even basic telephone services do not presently exist.

Currently, the basic HomePlug 1.0 protocol provides a solution for in-home networking, with Internet access still provided via DSL or cable modems. PLC Internet access seeks to extend the PLC channel all the way from the individual sockets within the home to Internet gateways located on the power line grid.

For example, MV power lines can be converted to carry PLC signals. This is possible by introducing a substation bridging device (SBD) between the Internet IP backbone network and the power grid that will make the power grid "live" in the Internet sense. SBD, as the name suggests will bridge the MV substation with multiple MV lines to the IP backbone Internet. MV lines can be further connected to repeater devices. MV bridging devices (MVBD) are then used to provide a data link between the LV and MV lines. Gateway devices (GD) at the customer's premise have a PLC interface, which then connects to all the electrical outlets. In addition to supporting the HomePlug protocols, the GD can support WiFi to enable in-house wireless networking. In this latter case, the PLC is used as the long-haul data link and the connection to the home is via WiFi or PLC.

All the PLC networking devices can support the simple network management protocol (SNMP) and services to enable network monitoring and management. Routers, gateways, high-speed network switches, and other networking devices should be customized to suit the power line distribution grid architecture. As shown in Figure 3.6, the MV lines are stepped down to LV lines at the distribution transformer. The LV lines emanating from this distribution transformer lead to the individual homes and finally to the electrical outlets. The issue to be addressed at the distribution transformer is whether to bypass the stepdown transformer completely or let the signal pass through the transformer to the LV line and to the home, where it is connected to the GD. The advantages of bypassing the transformers are its low costs, ease of installation, and ease of maintenance [Jee03].

Another option is to completely bypass the substation and eliminate the SBD. The PLC network would then be bridged to the IP network backbone at the MV lines through the MVBD. WiFi transceivers can be installed at the LV transformer pole. At the home site, the WiFi can be again bridged with a WiFi-PLC access point; thus, Internet access can be provided to every electrical outlet as well as to WiFi devices. This enables distribution of the broadband communication effectively through WiFi, creating a WiFi hot spot near the transformer site [Amperion03].

In the above solution, the transformer site will host the administration gateway and will employ an SNMP agent to manage the network. To provide home networking using hybrid PLC and WiFi in every corner of the home and every electrical plug, a PLC-WiFi access point or router is installed at the customer's location.*

3.8 SECURITY IN PLC

Like WiFi, the PLC channel is a shared channel. This calls for the implementation of a robust security mechanism to safeguard all the data transmitted over the PLC channel. Numerous techniques can be applied to encrypt the data before putting it on the line. The encryption technique should have a good trade-off between security and complexity. Complex techniques require more computation capacity. Rivest is a candidate encryption algorithm that includes a 128-bit encryption key. The key exchange can be achieved by using the Diffie-Hellman's algorithms [Tannenbaum96]. HomePlug 1.0 implements the Data Encryphen Standards algorithm with 56-bit keys.

Another major security issue pertaining to in-home PLC networks is the possibility of intrusion and interference from adjacent subnetworks. This type of intrusion can be observed at a typical apartment complex where adjacent apartments have their own small home network. As the PLC is a shared medium and HomePlug 1.0 has a contention-based MAC algorithm, every node contends for the channel and collisions are mitigated using a MAC-based on CSMA/CA. On collisions, the packets are retransmitted by the contending nodes. Intrusion increases the number of nodes contending in the subnetwork, thereby reducing the overall throughput of the system. In addition, such adjacent networks increase the probability of multiple levels of hidden nodes, leading to further network performance degradation. A home network implementation that can prevent such an intrusion involves the use of PLC decoupling filters. These filters may be used to isolate each electrical circuit at the meter panel for each household or apartment, thus reducing signal propagation across PLC subnetworks and avoiding unwanted

---

*In contrast to in-building PLC LANS, PLC-Internet Access via LV or MV powerlines may result in interference to shortwave and amateur radio operations.

signal interference. Further, a WiFi or wired router can be connected between the power line at the location where the decoupling filter separates the line physically to achieve a logical connection between the separated power lines, if desired. Because there is no signal transfer on the power line due to isolation, the router is the only path for the data packets to travel around the decoupling filter. The advantage of a wireless router is that wireless devices using 802.11x standards would also be supported, thus providing wired (no new wires) and wireless connectivity to the apartment. In the future, the connectivities provided by power-line and wireless devices will complement each other, providing ubiquitous networking.

3.9 SUMMARY

PLC technologies have tremendous potential for growth in providing a networking infrastructure to support smart environments such as the smart home. Many companies across Europe, North America, South East Asia, Japan, and elsewhere are identifying this potential and investing in improving the technology. Research is being conducted to improve PLC channel utilization and make the PLC networks faster, more robust, and more reliable. Due to the low cost of installation of PLC equipment modules in the existing power grid infrastructure, PLC technology is cost-effective, as opposed to cable or public switched telephone technology. Smart homes of the future will have various internetworking devices and home appliances such as Internet-enabled refrigerators, an integrated home security system, home computers, game stations, HDTVs, and other multimedia systems. These systems may interconnect with each other using different interconnect protocols like Infra Red Data Access (IRDA), Bluetooth, WiFi, Firewire, etc. PLC networking can provide a robust, high-speed backbone network to such devices to achieve seamless connectivity.

With further improvement in security for PLC networks, enhancement of signal conditioning to mitigate interference and noise, and maturation of PLC product development and deployment, PLC promises to be a cost-effective networking technology for future smart environments.

REFERENCES

[Amperion03] Amperion.com homepage as of October 20, 2003: http://www.amperion.com

[Cañete03] F.J. Cañete, J.A. Cortés, L. Díez, J.T. Entrambasaguas, "Modeling and Evaluation of the Indoor Power Line Transmission Medium." *IEEE Communications Magazine*, April 2003.

[Dai03] H. Dai, H. Vincent Poor, "Advanced Signal Processing for Power Line Communications." *IEEE Communications Magazine*, May 2003.

[Galli03] S. Galli, A. Scaglione, K. Dostert, "Broadband Is Power: Internet Access Through the Power Line Network." *IEEE Communications Magazine*, May 2003.

[Gebhardt03] M. Gebhardt, F. Weinmann, K. Dostert, "Physical and Regulatory Constraints for Communication Over the Power Supply Grid." *IEEE Communications Magazine*, May 2003.

[Homeplug03] HomePlug alliance homepage as of October 20, 2003: http://www.homeplug.org

[Intellon03] Intellon Corporation homepage as of October 20, 2003: http://www.intellon.com

[Jee03] G. Jee, R.D. Rao, Y. Cern, "Demonstration of the Technical Viability of PLC Systems on Medium- and Low-Voltage Lines in the United States." *IEEE Communications Magazine*, May 2003.

[Katar00] S. Katar, "Analysis of Tone Allocated Multiple Access Protocol." Masters thesis, University of Florida, 2000.

[Latchman03] H.A. Latchman, L.W. Yonge, "Power Line Local Area Networking." *IEEE Communications Magazine*, April 2003.

[Lee03] M.K. Lee, R.E. Newman, H.A. Latchnman, S. Katar, L. Yonge "HomePlug 1.0 Power Line Communication LANs—Protocol Description and Performance Results." *International Journal of Communication Systems*, 2003.

[Lin03] Y.-J. Lin, H.A. Latchman, R.E. Newman, S. Katar, "A Comparative Performance Study of Wireless and Power Line Networks." *IEEE Communications Magazine*, April 2003.

[Liu03] W. Liu, H. Widmer, P. Raffin, "Broadband PLC Access Systems and Field Deployment in European Power Line Networks." *IEEE Communications Magazine*, May 2003.

[Tannenbaum96] A.S. Tannenbaum, *Computer Networks*, 3rd ed., Prentice-Hall, 1996.

CHAPTER 4

Wireless Communications and Pervasive Technology

MARCO CONTI

Istituto di Informatica e Telematica
Pisa, Italy

4.1 INTRODUCTION

The 1990s were the *mobile computing age*. The proliferation of mobile computing devices [e.g., laptops, handheld digital devices, personal digital assistants (PDAs)] produced a revolution in the computing model. Individuals use, at the same time, several electronic platforms through which they can access all the information they require whenever and wherever needed. Mobile users can use their cellular phone to check e-mail and browse the Internet; travelers with portable computers can surf the Internet from airports, railway stations, and other public locations; tourists can use Global Positioning System (GPS) terminals installed in rental cars to locate driving maps and tourist attractions; researchers can exchange files and other information by connecting portable computers via wireless local area networks (LANs) while attending conferences; at home, users can synchronize data and transfer files between portable devices and desktops.

A decade of hardware and software development (PDAs, wearable computers, wireless networks, devices for sensing and remote control) provided the basic elements for progressing from the mobile to the *ubiquitous computing age* [Weiser 1991], now also called the *pervasive computing age* [Satyanarayanan 2002]. According to Mark Weiser, the environment is saturated with computing and communication capabilities that are hidden, designed to help users in everyday life without requiring any major change in their behavior. In this environment, virtually everything (from key chains to computers and PDAs) is connected to the network, and can originate and respond to appropriate communications. We can envision a physical world with pervasive, sensor-rich, network-interconnected devices embedded in the environment [Estrin et al. 2002]. The nature of ubiquitous devices makes wireless

---

Smart Environments: Technologies, Protocols, and Applications, edited by D.J. Cook and S.K. Das
ISBN 0-471-54448-5   © 2005 John Wiley & Sons, Inc.

networks the easiest solution for their interconnection. Furthermore, mobility is a fundamental part of everyday life. Hence, wireless and mobile communications are fundamental building blocks of smart computing environments. In these scenarios, connectivity is currently provided by wireless LANs (e.g., the 802.11 WLAN standard) or somewhat smaller, less expensive Bluetooth devices. However, to provide network connectivity to all consumer electronics devices, Bluetooth and 802.11 are not adequate. There is a need for cheaper, simpler, lighter, and lower-power technologies. These solutions should be able to support low bit rates (e.g., less than 100 kbps), short ranges (a few meters), and low power requirements; above all, they must be extremely inexpensive. The IEEE 802.15.4 specification is one of the most promising solutions for short-range, low data rate (<250 kbps) personal area networking (PAN). Specifically, 802.15.4 is designed to address wireless networking requirements for industrial control, home automation and control, and inventory management, as well as wireless sensor networks [Callaway et al. 2002].

Ambient intelligence represents the long-term (2010 and beyond) evolution of the ubiquitous computing concept [Ahola 2001]. In this vision, the world around us (homes, offices, cars, and cities) is organized as a pervasive network of intelligent devices that will cooperatively gather, process, and transport information. A virtual world (cyberworld) filled with avatars and cymans (our synthetic counterparts in the cyberworld) will be superimposed on the real world to provide a natural, enhanced living environment [Davide et al. 2002]. In the cyberworld, users' avatars will stay in touch with other synthetic agents to obtain services and perform transactions. Virtual immersive communications will constitute the basis for bridging the real and virtual worlds. In this environment, cheap, low-rate data communications will coexist with ultra-high-speed multimedia communications required to support, in the most natural way, the interactions between real users and avatars. The IEEE 802.15.3 task group has already defined a draft standard for high-speed wireless PANs (up to 55 Mbps). However, 802.15.3 data rates are not sufficient to support demanding multimedia applications. For this reason, a new task group, 802.15.3a, has been created to specify short-range, very-high-speed (100 Mbps or more) wireless solutions for the last mile. The Ultra wideband (UWB) communication technique is currently the best candidate technology for 802.15.3a ([Porcino et al. 2003] and [UCAN]).

In this chapter, we analyze the status of wireless communications and discuss their evolution with respect to the requirements for pervasive computing environments. The chapter is organized as follows: In Section 4.2 we discuss wireless networking for pervasive communications, and in Section 4.3 we introduce existing and emerging technologies for body, personal, and local wireless communications. In Sections 4.4 and 4.5 we present the 802.11 and 802.15 standard families, respectively. In Section 4.6 we draw our conclusions.

4.2 WIRELESS NETWORKS AND SMART SPACES

The evolution of pervasive computing is tightly coupled with 4G wireless and mobile communications. A 4G network is envisioned as a global network integrating heterogeneous wireless networks with varying transmission characteristics such as

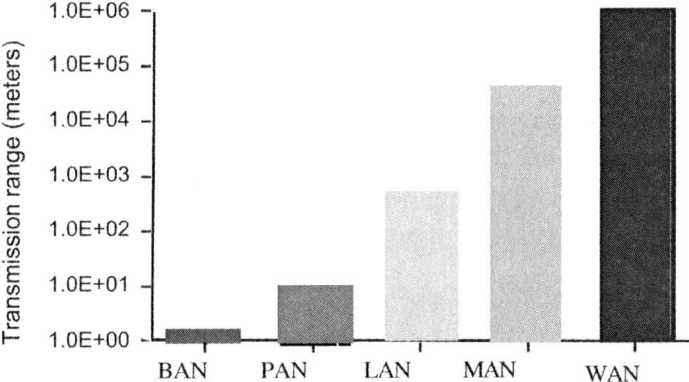

Figure 4.1 Networks taxonomy.

public cellular networks and private wireless LANs, as well as mobile ad hoc networks [Chlamtac et al. 2003]. In detail, as shown in Figure 4.1, we can classify future wireless networks, depending on their coverage area, into five main classes: body (BAN), personal (PAN), local (LAN), metropolitan (MAN), and wide area networks (WAN).

The first step in the pervasive computing age is the development of smart spaces. A smart space may be an enclosed area, such as a meeting room or corridor, or an open, well-defined area such as a courtyard [Satyanarayanan 2001]. BAN, PAN, and LAN wireless networks constitute the natural solution for supporting user-environment interactions in a smart space. For this reason, in this chapter we will focus on technologies for implementing these wireless networks. MAN and WAN are typically public networks used by service providers to implement wireless access services on a metropolitan or national scale. For this reason, they are not first-choice technologies for implementing smart environments.[1] Eventually, they can be used for interconnection of smart spaces if fixed networks are not available.

Inside a smart space, wireless sensor networks have a special role. A sensor network is composed of a large number of small sensor nodes, which are typically densely (and randomly) deployed inside the area in which a phenomenon is being monitored. Wireless networking techniques also constitute the basis for sensor networks. However, the special constraints imposed by the unique characteristics of sensing devices, and by the application requirements, make many of the solutions designed for wireless networks (generally) not suitable for sensor networks [Akyildiz et al. 2002]. This places extensive literature dedicated to sensor networks, which would require an entire chapter devoted to this topic. In this chapter, we will not specifically address wireless sensor networks. However, it is worth pointing out that one purpose of the IEEE 802.15.4 specification is to provide an effective solution for wireless sensor networks.

---

[1] In a second phase, wireless MANs (WMANs) can be used to construct large smart spaces covering a city.

4.2.1 WLAN, WPAN, and WBAN

Like a wired LAN, a WLAN has a communication range typical of a single building or a cluster of buildings, i.e., 100–500 m. A WLAN should satisfy the same requirements as any LAN, including high capacity, full connectivity among attached stations, and broadcast capability. However, to meet these objectives, WLANs must be designed to deal with issues specific to the wireless environment, like security on the air, power consumption, mobility, and bandwidth limitation of the air interface [Stallings 1996].

WLAN products consume too much power and have an excessive range for many personal consumer electronic and computer devices ([Stemm et al. 1997] and [Estrin et al. 2002]). This generates a strong push for a new class of networks: the *personal area network* (PAN). The communication range of a PAN is typically up to 10 m, enabling proximal devices to share information dynamically with minimum power consumption [Zimmerman 1999]. Wireless communications constitute the basis for PANs. Wireless PANs (WPANs) offer a wide space for innovative pervasive applications. For example, let us imagine a PDA (with a PAN interface) that, on arrival at a place (e.g., home, office, airport), automatically synchronizes (via the PAN network interface) with all the electronic devices in its 10-m range.

LANs and PANs do not meet all the networking requirements of ubiquitous computing. There are situations in which carrying and holding a computer is not practical, e.g., working on an assembly line. A wearable computer solves these problems by distributing computer components (e.g., head-mounted displays, microphones, earphones, processors, and mass storage) on the body ([Ditlea 2000] and [Zimmerman 1999]). A network with the transmission range of a human body, i.e., a *body area network* (BAN) is the best solution for connecting wearable devices. The concept of a wearable computer is not new. However, most of the required technologies were not mature enough for its successful deployment. Network technologies have been one of the main obstacles to wearable computing, as wiring a body is generally cumbersome.[2] To cope with this problem, fancy but less practical solutions have been proposed. Among these is the BAN prototype developed by T.G. Zimmerman [Zimmerman 1996]. Zimmerman's system provides data communications (with rates of up to 400,000 bits/s) by exploiting the body as the channel.[3] Recent advances in short-range, low-power wireless connectivity provide the basis for elegant and efficient solution for BANs.

To summarize, wireless LAN, PAN, and BAN networks (WLAN, WPAN and WBAN in the following discussion) provide elegant and effective solutions for communications in pervasive computing environments. However, the characteristics of

---

[2] For example, see the BAN prototype developed in the framework of the MIThril project, where a wired Ethernet network was adopted to interconnect wearable devices [MIT].

[3] Zimmerman showed that data can be transferred through the skin by exploiting a very small current (one-billionth of an amp). Data transfer between two persons (i.e., BANs interconnection) is achieved through a simple handshake.

the wireless medium and the constraints of mobile devices make the design of such networks fundamentally different from that of their wired counterparts. Specifically, the following characteristics introduce big challenges in the design and operations of these networks:

- The wireless medium has neither absolute nor readily observable boundaries outside of which stations are known to be unable to receive network frames.
- The channel is unprotected from outside signals, and interference results in low reliability.
- The wireless medium is significantly less reliable than wired media.
- The channel has time-varying and asymmetric propagation properties.
- The transmission resources are limited, since the spectrum is scarce and expensive.
- Security is weak because radio interface is accessible to everyone; network security is more difficult to implement, as attackers can interface more easily.

In addition, in wireless networks that rely on a carrier-sensing random access protocol, such as the IEEE 802.11, complex phenomena such as the hidden-station and exposed-station problems[4] may occur. These phenomena occur more frequently in the infrastructure-less networks, but the hidden-station phenomenon may be critical in infrastructure networks, too. The hidden-station problem occurs when two (or more) stations cannot detect each other's transmissions (due to being outside of each other's transmission range) but their transmission ranges are not disjoint [Tobagi et al. 1975]. The exposed-station problem results from situations in which a permissible transmission from a mobile station (sender) to another station has to be delayed due to the irrelevant transmission activity between two other mobile stations within the sender's transmission range. For more details see [Chlamtac et al. 2003] and [Anastasi et al. 2004].

4.3 TECHNOLOGIES FOR WIRELESS BAN, PAN AND LAN

The success of a network technology is connected to the development of networking products at a competitive price. A major factor in achieving this goal is the availability of appropriate networking standards [Marks et al. 2002].

The IEEE 802 committees, starting in the 1980s, specified the reference standards for connectivity in distributed computing environment. Specifically, IEEE 802 specifies standards for the *Physical* (PHY) layer and the *Medium Access Control* (MAC) layer for both wired and wireless LANs and MANs. Currently, the IEEE 802 committees are developing standard specifications that constitute the basis for

---

[4]Hereafter, the terms *hidden terminal* and *exposed terminal* will be used interchangeably with the terms *hidden station* and *exposed station*, respectively.

wireless communications in pervasive computing environments. These standards include:

- the IEEE 802.11 standards for WLANs [802.11] that support wireless connectivity within the home, office buildings, and prespecified locations in airports, campuses, hotels, etc.
- the IEEE 802.15 standards for WPANs [802.15] for short-range wireless communications among computers, peripherals, and (wearable) consumer electronic devices. These standards provide suitable solutions for both WPANs and WBANs.
- the IEEE 802.16 standards for broadband WMAN [802.16]. This body is concerned with fixed broadband wireless access systems, also known as *last mile* access networks.

Below, we present and discuss the solutions emerging in the 802.11 and 802.15 standardization groups; the analysis of WMAN standards is beyond the scope of this chapter. The 802.11 technology is more mature than the 802.15 technology; hence, we will dedicate more space to this technology.

Two different approaches can be followed in the implementation of a WLAN and a WPAN: infrastructure-based and infrastructure-less (also referred to as *ad hoc mode* or *peer-to-peer*).

4.3.1 Infrastructure-Based Networks

An infrastructure-based architecture requires a centralized controller for each cell, often referred to as an *access point* (AP) or *base station*. The AP controls all the communications within its transmission range, i.e., its *service area*. All mobile devices inside the service area can communicate directly with the AP, while communications among mobile devices must go through the AP. The AP is normally connected to the wired network, thus providing Internet access to mobile devices as well. Infrastructure-based is the mode commonly used to construct the so-called Wi-Fi hot spots, i.e., to provide wireless access to the Internet ([Kaczman 2002] and [Varshney 2003]).

4.3.2 Infrastructure-less Wireless Networks

Currently, most of the connections among wireless devices are achieved via fixed infrastructure-based service provider or private networks. The drawbacks of an infrastructure-based WLAN are the costs and time associated with purchasing and installing the infrastructure. These costs may not be acceptable for dynamic environments where people and/or vehicles need to be interconnected temporarily in areas without a preexisting communication infrastructure (e.g., intervehicular and disaster networks) or where the cost of the infrastructure is not justified (e.g., in-building networks, specific residential community networks, etc.). In these cases, the infrastructure-less or ad hoc networks are a more efficient solution. An ad hoc network is a peer-to-peer network formed by a set of stations within the range of each other that dynamically configure themselves to set up a temporary network; no fixed controller (AP) is required. The wireless networks ad hoc mode is the basis for a new networking paradigm, often referred to as *Mobile Ad hoc NETwork* (MANET), in which the users' mobile devices are the network, and they must cooperatively provide the functionality that is usually provided by the network infrastructure, e.g., routers, switches, and servers [Chlamtac et al. 2003]. Even though large-scale multi-hop ad hoc networks will not be available in the near future, smaller-scale mobile ad hoc networks are starting to appear, extending the range of WLANs over multiple radio hops. Most of the existing multi-hop ad hoc networks have been developed in the academic environment, but recently even commercial solutions have been proposed (see, e.g., MeshNetworks[5] and SPANworks[6]).

In a pure ad hoc networking environment, the users' mobile devices *are* the network. This approach requires a high density of users to guarantee the packets moving between the sender and the receiver. When the users' density is low, networking may become unfeasible. Apart from being a solution for pure ad hoc networking, the wireless-network ad hoc mode is also an important building block for solving the first mile problem in hot spots instead of using a large number of uniform, closely spaced APs. Multi-hop wireless networks can be used to increase the APs' coverage area by providing access to the wired backbone via multiple wireless hops ([Acharya et al. 2002] and [Chlamtac et al. 2003]).

4.4 IEEE 802.11 STANDARDS

The IEEE 802.11 working group is responsible for wireless local area network (WLAN) standards to provide connectivity in homes, factories, and hot spots. In 1997, the IEEE adopted the first wireless LAN standard, named IEEE 802.11, with data rates of up to 2 Mbps [Std802.11]. Since then, several task groups (designated by the letters a, b, c, etc.) have worked to extend the IEEE 802.11 standard. Task groups a, b, and g provided relevant extensions to the original standard [802.11], which are also known as *Wireless Fidelity* (WiFi). The 802.11b task group produced a standard for WLAN operations in the 2.4 GHz band, with data rates of up to 11 Mbps [Std802.11b]. This standard, published in 1999, has been very successful. In the same period, the 802.11a task group specified a standard for WLAN operations in the 5 GHz band, with data rates of up to 54 Mbps [Std802.11a]. Finally, the 802.11g task group has just completed a specification for a higher-speed extension of the 802.11b [Std802.11g]. Table 4.1 summarizes the current status of the IEEE 802.11 standards family and the relationships among the standards. As it clearly shows, 802.11, 802.11b, and 802.11g are all operating in the 2.4 GHz band, enabling some forms of backward compatibility. On the

---

[5]http://www.meshnetworks.com
[6]http://www.spanworks.com

TABLE 4.1 Comparison of 802.11 Standards

Standard	Spectrum	Transmission Technique	Maximum Rate	Compatible With:
802.11		FHSS/DSSS[7]	2 Mbps	—
802.11b	2.4 GHz	DSSS	11 Mbps	802.11
802.11g		OFDM	54 Mbps	802.11, 802.11b
802.11a	5 GHz	OFDM	54 Mbps	—

other hand, 802.11a operates in a completely different portion of the spectrum, and it cannot interoperate with the other standards.

Hereafter, we will provide an overview of the state of the art of the IEEE 802.11 standard family by focusing on the original 802.11 standard and its enhancements (a, b, and g). Special attention will be devoted to IEEE 802.11b, which is currently the reference technology for wireless networking. We will also discuss the performance and current limitations of this technology. In addition, we will present the activities of 802.11e task group, which has attempted to enhance the MAC with quality of service (QoS) features to support voice and video over 802.11 networks.

Several other task groups are currently active in the 802.11 working group to solve technical and regulatory problems in order to promote worldwide use of 802.11 technology [Varshney 2003]. For example, the 802.11h task group is working to comply with European regulations for 5 GHz WLANs, while the 802.11d task group is developing an auto-configuration protocol through which an 802.11 device can receive the regulatory information related to the country in which it is operating.

The current activities of the 802.11i task group deserve special attention. This task group is working to improve 802.11 security. Wireless communications obviously involve potential security issues, since an intruder does not need physical access to the traditional wired network to gain access to data communications. The IEEE 802.11 working group addressed security issues by defining an optional extension to 802.11: the Wired Equivalent Privacy (WEP). WEP is a form of encryption that should provide privacy comparable to that of a traditional wired network. If the wireless network has information that should be secure, WEP should be used. WEP supports both data encryption and integrity. The security is based on a 40-bit secret key. The secret key can either be a default key shared by all the devices of a WLAN or a pairwise secret key shared only by two communicating devices. Since WEP does not provide support for the exchange of secret keys, the key must be manually installed on each device. Cryptographers have identified many flaws and weaknesses in WEP; see, e.g., [Gast 2002 and Michiardi et al. 2004]. These studies pointed out that WEP is useful to prevent casual traffic capture only. To address these security issues, the 802.11i task group has been set up. It will apply to 802.11 physical standards a, b, and g by providing new encryption methods and authentication procedures. IEEE 802.1x forms a key part of 802.11i. 802.1x is based on the IETF Extensible Authentication Protocol (EAP) [RFC2284].

---

[7] As explained hereafter, 802.11 also specifies an infrared-based PHY.

4.4.1 Architecture

The IEEE 802.11 original standard, and standards developed by task groups a, b, and g, use the same CSMA/CA MAC protocol, while the physical layers depends on the standard version. For this reason, we present the 802.11 MAC in the section devoted to 802.11 specifications. PHY standards will be discussed separately.

An IEEE 802.11 WLAN can be implemented with the infrastructure-based or ad hoc paradigm. In the IEEE 802.11 standards' family, infrastructure-based and ad hoc networks are named *Basic Service Set* (BSS) and *Independent Basic Service Set* (IBSS), respectively.

In a BSS the AP periodically sends beacon frames to announce the existence of an 802.11 network. The beacon frames contain the BSS parameters (e.g., clock synchronization) and are used to implement functions within the BSS (e.g., power management). Mobile devices can join an 802.11 network by using the information contained in the beacon.

An IBSS enables two or more IEEE 802.11 stations to communicate directly without requiring the intervention of a centralized AP. Due to the flexibility of the CSMA/CA algorithm, synchronization (to a common clock) of the stations belonging to an IBSS is sufficient to receive or transmit data correctly [Anastasi et al. 2004]. In IBBSs, no centralized controller exists and beacon frames, which contain timing information, are managed through a distributed process. All stations in an IBSS schedule the transmission of a beacon frame at a random time just after the target time identified by the beacon interval. After the first successful transmission of the beacon, all the other transmissions are cancelled.

Currently, the widespread use of IEEE 802.11 cards makes this technology the most interesting off-the-shelf enabler for ad hoc networks [Zaruba et al. 2004]. However, 802.11 standardization efforts concentrated on solutions for infrastructure-based WLANs, while little or no attention was given to the ad hoc mode. This generated extensive investigations of the performance of the 802.11 standards (mainly 802.11 and 802.11b) in the ad hoc environment and proposed solutions to fix 802.11 problems when this standard operates in ad hoc mode. Most of the problems are due to the interaction of wireless channel characteristics (e.g., hidden- and exposed-station problems), the 802.11 MAC protocol (mainly the back-off scheme), and TCP mechanisms (congestion control and time-out). Discussion of these issues is beyond the scope of this chapter. The interested reader can found a survey of MANET technologies in [Chlamtac et al. 2003], while [Anastasi et al. 2004] present a detailed analysis of the problems and solutions in 802.11-based MANETs. Hereafter, if not explicitly stated, we will assume reference to IEEE 802.11 infrastructure-based networks.

4.4.2 IEEE 802.11 Specification

The IEEE 802.11 standard specifies a MAC layer and three PHY layers for WLANs. The 802.11 PHY layer specifications include an infrared, 1–2 Mbps frequency hopping spread spectrum (FHSS) and a 1–2 Mbps direct sequence spread spectrum (DSSS). FHSS and DSSS operate in the 2.4 GHz band. The infrared PHY uses near-visible light in the 850–950 nm range to transmit data at 1 and optionally at 2 Mbps. Hereafter, we concentrate on DSSS PHY; the others PHYs have been abandoned in the 802.11 enhanced versions.

4.4.2.1 DSSS PHY Layer The DSSS PHY operates in the 2.4–2.4835 GHz domain, which is subdivided into a set of 14 overlapping channels (see Table 64 in [Std802.11]). The channels' center frequencies are spaced of 5 MHz starting from the 2.412 GHz of Channel 1. Within a channel, most energy is spread across a 22 MHz band; hence, in a network topology with overlapping cells, the channels must be at a distance of 25 MHz (or greater) to operate without interference.[8] Regulatory bodies in each country specify the channels in which the DSSS PHY can operate, e.g., Channels 1 to 11 in the United States and Channels 1 to 13 in Europe, except for Spain and France. This means that in the United States and Europe, we can have up to three noninterfering base stations in the same area using, for example, Channels 1, 6 and 11.

The 802.11 DSSS standard uses the Barker sequence to spread data over the air. The Barker sequence is an 11-bit chipping sequence that is used to code a single data bit (1 or 0) in a symbol to be transmitted. The symbols are transmitted at a rate of 1 million symbols per second (MSps) by using two modulation techniques: Differential Binary Phase Shift Keying (DBPSK) and Differential Quadrature Phase Shift Keying (DQPSK). DBPSK represents one bit per symbol transmitted, resulting in a 1 Mbps transmission. DQPSK doubles the data rate by using four phases instead of two to modulate the phase of the signal.

The 802.11 DSSS PHY layer adds to MAC frames before transmission a preamble and a header. The preamble synchronizes the transmitter and the receivers, while the header contains the values of PHY parameters, e.g., the transmission rate of the MAC frame. The preamble and the PHY header are always transmitted at 1 Mbps so that all stations can read it, while the data field (MAC frame) is transmitted at 1 or 2 Mbps, as specified in the header.

In the 802.11 DSSS PHY, the duration of the preamble and the PHY header is 144 and 48 µs, respectively. In addition, the duration of the slot time is 20 µs and that of the SIFS is 10 µs.

4.4.2.2 MAC Layer The MAC layer provides its users both contention-based and contention-free access. The basic access method in the IEEE 802.11 MAC protocol is the *Distributed Coordination Function* (DCF), which is a contention-based CSMA/CA MAC protocol. The DCF mechanism has been extensively surveyed in the literature; hence, we present only a brief summary to introduce the relevant terminology. The interested reader can found detailed presentations in [Conti 2003a] and [Anastasi et al. 2004].

The DCF access method, hereafter referred to as *Basic Access*, is summarized in Figure 4.2. A station, before transmitting, listens (*carrier senses*) to the channel to

---

[8]The standard [Std802.11] indicates a 30 MHz distance among the center of the frequencies, i.e., a distance of 6-channel distance.

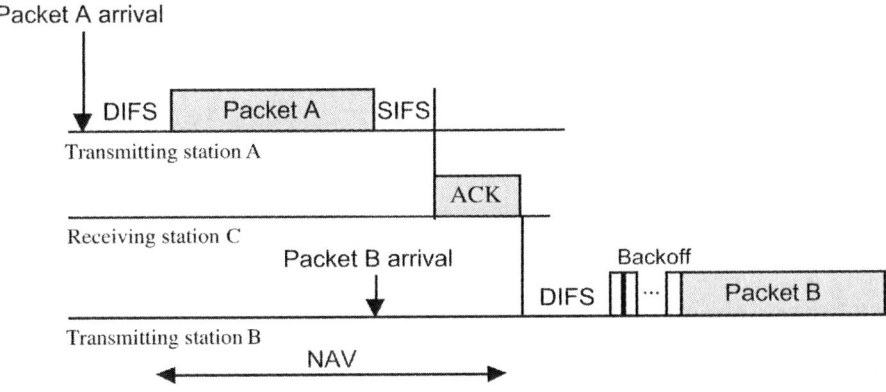

Figure 4.2 DCF basic operations.

determine whether another station is already transmitting. If the medium is found to be idle for an interval exceeding the *Distributed Inter Frame Space* (DIFS), the station (Station A in the figure) starts its transmission. Otherwise (i.e., the medium is busy), the transmission is deferred until the ongoing transmission terminates, and then the Collision Avoidance mechanism is applied (see Station B in Figure 4.2). The IEEE 802.11 Collision Avoidance mechanism uses the *Binary Exponential Backoff* scheme ([Std802.11] and [Conti 2003a]) to guarantee a time spreading of the transmissions, thus reducing the probability of collision.

Since more than one station can start transmitting at the same time, collisions may occur. DCF does not rely on the ability of the stations to detect a collision by hearing their own transmissions. Hence, immediate positive acknowledgments are employed to ascertain the successful reception of each packet transmission. Specifically, after reception of the data frame, the receiver waits for a time interval, named the *Short Inter Frame Space* (SIFS), which is less than the DIFS, and then initiates the transmission of an acknowledgment (ACK) frame. If an acknowledgment is not received, the transmitting station waits up to an *Extended Inter Frame Space* (EIFS) channel idle period (EIFS > DIFS), and then a new transmission is attempted according to the Collision Avoidance mechanism.

In addition to the DCF, the IEEE 802.11 incorporates an alternative access method known as the *Point Coordination Function* (PCF), which is implemented by exploiting the DCF mechanisms. The PCF operates similarly to a polling system: a point coordinator provides (through a polling mechanism) the transmission rights at a single station at time. The PCF guarantees frame transmissions in a contention-free way. To determine which station can transmit, the PCF uses a centralized coordinator, the *Point Coordinator* (PC), which can be used only in infrastructure networks. The PC is usually implemented in the AP. Stations that use PCF are recorded in a list managed by the PC, which, through polling techniques, guarantees these stations contention-free access to the channel. In an IEEE 802.11 WLAN, periods under the DCF functionality can be interleaved to periods in which control is entrusted to the PCF modality. Every contention-free period begins with the transmission of a beacon frame (by the PC) whose main purpose is stations' synchronization. The beacon transmission has higher priority than data transmission. This is obtained by adopting for the beacon transmission an Inter Frame Space, named *PIFS*, which is shorter than the DIFS. For more details see [Std802.11] and [Bruno et al. 2002a].

Although PCF has been designed to support time-bounded multimedia applications (see, e.g., [Coutras et al. 2000] and [Veeraraghavan et al. 2001]), this mode has several problems that lead to poor QoS performance ([Mangold et al. 2002] and [Ni et al. 2002]). Among these are (1) unpredictable delays before the beginning of the contention free periods[9] and (2) unknown duration of the transmission time of each polled station.

1. The former problem occurs if the channel is busy when the contention-free periods should start; as a consequence, the transmission of frames belonging to time-bounded multimedia applications is deferred, with QoS degradation.
2. A polled station is allowed to send a frame whose transmission time is not under the control of the PC, as it depends on several factors. This may prevent the PC from providing QoS guarantees to other stations that are polled during the remaining CFP.

PCF QoS problems led the IEEE 802.11 working group to set up task group e to specify solutions for introducing QoS guarantees in 802.11 WLANs; see Section 4.4.5.

4.4.2.3 Power Saving

In pervasive computing environments, most communications are wireless and nodes have to rely on batteries as the energy supply. Battery power is finite and represents one of the greatest constraints in designing pervasive computing algorithms for mobile devices, as battery replacement is often difficult or impossible. Even though energy-storage technology has advanced substantially, it is not improving at the same rate as the other components of mobile devices [Estrin et al. 2002]. For these reasons, it is vital that power is managed efficiently by identifying ways to use less power, preferably with no impact on the applications.[10] Results show that as the system layers become optimized for energy, the battery lifetime can be increased by (at least) one order of magnitude [Doherty et al. 2001].

In small mobile devices, networking activities have a major impact on energy consumption. Experimental results show that power consumption related to networking activities is approximately 10% of the overall power consumption of a laptop computer, but it is up to 50% in handheld devices [Kravets et al. 1998]. The impact of network technologies on power consumption has been investigated

---

[9]Up to 4.9 ms in IEEE 802.11a.
[10]Limitations on battery lifetime and the additional energy requirements for supporting network operations inside each node (e.g., routing) make energy conservation one of the main concern in ad hoc networking (Feeney 2004, Chlamtac et al. 2003).

TABLE 4.2 802.11 Interface Power Consumption Measurements

Interface Type	Interface Status			
	Transmit	Receive	Idle	Sleep
Aironet PC4800	1.4–1.9 W	1.3–1.4 W	1.34 W	0.075 W
Lucent Bronze	1.3 W	0.97 W	0.84 W	0.066 W
Lucent Silver	1.3 W	0.90 W	0.74 W	0.048 W
Cabletron Roamabout	1.4 W	1.0 W	0.83 W	0.13 W

in depth by [Stemm et al. 1997]. The key point in energy-aware networking is that often a wireless interface consumes nearly the same amount of energy in the receive, transmit, and idle states; in the sleep state, an interface cannot transmit or receive, and its power consumption is highly reduced. In IEEE 802.11 the cards can be in different states from the power-saving standpoint. Specifically, we must distinguish between transmit, receive, idle, sleep, and OFF states. Table 4.2 presents some experimental measurements of the average power consumption of various 802.11 network interfaces; see [Feeney 2004] for more details. Even though these results depend on the type of card, from a qualitative standpoint they provide the same picture. Relatively small power consumption differences exist between transmit, receive, and idle states (referred in the following discussion as ON states), while their power consumption is about one order greater than that in the sleep state. In the sleep state, an interface can neither transmit nor receive, so it consumes very little energy; however, to transmit or receive, an interface must change its status from sleep to idle, and this requires both time and energy. Typically, less than 1 ms is necessary to switch an IEEE 802.11 card from/to an ON state to/from the sleep state. On the other hand, about 100 ms are necessary to switch the card from/to the OFF state to/from the idle state. Hence, even though the OFF state has zero power consumption, moving the cards to/from this state introduces significant delays in networking operations. For these reasons, the 802.11 power-saving policy is based on the sleep state. The basic idea for implementing the power-saving policy is the same in the infrastructure and infrastructure-less networks: stations operating in power-saving mode spend most of their time in the sleep mode and periodically wake up to receive data. In BSS the power management mechanism is centralized in the AP, while in IBSS, power management is a fully distributed process managed by all mobile stations. In the next section, details on BSS and IBSS power management are given.

Power Management in an Infrastructure WLAN The existence of the AP makes power management very effective, as it assumes the full burden of buffering data frames for power-saving stations and delivering them at the stations' request. This allows the mobile stations to remain in their power-saving state for long periods. Specifically, the AP periodically (typically, every 100 ms) sends a beacon containing a map (traffic indication map, TIM) of the power-saving stations for which it has some buffered frame. Stations working in power-saving mode periodically wake up to receive the AP beacon. If they have pending traffic on the AP, they send a poll message to the AP that will finally send them their frames. A power-saving station does not need to wake up every beacon, but it may remain in the sleep state for several consecutive beacon periods whose length is communicated to the AP.

Power Management in Infrastructure-less WLANS In an IBSS, power management is a fully distributed process managed by the individual mobile stations. The station that initializes the IBSS defines the beacon interval. At the beginning of the beacon interval, all nodes wake up and randomly contend to transmit the synchronization beacon. Nodes synchronize themselves with the first beacon they receive. For power management, a fixed-length ATIM (Ad hoc Traffic Indication Message) window is associated with the IBSS. All stations must stay awake for an ATIM window after each beacon. During the ATIM window, every node sends an ATIM message to every other node for which it has pending traffic. Each node that receives an ATIM message responds with an ATIM acknowledgment.[11] These transmissions follow the basic 802.11 mechanisms. At the end of the ATIM window, nodes that have not sent or received ATIM announcements go back to sleep. All other nodes remain awake throughout the remainder of the beacon interval in order to send and receive the announced traffic.

The efficiency of 802.11 power management mechanisms depends strongly on the values selected for the beacon intervals, the offered load, and, in the IBSS case, the length of the ATIM window. Energy consumption is the main criterion in evaluating a power-saving protocol, but factors such as latency, throughput, and distribution of power consumption must also be taken into account. Currently, relatively few studies have examined the effectiveness of 802.11 power management; see, e.g., [Krashinsky et al. 2002] and [Woesner et al. 1998] for BSS and IBSS, respectively. Results presented in these works point out performance problems. In [Krashinsky et al. 2002] the authors investigated the interaction between the 802.11 power-saving protocol and TCP performance, assuming Web-like traffic. The results pointed out performance problems due to the static nature of the IEEE 802.11 power-saving mode (the TIM is delivered at fixed intervals). More precisely, the 802.11 protocol can degrade performance (1) by increasing round-trip times (RTTs) of fast connections by up to 100 ms and (2) by introducing unnecessary energy consumption by waking up the interface during long idle periods. To solve these problems, the authors propose a dynamic power management protocol that adapts to network activity [Krashinsky et al. 2002]. [Anastasi et al. 2003b] and [Anastasi et al. 2003c] present and evaluate solutions, based on the indirect TCP model, for the joint optimization of TCP performance and power saving in Wi-Fi hot spots.

The effectiveness of the IEEE 802.11 power-saving mechanism in IBSS was investigated in [Woesner et al. 1998] by analyzing a fully connected eight-node

---

[11]To avoid contention with data traffic, only beacons, frame announcements, and acknowledgments are transmitted during the ATIM window.

ad hoc network. The results indicate that power savings are obtained only at moderate loads; as the offered load increases, the savings decline; substantially. The offered load also influences the choice of the parameter (e.g., the ATIM interval); hence, the authors recommend adopting an adaptive ATIM window.

4.4.3 IEEE 802.11b Specification

The 802.11b standard extends the 802.11 standard by introducing a higher-speed PHY in the ISM band, still guaranteeing interoperability with 802.11 cards. Specifically, 802.11b adds two higher speeds to the 802.11 DSSS PHY: 5.5 and 11 Mbps. This means that 802.11b systems will interoperate with 802.11 DSSS systems but will not work with the 1 and 2 Mbps 802.11 FHSS systems.

To increase the data rate beyond 2 Mbps, in the 802.11b standard the eight-chip Complementary Code Keying (CCK) technique is used instead of the 11-bit Barker sequence. Table 4.3 summarizes the characteristics of 802.11b PHY.

To ensure coexistence and interoperability among multirate-capable stations and with 802.11 cards, the standard defines a set of rules that must be followed by all stations in a WLAN:

- The 802.11b PHY uses the same preamble and header as the 802.11 DSSS PHY. The preamble and header are always transmitted at 1 Mbps.
- All stations must be able to detect all control frames. To this end, a *basic rate set* for each WLAN is defined that contains the data transfer rates that all stations within the WLAN will be capable of using to receive and transmit. RTS, CTS, and ACK frames must be transmitted at a rate included in the basic rate set.
- Frames with multicast or broadcast destination addresses must be transmitted at a rate belonging to the basic rate set.

These design choices significantly affect the effective bandwidth and the transmission ranges of an 802.11b network. The effective bandwidth for an 802.11b network has been analyzed in detail in [Anastasi et al. 2004] and [Anastasi et al. 2003a] by studying the maximum amount of traffic that can be delivered between two 802.11b stations (e.g., a station and the AP). The analysis was performed by considering both UDP and TCP traffic. Results obtained for UDP traffic are summarized in

TABLE 4.3 802.11b PHY Characteristics

Data Rate	Code	Modulation	Symbol Rate	Bits/Symbol
1 Mbps	Barker sequence	DBPSK	1 MSps	1
2 Mbps	Barker sequence	DQPSK	1 MSps	2
5.5 Mbps	CCK	DQPSK	1.375 MSps	4
11 Mbps	CCK	DQPSK	1.375 MSps	8

TABLE 4.4 Maximum Throughput at Different Data Rates (UDP Traffic)

	$m = 512$ Bytes		$m = 1024$ Bytes	
	No RTS/CTS	RTS/CTS	No RTS/CTS	RTS/CTS
11 Mbps	3.337 Mbps	2.739 Mbps	5.120 Mbps	4.386 Mbps
5.5 Mbps	2.490 Mbps	2.141 Mbps	3.428 Mbps	3.082 Mbps
2 Mbps	1.319 Mbps	1.214 Mbps	1.589 Mbps	1.511 Mbps
1 Mbps	0.758 Mbps	0.738 Mbps	0.862 Mbps	0.839 Mbps

Table 4.4. These results show that even with large packet sizes (e.g., $m = 1024$ bytes) only 47% of the 11 Mbps bandwidth can be used for user data transfer. The differences in the rates used for transmitting (unicast) data and control frames have a big impact on the system behavior. Since 802.11 cards transmit at a constant power, lowering the transmission rate permits the packaging of more energy per symbol, thus increasing the transmission range. To consider this issue in more detail, it is useful to make a distinction between the transmission range, the interference range, and the carrier sensing range. The following definitions can be given:

- The *transmission range* (*TX_range*) is the range (with respect to the transmitting station) within which a transmitted frame can be successfully received. It is mainly determined by the transmission power, the data rate, and the radio propagation properties.
- The *physical carrier sensing range* (*PCS_range*) is the range (with respect to the transmitting station) within which the other stations detect a busy channel. It mainly depends on the power sensitivity of the receiver (the receive threshold) and the radio propagation properties.
- The *interference range* (*IF_range*) is the range within which stations in receive mode will be 'interfered with' by a transmitter and thus suffer a loss. It is usually larger than the TX_range, and is a function of the distance between the sender and receiver, and of the path loss model.

The relationships among *TX_range*, *PCS_range*, and *IF_range* and their impact on 802.11 performance have been investigated through measurements on a real testbed in [Anastasi et al. 2004]. Hereafter, the main results are summarized.

4.4.3.1 Transmission Range The dependency between the data rate and TX_range was investigated by measuring the packet loss rate experienced by two communicating stations whose network interfaces transmit at a constant (preset) data rate. Specifically, four sets of measurements were performed corresponding to the different data rates: 1, 2, 5.5, and 11 Mbps. In each set of experiments, the packet loss rate was recorded as a function of the distance between the

TABLE 4.5 Estimates of the Transmission Ranges at Different Data Rates

	11 Mbps	5.5 Mbps	2 Mbps	1 Mbps
TX_range	30 m	70 m	90–100 m	110–130 m

communicating stations. The results averaged on several experiments are summarized in Table 4.5.

In [Anastasi et al. 2004] it is also pointed out that TX_range values also depend on the mobile devices' height from the ground.

4.4.3.2 Physical Carrier Sensing Range

A direct measure of the PCS_range is difficult to achieve because 802.11b cards generally do not provide to the higher layers information about channel carrier sensing. To tackle this problem, an indirect way to estimate the PCS_range was defined [Anastasi et al. 2004]. Specifically, a set of measurements was performed in the scenario shown in Figure 4.3. In this scenario, there are two active communications flows, one between S1 and S2 and the other between S3 and S4. The distance between each couple of communicating stations is fixed (d(1, 2) = d(3, 4) = 10 m), while the distance between the two couples, i.e., d(2, 3), is variable. In each experiment, all stations transmit at the same constant (preset) data rate.

The idea was to investigate the correlation between the two sessions while increasing the distance d(2, 3). The results indicated two thresholds for the correlation that are (almost) independent on the data rate:

1. The correlation sharply decreases when d(2, 3) is increased from 180 to 200 m.
2. The correlation almost disappears when d(2, 3) is increased from 250 to 300 m.

This behavior can be explained as follows. Taking a session as a reference, the presence of the other session may have two possible effects on the performance of the reference session: (1) if the two sessions are within the same physical carrier sensing range, they share the same physical channel; (2) if they are outside their respective physical carrier sensing ranges, the radiated energy from one session may still affect the quality of the channel observed by the other session. From the obtained results, it can be expected that the first step in the two-session correlation

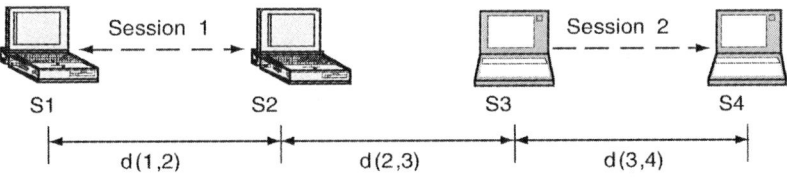

Figure 4.3 Reference network scenario.

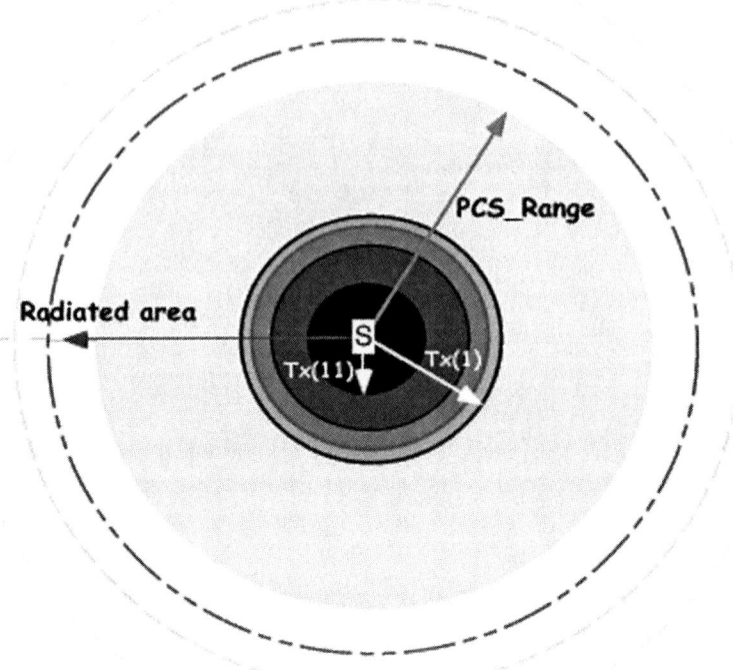

Figure 4.4 802.11b channel model.

occurs at the boundary of the physical carrier sensing range (i.e., 180 m < PCS_range ≤ 200 m), while the second step (i.e., d(2, 3) approximately 300 m) occurs when the radiated energy from one session has almost no effect on the other. A more detailed discussion on the physical carrier sensing range can be found in [Anastasi et al. 2004].

To summarize the above results, in [Anastasi et al. 2004] the channel model shown in Figure 4.4 to characterize an IEEE 802.11b WLAN is proposed. The channel model describes how a transmitting station S affects the stations around it, depending on the distance, d, from S and the rate j ($j = 1, 2, 5.5, 11$ Mbps) used by S for its transmissions. In the figure, $Tx(j)$ denotes the station S transmission range when it is transmitting at rate j. As shown in Figure 4.4, stations at a distance lower than $Tx(j)$ are able to receive the S data. Nodes at a distance $Tx(j) < d < 200$ m are in the S physical carrier sensing range, and hence observe that the channel is busy when S is transmitting. Finally, nodes at a distance $200 \leq d < 300$ m are affected by the energy radiated by S. From this channel model it follows that the hidden-station phenomenon, as it is usually defined in the literature (see Section 4.2.1), is almost impossible with the above ranges. Indeed, the PCS_range is about twice TX_range(1), i.e., the larger transmission range. Furthermore, two stations, say $S1$ and $S2$, that can start transmitting toward the same receiver, R, must be at a distance $\leq 2 \bullet TX\_range(1)$; thus, they are inside the physical carrier sensing range of each other. Hence, if S1 has an ongoing transmission with R, S2 will observe a busy channel and thus will defer its own transmission. This means that in this scenario, virtual carrier sensing is not necessary and the RTS/CTS mechanism only introduces additional overhead.

4.4.4 High-Speed WLANs: IEEE 802.11a and IEEE 802.11g

The success of 802.11b WLANs increased the bandwidth requests. To tackle this issue, IEEE 802 working groups defined two standards, 802.11a and 802.11g, both providing a maximum data rate of 54 Mbps.

The 802.11a standard operates in the 5 GHz band. This band, called the *Universal Networking Infrastructure* (UNII) band, is divided into three subbands with different transmission constraints. Of these, the UNII-1 (5.15–5.25 GHz) and UNII-2 (5.25–5.35 GHz) subbands can be used for WLANs.[12] Specifically, UNII-1 is reserved for indoor use, while UNII-2 is both indoor and outdoor. Each subband provides four nonoverlapping channels. This contributes greatly to WLANs' deployment, as eight channels are available for WLANs instead of the (up to) three nonoverlapping channels of 802.11b [Kapp 2002]. The 802.11a standard uses the Orthogonal Frequency Division Multiplexed (OFDM) modulation technique. In traditional frequency division multiplex (FDM) systems, the spacing between channels is greater than the symbol rate to avoid overlapping. OFDM distributes the data over multiple carriers spaced at precise frequencies. The spacing provides orthogonality among carriers so that they can be uniquely identified. Hence guard bands are eliminated, thus increasing efficiency [Kapp 2002]. OFDM distributes the data over 48 subcarriers. This reduces the data rate and increases transmission robustness.

The 802.11a standard provides data rates of up to 54 Mbps. Multirate stations can operate at the following throughput steps: 6, 9, 12, 18, 24, 36, 48, and 54, where 9 and 18 are optional. The throughput increments are obtained at the cost of reducing the transmission ranges. Furthermore, by using the 5 GHz spectrum, the reduction of the transmission ranges are more marked than the corresponding reductions in the 2.4 GHz spectrum [Kapp 2002].

The 802.11g standard will operate at 2.4 GHz by using the modulation techniques of both a and b systems. Hence, it allows interoperability with 802.11b systems and provides the higher data rates of the 802.11a standard. Specifically, it defines a physical layer standard for 2.4 GHz WLANs with a maximum link rate of 54 Mbps. The 802.11g standard uses OFDM modulation but, for backward compatibility with 802.11b, it also supports CCK modulation (see Table 4.6).

4.4.5 Quality of Service: IEEE 802.11e

Applications may have very different QoS requirements in terms of bandwidth, delay, jitter, etc. On the other hand, the DCF access mode does not provide any mechanism to differentiate among data flows. Furthermore, as explained before, the PCF access mode may introduce QoS degradations.

---

[12]UNII-3 is reserved for outdoor bridging.

TABLE 4.6 Relationship Between Standards 802.11b, 802.11g, and 802.11a

Rate (Mbps)	Single/Multicarrier	802.11b	802.11g	802.11a
1	Single carrier	Barker	Barker	
2	Single carrier	Barker	Barker	
5.5	Single carrier	CCK	CCK	
6	Multicarrier		OFDM	OFDM
9	Multicarrier		OFDM	OFDM
11	Single carrier	CCK	CCK	
12	Multicarrier		OFDM	OFDM
18	Multicarrier		OFDM	OFDM
24	Multicarrier		OFDM	OFDM
36	Multicarrier		OFDM	OFDM
48	Multicarrier		OFDM	OFDM
54	Multicarrier		OFDM	OFDM

To support applications with QoS requirements, the IEEE 802.11e WG is developing a supplementary to the MAC layer to provide QoS support for LAN applications. It will apply to 802.11 physical standards a, b, and g to give them the ability to support time-critical multimedia data. All the details have not yet been finalized, but the basic elements have been selected. Specifically, the e standard defines two main access modes that are backward compatible with DCF and PCF:

- *Enhanced DCF* (EDCF) that extends DCF to provide service differentiation.
- *Hybrid Coordination Function* (HCF) that modifies the PCF to have more efficient polling.[13] This method is under the control of the *Hybrid Coordinator* (HC), which is typically located in the AP. Similarly to the 802.11, the channel access is subdivided into *Contention Periods* (CPs) and *Contention Free Periods* (CFPs). EDCF is used during CPs only, while the HCF can operate in both periods.

4.4.5.1 Enhanced DCF EDCF enhances the DCF access scheme to support service differentiation by introducing, in each station, four *Access Categories* (ACs) that are used to support user traffics with eight different priorities. Each AC operates as a *virtual station* following the DCF-like rules with its own parameters for Inter-Frame Spacing—the *Arbitration Inter-Frame Spacing* [AIFS(AC)]—and contention parameters [i.e., *CW_Size_min*(AC), *CW_Size_MAX*(AC)]. The AIFS(AC) is equal to DIFS plus some (possibly zero) time slots. The values of these parameters are selected to give the highest access probability to the traffic with the stringent requirements.[14]

---

[13] While PCF is optional, HCF is an 802.11e mandatory mechanism.
[14] The priority of a class increases by decreasing AIFS(AC), *CW_Size_min*(AC), and *CW_Size_MAX*(AC).

TABLE 4.7   Contention Parameters

AC	AIFS(AC)*	CW_Size_min(AC)	CW_Size_MAX(AC)	Traffic Type
0	2	CW_{min}	CW_{max}	Best effort
1	1	CW_{min}	CW_{max}	Video probe
2	1	$(CW_{min} + 1)/2$	CW_{min}	Video
3	1	$(CW_{min} + 1)/4$-1	$(CW_{min} + 1)/2 - 1$	Voice

*The value indicates the number of time slots.

Table 4.7 reports the typical parameter values for the four ACs [Gu et al. 2003]. These values are selected to give the highest access probability to the traffic with the most stringent requirements. The CW_{min} and CW_{max} values depend on the physical layer; for example for 802.11a PHY, $CW_{min} = 15$ and $CW_{max} = 1023$. Specifically, an AC virtual station with a frame to transmit senses the channel. If the channel is idle for an AIFS(AC) long interval, the station starts the transmission; otherwise, the station defers the transmission until the channel is idle for an AIFS(AC) interval. At this point, it starts the backoff procedure: it uniformly selects an integer number of slots in the interval [1, CW(AC) + 1], where CW(AC) is the current size of the virtual station contention window: CW_Size_min(AC) $\leq$ CW(AC) $\leq$ CW_Size_MAX(AC).

As each AC corresponds to a separate virtual station, a station with multiple ACs will have an internal contention among its ACs (besides the access contention with the other stations). Contentions among ACs within the same station are locally managed: the highest AC performs the transmission attempt (which may collide with those of the other stations), while the other ACs behave as they do when a collision occurs (virtual collision). As in DCF, a real collision occurs if more stations start transmitting at the same time.

After a (virtual or real) collision, the CW(AC) is enlarged to reduce the probability of a new collision. However, whereas in legacy 802.11 CW is always doubled after any unsuccessful transmission, in EDCF a new CW, say CW_{new}(AC), is calculated with the help of the persistence factor PF(AC). In detail [Mangold et al. 2002]:

$$CW_{new}(AC) \geq [CW(AC) + 1]^*PF(AC) - 1$$

The PF value can be set to any value in the range [1, 16], where PF $= 2$ corresponds to the legacy 802.11 algorithm.

As in DCF, to reduce the duration of a collision when long frames are transmitted, a virtual station may reserve the channel through the RTS/CTS mechanism.

4.4.5.2 Hybrid Coordination Function

Some types of interactive and synchronous traffic may require QoS guarantees (e.g., bounded delays) more stringent than those provided by EDCF service differentiation. To manage these classes of traffic, the HCF access mode is included in the 802.11e standard. The HCF access mode uses an HC generally located in the AP that is in charge to start, when necessary, controlled access periods in the channel access.

The HC performs bandwidth management by allocating the Transmission Opportunities (TXOPs) to 802.11e stations. A TXOP defines the time interval in which a station can transmit; it is characterized by a starting time and a maximum duration.

The HCF access method operates during both CPs and CFPs by initiating and managing time intervals during which only the Hybrid Coordinator and the polled stations can access the channel.

A CFP starts after the beacon and ends either when (1) the HC sends a CF-End frame or when (2) the time interval specified in the beacon expires. During a CFP, the HC sends CF-Poll frames to give the transmission right to the stations. The station addressed by the CF-Poll receives a TXOP and start transmitting within a SIFS. If no transmission starts after a PIFS, the HC can issue another CF-Poll.

During CPs, the HC can start controlled access periods in which bursts of frames are transmitted using the polling-based channel access mechanism. This also provides guaranteed services under heavy loads conditions. To start a controlled access period, the HC issues a polls message as soon as the channel is idle for a PIFS.

A signaling protocol is used by HC to learn which stations must be polled. Specifically, the stations signal to the HC the requirements of their traffic streams (e.g., required bandwidth, maximum delay) during controlled CPs that are started on the channel by the HC sending a special control frame. Using this information, the HC determines the time instants at which stations must be polled.

4.5 TECHNOLOGIES FOR WBAN AND WPAN: 802.15 STANDARDS

Wireless personal area networks (WPANs) are used to convey information over relatively short distances (<10 m) among relatively few participants. Unlike WLANs, WPANs involve little or no infrastructure. This allows small, power-efficient, inexpensive solutions to be implemented for a wide range of devices.

The development of standards for short-distance wireless networks is currently ongoing within the IEEE 802.15 working group for WPANs. The aim is to develop standards for wireless networking of portable and mobile computing devices such as PCs, PDAs, peripherals, cell phones, pagers, and consumer electronics [802.15].

From the beginning, 802.15 activities have been strongly correlated with pervasive computing. Indeed, this working group was set up as a result of the decision of the IEEE Ad Hoc Wearable Standard Committee to focus on wireless PANs for supporting wearable computing environments [Marks et al. 2002].

Currently, four task groups (TGs) are active within the IEEE 802.15 working group:

- Which TG 1, in 2002 approved a WPAN standard based on the Bluetooth v1.1 specifications ([Bisdikian 2001], [Blue]).
- TG 2, which is developing recommendations to guarantee the coexistence between 802.11 and 802.15 devices.

- TG 3, which has just produced a draft standard for high-rate (20 Mbit/s or more) WPANs. TG3 also contains an Alternative PHY Task Group (TG 3a) that is working to define a higher-speed physical layer enhancement to 802.15.3 for applications involving imaging and multimedia. All the alternative physical layers under consideration employ UWB communications.
- TG 4, which is investigating a low-data-rate, low-cost, low-power solution for WPANs operating in an unlicensed frequency band. Potential applications are sensors, interactive toys, smart badges, remote controls, and home automation.

TG 3 and TG 4 activities are currently ongoing. For this reason, only the basic concepts of 802.15.3 and 802.15.4 WPANs will be discussed.

4.5.1 IEEE 802.15.1: a Bluetooth Based WPAN

In 2002, the IEEE 802.15 working group for WPANs approved its first WPAN standard, which is based on the lower portions of the Bluetooth v1.1 specification. Bluetooth specifications are released by the Bluetooth Special Interest Group (SIG), which consists of industrial leaders in telecommunications, computing, and networking [Blue]. Bluetooth SIG aims to define specifications for low-cost, short-range radio links between mobile PCs, mobile phones, and other portable devices.

The complete Bluetooth protocol stack (see Figure 4.5) contains several protocol layers. Of these, the Bluetooth radio, Baseband, Link Manager Protocol (LMP), and Logical Link Control and Adaptation protocol (L2CAP) form the 802.15.1 MAC and PHY layers. We will focus only on the Bluetooth radio, Baseband, and

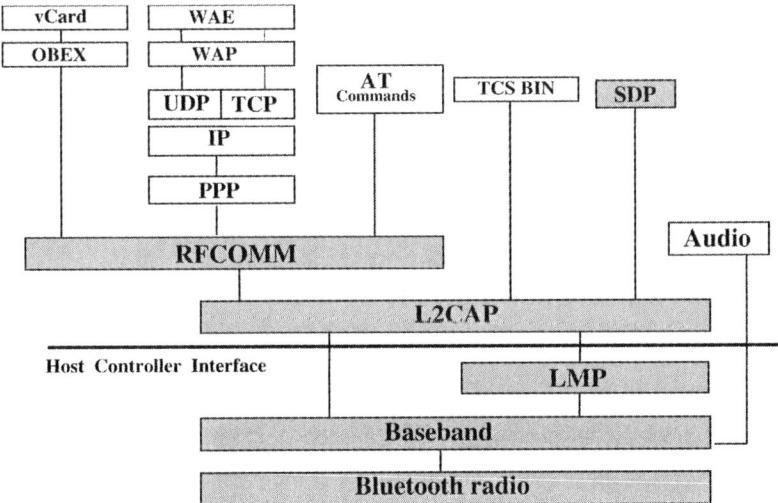

Figure 4.5 Bluetooth protocol stack.

(partially) L2CAP protocols. More details on the Bluetooth architecture and protocols can be found in [Bruno et al. 2002a] and [Bruno et al. 2002b].

Bluetooth radio provides the physical links among Bluetooth devices, while the Baseband layer provides a transport service of packets over the physical links. In the following, these layers will be presented. The L2CAP services are used only for data transmissions. The main features supported by L2CAP are *protocol multiplexing* (the L2CAP uses a protocol-type field to distinguish between upper-layer protocols), and *segmentation-reassembly*. The last feature is required because the Baseband packet is smaller than the usual packets used by higher-layer protocols.

A *piconet* is the fundamental building block of a Bluetooth network. A complex procedure is defined in the Bluetooth specifications for setting up a piconet and for enrolling devices to it [Bruno et al. 2003]. A piconet contains up to eight active (i.e., participating in data exchange) stations; one station is the master, while the other stations are slaves.

The units belonging to a piconet share the same channel (i.e., are synchronized to the same master). The master decides which slave has access to the channel. A Bluetooth piconet has a small coverage area (i.e., an area up to 10 m around the master) that can be extended by interconnecting independent piconets with overlapping coverage areas. The Bluetooth specification defines a method for piconet interconnection: the *scatternet*. A scatternet can be dynamically constructed, in an ad hoc fashion, when some nodes belong to more than one piconet at the same time (interpiconet units). For example, the two piconets in Figure 4.6 are partially overlapping and share a slave; hence, they may form a scatternet. In this figure, a master and a slave are denoted by *M* and *S*, respectively. Stations marked *P* (*Parking* state) are synchronized with the master but are not participating in any data exchange.

In general, a scatternet exists when a unit is active in more than one piconet[15] at the same time. Scatternets can be useful in several scenarios. For example, we can

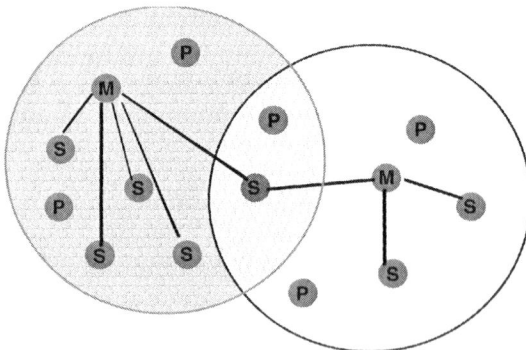

Figure 4.6 Two partially overlapping piconets.

---

[15] A unit can be master into only one piconet.

have a piconet that contains a laptop and a cellular phone. The cellular phone provides access to the Internet. A second piconet contains the laptop itself and several PDAs. In this case, a Scatternet can be formed with the laptop as the interpiconet unit. By exploiting the scatternet, the PDAs can exploit the cellular phone services to access the Internet. The current Bluetooth specification defines the notion of a scatternet but does not provide the mechanisms to construct it. This has generated an extensive literature about scatternet formation algorithms; see [Chlamtac et al. 2003] and the references therein.

A Bluetooth unit integrated into a microchip enables wireless ad hoc communications of voice and data in stationary and mobile environments ([Bisdikian 2001] and [Miller et al. 2000]) using a radio operating in the 2.4 GHz band. In this band are defined 79 different radio frequency (RF) channels that are spaced at 1 MHz. The radio layer utilizes as a transmission technique the *Frequency Hopping Spread Spectrum* (FHSS). The hopping sequence is a pseudorandom sequence of 79-hop length, and it is unique for each piconet (it depends on the master's local parameters). The FHSS system has been chosen to reduce the interference of nearby systems operating in the same frequency range (e.g., the IEEE 802.11 WLAN) and to make the link robust. The nominal rate of hopping between two consecutive RF is 1600 hops/s.

A *Time Division Duplex* (TDD) transmission scheme has been adopted. The channel is divided into time slots, each 625 μs in length, and each slot corresponds to a different RF hop frequency. The time slots are numbered according to the Bluetooth clock of the master. The master has to begin its transmissions in even-numbered time slots. Odd-numbered time slots are reserved for the beginning of slaves' transmissions. The transmission of a packet nominally covers a single slot, but it may also last for three or five consecutive time slots. For multislots packets the RF hop frequency to be used for the entire packet is the RF hopping frequency assigned to the time slot in which the transmission has begun.

Two types of physical links can be established between Bluetooth devices: a *Synchronous Connection-Oriented* (SCO) link and an *Asynchronous Connection-Less* (ACL) link. The SCO link is a point-to-point, symmetric connection between the master and a specific slave. It is used to deliver delay-sensitive traffic, mainly voice. The SCO link rate is 64 kbit/s, and it is settled by reserving a couple of consecutive slots for master-to-slave transmission and immediate slave-to-master response. The SCO link can be considered a circuit-switched connection between the master and the slave. The ACL link is a connection between the master and all slaves participating to the piconet. It can be considered a packet-switched connection between Bluetooth devices. It supports the reliable delivery of data by exploiting a fast *Automatic Repeat Request* (ARQ) scheme. An ACL channel supports point-to-multipoint transmissions from the master to the slaves.

As stated before, channel access is managed according to a polling scheme. The master decides which slave should have access to the channel by sending it a packet. The master packet may contain data or can simply be a polling packet (NULL packet). When the slave receives a packet from the master, it is authorized to transmit in the next time slot. For SCO links, the master periodically polls the corresponding slave. Polling is asynchronous for ACL links.

A piconet has a gross bit rate of 1 Mbps. The polling scheme and the protocols control information, reducing the amount of user data that can be delivered by a piconet. Inside a piconet, Bluetooth stations can establish up to three 64 kbit/s synchronous (voice) channels or an asynchronous (data) channel supporting maximal data rates of 723 kbit/s asymmetric or 433 kbit/s symmetric. The limiting throughput performances of a piconet are discussed in [Bruno et al. 2002b] analyzing a single master-slave link in which both stations operate under *asymptotic conditions*, i.e., the stations always have a packet ready for transmission. The same work also presents a more realistic analysis of Bluetooth performance when several slaves are active inside a piconet. In this case, the master must implement a scheduling algorithm to decide the polling order of the slaves. The Bluetooth specification indicates the *Round Robin* (RR) polling algorithm as a possible solution: slaves are polled in a cyclic order. Results presented in [Bruno et al. 2002b] indicate that, under unbalanced traffic conditions, the RR algorithm may cause severe bandwidth wastage (due to a large number of NULL packets). Several authors have proposed new schedulers suitable for Bluetooth (see [Bruno et al. 2002b] and references therein). An effective scheduling algorithm, named *Efficient Double Cycle* (EDC), was proposed in [Bruno et al. 2002b] and [Bruno et al. 2001]. EDC tunes the polling order to the network traffic conditions to limit the channel-bandwidth wastage caused by the polling of empty stations.

Bluetooth uses cryptographic security mechanisms implemented in the data link layer. A key management service provides each device with a set of symmetric cryptographic keys required for the initialization of a secret channel with another device, the execution of an authentication protocol, and the exchange of encrypted data on the secret channel. A detailed presentation of Bluetooth security mechanisms, together with an analysis of the weaknesses of the Bluetooth key management scheme, can be found in [Michiardi et al. 2004].

4.5.2 High-Rate WPAN: IEEE 802.15.3

The aim of TG 3[16] is to provide the specification for high-rate WPANs able to meet the requirements of applications performing video and audio distribution (e.g., high-speed digital video transfer from a digital camcorder to a TV screen, home theater, interactive video gaming) and/or high-speed data transfer (e.g., kiosks for still images, MP3 players, printers and scanners). This task group has already defined the draft version of MAC and 2.4 GHz PHY layers for WPANs with data rates of up to 55 Mbps. With the current PHY, five data rates are possible: 11, 22, 33, 44, and 55 Mb/s with a short-range coverage ($\approx$10 m). Due to the bandwidth needs of multimedia applications, an alternative task group (TG 3a) has been established to define an alternative PHY for high-data-rate WPANs. TG 3a PHY will use the MAC layer defined in the 802.15.3 standard.

The basic building block of an 802.15.3 WPAN is the piconet formed by two or more devices (DEVs) communicating on the same physical channel within a

[16]www.ieee802.org/15/pub/TG3.html

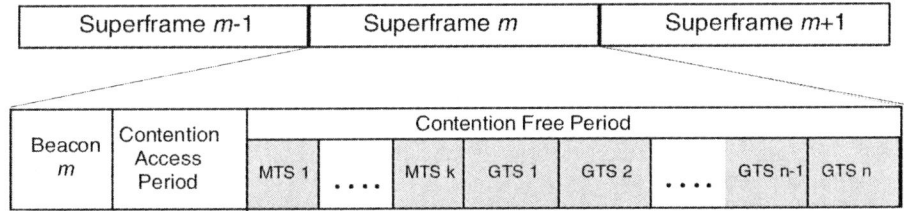

Figure 4.7 Superframe structure.

personal operating space (POS). In a piconet, one DEV must assume the role of the *piconet coordinator* (PNC).[17] The PCN provides the basic timing for the WPAN and manages the QoS requirements within the WPAN. To this end, the PCN periodically transmits a beacon containing, in addition to timing, other information useful managing the WPAN.

The MAC protocol controls PAN construction and operations. Among other things, it is in charge of forming and terminating PANs, transporting data between devices, and providing authentication and power management.

As shown in Figure 4.7, the channel is organized into superframes; each superframe is the interval between consecutive beacons. A superframe is made up of three parts: (1) beacon, (2) *Contention Access Period* (CAP); and (3) *Contention Free Period* (CFP). The beacon contains the channels' allocation for the current superframe. The CFP is used for asynchronous and synchronous data streams with QoS requirements, while the CAP is used for (small amounts of) non-QoS frames, i.e., asynchronous exchange. A CSMA/CA protocol is used to access the channel during the CAP. The CAP is an optional part of the frame that is also used to transmit PNC-DEV commands. The CFP is organized in TDMA style, with each slot having a fixed start time. Guaranteed start times enable both power saving (each device knows when it must be active to send-receive data) and good QoS characteristics.

In Figure 4.7, the CFP is composed of *Guaranteed Time Slots* (GTS) and *Management Time Slots* (MTS). MTS are used for PNC-DEV communications, while GTS slots are used for data communications. These communications are connection-based under the control of the PNC that assigns time slots for the connections. Nevertheless, connections and data transfer are made with peer-to-peer connections. GTS slots for synchronous data streams (e.g., voice) have a pseudo-static allocation[18], while slots for asynchronous (nonstream) connections are dynamically allocated.

Several levels of authentication and security can be defined in a piconet. Authentication uses a public/private key model. Data encryption uses a symmetric key that is generated by the PNC and is securely distributed to authenticated devices in the piconet.

---

[17]The specification includes a procedure for passing, if necessary, the coordination role to another DEV.
[18]PNCs may change their positions, but they need to communicate and confirm with both transmitter and receiver DEVs.

4.5.2.1 UWB: a Technology for a Very High Data Rate Wireless PAN

The 802.15.3 data rate is not sufficient to support demanding multimedia applications such as home theater, interactive applications (e.g., gaming), and high-rate content downloading. For this reason, an additional task group, IEEE 802.15.3a, was created inside TG 3 to investigate a physical layer alternative to the 802.15.3 PHY. The aim is to develop a very-high-rate PHY that will replace the IEEE 802.15.3 PHY while maintaining the same MAC layer. Specifically, TG 3a is working to define a physical layer able to support transmission of very high data rates over short distances, i.e., 110 Mbps at 10 m, 200 Mbps at 4 m, and 480 Mbps at unspecified distances.

Currently, TG 3a is comparing and contrasting several alternative proposals for a very-high-speed PHY. In the meantime, the Federal Communication Commission (FCC) has approved UWB devices, making UWB the most promising technology for the 802.15.3a PHY. Indeed, many manufacturers have proposed to 802.15.3a an UWB-based physical layer ([Porcino et al. 2003] and [UCAN]). For this reason, it is worthwhile to briefly sketch the main features of this technology.

UWB is a technique used to spread the signal over an exceptionally large bandwidth (well beyond that of CDMA systems). In its original form, UWB is based on impulse radio: it uses very-short-duration (a few nanoseconds) baseband pulses that use a bandwidth of several gigahertz.

Pulse repetition frequency (PRF) can range from hundreds of thousands to billions of pulses per second.

As shown in Figure 4.8, UWB has an extremely widespread spectrum; the energy is spread over several gigahertz. This has the following consequences:

- UWB is wider than any narrowband system by orders of magnitude.
- The power seen by a narrowband system is a fraction of the total.
- UWB signals can be designed to look like imperceptible random noise to conventional radios.

The FCC has ruled that UWB devices can operate with low power in the unlicensed spectrum from 3.1 to 10.6 GHz. The low emission limit ensures that UWB

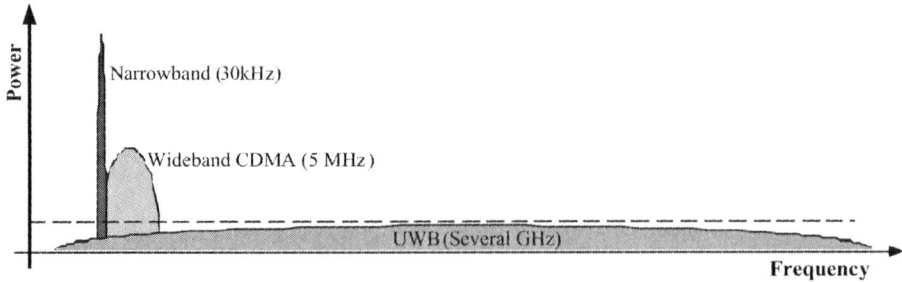

Figure 4.8 UWB spectrum.

devices do not cause harmful interference with other important radios, e.g., IEEE 802.11a. To further reduce coexistence problems with existing systems, a new approach to UWB is based on a multibanded system. In this system, the UWB band (3.1–10.6 GHz) is subdivided into smaller band (each greater than 500 MHz, according to FCC requirements), and UWB communications occur inside each band. Coexistence with other systems is easily achieved by not using bands where other systems are already present. The multibanded approach has two additional benefits: (1) it reduces the technical challenges and (2) it makes it easier to adapt to the regulatory requirements of different countries. For all these reasons, multibanded UWB is currently the manufacturers' preferred choice.

As stated before, TG 3a is working with the constraint of using the 802.15.3 MAC on top of 802.15.3a PHY. However, the MAC has several functionalities that are not easily supported with a UWB-based PHY, such as identification of idle channels (in UWB the energy is not a good measurement for a busy channel), supporting asynchronous broadcast frames in the CAP, scalability issues (how to extend the size of piconet by interconnecting two or more piconets), etc. These problems and possible solutions are discussed in [UCAN].

4.5.3 Low-Rate WPAN: IEEE 802.15.4

The aim of TG 4[19] is to define MAC and PHY specifications for a low-rate WPAN (LR-WPAN) that (1) has long battery life (months or years with one AAA cell); (2) is low in cost; and (3) is suitable for applications/systems with moderate data throughput (<250 kbit/s) and relaxed QoS requirements [Callaway et al. 2002]. These features make the IEEE 802.15.4 standard suitable for smart environments including sensing and location determination, smart badges, control and monitoring, home automation, etc. Bluetooth was initially conceived with similar aims, but its high-complexity specifications make it unsuitable for low-power consumption environments, and its costs exceed those for widespread use in consumer electronics [Callaway et al. 2002].

A LR-PAN is designed to provide wireless communications to/from very simple devices (e.g., tags) that may have small resources and provide little (or no) support to network functions. Inside a PAN, a distinction is therefore made among devices, depending on their resources. An LR-PAN can contain two devices: a *Full Function Device* (FFD) and a *Reduced Function Device* (RFD). The latter cannot control the network; it can only send small amounts of data to an FDD.[20] An FDD device can talk to RFDs and FFDs, and can operate both as a PAN coordinator and as a network device. A PAN must contain at least one FFD. It is expected that RFDs will spend most of their operational life in a sleep state to save their batteries, and will wake up only periodically to listen to the channel to determine whether a message is pending.

---
[19]www.ieee802.org/15/pub/TG4.html
[20]It is typically used for simple applications like light switches.

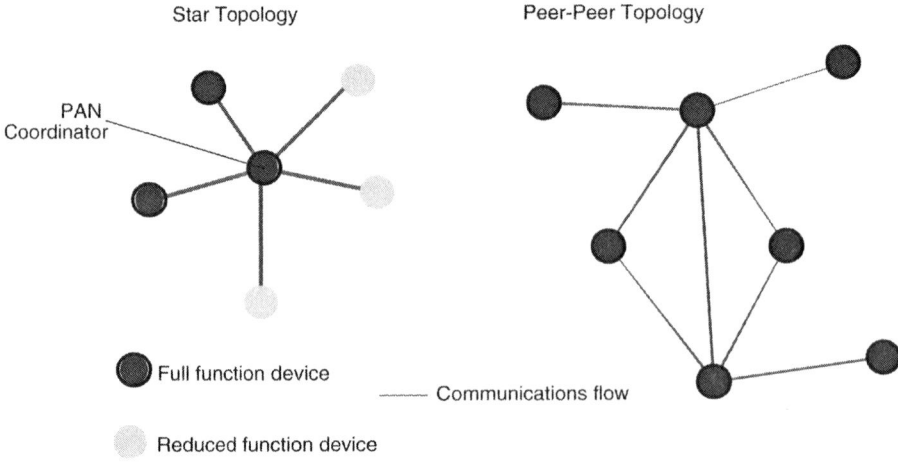

Figure 4.9 802.15.4 PAN topologies.

As shown in Figure 4.9, an IEEE 802.15.4 PAN can be organized as a centralized (star topology) or as a peer-to-peer network, depending on the application requirements. In the star topology, similar to a Bluetooth piconet, the PAN is organized around a coordinator and all communications are between a device and the coordinator. The standard specifies a transmit power of 1 mW, implying an expected transmission range of 10–20 m around the coordinator. The star topology is the best choice for low-latency communications between a PC and its peripherals. On the other hand, in a peer-to-peer topology, the network is organized as a multi-hop ad hoc network in which each device communicates directly with devices within its transmission range. In addition, a multi-hop capability is used to cover large areas.[21] A peer-to-peer organization seems suitable for networks that cover a large physical area, such as sensor networks for perimeter security, in which a single device does not have enough power to communicate with all other devices. A special peer-to-peer network is the cluster-tree network, in which a clustering algorithm is superimposed on the peer-to-peer network. The simple form is a single-cluster network, but it is also possible to form a multicluster structure to cover a large area by interconnecting neighboring clusters.

Currently, the standardization of the MAC and PHY layers is almost complete and the focus is mainly on upper-layer protocols. These latter activities are coordinated by the ZigBee Alliance,[22] which is working to define the network, security, and application layers that will reside on top of the 802.15.4 MAC.

---

[21]Multi-hop routing and forwarding functions should be performed at the network layer and are beyond the scope of this standard.
[22]The ZigBee Alliance is an association of companies working together to develop reliable, cost-effective, low-power, wireless networking products based on an open global standard. (http://www.zigbee.org).

4.5.3.1 Physical Layer The 802.15.4 standard uses two physical layers based on the direct sequence spread spectrum. The main difference between the two physical layers is the frequency. One physical layer operates in the 2.4 GHz band, while the other specifies operations in the 868 and 915 MHz bands in Europe and the United States, respectively. The 2.4 GHz band supports 16 transmission channels (with a 5 MHz channel spacing) between 2.4 and 2.4835 GHz, while the 915 MHz band supports 10 channels between 902.0 and 928.0 MHz (with a 2 MHz channel spacing). Finally, a single channel (between 868.0 and 868.6 MHz) is supported by the 868 MHz physical layer. The sixteen 2.4 GHz channels provide a 250 kbps transmission rate each, while 20 and 40 kbps are the transmission rates for the 868 and 915 MHz physical channels, respectively.

4.5.3.2 MAC Layer Similarly to standard IEEE 802.11, CSMA/CA-based mechanisms are used to control access to the channel. A distinction must be made between *beacon-enabled* and *non-beacon-enabled* networks. Beacon-enabled networks are used to support applications with stringent QoS requirements (low latency or guaranteed bandwidth) and can be organized only according to a star topology.

Non-Beacon-Enabled Networks The access policy is very close to that of the IEEE 802.11 DCF. The main differences are:

- a single interframe spacing, named *Short Inter-Frame Spacing* (SIFS), is used; and
- three different policies can be used to acknowledge MAC frames: *no acknowledgment, immediate acknowledgment,* or *delayed acknowledgment.*

To summarize, when a device wishes to transmit a frame, it senses the channel to determine whether another station is transmitting. If the medium is found to be idle for a SIFS interval, the station continues with its transmission; otherwise, it backs off for a random period before trying again. Collision management is similar to that used in 802.11 DCF; (see [Callaway et al. 2002]).

Beacon-Enabled Networks In this network, the channel is organized in superframes. The PAN coordinator periodically transmits superframe beacons, and the channel between two consecutive beacons is subdivided into a fixed number of time slots. The superframe is subdivided into two parts: a CAP, and a CFP. The latter contains (if any) the slots reserved for single applications. The length of the superframe is constant. The length depends on the beacon interval, and this determines the time slot duration. During the superframe, devices access the channel using a slotted-access CMSA/CA mechanism. The transmissions must be completed before the beginning of the next superframe. To support applications with stringent QoS requirements, the PAN coordinator may reserve some slots for them at the end of each superframe. These slots are called *guaranteed time slots*, and the CSMA/CA is not used to access them.

4.6 SUMMARY AND CONCLUSIONS

The number of microprocessors residing in everyday electronics is continuously increasing, offering the possibility of integrating them to create smart spaces and other intelligent human environments (e.g., intelligent homes), providing new, advanced forms of cooperation between humans and devices. The integration of all devices through a network infrastructure is one of the main elements of pervasive computing. Wireless solutions are the natural choice because they offer mobility and avoid wiring problems. Radio solutions operating in the unlicensed bandwidth (thus avoiding extra costs and bureaucracy) are the preferred choice. Solutions should be standardized to construct interoperable systems. On the other hand, the heterogeneity of devices to be interconnected (from small sensors and actuators to multimedia PDAs) results in a wide variety of requirements; hence, agreement on a single technology seems impossible. At one extreme, are very simple devices for which small size, low cost, and low energy consumption are the main constraints; a high data rate is not necessary. At the other extreme are devices that need to exchange multimedia information; here, a high data rate is a must. Also, coverage requirements may vary significantly (from a few meters to an entire building). This requires a large set of standard specifications for WPANs and WLANs, where each specification covers a specific scenario. In this chapter, we have presented and analyzed the two main families of standards for PANs and LANs: the specifications emerging from the IEEE working groups 802.11 and 802.15 for WLANs and WPANs, respectively. Figure 4.10 summarizes the technologies we have analyzed and highlights the main design requirements of each (data rate vs. cost). In addition, the figure shows the HiperLAN (High Performance Radio Local Area Network) technology. HiperLAN is a family of standards developed by the European Telecommunications Standardization Institute [ETSI]. Among these, the most interesting standard for WLAN is HiperLAN/2. The HiperLAN/2 technology addresses high-speed wireless networks with data rates ranging from 6 to 54 Mbit/s. Infrastructure-based and ad hoc networking configurations are both supported in HiperLAN/2. HiperLAN/2 is similar to IEEE 802.11a in that both operate in the 5 GHz band and both use OFDM. Differences between the two standards exist mainly in the MAC portion of the systems: HiperLAN/2 is connection oriented and uses a time division multiplexing scheme. Each channel, or connection, can be assigned an appropriate QoS based on need (type of data being transmitted, such as voice or video). More details on HiperLAN/2 can be found in [Mingozzi 2002]. In Europe the UNI band is reserved for HiperLAN operations. Currently, the IEEE 802.11 Task Group h is investigating means to make the 802.11 and HiperLAN standards coexist in the same 5 GHz band.

Figure 4.10 compares the various technologies, taking into consideration the cost-performance trade-off. As the figure shows, the market is changing this trade-off, and hence the applicative scenarios. Standard 802.11 was initially

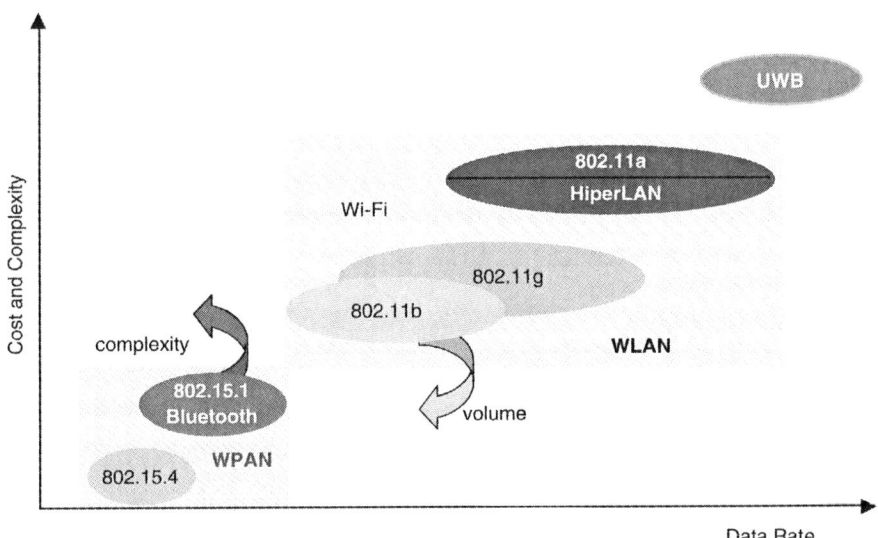

Figure 4.10 WBAN, WPAN, and WLAN technologies.

designed for office environments and was relatively costly, but the success of 802.11b reduced the costs and it is becoming an important technology for smart environments.[23] On the other end, the complexity of Bluetooth implementation is making this technology unavailable for all consumer electronics. It is expected that the role of Bluetooth in scenarios requiring short-range, low-cost, low-power wireless communications will be replaced by 802.15.4 solutions.

Throughout the chapter, we have focused on low-level network technologies for communications in pervasive computing environments. However, the characteristics of devices used in smart spaces require a new design for the overall network architecture and protocols. In pervasive environments, most of the communicating devices can be very small and have power, size, and weight restrictions that significantly limit their physical and link layer functionality and performance. Upper layers of the network protocol stack must therefore compensate. This is in contrast to the legacy networking approach, where the medium's performance challenges are hidden as much as possible from upper-layer protocols [Satyanarayanan 2001]. In general, this masking is desirable to minimize performance degradation of upper-level protocols designed for a more stable, low-loss wired environment. In the case of micro radios, this redundancy may be too expensive, and a different approach, involving tighter integration of the MAC layer with the layers above and below it, might be appropriate. This tendency is mainly emerging in ad hoc networking environments where a cross-layer design has been proposed in contrast to the legacy layered approach [Conti 2003b]. In the cross-layer approach,

---

[23]Currently, security concerns are probably the biggest barrier to acceptance of 802.11 technology. The weaknesses of 802.11 WEP are damaging the perception of the 802.11 standard in the market.

control information is continuously flowing top down and bottom up through the protocol stack, and a protocol behavior adapts to the status of both higher and lower protocols. With a cross-layer architecture, all protocols can access the information produced by/collected from the other protocols. This avoids duplication of the layers' efforts to collect network-status information, leading to a more efficient system design ([Goldsmith et al. 2002] and [MobileMAN]).

ACKNOWLEDGMENTS

This work was partially funded by the Information Society Technologies program of the European Commission, Future and Emerging Technologies under the IST-2001–38113 MobileMAN project, and by the Italian Ministry for Education and Scientific Research within the framework of the FIRB-VICOM project.

REFERENCES

[Acharya et al. 2002] A. Acharya, A. Misra, S. Bensal, "A Label-Switching Packet Forwarding Architecture for Multi-hop Wireless LANs," *Proceedings of the ACM Workshop on Mobile Multimedia (WoWMoM 2002)*, M. Conti and D. Raychaudhuri (Editors), Atlanta, September 28, 2002,

[Ahola 2001] J. Ahola, "Ambient Intelligence," *ERCIM News*, No. 47, October 2001, http://www.ercim.org/publication/Ercim_News/enw47/intro.html

[Akyildiz et al. 2002] I.F. Akyildiz, W. Su, Y. Sankarasubramaniam, E. Cayirci, "Wireless Sensor Networks: A Survey," *Computer Networks*, Vol. 38, 2002, pp. 393–422.

[Anastasi et al. 2003a] A. Anastasi, E. Borgia, M. Conti, E. Gregari, "IEEE 802.11 Ad Hoc Networks: Performance Measurements," *Cluster Computing Journal*, Special Issue on Ad Hoc Networks.

[Anastasi et al. 2003b] G. Anastasi, M. Conti, E. Gregori, A. Passarella, "Balancing Energy Saving and QoS in the Mobile Internet: An Application-Independent Approach," *Proceedings of the 36th Hawaii International Conference on System Sciences (HICSS-36)*, 2003, pp. 305–314.

[Anastasi et al. 2003c] G. Anastasi, M. Conti, E. Gregori, A. Passarella, "Performance Comparison of Power-Saving Strategies for Mobile Web Access," *Performance Evaluation Journal*, Vol. 53, No. 3–4, August 2003, pp. 273–294.

[Anastasi et al. 2004] G. Anastasi, M. Conti, E. Gregori, "IEEE 802.11 Ad Hoc Networks: Protocols, Performance and Open Issues," in *Mobile Ad Hoc Networking* (S. Basagni, M. Conti, S. Giordano, I. Stojmenovic, Editors), IEEE Press and John Wiley & Sons, New York, 2004.

[Bisdikian 2001] C. Bisdikian, "An Overview of the Bluetooth Wireless Technology," *IEEE Communication Magazine*, December 2001, pp. 86–94.

[Blue] Website of the Bluetooth Special Interest Group: http://www.bluetooth.com

[Bruno et al. 2001] R. Bruno, M. Conti, E. Gregori, "Wireless Access to Internet Via Bluetooth: Performance Evaluation of the EDC Scheduling Algorithm," *Proceedings of the First ACM Workshop on Wireless Mobile Internet*, Rome, 2001, pp. 43–49.

[Bruno et al. 2002a] R. Bruno, M. Conti, E. Gregori, "Traffic Integration in Personal, Local and Geographical Wireless Networks," in *Handbook of Wireless Networks and Mobile Computing* (I. Stojmenovic, Editor), John Wiley & Sons, New York, 2002.

[Bruno et al. 2002b] R. Bruno, M. Conti, E. Gregori, "Bluetooth: Architecture, Protocols and Scheduling Algorithms," *Cluster Computing Journal,* Vol. 5, No. 2, April 2002, pp. 117–131.

[Bruno et al. 2003] R. Bruno, F. Delmastro, "Design and Analysis of a Bluetooth-Based Indoor Localization System," *2003*, LNCS 2775, pp. 698–712.

[Callaway et al. 2002] E. Callaway, P. Gorday, L. Hester, J.A. Gutierrez, M. Naeve, "Home Networking with IEEE 802.15.4: A Developing Standard for Low-Rate Wireless Personal Area Networks," *IEEE Communications Magazine*, August 2002, pp. 70–77.

[Chlamtac et al. 2003] I. Chlamtac, M. Conti, J. Liu, "Mobile Ad Hoc Networking: Imperatives and Challenges," *Ad Hoc Networks Journal*, Vol. 1, No.1, January–March 2003, pp. 13–64.

[Conti 2003a] M. Conti, "Body, Personal, and Local Wireless Ad Hoc Networks," in *Handbook of Ad Hoc Networks* (M. Ilyas, Editor), CRC Press, New York, 2003.

[Conti 2003b] M. Conti, "Cross Layering in MANETs' Design" (extended abstract), *NeXtworking'03: The First COST(EU)-NSF(USA) Workshop on Exchanges and Trends in Networking*, June 23–25, 2003, Chania, Greece.

[Coutras et al. 2000] C. Coutras, S. Gupta, N.B. Shroff, "Scheduling of Realtime Traffic in IEEE 802.11 Wireless LANs," *ACM Wireless Networks,* Vol. 6, December 2000, pp. 457–466.

[Davide et al. 2002] F. Davide, P. Loreti, M. Lunghi, G. Riva, F. Vatalaro, "Communications Through Virtual Technologies," in *Advanced Lectures on Networking* (E. Gregori, G. Anastasi, S. Basagni, Editors), 2002.

[Ditlea 2000] S. Ditlea, "The PC Goes Ready to Wear," *IEEE Spectrum*, Vol. 37, No. 10, October 2000, pp. 34–39.

[Doherty et al. 2001] L. Doherty, B.A. Warneke, B.E. Boser, K.S.J. Pister, "Energy and Performance Considerations for Smart Dust," *Journal of Parallel Distributed Systems and Networks*, Vol. 4, No. 3, 2001, pp. 121–133.

[Estrin et al. 2002] D. Estrin, D. Culler, K. Pister, G. Sukhatme, "Connecting the Physical World with Pervasive Networks," *IEEE Pervasive Computing*, Vol. 1, No. 1, 2002, pp. 59–69.

[ETSI] ETSI Technical Report 101 683, V1.1.1, "Broadband Radio Access Networks (BRAN): High Performance Local Area Network (HiperLAN) Type 2; System Overview."

[Feeney 2004] L. Feeney, "Energy Efficient Communication in Ad Hoc Wireless Networks," in *Mobile Ad Hoc Networking* (S. Basagni, M. Conti, S. Giordano, I. Stojmenovic, Editors), IEEE Press and John Wiley & Sons, New York, 2004.

[Gast 2002] M.S. Gast, *802.11 Wireless Networks—The Definitive Guide*, O'Reilly & Associates, 2002.

[Goldsmith et al. 2002] A.J. Goldsmith, S.B. Wicker, "Design Challenges for Energy-Constrained Ad Hoc Wireless Networks," *IEEE Wireless Communications*, Vol. 9, No. 4, August 2002, pp. 8–27.

[Gu et al. 2003] D. Gu, J. Zhang, "QoS Enhancements in IEEE 802.11 Wireless Local Area Networks," *IEEE Communications Magazine*, June 2003, pp. 120–124.

[Kaczman 2002] J. Kaczman "Wi-Fi Hotspot Networks Sprout Like Mushrooms," *IEEE Spectrum*, September 2002, http://www.spectrum.ieee.org/WEBONLY/resource/sep02/nwi.html

[Kapp 2002] S. Kapp, "802.11a More Bandwidth without the Wires," *IEEE Internet Computing*, July–August 2002, pp. 75–79.

[Krashinsky et al. 2002] R. Krashinsky, H. Balakrishnan, "Minimizing Energy for Wireless Web Access Using Bounded Slowdown," *Proceedings of the ACM MOBICOM 2002 Conference*, Atlanta, September 2002, pp. 119–130.

[Kravets et al. 1998] R. Kravets, P. Krishnan, "Power Management Techniques for Mobile Communication," *Proceedings of the ACM/IEEE MOBICOM 98*, October 25–30, 1998, Dallas, Texas, pp. 157–168.

[Mangold et al. 2002] S. Mangold, S. Choi, P. May, O. Klein, G. Hiertz, L. Stibor, "IEEE 802.11e Wireless LAN for Quality of Service," *Proceedings of the European Wireless 2002 Conference*, Florence, February 2002, pp. 32–39.

[Marks et al. 2002] R.B. Marks, I.C. Gifford, B. O'Hara, "Standards from IEEE 802 Unleash the Wireless Internet," *IEEE Microwave*, June 2002, pp. 46–56.

[Michiardi et al. 2004] P. Michiardi, R. Molva, "Ad Hoc Networks Security," in *Mobile Ad Hoc Networking* (S. Basagni, M. Conti, S. Giordano, I. Stojmenovic, Editors), IEEE Press and John Wiley & Sons, New York, 2004.

[Miller et al. 2000] B.A. Miller, C. Bisdikian, *Bluetooth Revealed*, Prentice Hall, 2000.

[Mingozzi 2002] E. Mingozzi, "QoS Support by the HiperLAN/2 MAC Protocol: A Performance Evaluation," *Cluster Computing Journal*, Vol. 5, No. 2, April 2002, pp.145–155.

[MIT] The MIThril Home Page: http://www.media.mit.edu/wearables//mithril/index.html

[MobileMAN] European Commission, FET-IST Programme, *MobileMAN Project* (IST-2001–38113), "Deliverable D5": http://cnd.iit.cnr.it/mobileMAN

[Ni et al. 2002] Q. Ni, L. Romdhani, T. Turletti, I. Aad, "QoS Issues and Enhancements for IEEE 802.11 Wireless LAN," INRIA Research Report 4612, November 2002.

[P802.15.3] IEEE Draft P802.15.3/D15, "Wireless Medium Access Control (MAC) and Physical Layer (PHY) Specifications for High Rate Wireless Personal Area Networks (WPAN),"

[P802.15.4] IEEE Draft P802.15.3/D14, "Wireless Medium Access Control (MAC) and Physical Layer (PHY) Specifications for Low Rate Wireless Personal Area Networks (LR-WPANs),"

[Porcino et al. 2003] D. Porcino, W. Hirt, "Ultra-Wideband Radio Technology: Potential and Challenges Ahead," *IEEE Communications Magazine*, July 2003, pp. 66–74.

[RFC2284] PPP Extensible Authentication Protocol (EAP), RFC 2284, 1998: ftp://ftp.rfc-editor.org/in-notes/rfc2284.txt

[Satyanarayanan 2001] M. Satyanarayanan, "Pervasive Computing: Vision and Challenges," *IEEE Personal Communications*, August, 2001, pp. 10–17.

[Satyanarayanan 2002] M. Satyanarayanan, "A Catalyst for Mobile and Ubiquitous Computing," *IEEE Pervasive Computing*, Vol. 1, Issue 1, January–March 2002, pp. 2–5.

[Stallings 1996] W. Stallings, *Local and Metropolitan Area Networks*, Prentice Hall, Englewood Cliff, NJ: 1996.

REFERENCES

[Std802.11] ANSI/IEEE Std 802.11, 1999 edition, Wireless LAN Medium Access Control (MAC) and Physical Layer (PHY) Specifications.

[Std802.11a] IEEE Std 802.11a, 1999 edition (Supplement to IEEE Std 802.11, 1999 edition), Wireless LAN Medium Access Control (MAC) and Physical Layer (PHY) Specifications: High-Speed Physical Layer in the 5 GHZ Band.

[Std802.11b] IEEE Std 802.11b, 1999 edition (Supplement to ANSI/IEEE Std 802.11, 1999 edition): Wireless LAN Medium Access Control (MAC) and Physical Layer (PHY) Specifications: Higher-Speed Physical Layer Extension in the 2.4 GHz Band.

[Std802.11g] IEEE Std 802.11g-2003 (Amendment to IEEE Std 802.11, 1999 edition), Wireless LAN Medium Access Control (MAC) and Physical Layer (PHY) Specifications Amendment 4: Further Higher Data Rate Extension in the 2.4 GHz Band.

[Stemm et al. 1997] M. Stemm, R.H. Katz, "Measuring and Reducing Energy Consumption of Network Interfaces in Handheld Devices," *IEICE Transactions on Fundamentals of Electronics, Communications and Computer Science*, Special Issue on Mobile Computing, Vol. 80, No. 8, 1997, pp. 1125–1131.

[Tobagi et al. 1975] F.A. Tobagi, L. Kleinrock, "Packet Switching in Radio Channels: Part II," *IEEE Transactions on Communications*, Vol. 23, 1975, pp. 1417–1433.

[UCAN] European funded U.C.A.N. (Ultra Wideband Concepts for Ad-hoc Networks) project, IST program (IST-2001-32710), Deliverable number: D42–1.

[Varshney 2003] U. Varshney, "The Status and Future of 802.11-Based WLANs," *IEEE Computer*, June 2003, pp. 102–105.

[Veeraraghavan et al. 2001] M. Veeraraghavan, N. Cocker, T. Moors, "Support of Voice Services in IEEE 802.11 Wireless LANs," *Proceedings of INFOCOM 2001*, pp. 488–497.

[Weiser 1991] M. Weiser, "The Computer for the Twenty-First Century," *Scientific American*, September 1991, pp. 94–100.

[Woesner et al. 1998] H. Woesner, J.-P. Ebert, M. Schlager, A. Wolisz, "Power Saving Mechanisms in Emerging Standards for Wireless LANs: The MAC Level Perspective," *IEEE Personal Communications*, Vol. 5, No. 3, June 1998, pp. 40–48.

[Zaruba et al. 2004] G. Zaruba, S.K. Das, "Off-the-Shelf Enablers of Ad Hoc Networks," in *Mobile Ad Hoc Networking* (S. Basagni, M. Conti, S. Giordano, I. Stojmenovic, Editors), IEEE Press and John Wiley & Sons, New York, 2004.

[Zimmerman 1996] T.G. Zimmerman, "Personal Area Networks: Near-Field Intrabody Communication," *IBM Systems Journal*, Vol. 35, No. 3–4, 1996, pp. 609–617.

[Zimmerman 1999] T.G. Zimmerman, "Wireless Networked Devices: A New Paradigm for Computing and Communication," *IBM Systems Journal*, Vol. 38, No. 4, 1999, pp. 566–574.

[802.11] Website of the IEEE 802.11 WLAN: http://grouper.ieee.org/grups/802/11/main.html

[802.15] Website of the IEEE 802.15 WPA.N: http://www.ieee802.org/15/pub/main.html

[802.16] Website of the IEEE 802.16 WMA.N: http://www.ieee802.org/16/pub/main.html

CHAPTER 5

Middleware

G. MICHAEL YOUNGBLOOD

Department of Computer Science and Engineering
The University of Texas at Arlington

5.1 INTRODUCTION

Developing systems and software for a smart environment is a daunting task. Like any large endeavor, modern smart environments have many components. There is sensor hardware and software perceiving the environment, application software that interprets and reasons about that perception data, and effector control software acting on the environment, as well as many support systems. Most of these components work with an operating system on hardware that makes computation possible with the goal of making the environment 'smart.' Here lies the opportunity for software that can provide important services to facilitate rapid development, ease of integration, improved reliability, and increased scalability of systems that make smart environments possible. This software is commonly called *middleware*, and this chapter describes the search for the ideal smart environments middleware.

Middleware is connectivity software that joins applications through communication mechanisms creating transparency, scalability, and interoperability. It lies between the software applications it assists and the platform it is based on. Middleware typically resides in a layer built directly on the operating system of the target hardware platform, but it may be built on other layers of middleware, typically forming higher abstractions with each additional layer. Middleware is defined by the API (Application Programming Interface) it provides to applications that utilize it and the protocol(s) it supports [Ber96]. Middleware should be designed to reduce the complexities of the network, the host operating system, and any available resource servers creating value in simplifying these for the applications using it and the developers who write them [Lin97]. Middleware should provide a cross-platform infrastructure that facilitates rapid development by providing services and features that would normally have to be developed if not provided by the operating

---

Smart Environments: Technologies, Protocols, and Applications, edited by D.J. Cook and S.K. Das
ISBN 0-471-54448-5 © 2005 John Wiley & Sons, Inc.

system, as well as providing a consistent and natural extension to the development of software applications. Overall, middleware should improve the desired characteristics of the target application and the developed system.

The goals of this chapter are to provide an understanding of the concept of middleware, present its desirable characteristics, and discuss its forms as well as the advantages and disadvantages of each form. We will introduce some of the technologies in current use, develop an understanding of the importance of standards and where to find them, and present design issues to consider in choosing the proper form and technology for a project. We hope to develop an understanding of the benefits of middleware and will present what current intelligent environments use for middleware that may provide some insight, ideas, and options for other smart environment projects. To accomplish these goals, we will start by discussing some basic software architecture and the desirable characteristics of middleware that enhance system designs. Then the current forms and trends will be presented and discussed, leading to a further discussion on middleware standards. Following that discussion, we will expand on design considerations before considering what middleware systems are being utilized in current smart environment projects. We will end with a discussion summarizing what we have covered.

This is an information chapter. Every smart environment project is slightly different; each has unique requirements, architecture, systems, and goals. We wish that we could give a definitive answer to the question of which middleware solution, if any, best fits a set of given project needs, but this would be a very large undertaking and the subject of a book in itself. Our goal in this chapter is to provide a working knowledge base for the smart environment designer, system architect, and developer so that they will have the basic tools to begin an examination of their system needs against possible middleware solutions. We are commited to the search for the ideal middleware for smart environments, but we realize that there is no silver bullet [Bro95] and that this will be a limited breadth-first search. This chapter is a survey of what is currently in common use, but it is by no means comprehensive. The reader is strongly encouraged to use this chapter as a knowledge base from which to explore more deeply and broadly the world of middleware.

Before we get started, we will build an analogy that we can apply as we discover more about middleware. Since we are more than likely developing a smart environment, or at least thinking about it, we use the analogy of a structure—a house. The hardware platform will be represented by the foundation of the house, and the operating system will be the general structure of the house (i.e., outside veneer, frame, walls, doors, windows, roof). In this house we will place the standard home appliances, such as a telephone, television, stereo system, refrigerator, gas oven, microwave oven, telephone, and so forth. In setting up this home, everything seems in place. What would represent the middleware in this house? We haven't introduced any extra technology in the home, and this is not a smart environment as described, but there is a layer of nonsoftware middleware.

Using our home analogy, we shall add a telephone. The telephone can be used to communicate (among other things) with people on other telephones across the Earth. The telephone represents an application. The middleware is defined by its interface, the telephone wire (RJ-11), and its protocol, analog voice waveform. The middleware can be extended to the local coder-decoder (codec) that forms the boundary for the operating system and networking (i.e., the digital telephone system). The middleware converts the analog signal to a digital signal handling a complex conversion so that the phone does not have to do so, and it supplies the signal and routing information to the telephone company infrastructure; conversely, the middleware will in full-duplex fashion decode digital signals into analog signals for playback through the phone. Thus, middleware greatly simplifies the application's required resources, provides a clear protocol and a standard and natural interface (humankind is now very familiar with plugging in wired appliances). Many middleware products facilitate the client-server relationship where there is a consumer and a producer or the peer-to-peer relationship where there is an exchange of information/services. This home analogy extends to all basic services. For example, the gas stove is the client application, the gas company is the server, and the middleware is the gas piping where the interface is the gas adapter fittings and the protocol is natural gas (mostly methane). Middleware provides an interface and a protocol, but what other characteristics can it possess?

5.2 NEEDS, WANTS, AND DESIRES

There may be an infinite number of approaches and paradigm combinations to explore when building smart environments, but we shall use a basic perceive-reason-act AI (artificial intelligence) approach [RN95] as a building block to identify a typical set of software needs, add some wants, and define desirable characteristics for middleware we might consider.

Start with a basic house. In this house we are going to place sensors (e.g., for temperature, humidity, light); these will be our senses or perceptory input through which we *perceive*. Logically, each sensor or group of sensors is represented in a computer by a simple application that allows a specific sensor to be read, produce a continuous reading, initiates calibration, and performs other appropriate operations. Next, we add some software AI applications (more than one) to *reason* about this environment based on perception in order to provide an action to change the system's state—hopefully for the better. We arrange these so that there are three AI applications, two of which receive sensor data as inputs, perform some independent reasoning on this data, and then pass abstract data to a single decision-making application that will decide whether to take an action by doing nothing or passing information on to a controller application. Finally, we add some controls over the environment (e.g., power control, light control, water flow control), as mentioned previously. These are actions that we can take to affect the environment through which we *act*. Figure 5.1 provides a graphical representation of this design.

The basics are put forth, but there are still many unanswered questions about this design and how it should work. We are working to build an architecture composed of several different components that, when working together and with each component

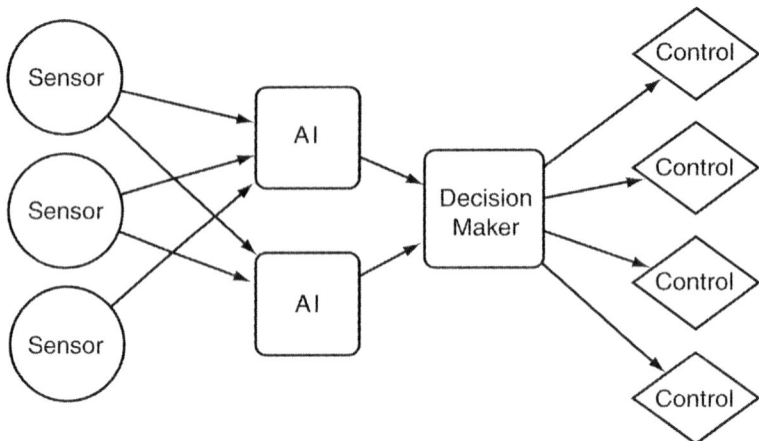

Figure 5.1 Basic perceive-reason-act design.

performing as designed, comprise a complete perceive-reason-act-based system to control an environment. However, in this chapter we are not concerned with the inner workings of each component, but rather with their communication requirements and features that can improve this system's functionality, preferably with little extra work by the developer.

The needs of this system are defined, first, by the need for application interoperability—the ability of two or more entities to exchange and interpret information [IoEEE90]. The sensors need to provide information to the input AI applications, the AI applications need to provide information to the decision maker, and the decision maker needs to pass information to a controller. The act of communication alone creates further needs. We want to ensure that when communication occurs the messages have a delivery guarantee, so the mechanism must be reliable. The communication process should minimize resource consumption and time of delivery, so it must be efficient. These applications may provide a large amount of data traffic in their intercommunication, so the middleware should have a high level of throughput. The middleware should hopefully not be the bottleneck in any system unless that is inherent in the problem—in which case it should provide a clear advantage over other solutions. In addition to our basic interoperability need, all of these applications should not have to reside on a single piece of hardware. Middleware should allow this communication to occur among these applications through a network, with the possibility of all components being on the same machine, all on different machines, or a combination of both (i.e., distributed computing support). These machines may be in the same area or geographically distributed. Reliable, efficient, and distributed communication is our basic need.

In addition to these needs, we would want middleware that provides for future extensions and contingencies. If we decide to add more sensors or controllers to our system, we want the system to scale up appropriately and easily to accommodate larger systems. Furthermore, if we decide to replace an existing application in the system, the middleware should allow for hot-swappable components so that the system does not have to be shut down in order to replace an application component. If important data is transmitted between applications, there should be a secure means of communication to protect the data. While middleware provides these features, we want such a system to be highly available, always running and accessible to applications in need of the middleware services, and to be fault-tolerant, continuing operations despite failures in hardware or software components [IoEEE90]. We certainly do not want a fragile system or one prone to complete failure if one of the distributed component applications fails. The addition of scalability, hot swapability, and security in a highly available, fault-tolerant middleware system increases the value that a middleware solution can provide.

Given the mentioned needs and wants, we add some additional desirable characteristics. The developers want simplicity and power. Middleware (APIs) should provide simple (low-complexity) but powerful interfaces with a high level of transparency—interfaces that follow the same form and function as other integral parts of the implementation (e.g., in C++ a transparent API may simply add additional classes that, when instantiated, appear as any other object in the system to which standard means of use apply, such as using the stream insertion operator to pass information to that object). A middleware solution should feel like a natural and seamless extension of the development environment for the implementer and should not present an overly complex system that removes the focus from the purpose of the system under development. The middleware interface should offer flexibility to allow easy modification of software components so that they can interact in different environments. Middleware that provides means for developing well-defined interfaces while keeping a separation from the implementation greatly aids in maintaining many programming paradigms, as well as aiding flexibility, and provides interface maintainability and reusability. Maintainability is important to development and for the future life of a system. The interface must have the ability to be modified in order to correct errors, make improvements, or be adapted to environmental changes [IoEEE90]. Reusability is also important to developers who like to create common solutions to problems and use them in different systems. Middleware should make reusability easier and perhaps more intuitive. That reusability would be greatly enhanced by a high degree of portability. Middleware should be available on many platforms and provide a consistent interface across them, allowing the same development code to be used in multiple environments. It is desirable for middleware solutions to have low complexity and transparent interfaces while providing flexibility, maintainability, reusability, and portability for developers to more easily adopt, integrate, and utilize these solutions to improve their systems and applications.

This is just an overview of the process that system architects and developers should go through when designing smart environments and choosing middleware. There is much to consider in designing and building these systems. Every uniquely designed system will have a set of unique requirements. System architects should carefully evaluate the system requirements when considering a fit for middleware solutions. At a minimum, the benefits that middleware should provide are improved functionality, reliability, and development cycles through simple, natural interfaces and common services. System needs, wants, and desires are creating the demand for middleware that provides efficient, reliable, interoperable, flexible, portable, secure, scalable, maintainable, reusable, adaptable, and transparent services. For the interested reader, the Software Engineering Institute at Carnegie-Mellon University provides more information concerning software characteristics and design [Ins03].

5.3 BETWEEN THE OPERATING SYSTEM AND THE APPLICATION

Now that we have a better understanding of what middleware is and what we are looking for in a middleware solution, we will explore these systems that reside between the operating system and the using applications. In this section we will discuss some architecture basics before talking about the forms of middleware, followed by a discussion of frameworks, middleware services, and ubicomp initiatives.

5.3.1 Architecture Basics

Middleware is mostly about communication. Before we begin discussing the forms of middleware, we shall review some basic communication paradigms. Computing began with close human-computer interfaces requiring rewiring of the computer, using punch cards or paper tape and even flipping switches before the field advanced to teletype interfaces. Eventually computing moved to the mainframe architecture, which consists of a central mainframe computer where all computation is performed and users interacting with the system through terminals that capture keystrokes and relay the information to the mainframe. Over time and with the advent of personal computers (PCs), computing moved toward a file-sharing architecture utilizing these new PCs to download files from shared locations to the local desktop where user jobs were run. In the 1990s, when more and more people began using PCs, the PC local area networks (LANs) became too overloaded for this paradigm [Ede94].

The limitations of the file-sharing architecture gave birth to the client-server architecture. The file server was replaced by a database server that responds to queries by returning only requested information instead of whole files. This reduced the network traffic load and made way for incorporating graphical-based clients to provide a consistent desktop experience [Ede94, Sch95]. Client-server architectures are typically implemented in two- or three-tier architectures.

Two-tier client-server architectures are defined by a client layer and a server layer, as shown in Figure 5.2. This design assigns the system interface (e.g., session management, display interface, input/output) to the client and the database management system (DBMS) to the server. There is an additional component of the system that is shared between the two tiers—processing management that manages the initiation, conduct, and publication of the results from work to be performed. This migration to a more specialized system of services that perform specific work and

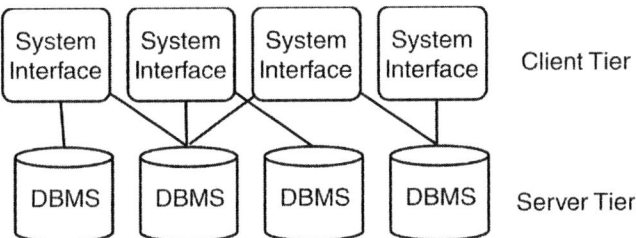

Figure 5.2 Two-tier client-server architecture [Ins03].

clients that request work utilizes resources more effectively and efficiently. It also allows for greater specialization of the server to perform work and of the client to be more tailored to the capabilities of the client platform. This provides scalability and flexibility over the file-sharing architecture and performs well in light traffic conditions [Ins03].

The three-tier client-server architecture shown in Figure 5.3 was designed to compensate for the two-tier architecture's shortcomings. A middle tier is added between the system interface and the DBMS. This tier takes over process management by providing logic and rules to control job processing and adds features such as queueing of messages. The addition of this layer and the features it provides increases the number of clients the system can handle (increased performance) and improves the system's flexibility, maintainability, reusability, and scalability [Ins03]. This architecture has become the basis for many middleware solutions.

Given the background information on communication architectures, we are now ready to examine how middleware has grown from this architectural beginning as our worldwide information systems have grown in size and complexity.

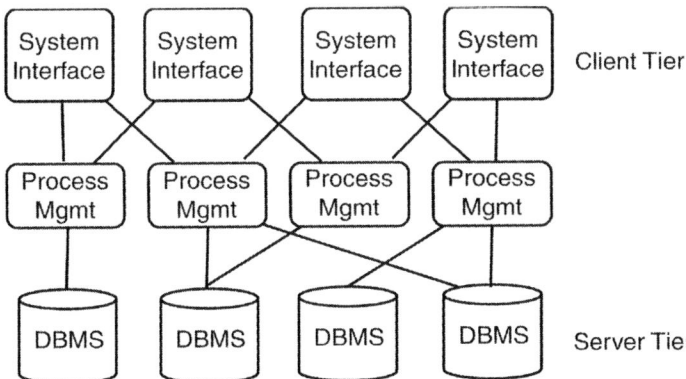

Figure 5.3 Three-tier client-server architecture [Ins03].

5.3.2 Forms of Middleware

Middleware comes in many forms; the ones presented here are the most typical architectures being utilized currently. The number of middleware products is staggering, and many in this field have slightly different views about the role, terminology, and composition of these systems. This is the nature of the area of middleware and is a sign of how rapidly it is advancing. After all, when programmers wrote machine code for specific platforms and those were the only programs that ran on a machine (one at a time), along came the idea of a novel piece of middleware, the operating system, which sat between the hardware and the application to allow programmers to write code for an operating system instead of a specific hardware platform. In the next sections, we will present the basic forms in high-level categories of middleware. In each section we will present an overview of the technology, discuss its strengths and weaknesses, and then list some implementation examples for the reader's reference.

5.3.2.1 Transaction Processing Transaction processing (TP) monitor technology is involved with creating a middle tier of processing routines between a system that provides transaction-based services (e.g., financial, sales) and clients making those transactions. Many TP systems utilize the two-phase commit protocol [LS79], which can be demanding on a high-use system. Introducing a layer of processing routines to manage the transactions more loosely with the clients in a stateless manner while being statefully coupled to the transaction server allows the system to serve orders of magnitude more clients while satisfying the rigid transaction protocols. Figure 5.4 illustrates this technology.

TP monitor technology usually includes the ability to handle client disconnects and reconnects seamlessly, restart failed processes to maintain availability, marshal data from various types of clients into a consistent form for TP, perform load balancing, and provide consistent logic across clients.

The advantages of this type of middleware includes independence of the key layers. The client is independent and can be customized for specific platforms, the TP monitor is independent; it can take any clients that communicate with the proper transaction protocols and can communicate with a transaction server over a defined transaction protocol. The transaction server and underlying database are transparent to the TP monitor. This system is efficient and reliable in creating a flexible transaction-based system. It is very mature and well tested in large-scale deployments servicing millions of transactions per day.

One disadvantage of this type of middleware is its limited scalability because each client incurs a small amount of system overhead on the TP monitor. Also, because it is an older form of middleware, most of these systems are written in and for lower-level programming languages.

Examples of TP monitoring technology implementations are IBM's CICS TP monitor and BEA TUXEDO.

5.3.2.2 Message-Oriented Message-oriented middleware (MOM) is a layer of software that resides on the operating system and provides communication

5.3 BETWEEN THE OPERATING SYSTEM AND THE APPLICATION

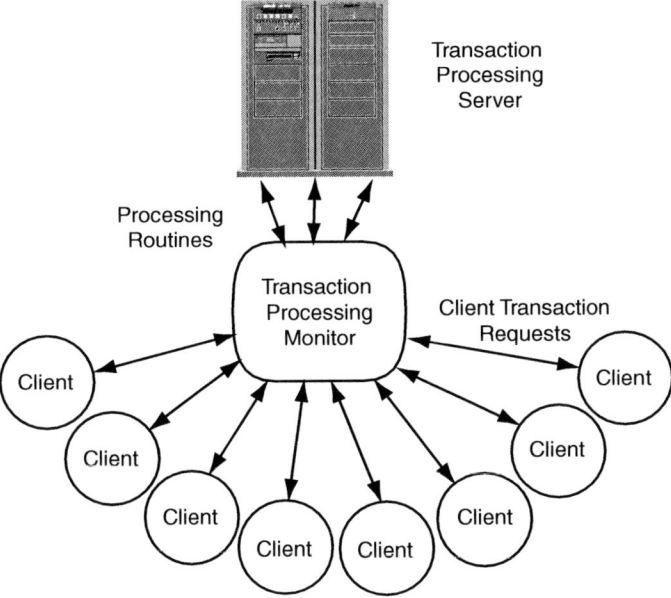

Figure 5.4 TP monitor technology [Ins03].

services between applications either on the same machine or on other machines on possibly different platforms. These messages are generally asynchronous but could be synchronous (sometimes, if desired), and the middleware usually provides message queueing and persistence for those times when the message recipient is unavailable and delivery is postponed until the recipient is available. MOM establishes a peer-to-peer level of connectivity between applications, breaking down the strict client-server relationship that sometimes forces master-slave relationships. The messages can follow agreed-upon protocols and may include structure and forms freeing the developer from cross-platform issues such as endianess [Ste95]. Figure 5.5 illustrates a typical MOM system.

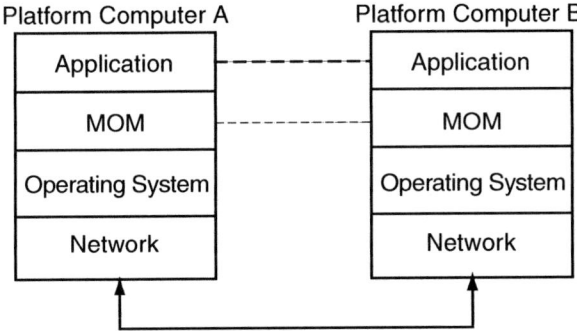

Figure 5.5 Message-oriented middleware [Ins03].

MOM provides the advantages of abstracting away cross-platform and local communication complexities, increased interoperability between applications through communication, cross-platform portability for messaging, and increased flexibility. MOM is a good fit for event-driven applications and peer-to-peer communications. Asynchronous communications allow continued operations of the system instead of waiting on message delivery and response. MOM has been around since the 1980s and is a mature technology.

The disadvantages of MOM are that with asynchronous communications it is easy for a client to overload the network and the server that is not processing the messages quickly. MOM must run on every platform in a system, and if there is no implementation for a platform, the system will not work. There may also be limitations on protocol support with less popular platforms.

Examples of MOM systems are Oracle Advanced Queueing, Arjuna Messaging, IBM MQSeries, and Microsoft MSMQ.

5.3.2.3 Object-Oriented Object-oriented middleware or object-request brokers (ORB) are middleware technologies that extend the object-oriented development and communication paradigms to middleware. ORBs support interface definition languages, object communication mechanisms, and object activation and location mechanisms. ORBs facilitate locating objects and establishing communication with those objects in a manner similar to that of MOM technology. ORB interfaces and object communications usually appear as transparent extensions to the object-oriented development environment. Objects that may be remotely located seem local to the objects communicating with them. Figure 5.6 illustrates an ORB system.

The advantages of ORB technology are those of MOM. In addition, the interface is usually a natural extension of the object-oriented development environment. Interface description languages employed by ORB systems provide a clear mechanism

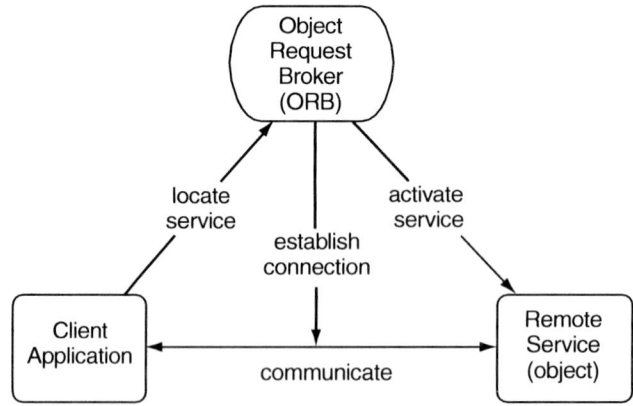

Figure 5.6 Object request broker [Ins03].

for providing contractual interfaces between objects, provide for rapid integration, and preserve implementation and interface separation.

The disadvantages of ORB technology include the fact that different ORBs provide different levels of service, support ranges of platforms, and often support only certain OO languages. Finding the ORB to meet all of the software needs requires careful examination of the available ORB implementations [AEGO96].

Examples of object-oriented middleware include OMG's CORBA, Microsoft's COM/DCOM, and Sun's Java RMI.

5.3.2.4 Database Database connectivity issues can be complicated. Middleware products have been developed to provide API access to standard database interfaces in an effort to answer the call for simplified, robust database connectivity. This layer takes the form of development connectivity tools and language extensions that facilitate the application to database communications.

The advantages of this middleware come from its standard and simplified database connectivity. The disadvantages are that many solutions are not cross-platform, may not support advanced database features (especially proprietary ones), and may provide blocking, synchronous connections.

Examples of database middleware include Microsoft's ODBC, Sun's JDBC, and Rogue Wave Software Inc.'s DBTools.h + + [Lin97].

5.3.2.5 Remote Procedure Call A more discrete form of middleware lies in Remote Procedure Call (RPC) technology. RPCs are stubs embedded in the client-server applications at compile time. The stubs facilitate procedure calls between client and server. Figure 5.7 shows the structure of RPC middleware [Ste95].

The advantages of RPCs include providing a level of consistency in procedure calls both locally and remotely, a natural extension for remotely calling server functions, and network transparency of the client-server locations.

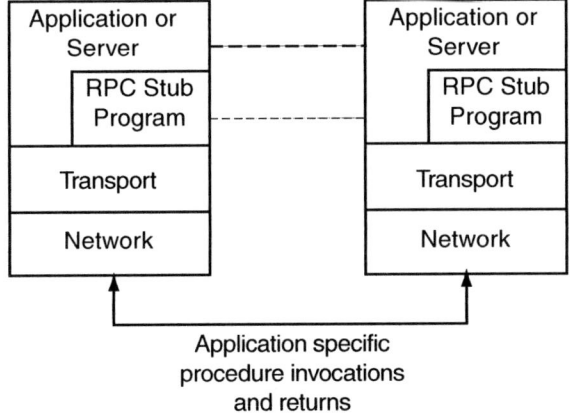

Figure 5.7 Remote procedure calls [Ste95].

The disadvantages of RPCs stem from the fact that the majority of them are implemented using synchronous communications, forcing a call-wait scenario that can cause blockages in the flow of an application. Even in cases where RPCs include asynchronous mechanisms, they add significant complexity to the development [Rao95].

Synchronous RPC can keep a system simple and prevent network overloading. However, it makes the technology a poor choice for object-oriented systems or peer-to-peer implementations.

The Open Group's Distributed Computing Environment is an example of an RPC system [TOG03, Blo92].

5.3.2.6 Web Services Web services are popular because they bridge the interface gap between applications that are often hidden by network security features such as firewalls. Leveraging the basics of technologies that have created the ubiquitous World Wide Web, a web service is simply a network accessible interface to an application using web-based protocols (e.g., HTTP, XML) [STK02]. Typically, the interface is provided by ASCII text-based XML (eXtensible Markup Language) communicated between applications via HTTP (Hyper-Text Transport Protocol). XML merely specifies a format language; however, the true definition of the interface is molded by other emerging technologies such as SOAP (Simple Object Access Protocol) that add object-oriented mechanisms to web services and WSDL (Web Services Definition Language), which provides communication descriptions between web service endpoints. Figure 5.8 illustrates how web services work.

The advantages of web services are that, due to the ubiquitous nature of web servers and browser APIs of which they take advantage, there is a wealth of software to facilitate infrastructure development and implementation. Communication over an ASCII-based message protocol improves troubleshooting due to complete message transparency and almost human-readable message traffic. Since most corporate security systems already allow web traffic into and out of the enterprise, communication barriers for web services are few. Network administrators can easily ensure that web traffic channels are available.

The ability to easily pass XML traffic through HTTP traffic channels on the network has led to potential security holes and the implementation of network equipment that can filter by traffic content. Another weakness of web services is that the conversion of data structures into XML and the subsequent parsing are

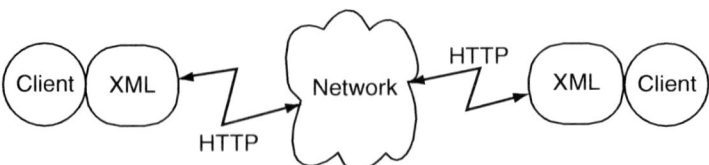

Figure 5.8 Example of web service structure.

computationally expensive compared to more native binary data formats; thus, web services tend to be slow. Describing data in XML also greatly expands the data structure size, utilizing more bandwidth for communications.

Examples of web service building tools and infrastructure support include Apple Computer's WebObjects, IBM's Websphere, Microsoft's .NET Framework, and Sun's Open Net Environment.

5.3.2.7 Agent-Oriented Agent research being conducted in universities around the world is the basis for the emergence for a new type of middleware—one that focuses on intelligent software agents. Agents are autonomous, intelligent software entities that have the ability to perceive their environment, reason about what they observe, and act to change that environment to accomplish their goals [RN95, ISAG03]. Agent technologies are being used to solve financial management, military logistics, personal information management, and other problems [ISAG03]. Since agents need to perceive and act on their environment, communicate with outside entities and other agents, and may have platform and network mobility middleware components, multiagent systems (MAS) have emerged to serve agents' needs. These packages typically appear more as frameworks (to be discussed later) and provide means for interagent communication, load balancing, and mobility (moving agents between machines), but some systems utilize extensions to MOM and object-oriented middleware systems creating higher levels of middleware solutions. Agent middleware may be one of the areas of growth in this field as this paradigm expands.

Examples of agent frameworks are HIVE [MGR+99] and CMU's RETSINA [SDP+96].

5.3.3 Frameworks

Not to be confused with the middleware forms discussed previously but worth mentioning is the area of frameworks. Frameworks are targeted at specific domains and consist of software environments that provide an API, a user interface, and tools for application development and system management [Ber96]. Frameworks may provide their own private middleware services and may utilize other common middleware services. For specific domains, frameworks may provide better solutions than general middleware and may be accurately called middleware themselves.

Examples of some frameworks include Lotus Notes, Microsoft Office, Transarc's Encina, Cognos, and HP's OpenView [Ber96].

5.3.4 Middleware Services

This may be an area of definitional debate; some people consider the types of middleware described previously to be middleware services and middleware itself to be those services and/or frameworks [Ber96]. We choose to refer to distributed system services as middleware under the premise that good middleware is never seen (transparent) and tends to be useless unless used by an application, whereas frameworks usually provide a user interface and environment and are therefore visible to the user. For now, we will refer to them as frameworks, defining *middleware services* as service components that provide value-added work to other middleware clients. Such middleware services include naming services, directory services, interface repositories, and data libraries.

As middleware evolves, abstracting commonly implemented components into the middleware adds value and functionality that reduces the development burden and creates portable, common solutions to commonly occurring problems. We will not discuss all of the middleware services available today; instead, we will focus on the trend of services provided.

When distributing components across the network, it is often difficult to locate those components and, more importantly, to locate useful components. Naming services create central repository locations for performing name lookups from common names to resource names that provide location and connection information. When a component is not sure of the name of another component it seeks to connect to, but knows what type of component it is, a trading service can broker the connection by providing matching names based on desired characteristics to requesting clients; these are also known as *discovery services* [HV99].

Services may even provide modified communication schemes, such as an event service that can provide a more decoupled publish-subscribe communication method augmenting or replacing point-to-point communications [HV99]. Services can add value and flexibility to middleware.

5.3.5 Ubicomp Initiatives

In a world soon to be dominated by ubiquitous computing (ubicomp), several initiatives have emerged to tame the potential madness. In the current state of technology, when a user purchases new computer peripheral devices (e.g., printers, scanners, PDAs), the user has to load in drivers and configure items before being able to fully utilize those new devices. As more and more items have embedded microchips placed in them and gain features that allow them to become managed or peer computing peripherals, the user-required configuration scheme may become unmanageable. Technologies such as ZEROCONF [Che03] and Universal Plug and Play (UPnP) [UPn03] seek to alleviate the problem through zero configuration technologies that allow devices to self-integrate and configure in their local environments. These technologies may become part of the middleware infrastructure and are already embedded in the operating systems of Apple (Rendezvous branded ZEROCONF) and Microsoft (UPnP). Zero configuration technologies are poised to replace name and service discovery middleware services.

5.4 STANDARDS

A common mistake of new designers is to think that they are the first to solve a problem or that their solution is better than anyone else's. This type of thinking leads to islands of technology and repetition of research and effort. By introducing some standards and sources, we hope that readers will utilize existing standards and strive to improve them to allow scientific and engineering progress to continue and avoid repetition of work. To this end, we will start by discussing some of the middleware standards in common use and introduce the organizations leading the standardization effort. Following this will be a discussion of protocol standards.

5.4.1 Middleware Standards and Implementations

The growth of middleware and its core communication-based underpinnings has caused the need for commonality in functionality, interfaces, and protocols so that even though different implementers provide different solutions, they should still be able to interoperate. Some standards are led by industry-independent organizations that act as consortiums for collaboration and compromise producing open, well-defined standards, while others coming from proprietary corporations become de facto standards due to their large market share and heavy corporate influence.

5.4.1.1 COM/DCOM An example of a de facto standard is the Component Object Model (COM), Distributed COM (DCOM) middleware from Microsoft. COM, originally a Windows technology that has since migrated to other platforms, provides a model for interface definition through the IDL (Interface Description Language) and a protocol for communication between objects. DCOM extends this to components across the network.

5.4.1.2 CORBA A more open standard has been defined by the Object Management Group [OMG03] in CORBA (Common Object Request Broker Architecture). CORBA is part of a larger standard called the Object Management Architecture (OMA), which defines how application interfaces, domain interfaces, ORBs, and object services interact. CORBA uses IDL-to-programming language mapping for the large number of object-oriented languages supported. Skeleton and stub code are generated and compiled into developer code that interacts with an ORB on each machine. The ORBs talk to each other in a distributed system through the network using an inter-ORB protocol (e.g., IIOP, the Internet Inter-ORB Protocol) to facilitate a complete communication infrastructure. Services such as naming, trading, and event as well as IDL repositories and dynamic capabilities make CORBA a powerful and widely used middleware standard.

5.4.1.3 DCE Another open standard is the Open Group's Distributed Computing Environment (DCE) [TOG03]. DCE is composed of a set of integrated system service specifications that are operating system, network, and platform independent. DCE provides fundamental distributed services such as remote procedure calls (RPC), security, directory, time, and threads, as well as data-sharing services such as a distributed file system and diskless workstation support [Ins03]. DCE has been very popular and forms the basis of many other middleware layers. Recent extensions to improve object and web compatibility create continued use and growth opportunities for DCE.

5.4.1.4 Java Middleware Technologies Sun Microsystems' Java language was originally designed for embedded devices and found quick adoption during the growing use of the Internet by providing a mechanism to distribute operational code over the network via applets. Java was also capable of creating applications, and due to its portability its use has been growing. JIT (Just in-time) compilers and optimizers have improved the interpreted language's speed and efficiency.

The Java platform hosts a number of middleware initiatives and support. Java supports CORBA as part of its platform and also from many vendor products. Java also offers the proprietary Java Remote Method Invocation (RMI) mechanisms that provide a CORBA-like object-oriented middleware layer for distributed inter Java-object communication. In cooperation with industry partners, Sun has developed the Java Message Service (JMS) API as part of the Java 2 Enterprise Edition to provide MOM to enterprise Java systems. Java also participates in the web services realm by offering the Java Web Services Developer Pack (Java WSDP) to facilitate easy integration of web services into Java applications. Java Servlet technology and Java Server Pages (JSP) provide the means to extend web server functionality and provide dynamic content to support web service serving applications. And if that is not enough, Java Jini technology is being deployed to provide adaptive network-centric applications and services from dynamic networked components through middleware that offers code mobility, open protocols, fault tolerance, and ease of integration [SM03]. The Java platform is poised to offer all of this as long as the developer adopts programming in Java and does not mind being completely dependent on technologies from a single source.

5.4.2 Web Services Standards

The World Wide Web Consortium (W3C), fueled by a strong industry focus on web services, is leading the way to provide standards for web interoperable technologies—specifications, guidelines, software, and tools [WWWC03]. Specifications for HTML, HTTP, XML, SOAP/XMLP, WSDL, and other key technologies can be found on their website.

In addition to the W3C there is the Organization for the Advancement of Structured Information Standards (OASIS). OASIS is another membership-driven standards body that is currently offering specifications for DocBook (a documentation standard), Directory Services Markup Language (DSML), ebXML (eBusiness XML), Security Assertion Markup Language (SAML), and the Universal Description, Discovery and Integration of Web Services (UDDI) standard, among others [OAS03a]. UDDI is bringing trading services to web services [OAS03b].

As mentioned in the previous section, many vendors are also providing development tools, APIs, and services that facilitate faster web service development. As this area matures, many may fall out of use and dominant forms may become de facto standards.

5.4.3 Databases

Databases play an important role in modern systems as storage caches for often vast amounts of information that is the key component of processing systems. Structured Query Language (SQL), created by Oracle based on SEQUEL by IBM in the mid-1970s, has become the de facto database communication language even though many vendors provide nonstandard extensions [Web03]. Open DataBase Connectivity (ODBC), developed by Microsoft, provides a middleware database driver to facilitate standard database communications between applications and a database. Many database vendors produce ODBC-compliant databases. Sun provides ODBC for Java in the form of JDBC.

5.4.4 Protocols

There are protocols for just about everything one can imagine in computing. This chapter has already mentioned many protocols and sources for information, but in addition to communication negotiation protocols, there are specifications for many of the intricate information transactions that take place between applications and/or systems. A good source for protocol information is the Internet Engineering Task Force's (IETF) Request For Comments (RFC) website [IET03], where authors submit protocol specifications for comments and opinions, or the Internet Assigned Numbers Authority (IANA) website [IAN03], where port numbers are assigned to services that can be traced to the protocols used by those services. As stated in Section 5.4.2, W3C [WWWC03] and OASIS [OAS03a] provide protocol standards. The Open Group [TOG03] and Object Management Group [OMG03] provide them as well. Standards bodies such as the ISO [IOfS03] and ANSI [ANSI03] may provide internationally or United States approved standards. For mobile communications there is the Open Mobile Alliance (OMA) [OMA03]. More broadly for telecommunications, there is the International Telecommunication Union Telecommunication Standardization Sector (ITU-T) [ITU03].

Utilizing standards and providing feedback and participation to the users community of those standards helps them meet their intended goals and become mature technologies. Standards provide contracts for interoperability and allow powerful systems to be built.

5.5 DESIGN CONSIDERATIONS

In Section 5.2 we discussed our needs, wants, and desires as architects and developers of smart environment systems. In Sections 5.3 and 5.4 we covered middleware basics, forms, implementations, and standards. Now we revisit those design discussions.

Users may have determined that they do not need middleware for their work. That argument has been made many times, to the detriment of everyone who could have used someone's work had it been more easily integrated into theirs. Researchers tend to be the worst offenders since they often prefer to work in isolation and often have project tunnel vision. Consider that if there is even a remote possibility that others may benefit from using a system, that system should be easy to integrate. Middleware can help, and this is why middleware is important.

Middleware should complement a project, making it easier to design, develop, and maintain. It should provide interoperability, reliability, efficiency, and throughput handling to applications using it. It should also afford security, scalability, adaptability, dynamism, availability, and fault tolerance. For the future life of the application, middleware should also allow flexibility, portability, maintainability, and reusability. Designers should know what they are looking for, what the limitations and requirements are, and choose middleware that best fits the goals of the application, but they should also be careful.

Caveat emptor! Middleware can also be plagued with pitfalls. Many middleware solutions can add a large amount of infrastructure to a project. This may incur more system administration and problems than benefits. Many solutions are completely proprietary to a single vendor, which makes a project risky if that vendor goes out of business or decides to discontinue the product. Even with standardized middleware, many vendors extend the standards to include their own proprietary extensions, which may add value but will make the project dependent on that particular vendor's solution (the same problem as with a completely proprietary solution). Even if they are very tempting and offer an improvement, developers should try to avoid using proprietary API extensions. As an alternative, open source projects often seem tempting and may provide some good middleware solutions (e.g., the fastest CORBA implementation, omniORB, is an open source project [Gri03]), but many open source projects do not last long, because development is on a volunteer basis and many authors move on to paying work. Open source dependence may lead to middleware maturity issues that may force the development team to work on the middleware instead of the target project. Open source licensing may make it difficult to sell a product for profit or may require that source code be distributed. However, open source projects may provide excellent immediate solutions, and if an organization is willing to contribute to the middleware project, they may provide more long-term solutions.

Middleware is defined by its API and the protocols it uses [Ber96]. We have said that to stay standard one should avoid proprietary API extensions, but there is another concern. Protocols can change or even have dialects—more vendor extensions. The same rules should apply for protocols as for APIs: Do not use the proprietary protocol extensions; stay with the standard specified protocol. This is not to say that these extensions are evil or that they do not add value; some proprietary extensions even become part of the standard (e.g., Netscapisms that were added to the HTML specification). Middleware should grow with the standards they are based on and implement the newest features of their design and protocol specifications. Users of proprietary extensions need to consider the benefits of use over the retooling of the software if the middleware vendor is changed or if the middleware solution ceases to exist. They must also consider the impact on interoperability with other applications.

As projects use more and more middleware products, there is a dependence shift from the operating system and platform services to the middleware and its services. Projects should look for middleware that provides for their needs, wants, and desires, but that also follows an open standard that has many vendor implementations (both commercial and open source) and multiple platform support. Focus should be on what the project really needs for a middleware solution and what can best provide those needs.

Going back to the basic perceive-reason-act system presented in Section 5.2 Figure 5.1, we can apply some of our knowledge acquired there to the design. This is just one possible design solution and not necessarily the best. Our purpose is just to illustrate the process of middleware selection. The needs of the system, as stated previously, are basic reliable, efficient, and distributed communication between the components. We will forego our wants and desires for now and leave them as exercises for the reader. Based on our basic needs, we have several options: a MOM solution, an object-oriented solution, an RPC solution, or a web services solution. There is no obvious transaction processing, database, or agent-oriented need. Given what we know, any of the solution options is viable, but if we add that we will be developing on the Linux platform using C++ on a closed network, we can narrow our solution choices. These additional system requirements lead us to eliminate the web services and MOM solution because XML over HTTP is too communication and processing inefficient and MOM APIs are programming inefficient with C++. Web services could also be eliminated because there is no need to bridge across the Internet. RPC would be a good choice if we were using Java because of the built-in RPC mechanisms (it is also easy using C++ on Linux), but an object-oriented solution fits better, with C++. We now choose CORBA as our object-oriented middleware solution because we are using Linux, if we were using Microsoft Windows, we may have chosen COM/DCOM. CORBA IDL will provide a good environment for defining our own interfaces between the custom system components and has the benefit of not locking us into C++ if we decide to replace a component with a Java, Python, or other CORBA-supported language component. CORBA provides a reliable, efficient, and distributed communication middleware system that fulfills our basic needs. CORBA is also object-oriented and available on Linux, meeting our development language and OS requirements. We could further delve into CORBA ORB selection, and so forth, but it should be obvious to the reader that proper selection of middleware is merely a function of knowing all of the system requirements and matching them with the middleware solution that best satisfies them. It should be noted that in some cases several middleware solutions will be needed to meet a single system's needs.

5.6 MIDDLEWARE FOR SMART ENVIRONMENTS

Creating new technologies and solving the outstanding research questions associated with smart environments required new, viable middleware solutions. The unique real-time, sensory, control, and data flow issues presented by these environments can be a significant problems when working in this area [Coe98]. To provide possible solutions, we present a brief survey of older and newer middleware solutions used in various smart environment projects. The projects are presented in alphabetical order by name. We strongly encourage the reader to further investigate these and other projects to learn from their successes and failures.

5.6.1 AIRE, MIT Artificial Intelligence Lab

Out of the MIT Artificial Intelligence Lab comes the AIRE (Agent-based Intelligent Reactive Environments) group. The AIRE group is engaged in research involving pervasive computing designs and people-centic applications, and they have constructed 'AIRE spaces' in the forms of an intelligent conference room, intelligent workspaces, kiosks, and 'oxgenated' offices. To assist in their research and to integrate their technologies, they have developed middleware called Metaglue and an extension, Hyperglue [Gro03].

Metaglue is an extension to the Java programming language to allow the creation of intelligent environments controlling software agents. It provides *linguistic primitives* that facilitate the interconnection and management of a large number of disparate components (hardware and software), real-time operations, agent management, resource allocation, dynamic configuration, dynamic components, and state capture mechanisms. Metaglue provides an inherited *agent* class to Java objects, a post-compiler to generate new Metaglue agents from Java-compiled classes, and a *Metaglue Virtual Machine* infrastructure to be run on all supporting computing equipment. The Metaglue authors claim that the infrastructure creates a negligible amount of overhead and is more efficient than CORBA or KQML (Knowledge Query and Manipulation Language) because it provides both communication and control with a lighter-weight solution [CPW$^+$99].

Hyperglue extends Metaglue by providing a society communication model and discovery system for Metaglue agents in a new infrastructure layer. Metaglue allows agents to be segmented into small groups called *societies*. Hyperglue provides a communication layer for societies to communicate with each other and to find needed service-providing societies through resource managers and society ambassadors [PLQ$^+$03].

5.6.2 The Aware Home, Georgia Tech

The Aware Home Research Initiative (AHRI) at the Georgia Institute of Technology is conducting research to answer the question "Is it possible to create a home environment that is aware of its occupants' whereabouts and activities?" [AHR03]. Although not specifically focused on middleware systems, they have developed two toolkits, INCA and the Context Toolkit, as well as a location service that may be of interest to system designers and integrators. INCA (Infrastructure for Capture and Access) provides the means for creating systems that capture life experience details and preserve them for future access. INCA provides capture, storage, format-conversion, and access support [TA02]. The Context Toolkit provides abstractions and support for context-aware development. This Java toolkit consists of widgets as encapsulation objects, aggregators to create meta-widgets, and interpreters to translate low-level context information into higher levels all communicating via XML over HTTP [SDA99]. AHRI has focused on the problem of sensing location and, as a by-product, has produced the Location Service infrastructure, which seeks to provide a robust and accurate location service, performs sensor fusion transparently for the user, and supplies reusable and extensible techniques to application programmers so that they can utilize location information in application-relevant ways [ABO02].

5.6.3 Counter Intelligence, MIT Media Lab

MIT Media Lab's Consortia on Things That Think (TTT) and their special-interest group on Counter Intelligence are primarily focused on single applications such as Smart Architectural Surfaces, Public Anemone, and an intelligent spoon, but have also produced a distributed agents platform called Hive [ML03]. Hive is a Java-based framework that provides ad hoc agent interactions, mobility, ontologies, and a graphical user interface to the entire distributed system. Hive is composed of three elements: *cells* that exist on each machine in the distributed system and provide the infrastructure connectivity, *shadows* that are the local resource encapsulation mechanism in each cell, and *agents* that utilize local resources through shadows and exist in one cell at a time. Hive has been used to develop a smart kitchen, a jukebox, and other applications and utilizes Java RMI for communication [MGR$^+$99].

5.6.4 IBM Pervasive Computing Lab, IBM Research

The Pervasive Computing Lab under the direction of Bill Bodin at IBM Research in Austin, Texas, is performing work involving speculative integration to create *proof of concept* demonstrations, utilizing modern technology to create such things as an advanced media living room, a networked kitchen, and integrated automobiles. Although these workers are not developing new technologies, they are combining existing technologies in new and interesting ways to show what is possible. For the designer and integrator, it should be of interest that they use IBM Websphere, Java servlet technology, and Lotus Notes [Yor03].

5.6.5 i-LAND, AMBIENTE

The AMBIENTE division of the Fraunhofer-IPSI Research Institute in Germany is working on i-LAND, an Interactive LANDscape for creativity and innovation, to create cooperative buildings out of *roomware* components such as an interactive electronic wall, an interactive table, and computer-enhanced chairs in order to create the offices of the future [AMB03]. The research focus is on these *roomware* components, but they are connected through integration on the COAST [SKSH96] cooperative hypermedia framework. COAST is groupware and comes from research done in the Computer Supported Cooperative Work (CSCW) field. COAST is an object-oriented (SmallTalk) toolkit that supports the creation of synchronous groupware.

5.6.6 Interactive Workspaces, Stanford University

At Stanford University, the Interactive Workspaces Project is exploring work collaboration technologies in technology-rich environments with a focus on task-oriented work such as design reviews or brainstorming sessions. Their experimental facility is called 'iRoom,' where they are investigating integration issues with multiple-device, multiple-user applications, interaction technologies, deployment software, and component integration [SIL03]. To meet the integration and interactive workspace building challenge, they have developed iROS, a middleware system for interactive workspaces. iROS is composed of three subsystems: the *EventHeap*, which provides coordination; the *DataHeap*, which provides data movement and transformation; and *ICrafter*, which provides user resource control. Through iROS they seek to provide a middleware layer that provides a true platform portability, application portability and extensibility, robustness, and simplicity [PJKF03].

5.6.7 MavHome, The University of Texas at Arlington

The MavHome [You03] (Managing an Adaptive Versatile Home) project at the University of Texas at Arlington is focused on research involving the home as an intelligent agent that seeks to maximize the comfort of its inhabitants while minimizing resource consumption (e.g., power, water, natural gas) and maintaining safety and data security. MavHome environments currently include the MavLab where research is conducted daily, MavKitchen for kitchen environment experiments, and the MavPad, an on-campus apartment where the researchers perform human-in-the-loop experiments. MavHome is composed of many independent components written in C++ and Java integrated with CORBA, mixing in ZEROCONF technology to replace the naming service and allowing self-publication and discovery services. The MavHome approach leverages existing technologies so that workers can concentrate on the main AI focus of their project.

5.6.8 Microsoft Easy Living, Microsoft Research

The Vision Group at Microsoft Research is developing a prototype architecture and associated technologies for intelligent environments in their Easy Living project. Their research is concerned with using computer vision for inhabitant tracking and visual gesture recognition, sensor fusion, context-aware computing using geometric models, automatic sensor calibration, dynamic and adaptable user interfaces, generalized communication and data protocols, and system extensibility [MRVG03]. To provide integration for their research systems, the Easy Living project is using middleware called InConcert that is being developed at Microsoft Research in conjunction with other groups there. InConcert was created out of the need for middleware that can provide communication in a distributed environment, but the workers believe it is better suited for the real-time and unusual needs of an intelligent environment than DCOM, Java, or CORBA. InConcert provides an asynchronous message-passing system with machine-independent addressing and XML-based message protocols. Unique to this system is that the naming service is integrated in the message delivery [BMK+00].

5.6.9 Sentient Computing, Cambridge University

The Laboratory for Communication Engineering (LCE) at Cambridge University (originally in conjunction with AT&T Laboratories Cambridge, now shut down) is pursuing its Sentient Computing Project and is focused on simulating computer perception in computing systems that detect, interpret, and respond to facets of a user's environment [Ber03]. Research has involved a deployed ultrasonic location system, advances in world modeling including spatial considerations, and sentient computing applications such as world model browsing, remote desktop displays that follow users, smart posters using context-aware information retrieval, and ubiquitous user interfaces [LC01]. The omniORB CORBA package and VNC (Virtual Network Computing) both originated from LCE's research.

The Sentient Computing group has replaced omniORB with middleware that can support context-aware multimedia applications called QoSDREAM, also under research and development at the LCE. QoSDREAM supports multiple types of sensors and provides a simple spatial model for representing *locatable entities*, real-time model and sensor data integration, an event mechanism for notifying applications of location information, a query-able location database, and ease of extensibility. Like many others, this project is also developed in Java and with Java technologies. QoSDREAM is based on providing quality of service guarantees and takes a location-centric approach to the services it provides [NCM01].

5.6.10 Smart Space Lab, NIST

In the United States, the National Institute of Standards and Technology (NIST) has set up the Smart Space Laboratory to "address the measurement, standards, and interoperability challenges" [NIS03] for *smart spaces*. This group is using a two-phase approach to addressing their interests in pervasive computing. In the first phase they are identifying areas for standardization, creating real experiences in which to identify applicable measurements, and identifying security measures to ensure the privacy and integrity of systems. The second phase involves developing specific metrics, tests, and comparative data sets for the community, providing reference implementations of designed system ideas, collaborating with industry to form standard specifications, establishing industry and academic partnerships, and integrating the phase 1 technologies to explore distributed issues with the technologies. Using these goals, they are working to create a test bed containing a defined middleware component that provides real-time data communications, a connection broker for sensors, and containers for processing data. NIST has already released their

Smart Flow System, which provides a data flow server, graphical interface, and control console as well as audio, video, and voice recognition interfaces [NIS03].

5.7 CONCLUSIONS

Perfection in software systems is a goal of many system architects and developers. Whether it can be obtained is an open question. Much comes down to what the project needs, wants, and desires. This is why requirement analysis is a key part of software engineering. Simple and elegant designs seem to provide better solutions than complex ones. Middleware can certainly alleviate complexity in designs, development, and maintenance, but there is no silver bullet [Bro95].

Middleware should complement a project, making it easier to design, develop, and maintain. It should provide interoperability, reliability, efficiency, throughput, security, scalability, adaptability, dynamism, availability, fault tolerance, flexibility, portability, maintainability, and reusability. Architects should know what the limitations and requirements are and choose middleware that best fits the goals of the application while watching out for proprietary and nonstandard solutions that may leave the project trapped in certain technologies.

In this chapter we have discussed the concept of middleware, presented its desirable characteristics, and discussed its forms, as well as the advantages and disadvantages of each form. We introduced some of the technologies in current use, developed an understanding of the importance of standards and where to find them, and presented design issues to consider in choosing the proper form and technology for a project. We hope we have developed an understanding of the benefits of middleware. We ended by presenting the middleware used in current intelligent environments to provide insights, ideas, and options for other smart environment projects.

In conclusion, middleware solutions can provide a solid platform on which to develop smart environment systems given a thorough knowledge of requirements and middleware solution options.

REFERENCES

[ABO02] G.D. Abowd, A. Battestini, and T. O'Connell. The Location Service: A framework for handling multiple location sensing technologies, 2002. Website: www.cc.gatech.edu/fce/ahri/publications/location_service.pdf

[AEGO96] G. Abowd, J. Engelsma, L. Guadagno, and O. Okon. Architectural Analysis of Object Request Brokers. *Object Magazine*, special issue on distributed systems, 1996.

[AHR03] AHRI. AHRI—Aware Home Research Initiative, Oct. 2003. Website: www.cc.gatech.edu/fce/ahri/index.html

[AMB03] AMBIENTE. AMBIENTE Activity: i-LAND, Oct. 2003. Website: www.darmstadt.gmd.de/ambiente/i-land.html

[ANSI03] American National Standards Institute, Oct. 2003. Website: www.ansi.org

[Ber96]   P.A. Bernstein. Middleware: a model for distributed system services. *Communications of the ACM*, 39(2):86–98, 1996.

[Ber03]   A. Beresford. CUED: Laboratory for Communication Engineering, Oct. 2003. Website: www-lce.eng.cam.ac.uk/research/?view = 2&id = 7

[Blo92]   J. Bloomer. *Power Programming with RPG*. O'Reilly & Associates, Inc., Sebastopol, CA, February 1992.

[BMK+00]   B. Brumitt, B. Meyers, J. Krumm, A. Kern and S.A. Shafer. EasyLiving: Technologies for Intelligent Environments. In *Proceedings of the Second International Symposium for Handheld and Ubiquitous Computing (HUC)*, pages 12–29. Springer, 2000.

[Bro95]   F. Brooks. *The Mythical Man-Month*. Addison-Wesley, 1995.

[Che03]   S. Cheshire. Zero Configuration Networking (Zeroconf), Oct. 2003. Website: www.zerconf.org

[Coe98]   M.H. Coen. Design Principles for Intelligent Environments. In *Proceedings of the Fifteenth National Conference on Artificial Intelligence*, pages 547–554, 1998. Website: citeseer.nj.nec.com/coen98design.html

[CPW+99]   M.H. Coen, B. Phillips, N. Warshawsky, L. Weisman, S. Peters, and P. Finin. Meeting the Computational Needs of Intelligent Environments: The Metaglue System. In *Proceedings of MANSE'99*, Dublin, Ireland, 1999. Website: citeseer.nj.nec.com/coen99meeting.html

[Ede94]   H. Edelstein. Unraveling Client/Server Architecture. *DBMS*, 34(7), 1994.

[Gri03]   D. Grisby. omniORB, Oct. 2003. Website: omniorb.sourceforge.net

[Gro03]   AIRE Group. MIT Project AIRE—About Us, Oct. 2003. Website: www.ai.mit.edu/projects/aire

[HV99]   M. Henning and S. Vinoski. *Advanced CORBA Programming with C++*. Addison-Wesley, 1999.

[IAN03]   IANA. IANA Home Page, Oct. 2003. Website: www.iana.org

[IET03]   IETF. IETF RFC Page, Oct. 2003. Website: www.ietf.org/rfc.html

[Ins03]   Software Engineering Institute. Software Engineering Institute (SEI) Home page, Sept. 2003. Website: www.sei.cmu.edu/sei-home.html

[IoEEE90]   Institute of Electrical and Electronic Engineers. IEEE standard computer dictionary: A compilation of IEEE standard computer glossaries, 1990.

[IOfS03]   International Organization for Standardization. ISO—International Organization for Standardization, Oct. 2003. Website: www.iso.ch/iso/en/ISO Online.openerpage

[ISAG03]   CMU Intelligent Software Agents Group. Intelligent Software Agents, Oct. 2003. Website: www-2.cs.cmu.edu/softagents/intro.htm

[ITU03]   International Telecommunications Union. The ITU Telecommunications Standardization Sector (itu-t), Oct. 2003. Website:www.itu.int/ITU-T

[LC01]   AT&T Laboratories Cambridge. Sentient Computing Project Home Page, 2001. Website: www.uk.research.att.com/spirit

[Lin97]   D.S. Linthicum. Next Generation Middleware, July 1997. Website: www.dbmsmag.com/9709d14.html

[LS79]   B.W. Lampson and H.E. Sturgis. Crash recovery in a distributed data storage system. Technical report, XEROX Palo Alto Research Center, 1979. Website: citeseer.nj.nec.com/lampson79crash.html

[MGR+99] N. Minar, M. Gray, O. Roup, P. Krikorian, and P. Maes. Hive: Distributed Agents for Networking Things. In *First International Symposium on Agent Systems and Applications (ASA'99)/Third International Symposium on Mobile Agents (MA'99)*, Palm Springs, CA, 1999.

[ML03] MIT Media Lab. MIT Media Lab: Projects List Database, Oct. 2003. Website: www.media.mit.edu/research/index.html

[MRVG03] Microsoft Research Vision Group. Easy Living, Oct. 2003. Website: research.microsoft.com/easyliving

[NCM01] H. Naguib, G. Coulouris, and S. Mitchell. Middleware Support for Context-Aware Multimedia Applications. In *Proceedings of the Third International Working Conference on Distributed Applications and Interoperable Systems DAIS*, pages 9–22, 2001.

[NIS03] NIST. Welcome to the NIST Smart Space Laboratory Web Site, Oct. 2003. Website: www.nist.gov/smartspace

[OAS03a] OASIS. OASIS, Oct. 2003. Website: www.oasis-open.org

[OAS03b] OASIS. UDDI.org, Oct. 2003. Website: www.uddi.org

[OMA03] Open Mobile Alliance. Open Mobile Alliance, Oct. 2003. Website: www.openmobilealliance.org

[OMG03] Object Management Group. Object Management Group, Oct. 2003. Website: www.omg.org

[PJKF03] S.R. Ponnekanti, B. Johanson, E. Kiciman, and A. Fox. Portability, Extensibility and Robustness in iROS. In *Proceedings of IEEE International Conference on Pervasive Computing and Communications*, Mar. 2003.

[PLQ+03] S. Peters, G. Look, K. Quigley, H. Shrobe, and K. Gajos. Hyperglue: Designing High-Level Agent Communication for Distributed Applications, 2003. Website: citeseer.nj.nec.com/peters03hyperglue.html

[Rao95] B.R. Rao. Making the Most of Middleware. *Date Communications International*, 24(12):89–96, Sept. 1995.

[RN95] S.J. Russell and P. Norvig. *Artificial Intelligence: A Modern Approach*. Prentice Hall, Upper Saddle River, NJ, 1995.

[Sch95] G. Schussel. Client/Server Past, Present, and Future, 1995. Website: news.dci.com/geos/dbsejava.htm

[SDA99] D. Salber, A.K. Dey, and G.D. Abowd. The Context Toolkit: Aiding the Development of Context-Enabled Applications. In *Proceedings of the ACM SIGCHI Conference on Human Factors in Computing Systems (CHI)*, pages 434–441, 1999.

[SDP+96] K. Sycara, K. Decker, A. Pannu, M. Williamson, and D. Zeng. Distributed Intelligent Agents. *IEEE Expert*, 11(6):36–46, Dec. 1996.

[SIL03] Stanford Interactivity Lab. Interactive Workspaces, Oct. 2003. Website: iwork.stanford.edu

[SKSH96] C. Schuckmann, L. Kirchner, J. Schummer, and J.M. Haake. Designing Object-Oriented Synchronous Groupware with COAST. In *Computer Supported Cooperative Work*, pages 30–38, 1996.

[SM03] Sun Microsystems, Inc. The Source Java Technology, Oct. 2003. Website: java.sun.com.

[Ste95] S. Steinke. Middleware Meets the Network. *LAN: The Network Solutions Magazine*, 10(13):56, 1995.

[STK02]   J. Snell, D. Tidwell, and P. Kulchenko. *Programming Web Services with SOAP*. O'Reilly & Associates, Inc., Sebastopol, CA, 2002.

[TA02]   K.N. Truong and G.D. Abowd. INCA: Architectural Support for Building Automated Capture and Access Applications, 2002. Website: www.cc.gatech.edu/fce/ahri/publications/inca_final.pdf

[TOG03]   The Open Group. DCE Portal, Oct. 2003. Website: www.opengroup.org/dce

[UPn03]   UPnP Forum. Welcome to the UPnP Forum!, Oct. 2003. Website: www.upnp.org

[Web03]   Webopedia. SQL, Oct. 2003. Website: www.webopedia.com/TERM/S/SQL.html

[WWWC03]   World Wide Web Consortium, Oct. 2003. Website: www.w3c.org

[Yor03]   C.A. York. IBM's Advanced PvC Technology Laboratory, Oct. 2003.

[You03]   G.M. Youngblood. MavHome: Managing an Adaptive Versatile Home, Oct. 2003. Website: mavhome.uta.edu

CHAPTER 6

Home Networking and Appliances

DAVE MARPLES and STAN MOYER

Telcordia Technologies, Inc.

6.1 INTRODUCTION

This chapter discusses the emergence of networked appliances, what is driving this emergence, and what issues exist. What is a network appliance (NA)? For our purposes, it is a dedicated-function consumer device containing a networked processor. These devices are also referred to as *internet appliances* (IPs). These terms are, however, more specific in that they tend to constrain the physical network to which the appliance is connected. More correctly, we should probably use the term *network device* or *network consumer device* to describe the devices we are considering. However, *network appliance* has been adopted by the community, so this is the term we shall use in this chapter.

We focus on consumer NAs, since many special-application or vertical-market NAs have been available commercially for years. Then the cost/benefit trade-off is more able to support expensive equipment, provided that the benefit from its acquisition is commensurate with the outlay. When we first talk about NAs, our thoughts turn to personal digital assistants (PDAs), webpads, sophisticated mobile phones, and perhaps even the TV set top box. The fact is that many more devices can be considered NAs—the navigation computer in the car or the headlight azimuth adjustment, the picture frame[1] or weather-telling toaster[2] in the home, or the heart monitor strapped to a user's body. The fact is that NAs are already well established in some domains and are set to encroach on others over the next 5 to 10 years.

In this chapter we shall consider why NAs are emerging now, identify three example environments for NAs, and note the differences both in the character of those environments and in their adoption of NA technology. We shall then look at two of the main challenges facing long-term NA adoption—one with a proposed solution and one whose solution is still uncertain.

Smart Environments: Technologies, Protocols, and Applications, edited by D.J. Cook and S.K. Das
ISBN 0-471-54448-5 © 2005 John Wiley & Sons, Inc.

6.1.1 Emergence of the NA

Why are consumer NAs emerging now? There is no single reason, but a number of factors that together have fostered the environment in which NAs can be created. These factors include:

- **The decreasing cost of network-capable electronics:** Microcontrollers have revolutionized control systems, offering better performance, greater reliability, and less power consumption than was previously possible. Microcontrollers now come with integrated network interfaces for a wide variety of network technologies, including Ethernet,[3] Wireless,[4] and many other physical standards[5] at prices that make them suitable for use in consumer devices and that make the cost of a network connection negligible. We do not claim that communications interfaces were not previously available on microcontrollers; standards such as I2C,[6] CANBus,[7] and the ubiquitous USART (Universal Synchronous Asynchronous Receiver Transmitter) have been around since the earliest days of the microprocessor. However, the increasing ease with which network capability can be integrated into a product is driving the change to ubiquitous network connection for even the simplest devices.
- **The increase in online data availability:** Increasingly, users are finding information online—from yellow/white pages through recipes and maps. The personal computer (PC) is an increasingly inconvenient and constraining device that a user must employ to access this information. Users want to be able to access information on devices that are molded to their lifestyles. NAs can fulfill this need by acting as information access portals. Networking technologies that enable machines to directly interrogate each other, such as web services,[8] further enhance the capacity of small, user-centric devices to communicate with remote elements on behalf of users and deliver the information in a form they can understand.
- **Consumer demand for seamless integration of networked services into their lifestyle:** As noted above, users want information to be presented to them in a convenient fashion; they do not want to go out of their way to collect it.
- **Continuously available network connectivity:** Two factors are contributing to continuously available network connectivity: broadband access networks and home networking. The continuous connection that broadband access technologies like digital subscriber line (DSL) and cable modem (CM) offer are arguably more important than the bandwidth they deliver. The fact that a user can access information on demand, rather than having to wait for a dialup connection to be established, has fundamentally changed network usage patterns. Home networking and other local area networking technologies (described later in this chapter) are proliferating, making it easier to interconnect NAs and provide them with local and wide area network connectivity.
- **Emergence of mass market opportunities amenable to appliance technology:** Home power consumption control, service model sales for white goods, pay-per-use technologies, digital rights management, and many other application environments that demand network connectivity are significant drivers of appliance technology.

In this chapter, we shall investigate some of these drivers and their implications, together with the limitations of the available technology, in more detail. We begin with some examples of the kinds of devices we expect to see in consumer NA device environments.

6.2 TYPICAL CONSUMER NA DOMAINS AND EXAMPLES

By looking at the early devices in the consumer space, it is possible to identify some trends for NAs, but it is not possible to know all of the devices that will exist in these environments. Some of the general drivers for networking appliances together include local command, control and content distribution, the ability to share computational resources to reduce the cost of individual components (e.g., using your home PC to decode MP3s), the ability to provide new services on preexisting devices, and the creation of collaborative behaviors when multiple devices coordinate to offer a service.

6.2.1 Example Domains

NAs are applicable in any environment where a network is present and user-accessible devices connect to that network. However, in this chapter, we shall consider three environments where NA technology is starting to emerge. An environment is generally bordered by the security boundary, and a single environment is usually a single domain of authority. This does not mean that all the devices within the network have the same rights of access. Often a single environment uses a single access technology, but this is not always the case. A single environment may contain a variety of access technologies, depending on the characteristics of the NAs it is supporting and the devices with which it is required to interwork or represent to the outside world (e.g., a home with POTS, DSL, cable and cellular connectivity).

Different environments are subject to different constraints that have affected the rate of adoption in each. We consider three environments, each in a different phase of adoption of NA technology.

6.2.1.1 The Automotive Environment The automotive environment generally consists of a collection of networks separated for performance, safety, or cost reasons. There are distinct network infrastructures for car control, entertainment, and ancillary systems that may be connected via gateway devices or that may even be totally independent of each other. It is possible to consider the devices that attach to these networks as early examples of network appliances—dedicated-function, network-connected computational elements. These devices might range from the flasher module to the car stereo, from the engine sensor to the central locking controller.

Historically, connectivity to the wide area from the vehicle has been very constrained. Modern vehicles offer diagnostic and maintenance access to these networks via physical connections, but there is little remote access. This situation is now starting to change with systems like OnStar,[9] which offer access to onboard equipment via mobile phone network connections to give the vehicle user a level of functionality that was previously unavailable. A control center could, for example, unlock the doors of a suitably equipped vehicle remotely; it could also participate in accident remediation activity.

In the automobile, the user usually has no explicit access to the in-vehicle networks. These networks are provided only to make the vehicle functional. We argue that this should be the long-term aim of NA technology; users should not need to be aware that the devices are exploiting a network to deliver functionality. However, we are now starting to see external access to these systems, and in the future we might expect NAs to join an existing automotive network to exploit the functionality they offer—Personal Area Network (PAN) devices are good candidates. A Bluetooth-enabled mobile phone connecting to the in-vehicle stereo system to deliver loudspeech telephony is already offered as an option on some cars and will become common. We might also expect to see a PDA connecting to the in-vehicle systems to offer enhanced I/O capability using the display of the PDA rather than the constrained facilities of the automobile.

We classify the automotive market for NAs as *established*, since, with the appropriate definition of an NA, there are numerable examples of its use in most modern vehicles.

6.2.1.2 The PAN The PAN is specific to an individual user, and is intended to connect together the NAs that a typical user might have nearby area—a mobile phone, PDA, headphone, microphone, laptop PC, medical sensors, body area sensors (e.g., radiation, temperature), cameras, and other devices that augment the capabilities of the individual. By definition the individual user of a PAN is unambiguously identified, so the right of access can be more easily assumed than is the case for many other environments.

Access to Wide Area Networks (WANs) from the PAN is completely defined by the WAN access devices that are present. However, the requirement for universal access limits speed, or at least sets a maximum speed that can be guaranteed, according to the capabilities of the available pervasive networks. Typically, for a 2.5 G network this is in the order of 28 Kbps using General Packet Radio Service (GPRS) over GSM (a wireless communications standard), though GPRS can offer higher speeds in suitably configured environments. It might be expected that when the individual is in the range of higher-capability networks (e.g., an 802.11 hot spot), the network will adapt and higher speeds would then be possible. Thus, the amount of bandwidth and its characteristics that are available to a PAN will be dynamic, and PAN applications will need to be bandwidth agile. Note also that the WAN bandwidth available to the PAN will be statistically multiplexed among all local PAN users, so available bandwidth might be considerably lower than the headline speeds.

We classify the PAN market for NAs as *emergent*, since there are established standards and the market mass is starting to build, with the Bluetooth Special Interest Group (SIG) claiming more than 1 M units shipped per week.[10]

6.2.1.3 The Home Environment Like the automotive network, the home network is, in general, a collection of networks with interworking units between them,

6.2 TYPICAL CONSUMER NA DOMAINS AND EXAMPLES 133

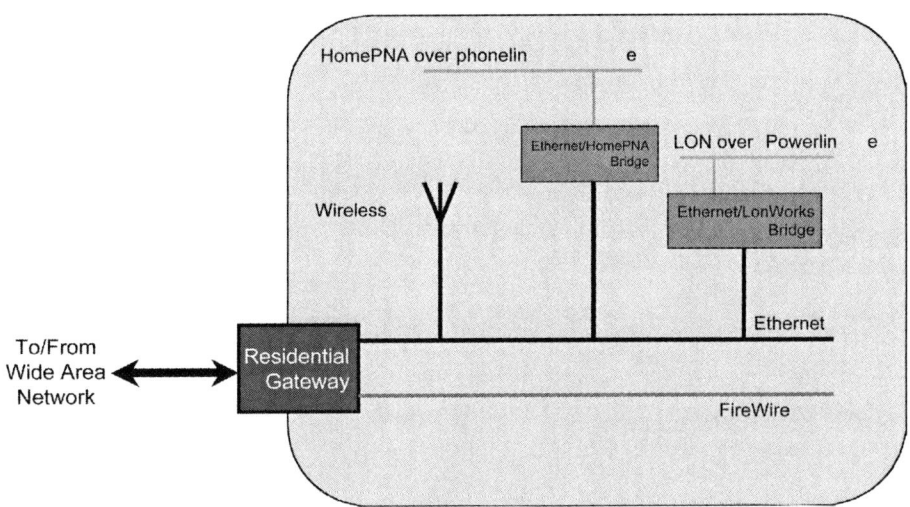

Figure 6.1 Typical arrangement in the home environment.

as shown in Figure 6.1. Different networks exist for reasons of physical connectivity (i.e., to minimize new wiring within the home) or to connect devices that have particular requirements (e.g., using IEEE1394 for a content network) and/or similar functionality [e.g., home security systems and heating. ventilation, and air conditioning (HVAC)]. For most networks one would expect to see relatively large amounts of bandwidth—at least in the order of megabits per second—and in the future we expect to see quality of service (QoS) overlays within the home. Today, however, they exist only on specific networks, and home routers do not generally support QoS.

The presence of multiple physical networks will lead to the home network's being *zoned.* Some zones might support Internet Protocol (IP), while others might support an alternative communication system that may be proprietary or based on another protocol suite, such as X10[11] or LonWorks.[12] For those zones that use an Ethernet style Media Access Controller (MAC), one would expect to see a Layer 2 switching capability between different physical networks: a zone of 100 Mb/s Ethernet, another of 802.11x wireless, another of powerline signaling, another of telephone cable signaling, and so on.

Network connectivity to the wide area from the home is usually quite good, with a permanent connection to a gateway or router providing at least 512 Kb/s to the home and 128 Kb/s away from it via an IPv4 address. Due to the IPv4 addressing constraints that Internet service providers (ISPs) are under, one must assume Network Address Translation (NAT)[13] to the wide area that limits the access from the wide area into the home. Devices within the home are not directly addressable except via explicit configuration of the home gateway or router.

Within the home there are multiple users with different rights and responsibilities; being a member of the home network does not automatically give the user a specific set of capabilities. Capabilities may vary from those of the owner/administrator of the home to those of a visitor who is using the network temporarily to access the Internet.

We classify the home market for NAs as *embryonic*. Although products for networking PCs in the home exist, there are relatively few NA-specific products and no clear consensus on standards.

6.2.2 Typical NAs

Given the incredible ingenuity of the human mind, it is impossible to even begin to identify the NAs that will emerge over the next few years. The best that we can hope to do is to identify some early opportunities and use them to identify key capabilities NAs should offer. NAs can be divided into extensions of conventional applications and novel applications. Among the extensions we consider devices that are already established in the home and are sometimes network connected. Video phones, set top boxes, webpads, PDAs, microwave ovens, and PCs are existing devices whose capability can be extended by networking technologies. Although these devices have already changed our lifestyles beyond all recognition, extending them with network-enabled functionality will further enhance them. In contrast, novel applications cannot be forecast as logical extensions of preexistent technology. As the cost of network connectivity tends toward zero and it becomes a standard feature of consumer products, interesting new applications will start to emerge. ZigBee[14] and BlueTooth[15] are two main driving technologies in this space today; one of the authors' mobile phone is now permanently connected to his PC, so that it automatically goes to screensaver when he moves away from it, pops the details of the calling party on the screen for incoming calls, and allows him to send and receive Short Message Service (SMS) messages without taking the phone out of his pocket! We cannot begin to guess the applications that will emerge for these new capabilities; BlueJacking[16] is a remarkable example of an early unintended consequence of PAN.

NAs can take advantage of:

- **On-demand data availability:** TV schedule updates, new recipes, or automatic firmware updates on devices that previously might have never been updated at all. It's not impossible that your TV remote might automatically have its firmware updated occasionally—perhaps to fix bugs in the original implementation or to extend its life with new functionality as part of an ongoing maintenance arrangement. Data availability can also aid the decision-making process—the NA that automatically slows your car because the one in front has braked suddenly or the heating system that switches on when you're a mile away from home.
- **Dynamic data and information exchange:** Sending a recorded TV show to a friend, automatically updating schedules, elements within the home communicating with the car to ensure that its stereo has the latest music collection, etc.

Much information exchange will be needed to observe the copyright laws covering such information. It is easy to see the network connectivity of the NA being exploited to ensure appropriate management of rights.

- **Remote command and control:** The ability to remotely address and excite devices leads to all sorts of interesting capabilities. The garage door opener is today's classic example, but imagine a world in which you can open the door for a repairman and then watch him at any point in the house as he performs his task or set the vacuum cleaner on its cleanup cycle while you're still at the office. These examples may be trite, but the power of remote command and control becomes more compelling when you consider having the ability to turn off the engine, lock the doors, and sound continuously the horn of your car that has just been stolen.
- **Remote reporting:** The ability of a device to deliver status updates anywhere in the world on demand or in response to exception conditions—a water pipe break, an automatic warning from your washing machine to the repair company that a bearing is running hot, a message to your car dealer that the car is ready for an oil change, or a warning that an elderly relative hasn't opened the refrigerator in the past 24 hours are all typical examples of remote reporting. In general, remote reporting allows humans to step out of the loop in exception reporting, thus rendering it automatic and more reliable.

Many, if not most, of the applications that we foresee for NAs require an appropriate sensor infrastructure to make them possible. The NA itself can be considered a collaboration of sensors, actuators, and network connectivity, optionally with some local processing as well. Of course, these components do not have to be located in the same physical package, and we foresee a huge opportunity for collaborative services in which multiple NAs work together to deliver functionality to the user.

6.2.3 An Example Scenario

All of the above possibilities are best demonstrated with the aid of an example.

Dave prepares to leave the office a little earlier than usual, since he managed to get some work wrapped up more quickly than expected. As he heads out of the door, his PC automatically locks and switches over to screensaver, the office lights dim, the air conditioner switches off, and the door locks shut behind him (*PAN device as personal talisman integrated with PC and office environmental systems*). As he walks out of the building, his "status" on the corporate phone directory automatically changes to "Out" (*PAN location tracking*). Reaching his car, he hits a key on his phone. The door unlocks automatically and the engine starts. The seat and steering wheel adjust to suit him as he sits down (his wife gave him a lift to work this morning, so the seat was set for her) (*automobile and PAN integration*). He notes that he needs gasoline and should get it on the way home. He calls his wife to let her know he has set off for home, using the hands-free capability built into the car stereo and the phone that's still in his pocket (*PAN dynamic integration with automobile*).

When he reaches the gas station, he gets out to use the pump. As he steps out of the car, he notices that his music collection is being updated using the local Wireless Fidelity (WiFi) cloud that exists around the pumps *(Automobile dynamic network integration with WiFi)*. He wonders if they'll send a software update for that irritating display bug in the car *(dynamic software update)*. After he gets the gas and drives off *(PAN talisman for payment applications)*, he arrives home to see the garage door rising just as he pulls around the corner. He parks the car and walks to the front door and into a warm, pleasant house with the smell of dinner wafting from the kitchen. It started cooking before he left the office, and the central heating turned on when he was about a mile away from home *(home environment and device control)*. His car, in the garage, syncs the music it got at the gas station with the other media devices in the house *(automobile and home network integration)*, and he settles down in front of the TV with his dinner.

6.3 CORE ISSUES WITH NA ADOPTION

There are many issues that need to be addressed before universal adoption of NAs is achieved.

6.3.1 Cost of Network Connectivity

As already noted, the cost of network connectivity has been dropping steadily over the past few years, and Moore's law ensures that more and more powerful computation devices will become available to fit into a typical NA profile. In the automotive environment these costs can be offset by the savings in interconnectivity achieved by the use of a network infrastructure, and in the PAN environment they can be absorbed by the price of relatively expensive mobile phones, PDAs, and similar equipment. In the home environment, however, the cost of network connectivity is an explicit line item that it is difficult to hide in other costs. Networks are starting to emerge for home use, but they are expensive, inconvenient, and relatively difficult to configure. There is considerably more work to be done here.

6.3.2 Diversity of Network Infrastructure

Cost, performance, security, power consumption, and various other constraints mean that frequently more than a single network infrastructure is in use, with gatewaying between them. Each of these networks may have its own independent addressing scheme and means of access. Methods are needed to ensure homogeneous access to these disparate physical systems.

6.3.3 Complexity of Configuration and Maintenance

As the number of devices with network connectivity increases, so does the amount of configuration and maintenance required. If devices are anything more than plug and play, limitations on uptake, configuration issues, security problems, and many other issues will arise. Our experience with telephony shows that it is possible to build secure networks, but so far this has been achieved only by means of a third party helping the user (i.e., the phone company maintaining the line). Already we see considerable difficulties in normal users configuring their home PCs and networks, and we can expect these problems to be multiplied many times as the number of devices increases. Means of relieving users of this administrative burden need to be found.

6.3.4 Security Requirements

Asking users to understand security and to make reasoned choices based on that knowledge is untenable; normal users simply don't have the sophistication to perform this function. For example, it is well known that telnet should not be used except in a very secure environment and that secure shell (ssh) should be preferred. How does a user reach an understanding of this? This requires the user have at least a passing understanding of IP, network sniffers, encryption, and many other technologies that those of us in the industry take for granted but others do not comprehend. Alternatively, we ask users to accept rules that we provide for them—telnet should not be an option. We need this same "default secure" configuration in NAs.

6.3.5 Collaborative Operation

Many network appliances will be single-function devices; indeed, that is the approach that experts in the field of human-computer interaction recommend[17] (within the constraints of fitness for purpose). However, if each of these devices can only work independently, then many opportunities for new, interesting behaviors based on collaboration of devices are lost. Consider a wakeup service for use in the home environment. An alarm clock monitors road conditions and weather status throughout the night to see if the user should be woken earlier than usual due to poor weather or road conditions. In itself, this is a useful service. But consider what would happen if this service could be integrated with other devices in and around the home:

- Integration with the car would allow the alarm clock to "know" if the level of fuel is low, making refueling necessary—perhaps making the wake-up time 10 minutes earlier.
- Integration with the heating system and the coffee maker could ensure that there's hot water for a shower and hot coffee to follow, no matter what time the user is awoken.
- Integration with body sensors could ensure that a diabetic is woken at any time during the night if his or her condition requires immediate attention.

We term these new behaviors that are enabled when multiple NAs work together *collaborative*. The term *emergent* has also been used, but this should be applied to behaviors that have not been explicitly programmed into the NAs to map to the terms' more conventional use in Artificial Intelligence.

There is still the question of where to run the code to implement these collaborative behaviors. It could potentially be in any one of the devices, but chances are that each of these has only limited capability that cannot be stretched to coordinate multiple NAs. It is much more probable that collaborative behavior will be implemented in a separate high-capability device that acts as a controller/coordinator of several individual devices. Given the nature of this coordinating activity, this functionality will probably be found in gateways or routers.

6.3.6 Feature Interaction

Consider an NA environment containing a heating system together with an air conditioning system in which the heating system has been set to 75°F and the aircon to 70°F. Both systems will be fighting the other, and wasting energy, in trying to achieve their goals, which are in conflict. Such conflicts were first identified in telecommunication systems,[18] where the conflicts between features involved in call processing were called *feature interactions*, a term we have borrowed to apply in the NA domain, where we expect to see many interactions of NAs in ways that have not been foreseen and that may, in many cases, be detrimental. We define feature interaction as *the change in operation of one feature that can be wholly or partially attributed to the presence of another feature in the environment.* Other definitions exist and can be found in the references, but this one has proven to be sufficient for our needs for a long time.

6.4 CURRENT STATE OF NA DEPLOYMENT

The deployment of NA technology today is largely dependant on the application domain; the automobile is, by many measures, far ahead of any other consumer domain. This may be something of a surprise given the issues associated with deploying processors in the automobile (a decidedly unfriendly environment, with heat, cold, vibration, and electrical noise and strict demands for highly reliable operation), but manufacturers are already reportedly claiming that their vehicles have "more computers than a jet fighter"[19] and we should expect this trend to continue. The automotive environment is aided by a number of factors that work to its advantage:

1. A single integration agency (the automobile manufacturer) for all of the devices in the environment.
2. Well-respected and accepted standards.
3. A safety critical environment demanding thorough testing.
4. A strong brand image that must be protected.

5. Imperative need for cost reduction.
   6. Good understanding of the technology developed over a number of years.
   7. User interfaces that are logical enhancements and extensions of existing uses.

In comparison with both the home and personal area markets, it is easy to see why the automobile has been an early success for the NA. The home, in particular, has few of the characteristics identified above.

6.5 ADDRESSING SOME OF THE KEY PROBLEMS

We examine two of the key issues that need to be solved for the widespread adoption of NA technology. These problems have been solved to varying degrees in each of the identified target domains and will be considered in turn.

6.5.1 Appliance Addressing and Access

In the home environment, the question of wide area appliance addressing and access is paramount. Devices, as already discussed, will use different bus and communication standards, which preclude a standard addressing scheme, and it will not be possible to access these devices from outside of the local domain in a standard fashion.

This problem exists to a slightly more limited degree in the PAN space (since there are fewer networking standards and less of a requirement for access from the wide area). It does not really exist in the automotive space due to the existence of a single integration entity and the more closed environment.

6.5.1.1 Requirements There are a number of core requirements for an appliance addressing and access scheme, including the following:

- **Security:** In-home communication has a level of physical security that is lost when arbitrary access from outside is permitted. Means must be found to ensure that exciting agents are appropriately identified.
- **Authentication:** The entity trying to enter the home needs to be clearly identified before access is permitted.
- **Reliability:** Because of the wide area nature of home access, there are more points of failure. The home should continue to operate independently of external systems when communication with them is lost.
- **Scaling:** There are many homes.
- **Protocol independence:** Although within a single home it is acceptable to use many different protocols for interdevice communication, a much more protocol-independent approach is required for the wide area, since the exact nature

of the devices comprising the in-home network may not (and, under most circumstances, should not) be known by outsiders.

- **Naming and location:** Devices within the home need to be unambiguously named and their location identified from the outside.

6.5.1.2 The Solution
The authors have done a significant amount of work in this area that was reported in a (now expired) Internet draft (ID). Much of the following section is taken from this ID with permission from Telcordia Technologies, (copyright 2001). The interested reader is directed to that document and its successors for a more detailed discussion of the proposed solution, including use cases that are not presented here for the sake of brevity.

For a networked appliance, in which the communication is frequently brief, the *location* of the endpoint and *communication with it* can be merged into a single activity. The requesting agent sends an instruction to perform an action on a named object in a message. The message contains the name of the object on which the action should be performed as its address and the action itself as the payload. This message is routed from agent to agent, resolving the name as it goes along. For example, the command "Switch on the lamp in the master bedroom in Dave's house" is first routed to the server that knows where Dave's house is located. Then the message is onward routed to the Dave's house firewall, where access control and authorization is performed. If this is successful, the message payload is then delivered to the device to perform whatever action has been requested. We observed that many of these concepts are already present in the Session Initiation Protocol (SIP).[20] SIP performs exactly this routing by name function in the INVITE process. An INVITE is sent first to an agent, or proxy, for the name. The proxy can rewrite the name and relay the INVITE, getting closer to the eventual destination for the message, delivering the payload [which is conventionally Session Description Protocol (SDP)[21]] once it arrives. The location and action processes are intertwined in the same procedure. A simplified version of the process, which ignores the handshaking and acknowledgments that are part of the real protocol, is shown in Figure 6.2.

In addition, the SIP security architecture enables verification based on these high-level names.

SIP was originally developed as an IETF (Internet Engineering Task Force) protocol for use in next-generation telephony, initially for voice calls over an IP infrastructure but intended to be general enough for adoption in many different environments. In SIP, endpoints are represented by User Agents (UAs). A UA forms a message for transport to another UA, which will decode and act it. Between the originating and terminating UAs there may be intervening proxies, which can optionally rewrite the messages from the originating UA to help them on their way to their eventual destination. Proxies can also redirect messages, duplicate them, authenticate endpoints and perform any number of other functionalities. On initial consideration, it appears that SIP is capable of performing the functions required of an appliance addressing and access scheme. There is, however, one

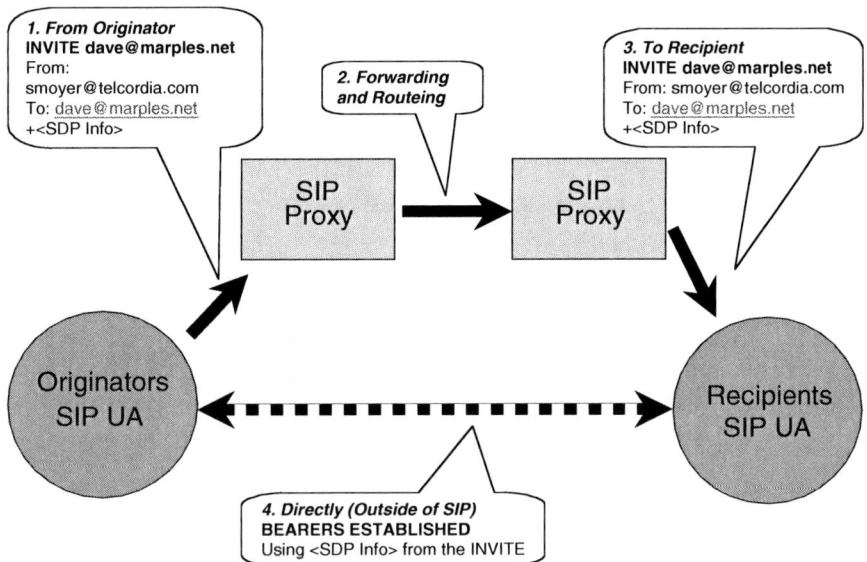

Figure 6.2 Simplified SIP session establishment.

essential difference between the capabilities of SIP and the identified requirements in respect to addressing—SIP (URIs) are, in practice, Internet (DNS) addresses. If this difference can be addressed, SIP becomes a practical method of communicating with appliances. We generically refer to this modified version of SIP to incorporate appliance functionality as *SIP for Appliances* (SIPa).

The question should be asked if there are any workable alternatives to SIP for this application. Simple Object Access Protocol (SOAP)[22] technology is one promising alternative, and accessing devices over a secure (http) session is also a possibility, but taken as a whole, there do not appear to be any well-developed alternatives to the SIPa proposal that exhibit the same architectural cleanliness, re-use of existing infrastructure, mobility, direct machine-to-machine communication capability, and security capacity. Thus, we feel that SIPa is the leading contender for this application. A more detailed analysis of alternatives has been completed.[23]

6.5.1.3 Addressing In SIP, the names found in the To: and From: fields are encoded as Universal Resource Locators (URLs). Current implementations support SIP and PHONE URLs. One could define a new type of URL without changing the nature of the protocol. This allows for "user-friendly" discovery of the appliance address. An example, could use a format similar to the service URL syntax defined in RFC2609,[24] but without the location information (which has already been determined via the SIP routing) and without the "slp: prefix it would be:

```
d = lamp, r = bedroom
```

By base64 encoding this URL (and potentially encrypting it to avoid revealing information about the types of devices contained in the domain), it is possible to structure this URL as part of a SIP URL;

```
sip:a458fauzu3k3z@stan.home.net
```

Thus, the existing structure of `<entity>@<location>` is maintained even when extended to accommodate appliances. However, it is not mandatory to use this proposed type of addressing scheme. A standard SIP URL addressing scheme in either plaintext (e.g., `toaster@stan.home.net`) or a URL with the portion to the left of the @ sign encrypted (e.g., `a3245dsfs234@stan.home.net`) are also valid addresses. A structured addressing scheme could even be used in standard SIP addressing, e.g., `lamp.bedroom@stan.home.net`.

6.5.1.4 Excitation SIP was initially created with call setup in mind. It is intended to establish a relationship, or session, between two endpoints such that ongoing bearer paths can be established between them. This structure could be generalized to cater to brief connections if the connection establishment phase is removed and the payload generalized. The difference between the current way in which SIP is used and the proposed modifications is analogous in many ways to the difference between (TCP) and (UDP) or other Session/Datagram protocols. Fortunately, this problem has also been identified when SIP is extended for use in Instant Messaging (IM) environments,[25] which has resulted in the definition of the MESSAGE extensions to SIP that carry the payload to the remote UA and bring back the response. This method meets the requirements identified above and can carry payloads other than SDP. Any MIME type could be used as the payload of a SIP command, and new MIME types could easily be defined for Action Languages for particular classes of appliances. MESSAGE would carry the command that is appropriate for the target appliance, such as Turn the Light On. The command would trigger a single response, indicative of its result, which would be carried by the standard SIP response mechanisms.

6.5.1.5 Notification/Events In addition to synchronous communication with networked appliances, there is a need for asynchronous communications—for example, to be notified when an alarm goes off in your home, when a certain temperature is reached, or when someone rings your doorbell. The SIP Event Notification draft defines two new primitives, SUBSCRIBE and NOTIFY, that can be used to achieve asynchronous communications. When these methods are used in conjunction with the proposed addressing scheme and the Device Messaging Protocol MIME type, event notification from and between networked appliances is enabled.

6.5.1.6 New Payload Type(s) The typical MIME payload for SIP INVITE messages is Session Description Protocol (SDP). For networked appliances, a payload type that is specific for communicating with devices is required. We therefore propose a new MIME type called *Device Messaging Protocol* (DMP). The details of

DMP are still under investigation, but we believe it will be an XML-based specification that may be similar to the Universal Plug 'n Play's Device Control Protocol.[26] In addition, when a device registers with a proxy (via the REGISTER message), a description of that device needs to be conveyed. We propose to use a *Device Description Protocol* (DDP) to carry this information. As with the DMP, the details are still under development, but it also will likely be XML-based and will leverage existing work in this area.

6.5.1.7 Advantages
Adopting SIP for NAs provides a number of advantages:

- The system leverages SIP, which is already well proven and offers security, authentication capabilities, high reliability, and scaling.
- The use of what amounts to an overlay naming scheme makes the approach independent of any particular naming or addressing regime that might be employed in a specific environment.
- The ability to "register" endpoints allows device mobility. The user can simply register an NA in the home domain; from that point on, messages will be routed to it.
- SIP is likely to be deployed for communication applications like voice over IP. Leveraging it to also support NAs extends both its utility and its early applicability; in short, SIP itself benefits from additional uses.

6.5.1.8 Disadvantages
The biggest disadvantage of SIPa is that it is not currently deployed, so establishment of the infrastructure to support it will take time. SIP is intended to carry unrecognized messages, so there is no need for proxies and other infrastructure equipment to be upgraded to support it. Any field SIP infrastructure should be capable of incorporating an appliances mode.

The other major disadvantage is that there are still a number of open issues; neither DDP nor DMP is fully defined, which limits deployment. It is hoped that their definition will be completed shortly. Provisioning, configuration, and other real-world issues still need to be addressed, as does the problem of transferring services to the devices that are available in a particular environment. It is hoped that these issues can be resolved so that the deployment of a SIPa system, with its considerable advantages, will be possible.

6.5.2 Feature Interaction

The second major problem with NA adoption, particularly as the number of devices in a given environment increases, is Feature Interaction (FI). As already noted, FI occurs when multiple entities make assumptions about the environment in which they are operating and those assumptions are rendered invalid by other entities of which they have no knowledge. A significant amount of FI work has been done in other domains. An investigation of FI in NA environments has been carried out

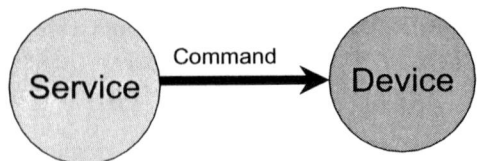

Figure 6.3 Asynchronous excitation.

by Kolberg[27] in collaboration with the authors and others, and some of this work is reported here.

6.5.2.1 Classification of Services In the above work, it was noted that there is a limited set of interaction patterns between devices and their controllers, and that a simple classification could be overlaid for these interactions.

6.5.2.2 Asynchronous Excitation In this scenario, a single service (perhaps implemented on an NA itself, although this is not important for this discussion) excites a single device with no feedback to the service (Figure 6.3). The stimulus that caused the service to perform the action is not known within the system. This is the simplest case. A typical example of this mode of operation is provided by the TV remote control, which simply instructs the TV on the actions that it is to perform. The excitation to perform this action is created by the human user and thus is outside of the system.

6.5.2.3 Notification followed by Excitation In this example, the stimulus that caused the service to generate an excitation event is known (Figure 6.4). This might be the case when a washing machine informs a service that the door has been closed and the service then instructs the washing machine to start the cycle. The difference between this and the previous case is that the excitation that started the process is known within the system and thus is potentially open to influence or modification.

6.5.2.4 Notification followed by Asynchronous Excitation In this case, a stimulus from one device causes the service to excite another device (Figure 6.5). Although this may not seem different from the preceding case, the key issue is that from the point of view of each individual device, the situation is different—the

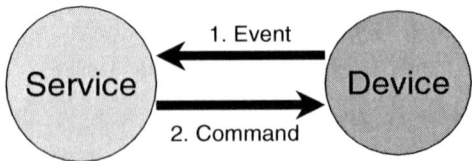

Figure 6.4 Notification followed by excitation.

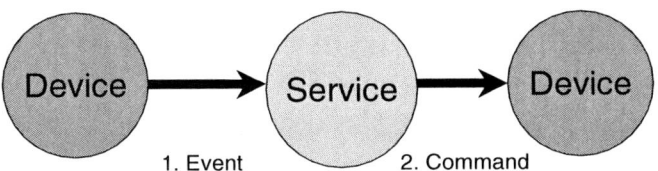

Figure 6.5 Notification followed by asynchronous excitation.

source device sees no consequence as a result of its action report, and the target device sees asynchronous excitation since it is not aware of the original notification, which originated elsewhere. We consider this case to be separate from the case of a normal notification/excitation event (with a null excitation) followed by an asynchronous excitation because it may be possible for some element with a higher-level "world view" than any of the individual components to perform some useful resolution action in this scenario.

6.5.2.5 Classification of Interactions Kolberg has provided numerous examples of the operation of systems using these abstractions in conjunction with a SIPa infrastructure. He also notes a few examples of typical interactions that might be expected to occur:

- The video recorder that is normally used to record TV programs, but that can be overridden to record footage from security cameras when a burglar is detected.
- An "away from home" service that replays previously recorded light switching sequence lights to give the impression that someone is home. Unfortunately, this triggers the burglar alarm.
- The air conditioning service interacting with the heating service, as described previously.

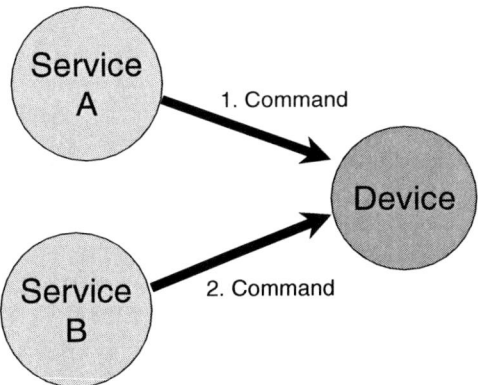

Figure 6.6 Shared action interaction.

Kolberg found that the types of interaction that appeared to occur had strong parallels to work that had been reported previously in the telecom domain:[28]

- **Shared action interactions:** Two or more services attempt to control the same device (Figure 6.6). Note that the two commands do not need to be temporarily associated. The fact that A has sent a command to the device may mean that it makes some assumption about the state of that device that is rendered invalid by B's activity.
- **Shared trigger interactions:** One event is passed to more than one service, which then performs conflicting actions is response to that triggering event (Figure 6.7).
- **Sequential action interactions:** A service performs an action on a device that generates a new event that is reported to the same or another service, causing it to perform a function (Figure 6.8). This can, for example, lead to looping conditions.
- **Missed trigger interaction:** The existence of one service prevents a device from producing an event that would cause a second service to operate. This is difficult to describe pictorially because it is an *absence* of functionality that leads to the interaction.

6.5.2.6 Current Status FI is a vital issue in telecommunication systems, with many academic studies dedicated to it. Interaction between features (or services in the NA environment) becomes a problem only when sufficient services are deployed in an environment for them to impact on each other. In the automotive domain this issue is handled by the design authority for the entire environment ($=$ car) that controls what elements can be used in the vehicle and how they interact with other elements. Thus, in this environment FI limits the speed of rollout of new products as interactions are resolved in the integrated platform, but it should not lead to system misoperation unless particular interactions have been missed during

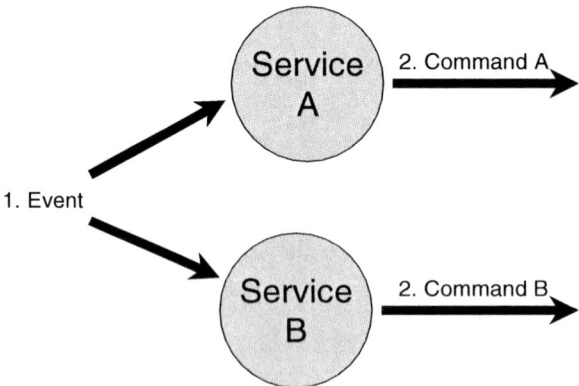

Figure 6.7 Shared trigger interaction.

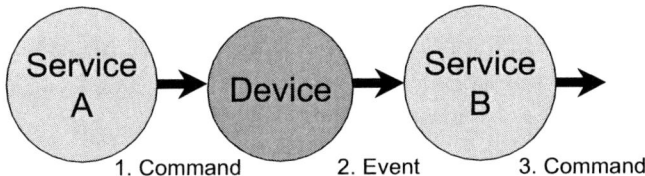

Figure 6.8 Sequential action interaction.

system integration. In the PAN space, we are just starting to see the emergence of FI—mobile phones that connect to only one other Bluetooth device at a time, PDAs that can't deliver audio to the headset because the phone is already bound to it, and many other similarly trivial but irritating issues. However, it is in the home environment that FI has the greatest potential to wreak havoc, with distributed services and devices being required to work together to deliver functionality to the homeowner. How FI management will be resolved in this domain is an open issue, but fortunately, given the slow rate of adoption of NAs in the home environment, we have time to address this problem.

6.6 THE FUTURE OF THE NA

In this chapter, we have given you a glimpse of the world of NA technology and its use in mainstream consumer electronics. Today network connectivity is increasingly the norm—in our homes, in our cars, and on our bodies. We can reasonably expect the devices that turn the electrical impulses of our communications networks into meaningful renderings that our brains can process to become more and more prevalent. These devices will adapt more and more to our ways of working, in contrast to earlier products that forced us to adapt to the limitations of the devices themselves. In other words, the user interface of the NA will change beyond all recognition.

This will happen in two different ways. First, we will start to see more sophisticated use of computer I/O techniques. Speech recognition will become pervasive. Direct eye projection, in-ear loudspeakers, throat microphones, direct electrical stimulation, and many other I/O enhancements will also emerge to help these devices align themselves more closely with their human masters. There will also be another class of user interfaces: those that hide the computing devices from the user in much the same way that the computers in the automobile are hidden. Products such as the Anoto pen[29] and the research work being done at Lancaster University[30] are already heading in this direction. Arguably, this is much more exciting that simply enhancing traditional I/O technologies that force us to change long-established work and interaction patterns to integrate with the technology.

We should also expect to see innovations in power delivery for these devices—on of the great problems at the moment, especially in PAN applications. Enhancements to battery power are the incremental approach, but revolutionary approaches, perhaps taking power from their human hosts in the form of parasitic (or perhaps symbiotic) relationships—kinetic generators exploiting muscle power or perhaps even taking power directly from the body's own power mechanisms, as some early experiments suggest[31]—will begin to free us from the need to service our appliances as distinct entities, and we can start to treat them as cybernetic enhancements to our own bodies.

Whatever the future holds, we can be certain that in our increasingly connected world, we are only at the start of the NA revolution.

It's going to be fun.

REFERENCES

1. http://www.ceiva.com
2. http://news.bbc.co.uk/1/hi/sci/tech/1264205.stm
3. http://www.rabbitsemiconductor.com
4. http://www.atmel.com/dyn/resources/prod_documents/doc4594.pdf
5. http://www.emjembedded.com/products/ieee1394/microcontroller.html
6. http://www.semiconductors.philips.com/buses/i2c/facts/index.html
7. http://www.can-cia.org/can
8. http://www.w3.org/2002/ws
9. http://www.onstar.com/us_english/jsp/index.jsp
10. http://www.bluetooth.com/news/press/sigpress.asp?A = 2&PID = 994
11. http://www.x10.com
12. http://www.echelon.com
13. http://www.faqs.org/rfcs/rfc2663.html
14. http://www.zigbee.org
15. http://www.bluetooth.com
16. http://www.bluejackq.com
17. D.A. Norman, *The Invisible Computer*, MIT Press, 1998.
18. E.J. Cameron, N.D. Griffeth, Y.J. Lin, M.E. Nilson, W.K. Schnure, and H. Velthuijsen, *A Feature Interaction Benchmark for IN and Beyond*, Proc. of the Second Workshop on Feature Interactions in Telecommunication Systems, pp. 178–196, 1994.
19. http://fox.rollins.edu/~tlairson/hightech/NYTCAR.HTML
20. http://www.ietf.org/rfc/rfc3261.txt
21. http://www.faqs.org/rfcs/rfc2327.html
22. http://www.soapware.org
23. S. Moyer, D. Marples, and S. Tsang, "A Protocol for Wide-Area Secure Networked Appliance Communication," *IEEE Communications Magazine*, October 2001.
24. http://www.faqs.org/rfcs/rfc2609.html
25. http://www.ietf.org/html.charters/simple-charter.html
26. http://www.upnp.org/standardizeddcps/basic.asp
27. M. Kolberg, E.H. Magill, and M. Wilson, Compatibility Issues between Services Supporting Networked Appliances, *IEEE Communications Magazine*, December 2003.

28. D.J. Marples, *Detection and Resolution of Feature Interactions in Telecommunication Systems during Runtime*, Ph.D. thesis, Communications Division, Department of Electrical and Electronic Engineering, University of Strathclyde, 2000.
29. http://www.anoto.com
30. http://ubicomp.lancs.ac.uk/portal/html/modules.php?name = Content&pa = showpage&pid = 6
31. Japanese experiments in blood powering.

PART 3
ALGORITHMS AND PROTOCOLS FOR SMART ENVIRONMENTS

CHAPTER 7

Designing for the Human Experience in Smart Environments

GREGORY D. ABOWD and ELIZABETH D. MYNATT
College of Computing and GVU Center
Georgia Institute of Technology

7.1 INTRODUCTION

Mark Weiser originated the term *ubiquitous computing* (ubicomp), creating a vision of people and smart environments augmented with computational resources that provide information and services when and where desired. Weiser's words emphasize the human-centered potential of these augmented environments:

> Machines that fit the human environment instead of forcing humans to enter theirs will make using a computer as refreshing as a walk in the woods.
>
> — (Weiser, 1991)

> We wanted to put computing back in its place, to reposition it into the environmental background, to concentrate on human-to-human interfaces and less on human-to-computer ones.
>
> — (Weiser et al., 1999)

Technologists have excitedly embraced this vision, but aspects of it have also inspired social scientists. Weiser describes the genesis of ubiquitous computing in the following terms:

> Inspired by the social scientists, philosophers, and anthropologists at PARC, we have been trying to take a radical look at what computing and networking ought to be like. We believe that people live through their practices and tacit knowledge so that the most powerful things are those that are effectively invisible in use. This is a challenge that affects all of computer science. Our preliminary approach: Activate the world. Provide hundreds of wireless computing devices per person per office, of all scales

---

Smart Environments: Technologies, Protocols, and Applications, edited by D.J. Cook and S.K. Das
ISBN 0-471-54448-5 © 2005 John Wiley & Sons, Inc.

(from 1" displays to wall sized). This has required new work in operating systems, user interfaces, networks, wireless, displays, and many other areas. We call our work "ubiquitous computing." This is different from PDA's, dynabooks, or information at your fingertips. It is invisible, everywhere computing that does not live on a personal device of any sort, but is in the woodwork everywhere.

— (Weiser, 1994)

What is clear from this original articulation of ubicomp is that people and their activities are central to this vision and that realizing the vision requires us to address a number of clear goals. First, the everyday practices of people need to be understood and supported. Second, the world needs to be augmented by providing of heterogeneous devices offering different forms of interactive experience. The networked devices must be orchestrated to provide for a holistic user experience.

In this chapter, we will describe how these human-centered goals have impacted research in three areas relevant to smart environments: the definition of the appropriate physical interaction experience; discovering general application features; and the evolution of theories and practices for designing and evaluating the human experience in smart environments. Though we will provide examples from many other research efforts, we will conclude with concrete examples from our own work in classrooms and the home.

7.2 DEFINING THE APPROPRIATE PHYSICAL INTERACTION EXPERIENCE

The vision of the smart environment eliminates any assumption about traditional locales for interaction, such as the computer desktop. In addition to suggesting freedom from a small number of well-defined interaction locales (e.g., the desktop), this vision assumes that physical interaction between humans and computation will be less like the current desktop keyboard/mouse/display paradigm and more like the way humans interact with the physical world. Humans speak, gesture, and use writing utensils to communicate with other humans and alter physical artifacts. Supporting human activity within a smart environment, therefore, has resulted in a variety of important changes to the input, output, and interactions that define the human experience with computing. We describe three of those changes in this section.

We have traditionally treated input as an explicit communication act. However, the advance of sensing and recognition technologies has challenged us to provide more human-like communications capabilities and to effectively incorporate implicit actions into the subset of meaningful system input. Similarly, communication from the environment to the user—the output—has become highly distributed and available in many form factors and modalities. The challenge is to coordinate across many output locations and modalities without overwhelming our limited attention spans. Finally, the relationship between input and output is important as we attempt to integrate smoothly between the physical and digital worlds.

7.2.1 Toward Implicit Input

Input has moved beyond the explicit nature of textual input from keyboards and selection from pointing devices to a greater variety of data types. This has resulted in not only a greater variety of input technologies, but also a shift from *explicit* means of human input to more *implicit* forms. By implicit input we mean that our natural interactions with the physical environment provide sufficient input to a variety of attendant services, without any further user intervention. For example, walking into a space is enough to announce one's presence and identity in that location.

Computer interfaces that support more natural human forms of communication (e.g., handwriting, speech, and gestures) are beginning to supplement or replace elements of the graphical user interface (GUI) interaction paradigm. The emerging area of perceptual interfaces is being driven by long-standing research on computer vision and multimodal recognition technologies (mainly handwriting and speech). Pen-based interaction, unsuccessfully rushed to the market in the early 1990s, is also experiencing a resurgence. Large-scale touch-interactive surfaces, using technologies such as capacitive coupling, have made it possible to create multiperson interactive surfaces on tables and walls (see Figure 7.1). Recognition of freehand writing is improving but, more significantly, mass adoption has followed the introduction of less sophisticated and more robust recognition technologies such as Grafitti. We have even seen compelling examples of how voice and pen input can be used effectively in applications without requiring any recognition at all (e.g., Hindus & Schmandt, 1992).

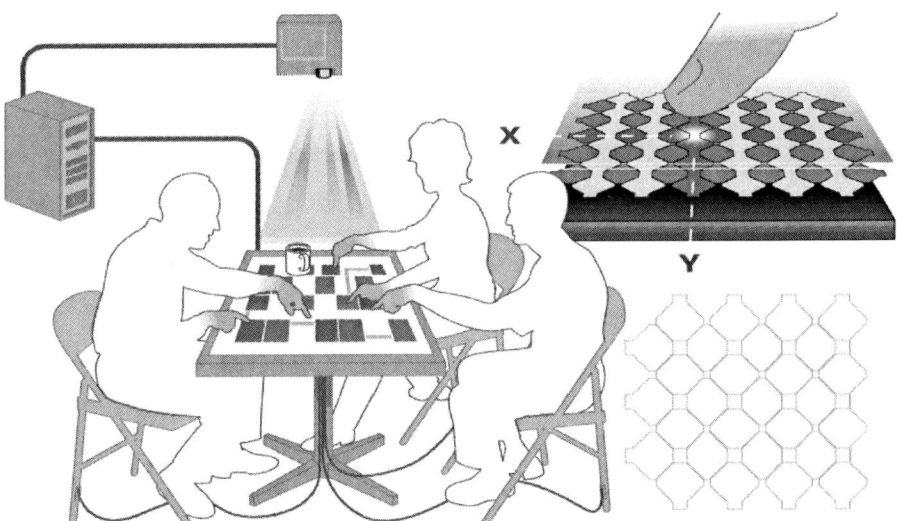

Figure 7.1 The DiamondTouch input technology from the Mitsubishi Electic Research Laboratory (MERL) uses capacitive coupling through humans to provide a large-scale input surface for multiple simultaneous users. See http://www.merl.com/projects/DiamondTouch for more details.

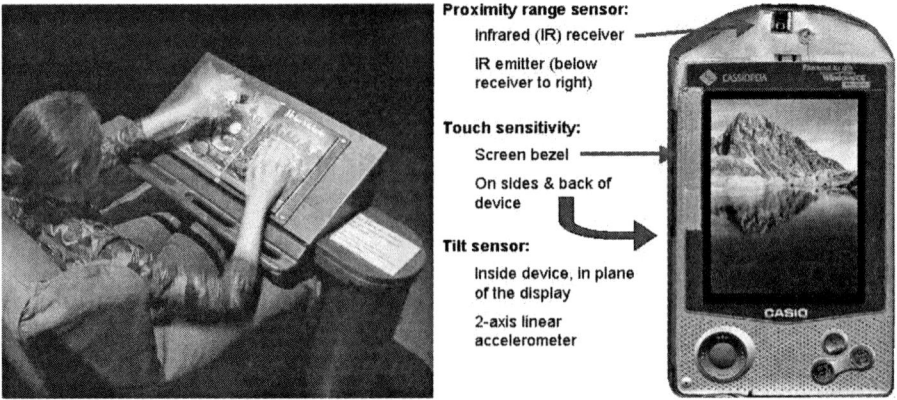

Figure 7.2 Two examples of simple sensing embedded into devices. On the left, the Listen reader from Xerox PARC (Back et al., 2001) uses electric field sensors located in the book binding to sense the proximity of the reader's hands and control audio parameters, while (RFID) tags embedded in each page allow fast, robust page identification. Picture courtesy of Xerox PARC. On the right is an experimental personal digital assistant platform used at Microsoft Research to investigate how a variety of simple sensors can improve the interaction between a user and various handheld applications (Hinckley et al., 2000). Picture courtesy of Ken Hinckley.

These recognition technologies are some examples of interpreting meaning from sensed signals of human activity. There are many other ways to obtain information about people and environments by sensing a variety of other physical signals. The significance here is that sensing and interpretation of human activity provides a more implicit notion of input to an interactive system. For example, many researchers have investigated how simple sensors such as radio frequency identification (RFID), accelerometers, tilt sensors, capacitive coupling, IR range finders, and others can be incorporated into artifacts to increase the language of input from the user to control that artifact, as shown in Figure 7.2 (Hinckley et al., 2000).

Invisibility of computing, from the human perspective, can start when we are able to determine an individual's identity, location, affect, or activity through her mere presence and natural interactions within an environment. The union of explicit and implicit input defines the *context* of interaction between the human and the environment, a theme we will return to in the next section on emergent application features.

7.2.2 Towards Multiscale and Distributed Output

The integration of ubiquitous computing capabilities into everyday life also requires novel output technologies and techniques. To start, the design of targeted information appliances, such as personal digital assistants (PDAS) and future home technologies, requires addressing the form of the technology, including its aesthetic appeal. Output is no longer exclusively in the form of self-contained desktop/laptop visual displays that demand our attention. A variety of sizes or scales, both smaller and larger than the desktop, of visual displays are being distributed throughout our environments. More importantly, we are seeing multiple modalities of information sources that lie at the periphery of our senses and provide qualitative, ambient forms of communication.

Weiser described the form factor ubicomp technology in three scales —the inch, the foot, and the yard. The middle (foot) scale is similar to the standard laptop and desktop displays. We all have one or a small number of these devices, and we use them largely in stationary settings. A new generation of tablet-like, portable, pen-based computers, devices that rival the experimental MPAD prototypes developed at Xerox PARC, hit the consumer market in late 2002. Pagers, cellular phones, and PDAs, handheld displays with relatively low resolution today, represent the small end of the scale (inch). We all carry an increasing number of these display devices at all times. The large end of the scale (yard) is now represented by high-resolution, wall-sized displays that are created by stitching together multiple low-resolution projected displays, such as the Stanford Interactive Mural (Humphreys & Hanrahan, 1999; see Figure 7.3) or the Princeton Display Wall (Chen et al., 2000).

As these displays have continued to proliferate in number and variety, two important trends have emerged. First, as initially motivated by Rekimoto's

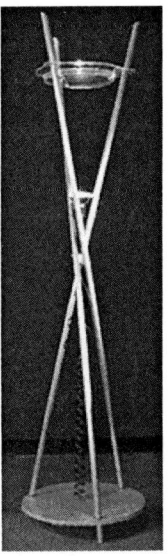

Figure 7.3 The figure on the left is the Stanford Interactive Mural, an example of a large-scale interactive display surface created by tiling multiple lower-resolution projectors. Picture courtesy of Françoise Guimbetrière. The figure on the right is an example of an ambient display, the Water Lamp, from Ishii's Tangible Media Group at the MIT Media Laboratory. Light shines up through a pan of water, actuated by digitally controlled solenoid that can tap the water and cause ripples. External information can be used to drive the tapping of the solenoids. Picture courtesy of Hiroshi Ishii.

"pick-and-drop" demonstration (1997) and further explored in the Stanford Interactive Room (Fox et al., 2000), we want to move information between separate displays easily and coordinate the interactions between multiple displays. Second, as displays proliferate, we want them to be less demanding of our attention. Weiserian invisibility comes through design of output that provides for peripheral awareness of information outside of our conscious attention.

The trend toward peripheral output has been explored for a particular class of displays called *ambient*. Ambient displays require minimal attention and cognitive effort, and are thus more easily integrated into a persistent physical space. One of the first ambient displays, the Dangling String (Weiser & Brown, 1995), was invented at Xerox PARC by the artist Natalie Jeremijenko. Using analog sensing of network traffic from the cabling in the ceiling, a motor drove the spin of a long string. The heavier the traffic, the faster the rotation. During high-traffic periods, the whir of the string was faintly audible as well.

The Dangling String has many of the features of subsequent efforts in ambient displays. A data source drives the abstract representation such that the output can be monitored by the user's peripheral perception. The data source is generally information of medium to low priority, but it is beneficial for the user to be aware of, perhaps for some opportunistic action. As these displays are meant to be persistently available in the environment, they are often designed to be aesthetically appealing and novel. Other examples of ambient displays include ambientROOM, which projects information about colleagues as pinpoints of light on the wall (Ishii et al., 1998); Audio Aura, which encodes the arrival of incoming e-mail as auditory cues in a mobile device (Mynatt et al. 1998); and Kandinsky, which assembles images triggered from keywords in information bulletins into an aesthetically pleasing and intriguing collage (Fogarty et al., 2001).

Though our experience with computing output is dominated by the use of the visual channel, examples such as Audio Aura demonstrate how other modes of output can be effective in communicating ambient information. Other forms of output include actuation of small devices. With the introduction of simple programming tools for dealing with motors and other actuators, such as Phidgets (Greenberg & Fitchett, 2001), mechanical actuation to drive distributed output devices will increase.

7.2.3 Seamless Integration of Physical and Virtual Worlds

An important feature of ubicomp technology is that it attempts to merge computational artifacts smoothly with the world of physical artifacts. There have been plenty of examples demonstrating how electronic information can be overlaid on the real world, producing an augmented reality (Feiner et al., 1993). An example of such augmented reality is NaviCam, a portable camera/TV that recognizes two-dimensional glyphs placed on objects and can then superimpose relevant information over the objects for display on the TV screen (see Figure 7.4). This form of augmented reality only affects the output. When both input and output are intermixed, as with the DigitalDesk (shown in Figure 7.4) (Wellner, 1993), we begin

Figure 7.4 On the left is the DigitalDesk prototype integrating physical and virtual desktop environments with the aid of projection and vision technology (Wellner, 1993). On the right is the NaviCam system, which recognizes two-dimensional glyphs on objects and then superimposes additional information on those objects (Rekimoto & Katashi, 1995). © 1994–1998, Sony Computer Science Laboratories, Inc.

to approach the seamless integration of the physical and virtual worlds. Researchers have suggested techniques for using objects in the physical world to manipulate electronic artifacts, creating so-called graspable (Fitzmaurice et al., 1995) or tangible (Ishii and Ullmer, 1997) user interfaces. Sensors attached to devices themselves provide ways for physical manipulations of those devices to be interpreted appropriately by the applications running on those devices (Harrison et al., 1998, 2000).

7.3 APPLICATION THEMES

Applications are of course the whole point of ubiquitous computing.
— (Weiser, 1993)

What is the "killer app" for a smart environment? We argue that it is not the value of any single service that will make a smart environment desirable. Rather, it is the combination of a large range of services, all of which are available when and as needed, and all of which work as desired without extraordinary human intervention. A major challenge for applications research is to discover an evolutionary path toward this idyllic interactive experience in a smart environment.

There are emergent features that appear across many applications. One feature is the ability to use implicitly sensed context from the physical and electronic environments to determine the correct behavior of any given service. Context-aware computing demonstrates promise for making our interactions with services more seamless and less distracting from our everyday activities. Applications can be made to work right when they are informed about the context of their use. Another feature of many ubicomp applications is the ability to easily capture and store memories of live experiences and serve them for later use. The trajectory of these two applications themes, coupled with the increasing exploration of ubiquitous computing of novel nonwork environments, points to the changing relationship between people and computing, and thus the changing purpose of ubicomp applications. We describe this newer trajectory, termed *everyday computing*, following a discussion of the two more established themes.

7.3.1 Context-Aware Computing

Two compelling early demonstrations of ubicomp were the Olivetti Research Lab's Active Badge (Want et al., 1992) and the Xerox PARCTab (Want et al., 1995), both location-aware appliances. These devices leverage a simple piece of context information, user location, and provide valuable services (automatic call forwarding for a phone system, automatically updated maps of user locations in an office). These simple location-aware appliances are perhaps the first demonstration of linking implicit human activity with computational services that serve to augment general human activity.

Location of identifiable entities (usually people) is a very common piece of context information used in ubicomp application development. The most widespread applications have been Global Positioning Sattelite (GPS)-based car navigation systems and handheld "tour guide" systems that vary the content displayed (video or audio) by a handheld unit given the user's physical location in an exhibit area (Abowd et al., 1997; Cheverst et al., 1998). The Sentient Computing Project demonstrates the most complex set of location-aware applications provides the most complex indoor location-aware infrastructure and applications development, as shown in Figure 7.5 (AT&T, 2002).

Of course, there is more to context than position (where) and identity (who). Although a complete definition of context remains an illusive research challenge, it is clear that in addition to who and where, context awareness involves questions of when things occur, what activities are being performed, and, ultimately, why those actions occur as they do.

Related to the definition of context is the question of how to represent context. This issue is important once we consider separating the context-sensing portion of an application from its context-aware behavior. Without good representations of context, applications developers are left to develop ad hoc, limited schemes for storing and manipulating this key information. The evolution of more sophisticated representations will enable a wider range of capabilities and a true separation of sensing context from the programmable reaction to that context.

An obvious challenge of context-aware computing is making it truly ubiquitous. Having certain context, in particular positioning information, has been shown to be useful. However, there are few truly ubiquitous, single-source context services. Positioning is a good example. GPS does not work indoors and is suspect in some urban regions as well. There are a variety of indoor positioning schemes as well,

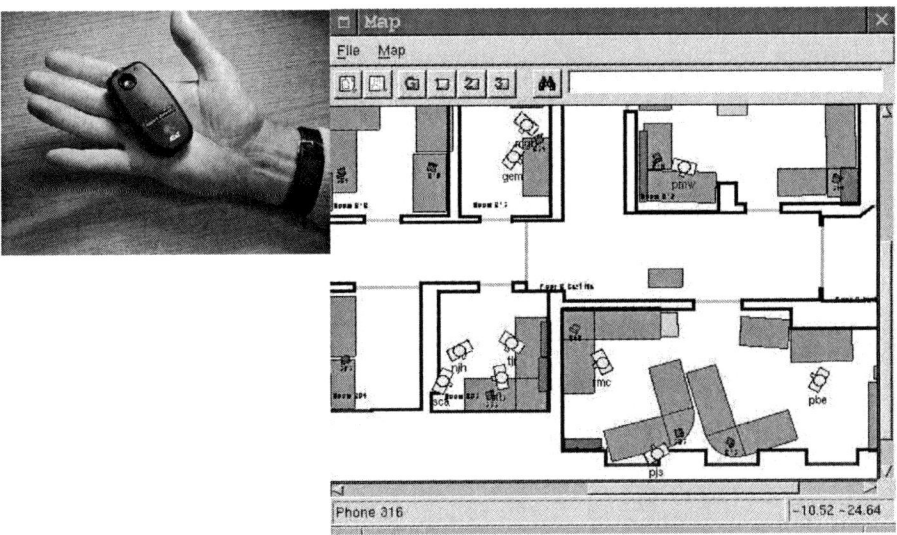

Figure 7.5 On the left is the AT&T Laboratories Bat device, part of a three-dimensional ultrasonic indoor location system. On the right is a map of office worker locations that helps coworkers find each other and talk by phone.

with differing characteristics in terms of cost, range, granularity, and requirements for tagging, and no single solution is likely to ever meet all requirements. The solution for obtaining ubiquitous context is to assemble context information from a combination of related context services. Such *context fusion* is similar in intent to the related, and well-researched, area of sensor fusion.

7.3.2 Automated Capture and Access

Much of our life in business and academia is spent listening to and recording, more or less accurately, the events that surround us and then trying to remember the important pieces of information from those events. There is clear value, and potential danger, in using computational resources to augment the inefficiency of human record taking, especially when there are multiple streams of related information that are virtually impossible to capture as a whole manually. Tools to support automated capture of and access to live experiences can remove the burden of doing something humans are not good at (i.e., recording) so that they can focus attention on activities they are good at (i.e., indicating relationships, summarizing, and interpreting).

We define capture and access as the task of preserving a record of a live experience that is then reviewed at some point in the future. Vannevar Bush was perhaps the first to write about the benefits of a generalized capture and access system when he introduced the concept of the memex (Bush, 1945). The memex was intended to store the artifacts that we come in contact with in our everyday lives and the associations that we create between them. Over the years, many researchers have worked toward this vision. As a result, many systems have been built to capture and access experiences in classrooms, meetings, and other live experiences.

The earliest work on automated capture was done at Xerox PARC to support meeting capture. Over the past decade, a number of capture applications have been explored in a variety of environments (later, we describe a classroom capture environment) in support of individuals or groups. A full review of automated capture is presented by Truong et al. (2001).

7.3.3 Toward Continuous Interaction

Providing continuous interaction transforms computing from a localized tool into a constant presence. A new thread of ubicomp research, everyday computing, promotes informal and unstructured activities typical of much of our everyday lives. Familiar examples are orchestrating daily routines, communicating with family and friends, and managing information.

The focus on activities as opposed to tasks is a crucial departure from traditional Human–Computer Interaction (HCI) design. The majority of computer applications support well-defined tasks that have a marked beginning and end, with multiple subtasks in between. Take word processing as an example. Word processing features are tuned for starting with a blank document (or a template), entering text, formatting, printing, and saving. These applications are not well suited to the more general activity of writing, encompassing multiple versions of documents where text is reused and content evolves over time.

The emphasis on designing for continuously available interaction requires addressing these features of informal, daily activities:

- They rarely have a clear beginning or end, so the design cannot assume a common starting or closing point, requiring greater flexibility and simplicity.
- Interruption is expected as users switch attention among competing concerns.
- Multiple activities operate concurrently and may need to be loosely coordinated.
- Time is an important discriminator in characterizing the ongoing relationship between people and computers.
- Associative models of information are needed, as information is reused from multiple perspectives.

Of course, activities and tasks are not unrelated to each other. Often an activity consists of a number of tasks, but the activity itself is more than these component parts for the reasons listed above. For example, communication activities contain well-defined tasks such as reading a message or composing a reply. The interaction falters when the task refers to the larger activity: How does this new message relate to previous messages from this person? What other issues should be included in the reply? The challenge in designing for activities is encompassing these tasks in an environment that supports continuous interaction.

7.4 THEORIES OF DESIGN AND EVALUATION

Traditional work in HCI has produced considerable human factors guidance for designing various kinds of computer interfaces (e.g., graphical displays, direct manipulation interfaces, multimedia systems, and websites). Although widely used, the majority of these guidelines tend to focus on the needs and demands of designing desktop computer interfaces. During the past few years, the emergence of ubicomp has led the research communities to ask whether these current approaches are appropriate to the design of interfaces where interaction extends beyond the traditional monitor, keyboard, and mouse arranged on a desk.

The particular concern for ubicomp is developing support for the design and assessment of systems that are appropriate when computing functionality becomes embedded in the surrounding environment, in specific physical objects, or even in objects that are carried. This movement away from the desktop, with its well-understood and fixed arrangement of devices, has been a catalyst for three broad research activities:

- the development of new models of interaction that incorporate the relationship of ubiquitous computing with the physical world;
- the emergence of methods that focus on gaining richer understandings of settings; and
- the development of approaches to assess the utility of ubiquitous computing.

7.4.1 New Models of Interaction

The shift in focus from the desktop to the surrounding environment inherent in ubicomp mirrors previous work in HCI and CSCW (Computer Supported Cooperative Work). As the computer has increasingly "reached out" in the organization, researchers have needed to shift their focus from a single machine engaging with an individual to a broader set of organizational and social arrangements and the cooperative interaction inherent in these arrangements. This shift has seen the development of new models of interaction to support the design process in broader organizational settings. Many of these models are applicable to ubicomp, with its emphasis on integrating numerous devices in one setting.

Traditionally, research and evaluation efforts in HCI have been informed by the Model Human Processor theory of human cognition and behavior (Card et al., 1983). This model focuses on internal cognition driven by the cooperation of three independent units of sensory, cognitive, and motor activity, where each unit maintains its own working store of information. As the application of computers has broadened, designers have turned to models that consider the nature of the relationship between the internal cognitive processes and the outside world. Designing for a balance between "knowledge in the world" and "knowledge in the head" is now a common maxim in the design community (Hutchins, 1995; Norman, 1990).

The ubicomp community is currently exploring three main models of cognition as guides for future design and evaluation.

Activity theory is the oldest of the three, building on work by Vygotsky (1981). The closest to traditional theories, activity theory recognizes concepts such as goals ("objects"), actions, and operations. However, both goals and actions are fluid, based on the changing physical state of the world instead of more fixed, a priori plans. Additionally, although operations require little or no explicit attention, such as an expert driver motoring home, the operation can shift to an action based on changing circumstances, such as difficult traffic and weather conditions. Activity theory also emphasizes the transformational properties of artifacts that implicitly carry knowledge and traditions, such as musical instruments, cars, and other tools. The behavior of the user is shaped by the capabilities of the tool itself (Nardi, 1996). Ubiquitous computing efforts informed by activity theory, therefore, focus on the transformational properties of artifacts and the fluid execution of actions and operations.

Situated action emphasizes the improvisational aspects of human behavior and deemphasizes a priori plans that are simply executed by the person. In this model, knowledge in the world continually shapes the ongoing interpretation and execution of a task. For example, a downhill skier constantly adjusts his behavior given the changing physical terrain, the presence of other people, and the signals from his own body. Any external plan, such as "ski to the bottom of the hill without falling," is vague and driven by the context of the ski resort itself (Suchman, 1987). Ubiquitous computing efforts informed by situated action also emphasize improvisational behavior and would not require or expect the user to follow a predefined script. The system would aim to add knowledge of the world that could effectively assist in shaping the user's action, hence an emphasis on continuously updated peripheral displays. Additionally, evaluation of this system would require watching authentic human behavior and would discount post-task interviews as rationalizations of behavior that is not necessarily rational.

Distributed cognition also deemphasizes internal human cognition, but in this case, it turns to a systems perspective in which humans are part of a larger system. This theory focuses on the collaborative process by which multiple people use multiple objects to achieve a larger systems goal, such as naval crew members using numerous tools to bring a ship into port (Hutchins, 1995). Of these three theories, distributed cognition plays the greatest attention to knowledge in the world, as much of the information needed to accomplish a system's goal is encoded in the individual objects. Cognition occurs as people translate this information in order to perform part of the larger task. Ubiquitous computing efforts informed by distributed cognition focus on designing for a larger system goal, in contrast to the use of an individual appliance, and emphasize how information is encoded in objects and how that information is translated, and perhaps transmitted, by different users.

7.4.2 Gaining Richer Understandings of Settings

The development of the cognitive models presented in the previous section is not without contention. Indeed, considerable debate exists within the social sciences about the nature of cognition and the observable world of everyday practices.

Suchman first highlighted the need to gain a rich understanding of the everyday world to inform the development of information technology (IT) (Suchman, 1987). In contrast to the development of abstract models, a number of researchers focus on gaining rich understandings of particular settings and conveying these understandings to the design process. Weiser also emphasized the importance of understanding these everyday practices to inform ubicomp research:

> We believe that *people live through their practices* and tacit knowledge so that the most powerful things are those that are *effectively invisible in use* [our emphasis].
> — (Weiser, 1994)

The challenge for ubicomp designers is to uncover the practices through which people live, and to make these invisible practices visible and available to the developers of ubiquitous computing environments. Ethnography has emerged as a primary approach to address the need to gain rich understandings of particular settings and the everyday practices that encompass these settings.

Ethnographic studies have their roots in anthropology and sociology and focus on uncovering everyday practices as they are understood by a particular community. Ethnography relies on an observer going into the field and "learning the ropes" through questioning, listening, watching, talking, etc., with practitioners. The task of the field worker is to immerse herself in the setting and its activities with a view to describing them as the skillful and socially organized accomplishments of the inhabitants of that setting.

In the context of ubicomp, the goal of an ethnographic investigation is to provide these descriptions and analyses of everyday life to the IT designers and developers so that ubicomp environments seamlessly mesh with the everyday practices that encapsulate the goals, attitudes, social relationships, knowledge, and language of the intended setting. These techniques have been applied to inform the design of social communications devices for the home (Hindus et al., 2001) and to enhance the social connection between seniors and their extended families (Mynatt et al., 2001).

Perhaps a more intriguing method to convey the nature of settings to developers of future technologies has emerged from an art and design tradition. The work of Gaver et al. (1999) has explored the use of cultural probes to collect information from settings in order to *inspire* the development of new digital devices.

7.4.3 Assessment of Use

In the previous sections, we considered models and theories to understand users and some of the methods researchers have used to uncover the needs and desires of users. However, we must also assess the utility of ubicomp solutions. Researchers have only recently begun to address the development of assessment and evaluation techniques that meet the demands of ubicomp. One reason for the relatively slow development of these techniques is the gradual evolution of the vision of ubiquitous use of technology. In order to understand the impact of ubicomp on everyday life, we maintain a delicate balance between prediction of how novel technologies will serve a real human need and observation of authentic use and subsequent coevolution of human activities and novel technologies.

Formative and summative evaluation of ubicomp systems is difficult and represents a real challenge for the ubicomp community. Scholtz and Consolvo (2004) have surveyed the state of the art in evaluation of ubiquitous computing applications, many of which qualify as smart environments projects.

7.4.3.1 The Need for New Measures
The shift away from the desktop inherent in the ubicomp vision also represents a shift away from the office and the managed structuring of work inherent in these environments. Much of our understanding of work has developed from Fordist and Taylorist principles on the structuring of activities and tasks. Evaluation within HCI reflects these roots and is often predicated on notions of tasks and the measurement of performance and efficiency in meeting these goals and tasks.

However, it is not clear that these measures can apply universally across activities when we move away from structured and paid work to other activities. For example, it is unclear how we can assess the domestic devices suggested by the Royal College of Art (Gaver and Dunne, 1999) or the broad range of devices to emerge from Philips' Vision of the Future (Philips, 1996). This shift away from the world of work means that there is still the question of how to apply qualitative or quantitative evaluation methods. Answering this question requires researchers to consider new representations of human activity and how to undertake assessment that goes beyond existing task-oriented approaches. Although many researchers have investigated the use of observational, and semistructured interviews, the lack of deployment of ubiquitous environments has hampered many of these activities.

7.4.3.2 The Need for Authentic Deployment
The technology used to create ubicomp systems is often on the cutting edge, and it is difficult to create reliable and robust systems that support some activity on a continuous basis. Consequently, a good portion of reported ubicomp applications work remains at this level of demonstrational prototypes that are not designed to be robust. Deeper empirical evaluation results cannot be obtained through controlled studies in the traditional, contained usability laboratory. Rather, the requirement is for real use of a system deployed in an authentic setting.

A number of researchers are seeking to roll out ubiquitous devices into a range of settings, such as museums, outdoor city centers, and the home. These researchers are creating "living laboratories" for ubicomp research by developing testbeds that support advanced research and development as well as use by a targeted user community.

7.5 TWO EXAMPLES OF LIVING LABORATORIES

Our own research at Georgia Tech has explored several living laboratories, and in this last section we will give brief overviews of two of those laboratories, for the classroom and for the home.

7.5.1 The Classroom

An influential case study in deployment and evaluation of a ubicomp application is the Classroom 2000 system, developed at Georgia Tech (Abowd, 1999). The project began in July 1995 with the intent of producing a system that would capture as much of the classroom experience as possible to facilitate later review by both students and teachers. In many lectures, students have their heads down, furiously writing down what they hear and see for future reference. While some of this writing activity is useful as a processing cue for the student, from both the student's and the teacher's perspective it was desirable to give students the opportunity to lift their heads occasionally and engage in the lecture experience. The capture system was seen as a way to relieve some of the note-taking burden.

To test the feasibility of this hypothesis quickly, an environment for capture was implemented within six months and used to support the capture of an entire course to determine whether the initial hypothesis was worth testing more vigorously. Some very valuable lessons were learned during this first extended experience. The initial experiments included student note-taking devices that were clear distractions to the students. Support for private student note-taking was abandoned, only to be resume two years later when the technology had caught up.

To understand the impact of this capture system on teaching and learning, it would have to be used by many more students and teachers in a wider variety of courses. This required significant engineering effort to create a robust and reliable capture system that, by early 1997, was able to support multiple classes simultaneously. During a three-year experimental period ending in mid-2000, over 100 courses were supported for 30 different instructors. In what will hopefully serve as a model for longitudinal study of ubicomp systems, Brotherton and Abowd (2004) reported on the extensive quantitative analysis that reveals how such an automated capture and access system impacts the educational experience *once it has been incorporated into everyday experience*. As a direct result of these deeper evaluations, we know that the system encourages 60% of its users to modify their in-class note-taking behavior. We also know that not all of this modified behavior is for the better. Taking no notes, for example, is not a good learning practice to reinforce. We know that it is time to reintroduce student note-taking units that can personalize the capture experience and also encourage better note-taking practices (Truong et al., 1999). We also know how to facilitate more content-based retrieval and synchronized playback of the lecture experience. These insights have motivated further research efforts and established a long-term research project, eClass, which stands as a model for ubicomp research and automated capture and access.

We also learned the importance of very-large-scale interactive surfaces. Current upright interactive surfaces are somewhat limited in size. Rear-projected displays have many nice interactive properties, yet they remain too costly for large-scale adoption. We have been developing an alternative virtual rear projection capability, that uses only front projection. With the assistance of computer vision, shadows and other undesirable features of front projection can be removed, providing an interactive experience that is demonstrably close to rear projection (Summet et al., 2003).

7.5.2 The Office

Designing ubiquitous computing applications require designers to determine how users will employ these new technologies in the future. Although designing for a currently impossible interaction is not a new HCI problem, it is made more difficult by the implied paradigm shift in HCI resulting from the distribution of computing capabilities into the physical environment and the new role of computing in highly informal activities. In the design work for Flatland (Mynatt et al., 1999), ethnographic observations of whiteboard use in the office were conducted, coupled with questionnaires and interviews, to understand how people used their whiteboards on a daily basis. The richness of the data from the observations was both inspirational in the design work and provided useful constraints. For example, many of the observations that characterized individual whiteboard use, in contrast to whiteboard use in meeting rooms, challenged assumptions about the design of augmented whiteboards and informed specific design features. The data from the observations was key in grounding more in-depth user studies through questionnaires and interviews. Without this data, discussions would too easily slip into wild speculation by users about what they might do. By referring to two weeks of observational data, we were able to uncover and examine the details of daily practice.

Flatland's design demonstrated a "walk up and write" informal interface, allowing users to manipulate multiple "segments" of whiteboard content, coupled with lightweight behaviors, e.g., "act like a map." All content was automatically stored, available for retrieval using multiple associative scan and search interfaces. Although long-term evaluation was not feasible, Flatland passed the "I want this in my office today" litmus test, not because of its gee-whiz technology, but because its design successfully mirrored informal office activities. This work has been incorporated into the Kimura project, an augmented office environment integrating a desktop computer, an electronic whiteboard, and a variety of physical and virtual context sensors (Voida et al., 2002).

7.5.3 The Home

Major shifts in emerging technologies can significantly alter the landscape of the home. Although computing technology has made inroads into home environments, it has yet to instigate a major shift in the design of homes or home activities. The convergence of television and the Internet is lagging expectations, and the combination of desktop computers, entertainment consoles, televisions, and cell phones has yet to form a cohesive whole. A revolution of technology in the home may very well arise from technologies aimed at helping older adults maintain their independence and quality of life while helping avoid the transition to a more expensive institutional setting. A coherent suite of technologies will eventually enable older adults to be proactive about their own health care, aid them in performing daily activities, and help them learn new skills. It will create new avenues for social communication and, of course, will help ensure their safety and well-being.

There is a spectrum of needs in which computational technologies can help older adults to maintain their quality of life and independence while aging in place. In the Aware Home Research Initiative we are examining the design, development, and evaluation of many technological possibilities along this spectrum in three different categories.

7.5.3.1 Compensating for Physical Decline

Ironically, the use of technology is also a potential barrier for older adults. Controls are typically difficult to see, operate, and remember. We have developed the Gesture Pendant, a wireless device that enables the residents of a smart home to give the house commands in the form of hand movements to perform particular tasks instead of physically performing these tasks themselves. For example, different gestures would close the blinds, lock the doors, open the front door, dim the light, or raise the thermostat. The gesture pendant is worn around the neck, similar to a necklace, and has a camera and motion sensors. It can take commands as well as monitor the physical activities of its user, and can even be used to get help in case of an emergency. A potential side benefit of this technology is that it can track tremors in the hand and possibly serve as an early indicator of neurological impairments such as those of Parkinson's disease.

7.5.3.2 Aiding Recall of Past Actions

Memory capabilities decline with age, including the ability to recall recent actions. This deficit hinders older adults in completing tasks when interrupted or distracted. We have been exploring memory lapses during a common household task, cooking. Cooking is a physical activity that is subject to distractions and interruptions. Mistakes are costly but, for the most part, are not life-threatening. The process is made up of specific activities (e.g., "add a cup of flour"), but rote cooking from a recipe is not the norm. Hence a predictive system (e.g., "next, do this") could often be wrong, but a capture system (e.g., "here's what you've been doing") could aid a user in remembering specific actions. Our current prototype system, the Cook's Collage, provides surrogate memory support for general cooking tasks. The current design emphasizes the temporal order of cooking events. Visual snapshots of cooking actions are arranged as a series of panels similar to a comic strip. The primary goal of the system is to provide an ongoing record of recent cooking activity. Its design is motivated by Norman's (1990) distinction between knowledge in the head and knowledge in the world. By adding information to the world in the form of a visual record, the system decreases the cognitive demands of the cooking task, namely, the recall of recent actions. Ideally, users would integrate these snapshots with existing information in the world, such as discarded eggshells or a measuring cup with a trace of flour, so that with little conscious effort, they would fill in any gaps in their retrospective memory.

7.5.3.3 Supporting Awareness for Extended Family Members

The desire of older adults to remain in the familiar setting of their family home frequently must be balanced with their extended family's desire to keep them safe. Clearly, this balance becomes more precarious as age increases. Geographic distance between extended family members exacerbates the problem by eliminating the casual daily contact that naturally occurs when family members live nearby. The Digital Family Portrait is an in-home monitoring system to inform family members about an older relative's daily activities, health status, and potential problems, as well as provide information about patterns of activities over a period of time (Mynatt et al., 2001). The Digital Family Portrait creates a visualization of the older person's day at home from available sensor information and displays the information to a family member in a. different location. We designed our current prototype by framing a flat panel display and connecting it to a standard PC. Various sensing technologies (e.g., radio frequency badge tracking and computer vision) can gather information about the individual pictured on the display and integrate it into the interface.

We have been particularly interested in understanding older adults' acceptance of these kinds of technological interventions in their home lives. Interviews of older adults to gauge their reactions to the prototypes in the Aware Home have revealed the trade-offs or tensions between the perceived utility of these services and the perceived value, costs, and stigma for older adults contemplating how to age in place (Sarkisian et al., 2003).

7.6 CONCLUSIONS

Weiser's vision of ubiquitous computing was human-centered, and over a decade later, it still presents a grand challenge for those who wish to address this new interaction paradigm. As discussed in this chapter, those challenges cover three main areas.

First, the physical interface between humans and a computationally enhanced environment requires a shift in emphasis for both input and output. Input is no longer just an explicit communication. It must include more implicit means of communications that are perceived and interpreted by the environment. For output, multiple form factors and modalities are becoming more widely distributed in our environments, with more opportunities to provide peripheral awareness. The line between the physical and virtual worlds is also purposely blurred.

Second, while a "killer app" for ubicomp has arrived in the form of person-person communication, the more interesting challenge is to understand what general features of ubicomp applications matter. The past decade has seen two emergent features—context awareness and automated capture. The next decade should see an increased focus on continuous services that support everyday activities.

Third, different theories of human cognition inform the design of ubicomp applications as knowledge in the world becomes even more important. The design process must better incorporate an understanding of the invisible meaning of everyday activities. Evaluation of the utility of ubicomp applications is harder in controlled usability laboratories, so we must build a new form of laboratory that facilitates observation and measurement as well as everyday activity.

A smart environment is a *real* environment, a place where people perform routine actions. In order to study the impact of smart environments, we must work to create realistic settings for the development *and evaluation* of our research. We have produced three such "living laboratories" in our work at Georgia Tech: the classroom, the office, and the home.

ACKNOWLEDGMENTS

This chapter has been adapted from a previous publication by Drs. Abowd and Mynatt, a survey article that appeared first in *ACM Transactions on Computer-Human Interaction* and was revised for the inaugural issue of *IEEE Pervasive Computing*. The authors would like to acknowledge all faculty and student colleagues at Georgia Tech who have participated in the Future Computing Environments effort since the mid-1990s. Support for this work has come from the National Science Foundation, DARPA, and various industrial sponsors for Classroom 2000/eClass, the Augmented Office, and the Aware Home Research Initiative.

REFERENCES

Abowd, G.D. 1999. Classroom 2000: An experiment with the instrumentation of a living educational environment. *IBM systems Journal*, special issue on human-computer interaction: A focus on pervasive computing, **38**(4):508–530.

Abowd, G.D., C.G. Atkeson, J. Hong, S. Long, R. Kooper, and M. Pinkerton. 1997. Cyberguide: A mobile context-aware tour guide. *ACM Wireless Networks*, **3**:421–433.

Abowd, G.D. and E.D. Mynatt. 2000. Charting past, present and future research in ubiquitous computing. *ACM Transactions on Computer-Human Interaction*, special issue on HCI in the new millenium, **7**(1):29–58.

AT&T Laboratories, Cambridge. 2002. Sentient Computing Project home page: http://www.uk.research.att.com/spirit

Back, M., J. Cohen, R. Gold, S. Harrison, and S. Minneman. 2001. Listen reader: An electronically augmented paper-based book. In *Proceedings of the 2001 ACM Conference on Human Factors in Computing Systems (CHI 2001)*, pp. 23–29.

Brotherton, J.A. and G.D. Abowd 2004. Lessons Learned from eClass: Assessing automated capture and access in the classroom. *ACM Transactions on Computer-Human Interaction (ToCHI)*, **1**(1).

Bush, V. 1945. As we may think. *Atlantic Monthly*, **176**(1), July: 101–108.

Card, S., T. Moran, and A. Newell. 1983. *The Psychology of Human-Computer Interaction*. Lawrence Erlbaum.

Chen, Y., D.W. Clark, P. Cook, S. Damianakis, G. Essl, A. Finkelstein, T. Funkhouser, A. Klein, Z. Liu, E. Praun, R. Samanta, B. Shedd, J.P. Singh, G. Tzanetakis, K. Li, H. Chen, and J. Zheng. 2000. Early experiences and challenges in building and using a scalable display wall system. *IEEE Computer Graphics and Applications*, **20**(4):671–680.

Cheverst, K, K. Mitchell, and N. Davies. 1998. Design of an object model for a context sensitive tourist guide. In *Proceedings of Interactive Applications of Mobile Computing—IMC'98*, Rostock, Germany, November. Available at http://www.egd.igd.fhg.de/~imc98/proceedings.html

Feiner, S., B. MacIntyre, and D. Seligmann. 1993. Knowledge-based augmented reality. *Communications of the ACM, 36*(7):53–62.

Fogarty, J., J. Forlizzi, and S.E. Hudson. 2001. Aesthetic information collages: Generating decorative displays that contain information. In *Proceedings of the 14th Annual ACM Symposium on User Interface Software and Technology (UIST 2001)*.

Fitzmaurice, G.W., H. Ishii, and W. Buxton. 1995. Bricks: Laying the foundations for graspable user interfaces. In *Proceedings of the 1995 ACM Conference on Human Factors in Computing Systems (CHI '95)*, pp. 442–449.

Fitzmaurice, G.W., S. Zhai, and S.H. Chignell. 1993. Virtual reality for palmtop computers, special issue on virtual worlds. *ACM Transactions on Information Systems*, **11**(3): 197–218.

Fox, A., B. Johanson, P. Hanrahan, and T. Winograd. 1992. Integrating information appliances into an interactive workspace. *IEEE Computer Graphics and Applications*, **20**(3).

Gaver, W. and A. Dunne. 1999. Projected realities: Conceptual design for cultural effect. In *Proceedings of the 1999 ACM Conference on Human Factors in Computing Systems (CHI '99)*, Pittsburgh, pp. 600–607.

Gaver, W., A. Dunne, and E. Pacenti. 1999. Design: Cultural probes. In *Interactions: New Visions of Human-Computer Interaction*. Danvers, MA: ACM, Inc.

Harrison, B.J., K.P. Fishkin, A. Gujar, C. Mochon, and R. Want. 1998. Squeeze me, hold me, tilt me! An exploration of manipulative user interfaces. In *Proceedings of the 1998 ACM Conference on Human Factors in Computing Systems (CHI '98)*, May, pp. 17–24.

Hinckley, K., J. Pierce, M. Sinclair, and E. Horvitz. 2000. Sensing techniques for mobile interaction. In *Proceedings of the 13th Annual ACM Symposium on User Interface Software and Technology (UIST 2000)*, pp. 91–100.

Hindus, D., S.D. Mainwaring, A.E. Hagstrom, N. Leduc, and O. Bayley. 2001. Casablanca: Designing social communications devices for the home. In *Proceedings of the 2001 ACM Conference on Human Factors in Computing Systems (CHI 2001)*, April, pp. 325–332.

Hindus, D. and C. Schmandt. 1992. Ubiquitous audio: Capturing spontaneous collaboration. In *Proceedings of the ACM Conference on Computer Supported Cooperative Work (CSCW '92)*, November pp. 210–217.

Humphreys, G. and P. Hanrahan. 1999. A distributed graphics system for large tiled displays. In *Proceedings of IEEE Visualization*.

Hutchins, E. 1995. *Cognition in the Wild.* Cambridge, MA: MIT Press.

Ishii, H. and B. Ullmer. 1997. Tangible bits: Towards seamless interfaces between people, bits and atoms. In *Proceedings of (CHI'97)*, May, pp. 234–241.

Ishii, H., C. Wisneski, S. Brave, A. Dahley, M. Gorbet, B. Ullmer, and P. Yarin. 1998. AmbientROOM: Integrating ambient media with architectural space. In *Proceedings of the 1998 ACM Conference on Human Factors in Computing Systems (CHI '98), Companion Proceedings*, pp. 173–174.

Mynatt, E.D. 1999. The writing on the wall. In *Human-Computer Interaction (INTERACT '99)* Angela Sasse and Chris Johnson (Eds.). IOS Press.

Mynatt, E.D., M. Back, R. Want, M. Baer, and J. Ellis. 1998. Designing Audio Aura. In *Proceedings of the 1998 ACM Conference on Human Factors in Computing Systems (CHI'98)*, Los Angeles, pp. 566–573.

Mynatt, E.D., T. Igarashi, W.K Edwards, and A. LaMarca. 1999. Flatland: New dimensions in office whiteboards. In *Proceedings of the 1999 ACM Conference on Human Factors in Computing Systems (CHI '99)*.

Mynatt, E.D., J. Rowan, S. Craighill, and A. Jacobs. 2001. Digital Family Portraits: Providing peace of mind for extended family members. In *Proceedings of the 2001 ACM Conference on Human Factors in Computing Systems (CHI 2001)*, April, pp. 333–340.

Nardi, B. (Ed.). 1996. *Context and Consciousness: Activity Theory and Human-Computer Interaction.* Cambridge, MA: MIT Press.

Norman, D.E. 1990. *The Design of Everyday Things.* New York: Doubleday/Currency.

Philips Corporate Design. 1996. Vision of the future. Available at http://www.design.philips.com/vof

Rekimoto, J. 1997. Pick-and-drop: A direct manipulation technique for multiple computer environments. In *Proceedings of the ACM Symposium on User Interface Software and Technology (UIST '97)*, pp. 31–39.

Rekimoto, J. and N. Katashi. 1995. The World through the computer: Computer augmented interaction with real world environments. In *Proceedings of the ACM Symposium on User Interface Software and Technology (UIST '95)*, pp. 29–36.

Sarkisian, G., A.S. Melenhorst, W.A. Rogers, and A.D. Fisk. 2003. Older adults' opinions of a technology-rich home environment: Conditional and unconditional device acceptance. *Proceedings of the 48th Annual Meeting of the Human Factors and Ergonomics Society.* Santa Monica, CA.

Scholtz, J. and S. Consolvo. (January 2004). Towards a discipline for evaluating ubiquitous computing applications." Intel Research Technical Report IRS-TR-04-004. Available at http://www.intel-research.net/seattle/publications.asp

Starner, T., J. Auxier, D. Ashbrook, and M. Gandy. 2000. The Gesture Pendant: A self-illuminating, wearable, infrared computer vision system for home automation control and medical monitoring. *Proceedings of the International Symposium on Wearable Computers*, Atlanta, pp. 87–94.

Stifelman, L.J., B. Arons, and C. Schmandt. 2001. The audio notebook: Paper and pen interaction with structured speech. In *Proceedings of ACM CHI 2001 Conference on Human Factors in Computing Systems*, pp. 182–189.

Suchman, L. 1987. *Plans and Situated Actions: The Problem of Human-Machine Communication.* Cambridge: Cambridge University Press.

Summet, J., G.D. Abowd, G. Corso, and J. Rehg. 2003. Virtual rear projection: A comparison study of projection technologies for large interactive displays. Georgia Institute of Technology, GVU Center Technical Report GIT-GVU-03-36, December 2003.

Truong, K.N., G.D. Abowd, and J.A. Brotherton. 1999. Personalizing the capture of public experiences. In *Proceedings of the 12th Annual ACM Symposium on User Interface Technology (UIST '99)*, Asheville, NC, pp. 121–130.

Truong, K.N., G.D. Abowd, and J.A. Brotherton. 2001. Who, what, when, where, how: Design issues of capture and access applications. In *Proceedings of Ubicomp 2001*, Atlanta, pp. 209–224.

Voida, S.A., E.D. Mynatt, B. MacIntyre, and G. Corso. 2002. Integrating virtual and physical context to support knowledge workers. *IEEE Pervasive Computing*, **1**(3):73–79.

Vygotsky, L. 1981. The instrumental method in psychology. In J. Wertsch (Ed.), *The Concept of Activity in Soviet Psychology.* Armonk, NY: Sharpe.

Want, R., A. Hopper, V. Falcao, and J. Gibbons. 1992. The active badge location system. *ACM Transactions on Information Systems*, **10**(1):91–102.

Want, R., B. Schilit, N. Adams, R. Gold, K. Petersen, J. Ellis, D. Goldberg, and M. Weiser. 1995. The PARCTab ubiquitous computing experiment. Polo alto, CA: Xerox Palo Alto Research Center, Technical Report CSL-95-1.

Weiser, M. 1991. The computer of the 21st century. *Scientific American*, September **265**(3):66–75.

Weiser, M. 1993. Some computer science issues in ubiquitous computing. *Communications of the ACM*, **36**(7):75–84.

Weiser, M. 1994. The world is not a desktop, *ACM Interactions*, 7–8.

Weiser, M. and J.S. Brown. 1995. Designing calm technology. Available at *PowerGrid Journal*: http://www.ubiq.com/hypertext/weiser/calmtech/calmtech.htm

Weiser, M., R. Gold, and J.S. Brown. 1999. The origins of ubiquitous computing research at PARC in the late 1980s. *IBM Systems Journal*, special issue on human-computer interaction: a focus on pervasive computing, **38**(4):693–696.

Wellner, P. 1993. Interacting with Paper on the digital desk. *Communications of the ACM*, **36**(7):87–96.

CHAPTER 8

Prediction Algorithms for Smart Environments

DIANE J. COOK

Department of Computer Science and Engineering
The University of Texas at Arlington

8.1 INTRODUCTION

We live in an increasingly connected and automated society. Smart environments embody this trend by linking computers to everyday tasks and settings. Important features of such environments are that they possess a degree of autonomy, adapt themselves to changing conditions, and communicate with humans in a natural way.

Designing and implementing smart environments requires a breadth of knowledge not limited to a single discipline, but integrating aspects of machine learning, decision making, human-machine interfaces, wireless networking, mobile communications, databases, sensor networks, and pervasive computing. With these capabilities, the home can control many aspects of the environment, as shown in Figure 8.1. Intelligent automation of these activities can reduce the amount of interaction required by inhabitants, as well as reducing energy consumption and other potential wastages. The same capabilities can be used to provide important features such as detection of unusual behaviors for health monitoring and home security.

The benefits of automation can influence every environment in which we interact. For example, operations in a smart home may include the following scenario. To minimize energy consumption, the home keeps the temperature cool throughout the night. At 6:45 am, the home turns up the heat because it has learned that it needs 15 minutes to warm to Bob's desired waking temperature. The alarm sounds at 7:00 am, after which the bedroom light and kitchen coffee maker turn on. Bob steps into the bathroom and turns on the light. The home records this manual interaction, displays the morning news on the bathroom video screen, and turns on the shower. When Bob finishes grooming, the bathroom light turns off while the kitchen light and display

---

Smart Environments: Technologies, Protocols, and Applications, edited by D.J. Cook and S.K. Das
ISBN 0-471-54448-5 © 2005 John Wiley & Sons, Inc.

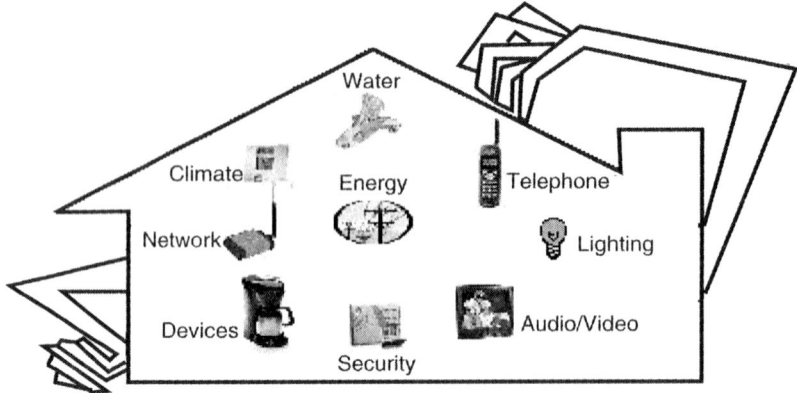

Figure 8.1 Features of a smart environment.

turn on. Bob's current weight and other statistics are added to previously collected data to determine health trends that may merit Bob's attention. When Bob leaves for work, the home secures all of the doors and windows behind him and starts the lawn sprinklers. Because there is a 30% chance of rain, the sprinklers will run for a shorter time to lessen water usage. During the day, a movie is shown on TV that is similar to those Bob enjoys, so the home records the movie for him. Because the refrigerator is low on milk and cheese, the home places a grocery order. To reduce energy costs, the house turns down the heat until 15 minutes before Bob is due home. When Bob arrives home, his grocery order has arrived, the house is back at Bob's desired temperature, and the hot tub is waiting for him.

8.2 THE ROLE OF PREDICTION ALGORITHMS IN SMART ENVIRONMENTS

In order to maximize comfort, minimize costs, and adapt to inhabitants, a smart environment must rely on tools from artificial intelligence such as prediction and automated decision making. Prediction plays an important part in many aspects of smart environments. First, models of various devices can be learned from observation and used to predict their behaviors in the future. As an example, predicting the amount of time required to warm a home to Bob's desired temperature requires an algorithm that can effectively make use of past performance of the heating unit, the current internal and external temperatures, and thermal flow within the house. Similar models of behavior can be learned for other devices, such as the time required to dry a load of clothes, the effect of a 400°F oven on the house temperature, and the time it takes to brew a pot of coffee.

Given the predicted behavior of a device, utilization of resources such as energy and water can be predicted and used to select an appropriate control strategy for the home. For example, a number of methods can be used to raise or lower the temperature of an environment, as shown in Figure 8.2. The ceiling fan can be turned on,

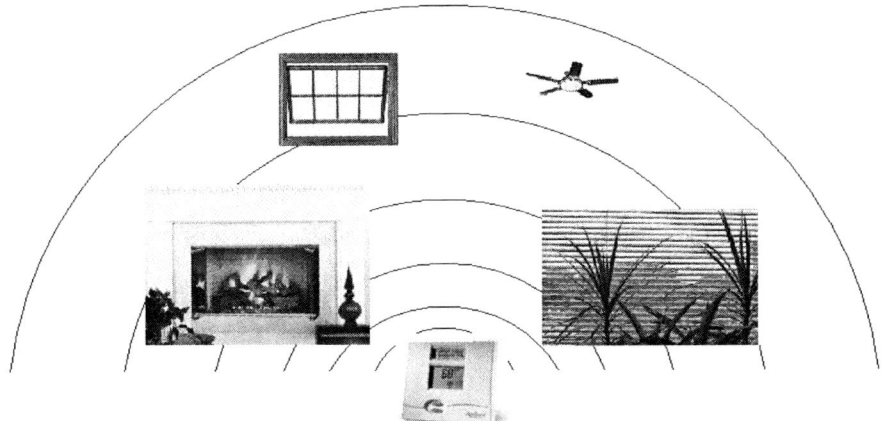

Figure 8.2 Methods of controlling the temperature of a smart environment.

window blinds can be opened or shut, a fire can be built, a window can be opened, or a central heating/air conditioning unit can be activated. The choice among alternatives may depend on the effectiveness of the device in achieving the desired temperature, the time required to achieve the change, and the resulting energy usage.

In addition to predicting the behavior of devices in an environment, predicting an inhabitant's next action may be needed for the environment to automate selected repetitive tasks for the inhabitant, to detect anomalies that could indicate security or health concerns, and to identify ways of improving control of the environment.

The information available from which to build models and make predictions will vary based on the environment and may include video, power meters, motion detectors, load sensors, device controllers, and vital sign monitors. A prediction algorithm must be able to determine which features are relevant to the model being learned and make maximal use of the information provided. The number of prediction errors must be minimal, and the algorithms must be able to deliver predictions with minimal delays for computation. The results of a prediction algorithm may ultimately be input to a decision-making algorithm that selects actions for the house to execute.

8.3 PREDICTION ALGORITHMS

A number of prediction algorithms have been developed for many different application domains in recent years. We define the prediction task as the process of forming a hypothesis representing the future value of a target variable for a given data point. Prediction algorithms thus learn a function that maps known information about the problem, collected from past and current observations, to a hypothesized value for a future point in time.

In our usage discussion, we assume that a sequential ordering of events (e.g., the inhabitant's actions) is input to the algorithm, for which actual timing information may or may not be provided. Algorithms that make use of historical information as well as current state information thus provide the greatest leverage for addressing the problem. We summarize the techniques developed for this purpose and then provide an in-depth look at the prediction algorithms used for the MavHome smart home.

8.3.1 Prediction Using Sequence Matching

The first approach to prediction we examine is based on pattern-matching techniques. These algorithms use historical event information to predict the next event in the sequence. Consider a sequence of events being generated by an arbitrary deterministic source, which can be represented by the stochastic process $X = \{x_i\}$. The sequential prediction problem can then be stated as follows. Given the sequence of events $\{x_1, x_2, \ldots, x_i\}$, what is the next event x_{i+1}?

The IPAM system of Davison and Hirsch [1998] collects sequential pairs of events and encodes the likelihood of transitioning from one event to the next in a table. Transition probabilities are initialized using a uniform probability distribution. When a new event x_{i+1} is observed, the probability of transitioning from x_i to x_{i+1} is increased by a factor of $1 - \alpha$, where α is a constant between 0 and 1. In contrast, the probability of transitioning to any event other than x_{i+1} is decremented by a factor α. This update method thus weights recent events more heavily than older events. When predicting the next event, all possible choices are ranked according to the estimated probability given the previous observed event, or $P(X_{i+1}|X_i)$, and the choice with the highest estimated probability is output as the predicted next event. Korvemaker and Greiner [2000] use a "mixture of experts" approach to combine evidence supplied by various refinements to the basic matching algorithm.

In a separate approach, Gorniak and Poole [2000] employ a k-nearest-neighbor scheme to form a prediction in the ONISI system, where the sequence match length between the immediate event history and earlier history subsequences is used as the distance criterion. To balance the effects of match length and match frequency, ONISI weights the two factors by α and $1 - \alpha$, respectively, and when the highest-ranked match is found, the event that occurs just after the matched pattern is output as the predicted next event for the current situation. This approach is enhanced in the SHIP system [Das et al., 2003] to adapt to changing behavioral patterns.

All of these matching-based prediction algorithms have been applied to the UNIX command prediction problem following the hypothesis that computer users tend to exhibit common interaction patterns. These patterns can be used to identify the most likely next computer command, which can in turn be used to assist the user in the intended task. However, all of these techniques can be also used to perform prediction in a smart environment. Consider the case where the most recent sequence of inhabitant actions consists of {AlarmOff, BedroomLightOn, CoffeeMakerOn, BathroomLightOn, BathroomVideoOn}. The IPAM system would find the pair (BathroomVideoOn, *action*) that was assigned the greatest probability in the transition table and output the corresponding *action* as its prediction. In contrast, ONISI would look through the entire event history to find event sequences that match this sequence. The action following BathroomVideoOn in the highest-ranked matched sequence would be output as the predicted next event, or action, in the smart environment.

8.3.2 Prediction as a Markov Decision Process

Faced with the fact that the actions of an agent often have uncertain effects on an environment, we can model these actions as a Markov Decision Process (MDP). At each time step of an MDP, the agent perceives the current environment state and selects an action to execute. The result of the action is modeled as a probability distribution over states and possibly yields a reward from the environment. In contrast to the sequence-matching approaches, MDPs considers only the last few states to predict the next state of the environment, following the Markov assumption.

The next state of an agent in a smart environment may depend on *observable states* that can be directly monitored such as time of day, internal temperature, and the status of devices. However, the pattern may also depend on other factors that cannot be directly observed and thus can be modeled as *hidden states* such as the task that the inhabitant is performing and the health status of the individual. Hidden states may have probabilistic relationships with the observable states, modeled by Hidden Markov Models (HMMs) such as the one shown in Figure 8.3.

Given an HMM, standard algorithms can be used to determine the probability of an observed sequence of events and to find the sequence of hidden states that most likely generated the observed sequence. HMMs have been used for a number of modeling tasks, including speech recognition [Rabiner, 1989] and anomaly detection [Lane, 1999]. The work of Luhr et al. [2003] uses this model to recognize human activities in a smart environment. Gorniak and Poole [2000] view an agent as trying to solve a Markov Decision Problem by maximizing the expected

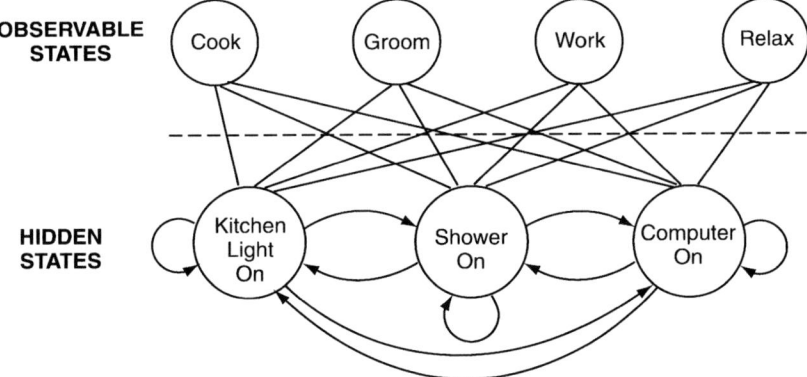

Figure 8.3 Hidden Markov Model for a smart environment prediction task.

reward given an MDP model, and uses this view to predict the agent's next action. Rao and Cook [2003] use clustering techniques to automatically generate the hidden states for an HMM in order to improve such activity prediction.

8.3.3 Prediction Using Plan Recognition

Yet another technology that contributes to the prediction task in smart environments is plan recognition. Assuming that agents in such an environment are performing actions to achieve a particular set of goals, plan recognition can be used to identify the possible plans, or sequences of actions, that are known to achieve those goals. To perform this recognition task, a common approach is to build a belief network representing the set of known plans [Bui, 2003; Huber et al., 1994; Huber and Simpson, 2003].

A belief network is a directed acyclic graph where nodes represent a set of random variables, and a directed edge from node X to node Y indicates that X has an influence on Y. Associated with each node is a conditional probability table that quantifies the probabilistic effects the parents have on the node. For plan recognition, a node is created representing the goal to be achieved, all possible actions, and contexts in which a particular plan is likely to be executed. In Figure 8.4, a node is created for the goal "Order Supper," which can be achieved by the action sequence "Select Restaurant," "Lookup Number," and "Order Food." This particular plan is generally executed when the context "Refrigerator Empty" is true. When an action (such as "Lookup Number") is observed, this is added as evidence in support of one or more goals in the network. The plan recognizer can then adjust its belief that a particular plan is being executed to achieve a selected goal and can use knowledge of the plan steps to predict the next action with an associated level of confidence.

As an additional note, *plan generation* has also been used in the context of the Autominder system designed by Pollack et al. [2003]. Autominder generates plans consistent with the inhabitant's tasks and time constraints, and can provide gentle reminders for actions such as taking medication when the inhabitant appears to have forgotten this important task.

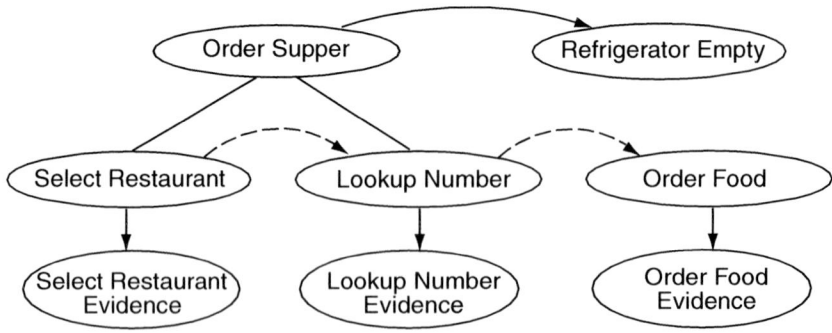

Figure 8.4 Belief network for the goal "Order Supper."

8.3.4 Other Approaches to Prediction

The field of machine learning offers many techniques that are useful for the smart environment prediction problem. In particular, inductive learning methods such as decision trees, neural networks, Bayesian classifiers, nearest neighbor algorithms, and support vector machines all generate a function that approximates f, a mapping between a data point and an associated output value. In the case of action prediction, the input x can contain pertinent information such as the previous action, the state of devices in the environment, and the time of day. The output $f(x)$ could be the action that the inhabitant will execute next. These techniques have been used to great effect for classification problems. The challenge for prediction is to be able to represent an arbitrary amount of prior history information in the input vector, which is generally fixed in length. These methods are described in detail in current textbooks and articles [Cristiani and Scholkopf, 2002; Mitchell, 1997].

8.4 CASE STUDY: THE MAVHOME SMART HOME

The MavHome smart home at the University of Texas at Arlington represents an environment that acts as an intelligent agent, perceiving the state of the home through sensors and acting on the environment through device controllers, as shown in Figure 8.5. The agent's goal is to ensure the inhabitants' comfort while minimizing the cost of running the home. To achieve this goal, the house must be able to predict, reason about, and adapt to its inhabitants.

The desired smart home capabilities must be organized into a software architecture that seamlessly connects these components while allowing improvements to be made to any of the supporting technologies. Figure 8.6 shows the architecture of a MavHome agent. Technologies are separated into four cooperating layers. The *Decision* layer selects actions for the agent to execute. The *Information* layer collects information and generates inferences useful for decision making. The *Communication* layer routes information and requests between agents. The *Physical* layer contains the environment hardware, including devices, transducers, and

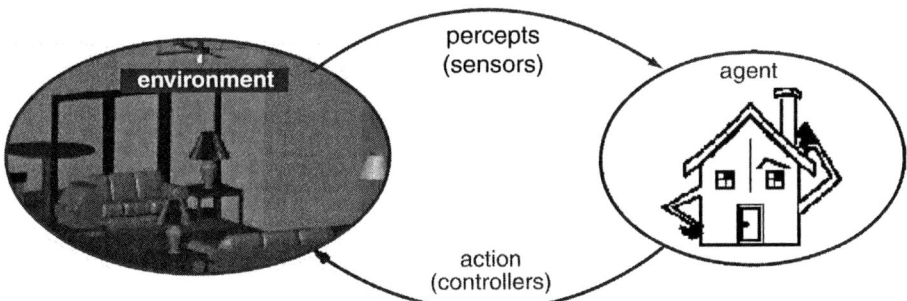

Figure 8.5 Design of a smart home as an intelligent agent.

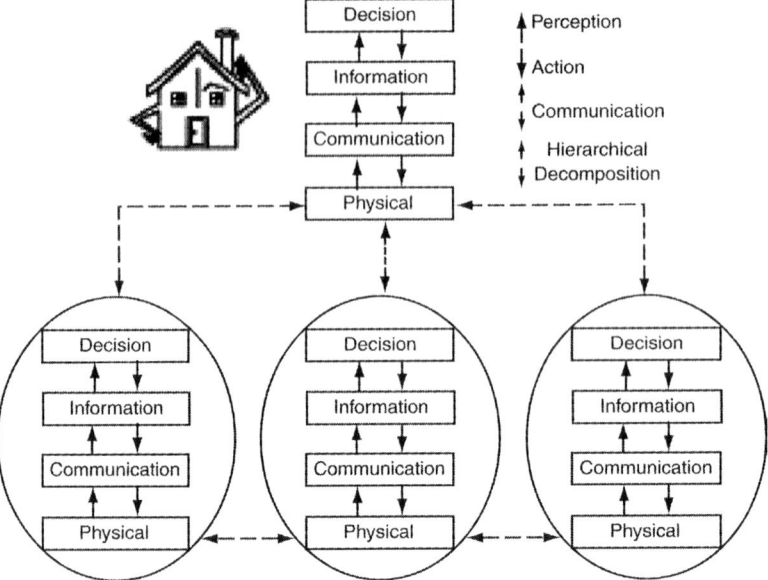

Figure 8.6 MavHome agent architecture.

network equipment. The MavHome software components are connected using a Common Object Request Broker Architecture (CORBA) interface.

Because controlling an entire house is a very large, complex learning and reasoning problem, the problem is decomposed into reconfigurable subareas or tasks. Thus the Physical layer for one agent may in actuality represent another agent somewhere in the hierarchy that is capable of executing the task selected by the requesting agent.

Perception is modeled here as a bottom-up process. Sensors monitor the environment (e.g., lawn moisture level) and possibly transmit the information to another agent through the Communication layer. The database records the information in the Information layer, updates its learned concepts accordingly, and alerts the Decision layer to the presence of new data. During action execution, information flows top down. The Decision layer selects an action (e.g., run the sprinklers) and relates the decision to the Information layer. After updating the database, the Communication layer routes the action to the appropriate effector to execute. If the effector is actually another, more specialized agent, the agent receives the command through its effector as perceived information and must decide on the best method of executing the desired action. Agents can communicate with each other using the hierarchical flow shown in Figure 8.6.

8.4.1 Learning to Identify Significant Episodes

MavHome needs to identify repetitive tasks performed by inhabitants that warrant potential automation by the home, and must predict the inhabitant's next action in order to automate such selected repetitive tasks for the inhabitant. MavHome currently generates this prediction based solely on previously seen inhabitant interactions with various devices and the current state of the inhabitant and the house. The prediction is given to a decision-making algorithm that selects actions for the house to execute in order to meet its goals.

A smart home inhabitant typically interacts with various devices as part of his routine activities. These interactions may be considered as a sequence of events with some inherent pattern of recurrence. This repeatability leads us to the conclusion that the sequence can be modeled as a stationary stochastic process. Here we introduce three algorithms that play important roles in selecting significant sequences, predicting events within the sequences, and automating such sequences within a smart home. We perform inhabitant action prediction, first, by mining the data [using Episode Discovery (ED)] to identify sequences of actions that are regular and repeatable enough to generate predictions and, second, by using a sequence-matching approach (Active LeZi) to predict the next action in one of these sequences.

Our ED data mining algorithm is based on the work of Agrawal and Srikant [1995] for mining sequential patterns from time-ordered transactions. We move a window in a single pass through the history of inhabitant actions, looking for significant episodes (sequences) within the window. Each inhabitant-home interaction event is characterized as a triple consisting of the manipulated device, the resulting change that occurred in that device, and the time of interaction. The input sequence is partitioned based on a specified episode maximum time frame, and all possible maximal episodes are created from this information.

To evaluate candidate episodes, ED uses the Minimum Description Length (MDL) principle [Rissanen, 1989]. The MDL principle targets patterns that can be used to minimize the description length of a database by replacing each instance of the pattern with a pointer to the pattern definition. Our MDL-based evaluation measure thus identifies patterns that balance frequency and length. Instances of a regular (daily, weekly) sequence can be removed without storing a pointer to the sequence definition, because the regularity of the sequence is stored with the sequence definition. Regular sequences thus further compress the description length of the original interaction history. Deviations from the pattern definition in terms of missing events, extra events, or changes in the periodicity of the occurrence add to the description length because extra bits must be used to encode the change, thus lowering the value of the pattern. The larger the potential amount of description length compression a pattern provides, the greater the impact that results from automating the pattern. Candidate episodes are evaluated, and the episodes with values above a minimum acceptable compression amount are reported [Heierman and Cook, 2003].

Based on 30 days of data consistent with the MavHome scenario described earlier (along with spurious noisy events), ED discovers the following significant episodes:

- HeatOn (daily)
- AlarmOn, AlarmOff, BedroomLightOn, CoffeeMakerOn, BathroomLightOn, BathroomVideoOn, ShowerOn, HeatOff (daily)

- BedroomLightOff, BathroomLightOff, BathroomVideoOff, ShowerOff, KitchenLightOn, KitchenScreenOn (daily)
- CoffeeMakerOff, KitchenLightOff, KitchenScreenOff (daily)
- HotTubOn, HotTubOff (daily)
- SprinklerOn (biweekly)

The knowledge that ED obtains by mining the user action history can be used in a variety of ways. First, the mined patterns provide information regarding the nature of the activities in the home, which can be used to better understand lifestyle patterns and aid in designing homes and software for the home. Second, the discovered patterns can be used in the decision-making process to determine whether this task is worth attempting to automate. Third, knowledge of the mined sequences can improve the accuracy of predicting the next action by performing prediction only for events known to be part of a common pattern.

We demonstrate the ability of ED to perform the third task, improving the accuracy of prediction algorithms, by filtering action sequences by the mined sequences. If a sequence is considered significant by the mining algorithm, then predictions can be made for events within the sequence window. A case study was conducted on the IPAM sequence matching predictor [Davison and Hisrch, 1998] and a backpropagation neural network (BPNN). Both algorithms could be used to predict the next action that might occur in a home environment but might not fare well due to noisy data. Our goal was to determine if ED could consistently improve the predictive accuracy of the algorithms by training each algorithm on filtered data and using the mined pattern information to only predict events contained within significant episodes.

Using a synthetic data generator, we created five randomly generated scenarios executing over a 6-month period. Our scenarios utilize 22 devices with on and off states, including several lamps, a garage door opener, lights, and a radio. Fourteen daily and weekly episodes were defined that ED should discover, as well as 68 noisy patterns. Each scenario contains close to 13,000 device interactions, of which fewer than 5,000 are part of a regularly occurring pattern. We set the parameters for IPAM to be the same as reported in the literature and trained the neural network on the states of all devices for the previous five events. ED was able to correctly discover the significant episodes in all of the data sets, and appreciably improved the accuracy of both algorithms across all five scenarios, as can be seen in Table 8.1.

We see that the knowledge ED discovers can be used to consistently improve the predictive accuracy of the case study algorithms. One reason for the improvement was that the algorithms were trained on data that was significant, rather than on data that also contained noise. In addition, the predictions were filtered so that predictions were not performed on data that was considered noise. By using ED, we not only improved the accuracy of the algorithms, but also significantly reduced the total number of false predictions each algorithm made. Limiting the number of incorrect predictions will be important in a home environment to ensure that the home will not erroneously attempt to automate anomalous and highly variable activities.

TABLE 8.1 Prediction Improvement Results

Scenario	1	2	3	4	5	Average
Events	12,958	12,884	12,848	13,058	12,668	12,883
Episode candidates	5,745	5,608	5,619	5,655	5,496	5,625
Significant episodes	13	13	13	13	13	13
IPAM percentage correct	39%	42%	43%	40%	41%	41%
IPAM + ED percentage correct	77%	84%	69%	73%	65%	74%
BPNN percentage correct	62%	64%	66%	62%	64%	64%
BPNN + ED percentage correct	84%	88%	84%	84%	88%	86%
Processing time (s)	11	9	10	9	9	10

8.4.2 Learning to Predict Inhabitant Actions

Our prediction algorithm is based on the LZ78 text compression algorithm [Ziv and Lempel, 1978]. Good text compression algorithms have also been established as good predictors. According to information theory, a predictor with an order (size of history used) that grows at a rate approximating the entropy rate of the source is an optimal predictor [Feder et al., 1992].

LZ78 processes an input string of characters, which in our case is a string representing the history of inhabitant actions interacting with devices in the home. The prediction algorithm parses the input string $x_1, x_2, \ldots, x_i$ into $c(i)$ substrings, or phrases, $w_1, w_2, \ldots, w_{c(i)}$ such that for all $j > 0$, the prefix of the substring w_j (i.e., all but the last character of w_j) is equal to some w_i for $1 < i < j$. Because of the prefix property used by the algorithm, parsed substrings can be efficiently maintained in a trie along with frequency information.

Consider the sequence of input symbols *aaababbbbbaabccddcbaaa*. An LZ78 parsing of this input string would yield the following set of phrases: *a,aa,b,ab, bb,bba,abc,c,d,dc,ba,aaa*. As described above, this algorithm maintains statistics for all contexts seen within each phrase w_i. For example, the context *a* occurs five times (at the beginning of the phrases *a, aa, ab, abc, aaa*), the context *bb* is seen two times (*bb, bba*), etc. These context statistics are stored in a trie.

Because it is designed as a text compression algorithm, LZ78 requires some enhancements to perform effective prediction. For example, we can see that the amount of information being lost across phrase boundaries grows with the number of possible states in the input sequence. In our Active LeZi (ALZ) algorithm, we enhance the original LZ78 to recapture information lost across phrase boundaries [Gopalratnam and Cook, 2003]. Specifically, we maintain a window of previously seen symbols, with a length equal to the length of the longest phrase seen in a classical LZ78 parsing. The reason for selecting this window size is that the LZ78 algorithm is essentially constructing an (approximation to an) order-k Markov model, where k is equal to the length of the longest LZ78 phrase seen so far. This refined approach builds a better approximation to the order-k Markov model, because it has captured information normally lost across phrase boundaries. As a result, we gain a better convergence rate to optimal predictability as well as achieve greater predictive accuracy. Figure 8.7 shows the trie formed by the Active LeZi parsing of the input sequence *aaababbbbbaabccddcbaaa*.

When performing prediction, the algorithm calculates the probability of each symbol (action) occurring in the parsed sequence and predicts the action with the highest probability. To achieve optimal predictability, we must use a mixture of all possible order models (phrase sizes) when determining the probability estimate. Active LeZi performs a second refinement of the LZ78 algorithm to combine this predictive information. To accomplish this, we incorporate ideas from the Prediction by Partial Match (PPM) family of predictors, which has been applied to great effect in the mobility prediction work of Bhattacharya and Das [2002].

PPM algorithms consider different order Markov models to build a probability distribution. This blending strategy assigns greater weight to higher-order models in keeping with the advisability of making the most informed decision. We employ the PPM *exclusion* strategy [Bell et al., 1990] to gather information from the $1 \ldots k$ order models in assigning a probability to the next symbol.

As an example, consider our example string *aaababbbbbaabccddcbaaa*, ending in the phrase *aaa*. Within this phrase, the contexts that can be used for prediction are all suffixes, except itself (i.e., *aa*, *a*, and the null context). From Figure 8.7, we see that an *a* occurs 2 out of the 5 times that the context *aa* appears, the other cases producing two null outcomes and one *b*. Therefore, the probability of encountering *a* at the context *aa* is 2/5, and we now fall back (escape) to the order-1 context (i.e., the next lower order model) with probability 2/5. At the order-1 context, we see an *a* 5 out of the 10 times that we see the *a* context, and of the remaining cases, we see two null outcomes. Therefore, we predict symbol *a* at the order-1 context with probability 5/10 and escape to the order-0 model with probability 2/10. At the order 0 model, we see the *a* 10 out of 23 symbols seen so far, and we therefore predict *a* with probability 10/23 at the null context. The *blended* probability of seeing *a* as the next symbol is therefore $2/5 + 2/5\{5/10 + 2/10(10/23)\}$.

Using the synthetic data generator, we created 30 days of activities using six different scenarios and tested the ability of Active LeZi to generate correct predictions, given a model built from all previous events, for the next 100 events. In the first experiment, the data consists only of events drawn from the scenario definitions. The predictive accuracy in this case converges to 100%, as shown in Figure 8.8. For the second experiment, we introduced noise in the form of events not part of any

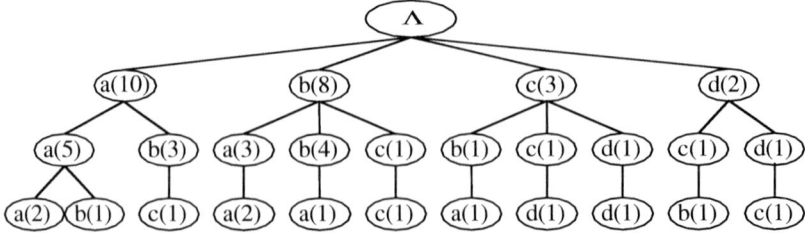

Figure 8.7 Trie formed by sample history sequence.

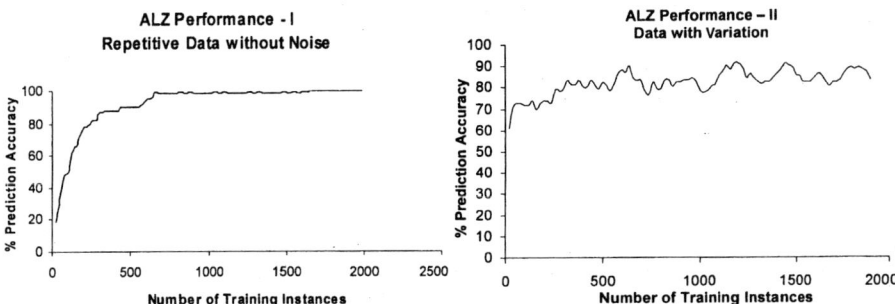

Figure 8.8 Prediction performance on sample smart home data.

scenario and variations in event orderings. In this case, the predictive accuracy does improve with the amount of training data, but reaches only 86% accuracy.

We also tested the ability of Active LeZi to perform prediction on the sampled real data collected in the MavHome environment. As shown in Figure 8.9, the accuracy of the model does improve with the amount of training data but converges to only 48%. However, this represents an improvement over random choice, which for this data would result in an average accuracy of 2%. Combining ALZ with ED yields a 14% improvement in predictive accuracy for this data.

In an agent-based smart home architecture, the responses of the home to various situations are determined by the decision-making agent, which is aided in making the appropriate decision by various prediction agents, such as ALZ. The decision-making agent benefits from knowing not only what the next action is but also when it will occur, in order that the action may be more effectively automated.

In many situations, the time between one inhabitant action and the next depends on the particular sequence, or history of previous interactions. Given the assumption that such a dependency does indeed exist in certain sequential processes of events, a sequential predictor such as ALZ can be used to learn a relative time interval between events. In our model, the next event to occur is already predicted, and given that information, the decision maker requires an estimate of the time interval that will elapse before that event takes place. We represent these time intervals as Gaussian distributions characterized mean μ and standard deviation σ.

Here, the relative frequency counts of the various phrases are stored as before in the trie. In addition, each node in the trie incrementally builds a Gaussian that represents the observed normal distribution of the relative time of occurrence of the last event in that phrase. The mean is easily constructed incrementally, and the standard deviation can be recursively defined for n data points in terms of the mean and standard deviation for the previous $n - 1$ data points as $\sigma_n = 1/n\{(n - 1)[\sigma_{n-1}^2 + (\mu_n - \mu_{n-1})^2] + (t_n - \mu_n)^2\}$, where t_n represents the new data point. Given a predicted event, the time of occurrence of that event is to be computed using the model of time built as discussed above. As with the prediction of the event itself, information stored at various orders of the trie is blended to strengthen the resulting prediction.

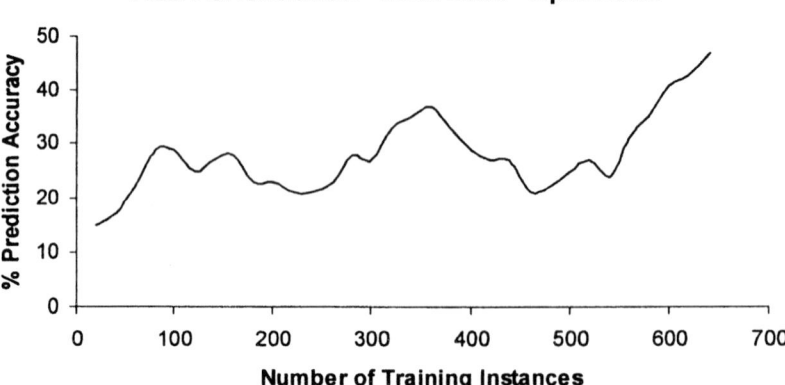

Figure 8.9 Prediction performance on actual MavHome data.

ALZ effectively models sequential processes, and is extremely useful for prediction of processes where events are dependent on the previous event history. This is because of the ability of the algorithm to build an accurate model of the source of the events being generated, a feature inherited from its information theoretic background. The effectiveness of the method for learning a measure of time can also be attributed to the fact that ALZ is a strong sequential predictor. The sound theoretical principles on which ALZ is founded mean that ALZ is an optimal Universal Predictor and can be used for a variety of prediction tasks.

8.4.3 Improving Decision Making Through Prediction

The goal of MavHome's decision-making algorithm is to enable the home to automate basic functions in order to maximize the comfort of the inhabitants and minimize the cost of operating the home. Initially, we measure comfort as minimizing the number of manual interactions with the home and measure operating cost as energy usage by the home.

To achieve its goal, MavHome uses reinforcement learning to acquire an optimal decision policy. In this framework, the agent learns autonomously from potentially delayed rewards rather than from a teacher, as described in Chapter 10. The decision algorithm uses prediction of inhabitant activities as one of the state space features that are used to influence the action taken by the environment.

8.4.4 MavHome Components

The MavHome smart home project is currently functioning at the University of Texas at Arlington. Visitors can register their presence in the environment using a fingerprint reader (Figure 8.10), and data is collected continuously based on their interactions with devices in the environment. Off-the-shelf X10 controllers automate most devices.

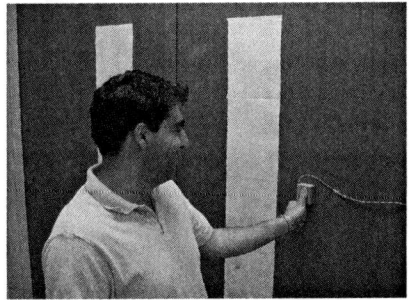

Figure 8.10 Current MavHome devices include fingerprint reader and automated blinds.

Using the ResiSim simulator, a graphical model has been constructed of the environment that allows a remote visitor to monitor or change the status of devices in MavHome. Images in the left column of Figure 8.11 show the actual environment, and the simulator visualization is shown on the right. The "Information" window at the lower right indicates that devices have recently been manipulated, either manually or by MavHome. Figure 8.12 reflects the fact that the entryway light (upper left) is illuminated once Darin enters the environment and the lamp on Ryan's desk (lower left) turns on to assist him with work. The updated status of the lamp is shown by the yellow circle in the ResiSim model (right). ResiSim indicates the status of sensors as well; the orbs in Figure 8.13 show two areas of activity captured by motion sensors.

Figure 8.11 Web camera views of MavHome (left) and ResiSim visualization (right).

PREDICTION ALGORITHMS FOR SMART ENVIRONMENTS

Figure 8.12 Environment after desk lamp (lower left) is turned on.

A live demonstration of MavHome was conducted in the fall of 2002. Activity data was collected for one of the project participants ("MavHome Bob"). Actions included turning on lights en route to his desk in the morning, watching a live news feed on the computer, taking a coffee and TV break, and turning off devices

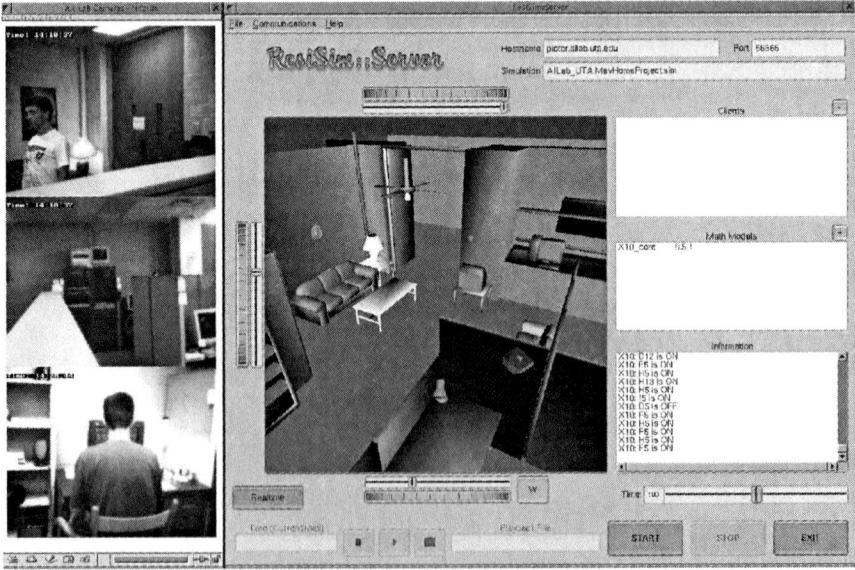

Figure 8.13 ResiSim indicates activated motion sensors with green orbs.

Figure 8.14 Bob's movements in MavHome. Bob's position is indicated by a dashed box.

on the way out at the end of the day. Despite the presence of approximately 50 people during the live demonstration (who were setting off motion sensors throughout the environment), MavHome employed the algorithms described in this chapter to correctly predict and automate each activity. Figure 8.14 reflects the movements of MavHome Bob during the demonstration as he moves through the environment, and lights reflecting his typical activities are illuminated.

8.5 CONCLUSIONS

This chapter highlights the need for prediction algorithms in smart environments. Prediction algorithms provide information useful for automating activities, optimizing design and control methods for individual devices and tasks within the environment, and identifying anomalies. Here, prediction is based on data collected within a single environment and is, in turn, used to control and adapt that same environment. However, the same algorithms can be used on a larger scale. Data collected from an entire city can be used, for example, to characterize power usage patterns. The resulting models will allow individual environments to make better decisions, avoiding situations such as blackouts and providing better control of the smart environment.

ACKNOWLEDGMENTS

This research was supported by National Science Foundation grants IIS-0121297 and MRI-0115885.

REFERENCES

R. Agrawal and R. Srikant, Mining sequential patterns. *Proceedings of the Conference on Data Engineering*, pp. 3–13, 1995.

T.C. Bell, J.G. Cleary, and I.H. Witten, *Text Compression*. Prentice Hall Advanced Reference Series, 1990.

A. Bhattacharya and S.K. Das, LeZi-Update: An information-theoretic framework for personal mobility tracking in PCS networks. *ACM/Kluwer Wireless Networks Journal*, 8(2–3):121–135, 2002.

H.H. Bui, A general model for online probabilistic plan recognition. *Proceedings of the International Joint Conference on Artificial Intelligence*, pp. 1309–1318, 2003.

N. Cristiani and B. Scholkopf, Support vector machines and kernel methods: The new generation of learning machines. *AI Magazine*, 2002.

S.K. Das, D.J. Cook, A. Bhattacharya, E.O. Heierman III, and T.-Y. Lin, The role of prediction algorithms in the MavHome smart home architecture. *IEEE Wireless Communications*, 9(6):77–84, 2003.

B.D. Davison and H. Hisrch, Probabilistic online action prediction. *Proceedings of the AAAI Spring Symposium on Intelligent Environments*, 1998.

M. Feder, N. Merhav, and M. Gutman, Universal prediction of individual sequences. *IEEE Transactions on Information Theory*, 38(4): 1992.

K. Gopalratnam and D.J. Cook, Active LeZi: An incremental parsing algorithm for device usage prediction in the smart home. *Proceedings of the Florida Artificial Intelligence Research Symposium*, pp. 38–42, 2003.

P. Gorniak and D. Poole, Predicting future user actions by observing unmodified applications. Proceedings of the *National Conference on Artificial Intelligence*, pp. 217–222, 2000.

P. Gorniak and D. Poole, Building a stochastic dynamic model of application use. *Proceedings of the Sixteenth Conference on Uncertainty in Artificial Intelligence*, pp. 230–237, 2000.

E. Heierman and D.J. Cook, Improving home automation by discovering regularly occurring device usage patterns. *Proceedings of the International Conference on Data Mining*, 2003.

M.J. Huber, E.H. Durfee, and M.P. Wellman, The automated mapping of plans for plan recognition. *Proceedings of the Conference on Uncertainty in Artificial Intelligence*, 1994.

M.J. Huber and R. Simpson, Plan recognition to aid the visually impaired. *Proceedings of the Conference on User Modeling*, 2003.

B. Korvemaker and R. Greiner, Predicting UNIX command lines: Adjusting to user patterns. *Proceedings of the National Conference on Artificial Intelligence*, pp. 230–235, 2000.

T. Lane, Hidden Markov models for human/computer interface modeling. *Proceedings of the IJCAI 99 Workshop on Learning about Users*, pp. 35–44, 1999.

S. Luhr, H.H. Bui, S. Venkatesh, and G.A.W. West, Recognition of human activity through hierarchical stochastic learning. *Proceedings of the First IEEE International Conference on Pervasive Computing and Communications*, pp. 416–422, 2003.

T. Mitchell, *Machine Learning*. McGraw-Hill, 1997.

M.E. Pollack, L. Brown, D. Colbry, C.E. McCarthy, C. Orosz, B. Peintner, S. Ramakrishnan, and I. Tsamardinos, Autominder: An intelligent cognitive orthotic system for people with memory impairment. *Robotics and Autonomous Systems*, 44(3–4):273–282, 2003.

L.R. Rabiner, A tutorial on hidden Markov models and selected applications in speech recognition. *Proceedings of the IEEE*, 77(2):257–285, 1989.

S. Rao and D.J. Cook, Identifying tasks and predicting actions in smart homes using unlabeled data. *Proceedings of the Machine Learning on the Continuum from Labeled to Unlabeled Data*, 2003.

J. Rissanen, *Stochastic Complexity in Statistical Inquiry*. World Scientific Publishing Company, 1989.

J. Ziv and A. Lempel, Compression of individual sequences via variable rate coding. *IEEE Transactions on Information Theory*, IT-24:530–536, 1978.

CHAPTER 9

Location Estimation (Determination and Prediction) Techniques in Smart Environments

ARCHAN MISRA
Pervasive Security and Network Department
IBM T.J. Watson Research Center

SAJAL K DAS
Department of Computer Science and Engineering
The University of Texas at Arlington

9.1 INTRODUCTION

A smart environment is, by definition, *context-aware*: by combining inputs from multiple pervasive sensing devices, applications in the smart infrastructure should be able to intelligently deduce the intent or attributes of an individual without explicit manual input. Location is perhaps one of the earliest, and still most common, examples of such context. There are myriad examples of pervasive applications where the system uses the location of a mobile individual, or sometimes groups of individuals, to customize the computing environment. For example, knowing that the user is at the office, instead of home, allows the intelligent telecommunication infrastructure to automatically reroute an appropriate subset of calls made to the home phone number to the office phone. As an extended example, this redirection could make use of finer-grained location information to optimize rerouting further by hypothetically redirecting the call to the correct conference room if the individual is currently participating in a meeting.

By definition, a smart environment must be able to both *determine* and *predict* the location of an individual. In the conventional cellular telephony environment (for which most of the early work on location management was carried out), location prediction is used only as an intermediate step to improve the efficiency of the location

---

Smart Environments: Technologies, Protocols, and Applications, edited by D.J. Cook and S.K. Das
ISBN 0-471-54448-5 © 2005 John Wiley & Sons, Inc.

determination process. For example, to correctly route a call to a mobile phone, the cellular infrastructure must determine the current base station to which a mobile phone is attached. To avoid having to search the entire coverage area for the current location of the mobile phone, the location management system uses a variety of signaling protocols to predict a smaller subset of cells within which it can confidently localize the search process. For more advanced location management functions, such as fast handoff, location prediction is, however, not merely an intermediate step but an absolutely essential component. *In an abstract sense, prediction is necessary to appropriately allocate resources or activate effectors in advance, especially when the resource allocation or the effector activation process imposes an unacceptable latency on the user's experience.* In many smart environments, the need for allocating resources or actuating effectors in advance, before the actual occurrence of a location-related event, goes well beyond the basic goal of optimizing the allocation of networking resources: *it may be fundamental to the functioning of the smart environment itself.* Consider, for example, an intelligent home where the home controller wishes to warm up the rooms to the appropriately customized temperature setting when the inhabitant returns home. The process of warming up is not instantaneous, and may involve a latency of not just a few minutes but possibly an even longer time span. Accordingly, it is not enough to merely detect the presence of the individual through specific link-layer technologies (such as the Active Badge [Harter:1994], to be discussed shortly). It is necessary to *correlate* multiple context sources to *predict* the mobile user's future location over a much longer time scale. Given the need to tailor the behavior of a smart environment to each individual's habits and behavioral preferences, this predictive capability must also be *customizable* on a per-user basis.

Before proceeding further, let us provide a very brief overview of location management techniques employed in wireless cellular environments. While the location management algorithms of wide-area cellular networks are largely beyond the scope of our discussion, the techniques and principles of such wide-area location management are the foundation on which location algorithms for emerging smart environments (e.g., homes) are based. Algorithms for tracking the location of a mobile user or device use a combination of two fundamental operations:

1. *Location Update or Registration*: a mobile node (MN) proactively informs the network of its location information (e.g., current cell ID), thereby reducing its location uncertainty.
2. *Paging*: the infrastructure (cellular network elements) potentially searches for the MN in all plausible locations, i.e., those cells in which the MN has a nonzero probability of residence.

Current Personal Communication Systems (PCS)–based cellular networks, for instance, cluster groups of individual cells into *registration areas* (RA), such that an MN's location uncertainty is confined to its last reported RA. The MN performs proactive location updates whenever it changes its current RA (not on every cell change). As a result of this proactive registration by the MN, the system can be certain that an idle MN's location can be confined to all cells in the last reported RA. To resolve the MN's precise location within this RA, the system then simultaneously pages (searches for) the MN in all the cells belonging to that RA.

Although the literature related to the location management problem in cellular environments is immense and diverse, all this work can be fundamentally classified as strategies and techniques for improving either or both the update and paging processes. For example, strategies for location update include timer-based updates [BarNoy:1995] (where the MN generates periodic updates), distance-based updates [BarNoy:1995] (where the MN generates updates when its distance changes by a specified threshold), movement-based updates [BarNoy:1995] (where the MN generates updates after moving a certain amount), and reporting center–based updates [BarNoy:1993] (where the MN updates only when it visits certain designated cells). Similarly, improved paging schemes include the computation and use of residency probabilities in an efficient manner (e.g., [Rose:1995]). For example, directional paging [BarNoy:1995][Birk:1995] strategies assume that the residency probabilities decrease omnidirectionally from the last known (updated) position and then page cells sequentially in the decreasing order of these residency probabilities. The mobility management literature for cellular networks can also be classified as either *global* schemes (such as the current PCS architecture), where the update thresholds or paging schemes are common to all (or sets of) mobile nodes, or *individualized* schemes (such as profile-based paging [Tabbane:1995]), where the tracking algorithm adapts to the unique characteristics of each MN. While the goal of such cellular tracking algorithms is usually to determine an MN's cellular point of attachment, many of these algorithms implicitly perform location prediction as well. For example, computing residency probabilities is nothing but a statistical way of predicting a parameter currently unknown to the network—namely, the MN's present location.

In this chapter, we shall look at the various protocols, algorithms, and technologies used for effective location prediction in smart environments. In particular, we shall evaluate how the variety of cellular location tracking algorithms, with or without location prediction, have been customized to the unique characteristics of emerging smart environments. We shall observe that the raw network layer measurements (such as radio signal strength) used for inferring location in various location-determination prototypes are often error-prone. Accordingly, location determination often involves the use of not only customized wireless link-layers, but also *statistical estimation* algorithms and protocols for processing the raw data streams to extract location parameters with an acceptable degree of confidence. Viewed in this light, the location prediction problem is fundamentally nothing but an *estimation problem*, except that, unlike location determination, we now seek to estimate either a future location of a mobile entity based on currently available data or a current location based on previously collected location data. The chapter thus presents both the location determination and prediction techniques within this unifying *estimation theory* framework. For ease of discussion, the bulk of this chapter has been divided into three distinct components:

1. We shall first study the various research prototypes and techniques used to obtain the location information of a mobile user or device in a smart

environment. As stated earlier, *location determination* is often the first step in predicting future location values. We shall study a wide variety of location determination technologies, which differ in various characteristics such as the range and resolution of the location data, the energy characteristics of the link-layer technology employed and their operating environment, and the specific statistical algorithms used to derive location coordinates from a set of measurement values.

2. Given the wide diversity of location-reporting technologies, it is natural to ask if the prediction techniques in a smart environment will also vary with the choice of technology. Indeed, attempts to develop a useful location prediction framework will be futile unless we can find a common set of technology-independent algorithms and approaches for predicting the future location. This chapter is in fact an effort to develop one or more such unifying approaches to location prediction. As part of this effort, we shall borrow from the taxonomy of Leonhardt and Magee [Leonhardt:1996] and show how the entire spectrum of location determination technologies can be classified into two distinct conceptual groups—*geometric* or *symbolic*—depending on the coordinate frame in which the location datum is expressed. We shall also map each of the location determination prototypes to either of these two abstract groups.

3. Finally, we shall concentrate on the problem of location prediction for both the geometric and symbolic groups of location-reporting technologies. The set of techniques, advantages, and problems for each approach will then become clear. In particular, we shall elaborate on why, contrary to popular expectation, the symbolic location representation approach sometimes offers more powerful location prediction techniques than the geometric representation approach.

The rest of the chapter is organized as follows. In Section 9.2, we survey techniques, algorithms, and prototype implementations for computing the current location of a mobile user or object by using a variety of sensing technologies. Section 9.3 shows how the variety of prototype implementations can be grouped into two different camps corresponding to two distinct ways in which the location data is represented. Then, in Section 9.4, we describe algorithms and protocols for predicting (estimating the future) location, highlighting techniques used for the two different representations of location data. We conclude the chapter with a set of open problems and pointers to ongoing work.

9.2 LOCATION DETERMINATION TECHNIQUES (FOR ESTIMATING CURRENT LOCATION)

We first look at the various research prototypes and techniques for obtaining the location of mobile users and devices in a smart environment. As we shall see, these prototypes differ widely in the type of link-layer technology [e.g., radio frequency (RF), infrared] employed, their applicability to indoor and/or outdoor environments, and the resolution offered by the location reporting technology. Some of the more advanced location determination techniques also use estimation algorithms to filter multiple sets of location reading values to derive a more accurate location estimation. Broadly speaking, the location tracking technologies can be classified into two groups:

1. *Device-oriented*, where the location is principally determined by measurements of signals emitted from the infrastructure and received by the mobile device.
2. *Network-oriented*, where the location is principally determined by measuring signals emitted from the mobile device and received by sensors within the network infrastructure.

We shall use this broad classification to categorize the various location determination technologies. Moreover, to keep the chapter concise, we shall focus on the relatively well-known and popular location technologies. For a more comprehensive, although slightly dated, review of location technologies, refer to the excellent review article in [Hightower:2001].

9.2.1 Device-Oriented Technologies

Device-oriented technologies have been used or proposed for location tracking in both outdoor and indoor environments. Since the location determination is performed by the mobile device, this approach imposes greater hardware and processing requirements on the mobile device than does the network-oriented approach. The biggest advantage of this family of technologies is that it allows the mobile device to control the exposure of its location information—since the location is determined by the mobile device, and not by the infrastructure, the location coordinates can be exposed only with the consent of the mobile device.

9.2.1.1 GPS The Global Positioning System (GPS) [Kaplan:1996] is perhaps the most popular and well-known location determination system and has been deployed in many outdoor location-based applications, such as tracking of fleet vehicles by trucking companies or vehicular on-board driving directions. The GPS approach utilizes a set of nominally 24 orbiting satellites to provide a set of reference points over the entire globe. These satellites are maintained and operated by the U.S. Department of Defense. The satellite constellations are designed such that each satellite has an orbiting time of approximately 1 day, and any point on the Earth's surface has a line-of-sight connectivity concurrently to at least five satellites. Each satellite transmits "beacon" signals that are used by receivers in its footprint to determine their own location. Each GPS signal transmitted consists of a specific code, called a *course/acquisition* (CA) code, which includes the satellite's location (with reference to the Earth's coordinates), the GPS system time (as measured at the satellite), and its clock error. To provide accurate and synchronized time estimates, the GPS transmitters on the satellites utilize very sensitive atomic clocks. The GPS satellites actually send out two different kinds of beacons, one intended for public (civilian) usage and the other reserved for use under the authorization of the U.S. Department of Defense. The Standard Position Signal (SPS) can be received by all receivers without any restrictions, and the quality of this signal is intentionally degraded to ensure that the GPS receiver is unable to resolve it location to less than 100 m. The Precise Positioning Service (PPS) is transmitted using proprietary encryption and can be used by authorized receivers to resolve locations up to the granularity of 22 m.

The GPS receiver uses a mechanism called *triangulation*, whereby a set of signals from multiple satellites is used to derive the location of the receiver. The GPS receiver on the mobile device first matches the CA code sent by a satellite with an identical copy in its local database by progressively shifting this code and measuring the clock shift in its internal clock. The required clock shift equals the propagation delay from the transmitter to the receiver, which is then converted to an equivalent distance estimate (since the speed of light is a well-known constant). In practice, this estimate can deviate from the true value due to changes in the propagation speed of the signal (due to ionospheric changes) and errors in clock synchronization. In theory, by combining the information about the distance and orientation of three or more satellites, the GPS receiver can find its own location (as the intersection of these three spheres). In addition, the GPS receiver can combine these position readings with additional information in its local database (such as previous GPS readings) to determine other parameters, such as its velocity or bearing toward a particular reference point. In practice, however, due to errors in the distance computation, four satellite signals are typically needed to resolve the location information, and five or more satellites are used to obtain both accurate position and time estimations and to provide robustness against individual measurement errors. Due to the line-of-sight communication needed with the satellites, GPS is useful as a location resolution technology only in outdoor environments, and is thus of relatively little use for smart indoor environments.

9.2.1.2 Device-Centric E.911 in PCS Cellular Networks
The U.S. Federal Communications Commission's (FCC) E911 initiative has made it mandatory for wireless cellular service providers to track the location of phones making emergency 911 calls to an accuracy of 100 yards. While GPS information provides the easiest form of location determination, most cell phones do not currently possess such technology. Several alternative approaches have been studied and, to various degrees, adopted to obtain the location information of phones using the cellular infrastructure. Broadly speaking, these technologies include the Enhanced Observed Time Difference (E-OTD), Time Difference of Arrival (TDOA), Angle of Arrival (AOA), and Assisted GPS (A-GPS) methods. Of these, the A-GPS and E-OTD methods are device-centric, while the other two, namely, the TDOA and AOA

methods, are network-centric. In this section, we briefly survey the A-GPS and E-OTD techniques for E911 support.

The A-GPS method presumes the availability of a GPS receiver on the handset. In the basic GPS approach, the GPS receiver is responsible for obtaining all the timing and location parameters from the signals transmitted by the satellites. In many cellular environments, the received signals are either too noisy or too distorted by multipath fading to be reliably used for ranging operations. In the A-GPS method [Syrjarinne:2001], these limitations are overcome by having the cellular service provider provide additional GPS information to the handset. This information is sent in an "aiding" message on the detection of an incoming 911 call and typically consists of a list of satellites within range of the handset, their relative Doppler offsets, and orbital parameters. The network itself can obtain this information by deploying a set of GPS receivers at designated reference points. The handset can then combine this network-provided information with its short snapshot of GPS data to accurately determine "pseudo-range" information (relative to the reference points). After determining its precise location, the handset sends this information to the cellular service provider, which is then responsible for forwarding it to a designated Public Service Answering Point (PSAP), a special node that will respond to such emergency 911 calls.

The E-OTD method, on the other hand, relies on the measurement of reference signals (pulsed beacons) emitted by the base stations of the cellular network. This method is quite similar in philosophy to the A-GPS technique, except that the beacons or pulses are now generated from terrestrial base stations over the communication channel rather than by satellites operating in a separate band. This technology also uses a set of Location Measurement Unit (LMU) receivers, which are dispersed over the geographic region and provide a set of well-known reference points for measuring these pulsed beacons. Special hardware on the base stations ensures that the pulses are generated in a synchronized manner with high accuracy. The E-OTD method relies on a modified form of trilateration, with the handset receiving the pulses from three or more base stations and measuring the propagation delay in the arrival of the pulses from different base stations. The handset then reports these delay readings back to a Serving Mobile Location Center (SMLC), which also receives similar propagation delay reports from the LMU devices located at the reference points. By comparing the difference in the time of arrival of the signal from a particular base station at the handset and at an LMU, the SMLC is able to estimate a radial distance between the handset and an LMU. By using readings from multiple LMUs and by using signals from multiple base stations, the SMLC can then determine the precise location of the handset.

9.2.1.3 Cricket
MIT's Cricket Location Support System [Priyantha:2000] uses a combination of RF and ultrasound technologies to track the location of mobile objects in an indoor environment. Unlike several other prototypes (such as Active Bats, to be discussed later) for indoor location tracking, Cricket delegates the responsibility for location reporting to the mobile object itself. Moreover, in the Cricket infrastructure, it is the individual mobile device, rather than a centralized

server in the network, that is responsible for computing its own location, using information gleaned from beacons emitted by wall or ceiling transmitters. As an additional feature, Cricket is also designed to provide orientation information, i.e., the direction toward which a mobile device is pointing. A combination of ultrasonic and RF technologies was needed, since experiments [Chakraborty:2000] showed that the channel quality of an RF path exhibits significant fluctuation (even in static indoor experiments), making any reference calibration of RF signal strengths extremely difficult.

The Cricket infrastructure consists of active (transmitting) beacons, which are static and located at well-known reference positions, and passive (receiving) mobile units mounted on the mobile device being tracked. Cricket's philosophy for passive receivers is driven primarily by energy efficiency and privacy concerns: in Cricket, each mobile device generates a location update only proactively (whenever it wants to), and may thus independently control the degree to which it exposes its own location coordinates. Each beaconing device periodically transmits a beacon, concurrently, on both the RF and ultrasonic channels. Due to the difference in the speed of propagation between light and sound waves, a receiver will perceive a distance-dependent lag between the reception of the RF and ultrasonic signals. It is easy to see that if v_l is the velocity of electromagnetic waves in air, v_s is the velocity of sound in the same medium, and Δt is the time difference between the arrival of the two signals, then the distance, D, of the receiver from the beacon is governed by the relationship

$$\Delta t = \frac{D}{v_s} - \frac{D}{v_l} \quad (1)$$

In particular, if $v_l \gg v_s$, we see that this distance may be closely approximated as

$$D = \Delta t^* v_s \quad (2)$$

Since the signals emitted by different beacons may collide with one another, Cricket uses a randomization mechanism to randomly distribute the interval between consecutive beacons over a reasonably wide range. Such randomization ensures that while multiple beacons may occasionally collide due to the absence of a multiple-access resolution mechanism on the RF channel, these collisions are only transient.

Cricket receivers essentially compute their location by determining the relative distance of the receiver from one or more beacons within its communication range and then associating its identity with the identity of the closest receiver. Note that, unlike GPS receivers, Cricket receivers do not correlate distance readings from multiple receivers (for example, by trilateration) to determine their precise location; instead, they merely identify their location by indirect association with the nearest beacon. Such trilateration is not always feasible, since Cricket does not define a uniform coordinate system to be used by all beacons. While beacons for some application scenarios, such as Active Maps [Schilit:1994], may provide their reference location in terms of a geometric location system such as an (x, y)

the reference location of the mobile node and the associated set of signal strength measurements obtained from the set of access points. Thus, in an environment with N access points, the ith entry in the Map would appear as $(x_i, y_i, SS^i_1, SS^i_2, \ldots, SS^i_N)$, where (x_i, y_i) refers to the coordinates of the ith reference location and SS^i_j ($j = 1, \ldots, N$) refers to the signal strength reading received from the jth access point at the ith reference location.

To locate the position of a mobile user, the mobile first measures the signal strength readings from all access points within its communication range. It then searches through the Radio Map to determine the signal strength tuple that offers the closest match to its current readings and estimates its own location to be given by the (x, y) coordinates of the closest matching tuple. To determine the nearest matching tuple, the original RADAR algorithm essentially looked for the nearest neighbor in the N-tuple space; that is, given a measurement tuple $(SS^m_1, SS^m_2, \ldots, SS^m_N)$ obtained by the mobile M, it searched for the Map entry e such that

$$e = \arg \min_i \sum_{j=1}^{N} \left(SS^m_k - SS^i_j \right)^2 \tag{4}$$

While the basic RADAR implementations focused solely on location determination based on instantaneous measurements, a later implementation of RADAR [Bahl:2000a] uses movement history to further reduce errors in location estimation. The continuous-tracking mode of RADAR keeps track of the movement history of the mobile in the coordinate space, and then uses a modification of the Viterbi algorithm (used for trellis decoding in wireless receivers) to determine the most likely path (and, hence, the most likely current location) taken by the mobile, given the sequence of h most recent measured signal strength readings. To develop the transition probabilities, the RADAR algorithm first obtains a set of k most likely locations (the k Map entries that are closest to the current signal strength tuple in the signal space) for each reading, called the *k-Set*. It then associates a transition weight between each element pair in successive *k-Sets*, corresponding to the Euclidean distance between the two points. Determining the most likely position then reduces to computing the least-cost path between any member of the first set of locations (obtained h samples ago) and any member of the current set of feasible locations. The system then estimates the location of the MN to be the first node (a Map entry from the set obtained h samples ago) in this least-cost path. Figure 9.2 shows the basic operation of the Viterbi decoding algorithm for computing the mobile's current position. The choice of a Map entry from the *k-Set* computed h samples ago implies that the system's measurement of the MN's true location lags the MN's current location by h samples. By increasing the frequency with which samples are measured (essentially moving to a continuous tracking mode), the modified RADAR implementation can predict the MN's location with a very small lag, but with greatly improved accuracy. While focused purely on location determination, the algorithm does perform a form of *location*

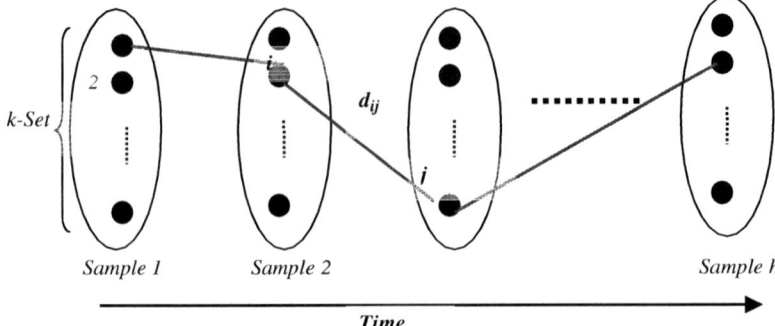

Figure 9.2 Viterbi decoding approach in RADAR. The algorithm computes the shortest path between h k-Sets, where the weight of an edge d_{ij} between nodes i and j in adjacent k-Sets is the Euclidean distance between the corresponding Map entries.

prediction: past samples of location readings are used to implicitly associate likelihood values with the location information of future samples.

The RADAR system offers two advantages: it requires only a few base stations, and it uses the same infrastructure that provides the general-purpose wireless networking of the building. However, it suffers from two drawbacks: the object being tracked must support a wireless LAN, which is impractical on small, power-constrained devices, and its generalization to multifloored buildings or to three dimensions presents a nontrivial problem. Experiments with RADAR's lateration implementation in [Bahl:2000a] indicated ∼4 m resolution accuracy at the 50% probability level. However, significant changes in the environment, such as moving metal file cabinets or congregation of large groups of people in rooms, often necessitate reconstruction of the predefined signal-strength database.

Alternative estimation techniques for deriving the location of an 802.11-equipped mobile device, based on estimates of radio signal strength, have also been reported in the literature. For example, Nibble [Castro:2001] provides a probabilistic estimation of the location coordinates by incorporating a Bayesian model for predicting the likely origin of a signal based on the signal quality observed at multiple access points. In this approach, it is the mobile's signal strength that is measured at each access point; readings from different access points are then correlated to obtain different possible locations (with different likelihood values) for the mobile. On the other hand, the SpotON system [Hightower:2000] was designed specifically to obtain three-dimensional location estimation based on signal strength readings.

9.2.2 Network-Centric Technologies

We now survey the technologies and prototypes where the location is determined by the measurement of signal strengths or beacons emitted by the mobile device. In contrast to the device-centric technologies, these approaches require relatively less sophisticated equipment on the tracked device, since the device merely needs to generate appropriate beacons or pulses. In many cases [e.g., the technologies based on Active (RFID) tags], the mobile device does not directly generate the beacons, but simply relays back appropriately modulated "echoes" of beacons transmitted by the infrastructure nodes. On the flip side, this approach can raise important issues about location privacy, since the mobile device no longer has direct control over the exposure of its location information.

9.2.2.1 Active Badge

Active Badge was one of the first indoor location tracking systems targeted specifically for indoor office environments and was first conceived [Weiser:1993] at the Xerox Palo Alto Research Center. This experimental system underwent further development after migrating first to the Olivetti Research Laboratory and later to the AT&T Cambridge Laboratory [Harter:1994], [Want:1992]. Active badges are essentially low-cost, low-power *infrared* beacon-emitting devices designed to be worn by employees in an office environment. Each active badge is associated with a unique identity (ID), which is broadcast as part of the beacons emitted by the badge worn by a user. The beacons are transmitted intermittently, with a beacon period being implementation-dependent and varying from around 10 s to 6 min. The Active Badge infrastructure consists of a group of Badge readers (sensors) that are deployed in various locations in the smart environment. As the walls or partitions in a room reflect the modulated IR signals, the Active Badge system allows a badge and a receiving sensor to operate in a reasonably omnidirectional mode. Since the IR technology does not pass through walls or partitions, the range of a particular sensor can be localized to a single physically enclosed environment, thereby reducing the uncertainty of location associated with a particular badge. A separate location management database contains the location information of each deployed sensor, and is thus able to provide a map indicating the current zone within which the location of a particular active badge may be localized.

In the Active Badge location management infrastructure, the location of a particular active badge (mobile user) is associated with the sensor that currently reports a reading from the badge. This reading does not provide additional information about the relative signal strength or some other indicator of the distance of the communication channel. Accordingly, the resolution of an Active Badge location report is essentially governed by the communication range, CR, of the active badge. If the reporting sensor is located at a point (x, y, z) in a three-dimensional coordinate space, the actual location of the MN lies anywhere within a sphere of radius CR centered on (x, y, z). As the active badge cannot communicate with any sensor across a partition, the location of an active badge can be localized to the room/partition in which the currently reporting sensor lies. Accordingly, the Active Badge infrastructure is unable to provide information at a finer granularity in environments, such as large conference halls, where the room partitions can be a few hundred feet apart. At any instant, an active badge is associated with only one sensor; accordingly, the Active Badge technology does not use any correlation technique (such as triangulation) to over multiple signal receptions to further refine the location of a specific badge.

The Active Badge technology is primarily *push-based*: each active badge is responsible for periodically generating beacons that provide location markers for the associated mobile user. An active badge does not directly have an idle mode. However, users wearing an active badge can manually turn off the badge, effectively shutting off the periodic updates and making the location information unavailable to the Active Badge system. While this form of manually controlled active badge reporting satisfies potential privacy concerns, it does not provide any means for the Active Badge sensors to initiate communication with a powered-off badge. Some Active Badge technologies incorporate an additional light sensor that detects ambient lighting conditions and increases the beacon periods in dark environments. The motivation here is to reduce the energy consumption in environments (such as a darkened office room at night) that are unlikely to require active location tracking. Even without the use of a specific idle mode, the relatively low power consumption of the infrared channel allows active badges to possess a reasonably long operational lifetime (typically ~ 1 year) with the associated battery.

Most modern implementations of an active badge do, however, have some receive capabilities, so that they can interpret a range of messages, including a paging message. A paging message is generated by the Active Badge infrastructure to proactively locate the current point of attachment of an active badge. Since the Active Badge infrastructure does not cluster sensors into registration areas, this paging message is sent to all sensors that are part of the deployed infrastructure, and are essentially broadcast over the entire Active Badge space. In fact, the active badges were initially designed as a technique for obtaining the location of a user so that location-specific data (such as maps or alerts) could be forwarded to the user's personal computing device [the PARCTab, which was the precursor of the current personal digital assistants (PDAs)]. The active badge thus served as *a surrogate location resolver* for the mobile user's personal device. Due to this primary focus on location resolution, the Active Badge infrastructure was not concerned with location prediction, and thus did not attempt to derive or exploit any predictability or constraints on the MN's movement pattern.

9.2.2.2 *Active Bat*
As we have seen, the confinement properties of infrared signals imply that an active badge can be tracked at the granularity of individual rooms by identifying the unique sensor that is currently receiving beacons from the badge. However, this level of resolution may not be appropriate for many applications, which require even finer granularity. For example, consider a large conference room or exhibition hall, where the location resolution must be able to distinguish between different segments and zones within the same room. Such a fine-grained resolution would be especially important when the resolution is used to primarily identify the nearest point of connectivity for devices using very-low-range communication links (e.g., Bluetooth-equipped devices with ranges as low as 5–10 m). This level of resolution would also be important for applications such as active maps [Schilit:1994] (e.g., where the high-resolution map of electrical wiring near a technician's current location in the room is provided to the technician's handheld device).

9.2 LOCATION DETERMINATION TECHNIQUES

The Active Bat [Harter:1999] technology was developed as a follow-on to the Active Badge system to obtain such higher-resolution location information. In contrast to active badges, active bats employ ultrasonic (sound waves) technology. Each active bat essentially emits short ultrasonic beacons (pulses), which are then captured at multiple (a minimum of three) receivers or sensors mounted at well-defined reference locations on the ceiling. By accurately synchronizing the clocks between the sensors and an active bat and measuring the time of flight of the ultrasonic signal, each receiving sensor can compute the distance between itself and the bat being tracked. (This distance estimation is possible since the speed of sound in air is assumed to be a well-known constant. Moreover, ultrasonic signals are employed since the relatively low speed of propagation of sound waves, compared to electromagnetic waves, makes the time of flight sufficiently larger than the minimum resolution capability that can be provided by these relatively cheap and ubiquitous sensor devices.) To subsequently determine the precise location of an Active Bat, the technology uses trilateration among the three or more sensors. Trilateration (see Figure 9.3) essentially finds the common point of intersection between three or more spherical surfaces, each centered at the appropriate sensor location and having the corresponding radial distance. The centralized Active Bat location tracking software retrieves the distance estimates from each sensor and then uses the static location information of these sensors to trilaterate the precise location of an individual active bat. Current experiments [Addlesse:2001] with the Active Bat system indicate that the trilateration techniques, which may also exploit additional statistical techniques and reflection elimination algorithms to filter out spurious measurements, can provide readings with an accuracy of $\sim 5-10$ cm in 95% of cases.

Location tracking in the Active Bat infrastructure is principally initiated by the sensors, i.e., the wired infrastructure. To enable such system-initiated location tracking, active bats not only have an ultrasonic transmitter, but also a separate 433 MHz radio transceiver. These receivers are connected to a wireless base station that

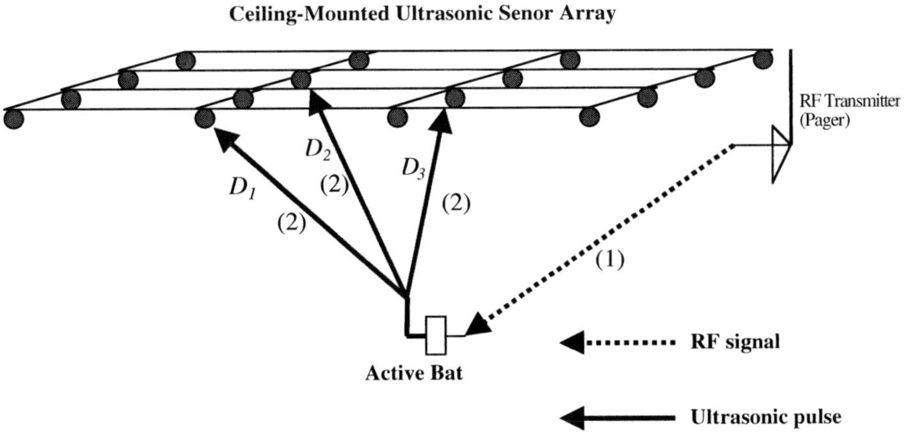

Figure 9.3 Active Bat trilateration.

coordinates the schedules at which individual bats are tracked. To trilaterate the location of a particular active bat, the wireless base station broadcasts a "paging" message (step 1 in Figure 9.3) to it over this radio link, triggering the generation of the ultrasonic pulse (step 2 in Figure 9.3) from the bat to the sensor array. This wireless link is also used to periodically synchronize the clocks on the sensors (receivers) and the active bats, since a reasonably accurate estimation of the time of flight requires good synchronization between the receiver and sender clocks. From a conceptual level, we can thus see that the Active Badge location update system is *purely paging-driven*—an individual bat never generates a location update proactively. To reduce the energy consumption on an active bat, the infrastructure may also indicate a future time when the bat is likely to be addressed or paged (i.e., timer-based paging), allowing the bat to turn off its radio transceiver for the intermediate interval. To aid the system in determining an appropriate inter-page period, a motion detector on an active bat is used to inform the base station whether the bat is stationary or in motion. The Active Bat wired infrastructure can then adjust the inter-paging interval appropriately, as stationary objects usually need to be tracked less frequently than mobile objects. The software module with the Active Bat infrastructure also allows users to customize the tracking frequency based on various quality-of-service (QoS) classes. Thus, the bats of some users participating in an application requiring low-latency position updates would be paged more frequently and preferentially over bats belonging to users utilizing less sensitive applications. As a pointer to our subsequent discussion on algorithms for mobility prediction, it should be noted that this paging frequency is *not adaptive*, i.e., it does not learn from or exploit past patterns of individual bat or user behavior.

9.2.2.3 3D-iD Pinpoint's 3D-iD [RFI] is a location resolution system that employs active RF-ID tags and proprietary base stations. In the 3D-iD system, the base station antennas placed at well-known reference points emit RF signals at 2.4 GHz [within the unregulated (ISM) band]. Tags located on the mobile devices respond to these signals, with an identification code uniquely identifying the mobile device. While the overall philosophy is similar to that of the RADAR approach, the active RF-ID tags are not part of the data communication infrastructure and do not respond over the same channel (the response is relayed back at 5.8 GHz). The RF-ID tags can be considered mirrors, simply reflecting back the original signal transmitted by the base stations. These response signals are measured by multiple receiving antennas (similar to the Active Bat technology) and are then triangulated at a centralized server to resolve the location of the mobile device. The triangulation technology achieves 1–3 m accuracy and offers easier deployment and administration than many other research systems.

The 3D-iD system suffers from the disadvantage that each receiving antenna has a narrow cone of influence, which makes ubiquitous deployment quite expensive. Thus, it is best suitable for large indoor spaces like hospitals or warehouses. Moreover, the Pinpoint system is *essentially paging-based*, with the network polling the mobile devices according to some schedule and the targeted mobile device reflecting back a response to each such poll. The tracking algorithms also do not currently engage in any mobility prediction, and do not learn from or adapt to any movement patterns of the individual mobile devices.

9.2.2.4 LANDMARC The LANDMARC (Location Identification Based on Dynamic Active RFID Calibration) prototype [Ni:2003] is another location tracking system that employs Active RFID tags. It deploys a group of Active RFID readers over the smart environment with partial overlap between the coverage area of different readers, governed by the power levels associated with each reader. By properly placing the readers in appropriate reference locations, the entire smart environment can be conceptually divided into multiple *zones*, each consisting of a unique collection of RFID readers that are within communication region of that entire zone. For example, given five readers, R_1, R_2, R_3, R_4 and R_5, we may set the power levels to define two zones: Z_1 comprising (R_1, R_3, R_5) and Z_2 comprising (R_2, R_3, R_4, R_5).

To determine the location of a particular RFID tag, the system can then merely look up the identity of the readers that receive a location update from the RFID tag. The location of the tag can then be localized to the zone corresponding to the set of active readers that detect the beacon from the tag. However, this naive approach is not very useful, since the propagation characteristics of the indoor environment change very rapidly, making it impossible to associate a set of RFID tags with a physical zone in any meaningful way.

To overcome this problem, the LANDMARC system uses a set of *RT* reference tags (called *landmarks*) in a manner similar to RADAR's use of reference locations. The LANDMARC readers receive updates not only from the tag being tracked, but also from this set of static reference tags, whose location is well known. If there are *N* readers in the environment, each update from the tracked tag *M* can be represented as a vector $S = (SS_1^m, SS_2^m, \ldots, SS_N^m)$, where S_i^m denotes the signal strength reading of tag *M* at the *i*th reader. In a similar manner, the *i*th reference tag, located at the coordinates (x_i, y_i), also generates a vector $\theta_i = (SS_1^i, SS_2^i, \ldots, SS_N^i)$ at the readers. The location resolution algorithm first computes the Euclidean distance E_i, between the vector **S** and θ_i, for each of the *RT* different values of *i* (the vectors of each of the landmark tags). The actual estimated location is then computed as a weighted sum of the location of the *k-nearest* landmark tags, i.e., the location of the *k* landmark tags with the smallest *E*-values. As the tracked tag is assumed to be "closer" to the landmark with the smallest *E*-value, the weighing algorithm must assign greater weight to landmarks with smaller *E*-values. In LANDMARC, the weight is assigned in inverse proportion to the square of the Euclidean distance. In other words:

$$(x, y) = \sum_{i=1}^{k} w_i \times (x_i, y_i) \quad \text{where} \quad w_i = \frac{(1/E_i^2)}{\sum_{j=1}^{k} (1/E_j^2)} \qquad (5)$$

Experimental results reported in [Ni:2003] demonstrate that the maximum location estimation error using this technique is only around 1–2 m. LANDMARC's use of reference active tags as landmarks helps to significantly reduce the errors caused by the variability of the indoor operating environment; since both the tracked and reference tags are subject to the same environmental effects, the E-values should be reasonably insensitive to specific channel conditions. The accuracy of LANDMARC, however, depends on the appropriate a priori positioning of the reference tags; determining a good set of locations for a group of RT reference tags is still an open problem.

9.2.2.5 Network-Centric E.911 in PCS Cellular Networks
Both the A-GPS and E-OTD techniques described in Section 9.2.1.2 require enhancements on the mobile handsets to process differences in the arrival times of reference beacons. Accordingly, these approaches are unsuitable for providing E911 location resolution for existing handsets, which do not possess this enhanced functionality. The two network-assisted techniques, TDOA and AOA, which we discuss now, can both be used for backward-compatible location resolution support, since they rely only on measurements and processing within the network infrastructure.

The TDOA (Time Difference of Arrival) technique works by measuring the relative arrival times of a handset radio signal at three or more separate base stations. By measuring the difference in the arrival times at different sites, it is possible to obtain the location of the mobile device relative to the base station locations. This approach is thus similar in philosophy to the Active Bat approach, except that the handset clock need not be exactly synchronized with the base station clocks. Accordingly, the TDOA approach does not aim to calculate directly the distance between the handset and each base station, but rather the relative distance of the handset from a pair of base stations. Since the speed of propagation in the wireless medium is a known constant, the difference in the arrival time of a signal at two reference points (whose clocks are accurately synchronized) can be translated into a differential distance of the transmitter from each reference point. It is then easy to see that the locus of the transmitter's location is described by a hyperbolic surface with the two reference points (the base stations) as the foci. By obtaining the TDOA for multiple pairs of base stations, one can reduce the location uncertainty of the transmitting handset to the intersection of the corresponding hyperbolic surfaces.

The AOA (Angle of Arrival) approach works by triangulation (as opposed to TDOA, which uses trilateration). In this technique, each base station is equipped with an antenna array consisting of multiple antenna elements, and has specialized software to measure the phase difference between the arrival of the same signal at different elements. By measuring this phase difference of a signal generated from the handset, each base station can then compute the angle (or cone) from which the original signal was transmitted. By obtaining the estimated angular orientation of the handset relative to multiple base stations, one can localize the potential location of the handset to the common intersecting region between the corresponding cones. Additional details on the use of these network-centric location estimation techniques, especially for cellular layouts along highways, can be found in [Rappaport:1996]. More recently, the basic location determination has been augmented by the use of additional statistical estimators, such as the maximum likelihood estimator reported in [Zagami:1998].

9.2.3 Other Location Determination Techniques

All the location determination techniques discussed so far employ some form of triangulation, trilateration, or measurement of radio, infrared, or ultrasonic signals. Clearly, radio- or sound-wave-based technologies are more popular, since the hardware for measuring or modulating these signals is relatively inexpensive and requires little modification of standard hardware used in wireless communications. There are, however, several alternative location tracking technologies that use other techniques, such as electromagnetic sensing or image recognition, to determine the location and identity of mobile devices. To a large extent, these technologies are not universal, but are designed to operate in a specific targeted environment. We now briefly survey a few of these nonradio technologies for location determination.

Electromagnetic sensing [Raab:1979] is a classical way of detecting the presence of mobile objects around designated reference points. These tracking systems generate axial magnetic field pulses from a transmitting antenna in a fixed location. The system computes the position and orientation of the receiving antennas by measuring the response in three orthogonal axes to the transmitted field pulse, combined with the constant effect of the Earth's magnetic field. Tracking systems such as MotionStar [Ascension:2001] sense precise physical positions relative to the magnetic transmitting antenna. Electromagnetic sensing offers the advantages of very high precision and accuracy, on the order of less than 1 mm spatial resolution, 1 ms time resolution, and $0.1°$ orientation capability. Disadvantages include high implementation costs and the need to tether the tracked object to a control unit. Further, the sensors need to remain within 1 to 3 m of the transmitter, and accuracy degrades with the presence of metallic objects in the environment. Accordingly, this form of location estimation is predominantly suited for outdoor environments and often generates significant errors in indoor office scenarios.

Some research groups have explored the use of computer vision technology to figure out the exact location of mobile objects. One such effort is the Easy Living project [Krumm:2000] at Microsoft Research, which uses the Digiclops real-time three-dimensional cameras to provide stereo-vision positioning capability in a home environment. Although it uses high-performance cameras, the vision system typically uses substantial amount of processing power to analyze frames captured with comparatively low-complexity hardware. State-of-the-art systems demonstrate that multimodal processing of silhouette, skin color, and face pattern can significantly enhance accuracy [Darrell:1998]. Vision location systems must, however, constantly struggle to maintain analysis accuracy as scene complexity increases and more occlusive motion occurs. In general, computer vision–based location determination systems are not yet cheap enough to be considered for ubiquitous deployment in a smart environment. Such vision-based systems may, however, be legitimate candidates for monitoring and detecting the presence of users in specific portions of the smart environment, e.g., at the entrance to a corporate office. Another recent example of such vision-based location tracking is the use of arrays of video cameras [Huang:2003] to track the movement of the head or face of an individual inside a single intelligent room.

In Georgia Tech's Smart Floor proximity location system [Orr:2000], embedded pressure sensors capture footfalls, and the system uses *pressure-based data* for position tracking and pedestrian recognition. The system works on the principle that the foot pressure of an individual acts as a biometric indicator, much in the same manner as fingerprints. Whenever the individual steps on the embedded pressure sensors, the reading is matched against a database to identify the individual currently located in the vicinity of the pressure sensor. This unobtrusive direct physical contact system does not require people to carry a device or tag. However, the system has the disadvantages of poor scalability and high incremental costs, since the floor of each building in which the Smart Floor is deployed must be physically altered to install the pressure sensor grids. This technology may, however, be appealing in the construction of smart homes in the future; such piezoelectric crystals may be embedded in the house during the construction process.

9.3 LOCATION REPRESENTATION SCHEMAS: GEOMETRIC OR SYMBOLIC?

We have already seen that the various location-aware computing prototypes utilize a variety of location-tracking strategies and determine the location of a mobile user at different levels of granularity. It should thus be clear that each networking technology is likely to have its own mechanism for specifying location. However, a little thought will show that all the mechanisms we have discussed essentially represent a mobile user's location using one of the following two representations: geometric or symbolic (taxonomy clarified by Leonhardt and Magee [Leonhardt:1996]).

9.3.1 Geometric Representation

In this approach, the location of the mobile object is specified as an *n-dimensional* coordinate. This representation is thus *absolute* in that it specifies the location of a mobile with respect to a geographical coordinate system. The most common form of geometric data representation in location-aware computing systems involves the use of GPS data, which resolves the latitude and longitude of a mobile on the Earth's surface using a satellite-based triangulation system.

The main advantage of geometric representation is that it is typically invariant: the location information does not depend on the topology of the underlying network but is an intrinsic property of the mobile device. Accordingly, as long as the different access technologies use the same frame of reference (such as the Earth's geographical coordinates), this location information can be uniformly interpreted across heterogeneous networks. The accuracy of the location information is also well preserved unless the mapping between two coordinates systems is lossy. Geometric coordinates also provide a natural primitive to support a range of spatial queries, such as containment. For example, if we define a polygonal region by specifying the vertices of the polygon in geometric coordinates, it is very easy to compute if a particular (x, y, z) location coordinate lies inside or outside the polygon. Similarly, geometric coordinates are especially useful in determining proximity measures in the physical world, e.g., determining the geographically closest cafeteria or Chinese restaurant.

In spite of this seeming attractiveness, geometric representation may not always be the most convenient representation for context-aware applications in smart environments. For one thing, the same reference coordinate system is not universally applicable. As an example, while an outdoor positioning system such as GPS may be appropriate outdoors, ultrasonic- or infrared-based indoor positioning systems may not be equipped to use the same location coordinates. Moreover, it should be quite clear that heterogeneous access technologies and location tracking systems will require and resolve the location of a mobile device at varying depths of granularity. Thus, while GPS information may be accurate up to $\sim$20 m resolution, indoor office applications may require tracking at sub-meter resolutions. When different technologies use different reference systems, coordinate translation mechanisms will be needed to transfer location information from one system to another. Since geometric data is weakly structured, frequent coordinate translation will burden both the location-aware applications and the network-signaling infrastructure. The basic problem with geometric data is that it cannot reflect the notion of containment without numerical computation.

Additionally, geometric location information may not be universally available in all access technologies. For example, while GPS is certainly a useful location-tracking technology, we cannot expect GPS radio interfaces to be universally deployed on all pervasive devices (due to restrictions in cost and form factors). Similarly, technologies such as Active Bats require the deployment of additional location-specific infrastructure components. Mandating the use of geometric coordinates for location tracking can thus exclude a wide variety of indoor and outdoor technologies (e.g., if the Cricket system uses a virtual name space instead of geometric coordinates).

9.3.2 Symbolic Representation

In the symbolic representation of location data, the user's data is specified not in absolute terms, but relative to the topology of the corresponding access infrastructure. A little thought will show that this form of representation is in widespread use. For example, the PCS/cellular systems identify the mobile phone using the identity of its current serving mobile switching center (MSC); in the Internet, the IP address associated with a mobile device (implicitly) identifies the subnet/domain/service provider to which it is currently attached. In the symbolic approach, the location space is divided into named zones, such as the cells in a cellular network. An area of coverage is associated with the symbolic information, but the mapping may be much more subtle than a mere geometric relationship.

Perhaps the biggest advantage of a symbolic representation is its almost universal applicability. A symbolic representation of a user location is available in a wide variety of technologies, such as cellular/PCS, wireless LANs, Bluetooth, Home RF, etc., thus making symbolic location representation truly universal. *Moreover, it is important to realize that any geometric coordinate can be easily converted into a symbolic namespace simply by treating the physical coordinate space as the symbolic namespace.* Of course, since most symbolic namespaces have a finite alphabet size, we would need to discretize the continuous-valued geometric coordinates. For example, we could treat each ZIP code in the United States as a separate symbol and map each geometric coordinate to its ZIP code. Such ideas have already been used in different spatial databases; for example, the Mobiscope architecture [Denny:2003] encodes the location of vehicles to a symbolic key that is then mapped to a distributed query-processing database.

The geometric representation may be more natural for applications where the physical coordinates of the mobile node is of principal interest (such as the E911 initiative for emergency response). Also, applications that require extremely fine-grained location may find the symbolic namespace to be unacceptably coarse. For example, for a follow-me application wishing to activate wall-mounted displays based on user head motion, merely obtaining the ID of the nearest Active Badge sensor may not be good enough. There are, however, location-aware applications that do not need the exact location of the mobile node, but merely the location of the mobile node relative to the available access infrastructure. For example, consider local computing applications such as Electronic Tourist Guides [Cheverst:1999]. Clearly, the local data needed by a user is implicitly defined by his or her current point of attachment to the network; a museum system proactively pushing floor plans to user devices only needs to know the floor location of the current access point that is serving the mobile visitor. Similarly, ubiquitous connectivity can be assured as long as the system can ascertain the current and future points of attachment of the mobile device, and thus obtain the optimal network path to use in communicating with the mobile endpoint. Finally, there are many proximity-based applications where "nearness" is not defined in terms of physical distances, but by other measures in a more abstract space. For example, the physically nearest printer may be located on the floor above or in the next room, both of which may be geometrically closer than the printer in the current room. To usefully define closeness for such a nearest-printer application, Cricket [Priyantha:2000] described the use of virtual spaces in conjunction with the INS (Intentional Naming System) [Winoto:1999] discovery framework. For example, by defining each room as a unique virtual space, the problem of determining the nearest printer can be reduced to finding one that shares a common virtual coordinate with the user.

Having explained the basic classification of location management algorithms, we shall now return to the location determination strategies and technologies discussed earlier and see how they can be classified into these two camps. Table 9.1 provides an overview of the various technologies we have discussed and the form of representation they use. In the next section, we shall look at the various proposals for predicting the future or current location of a mobile user or device from past location-related values. During this discussion, we shall discover how different algorithms work on either the geometric or symbolic location format. The main motivation for developing or employing this classification system should now be clear. *By employing this classification, we can make the prediction algorithms*

TABLE 9.1 Location Determination Technologies and Use of Symbolic/Geometric Coordinates

Product/Research Prototype	Primary Goal	Underlying Physical Technology	Techniques Employed	Location Representation
GPS	Outdoor tracking	RF	Triangulation	Geometric
Active Badge	Indoor tracking	Infrared	Vicinity-based reporting	Symbolic
Active Bats	Follow-me indoor computing	Ultrasonic	Paging	Geometric
Cricket	Indoor location tracking	RF and ultrasonic	Location updates	Geometric/symbolic
RADAR	Indoor location tracking	802.11 WLAN	Triangulation, location updates	Geometric
3D-iD	Indoor location tracking	Active RFID	Triangulation, paging	Geometric
LANDMARC	Indoor location tracking	Active RFID	Multilateration, minimum distance estimation	Geometric
Smart floor	Indoor user tracking	Foot pressure	Location updates	Geometric

technology-independent; while different technologies may differ in some specific parameters associated with a particular location prediction strategy, the fundamental principles of the strategy will apply uniformly across all technologies using the same form of location representation.

9.4 PREDICTING FUTURE LOCATION

So far, we have covered different techniques for determining the location of mobile objects in a smart environment and have seen how the various technologies differ in their location resolution capability, infrastructure deployment requirements, and tracking algorithms. As the third component of this chapter, we now look at techniques for predicting the future location of mobile devices. At a conceptual level, prediction involves some form of statistical, or occasionally deterministic, *inferencing*, where a sample of the mobile's past movement history is used to provide intelligent estimates of its future location. Moreover, the system's ability to predict the location of a mobile device, and the uncertainty bound associated with this prediction, are closely coupled to the mobile's reporting policy, i.e., the set of events under which a mobile provides a location update, thereby resolving its location ambiguity. Accordingly, the description of any prediction algorithm must include the specification of the associated location update strategy employed by a mobile device or user. While there is an enormous amount of research on location prediction algorithms, we shall highlight some of the key approaches, taking care to specify their reliance on either the symbolic or the geometric form of location representation.

9.4.1 Distance-Based Prediction Strategies

Perhaps the simplest form of location management is one in which the mobile user guarantees that his current location does not deviate from his previously reported value by more than a prespecified distance. Note that the term *distance* can refer to a measure in either geometric or symbolic coordinates. For geometric coordinates, the distance measure is almost always Euclidean. As an example of a symbolic distance measure, consider cellular PCS networks where a mobile device is required to generate an update whenever it changes cell towers (base station) more than twice from the previously reported base station. In this case, the location management system can confidently predict that the mobile device is currently located somewhere within the set of all base stations that are no more than two hops (where the hop is defined by the topology of the associated cells) away from the previously reported base station. Indeed, if the mobile is guaranteed to update its location when it changes by a value D_{th}, the location prediction can guarantee that the mobile is currently located within a radial area (or, in general, within a spherical region) of radius D_{th}, centered at the location of its last update. The prediction algorithm cannot reduce the uncertainty further, since it does not attempt to utilize or derive any higher-order information (such as speed or direction) about the mobile's movement.

The basic framework of *distance-based* location update strategies was explored in [BarNoy:1995], which compared this form of location update with two alternative strategies, namely, *timer-based* (periodic updates) and *movement-based* (where the threshold is specified as a certain number of cell crossings). The work shows that the distance-based strategy is the best, and the timer-based strategy the worst (causes the highest number of update messages), if the user's movement follows a memory-less movement pattern (no correlation between the last movement and the current movement). In the case of correlated movement models, the difference between the strategies is dependent on the precise model parameters, with the movement-based strategy sometimes faring worse than the timer-based model. In general, the distance-based movement model is the most preferable strategy. As we have already noted, the distance-based location update and prediction strategy cannot resolve the uncertainty beyond the region of radius D_{th}. To provide high-fidelity location prediction in smart environments, the distance threshold D_{th} must be set to a very small value. This would lead to an extremely high update rate and high communication overhead on the mobile devices, reducing their operational lifetime between battery recharges to an unacceptably low value. Many smart environments, especially indoor ones such as homes and offices, however, permit only a relatively small set of feasible movement patterns (e.g., one can move only along an office corridor, not across walls). The set of location update strategies described next attempt to exploit such constraints on feasible movement patterns to significantly reduce the location update cost and simultaneously improve the prediction accuracy.

9.4.2 Dead Reckoning

In the dead-reckoning class of location prediction strategies, the mobile node not only provides its current location but also transmits an expected *route* to the location-tracking infrastructure as part of the update process. The location prediction infrastructure then assumes that the mobile continues on this route until it issues a fresh update. In the most common form of dead-reckoning strategies, the mobile device or user essentially transmits its *current position, direction, and velocity of motion* to the location management system. Based on the direction of motion and its velocity, as well as the time elapsed since the last update, the system can then predict a future location of the mobile user or device. To ensure that the prediction error stays within a specified tolerance bound, the mobile continuously tracks its evolving position, and is required to generate a fresh update when its location deviates from the predicted value by a specified threshold. Since the expected route is described in geometric coordinates in dead-reckoning algorithms, this class of algorithms requires the mobile device location to be specified in geometric coordinates.

To mathematically describe the basic principles of this approach, let us assume that the MN's current position is CR and its velocity (in general, as a three-dimensional) vector is v^m. Accordingly, after a time Δt since the last update, the mobile's predicted position PR can be obtained as

$$PR = LR + v^{m*}\Delta t, \qquad (6)$$

where LR denotes the MN's position at the last update. At any time Δt since the last update, the MN can then compute the difference in position between its current value $CR(\Delta t)$ and the predicted value as

$$Diff(\Delta t) = CR(\Delta t) - (LR + v^{m*}\Delta t). \qquad (7)$$

If the difference $Diff$ exceeds a specified threshold, D_{th}, the MN generates a fresh update. This threshold may be specified as a static constant or may be an adaptive value that changes based on the mobiles' movement pattern and a prespecified cost trade-off between the update cost and the uncertainty penalty [Wolfson:1999a]. Dead reckoning–based location update and prediction algorithms were an integral component of the DOMINO project [Wolfson:1999b] for tracking the location of mobile objects in a moving-object database.

Different dead-reckoning policies can be distinguished by the richness of the parameters used to specify a mobile node's expected path. The simplest *linear* model assumes that the MN essentially moves along straight-line segments (indicated by the specified direction) at the specified speed. This form of path specification is particularly suited to outdoor vehicular movements, where the mobile is constrained to move in straight-line segments (such as a highway) over reasonably long periods of time. An update becomes necessary whenever the mobile changes either its direction or its speed by a significant amount. As further refinements of this model, the mobile's expected path can be specified with higher-order models (such as splines) to capture, for example, curves in the road. In a similar manner, the mobile's speed itself can be defined via higher-order models to capture, for example, attributes such as acceleration. One example of such a higher-order model for movement is proposed in [Liang:1999], which models the velocity of the mobile node as a Gauss-Markov process. In this model, the mobile's velocity at a discrete time instant n can be related to its prior velocity at time instant $n-1$ by the equation

$$v_n^m = \alpha v_{n-1}^m + (1-\alpha)\mu + \sqrt{1-\alpha^2}\sigma_{n-1} \qquad (8)$$

where v_n^m is the mobile nodes' velocity at time instant n, α lies between 0 and 1 and expresses the correlation between current and past velocity values, μ is the asymptotic mean of the velocity v_n^m (as $n \to \infty$), and σ_n is an independent, uncorrelated Gaussian process with zero mean and standard deviation equal to the asymptotic standard deviation of v_n^m (as $n \to \infty$). Different techniques for computing the position and velocity of a moving object (within the cellular network environment) have been discussed in [Hellebrandt:1997].

Modifications to the basic dead-reckoning strategies have been proposed to reduce the prediction error below the specified threshold with the help of additional knowledge about the smart environment. One approach (e.g., [Leonhardi:2002]) is to integrate a map of the environment with the dead-reckoning algorithms to further constrain the possible directions or positions in which a mobile object can be located. For example, in an indoor office environment, one can constrain an object to lie either within each office room or on specific straight-line segments corresponding to aisles. The dead-reckoning algorithms can then associate a path with one of the map objects (such as an aisle), thereby removing the need to explicitly specify the mobile's precise direction of motion (which is now constrained to lie along the aisle).

A principal characteristic of dead-reckoning algorithms is that their performance is model-dependent. In other words, the choice of thresholds or the parameters used to model the mobile's expected path depend on some a priori assumptions about the mobile's movement pattern. A particular dead-reckoning approach, tuned for a specific mobile movement model, may turn out to be inappropriate for a mobile node exhibiting a different movement pattern. For effective location tracking, the system must then build up a mobility profile for each user (based on a trace of the user's movement pattern) and obtain the most appropriate parameters for each mobility profile. Thus, the ability to optimally customize the dead-reckoning parameters in a multiuser smart environment is an issue that requires further research.

9.4.3 Profile-Based Prediction Algorithms

An alternative to the movement-based update model used by dead reckoning is to explicitly associate a list of candidate locations (or areas) with a particular mobile. This list of areas is referred to as the *mobility profile* associated with the mobile device. As long as the mobile moves within an area belonging to its current list, it does not need to generate a new location update. However, if the mobile moves into a new area not included in its current mobility profile, it will generate a new update. As will be apparent shortly, this profile-based location prediction strategy is particularly appropriate for symbolic location representations, since each member of the list would then correspond to a specific identifier in the virtual space.

The basic idea of this profile-based approach and its application to the cellular PCS environment was presented in [Tabbane:1995], where the mobility profile was simply a collection of cells. In this approach, each such cell was also associated with a residency probability, indicating the likelihood that the mobile was currently located in that cell. Based on the fundamental results demonstrated in [Rose:1995], [Tabbane:1995] suggested that the paging algorithm for locating the MN's precise location would consist of paging each cell in the mobility profile in the decreasing order of these residency probabilities. The key challenge of such a profile-based approach is the construction of a mobility profile—i.e., the development of an algorithm for determining an appropriate list of possible cells and the right residence probabilities. Most profile creation techniques assume that the user movement exhibits repeatable patterns: by constructing the mobility profile set from observations of the user's past behavior, we can reduce the prediction error at future instants. As one possible technique for constructing a mobility profile, let us look at a temporal profile—one that creates a mobility profile for different time instants. Let $(t1, t2)$ represent a particular interval, which will be represented by a single mobility profile. For example, $(t1, t2)$ can refer to a specific day and time (say, Tuesdays from 8 a.m. to 5 p.m.) of the week. Then the mobility profile for $(t1, t2)$ can be constructed by observing all the cellular locations that a particular MN visits every Tuesday between 8 a.m. and 5 p.m. For example, if an MN's residency pattern over a 5-week period for $(t1, t2)$ consists of cells: C_1, C_3, C_5, C_1, C_2, C_3, C_1, C_5, C_6, C_3, C_1, C_3, the mobility profile will be the list $\{C_1, C_2, C_3, C_5, C_6\}$. Moreover, the residency probabilities can be derived by observing the fraction of time spent in each cell. Thus, in the previous example, each symbol in the pattern represents an equal interval of time, then it follows that the residency probability for C_1 equals $4/12$, whereas that for C_2 equals $1/12$. If the MN follows a regular routine every Tuesday during the workday, then this history-dependent mobility profile can be very useful in restricting the MN's set of possible locations to a very small subset. Of course, in practice, more elaborate profiles will consider spatiotemporal combinations based on both the time and location history of the MN.

The location profile–based framework was further investigated in [Pollini:1997], which not only considered the update and paging costs of this approach, but also the overhead for constructing and maintaining the profile list. Several subsequent publications have described novel ways of constructing this mobility profile. A data-mining approach to the construction of the mobility profile is presented in [Wu:2001]. In this approach, a set of data-mining techniques is used to mine the patterns of the user's movement from a long-term log of the user's detailed movement pattern. The mined information is then used to construct time-varying estimates of the individual residency probabilities of cells in the mobility profile. The use of spatial profiles in conjunction with the temporal profiles has been described in [Zhang:2002].

While the profile creation approaches described here often result in significant savings in the update rate, *they are still model-dependent.* In particular, the creation of a mobility profile is driven by a priori knowledge of the spatiotemporal parameters over which individual profiles are constructed. In our earlier example, an external decision (that the user will exhibit similar behavior between 8 a.m. and 5 p.m. on Tuesdays) is needed before the profile for that time interval is determined. Clearly, such human knowledge may not be available or may be inaccurate in many practical smart environments. For example, would it be more sensible to define a profile for 8 a.m. to 7 p.m. instead of 8 a.m. to 5 p.m. for a user who starts work later? Would it be better to maintain a single profile for all workdays instead of one profile for each day of the week? Similarly, in a smart home, it may not be possible to make a priori decisions about the spatiotemporal regions over which individual users show similar (repeatable) patterns. Accordingly, it would be preferable to have an online learning algorithm that is model-independent—one that does not make any prior assumptions about the user's movement pattern but learns them in an online fashion from the user's evolving movement history. We now describe such an on-line prediction approach.

9.4.4 The LeZi-Update Prediction Algorithm

LeZi-Update [Bhattacharya:2002] is an information-theoretic algorithm that provides a model-independent technique for implicitly creating a location profile. In this algorithm, the system uses an on-line learning technique for gradually discovering the various patterns of (arbitrary) length in the user's update sequence. LeZi-Update is driven by the observation that location prediction can be viewed as prediction of the outcome of a random process (the user's movement). For example, the movement of a user through a particular cellular infrastructure can be represented by the sample sequence *aaababbbbbaabccddcbaaaa* ..., where the individual symbols refer to the different cells of the network. As long as the movement of the mobile device conforms to a stationary or piecewise stationary process, the field of information theory suggests a fundamental bound on the signaling overhead needed to accurately capture the uncertainty of the mobile. This bound is called the *entropy*, denoted as $H(X)$ for a random variable X, and is defined in terms of its distribution as

$$H(X) = -\sum_{i=1}^{|X|} p_i^* \log(p_i), \qquad (9)$$

where p_i is the probability that X equals the ith symbol and $|X|$ denotes the cardinality (number of symbols) of X. More generally, when we seek to capture the outcome of a random process $X = \{X_i\}$, the entropy is defined in terms of its asymptotic marginal entropy as

$$H(X) = \lim_{n \to \infty} H(X_n \mid X_{n-1}, X_{n-2}, \ldots, X_1).$$

Shannon's theory of communication states that the information about the random process X cannot be transmitted at a lower cost per symbol than $H(X)$. In other words, $H(X)$ provides a lower bound on the update cost associated with any feasible location management algorithm. LeZi-Update employs the Lempel-Ziv [Ziv:1978] entropy coding algorithm, LZ78, to asymptotically reduce the update cost to this fundamental bound. The key characteristic of the LZ78 algorithm is its ability to incorporate on-line learning; that is, the update symbols transmitted over the wireless network adapt to the actual movement pattern of the mobile node. Thus, the algorithm is model-independent (makes no assumption about the specific statistics of the MN's movement pattern), yet asymptotically outperforms all model-based prediction schemes.

The LeZi-update algorithm can be represented as an encoder-decoder duo, as shown in Figure 9.4. The encoder part, residing in the mobile terminal, intercepts the update sequence generated by the mobile (whether it is distance-, movement-, or time-based) and transmits it as chunks of nonoverlapping strings. The coded update message is sent to the location management infrastructure, where the decoder can use the on-line dictionary to retrieve the original symbol sequence. As an

```
initialize dictionary := null
initialize phrase w := null

loop
        wait for next symbol v
        if (w.v in dictionary)

                w := w.v

        else
                encode <index(w),v>
                add w.v to dictionary
                w := null
        endif
```

Encoder at Mobile

```
Initialize dictionary :=null
loop
wait for next codeword <i,s>
        decode phrase := dictionary [i].s
        add phrase to dictionary
        increment frequency for every
                        prefix of phrase
forever;
```

Decoder in the Location Tracking System

Figure 9.4 Encoding and decoding of update strings in LeZi-Update.

example, the symbol sequence *aaababbbbbaabccddcbaaaa* considered earlier, gets parsed as *a,aa,b,ab,bb,bba,abc,c,d,dc,ba,aaa* by the encoder, where commas indicate the points of updates separating the updated path segments. The symbol sequences (actually user path segments) can easily be maintained in a trie, as shown in Figure 9.5, which captures all the relevant history of the user in a compact form. In addition to representing the dictionary, the trie can store statistics for context explored, resulting in a symbolwise model for LZ78. Using the stored frequencies, the trie can be used to predict the probability of future occupancy in the cell geometry (symbolic space). The associated paging process only needs to page in the decreasing sequence of these probabilities.

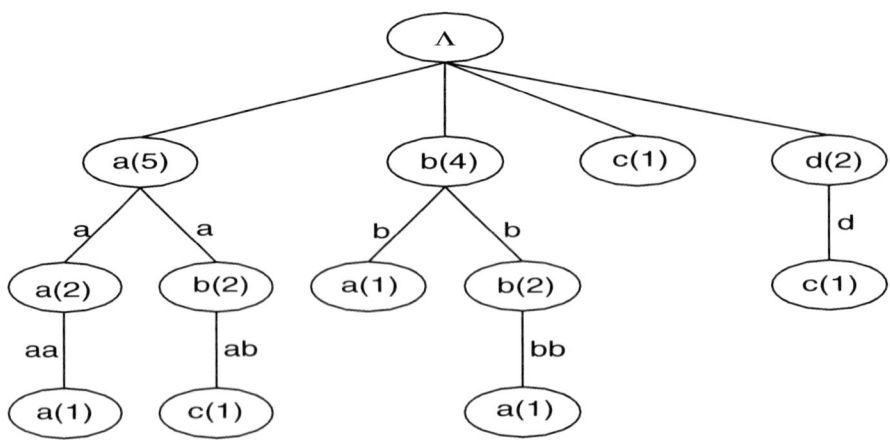

Figure 9.5 Trie-based path storage in LeZi-Update.

While the basic LeZi-Update algorithm was used to predict only the current location from past movement patterns, this approach has recently been extended in [Roy:2003] to predict the likely future paths (or trajectories) of residents in smart homes. This approach exploits the Asymptotic Equipartition Property, which asserts that for a random process with entropy $H(X)$, the number of observed unique paths of length n (n-length strings) is $2^{nH(X)}$ with probability 1; that is, for reasonably large n, most of the probability mass is concentrated in a small subset (called the *typical set*) of paths, which encompasses the user's most likely paths and captures the *average nature of long-length sequences*. Accordingly, the algorithm simply predicts a relatively small set of likely paths, one of which the user will almost surely take next. A smart home environment can then act on this information by activating resources (e.g., by turning on the lights in corridors that constitute one or more of these paths) in a minimal and efficient manner rather than turning on all lights in the house. More recently, the LeZi-Update-based approach has been generalized in [Misra:2004] for optimal mobility tracking of users roaming in multisystem, heterogeneous wireless networks, where the same user has different movement profiles on different sets of alphabets corresponding to the component networks involved. This approach may be used to learn and predict the mobility profiles of an inhabitant spending some parts of the day (say, morning and evening) in a smart home, some time on smart roads while driving, and the rest of the time in a smart office.

9.4.5 Issues with Location Prediction Algorithms

On surveying the individual location determination technologies we have discussed, we observe that very few of them actually use one or more of the location prediction algorithms outlined here. Of course, the location management algorithm can, in some sense, be seen as a layer lying on top of the basic location determination techniques (such as RADAR or Active Badge). However, such prediction algorithms are conspicuous by their absence in most current system prototypes for location management (such as the Active Bat or Cricket). A major reason for this lies in the complexity of the update algorithm required in the mobile device, which is often constrained to be extremely lightweight and should have very low power consumption. In many prototypes, practical hardware constraints essentially reduce the inexpensive mobile device being tracked to a relatively dumb entity capable of performing only simple tasks such as periodic updates or response to system-initiated pages. To utilize techniques like distance-based updates or dead reckoning, these inexpensive devices must possess more advanced software capabilities, such as the ability to modify the update rates adaptively or compute parameters of various motion models. Of course, some prototypes (e.g., Cricket) have fairly sophisticated transceivers on the mobile device and could be enhanced by the adoption of appropriate prediction algorithms.

On inspecting the current prediction algorithms and prototypes, we realize that they also lack a systematic way of optimally adapting their parameters to either (1) different resolutions of the MN's location reports or (2) different fidelity bounds on the prediction errors. For example, applications in a context-aware intelligent environment should be able to specify queries such as "Tell me about the location of user X at a resolution of no less than 5 m, with a prediction accuracy of no less than 65%." The location estimation and motion prediction algorithms should then be *self-tuning*—automatically adjusting various parameters, such as the update rate, size of mobility profiles, or registration areas, in response to the user's true movement patterns and the limitations of the location-sensing technology employed. Further work on these sorts of location management primitives is needed to make the technologies suitable for easy deployment in nontraditional smart environments such as homes, warehouses, and shopping malls.

9.5 CONCLUSIONS

In this chapter, we have surveyed advances in algorithms and protocols for estimating location information about mobile objects in smart environments (a.k.a. smart spaces). The location estimation problem has two facets: one related to determining the appropriate current location based on a set of current readings and another related to estimating a location (or set of probable locations) in the future based on past readings. As the various approaches demonstrate, this problem of location estimation is often harder in smart indoor environments than outdoors due to the time-varying channel characteristics caused by unpredictable electromagnetic interference in offices, homes, and other indoor public spaces. Location determination prototypes not only employ a wide variety of technologies, such as infrared, ultrasonic, RF measurements, RFID tags, and pressure sensors, but also use a variety of statistical estimation techniques (Trellis decoding, Bayesian models, etc.) to obtain refined estimates from the raw measurement data. As a result of this variety, the location accuracy can vary from a few centimeters to tens of meters, with a corresponding trade-off in the infrastructure deployment cost. Clearly, the choice of one or more location resolution technologies depends on the accuracy required by the overlying applications and the degree to which the location resolution process should be network or user controlled.

We have also discussed a variety of techniques for predicting the location of mobile devices. Many of these techniques were originally developed to reduce the location uncertainty of mobile devices in a wide area cellular infrastructure. These techniques can, however, be easily adapted to an indoor smart environment. Other techniques, such as those that require velocity estimation by the mobile node, may impose requirements on the processing capability or device hardware that are currently at odds with the need to keep the cost of such ubiquitous devices fairly low. In particular, techniques that work with symbolic namespaces are more universal, since they can be easily adapted to work with geometric location information as well.

Future research in this area must address mechanisms to make these location determination technologies more adaptive to individual users' behavior without sacrificing the low-cost, low-energy operation of such devices. Another interesting area of research in location estimation for smart environments relates to the ability to infer location by using alternative contextual sources rather than relying on location-oriented sensors alone. For example, one can obtain relatively accurate estimates of a user's location (inside an office or in a city) by obtaining such information as recent use of the user's laptop (and its connectivity to an infrastructure) or his calendar schedule. The challenge in such smart computing scenarios is to be able to customize the location inferences to the activity pattern of each user of the smart environment. As one example, the ContextTailor project [Davis:2003] at IBM Research has recently developed an initial framework for automating this inferencing process for pervasive computing application scenarios. Another research challenge is how to manage movement or activity profiles of multiple inhabitants [e.g., living in the same smart home] in the same dictionary and predict or trigger events to meet the common goals of the house.

ACKNOWLEDGMENTS

The work of Sajal Das is supported by NSF ITR grants under award numbers IIS-0326505 and IIS-0121297.

REFERENCES

[Addlesse:2001] M. Addlesse, R. Curwen, S. Hodges, J. Newman, P. Steggles, A. Ward, and A. Hopper, "Implementing a Sentient Computing System," *IEEE Computer Magazine*, vol. 34, no. 8, pp. 50–56, August 2001.

[Winoto:1999] W. Adjie-Winoto, E. Schwartz, H. Balakrishnan, and J. Lilley, "The Design and Implementation of an Intentional Naming System," *Proceedings of the ACM Symposium on Operating Systems Principles*, pp. 186–201, December 1999.

[Ascension:2001] "Technical Description of DC Magnetic Trackers," Ascension Technology Corp., Burlington, Vt., 2001.

[Bahl:2000a] P. Bahl, A. Balachandran, and V. Padmanabhan, "Enhancements to the RADAR User Location and Tracking System," Technical Report MSR-TR-2000-12, Microsoft Research, February 2000.

[Bahl:2000b] P. Bahl and V. Padmanabhan, "RADAR: An in-Building RF-Based User Location and Tracking System," *Proceedings of IEEE Infocom*, vol. 2, IEEE CS Press, Los Alamitos, Calif., pp. 775–784, March 2000.

[BarNoy:1993] A. Bar-Noy and I. Kessler, "Tracking Mobile Users in Wireless Communication Networks," *IEEE/ACM Transactions on Information Theory*, vol. 39, no. 6, pp. 1877–1886, November 1993.

[BarNoy:1995] A. Bar-Noy, I. Kessler, and M. Sidi, "Mobile Users: To Update or Not to Update," *Wireless Networks Journal*, vol. 1, no. 2, pp. 175–186, July 1995.

[Bhattacharya:2002] A. Bhattacharya and S.K. Das, "LeZi-Update: An Information-Theoretic Approach for Personal Mobility Tracking in PCS Networks," *Wireless Networks Journal*, vol. 8, no. 2–3, pp. 121–135, March–May 2002.

[Birk:1995] Y. Birk and Y. Nachman, "User Direction and Elapsed-Time Information to Reduce the Wireless Cost of Location Mobile Users in Cellular Networks," *Wireless Networks Journal*, vol. 1, no. 4, pp. 403–412, December 1995.

[Castro:2001] P. Castro, P. Chiu, T. Kremenek, and R. Muntz, "A Probabilistic Room Location Service for Wireless Networked Environments," *Proceedings of Ubicomp 2001: Ubiquitous Computing*, pp. 18–34, October 2001.

[Chakraborty:2000] A. Chakraborty, "A Distributed Architecture for Mobile, Location-Dependent Applications," master's thesis, Massachussetts Institute of Technology, May 2000.

[Cheverst:1999] K. Cheverst, N. Davies, K. Mitchell, and A. Friday, "Experiences of Developing and Deploying a Context-Aware Tourist Guide: The GUIDE Project," *Proceedings of the 6th Annual International Conference on Mobile Computing and Networking*, pp. 1–12, August 1999.

[Darrell:1998] T. Darrell, G. Gordon, M. Harville, and J. Woodfill, "Integrated Person Tracking Using Stereo, Color and Pattern Detection," *Proceedings of the Conference of Computer Vision and Pattern Recognition*, Santa Barbara, Calif., pp. 601–609, June 1998.

[Davis:2003] J. Davis, D. Sow, M. Blount, and M. Ebling, "ContextTailor: Towards a Programming Model for Context-Aware Computing," *Proceedings of the First International Workshop on Middleware for Pervasive and Ad-Hoc Computing*, June 2003.

[Denny:2003] M. Denny, M. Franklin, P. Castro, and A. Purakayastha, "Mobiscope: A Spatial Discovery Service for Mobile Network Resources," *Proceedings of the 4th International Conference on Mobile Data Management (MDM)*, January 2003.

[Harter:1994] A. Harter and A. Hopper, "A Distributed Location System for the Active Office," *IEEE Network*, vol. 8, no. 1, pp. 62–70, January–February 1994.

[Harter:1999] A. Harter, A. Hopper, P. Steggles, A. Ward, and P. Webster, "The Anatomy of a Context-Aware Application," *Proceedings of the 5th Annual International Conference on Mobile Computing and Networking*, pp. 59–68, August 1999.

[Hellebrandt:1997] M. Hellebrandt, R. Mathar, and S. Scheibenbogen, "Estimating Position and Velocity of Mobiles in a Cellular Radio Network," *IEEE Transactions on Vehicular Technology*, vol. 46. no.1, pp. 65–71, February 1997.

[Hightower:2000] J. Hightower, G. Borriello, and R. Want, "SpotON: An Indoor 3D Location Sensing Technology Based on RF Signal Strength," Technical Report UW-2000-02-02, University of Washington, February 2000.

[Hightower:2001] J. Hightower and G. Borriello, "Location Systems for Ubiquitous Computing," *IEEE Computer*, vol. 34, no. 8, pp. 57–66, August 2001.

[Huang:2003] K. Huang and M. Trivedi, "Video Arrays for Real-Time Tracking of Person, Head and Face in an Intelligent Room," *Machine Vision and Applications*, Special Issue on Omnidirectional Vision and Its Applications, vol. 14, no. 2, June 2003.

[Kaplan:1996] E.D. Kaplan, editor, *Understanding GPS: Principles and Applications*, Artech House Publishers, February 1996.

[Krumm:2000] J. Krumm, S. Harris, B. Meyers, B. Brumitt, M. Hale, and S. Shafer, "Multi-Camera Multi-Person Tracking for Easy Living," *Proceedings of the 3rd IEEE International Workshop on Visual Surveillance*, IEEE Press, Piscataway, N.J., pp. 3–10, 2000.

[Leonhardi:2002] A. Leonhardi, C. Nicu, and K. Rothermel, "A Map-Based Dead Reckoning Protocol for Updating Location Information," *Proceedings of the International Parallel and Distributed Data Processing Symposium (IPDPS 2002) Workshops*, pp., April 2002.

[Leonhardt:1996] U. Leonhardt and J. Magee, "Towards a General Location Service for Mobile Environments," *Proceedings of the Workshop on Services in Distributed and Networked Environments*, pp. 43–50, June 1996.

[Liang:1999] B. Liang and Z. Haas, "Predictive Distance-Based Mobility Management for PCS Networks," *Proceedings of IEEE INFOCOM*, March 1999.

[Misra:2004] A. Misra, A. Roy, and S.K. Das, "An Information-Theoretic Framework for Optimal Location Tracking in Multi-System 4G Wireless Networks," *IEEE INFOCOM*, March 2004.

[Ni:2003] L. Ni, Y. Liu, Y.C. Lau, and A. Patil, "LANDMARC: Indoor Location Sensing Using Active RFID," *Proceedings of the First IEEE International Conference on Pervasive Computing and Communications (PERCOM'03)*, pp. 407–415, March 2003.

[Orr:2000] R.J. Orr and G.D. Abowd, "The Smart Floor: A Mechanism for Natural User Identification and Tracking," *Proceedings of the Conference on Human Factors in Computing Systems*, ACM Press, New York, 2000.

[Pollini:1997] G.P. Pollini and I.C. Li, "A Profile-Based Location Strategy and Its Performance," *IEEE Journal on Selected Areas in Communications*, vol. 15, no. 8, pp. 1415–1424, 1997.

[Priyantha:2000] N. Priyantha, A. Chakraborty, and H. Balakrishnan, "The Cricket Location Support System," *Proceedings of the 6th International Conference on Mobile Computing and Networking*, pp. 32–43, August 2000.

[Priyantha:2001] N. Priyantha, A. Miu, H. Balakrishnan, and S. Teller, "The Cricket Compass for Context-Aware Mobile Applications," *ACM Mobile Computing and Networking*, pp. 32–43, 2001.

[Raab:1979] F. Raab et al., "Magnetic Position and Orientation Tracking System," *IEEE Transactions on Aerospace and Electronic Systems*, pp. 775–784, September 1979.

[Rappaport:1996] T. Rappaport, J. Reed, and B. Woerner, "Position Location Using Wireles Communications on Highways of the Future," *IEEE Communications Magazine*, pp. 33–41, October 1996.

[RFI] RFI Technologies, "The PinPoint Local Positioning System"; available at http://www.rftechnologies.com/pinpoint/solutions.htm

[Rose:1995] C. Rose and R. Yates, "Minimizing the Average Cost of Paging Under Delay Constraints," *Wireless Networks Journal*, vol. 1, no. 2, pp. 211–219, July 1995.

[Roy:2003] A. Roy, S.K. Das Bhaumik, A. Bhattacharya, K. Basu, D. Cook, and S.K. Das, "Location Aware Resource Management in Smart Homes," *Proceedings of the First IEEE International Conference on Pervasive Computing and Communications (PERCOM'03)*, pp. 481–488, March 2003.

[Schilit:1994] B. Schilit and M. Theimer, "Disseminating Active Map Information to Mobile Hosts," *IEEE Network Magazine*, pp. 22–32, September–October 1994.

[Syrjarinne:2001] J. Syrjarinne, "Wireless-Assisted GPS: Keeping Time with Mobiles," *GPS World Magazine*, January 2001.

[Tabbane:1995] S. Tabbane, "An Alternative Strategy for Location Tracking," *IEEE Journal on Selected Areas in Communications*, vol. 12, no. 5, pp. 880–892, 1995.

[Want:1992] R. Want, A. Hopper, V. Falcao, and J. Gibbons, "The Active Badge Location System," *ACM Transactions on Information Systems*, vol. 10, no. 1, pp. 91–102, January 1992.

[Weiser:1993] M. Weiser, "Some Computer Science Issues in Ubiquitous Computing," *Communications of the ACM*, vol. 36, iss. 7, pp. 75–84, July 1993.

[Wolfson:1999a] O. Wolfson, A. Sislta, S. Chamberlain, and Y. Yesha, "Updating and Querying Databases That Track Mobile Units," *Distributed and Parallel Databases Journal*, vol. 7, no. 3, pp. 1–31, 1999.

[Wolfson:1999b] O. Wolfson, A. Sistla, B. Xu, J. Zhou, and S. Chamberlain, "DOMINO: Databases for Moving Objects Tracking," *Proceedings of the ACM SIGMOD Conference 1999*, pp. 547–549, June 1999.

[Wu:2001] H. Wu, M. Jin, J Horng, and C. Ye, "Personal Paging Area Design Based on Mobile's Moving Behaviors," *Proceedings of IEEE INFOCOM*, pp. 21–30, March 2001.

[Zagami:1998] J. Zagami, S. Parl, J. Bussgang, and K. Melilo, "Providing Universal Location Services Using a Wireless E911 Location Network," *IEEE Communications Magazine*, pp. 66–71, April 1998.

[Zhang:2002] J. Zhang and L. Gruenwald, "Spatial and Temporal Aware Trajectory Mobility Profile Based Location Management for Mobile Computing," *Proceedings of the International Database and Expert Systems Applications (DEXA) Workshop on Mobile Databases and Distributed Systems*, pp. 716–720, September 2002.

[Ziv:2003] J. Ziv and A. Lempel, "Compression of Individual Sequences Via Variable-Rate Coding," *IEEE Transactions on Information Theory*, vol. 24, no. 5, pp. 530–536, September 1978.

CHAPTER 10

Automated Decision Making

MANFRED HUBER

Department of Computer Science and Engineering
The University of Texas at Arlington

As everyday devices become increasingly computerized and connected, and as sensors become more prevalent in homes and in the workplace, the concept of a smart environment becomes more feasible and powerful. Equipped with sensor resources to monitor the state of the environment and of the inhabitants, and with active devices that permit the automation of tasks, such an environment can now provide services for the inhabitants and thus increase their comfort and productivity while preserving energy and other resources. Examples of such smart environments include smart homes, intelligent work spaces, and smart hospitals and health care facilities where different types of monitoring and automation can be useful. In a smart home, for example, tasks can include the automatic control of lighting, heating, and air conditioning, as well as the automation of multimedia devices, sprinkler systems, and other devices throughout the home. The main objective here would be to maximize the inhabitants' comfort while minimizing the required interactions with the home and optimizing energy consumption. In an intelligent work space, automated tasks might include setting up a video conference or providing information services in order to increase the productivity of the employees. Other types of services that can be provided by smart environments are surveillance and monitoring functions where the system detects unusual behavior and can then issue appropriate warnings. The major power of smart environments here stems from their ability to make a range of autonomous decisions and to adapt to the preferences and needs of the inhabitants.

Most automation technologies available today are concerned largely with providing easy and remote access to functions in the home. The most common automation functions are preprogrammed timers and set points. Only recently have the first devices become available that can perform limited tasks autonomously. These include robotic devices such as automated lawn mowers, pool cleaners, and

---

Smart Environments: Technologies, Protocols, and Applications, edited by D.J. Cook and S.K. Das
ISBN 0-471-54448-5 © 2005 John Wiley & Sons, Inc.

vacuum cleaners. Similarly, the first devices have been developed that provide customization to the user in order to automate tasks more effectively. The most notable example of this is the learning TV recorder. Here a service is provided that models the user's taping and TV viewing preferences and, as a result, records matching TV programs autonomously without requiring the user to program them. While these are the first steps on the way to automated services in smart environments, they are still very limited and require significant work on the part of the service provider.

To fully tap into the potential of smart environments, it is necessary to employ more comprehensive and complex decision-making technologies that can adapt to the environment's inhabitants and perform complex decisions in accordance with general performance metrics. In particular, the technologies must be able to handle the high complexity of these environments, which might include large numbers of sensors to determine the state of the environment.

This chapter provides an overview of several artificial intelligence techniques for decision making in the context of smart environments. A range of techniques and applications are summarized, followed by a more detailed discussion of the decision-making component used in the MavHome smart home project. Finally, the chapter discusses important issues and techniques related to ensuring safety in the presence of automated actions and introduces techniques aimed at scaling decision-making systems to more complex environments.

10.1 DECISION-MAKING APPROACHES

A wide range of techniques and formalisms for automatic decision making have been developed and used in different applications. The decision-making task is defined here as the process of determining the action that should be taken by the system in the given situation in order to optimize a given performance metric. Decision-making algorithms therefore establish a mapping from the known information about the state of the environment and the inhabitants, gathered from current and past observations, to a decision to be made at the current point in time.

Within smart environments, these processes can take multiple forms. For relatively independent parts of the environment, decision making can consist of making a single decision based on a limited set of local observations. An example of such a component is a sprinkler system, where once a day a decision is made on whether the lawn should be watered based on the moisture level of the soil and the chance of rain in the weather forecast.

A second type of decision that is common in smart environments involves a feedback control system that regulates a particular subsystem in order to achieve and maintain a setpoint for a particular variable. Typical examples of such components are low-level lighting and heating control systems where either the illumination level or the room temperature is to be held at a particular, predetermined level.

The third and most complex decision problem considered here involves the construction of a sequence of decisions that have to be taken in order to optimize a general performance metric such as inhabitant comfort and energy consumption.

Compared to the previous two decision problems, this case does not require a decomposition of the environment into independent components and thus is capable of optimizing the overall performance of the automation. For example, for a task where the inhabitant gets up in the morning, takes a shower, and then leaves the home, a sequential decision maker could determine that it should turn on the bathroom light when the alarm goes off, and that it should turn off all the lights and lower the temperature of the heating system after the inhabitant leaves the house. To be able to determine optimal sequences of actions for a given scenario, the decision algorithms used here have to reason based on a large amount of state information, as well as with a potentially enormous number of possible action combinations. This is particularly important when decisions are made in a time-driven fashion when the decision-making algorithm has to determine at regular intervals what action to perform. To reduce this problem, sequential decision problems are often better cast as event-driven systems where decisions have to be made only when an event such as an inhabitant's action or a significant change in the sensor values occurs. Mozer and Miller [MM98] illustrate the advantages of transforming a complex control problem into an event-driven scenario by demonstrating that an otherwise nearly intractable real-world control problem can be solved straight forwardly when cast in terms of an event-based segmentation of time. (See also Chapter 12.)

The following sections introduce some of the decision algorithms that have been developed. Particular emphasis is placed on techniques that have direct applications in intelligent environments.

10.1.1 Reactive and Rule-Based Decision Systems

One of the major drawbacks of current home automation devices that provide pre-programmable timer functions is that their activation is not context-dependent. For example, a timed heating system will turn up the temperature at the preset time even if the inhabitants are not at home. To provide more flexibility and better performance, it would thus be important that automated decisions are made with respect to the context of the home. In this situation, for example, the decision maker should turn up the temperature in the morning only if the inhabitants are at home.

One approach for the design of a context-specific decision maker is the use of rule-based programming. In such a system, decisions are based on a set of facts and rules, encoding the state of the environment and the inhabitants, and a set of condition-action mappings, respectively. A rule here fires if all of its conditions are covered by the facts in the database. Sensor readings and actions, in turn, change the set of facts. In an early version of the IRoom project at MIT, for example, a reactive rule-based system was used to make automated decisions [Kul02]. In this system, rules and facts encoded reactions of the room to particular contexts, and were constructed and evaluated using JESS [FH03], a rule-based programming language. For example, the system could contain a rule that would encode *if user enters the room then turn on lights*, which would cause the IRoom to turn on the lights every time a user enters. One of the main problems with rule-based systems is that they generally require large numbers of carefully designed rules in order to cover all possible contexts. Furthermore, when using condition-action rules, these systems rely on a conflict resolution mechanism to determine which rule to actually fire if multiple rules are active.

Another approach to capturing the environment control problem in terms of rules is the application of Fuzzy Logic [Zad65]. Fuzzy Logic permits representation of rules in terms of fuzzy membership functions and thus facilitates the construction of a rule-based system that maps real-valued inputs to real-valued outputs. While this framework has been applied successfully to many low-level control problems such as the control of microwave ovens or video cameras [Zim99], so far it does not scale well to more complex inferences and controls.

Influence diagrams [HM84] provide a mechanism to represent a decision system in the presence of uncertainty. In this model, state attributes are represented probabilistically, and decisions are made using probabilistic inference within the network. Figure 10.1 shows a simple inference network for a sprinkler system.

Here the oval nodes are chance nodes representing state attributes in the form of random variables, while the rectangle indicates a decision node containing all actions available to the decision maker. By using random variables for state attributes, this framework permits explicit capture of uncertainties present in the observations and actions. The diamond indicates a utility node and represents the system's utility function, which assigns a single number that corresponds to the desirability or quality of the given situation or situation/action pair. If the utility function is chosen in accordance with the principles of utility theory [How77] and integrated with the probabilistic state representation captured in the chance nodes, inference networks can make optimal decisions using the maximum expected utility principle [RN95]. To compute this value correctly, chance nodes are linked through

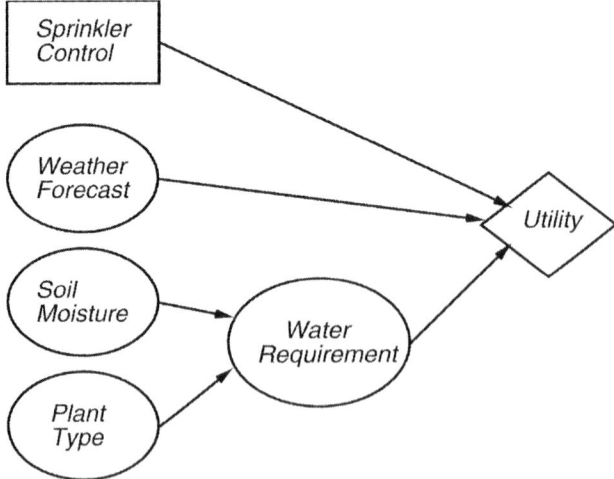

Figure 10.1 Simple inference network for sprinkler control.

conditional probabilities indicating the interrelation of the state attributes. Nodes are connected to the utility node through weights that define the particular node's influence on the quality of a system. Decisions in inference networks are made by evaluating the probabilities of all the chance nodes, computing the utility values corresponding to each of the action choices, and then selecting the action that results in the highest utility value. In the example in Figure 10.1, observations in terms of the soil moisture level and the type of grass on the lawn influence the water requirement. This, together with the likelihood of rain taken from the weather forecast, determines the utility of the sprinkler control actions. For example, if the likelihood of rain is high and the likelihood that the soil is wet is also high, the utility of the action to turn on the sprinkler system will be very low, while the utility of the action corresponding to leaving the sprinklers turned off is high. This, in turn, would cause the decision system to leave the sprinkler system turned off.

10.1.2 Planning Algorithms

The largest drawback of the techniques presented in the previous section is that the decision systems have to be constructed manually by the inhabitant of the environment or by a programmer. As a result, they are most useful for relatively simple and well-understood decision problems.

Planning provides a framework that permits decision-making agents to determine autonomously the best actions using an internal model of the environment. The planning system uses a model of the behavior of the environment and descriptions of the effects of the available actions in order to predict what the outcome of a particular sequence of actions would be. A solution in the form of a sequence of actions that leads to the desired task objective is generated using a planning mechanism.

Graphplan [BF95] is a popular and efficient planning algorithm that permits the construction of action sequences that perform a given task. It uses a plan graph to guide the search process, resulting in a significant speedup compared to traditional planners. [PC00] uses a decision theoretic version of graphplan to construct action sequences for a mobile robot to move a ball through an obstacle course.

Mozer et al. [MVD97] use a fixed-horizon search technique to plan optimal controls for a heating system in the Adaptive Home in order to optimize the comfort of the inhabitants while minimizing energy consumption. Using predictive models of room occupancy and of the thermal characteristics of the home, the planning algorithm searches for the sequence of actions that would minimize the accumulated cost function representing energy cost and occupant comfort. Models here are represented in the form of lookup tables and neural networks. (A more detailed description of this system can be found in Chapter 12.)

Another approach to planning optimal action sequences in situations where the overall objective is to optimize a known reward signal and where the system can be modeled as a Markov Decision Problem (MDP) is the use of dynamic programming [Ber87]. Here the known reward function is backed up through the state space to compute the utility function for each state and the associated optimal policy.

A wide range of other planning algorithms have been designed and used over the years. [RN95] provides a good overview of different planning approaches and discusses their advantages and disadvantages.

10.1.3 Learning Algorithms

One of the challenges arising in smart environments is that the optimal decision patterns are often dependent on the individual inhabitant and thus are hard to determine a priori. For example, temperature and lighting preferences vary across different users. Similarly, different inhabitants have very different expectations and preferences with respect to which parts of a larger application should be automated to increase their comfort. As a result, the previously described programming or planning approaches to decision making will generally not provide optimal control strategies unless the system designer or user is willing to construct customized models. This, in turn, puts a large burden on the inhabitant or the system programmer, who is required to determine the appropriate models.

Machine learning techniques provide a powerful means of addressing these challenges by introducing a mechanism through which the home can adapt autonomously to the inhabitants.

A wide range of supervised learning algorithms exist that permit a system to be trained to make decisions that conform to the ones specified in a training set. This enables the system to generalize from the training set to novel situations and can thus reduce the amount of time required to program the system. Such learning systems include decision tree classifiers, feedforward neural networks, nearest neighbor algorithms, and other learning techniques. Mitchell's book on machine learning [Mit97] provides a good overview of many of these approaches.

While these techniques are valuable due to their generalization abilities, they require the inhabitant to provide appropriate training data with the desired control actions. As a result, they either limit the system to make decisions that conform to the inhabitant's actions or require the inhabitant or programmer to have insight into the best control actions to be taken by the devices in the environment.

The following discussion concentrates on learning approaches that permit the system to acquire decision policies autonomously without the requirement for training data that includes the actual action to be learned.

In [DLRM94], Dodier et al. take advantage of the differentiability of neural networks to derive a lighting controller that learns appropriate device controls for a desired brightness level. Here, a neural network is constructed that learns a forward model that predicts how control settings on a bank of seven lights influence the brightness distribution in the room. Using this model, they use backpropagation to propagate the difference between the current brightness level and the desired setpoint in order to derive the optimal control settings for the lights. (See Chapter 12 for a more detailed description of this system.)

10.1.3.1 *Reinforcement Learning* Reinforcement learning [SB98, KLM96] is a learning framework in which action policies are learned from interactions with

the environment and a scalar reward function. In contrast to traditional supervised learning algorithms, reinforcement learning does not require knowledge of the appropriate control actions during training but instead relies on a simple, potentially delayed reward signal indicating its current performance within the given task. Furthermore, reinforcement learning can be performed with or without an existing model of the behavior of the environment. This makes it an appropriate learning framework for smart home environments where models are generally not available a priori and inhabitants often cannot provide appropriate preprogramming of optimal decisions. Rather, a reward function can be defined that captures energy cost and user comfort by monitoring the inhabitant's interactions with home devices.

Most reinforcement learning algorithms are built on the assumption that the underlying system is a Markov Decision Problem (MDP), and use either value or policy iteration techniques to estimate an optimal utility function and the corresponding policy through experimentation in the world. Sutton and Barto's book [SB98] provides an excellent introduction to different aspects of reinforcement learning algorithms and their applications.

Within the context of smart home applications, Mozer and Miller [MM98] used Q-learning [Wat89] to learn a control policy that optimally adjusts brightness setpoints for a lighting control system in accordance with user occupancy estimates. The reward function used is derived from the actual energy cost and a "discomfort cost" derived from the inhabitant's manual interactions with the lighting controls. Given this reward, the decision learner explores different setpoints and estimates their utility under the prevalent user movement patterns. In doing this, it learns an optimal control policy for the home's lighting system with respect to the particular user's preferences. (A more detailed description of this system can be found in Chapter 12.)

In [CB95], Crites and Barto used reinforcement learning to learn an optimal decision strategy for elevator scheduling in an office building. These experiments showed that with the correct representation, the reinforcement learning system performs comparably to the best available elevator scheduling programs without the need for complex modeling.

In addition to these domains, reinforcement learning has been applied to industrial tasks such as the control of a candy packing process, robot control [PVS03, SK02, Gul92], game playing [Tes95], and a wide range of other tasks.

10.2 AUGMENTING DECISION MAKING WITH PREDICTIVE MODELS

Predictive models of the behavior of the environment and of the inhabitants are an important component of all model-based decision-making approaches discussed here. While such models can sometimes be constructed by hand, they are frequently inhabitant-specific and thus require a considerable amount of work by the inhabitant or a programmer. As an alternative, such models can be learned from user interaction data using prediction algorithms.

In smart environments, two models are generally required. The first model captures the properties of the environment such as heat propagation, electricity costs, lighting parameters, etc. The second model captures the inhabitants' behavior and preferences by extracting their interaction patterns with the devices and the sensors in the environment. Particularly the latter model is generally difficult to construct a priori, illustrating the need for predictive modeling mechanism to complement the decision-making component. (A detailed introduction to prediction techniques is given in Chapter 8.)

Besides providing a model for use by the decision maker, the predictions of the inhabitant's interactions with the environment provide a valuable heuristic for planning approaches or a bootstrap mechanism for learning-based decision makers, since they include a basic profile of the user's task preferences.

10.3 CASE STUDY: DECISION MAKING IN MAVHOME

The goal of the decision-making component in MavHome is to enable the home to automate basic functions in order to optimize the overall utility of the home and the comfort of the inhabitants. One important aspect of this comfort is the number of tasks the inhabitants have to perform themselves.

While prediction algorithms can anticipate future actions performed by inhabitants and can thus form a basis for automating interactions, blind automation of all inhabitant actions is frequently not the desired solution. In particular, the action sequence performed by an inhabitant is often not the optimal strategy for an automated home. For example, an inhabitant might turn on the hallway light in the morning before opening the blinds in the living room. However, the act of turning on the light is necessary only because the inhabitant would otherwise have to reach the living room in the dark before being able to open the blinds. An automatic house agent, on the other hand, could open the blinds in the living room before the inhabitant leaves the bedroom, thus alleviating the need for the hallway lights. Similarly, turning down the air conditioning after the inhabitant leaves the house and turning it back up some time before he returns would be more energy efficient than turning the air conditioning to maximum after arriving at the house in order to cool it as fast as possible. As a result, the decision-making component should not directly mimic the actions of the inhabitant but rather learn to perform actions that optimize a given utility metric. In this process, it should use the inhabitant's predictions as a guide, since these predictions generally provide important information about the correct actions.

10.3.1 A Reinforcement Learning Agent for MavHome

To address these requirements, the decision-making component of MavHome uses reinforcement learning [KLM96] to acquire a policy that optimizes the comfort of the inhabitants while reducing energy usage. Here the agent learns autonomously from delayed rewards rather than from a teacher, thus reducing the requirement for the home's inhabitants to supervise or program the system. To learn a strategy, the decision maker explores the effects of its actions over time and uses this experience to construct control policies that optimize the expected future reward.

In the case of MavHome, the reinforcement learning algorithm is implemented in an event-driven framework where new decisions are made whenever a change in the state of the home occurs. To make correct decisions in terms of automating devices, the state of the decision-making component has to include not only the state of all the devices in the home, but also information about the behavior of the inhabitants. While the former can be easily determined in MavHome, the latter can generally only be inferred from the inhabitants' interactions with the sensors and devices in the home. To address this issue without the need for a prohibitively complex inhabitant tracking system, the approach proposed here uses the ALZ prediction algorithm [GC03] (see also Chapter 8) to determine the local dynamics of the inhabitants' behavior in terms of their device interactions. As a result, a policy is learned here on a state space $S = \{s_i\}$ consisting of the states of the devices in the home, d, and of the predictions of the inhabitants' behavior, p.

$$S: D \times P, \quad s_t = (d_t, p_t).$$

Inclusion of the prediction here serves as a representation of the inhabitants' state and intentions and assists in resolving state ambiguities.

To learn a control policy in this system, a reward function, r, has to be defined that captures user comfort and operating costs within the environment. Using this reward function, Q-learning [Wat89] is used to approximate an optimal action strategy by incrementally estimating the utility value, $Q(s_t, a_t)$, of state/action pairs. This value is the predicted future reward that will be achieved if the agent executes action a_t in state s_t. After each action, the utility is updated as

$$Q(s_t, a_t) \leftarrow Q(s_t, a_t) + \alpha[r_{t+1} + \gamma \max_{a \in A} Q(s_{t+1}, a) - Q(s_t, a_t)].$$

After learning, the optimal action, a_t, can be determined as

$$a_t = \arg\max_{a \in A} Q(s_t, a).$$

Since one of the measures of inhabitant comfort used here is the number of manual device interactions the inhabitant is required to perform, the user prediction algorithm ALZ can also be used here to bootstrap the learning algorithm such that its initial policy automates the interactions that the user would perform. Alternatively, the policy and value function could be initialized such that the automatic decision maker initially performs no actions. The reason for such an initialization is to reduce the amount of unwanted exploration during the initial learning of the value function. Furthermore, it provides an initial performance to the decision maker and thus limits the frustration of the inhabitants resulting from excessive requirements to correct counterproductive automations.

238 AUTOMATED DECISION MAKING

10.3.2 Experiments

To validate the basic concept of the decision maker in the context of MavHome, the basic reinforcement learning system was implemented, trained, and tested on data generated using an interactive version of the MavHome synthetic data generator. In these tests, a reward function, r, was defined that provides a negative reward of -1 for every manual interaction the user has to perform, a smaller negative reward of -0.2 for each action the decision maker performs, and a cost of -0.3 for each time interval in which a lamp is turned on. The reason for the negative reward associated with automated actions is to discourage irrelevant, spurious device automations by the learning system.

To apply the reinforcement learning agent in the particular home, a compact representation for the Q-value function is constructed, since the size of the state space grows exponentially in the number of devices in the home, making an exhaustive enumeration intractable even for moderately sized homes. To address this issue, tile coding (CMAC) with five tilings [Alb71] was used in these tests as an efficient function approximator. In addition, the actions returned by the prediction algorithm were used to initialize the policy of the decision maker.

Figure 10.2 shows a sample layout of the home environment used for the simulation experiment.

Here the environment contains 20 devices, all of which, with the exception of the doors, shower, and faucets, can be automated. In addition, the agent has a "noop" action that indicates that the learning system does not want to issue an action. This is particularly important in the event-driven framework used here, where the decision maker can perform multiple device actions in a sequence and thus requires an option to stop issuing control commands.

The user pattern used by the simulator in this experiment follows the following early morning scenario: At 7:45 a.m. the alarm clock in the bedroom goes off. Bob turns off the alarm and turns on the light on his night stand. He gets up, walks over to the bathroom, and opens the door. Then he turns on the bathroom light, closes the

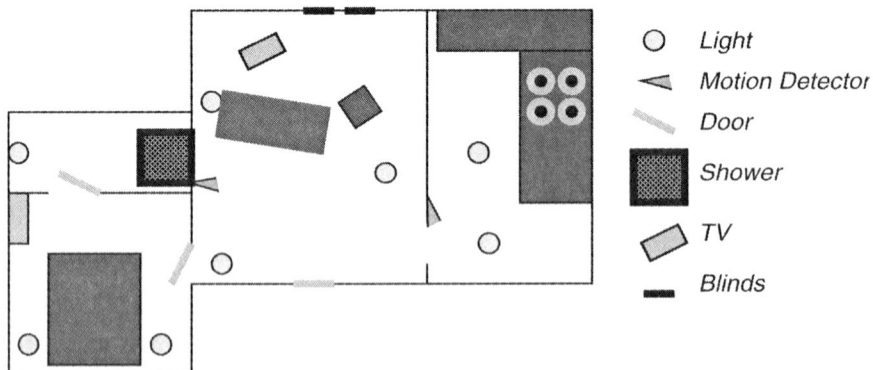

Figure 10.2 Home scenario for simulation experiment.

door, and takes a shower. After finishing his shower he opens the door, turns off the bathroom light, and goes to the closet to get dressed.

After a predictor is trained for this scenario, the Q-value function is initialized off-line to values representing the strategy that the inhabitant followed. This is achieved by repeatedly replaying the predictor's strategy and updating the Q-values appropriately. For all actions not present in the predicted strategy, Q-values are initialized to a slightly lower value than the one of the predicted user action, reducing spurious exploration of the decision maker.

After initialization, the reinforcement learning system is run with an ϵ-greedy exploration strategy in which the agent performs the best action 90% of the time and explores randomly with a probability of 10%. Figure 10.3 shows the learning curve for the decision maker.

For this graph, the learning process was repeated 20 times and the graph shows the average performance of the learning system in terms of the total reward obtained per trial. The intervals on the learning curve indicate the standard deviation between the 20 runs for the given trial. A trial here is one instance of the scenario described before. The other two curves show the performance of the predictor's policy and the reward obtained if all actions are left to the user. These graphs indicate that while the performance of the decision maker initially drops below the one of the pure predictor and even below a policy without automation, it eventually outperforms both of them in this scenario. In particular, the decision maker learns to perform the scenario in the following way: At 7:45 a.m. the alarm clock in the bedroom goes off. The decision maker turns off the alarm and turns on the light on the night stand. Bob gets up, walks to the bathroom, and opens the door. Once the door is opened, the decision learner turns on the light in the bathroom and turns off the light in the bedroom to preserve

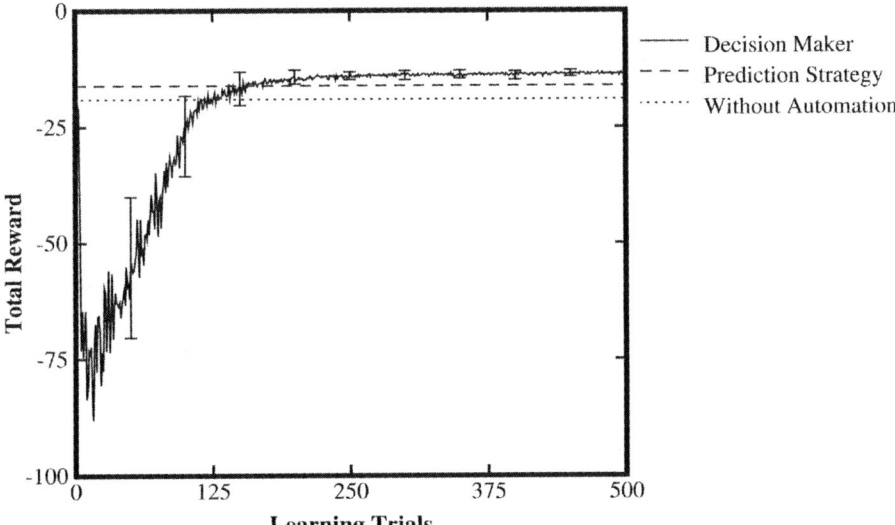

Figure 10.3 Learning performance of the system in the example scenario.

energy. Bob closes the door, takes a shower, and opens the bathroom door again. Once the door opens, the decision maker turns on the light in the bedroom and turns off the light in the bathroom. Then Bob goes to the closet to get dressed.

The performance gain is achieved here when the decision maker learns that the bedroom light is not necessary once Bob is in the bathroom and the bathroom light is turned on.

However, Figure 10.3 also shows that even though the decision maker is bootstrapped with the predictor's strategy, and thus initially performs in the same way as the predictor, the performance drops below both the predictor's and the purely manual strategy in the early stages of learning. To analyze the cause of this drop and to attempt to assess what effect the learning phase would have on the experience of an inhabitant, Figure 10.4 breaks the system performance into individual components. In particular, it shows the energy consumption and the number of required user-environment interactions throughout the learning process.

These graphs show that energy consumption drops immediately below the one achieved manually or with the predictor's strategy. The slightly higher energy consumption of the prediction-based system compared to manual control here results from the fact that the event-based decision maker has to turn on the lights slightly earlier than the inhabitant. The graph on the right-hand side of Figure 10.4 shows the number of actions that the inhabitant has to perform manually. To a certain degree this can be interpreted as a measure of discomfort, since the inhabitant is assumed to prefer not to have to activate any of the devices. In the scenario used in this experiment, the minimum number of interactions is three, since the doors and the shower are not automated. The predictor's strategy performs optimally with respect to this criterion, while the manual execution of the scenario requires seven actions. The learning curve of the decision maker here shows that during the initial learning phase the number of interactions required by the home's inhabitant increases but then rapidly drops and eventually (after approximately 1000 trials) converges to the minimum number possible. What is just as important in order to avoid inhabitant frustration with the system is that even in the initial phase, the number of required inhabitant interactions never rises above 10 and is thus not substantially higher than without automation. The main reason for this is the bootstrapping of the reinforcement learning system with the predictor's policy.

Since the reward function used here consists of energy consumption, inhabitant interactions, and a penalty for randomly issued actions, the observations from Figure 10.4 and closer analysis of the system's behavior during learning show that the majority of the initial drop in system performance seen in Figure 10.3 is due to spurious actions performed by the decision maker. As the number of user actions required shows, however, most of these spurious actions do not require a correction by the user, but rather are reversed immediately by the decision maker.

A second experiment was performed in the context of a live demonstration of MavHome in the fall of 2002. Here a simpler reward function was used that assigned a negative reward only to the manual interactions performed in the environment. Training occurred largely off-line on data collected beforehand. Despite the presence of a larger number of people during the demonstration, the

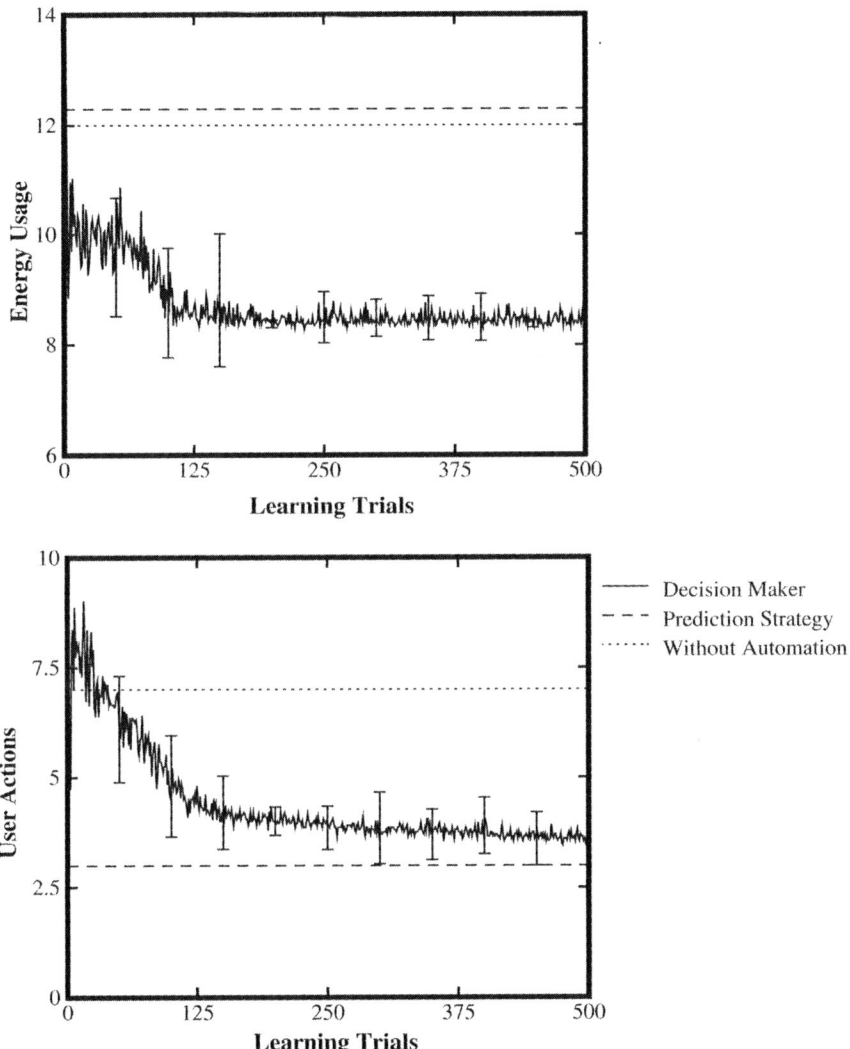

Figure 10.4 Energy consumption (left) and the number of user actions required (right).

decision-making framework and the prediction algorithm still succeeded in correctly predicting and activating the devices.

10.4 SAFETY IN AUTOMATED DECISION MAKING

An important issue that has to be addressed when applying decision making to smart environments is the assurance of safety for the inhabitants. Automation in the environment should not endanger the inhabitants or damage anything in the home. For example, it has to be assured that a computer that is in control of a heating and air conditioning system or that performs access control to the building always operates correctly and maintains the temperature within a safe range. Similarly, automatic doors or cleaning robots have to be equipped with mechanisms that prevent accidents involving the inhabitants. This is particularly important in reinforcement learning systems that have to explore their action potential in order to determine the correct control strategy.

A number of mechanisms to ensure safety constraints in control systems have been developed for different applications, including robotic systems.

Singh et al. [SCGB94] proposed a system for learning robot navigation that limits the range of learnable behavior to a set of parametric controllers, each of which is inherently safe. As a result, learned behavior cannot cause any collisions between the robot and obstacles in the environment.

For planning-based systems, separate execution monitoring and fault detection mechanisms [FHN72, Wil90] have been added during plan execution in order to detect unexpected and dangerous deviations from the expected behavior. Once a deviation is detected, a new strategy can be planned that avoids the dangerous situation.

While execution monitoring can predict potential failures, it would be desirable to reduce the risk that strategies containing dangerous actions or situations are generated at all. This is particularly important in exploration-based systems that frequently choose random actions. While limiting the system to control actions that are inherently safe would be the best solution, this is not possible in many situations, since actions that are dangerous in one context are often useful in a different situation. To address this issue, Discrete Event Systems (DES) theory [RW89, SOVG94] provides a formalism that permits constraints to be imposed on the admissible behavior a priori in order to avoid deadlock and unsafe behavior. In [HG97] this mechanism was used on a four-legged walking robot to ensure stability while the system was learning to walk. The constraints imposed here disabled all actions that could lead to a failure in the particular situation and made them inaccessible to the learning component.

When modeling a smart environment as event-driven, it might be possible to combine the DES mechanism with additional execution monitoring to enforce a set of safety and performance constraints in order to ensure correct operation of the system.

10.5 SCALING UP: DISTRIBUTED AND HIERARCHICAL DECISION-MAKING AGENTS

Another problem arising in smart environments is that the state space, and thus the complexity of the decision-making problem, increase exponentially with the number of devices in the environment. In a smart home scenario, where potentially hundreds of sensors and actuators can be present, this easily leads to an intractable problem.

To address this issue, it is necessary to develop technologies that permit smart environment components to scale gracefully to increasingly complex worlds. One possibility here is to hand-code sensor aggregation schemes to reduce the amount of data that has to be considered by the decision maker. However, this requires a thorough understanding of the details of the environment by the programmer or the inhabitant, and is thus frequently not achievable.

A second possible way to improve scaling is to decompose the problem into smaller problems to be solved. An alleviating factor is here that large-scale home or office environments can frequently be decomposed for decision-making purposes. For example, occupancy information on the second floor of a building is generally not related to light control in the kitchen on the first floor. Similarly, large ranges of sensors are unrelated to the temperature control component in the home, which can operate largely independently of the sprinkler and lighting control systems. As a result, the decision-making component can be broken into individual components that interact in order to achieve control of the complete home.

This decomposition can be performed in two ways: by modeling the system as a multiagent system where a number of individual decision makers control various aspects of the environment and interact through a communication mechanism, or by performing hierarchical decomposition, in which the home components are broken into subtasks that have to be performed in a sequence.

10.5.1 Multiagent Systems

In a multiagent system, a number of decision-making agents control different aspects of the environment and have to communicate in order to achieve the larger objective of the home. One of the main issues that has to be addressed in this framework is the distribution of shared resources. The problem arising here is that individual decision makers can interfere or rely on resources that might already be in use by a different agent. As a consequence, the agents have to compete for these resources and cooperate in achieving their objectives.

In the IHome project, Lesser et al. [LAB$^+$99] divided the environment according to individual appliances. Each appliance is associated with an agent that controls the actions for the device and potentially uses all available resources in the home. As a result, a number of agents have to cooperate in the home to perform given tasks. Cooperation and resource constraints are addressed using either a centralized or decentralized resource coordination protocol, depending on whether the resource is directly associated with one of the individual agents or not. For decentralized control, a priority-based reservation and allocation protocol called *SHARP* was developed and used.

The IRoom project at MIT also uses a mutliagent framework to address the complexity of the environment. However, here the decision maker is decomposed into applications, and each agent therefore represents a particular task [HKTH02]. In this system, a different resource manager, called Rascal, is used to coordinate the agents [Gaj01].

Weiss [Wei99] provides a good overview of multiagent systems and the associated communication and negotiation mechanisms.

10.5.2 Hierarchical Decision Systems

One of the challenges is how to decompose the environment into different parts. In multiagent systems, this is achieved by associating agents with particular resource sets. One of the problems arising with this decomposition is that a complete task in a home might involve the complete set of resources even though individual components of the task do not. A multiagent system with a device-specific decomposition must therefore achieve the complete task by means of a complex communication strategy that transfers the task objective between agents.

Hierarchical decompositions provide a different way to subdivide the environment and the task in order to reduce the complexity of the decision-making task. Here decisions are performed at varying levels of abstraction, each of which uses a more abstract set of resource representations. As a result, complete policies for the environment are represented at every level of the hierarchy.

A number of hierarchical planning systems have been developed in which strategies planned at higher levels ignore details of the task, which get subsequently refined. Examples of such systems include ABSTRIPS [Sac74] and Hierarchical Task Network Planners [EHN94].

10.5.2.1 Hierarchical Reinforcement Learning
Hierarchical reinforcement learning has created substantial interest lately, and a number of techniques have been derived to compute optimal value functions in the presence of extended actions that represent subtasks [PS97, PR97, Die98]. In this framework, the system is modeled as a Semi Markov Decision Problem (SMDP) in which decisions are made at two levels of abstraction. If an abstract action corresponding to a subtask is executed, primitive actions are selected according to the policy contained within the abstract action. Once the abstract action terminates, the next action (abstract or primitive) is picked according to the higher-level policy. Using these techniques, it has been shown that new tasks can frequently be learned faster if policies for subtasks are already available [PS97, MS98, Hub02].

While the learning algorithms have been thoroughly studied, mechanisms for the automatic construction of a subtask hierarchy, as well as hierarchical state representations, have received less attention. However, a number of techniques have been developed that attempt to determine subtasks on-line during the learning process [Dig96, MB01, GH03]. These techniques extract subgoals by examining the previous experiences and the reward function to determine which states in the underlying system are encountered repeatedly.

Similarly, a few techniques to minimize state space representations for learning have been proposed [DGL97, SV99, Die00, Asa03]. These techniques attempt to construct minimal representations that are sufficient to express the task at hand using the actions available to the decision learner.

Combining policy abstraction and state abstraction techniques can potentially lead to a system that could automatically detect subtasks that can be expressed in terms of small subsets of the system resources. For example, a decision policy for the "take shower" subtask used in the experiment in Section 10.3.2 could be learned and then used as a control decision at a higher level, dividing a morning task into "take shower," "have breakfast," and "leave for work," where each subtask consists of an entire action sequence.

10.6 CONCLUSIONS

This chapter illustrates the potential and challenges for decision-making algorithms in smart environments. These algorithm enable the environment to perform many useful tasks and improve inhabitant comfort and energy efficiency. However, they also pose many challenges in terms of safety considerations and computational efficiency in scaling to large environments. To fully utilize the potential of smart environments, these challenges will have to be tackled, possibly leading to hierarchical multiagent systems, permitting highly complex environments to be controlled according to the preferences of the inhabitants.

REFERENCES

Alb71 J.S. Albus. A theory of cerebellar Function. *Mathematical Biosciences*, 10:25–61, 1971.

Asa03 M. Asadi. State space reduction for hierarchical policy formation. Technical Report 2003–28, University of Texas at Arlington, 2003.

Ber87 D.P. Bertsekas, editor. *Dynamic Programming: Deterministic and Stochastic Models*. Prentice Hall, 1987.

BF95 A. Blum and M. Furst. Fast planning through planning graph analysis. In *Proceedings of the International Joint Conference on Artificial Intelligence*, pages 1636–1642. IJCAII, 1995.

CB95 R.H. Crites and A.G. Barto. Improving elevator performance using reinforcement learning. In *Advances in Neural Information Processing Systems 8*. Morgan Kaufmann, 1995.

DGL97 T. Dean, R. Givan, and S. Leach. Model reduction techniques for computing approximately optimal solutions for markov decision processes. In *Proceedings of CUAI*, pages 124–131, 1997.

Die98 T.G. Dietterich. *The Maxq Method for Hierarchical Reinforcement Learning*. Morgan Kaufmann, 1998.

Die00 T.G. Dietterich. State abstraction in maxq hierarchical reinforcement learning. In *Advances in Neural Information Processing Systems 12*, pages 994–1000. MIT Press, 2000.

Dig96 B. Digney. Emergent hierarchical control structures: Learning reactive/hierarchical relationships in reinforcement environments. In *From Animals to Animats*. MIT Press, pages 363–372, 1996.

DLRM94   R. Dodier, D. Lukianow, J. Ries, and M.C. Mozer. A comparison of neural net and conventional techniques for lighting control. *Applied Mathematics and Computer Science*, 4(3):447–462, 1994.

EHN94   K. Erol, J. Hendler, and D.S. Nau. HTN planning: Complexity and expressivity. In *Proceedings of the Twelfth National Conference on Artificial Intelligence (AAAI-94)*, pages 1123–1128. AAAI Press/MIT Press, 1994.

FH03   E. Friedman-Hill. *Jess in Action*. Manning Publications, 2003.

FHN72   R. Fikes, P.E. Hart, and N.J. Nilsson. Learning and executing generalized robot plans. *Artificial Intelligence*, 3(1–3):251–288, 1972.

Gaj01   K. Gajos. Rascal—a resource manager for multi agent systems in smart spaces. In *Proceedings of CEEMAS 2001*, pages 111–120, 2001.

GC03   K. Gopalratnam and D.J. Cook. Active Le Zi: An incremental parsing algorithm for device usage prediction in the smart home. In *Proceedings of the Florida Artificial Intelligence Research Symposium*, pages 38–42, 2003.

GH03   S. Goel and M. Huber. Subgoal discovery for hierarchical reinforcement learning using learned policies. In *Proceedings of the 16th International FLAIRS Conference*, pages 346–350, 2003.

Gul92   V. Gullapalli. Learning control under extreme uncertainty. In *Advances in Neural Information Processing Systems 5*, Morgan Kaufmann, pages 327–334, 1992.

HG97   M. Huber and R.A. Grupen. A feedback control structure for on-line learning tasks. *Robotics and Autonomous Systems*, 22(3–4):303–315, December 1997.

HKTH02   N. Hanssens, A. Kulkarni, R. Tuchinda, and T. Horton. Building agent-based intelligent workspaces. In *Proceedings of the ABA Conference*, pages 10–16, June 2002.

HM84   R.A. Howard and J.E. Matheson. Influence diagrams. In *The Principles and Applications of Decision Analysis*, pages 690–718. Strategic Decision Group, 1984.

How77   R.A. Howard. Risk preference. In Ronald A. Howard and James E. Matheson, editors, *Readings in Decision Analysis*, pages 429–465. Decision Analysis Group, 1977.

Hub02   M. Huber. Learning hierarchical control policies using closed-loop actions. In *Proceedings of the 6th IASTED International Conference on Artificial Intelligence and Soft Computing*, pages 356–361, July 2002.

KLM96   L.P. Kaelbling, M.L. Littman, and A.W. Moore. Reinforcement learning: A survey. *Journal of Artificial Intelligence Research*, 4: 237–285, 1996.

Kul02   A. Kulkarni. Design principles of a reactive behavioral system for the intelligent room. *Bit-stream: The MIT Journal of EECS Student Research*, pages 22–26, 2002.

LAB+99   V. Lesser, M. Atighetchi, B. Benyo, B. Horling, A. Raja, R. Vincent, T. Wagner, P. Xuan, and S.X.Q. Zhang. The UMASS intelligent home project. In *Proceedings of the Third International Conference on Autonomous Agents*, pages 291–298, January 1999.

MB01   A. McGovern and A.G. Barto. Accelerating reinforcement learning through the discovery of useful subgoals. In *Proceedings of the 6th International Symposium on Artificial Intelligence, Robotics and Automation in Space*, 2001.

Mit97   T. Mitchell, editor. *Machine Learning*. McGraw-Hill, 1997.

MM98   M.C. Mozer and D. Miller. Parsing the stream of time: The value of event-based segmentation in a complex real-world control problem. In C.L. Giles and M. Gori, editors, *Adaptive Processing of Temporal Sequences and Data Structures*, pages 370–388. Springer Verlag, 1998.

MS98 A. McGovern and R.S. Sutton. Macro-actions in reinforcement learning: An empirical analysis. Technical Report 98–70, University of Massachusetts, Amherst, 1998.

MVD97 M.C. Mozer, L. Vidmar, and R.H. Dodier. The neurothermostat: Predictive optimal control of residential heating systems. In Michael C. Mozer, Michael I. Jordan, and Thomas Petsche, editors, *Advances in Neural Information Processing Systems 9*, pages 953–959. MIT Press, 1997.

PC00 G. Peterson and D.J. Cook. Decision-theoretic planning in the graphplan framework. In *AIPC Workshop on Decision-Theoretic Planning*, 2000.

PR97 R. Parr and S. Russell. Reinforcement learning with hierarchies of machines. In *Advances in Neural Information Processing Systems 10*. MIT Press, pages 1043–1049, 1997.

PS97 D. Precup and R.S. Sutton. Multi-time models for temporally abstract planning. In *Advances in Neural Information Processing Systems 10*, pages 1050–1056. MIT Press, 1997.

PVS03 J. Peters, S. Vijayakumar, and S. Schaal. Reinforcement learning for humanoid robots. In *Third IEEE International Conference on Humanoid Robotics 2003*, 2003.

RN95 S. Russell and P. Norvig, editors. *Artificial Intelligence: A Modern Approach*, 2nd ed. Prentice Hall, 1995.

RW89 P.J.G. Ramadge and W.M. Wonham. The control of discrete event systems. *Proceedings of the IEEE*, 77(1):81–97, January 1989.

Sac74 E.D. Sacerdoti. Planning in a hierarchy of abstraction spaces. *Artificial Intelligence*, 5(2):115–135, 1974.

SB98 R.S. Sutton and A.G. Barto. *Reinforcement Learning: An Introduction*. MIT Press, 1998.

SCGB94 S. Singh, C. Connolly, R. Grupen, and A. Barto. Robust reinforcement learning in motion planning. In *Advances in Neural Information Processing Systems 6*. Morgan Kaufmann, pages 355–662, 1994.

SK02 W.D. Smart and L.P. Kaelbling. Effective reinforcement learning for mobile robots. In *Proceedings of the IEEE International Conference on Robotics and Automation*, pages 3404–3410, May 2002.

SOVG94 M. Sobh, J.C. Owen, K.P. Valvanis, and D. Gracani. A subject-indexed bibliography of discrete event dynamic systems. *IEEE Robotics and Automation Magazine*, 1(2):14–20, 1994.

SV99 P. Stone and M. Veloso. Team-partitioned, opaque-transition reinforcement learning. In *Third International Conference on Autonomous Agents*. Springer Verlag, pages 206–212, 1999.

Tes95 G. Tesauro. Temporal difference learning and td-gammon. *Communications of the ACM*, 38(3):58–67, 1995.

Wat89 C.J.C.H. Watkins. *Learning from Delayed Rewards*. PhD thesis, Cambridge University, 1989.

Wei99 G. Weiss, editor. *Multi-Agent Systems*. MIT Press, 1999.

Wil90 D.E. Wilkins. Can ai planners solve practical problems? *Computational Intelligence*, 6(4):232–246, 1990.

Zad65 L.A. Zadeh. Fuzzy sets. *Information and Control*, 8(3):338–353, 1965.

Zim99 H.-J. Zimmermann, editor. *Practical Applications of Fuzzy Technologies*. Kluwer Academic Publishers, 1999.

CHAPTER 11

Security, Privacy and Trust Issues in Smart Environments

P.A. NIXON, W. WAGEALLA, C. ENGLISH, and S. TERZIS
Department of Computer and Information Sciences
University of Strathclyde

11.1 INTRODUCTION

Recent advances in networking, handheld computing, and sensor technologies have driven research toward the realization of Mark Weiser's dream of calm and ubiquitous computing (variously called *pervasive computing*, *ambient computing*, *active spaces*, the *disappearing computer* or *context-aware computing*). In turn, this has led to the emergence of smart environments as one significant facet of research in this domain.

A *smart environment*, or *smart space*, is a region of the real world that is extensively equipped with sensors, actuators, and computing components [1]. In effect, the smart space becomes part of a larger information system: all actions within the space potentially affect the underlying computer applications, which may themselves affect the space through the actuators. Such smart environments have tremendous potential within many application areas to improve the utility of a space. Consider the potential offered by a smart environment that prolongs the time an elderly or infirm person can live an independent life or the potential offered by a smart environment that supports vicarious learning.

So, smart environments, by definition, are designed to exploit rich combinations of small distributed sensing/computational nodes to identify and deliver personalized services to the user when they are interacting and exchanging information with the environment. Within such environments solutions for users must be secure, private, and trustworthy. Security involves the cryptographic techniques used to secure the communications channels and required data. Privacy in this context encompasses reasoning about trust and the risk involved in interactions between users. Trust, therefore, controls the amount of information that can be

---

Smart Environments: Technologies, Protocols, and Applications, edited by D.J. Cook and S.K. Das
ISBN 0-471-54448-5 © 2005 John Wiley & Sons, Inc.

revealed, and risk analysis allows us to evaluate the expected benefit that would motivate users to participate in these interactions. In this chapter, we survey selected work in these three disparate, but related, areas and situate them in the unique problems of smart environments.

In particular, this domain of technology has at its core a collection of assorted contextual sensing information, such as the computers' context, the user context, and the physical context [2], that is subsequently used for the delivery of personalized services. A typical example of context gathering would be the placement of sensors in rooms and offices to enable the collection of data such as location of their inhabitants. The vast amount of personal information collected by such systems has led to growing concerns about the security, privacy, and trustworthiness of such systems and the data they hold. This is a core problem, as users concerned about their private information are likely to refuse participation in such systems, thus slowing or stopping the deployment of smart environments. Therefore, in this chapter we consider the broad issues of security, privacy, and trust in smart environments. We start by considering the characteristics that make smart environments unique, in terms of the requirements they place on security, privacy, and trust.

11.1.1 What Makes It Different?

In [3] the following question is asked in regard to privacy: *what makes ubiquitous computing any different from other computer science domains?* Langenheinrich goes on to identify four key motivators:

1. **Ubiquity:** The infrastructure will be everywhere, consequently affecting every aspect of life.
2. **Invisibility:** The infrastructure will be cognitively or physically invisible to the users; the users will have no idea of when or where they are using the computer.
3. **Sensing:** Input to the ever-present invisible computer will consist of everything the user does or says, rather than everything the user types.
4. **Memory amplification:** Every aspect of these interactions, no matter how personal, has the potential to be stored, queried, and replayed.

The descriptions of these four elements show that ubiquitous computing and smart environments will be characterized by massive numbers of almost invisible miniature sensing devices that can potentially observe and store information about our most personal experiences. It is worth noting that these observations are not merely an amplification of the current concerns of Internet users with desktop computers. These observations show the deep societal impact that such technology will have.

From a technological perspective, they also highlight a fundamental change. In most areas where security, privacy, and trust are investigated we can clearly identify the intended interaction endpoints. In an e-commerce transaction, it may be ones web browser and the shops website; in a targeted online communication, it may be between two or more specific people. However, in a smart environment, the interaction endpoints are not cognitively or physically visible; users may have no idea that they are engaging in a computer-mediated communication. In these situations, a password spoken aloud in an empty room could be a security hazard. We can imagine more personal situations in everyday living that would be equally uncomfortable and that would destroy our privacy or undermine our trust.

In addition to these operational characteristics, there are a number of technology-related characteristics that compound the problem. A smart environment [4] can be viewed as a composite space composed of many individual objects. These objects will be either fixed or mobile, and for our purposes can be broken down into the following categories:

- **Fixed sensors:** These are items that do not have computational or processing ability but do have state, which can be ascertained using sensors.[1] Examples range from simple door and window sensors (that can be open or shut), lights sensors (on, off, or dimmed), and thermostatic controls to rich sensors such as video surveillance systems. Such fixed sensors are used to provide a given environment its core *sense* of its surroundings.
- **Mobile sensors:** We differentiate fixed from mobile sensors for two reasons. First, certain types of sensing must be done on the move—such as gathering locational information from Global Positioning System (GPS)–like sensors. Second, an individual or a device may want to distinguish the sensed information it gathers from that supplied by a given environment.
- **Fixed computing elements:** These elements consist of objects that have processing and data storage ability but no method of moving. Obvious examples include servers, printers, desktop computers, coffee machines, photocopiers, and air conditioners.
- **Mobile computing elements:** These elements exhibit the properties of fixed computing entities but also have the freedom of movement. Examples include mobile communicators (phone/pda), intelligent wheelchairs, mobile personal computers, vehicles, and task-specific robots.

Campbell et al. [5] also identify a similar set of issues and characteristics. We have highlighted these four types of objects, as they emphasize the contrasting fixed and mobile computation and sensing elements that are now core, rather than peripheral, elements of the problem. Moreover, in identifying these characteristics, we hint at a fundamental part of the technology problem; in any given smart environment, no one part of the system has full knowledge or full control over what is stored, sensed, or communicated. In the following sections, we will consider each aspect of security, privacy, and trust in the light of these observations.

---
[1] http://www.sensormag.com has a comprehensive list of off-the-shelf sensors.

11.2 SECURITY

11.2.1 Motivation

The need for security in smart environments is identical, at some level, to the need for security in all other computing systems: to ensure that information is not stolen, modified, or access to it denied. The recurring argument we present in this chapter that differentiates smart environments is the massive diversity of information that can now be misused and thus needs to be protected. In smart environments, the carrier of a device with sensing and wireless network capabilities can become an unwitting spy by carrying information from one environment to another or by collecting information about third parties unintentionally. A comparable observation is also made in [6] about the increased context of operation for smart environments, referred to as the *trust context space* (Figure 11.1). In subsequent sections, we address design and good practice aspects of respecting privacy and decision processes to identify trustworthy interactions. In this section, we review some basic principles of security that must underpin the whole process.

11.2.2 Definitions

Security is not merely about cryptography [7,8]; it is also about assessing the risk of bad things happening in a given environment or situation and developing safeguards and countermeasures to militate against these risks. In this chapter, we have taken two security concerns, privacy and trust, and extracted them as important elements in their own right. However, security encompasses other issues as well. In its broadest definition security is widely accepted [7] to include the three main properties of confidentiality, integrity, and availability. Confidentiality is concerned with protecting the information/service from unauthorized access; integrity is concerned with

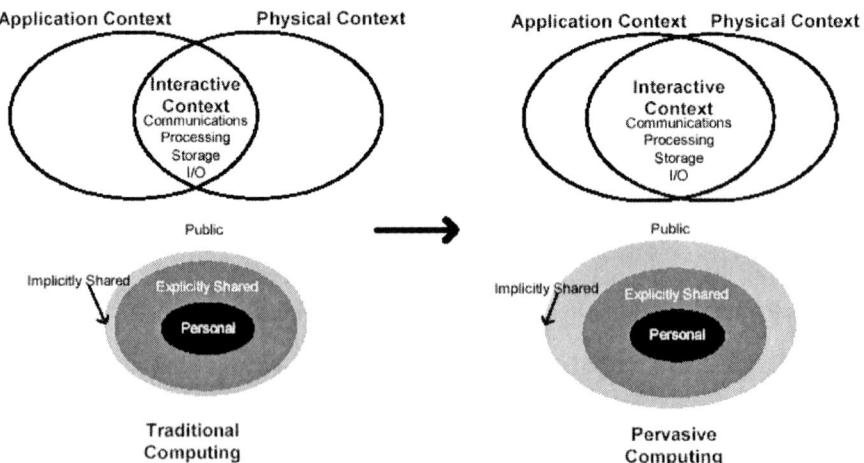

Figure 11.1 Trust context space [6].

protecting the information/service from unauthorized changes; and availability is concerned with ensuring that the information/service remains accessible. In the following section, we consider each of these aspects of the security problem and highlight a very small subset of the technologies. The interested reader is referred to [7,8] for broader coverage of technologies and the state of the art in security in pervasive computing, respectively.

11.2.3 Security in Smart Environments

Confidentiality and Integrity are essentially about encryption and decryption. Smart's book on cryptography [8] provides a thorough and detailed discussion of the many and varied cryptographic techniques. Encryption, decryption, and hence authentication in a smart space are complicated by the characteristics of the environment. Key to these environments is the largely decentralized and dynamic nature of the principals[2] and their interactions due to the transient nature of relationships among principals roaming among administrative domains. For authentication, Public Key Infrastructures (PKI) rely on a certification authority (a trusted third party) hierarchy that can verify that the principal carrying the key is the owner of the key. The rigid structure of this fixed hierarchy of authorities has limitations for a decentralized environment where two entities' certification hierarchies may not intersect. An approach to solving this problem originated with Pretty Good Privacy (PGP) [9], a tool intended to provide the general public with reliable e-mail cryptography by removing the need for hierarchies of certification authorities (CAs). The approach involves a decentralized *web of trust* in which individuals sign the key certificates of others, stating that the key in the certificate belongs to the person stated. These signatories, called *introducers*, are allocated specific trust levels with regard to their status as introducers, allowing for fine-grained evolution of the *trust in introducer* relationship. Chains (possibly multiple chains) of certificates can be formed based on these introducer relationships between entities, thereby propagating trust in the validity of the key in question from one end of the chain to the other. These intersecting chains of trust relationships form the web of trust. Local policies are defined in terms of the amount of each trust level required before a key certificate is considered valid. For example, two fully trusted introducers and one marginally trusted introducer claiming the validity of a key certificate may suffice to indicate that the key is valid. In this sense, each of these introducer trust relationships constitutes a piece of evidence or an indication of the validity of a key.

It is important to note, as pointed out by Germano Caronni [10], that although the web of trust approach is useful as a more generic solution than the hierarchical approach, it is potentially more difficult to manage. Because it is a more dynamic approach to authentication, there are no hard and fast rules regarding the formation of individual relationships. In PGP, this is done offline through user intervention, a principle at odds with Mark Weiser's vision of *calm technology*. The provision of

---

[2]*Principal* is the term used in security to signify the entities (people, agents, devices, etc.) of interest.

automated reasoning capabilities is hampered by the fact that portable devices may have limited processing and storage capabilities, which also affects the ability to provide suitable cryptographic security for confidentiality. In [11] it is also noted that the web of trust does not solve the problem of security for smart environments. In these environments, there may be no immediate recourse to the global infrastructure to establish trust in the introducers; hence, all introducers drop to a base trust value of unknown. Furthermore, as Phil Zimmermann, the creator of PGP, points out, "Trusting a key is not the same as trusting a key's owner," implying a shortcoming of PGP and PKIs: that trust in the identity of a principal is not the same as trust in that principal's behavior. This is a vital issue in environments that may be inhabited by principals unknown to the system. These problems highlight the need for more dynamic models of security/confidentiality that better reflect the properties of smart environments.

Security has traditionally focused on the integrity of messages in transit. Many techniques for this have been developed, and despite mobile device limitations, cryptography to all intents and purposes deals with this problem. While this obviously still holds for any smart environment, additional problems are introduced by the increasing use of wireless technologies within smart environments [12]. With these technologies being used for multiple access and dynamic connections, it becomes much more difficult to prevent eavesdropping on communications. In addition to this level of physical insecurity of the communication medium, many wireless protocol implementations fail to implement the security features of the protocol specification. Even when these features are implemented properly, the security protocols are not very resistant to attacks, as documented in work on Bluetooth's wireless security [13]. Concerns arise both for the security of wireless networks against attack from roaming devices and for the security of the roaming devices against a wireless network capable of malicious behavior. Furthermore, tracking malicious users becomes difficult in the case of mobile devices. Additional problems arise as computing becomes more invisible, and it becomes more difficult to ensure that the system is fulfilling the security needs of a user who may be unaware of its existence. Indeed, users are increasingly unaware of the security implications of such technology. To address these concerns, security configuration should be removed from the user as much as possible to avoid misunderstood security configurations causing problems for smart space integrity, allowing devices to be compromised.

Further security issues concern the integrity of the devices themselves; the devices are mobile and may arrive in a given smart environment from an unknown domain. The problem is that even if a given device has been seen before, it may have been altered during its absence. Theft of a device implies theft of the identity that the device represents; thus, a known device may behave very differently when controlled by a different and possibly malicious user. Consequently, no claims can be made about the device's integrity. Furthermore, there are concerns about the integrity of sensors. While cryptographic measures can be taken to protect data between the sensor and application, preventing a malicious user from masquerading as a sensor, the problem of protecting against false information entering the sensor itself must be addressed. This type of attack might be carried out much more easily if measures such as accurate biometric authentication are not used.

Availability also suffers from new problems in the smart environment. As well as typical denial-of-service attacks that might affect the communication channel, Stajano [7] observes that resource limitations on devices, such as limited battery power, could be the target of *sleep deprivation*. In this attack, the server or device may be kept awake until its battery power is dissipated completely. Intermittent service failure is likely on wireless connections and many wireless protocols do not require reauthentication [12], such that brief denial-of-service attacks may lead to man-in-the-middle attack vulnerabilities.

It should be clear from this discussion that there is a need for new security mechanisms to provide a more dynamic form of security for the environments under consideration here. Some promising approaches are being considered. In contrast to static access control lists, these approaches essentially classify users into categories based on certain properties, separating security policy from the allocation of users to categories and simplifying the policy definition. An example of this is Role Based Access Control (RBAC) where traditionally users are categorized according to their position in an organization's hierarchy. One approach that has been suggested to extend this paradigm to the smart environment is that of Covington et al. [14]. Instead of using organizational roles, they introduce the notion of *environmental roles*, categorizing users according to security-relevant environmental contexts, such as location and time, in conjunction with user information. Thus policies can vary, depending on, for example, which other users are in the same location or access requests outside of normal working hours. Another similar approach proposed by Mostéfaoui [15] is the use of adaptive, flexible smart security policies, in which contextual information is used as a constraint for real-time reconfiguration of policies. The user's preferences can be taken into consideration, but the user need not be directly involved in complex security decisions. These approaches provide access control while permitting access from any location, thus supporting user mobility. Furthermore, they demonstrate that even given the security and privacy implications of a sensor network, it is possible to use the contextual information that they provide to enhance security for smart environments.

A very promising approach, which we concentrate on in the later sections of this chapter, is trust management, and the application of trust and risk analysis to security problems in dynamic and decentralized environments with unknown entity interactions. We will provide a detailed analysis of this approach subsequently.

11.3 PRIVACY

11.3.1 Motivation

As discussed in the introduction to this chapter, the very features that allow smart environments to be personalized and dynamic are the features that contribute to the privacy problem. A smart environment will collect data from sensors and users. The manner of collection will not necessarily be obvious or active. The potential for collection and misuse of information is massive. As pointed out by Campbell et al. [5], this information could be used by the malicious or simply curious—for instance, to track and stalk unsuspecting users. This warning is echoed in [3], where we are reminded of the Orwellian Big Brother nightmare. For this reason, the demand for privacy is obvious—perhaps even more so than the demand for security or trust. Without a sense of individual privacy, users will simply not engage with the technology. Research in this area is very important for smart environments, where even previous solutions to privacy problems in online systems are inadequate.

11.3.2 Definition

According to Alan Westin [16], "privacy[3] is the claim of individuals, groups, or institutions to determine for themselves when, how and to what extent information is communicated to others." Privacy is about protecting users' personal information. Given the advances in technology in ubiquitous computing, the concern over privacy is greatly increased. The challenging question, which researchers have begun to tackle recently, is how to control and manage users' privacy. *Privacy control*, as the term states, encompasses both the notion of privacy and the notion of control or management. It relates not only to the process of setting rules and enforcing them, but also to the way privacy is managed/controlled adaptively according to changes in the degree of disclosure of personal information or user mobility from one smart space to another. The main point is that any good privacy solution should combine these two notions, as control is about justification of privacy and plays a role in the management of privacy [17].

As observed by Langeheinrich [3], the issues of privacy have been addressed in a number of domains. Langeheinrich identifies the significant recent historical aspects of privacy, showing its evolution as an issue for public concern from early arguments about privacy in the 19th century, notably by Warren and Brandeis [18], to their constitutional and legal impact in the late 1970s. He also points to the key open issue in privacy: information privacy. Information privacy is at the core of the privacy problem for smart environments. Westin [16] identifies this problem and refines some principles of fair information practices, which are summarized as [3]:

1. **Openness and transparency:** There is no secret record keeping.
2. **Individual participation:** The subject should be able to see the records.
3. **Collection limits:** Record collection should be appropriate for the application.
4. **Data quality:** Record collection should be accurate and relevant to the application.

---
[3]The word *privacy* originates from the latin word *privatus*, which means "apart from the public life."

5. **Use limits:** Records should be used only for specified purposes and only by authorized people.
6. **Appropriate security:** Reasonable efforts should be made to secure the records.
7. **Accountability:** Record keepers must be accountable.

These principles cover the smart environment. Only one minor modification is necessary. These principles implicitly assume one-way interaction (from system records to user). This is not the case in smart environments, where all parties in the process are both record keepers and the subjects of record keeping, although this does not change the validity of these seven principles. Furthermore, there is an issue of *awareness* from the user's point of view: users should be aware that interactions are taking place/in progress.

11.3.3 Privacy in Smart Environments

Privacy has been studied in the context of the Internet, with the most evident technology being the platform for privacy preferences (P3P) [19]. P3P aims to enhance user control by designing an open standard for a given website to describe how it uses personal information it collects during a session. This allows P3P-enabled browsers to interpret this machine-readable description, allowing users to decide how they use the site with reference to their own *privacy preferences*. This technology focuses on the service provider's annotating the *information* privacy policies and making these policies available. In addition to the standardization and adoption of P3P, there is a recent trend toward developing privacy-enhancing technologies that increase user privacy management. These technologies also provide solutions to the related problems of security and privacy, enabling information collectors and users to manage personal privacy in a flexible manner. The main concept behind these solutions is to use technical and organizational concepts to protect users' personal identities. Cryptographically, this is achieved through the use of digital signatures. Such solutions as P3P and privacy-enhancing technologies are aimed at facilitating control of privacy concerns in e-commerce, online systems, and Internet browsers. So far, they have not been successfully applied to smart environments, in part due to the bidirectional relationships between multiple principals and the difficulty of balancing the privacy requirements of all principals with the functionality of the smart space. This highlights a fundamental problem with privacy (and security in general) that is also observed in [3]: namely, we cannot achieve total privacy in any given system. It also shows that openness is the only way to develop a generic privacy infrastructure.

With this in mind, Langeheinrich [3] outlines a number of privacy guidelines for the design of ubiquitous computing systems (smart environments) inspired by Westin's principles. In describing these guidelines, rather than focus on the malicious invasion of privacy, he focuses on the more typical everyday aspects of accidental invasion of privacy.

11.3.3.1 Notice From the human perspective, it may be sufficient to make the user aware of the existence and activity of a smart environment. By giving notice to the user in a clean, open manner, we can transfer many of the privacy decisions to the user—which is the main aim in any case. This is essentially the approach taken in the P3P project. A P3P-compliant node announces its policies through a policy specification located at a well-known place. Such a service in a smart environment would have to include not only the environment policies but also the device policies (covering both fixed and mobile entities) because mobile devices may be collecting data that will leave the domain of control of the specific smart environment. It seems obvious that such an *awareness infrastructure* is a baseline technology for smart environments.

11.3.3.2 Choice and Consent As pointed in [3], legislation in some domains requires that explicit consent be obtained from a user before data is stored. Many of us, depending on our country of residence, never give any thought to the fact that we have consented to the logging of our web activity or e-mail traffic in the workplace. However, as already noted, the potential intrusiveness of the sensing smart environment requires more careful consideration. This second guideline is simple in essence: once the user has been notified of the activity in a space, allow the user to choose whether to engage and, if the user does interact, seek his or her consent. Tavani and Moor [20] stated that consent is a means of control that manages privacy and justifies what would be an invasion of privacy without it. Choice and consent are the main aspects of individual control, and they define a necessary trade-off in the human interaction with the smart environment. The premises of smart environments are *invisible* technology and *natural* interaction. But to deal with the user's privacy concerns, we have to make them *less invisible* and *less natural*.

11.3.3.3 Anonymity and Pseudonymity A solution often used to circumvent this trade-off and avoid seeking explicit consent is to provide mechanisms to hide the identity of a user. This guideline argues for offering anonymity but not mandating it. The problem encountered in smart environments is that the techniques used in the Internet context to provide anonymity[4] will not suit dynamic, real-time world activity. Moreover, the devices themselves may not have the computational power or network complexity to support such techniques. One system that addresses aspects of this issue is the Mist service of GAIA [5]. Finally, anonymity is again a trade-off in the privacy debate, as it may inhibit one of the core aims of a smart environment—to provide personalized interactions.

11.3.3.4 Proximity and Locality This guideline corresponds to the notions of filtering and multicasting in network communications: announcements of data or sensors should be distributed only to the interested parties that match some rules. The rules in this case are distance metrics from the source. In doing this, the guideline suggests a commonsense optimization of the previous three guidelines.

[4]http://www.anonymizer.com

11.3.3.5 Adequate Security The obvious answer to many problems of privacy is to encrypt the data in a manner that enforces the *provider's* privacy requirements. However, this again is a difficult trade-off. Simple, low-power devices will not be able to use robust encryption techniques because of the computational overhead. This guideline sensibly encourages the proportionate use of encryption in a given environment.

11.3.3.6 Access and Recourse This guideline echoes Westin's principles 3, 5, and 7, namely, collection limits, use limits, and accountability. Essentially it is a process and purpose guideline, rather than a technology guideline, which encourages good practice in the collection and dissemination of collected data or records.

In [21] a broadly similar set of guidelines are described. Interestingly, these guidelines focus strongly on the user and on one additional element. The notion of *making risky operation expensive* makes explicit the risk assessment that happens implicitly in most, if not all, interactions. This key point is considered in Section 11.4.

To summarize, this section has taken a guideline perspective on privacy, as described by Langeheinrich [3], rather than a technology implementation perspective. All of the emerging privacy technologies for ubiquitous computing [5,21–24] are encompassed in these guidelines.

11.4 TRUST

As mentioned in Section 11.1.1, mobile entities in a smart environment benefit from the ability to interact and collaborate in an ad hoc manner with other entities and services in the environment. Such entities may be from unfamiliar administrative domains and therefore may be completely unknown a priori. To safely take advantage of the whole range of possibilities such an environment creates, it is essential to provide support for secure autonomous decision making by its constituent entities. In such systems, spanning multiple administrative domains, autonomous operation is an essential characteristic of entities that cannot rely on specific security infrastructures or central control for help in making security-related decisions. Entities will have to deal with unforeseen circumstances ranging from unexpected interactions to disconnected operation, often with incomplete information about other principals and the environment. While security technologies such as cryptography can protect data and privacy concerns can be addressed, we are still left with the problem of deciding when a trust relationship between two or more principals should be initiated.

We believe that the process of decision making by the principals involves the estimation of likely behavior not explicitly covered by traditional security measures that focus on the identification/authentication of principals involved in an interaction. In addition to this unsuitable focus on identity, the hard-coded approach to centrally managed security domains is inflexible for environments with an unpredictable composition. The responsibility therefore falls on the entities themselves to make security-related decisions—for example, to protect their resources from misuse or to ensure that payment for service is received. Trust management attacks this part of the security problem—the process of decision making within a smart environment [11].

11.4.1 Definition

Beyond its basic dictionary definition, trust is notoriously difficult to define, with definitions challenging philosophers, psychologists, and sociologists. In his seminal thesis, Marsh [25] examines many of these definitions and determines certain generalities and principles of trust in a step toward his goal of developing a computational model for trust.

Firstly, trust is subjective and situation specific, based on observations made by an entity and on evidence made available to the entity in a particular situation or environment. Secondly, trust is inherently linked with risk; higher risk means that cooperation is less likely to occur, although the benefits of interaction are often worth the risk. This presupposition of risk is perhaps what differentiates trust from confidence or assurance. Thirdly, Marsh identifies trust as *intransitive*; if A trusts B and B trusts C, this does not necessarily imply that A trusts C. This, however, does not rule out the possibility of the transfer of trust information. It merely states that trust is not implicitly transitive; thus, when passing information, it is important to be sure that any trust in the information is explicit. The idea of the complex evolutionary nature of trust is also speculated on: trust is self-reinforcing such that it will not decrease below or above a certain threshold.

McKnight and Chervany [26] define six trust-related constructs that capture significant portions of the meaning of trust and help differentiate between trust and its consequences. These constructs are Trusting Intention, Trusting Behavior, Trusting Beliefs, System Trust, Dispositional Trust, and the Situational Decision to Trust.

Figure 11.2 shows how the constructs are related to one another such that beliefs lead to intentions, which in turn manifest in behaviors or the taking of the trusting

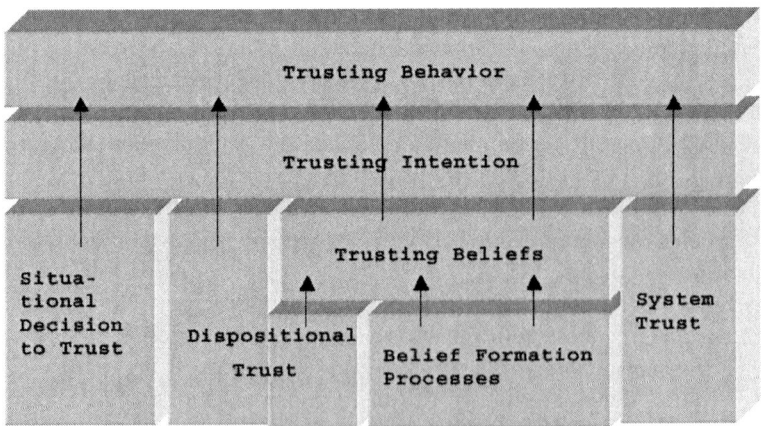

Figure 11.2 McKnight and Chervany's six trust constructs and interactions [26].

path in a decision situation. McKnight and Chevany feel that belief in another is based on benevolence, honesty, competence, and predictability, forming a solid foundation for the Trusting Intention. From a system point of view, it is therefore necessary to observe such characteristics in order to provide information for the formation and evolution of such trusting beliefs. Predictability here again implies that risk must be present before trusting is necessary, i.e., that perfect information is not available on which to base a decision. Important aspects of trust are included in the Situational Decision to Trust, Dispositional Trust, and System Trust. System Trust is the belief that the proper system measures are in place to encourage successful interactions, such as monitoring and dealing with improper behavior. Dispositional Trust relates to an entity's general expectations of the trustworthiness of others and should be consistent across a range of situations and entities. The disposition of an entity is an interesting idea in terms of trust dynamics as well, and might be used to determine how much an entity is affected by the available evidence. The Situational Decision to Trust construct highlights the situation-specific nature of trust and the formation of a trusting belief in relation to a specific entity. The constructs are deemed to have heuristic value rather than dictate a specific definition of trust itself by providing a means to discuss trust across a wide range of situations.

Other work by McKnight et al. [27] demonstrates that many of the definitions of trust in the literature are not explicit about its dynamic aspects, such as the formation of trusting relationships, instead focusing on what trust is used for in a static fashion. That work focuses on the initial meeting between two parties who depend on one another before they have interacted and built up experience between them. At first, interaction is supported by Dispositional Trust (particularly through lack of other support), a Situational Decision to Trust (perhaps irrespective of beliefs, because there is no other choice), System Trust, and categorization and illusionary mechanisms. Categorization and illusionary mechanisms underlie trust through their effects on trusting belief. In a new relationship, the authors claim that three types of categorization can occur: unit grouping (grouped due to common goals), reputation categorization (regarding the individual or group), and stereotyping (general biases). The authors claim that human trust is based not only on rational mechanisms, but also on illusions when information and logic to support categorization are not available. As such, a high level of confidence (not justified by the available evidence) about an entity may exist if we have great need of that entity's help. While the paper makes it clear that trust formation can be supported in many ways, it also points out that initial trust can be fragile, and that if experience and observation prove the initial trust incorrect, it may be rapidly revised downward. The authors further argue that trust is emotional and that modeling of an emotional concept is not well understood. For this reason, it may be more suitable to attempt to model the behavior of trust [25] rather than trust itself when considering trust in smart environments.

11.4.2 Trust Management in Smart Environments

Blaze et al. [28] define trust management as "a unified approach to specifying and interpreting security policies, credentials and relationships that allow direct authorization of security-critical actions." In such trust management systems, trust is viewed implicitly through the delegation of privileges to trusted entities via the use of credentials or certificates, which can be chained to represent the propagation of trust between entities. Examples of this type of trust management system are Blaze et al.'s PolicyMaker [28] and its later incarnation, KeyNote [29], applications that bind a key directly to access rights, moving away from identity-based certificates and static access control lists. Requestors of a service in a smart environment can prove directly that they have the credentials to authorize the requested service, integrating specification of policy with the key to privilege binding. Polices and credentials (assertions) are application-specific, essentially autonomous programs that do not communicate with or depend on one another or on externally defined data structures [30]. These systems appear to be similar to a database query engine to applications, accepting input of local policy statements, sets of credentials, and descriptions of the proposed actions. These are evaluated by a compliance checker [31] to provide a yes or no answer or conditions to be met before proceeding or, in the case of KeyNote, an application-defined string for flexible decision-making capabilities.

There have been extensions to this model of trust management. For example, the REFEREE Trust Management System [32] places all security-related decisions under direct policy control, including evaluation of compliance with policy. The dynamic loading of new credentials is made possible by making a trust management decision about the downloaded code. This allows credential discovery mechanisms to be developed, increasing the applicability of this approach to smart environments by seeking the necessary credentials to support access to some service. Kagal et al.'s work on security in ubiquitous computing [33] extends trust management with the notions of conditional delegation (imposing constraints), negotiable delegation, prohibition, and delegation requests to improve the evolutionary capabilities of trust relationships. Trust negotiation [34] takes trust management a step further by allowing the bilateral exchange of credentials between the negotiation participants as required to progress toward successful completion of the negotiation. The response to a request will communicate the credentials required to achieve the next step of the negotiation. Measures should be in place to allow credential chain discovery if locally cached credentials do not satisfy the policy. Li and Mitchell [35] have developed the RT role-based trust management framework for large, decentralized systems, combining role-based access control with trust management through a logic-programming approach based on Delegation Logic [36]. RT also incorporates credential chain discovery [37] and uses a goal-directed evaluation procedure for compliance checking and trust negotiation. Cross-domain vocabulary agreement ensures that the correct permissions are delegated by globally uniquely identified Application Domain Specific Documents declaring data types and role names (termed a *vocabulary*), allowing strongly typed credentials and policies, supported by a typed credential storage system.

In summary, all of the credential-based systems described in this section provide valuable insights into trust management and are useful in their own right, although not for the smart environments of interest here. Despite the advances outlined above, the systems are not flexible enough for general-purpose trust reasoning; basically, they describe measures for the exploitation of trust relationships for distributed security policy management. The fact that policy is evaluated with respect to delegation credentials means that if the necessary credentials cannot be discovered, access cannot be granted. This is a serious problem in an environment where unknown mobile entities cause only partial views of the system to exist and we cannot rely on a fixed security infrastructure. Furthermore, the implicit trust relationship established via credentials relies on entities with explicit knowledge of the trust subject to delegate privileges, assuming they have the authority to do so. There is no consideration of how relationships at this level are formed. At some stage, this comes down to administrative intervention, which is not consistent with calm computing. Given the limitations of credential-based trust management for our environment of interest, we advocate the use of trust management paradigms, which more closely mimic the nature of human trust, based on historical evidence evaluated from a subjective viewpoint.

11.4.3 A New Approach to Trust-Based Security in Smart Environments

Based on the properties of trust discussed in Section 11.4.2, it is clear that the credential-based approaches discussed not sufficiently flexible for smart environments due to their reliance, at least at some level, on complete information for policy evaluation. A new approach that is being actively researched is to define security policies in terms of a more humanly intuitive notion of trust. Due to the vast amount of research in this area, we can only briefly describe a few of the important contributions.

Marsh [25] made some early attempts to formalize the notion of trust for computational use in interactions between two autonomous agents. This approach takes into account many of the widely accepted aspects of trust as seen in the literature, defining basic or dispositional trust, general trust in another entity, and situational trust in another entity, combined with the notions of utility, risk, and importance. From this, simple linear equations allow the formation of trust values, which are represented in the range $[-1, 1)$ to allow for reasoning about distrust. Trust information (values representing payoff) from past interactions of an agent is stored, allowing evolution of trust, albeit in a rather arbitrary manner. More detailed evidence would be more useful in terms of evolution. The concept of a threshold for trusting behavior based on the perceived risk and competence in the situation demonstrates the important relationship between trust and risk. Although the model incorporates many of the important features of trust, implementations have encountered several problems due to the use of overly simple linear equations that fail to model trust intuitively. This work has made several useful contributions to the area of dynamic computational trust, but it is limited by a very basic trust model that fails to cope with certain values in a limited trust domain.

Abdul-Rahman [38] proposes a more comprehensive approach to decentralized trust management incorporating distinct trust levels and dynamics. This work focuses on the formation and evolution of trust rather than exploitation. Formation of trust relationships is based on reputation, comprising recommendations from third parties and experiences of the truster itself. The model defines *direct trust relationships*, which take a trust degree with locally defined semantics. At any given time, trust in an agent is evaluated from the relevant subset of experiences based on context. An experience is the result of either evaluating an interaction or relying on a recommendation from an agent, and it takes a value corresponding to the trust degree. By storing a count of each type of outcome, direct trust can be evaluated according to the trust degree that corresponds to the most frequent type of experience. *Recommender trust relationships* represent the belief that an agent provides good recommendations within a certain context, and *recommender trust* can give a weighting for recommendations based on the *semantic distance* of the experience from the recommendation. The context of a recommendation can be direct or a lead to a recommender, which means that chains can be omitted by contacting the final recommender directly. Recommendations from various sources can be combined. This work provides many valuable insights into the evaluation of trust, particularly the subjective evaluation of recommendations, a useful process for determining the trustworthiness of unknowns entering a smart environment. However, the notion of risk, which is important when determining the likelihood of desirable behavior, is not considered.

Josang [39] describes Subjective Logic as a logic that operates on subjective beliefs (opinions) about the world using standard and nonstandard logical operators. The representation of trust is based on probability metrics that represent a degree of uncertainty in beliefs represented as propositions. Logical operators are defined for propositional conjunction and disjunction for two propositions from distinct binary frames of discernment and for propositional negation. Two nontraditional operators are defined that depend on belief ownership. These allow discounting of opinions based on a view of the advice and also allow reaching a consensus opinion. It is only possible to reach a consensus with someone who retains some uncertainty (which can be introduced via discounting). An alternative representation of uncertain probabilities with respect to the evidence space is defined using probability density functions derived from the amount of evidence supporting the event and the amount of evidence supporting its negation. A mapping is easily defined between the evidence space and the opinion space to allow the use of results from one in the other. Propositional conjunction and disjunction are defined on the evidence space, as is the combination of evidence from two observers as if one entity had collected all of the evidence. This forms the basis for the opinion space consensus operator. This work is very important in the area of subjective reasoning, in particular, due to the fact that opinions can be represented with some uncertainty.

Jonker and Treur [40] have carried out some interesting work on the dynamics of trust in light of personal experience. Each event that can influence the degree of trust in a subject is interpreted as either trust-negative or trust-positive, reducing or increasing trust, respectively, although the degree to which the trust is changed depends on the trust model used by the agent. Trust dynamics affect how the agent is influenced by trust-positive and trust-negative experiences. For example, agents can be defined as slow-positive/fast-negative, meaning that it takes a lot of positive evidence to build trust and little negative evidence to reduce it. The dynamics of trust can be formalized by a trust evolution function, which relates sequences of experiences to trust representations, or in an inductive manner by a trust update function, which relates a current trust representation and a current experience to a new trust representation. This formal framework enables a variety of dynamic models to be developed to capture the individual characteristics of agents. This framework is not meant as a coherent approach to trust management, but rather as an analysis of trust dynamics; and as such, it does not address how trust might be used for decision making.

Grandison and Sloman [41] define a general-purpose trust management system developed as a trust specification that can be analyzed and evaluated for many uses. Example uses include a starting point for deriving Ponder security management policies or for making trust-based authorization decisions. SULTAN (Simple Universal Logic-oriented Trust Analysis Notation) is a notation with associated tools for specification, analysis, and management of trust relationships for Internet applications. SULTAN's trust management has several components. Trust Establishment defines protocols for negotiation and exchange of the evidence and credentials. Trust Analysis evaluates the trust and recommendation specifications to determine conflicts and implicit relationships. A Specification Server (with a Specification Editor) holds all the trust and recommendation specifications for the domain, while a Monitoring Service updates a State Information Server with state information for the scenario and system, experience information for direct alteration of trust levels (e.g., number of successful interactions), and risk information. The Risk Evaluation Service retrieves risk information from the state information server and performs a risk calculation using a list of common risks and their probabilities with a list of action dependencies and risk thresholds. The SULTAN framework is to be used both as a decision support tool to aid human managers or automated manager agents and to support on-line trust queries for security policy decisions. The model makes good use of context for effective use of evidence, considers risk factors, and allows propagation of trust through recommendations.

Examination of some of the influential trust management approaches reveals certain problems that must be addressed. In the systems considered, problems arise due to reliance on a global view of the system (through central storage or broadcast messages), which we assume cannot exist, even if desirable, from the privacy perspective. Furthermore, the provision of some form of centralized infrastructure, such as a storage or trust analysis engine, is common; this can be a problem for principals roaming between smart environments. A simple notion of evidence is used in most systems, such as quality of service feedback by the user, which leads to missing a great deal of information that could be gained from interaction via, for example, network monitoring. Furthermore, this simple evidence is not evaluated with respect to the trust value used to initiate a decision, and thus does not consider the behavior we expected to see. Limited evidence also leads to limited dynamics in terms of initial formation and evolution capabilities. In the exploitation of trust values, few systems take risk into account when making decisions, which is counterintuitive for trust-based decision making.

To address these inadequacies, a more comprehensive framework is required, such as that being developed in the SECURE project [42]. A comprehensive general framework is necessary to gather and evaluate detailed observational evidence [43] in an automated manner and to propagate source-weighted recommendations in a context-aware fashion. SECURE incorporates a general trust model [44], allowing application-specific trust domains to be used and providing the capability of incorporating many dimensions of trust; hence, it is less restrictive as a framework. The trust model also incorporates a notion of uncertainty to cope with unknown principals. Through the incorporation of uncertainty into our trust values, it is possible to assign unknown trust to news principal, yet still afford them the possibility of interaction. SECURE retains this notion of uncertainty throughout the dynamic life cycle of trust, even into the decision process, where the exploitation of trust occurs to facilitate risk assessment as part of a general risk model [45], which is also capable of representing uncertainty. This decision process based on the relationship between trust and risk allows the separation of policy evaluation from trust reasoning, since trust is used to categorize principals. By defining policy in terms of trust and risk, flexibility of decision making is retained, facilitating interaction in a smart environment even in the absence of full knowledge of a principal.

Furthermore, trust in SECURE is based on patterns of historical behavior rather than on separate pieces of evidence, and the trust evolution mechanisms essentially allow all the history to remain at some level within the trust values, albeit with decreasing influence over time. By explicitly modeling trust, it is possible to form and evolve trust relationships more intuitively based on observations and recommendations, whether negative or positive. Therefore, we can incorporate a range of opinions as evidence without leading to policy violations. This focus on evidence currently available for evaluation to predict likely behavior, coupled with risk analysis to incorporate other factors of the interaction, leads to an intuitively subjective notion of trust, supporting fine-grained trust evolution. Moreover, gathering evidence of past behavior can be automated and thus requires no user intervention, so that the principles of calm technology are maintained. Also, the same evidence can influence a variety of decisions through context mappings, although perhaps not to the same degree.

11.5 DISCUSSION

In this chapter we have attempted to describe the background and current status of security, privacy, and trust in smart environments. It is a difficult task, as for each aspect of the problem space there are many issues. Consequently, there are many areas we have simply not covered: access control, identity management, legal and sociotechnical issues, and biometric aspects, to name a few.

In considering security, we have been rather prosaic in revisiting and reusing the traditional definitions. However, this is an area perhaps best understood (although not yet solved) with much of the technology that is usable in some form in smart environments. Nevertheless, because of the characteristics of smart environments, new versions of old problems occur, such as denial-of-service attacks on battery power as well communication channels. The key problem identified is the lack of global reference, so that all secure interactions have to take place potentially in a zero knowledge environment [11].

In considering privacy, we have focused not on the technology aspects but on the guidelines for design derived from significant historical debate: these are exemplified by [3,21]. These demonstrate very clearly the importance of openness and accountability in establishing a privacy-preserving environment. One aspect we highlight from [28] is the importance of risk assessment, both implicit and explicit, in determining whether a user can engage in an activity. This aspect is reflected in some detail in our discussion of trust management.

Trust management is a key area for smart environments because of the user-centric nature of these systems. Encouraging users to engage while providing them with the ability to control their exposure to the system is a critical requirement. Existing trust management systems are not sufficient because they do not address fine-grained, dynamic trust evolution. This is a consequence of the lack of explicit models and representations for trust behaviors. Recent work [5,11,22,23,46] has begun to address this issue from a number of perspectives. However, we believe that trust, as a core enabling infrastructure, is the next step in balancing the complex trade-offs demanded by security and privacy in smart environments. In particular, each decision about encryption, access control, or information exchange implies a decision process. Trust-based infrastructure provides the mechanisms for users and systems to base this decision process on their view of the risks and benefits involved.

The authors believe that the issues of security, privacy, and trust are now among the most important challenges for smart environment research. We hope this chapter contributes to understanding in that area.

ACKNOWLEDGMENTS

This work was supported partly supported by the SECURE project (Secure Environments for Collaboration among Ubiquitous Roaming Entities, IST-2001-32486) and the GLOSS Project (Global Smart Environments, IST-2000-26070), both funded by the European Union Future and Emerging Technologies Programme.

REFERENCES

[1] P. Nixon, G. Lacey, and S. Dobson (eds.), *Managing Interactions in Smart Environments*, Springer-Verlag, p. 243, 1999.

[2] B. Schilit, N. Adams, and R. Want. "Context-Aware Computing Applications." In *Proceedings of the IEEE Workshop on Mobile Computing Systems and Applications*, pp. 85–90, Santa Cruz, California, December 1994. IEEE Computer Society Press, 1994.

[3] M. Langeheinrich. "Privacy by Design—Principles of Privacy Aware Ubiquitous Systems," In *UBICOMP 2001*, LNCS 2201, pp. 273–291.

[4] P. Nixon, G. Lacey, and S. Dobson. "Managing Smart Environments." In *Proceedings of the Workshop on Software Engineering for Wearable and Pervasive Computing*, June 2000, Limerick, Ireland.

[5] R. Campbell, J. Al-Muhtadi, P. Naldurg, G. Sampemane, and M.D. Mickunas. "Towards Security and Privacy for Pervasive Computing." In *Theories and Systems, Mext-NSF-JSPS International Symposium, ISSS 2002*, pp. 1–15. Tokyo, November 2002.

[6] P. Robinson and M. Beigl, "Trust Context Spaces: An Infrastructure for Pervasive Security." In *Proceedings of the First International Conference on Security in Pervasive Computing*, Springer-Verlag, pages 157–172, 2003.

[7] F. Stajano, *Security for Ubiquitous Computing*, Wiley, 2002.

[8] N. Smart, *Crytopgraphy*, McGraw-Hill, pages 157–172, 2003.

[9] A. Abdul-Rahman. "The PGP Trust Model," technical report, Department of Computer Science, University College, London, 1996.

[10] G. Caronni. "Walking the Web of Trust." In *Proceeding of WETICE*. IEEE Computer Society Press, 2000.

[11] V. Cahill, B. Shand, E. Gray, N. Dimmock, A. Twigg, J. Bacon, C. English, W. Wagealla, S. Terzis, P.A. Nixon, C. Bryce, G. Serugendo, J. Seigneur, M. Carbone, K. Krukow, C. Jensen, Y. Chen, and M. Nielsen. "Using Trust for Secure Collaboration in Uncertain Environments." *IEEE Pervasive Computing Magazine*, September 2003.

[12] A.K. Ghosh and T.M. Swaminatha. "Software Security and Privacy Risks in Mobile E-Commerce. *Communications of the ACM*, vol. 44, no. 2, pp. 51–57, February 2001.

[13] M. Jakobsson and S. Wetzel. "Security Weaknesses in Bluetooth." In *Proceedings of the RSA Cryptographer's Track (RSA CT '01)*, LNCS 2020, pp. 176–191. Springer-Verlag, 2001.

[14] M.J. Covington, W. Long, S. Srinivasan, A.K. Dev, M. Ahamad, and G.D. Abowd. "Securing Context-Aware Applications Using Environment Roles." *SACMAT 2001*, pp. 10–20.

[15] G.K. Mostéfaoui. "Security in Pervasive Environments: What's Next?" *In the proceedings of the 2003* Int. Conf. on Security & Management (SAM'03), Las Vegas, Nevada, USA, June 2003, pp. 93–98.

[16] A.F. Westin. *Privacy and Freedom.* Bodley Head, 1970.

[17] H.T. Tavani. "Informational Privacy, Data Mining, and the Internet." *Ethics and Information Technology*, vol. 1, no. 2, 1999, pp. 137–145.

[18] S. Warren, L. Brandeis, "The Right to Privacy." *Harvard Law Review*, vol. 4, pp. 193–220, 1890.

[19] http://www.w3.org/P3P/ and http://www.w3.org/2002/01/P3Pv1

[20] H.T. Tavani, and J.H. Moor. "Privacy Protection, Control of Information, and Privacy-Enhancing Technologies." *ACM SIGCAS Newsletter*, vol. 31, no. 1, pp. 6–11, 2001.

[21] S. Lahlou, and F. Jegou "Privacy Design Guidelines, Ambient-Agoras Project Deliverable D15.4", 2003 (http://www.ambient-agoras.org).

[22] W. Wagealla, S. Terzis, and C. English. "Trust-Based Model for Privacy Control in Context-Aware Systems." In the *UBICOM Workshop on Security in Ubiquitous Computing*, 2003.

[23] L. Kagal, J. Undercoffer, F. Perich, and T. Finin. "A Security Architecture Based on Trust Management for Pervasive Computing Systems." In *Proceedings of the Grace Hopper Celebration of Women in Computing*, 2002.

[24] M. Langheinrich. "A Privacy Awareness System for Ubiquitous Computing Environments." In *UBICOMP 2002*, LNCS 2498, pp. 237–245, 2002.

[25] S. Marsh. "Formalising Trust as a Computational Concept." Ph.D. thesis, University of Stirling, 1994.

[26] D. McKnight and N. Chervany. "The Meanings of Trust." Technical Report, Carlson School of Management, University of Minnesota, 1996.

[27] D. McKnight, L. Cummings, and N. Chevany. "Trust Formation in New Organisational Relationships." Carlson School of Management, University of Minnesota, 1995.

[28] M. Blaze, J. Feigenbaum, and J. Lacy. "Decentralized Trust Management." In *Proceedings of the 1996 IEEE Symposium on Security and Privacy*, pp. 164–173, May 1996.

[29] M. Blaze, J. Feigenbaum, J. Ioannidis, and A. Keromytis: "The KeyNote Trust Management System—Version 2." Internet Engineering Task Force, September 1999.

[30] M. Blaze, J. Feigenbaum, J. Ioannidis, and A. Keromytis. "The Role of Trust Management in Distributed Systems Security." In *Secure Internet Programming: Security Issues for Mobile and Distributed Objects* (J. Vitek and C. Jensen, eds.). Springer-Verlag, 1999.

[31] M. Blaze, J. Feigenbaum, and M. Strauss. "Compliance Checking in the Policymaker Trust Management System." In *Financial Cryptography*, vol. 1465 of Lecture Notes in Computer Science (R. Mischfeld, ed.), pp. 254–274. Springer-Verlag, 1998.

[32] Y.-H. Chu, J. Feigenbaum, B. LaMacchia, P. Resnick, and M. Strauss. "REFEREE: Trust Management for Web Applications." *World Wide Web Journal*, vol. 2, pp. 706–734, 1997.

[33] L. Kagal et al: "A Security Architecture Based on Trust Management for Pervasive Computing Systems." In *Proceedings of the Grace Hopper Celebration of Women in Computing*, 2002.

[34] K.E. Seamons, M. Winslett, T. Yu, B. Smith, E. Child, J. Jacobson, H. Mills, and L. Yu. "Requirements for Policy Languages for Trust Negotiation." In *3rd International Workshop on Policies for Distributed Systems and Networks (POLICY 2002)*, June 2002.

[35] N. Li and J.C. Mitchell: "RT: A Role-Based Trust-Management Framework." In *Proceedings of the Third DARPA Information Survivability Conference and Exposition (DISCEX III)*, pp. 201–212. IEEE Computer Society Press, 2003.

[36] N. Li, B.N. Grosof, and J. Feigenbaum. "Delegation Logic: A Logic-Based Approach to Distributed Authorization." *ACM Transactions on Information and System Security (TISSEC)*, vol. 6, no. 1, pp. 128–171, February 2003.

[37] N. Li, W.H. Winsborough, and J.C. Mitchell. "Distributed Credential Chain Discovery in Trust Management." *Journal of Computer Security*, vol. 11, no. 1, pp. 35–86, February 2003.

[38] A. Abdul-Rahman and S. Hailes. "Supporting Trust in Virtual Communities." In *Proceedings of the Hawaii International Conference on System Sciences*, January 2000.

[39] A. Jøsang. "A Logic for Uncertain Probabilities." *International Journal of Uncertainty, Fuzziness and Knowledge-Based Systems*, vol. 9, no. 3, pp. 279–311, June 2001.

[40] C.M. Jonker and J. Treur. "Formal Analysis of Models for the Dynamics of Trust Based on Experiences." In *Modelling Autonomous Agents in a Multi-Agent World, 1999 European Workshop on Multi-Agent Systems*, pp. 221–231, 1999.

[41] T. Grandison and M. Sloman. "Trust Management Tools for Internet Applications." In *Proceedings of the First International Conference on Trust Management*, Springer, LNCS 2692. May 2003.

[42] SECURE website: http://secure.dsg.cs.tcd.ie

[43] S. Terzis, W. Wagealla, C. English, and P. Nixon. "The SECURE Collaboration Model." Technical report 03, Department of Computer and Information Sciences, University of Strathclyde.

[44] M. Carbone, O. Danvy, I. Damgaard, K. Krukow, A. Møller, J.B. Nielsen, and M. Nielsen. "SECURE Deliverable 1.1: A Model for Trust." December 2002.

[45] J. Bacon, N. Dimmock, D. Ingram, K. Moody, B. Shand, and A. Twigg. "SECURE Deliverable 3.1: Definition of Risk Model." December 2002 (http://secure.dsg.cs.tcd.ie)-project website.

[46] P.A. Nixon and S. Terzis (editors). "Trust Management." *Lecture Notes in Computer Science*, vol. 2692. Springer-Verlag, 2003.

PART 4
APPLICATIONS

■ CHAPTER 12

Lessons from an Adaptive Home

MICHAEL C. MOZER
Department of Computer Science
University of Colorado

For the past four decades, the impending arrival of the smart home has been touted in the popular press. The newspaper copy hasn't changed much over the years. Consider this recent example:

> If time is money, then here's a definition of wealth for the 21st century: You're leaving the house for the day. You grab your things, hop into the car and back out of the garage. Then you pick up a device that looks like a four-button version of your car-lock remote control and punch a "goodbye" button. The garage door closes. Inside the house, all the exterior doors are bolted shut, all windows close and lock, drapes swing closed over west-facing windows, the temperature control adjusts to a more frugal level, and the lights are turned off.
> —('Smart home' technology creates true digital domain, *San Diego Union Tribune*, Aug. 4, 2003, p. C1)

Something is inherently wrong with this scenario. The operations described are initiated not by a smart home, but by smart inhabitants who indicate when they are leaving the home. Although the user interface is simple—the push of a button—it is not an action people easily remember to perform. If you doubt, read on.

> Before retiring for the night, ... the Alexanders will set a hello or morning mode, which will wake the family at 7 a.m. to lights, music, or television morning shows. Coffee begins brewing. The thermostat adjusts for family comfort. The hot water kicks in, and hot water fills the tub ...
>
> "Our biggest problem so far has been in forgetting to activate the home mode when we arrive home at the end of the day," says Alexander. "My wife, in particular, likes to take a hot bath at the end of her work day, but if she or I forget to press the home mode, there won't be any warm water in the hot water heater for her bath because we've turned off

---

Smart Environments: Technologies, Protocols, and Applications, edited by D.J. Cook and S.K. Das
ISBN 0-471-54448-5 © 2005 John Wiley & Sons, Inc.

the appliance during the day to conserve electricity."
—("Homes get smart with automation systems," *USA Today*, September 2, 1997, p.)

Even with touch screens and remote controls to simplify the user interface, home inhabitants have been less than satisfied with installed automation systems.

> Flipping a light switch, bumping down a thermostat and changing the channel on the TV are all exercises that homeowners around the world perform intuitively several times each and every day. You'd think that an automation system would magically eliminate these tasks completely from the daily routine. At least that's what Dave and Sharyl Faganel figured when they decided to have an automation system installed in their new ... home ... But as with any technology, it takes a good deal of time at the controls to feel completely comfortable living with and using an automated system. Unfortunately, a little too much time for the Faganels ... [A]fter weeks of wrestling with the setup menus, Dave and Sharyl realized that they and that particular automation system were simply a bad match. The only solution at this point was to tear out the system ... "We spent a good 40 hours showing them how to set up temperature schedules on the old keypad," says [home automation system installer] Michael.
> —("A period of adjustment," *Electronic House*, February 2003, pp. 52–59)

If Dave and Sharyl are technologically challenged, they have plenty of company:

> When I consider all the aggravation and the money, I wouldn't spend as much again the next time, said Tiburon homeowner Bob Becker. In 1991, he built a high-tech castle atop a hill ... with about $70,000 in electronic upgrades. "I use about half of it," said Becker ...
> —("The smart house, *San Francisco Examiner*, April 14, 1996, p.)

> The Christmas party at the ... house of Robert Soros ... was in full swing ... Children raced upstairs to experience ... a home theater screening of ... "Peter Pan." The large screen descended from the ceiling with an extraterrestrial hum, but the house lights refused to dim—despite a horde of caterers stabbing frantically at a panel of small buttons on the wall. As bright spots flashed and faded overhead, Mr. Soros ... bent prayerfully over a control panel, playing its glowing touch screen like a pipe organ as he tried to raise the volume on Tinkerbell. He had given up when the sound suddenly surged to IMAX level. Children screeched. "I would give anything to go back to good old toggle switches," his wife ... said later, sighing at the memory.
> —("When smart houses turn smart aleck," *New York Times*, January 13, 2000, p. 131)

> Elliot Fishkin ... is one of the new digital caretakers, on 24-hour call, seven days a week ... to indulge human frailty. Mr. Fishkin watched as one client sold a house lock, stock, and remotes soon after it was wired because he found the controls too daunting.
> —("When smart houses turn smart aleck," *New York Times*, January 13, 2000, p. 131)

Anecdotes like these are common. Smart homes have failed to become a reality for two reasons. First, inhabitants are fairly satisfied with traditional home controls. Second, the obstacle to understanding new interfaces is high. Technology will be adopted only if the perceived return outweighs the effort required to understand the new technology. Cell phones have become commonplace because they offer many benefits at a relatively minor cost to master. In contrast, personal digital assistants (PDAs) are not commonplace outside the business and academic communities, because the benefits to other individuals are small relative to the significant overhead required for mastery.

Even when designed by experts, user interfaces often fail due to the user's perception of benefit versus cost. For example, when I was a graduate student at the University of California at San Diego, my Ph.D. advisor, Donald Norman, well known for his popular books on the design of user interfaces and everyday consumer products, had a pet project to apply the principles proposed by his User-Centered System Design group to develop a novel interface for the lights in his laboratory. The original light panel was the standard row of a half dozen switches, and as with all such panels, one could not determine a priori which switch controlled which light, because there was no natural mapping between the switches and the lights. The innovative replacement involved cutting a wedge from the wall and laying an illuminated map of the lab horizontally in the wedge. Switches were placed at the locations on the map corresponding to the locations of the lights they controlled. Although this design was ingenious and innovative, it was only moderately successful. Because the lab layout was complex, the map was too, and reading the map was nontrivial, especially for someone unfamiliar with the lab. Further, the correspondence between corners of the map and the corners of the room depends on whether one perceives the map to be of the floor or ceiling; if it is perceived as a ceiling map, one could mentally flip the map around, reversing the coordinates by aligning the left edge of the map with the right edge of the ceiling. Because of these difficulties, it was easiest to simply tap all the switches simultaneously with a swipe of the hand. In a lab meeting, Dave Rumelhart suggested, tongue in cheek, that Don Norman write a user manual for the device and place it on the door leading to the switches.

Even if Don's effort was not fully appreciated, it was compelling relative to some commercially available lighting solutions. Figure 12.1 shows two different lighting

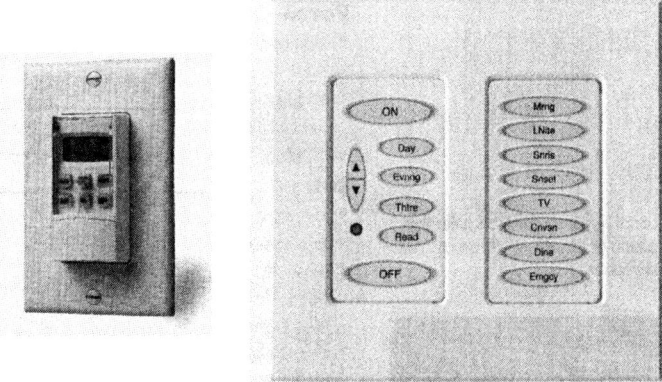

Figure 12.1 Examples of two lighting controls for residences.

controllers for residences. The controller on the left allows the inhabitant to program the lights to turn on based on the time of day and the day of the week—ideal if your weekly schedule is rigidly bound to the clock. The controller on the right allows for various lighting scenarios based on activities (e.g., watching TV or dining) as long as the user is willing to fish through the array of buttons to find the correct scenario.

For lights, stereos, TVs, and other devices we encounter in daily life, *any* sort of novel interface is likely to fail, simply because the benefits offered by smart control are unlikely to compensate for the fuss of learning to use the interface, especially when existing familiar interfaces are adequate for most purposes. Indeed, one might make the strong conjecture that the only way to improve an ordinary familiar environment is to eliminate the interface altogether.

Such an invisible interface is found in BMW (and perhaps other) automobiles. Vehicles have a memory for the configuration of the driver's seat, the steering wheel, and the outside mirrors. Three distinct memory settings are available, allowing for a customized configuration for up to three different drivers. A naive interface might require the drivers to identify themselves each time they enter the vehicle in order for the correct configuration to be chosen. Instead, the interface is hidden from the user by associating a different memory with each car key. Inserting the key in the ignition or pressing the remote entry button selects the memory configuration associated with the key.

Another example of an invisible interface is the *Internet Chair* (Cohen, 2003). The chair senses the direction that users are facing and adjusts the soundscape presentation appropriately so as to achieve orientation invariance: users hear the same binaural sound regardless of the direction they are facing, as if they were wearing headphones. The chair is noninvasive and does not require explicit user actions (such as pointing) or complex technology (such as computer vision).

12.1 THE ADAPTIVE HOUSE

During the past 8 years, we have proposed and implemented a smart home environment premised on the notion that there should be no user interface beyond the sorts of controls one ordinarily finds in a home—no touch pads, no speech input, no gaze tracking or hand gesturing, etc. The intelligence of the home arises from the home's ability to predict the behavior and needs of the inhabitants by having observed them over a period of time. We have focused on home comfort systems, specifically air temperature regulation, water temperature regulation, and lighting. Instead of being programmed to perform certain actions, the house essentially *programs itself* by monitoring the environment and sensing actions performed by the inhabitants (e.g., turning lights on and off, adjusting the thermostat), observing the occupancy and behavior patterns of the inhabitants, and learning to predict future states of the house. To the extent that the inhabitants' needs can be anticipated, the inhabitants are freed from manually controlling the environment via some type of interface. When the predictions are incorrect, the inhabitants can simply indicate their preferences via ordinary interfaces they are used to (e.g., using light switches or thermostats, or simply turning on the hot water).

Scenarios in the home include the following: On a rainy weekday when the inhabitant leaves the home at 8 a.m. and on the previous 3 days had returned by 7 p.m., the home predicts a return by 6:30 and runs the furnace in order to achieve a setpoint temperature by that time. When the inhabitant does return, he prepares dinner, and banks of lights in the kitchen and great room are turned on full intensity. The inhabitant then relaxes on a couch and watches TV in the great room; lights are turned off behind the TV and are dimmed elsewhere in the room. On a weekend, when the inhabitant leaves the house at 4 p.m., his return is not anticipated until past midnight, and the house is not heated before then. When the inhabitant does return home at 1 a.m., the prediction is made that only the master bedroom will be used for the next 7 hours, and instead of running the whole-house furnace, electric space heaters in the bedroom are used for generating heat; the hot water heater lowers its setpoint based on the prediction that hot water will not be required for at least another 7 hours. When the inhabitant awakens at 4 a.m. and climbs out of bed, the home predicts a trip to the bathroom, and the bathroom light is turned on at a low intensity before the inhabitant reaches the bathroom.

We have focused on home comfort systems because the correction involved in a misprediction is trivial; for example, if the house failed to anticipate the return of the inhabitants, it can simply turn on the heat or air conditioning when the inhabitants actually return; or if the house does not correctly turn on a light, the inhabitants can do so themselves. Predictions are based on statistical regularities in the behavior and preferences of inhabitants. If these regularities were based solely on time of day and day of the week, the accuracy of predictions would be severely limited. However, by basing predictions on dozens of variables (e.g., for predicting occupancy patterns, variables include recent room occupancy patterns, outside weather, times of recent departures and returns, home occupancy patterns on the same day of the week in recent weeks, and home occupancy patterns at the same time of day on recent days), subtle higher-order regularities can be discovered and exploited.

The *adaptive house* is an actual residence—my own—in Boulder, Colorado, that has been outfitted with over 75 sensors that monitor various aspects of the environment, including room temperature, ambient light, sound level, motion, door and window positions, and outside weather and insolation. Actuators control air heating via a whole-house furnace and electric space heaters, water heating, lighting, and ventilation. We call the control system in the adaptive house ACHE, an acronym for Adaptive Control of Home Environments. Our research involves several subprojects, each with its own challenges and peculiarities, but in this chapter I focus on the lighting control problem.

12.2 LIGHTING REGULATION

To regulate lighting, ACHE specifies the setpoint of 22 independently controlled banks of lights, each of which has 16 intensity settings. Most rooms have multiple banks of lights, e.g., the great room (containing the entertainment center, dining table, and kitchen) alone has seven banks of lights. ACHE is trained via actions taken by inhabitants to adjust the light setpoints (via dimming switches). ACHE is also influenced by energy consumption, in a manner we describe below. Figure 12.2 summarizes the framework in which ACHE operates.

12.2.1 What Makes Lighting Control Difficult?

Lighting control in the Adaptive House is a difficult task for a variety of reasons.

- More than simply turning lights on and off, lighting control involves setting lighting *moods*—the pattern and intensity of lighting. In a room used for multiple activities (e.g., a living room might be used for entertainment, reading, or watching television) and having several independently controlled banks of lights, determining the appropriate lighting mood is nontrivial.
- Although motion sensors can detect occupancy, it is not sufficient to simply switch on lights when motion is sensed. If one rolls over in bed at night, the lights should not go on. If one sits still in a chair while reading, the lights should not go off after a motion time-out period. Further, there is a 700 ms time lag between the firing of a motion sensor and the response of ACHE. This is due almost entirely to an inefficient and archaic protocol (X10) for sending commands to the lights. This lag is long enough to inconvenience the inhabitant.
- The range of time scales involved in lighting control spans many orders of magnitude. Control decisions must be responsive—in a fraction of a second—to changing environmental conditions. However, decisions can have implications that span many hours, e.g., in energy consumption.
- Two constraints must be satisfied simultaneously: maintaining lighting according to inhabitants' preferences and conserving energy. These two constraints often conflict. For example, leaving all lights on may be sufficient to satisfy the inhabitants, but it will be costly. Similarly, if minimizing energy consumption is the goal, lights will never be turned on.

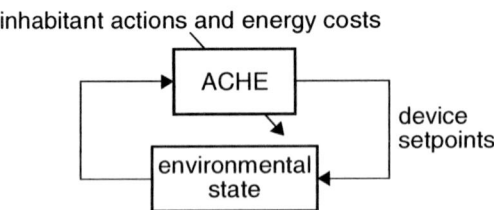

Figure 12.2 ACHE specifies device intensity setting (brightness), which affects the state of the environment, which in turn serves as input to ACHE. The training signals to ACHE are the actions taken by the inhabitants and energy costs.

12.3 OPTIMAL CONTROL

In what sort of framework can the two constraints—satisfying the inhabitants and conserving energy—be integrated? Supervised learning will not do: If lighting device settings chosen by the inhabitant serve as targets for a supervised learning system, energy costs will not be considered. Instead, we have adopted an *optimal control* framework in which failing to satisfy each constraint has an associated cost. A *discomfort cost* is incurred if inhabitant preferences are not met, i.e., if the inhabitant is not happy with the settings determined by ACHE and chooses to adjust the light settings manually. An *energy cost* is incurred based on the intensity setting of a bank of lights. The *expected average cost*, $J(t_0)$, starting at time t_0 can then be expressed as

$$J(t_0) = E\left[\lim_{\kappa \to \infty} \frac{1}{\kappa} \sum_{t=t_0+1}^{t_0+\kappa} d(x_t) + e(u_t)\right]d$$

where $d(x_t)$ is the discomfort cost associated with the environmental state x at t and $e(u_t)$ is the energy cost associated with the control decision u at t. The goal is to find an optimal control *policy*—a mapping from states x_t to decisions u_t—that minimizes the expected average cost.

This description of the control problem assumed a quantization of time into intervals indexed by t. Most research in optimal control treats these intervals as clock-based. However, the framework applies equally well to intervals produced by an event-based segmentation. We exploit this observation.

12.3.1 Reinforcement Learning

Although dynamic programming (Bellman, 1957) can be used to find a sequence of decisions u that minimize J, it has two significant drawbacks. First, it requires a model of the environment and the immediate cost function. Second, computing expectations over highly uncertain future states can be expensive. Consequently, we use *reinforcement learning*, a stochastic form of dynamic programming that samples trajectories in state space.

The particular version of reinforcement learning we consider is called *Q learning* (Watkins, 1992; Watkins & Dayan, 1992). Q learning provides an incremental update algorithm for determining the minimum expected discounted cost given that action u is taken in state x:

$$Q(x_t, u_t) \leftarrow (1 - \alpha)Q(x_t, u_t) + \alpha \max_{\hat{u}}[c_t + \lambda Q(x_{t+1}, \hat{u})]$$

where α is the learning rate, λ is the discount factor, c_t is the immediate cost incurred at t, and $\hat{u}$ is an index over all possible actions. Once this algorithm converges, the optimal action to take is the one that minimizes the Q value in the current state.

LESSONS FROM AN ADAPTIVE HOME

Because the algorithm requires that all states be visited to learn their Q values, the control policy, $\pi(x_t)$, requires exploration:

$$\pi(x_t) = \begin{cases} \mathrm{argmin}_u Q(x_t, u_t) & \text{with probability } (1-\theta) \\ \text{random} & \text{with probability } \theta \end{cases}$$

where θ is the exploration rate. Given a fully observable state and an infinite amount of time to explore the state space, Q learning is guaranteed to converge on an optimal policy.

12.3.2 Temporal Credit Assignment and the Issue of Time Scale

Figure 12.3 presents an alternative view of the sequential decision framework. At the beginning of each time interval, the current state is observed and a control decision must be made. Following the decision, a cost is observed. This cost can be attributed to the current decision or to any earlier decision, as depicted by the arrows. The *temporal credit assignment problem* involves determining which decision or decisions in the sequence are responsible for the observed costs. The challenge of learning is to correctly assign credit in time (Sutton & Barto, 1998).

On the surface, the temporal credit assignment problem for lighting control seems exacerbated due to the range of time scales involved. Because control decisions must be responsive to changing environmental conditions, the time interval between decisions must be brief, on the order of 200 ms. However, the shorter the time interval, the more difficult the temporal credit assignment problem becomes. Consider a decision to turn on lights when a room becomes occupied. As long as the room remains occupied, an energy cost is incurred at each time interval and must be attributed to the initial decision. With a 200 ms fixed interval and an hour-long occupancy period, this amounts to 18,000 time intervals over which credit assignment must be performed. Consider another scenario: The inhabitant enters a room, ACHE fails to switch on the light, and the inhabitant does so manually. The gap between the room entry and the manual override might be about 5 s, meaning that punishment for failing to turn on the light must be propagated back 25 time intervals.

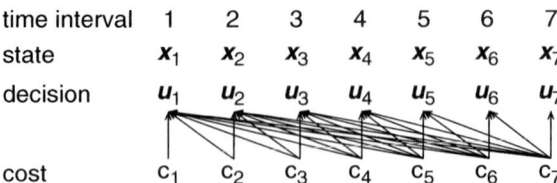

Figure 12.3 The temporal credit assignment problem.

12.4 MAKING THE LIGHTING CONTROL PROBLEM TRACTABLE

Although the standard approach to sequential decision problems using reinforcement learning involves a clock-based segmentation that divides the stream of time into uniform intervals whose durations correspond to the finest time grain of the domain, we have argued that this approach is unlikely to succeed for lighting control. ACHE would require orders of magnitude more training than any inhabitant would be willing to provide. For this reason, we were forced to consider an alternative to clock-based segmentation. Using event-based segmentation, along with three other techniques that take advantage of peculiarities of the lighting domain, the temporal credit assignment is eliminated and learning becomes almost trivial. In the following sections, we describe the key features of our solution that simplify the control problem.

12.4.1 Decomposing the Task Based on Lighting Zones

To a first order, the setting of a light in one *zone* (room) will not affect the ambient light level in another zone, nor will it affect inhabitant preferences in other zones. This is not strictly true, because light in one zone may spill into another, but by assuming independence of state and lighting decisions across zones, one can decompose the overall control problem into multiple smaller problems. This type of decomposition is extremely helpful because standard reinforcement learning methods do not have any way of taking advantage of compositional structure in the decision space, i.e., 22 banks of lights with 16 intensity settings each would result in a decision space of 16^{22} alternatives. The Adaptive House is naturally divided into eight lighting control zones, the largest of which has seven banks of lights and the smallest only one. In the remainder of this chapter, I focus on the control task for a particular zone.

12.4.2 Defining Time Intervals Using Event-Based Segmentation

The key to an event-based segmentation is an orienting mechanism that determines salient events. These events were defined to be:

- zone entry
- zone exit
- a significant change in the outdoor light level
- change in inhabitant activities (as indicated by the fact that the inhabitant manually adjusts light settings after having been satisfied with the previous settings for more than 2 min)
- in the largest zone, the great room, movement from one region of the zone to another
- anticipation of a zone entry

We discuss the mechanics of how these events are detected in later sections. When an event is detected, a lighting control decision is made. The window of time between events is treated as the basic interval. It is unitary in that only one lighting decision is made within the window, at the start of the window. Consequently, a discomfort cost—when the inhabitant manually overrides the device settings selected by ACHE—can be incurred at most one time within the window and is attributable to the decision made at the start of the window. Similarly, energy costs can be summed over the window and attributed to the decision made at the start of the window.

Because costs do not extend beyond the window, it might seem that the problem of temporal credit assignment is avoided. However, this is not necessarily the case, because a decision made at one time can affect the future state of the environment, which in turn can affect future decisions and hence future costs.

12.4.3 Eliminating Long-Term Consequences of Decisions

In the lighting control domain, the long-term consequences of decisions can in fact be eliminated due to three additional properties of the domain:

- The effect of a decision on a device is completely undone by a subsequent decision. This is true only if the decisions indicate absolute, not relative, device settings.
- Inhabitant activities are basically unaffected by ACHE's decisions. The inhabitant may have to switch on a light if ACHE fails to do so, but the inhabitant will not stop preparing dinner and instead watch television if a light doesn't turn on.
- The current device settings are irrelevant to decision making. Thus, they need not be considered part of the environmental state.

The net consequence of these properties is that the current environmental state does not depend on earlier decisions. By eliminating the long-term consequences of decisions and using event-based segmentation, we establish a finite horizon on the effect of a decision—the end of the event window. Lighting control thus becomes a single-stage decision problem, and the temporal credit assignment problem vanishes.

12.4.4 Getting the Most of Each Experience

In the standard reinforcement learning framework, a controller that makes some decision A will learn only about the consequences of A, not any other decision B. This is because the two decisions, A and B, are unrelated. However, in the case of lighting control, the decisions represent device intensity settings and hence have an intrinsic relationship to one another. With additional domain knowledge, ACHE can learn about some choices that were not selected.

Specifically, suppose that ACHE decides to set a device to intensity A, and the inhabitant overrides ACHE and sets the device to intensity C, thereby incurring a discomfort cost for decision A. If A was lower than C, then any B which is lower than A will also incur the discomfort cost. Similarly, if A was higher than C, then any B which is higher than A will also incur the discomfort cost. Because the total cost is the sum of the discomfort cost and the energy cost, and the energy cost can be computed based on trivial knowledge of the device, ACHE can determine the cost that *would have been incurred* had it made decision B. Thus, although reinforcement learning generally involves learning from experience, ACHE can learn about the consequences of some decisions it did *not* experience because it has a partial model of the cost function.

12.5 ACHE ARCHITECTURE

Figure 12.4 sketches the overall architecture of ACHE. Starting on the right side of the figure, the *Q learning controller* selects device intensity settings based on the current state. The *event-trigger mechanism* acts to gate the controller such that decisions are made only when salient events have been detected. The controller receives a training signal in the form of a total cost and depicted in the figure by the arrow cutting through the controller, from the *cost evaluator*. Cost evaluation is performed when an event is detected; hence the cost evaluator is also gated by the event-trigger mechanism. The cost evaluator needs to know when the inhabitant manually overrides the device settings produced by the controller, and hence it receives input in the figure from the light switches. The inhabitant can adjust the intensity of a device as well as switch it on or off; this information is also provided to the cost evaluator.

The state used for decision making is provided by the *state estimator*, which attempts to form a high-level state representation that explicitly encodes information relevant for decision making. In particular, we view two types of information as central: inhabitant activities and the level of natural light in the zone. Inhabitant activities cannot easily be determined from the available sensor data, but we can

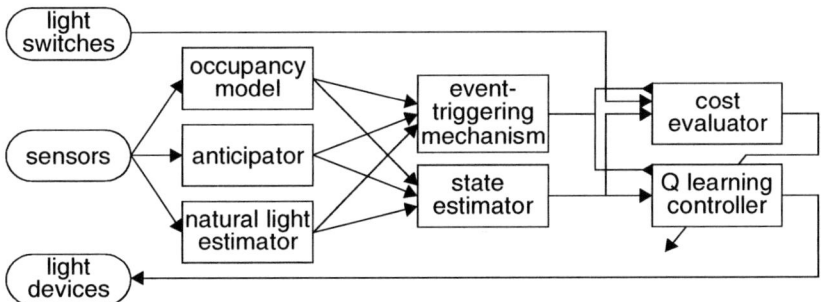

Figure 12.4 The ACHE architecture.

characterize the activities in a coarse way by observing short-term occupancy patterns across zones in the house. If the inhabitant is cleaning house, we would expect many zone changes in a short time; if the inhabitant is reading quietly in a corner, we would expect few zone changes; if the inhabitant is getting ready for work in the morning, we might expect an occupancy pattern that alternates between the bedroom and bathroom. An *occupancy model* and an *anticipator* provide information about these occupancy patterns to the state estimator. We discuss the occupancy model and the anticipator in a following section.

The second key bit of information useful for decision making is the level of natural light in the zone. This is a tricky problem, as light sensors in a zone measure the ambient light level, which depends on the current state of the lighting devices, the outside light level, and whether shades are open or closed. The *natural light estimator* attempts to determine the level of natural light in the zone if the lighting devices were turned off.

Although the state representation in ACHE attempts to recover some important information about the environment, the available sensor data does not contain all information relevant to the control task. For example, ACHE cannot determine the exact location of the inhabitants, their state of dark adaptation, or their intentions at the moment. Consequently, the state provided to the controller is non-Markovian (meaning that the instantaneous state is incomplete), and Q learning is not guaranteed to converge on an optimal policy.

12.5.1 Q-Learning Controller

As we indicated earlier, each zone is treated as an independent control task and has a separate Q controller. In addition, the control task for each *device* in each zone is treated as independent of the others. Although the optimal setting of one device in a zone certainly depends on the settings of others, the independent- controller approach still appears to capture these dependencies (Markey & Mozer, 1992).

The Q controller for a particular zone and a particular device in a zone is implemented as a pair of look-up tables—one for when the zone is occupied, one for when the zone is empty—that map a state and a decision to an expected cost. The occupied table takes as its state:

- natural light level (5 bins)
- number of zone changes by inhabitants in the last minute (0–1, 2–5, 6+)
- number of zone changes by inhabitants in the last 5 min (0–1, 2–5, 6+)
- if zone is great room, location in room (south, north, or moving) and allows five control decisions: intensity setting 0 (device off), 6, 9, 12, or 15 (device fully on). We might have allowed 16 decisions, corresponding to each of the 16 intensity settings our devices support, but subjectively many of these settings are indistinguishable. The empty table takes as its state:
- number of entries to zone under consideration in the last 5 min (0–1, 2+)
- number of entries to zone under consideration in the last 20 min (0–1, 2+)

- relative power consumption of device in its current state (5 bins) and allows for two control decisions: leave the device at its current setting or turn off the device.

12.5.2 Occupancy Model

The occupancy model determines which zones in the house are currently occupied based on motion detector signals and a finite-state model of the house. When motion is sensed in a currently unoccupied zone, the zone is flagged as occupied. It remains so until motion is sensed in a physically adjacent zone and no additional motion signals are received in the zone for at least k seconds. The occupancy model also uses opening and closing of the front and back doors, in conjunction with motion signals, to determine when an occupant enters or exits the house.

The value for k depends on whether a single or multiple occupants are in the home. It is necessary to be conservative in declaring a zone to be empty if the home contains multiple occupants for the following reason. If zone 1 is occupied and motion is sensed in adjacent zone 2, it could be that multiple inhabitants have moved from zone 1 to zone 2 and zone 1 is now empty, or it could be that a single inhabitant has moved from 1 to 2 and zone 1 is still occupied by another inhabitant who is stationary at the time. Thus, k is set to the conservative value of 600 s when the home contains multiple occupants, but only 10 s if the home contains a single occupant. The single/multiple status is also determined by the occupancy model: When multiple zones are occupied for longer than 10 s, the "multiple occupant" status is set, and remains set until the home becomes empty.

12.5.3 Anticipator

The occupancy model tags a zone as occupied when motion in that zone is first sensed. This is inadequate for lighting control, however, due to the fact that the motion detectors are sometimes sluggish—the inhabitant can walk halfway across a room before they fire—and once motion has been detected, the time to transmit commands to the lights is about 700 ms. Consequently, one would really like ACHE to predict an impending zone occupancy and to issue a lighting command shortly *before* the zone becomes occupied. A neural network, called the *anticipator*, is used for this purpose; it predicts which zone or zones will become occupied in the next 2 s.

One might argue that the anticipator is needed only because of limitations of the hardware in the Adaptive Home, and could be avoided with more expensive state-of-the-art sensors and actuators. We believe, however, that noisy and undependable sensors pose a constant challenge in real-world control, and prediction provides a means of increasing reliability in the face of noise.

The anticipator takes the following data as input:

- average value of the binary motion detector signal in a 1-, 3-, and 6-s window (36 inputs)

- instantaneous and 2-s average of the binary door status (20 inputs)
- instantaneous, 1-s, and 3-s averages of sound level (33 inputs)
- current zone occupancy status and durations (16 inputs)
- time of day (2 inputs in a circular 24 hour clock-based representation)

The purpose of including multiple time averages of sensor values is to encode information about the recent temporal history in a static representation. Although one could use a tapped-delay line to serve this purpose, the time-averaged values allow for a more compact and explicit representation of critical information. For example, one can determine that a door just opened by checking that the instantaneous door status is 1 (open) and the 2-s average is less than 1; and one can determine that motion just ceased if the 3-s average is larger than the 1-s average.

The output of the anticipator is interpreted as the probability, for each of the eight zones, that the zone will become occupied in the next 2 s, given that it is currently unoccupied. The output of the anticipator is ignored if the zone is currently occupied. The anticipator runs every 250 ms. It is a standard single-hidden-layer neural network with 107 inputs, 50 hidden units, 8 output units, direct input-output connections, and a symmetric sigmoidal activation function. The number of inputs is determined by the available data and the chosen state representation; the number of outputs is determined by the number of zones. The neural network architecture is fairly generic: including direct input-output connections allows for the linear structure of the domain to be easily captured. The number of hidden units used is generally crucial to the performance of a network (this is the problem of *model selection*), but because of the availability of large amounts of training data, the large number of free parameters in the network is justified and had less impact. (For further advice on building neural network models in practice, see Orr and Müller, 1998.)

The occupancy model provides the training signal to the anticipator. The anticipator's job is to detect cues in the environment that reliably predict the zone entry announced by the occupancy model. The training procedure is inductive: a partially trained anticipator net is run to make predictions, and when it produces an error, new data is added to the training set. When a sufficient quantity of new data is added (200 examples), the network is retrained. The anticipator can produce two types of errors: a *miss*, when a zone entry fails to be predicted within 2 s of the event, and a *false alarm*, when a zone entry is predicted and none in fact occurs. To avoid a miss in the future, a new training example is generated in which the sequence of eight input states leading up to the zone entry—corresponding to the states at $t - 2000$ ms, $t - 1750$ ms, ..., $t - 250$ ms—are all associated with the zone entry. To avoid a false alarm, a training example is generated in which the state at the time the entry is predicted is associated with no zone entry. A temporal difference training procedure (Sutton, 1988) is used for the sequence of states leading to the miss. This is appropriate because in the sequence, each state becomes an increasingly better predictor of the event. Using the temporal difference procedure yielded slightly better results than standard supervised learning.

Figure 12.5 shows a measure of performance of the anticipator as a function of the amount of collected training data. The horizontal axis also corresponds to time on the scale of about a month. The performance measure is the ratio of the number of *hits* (correct predictions of a zone entry) to the sum of misses plus false alarms collected in a small time window. Although the curve is noisy, performance is clearly improving as additional data is collected. Because the anticipator outputs a continuous probability, it is necessary to threshold the output to produce a definite prediction that can be used by ACHE. Through empirical tests, we found that a threshold of 0.7 roughly balanced the miss and false alarm rates.

Anecdotally, the anticipator net does seem to have captured important behavioral regularities of the house inhabitant. We illustrate several examples using the house floor plan shown in Figure 12.6. In the evening, when the inhabitant walks out of the great room and into the entry (trajectory *A*), the anticipator predicts that the master bedroom is about to become occupied. However, when the same pattern of movement occurs in the morning, the anticipator predicts that the inhabitant is headed toward bedroom 2, which is used as an office. At night, when the inhabitant gets out of bed and walks toward the master bath (trajectory *C*), the anticipator uses the onset of motion in the master bedroom, along with a sound produced by a creaky floor, to predict that the bathroom is about to become occupied. This combination of cues is apparently necessary, as sound alone (e.g., a telephone ringing) or motion alone (e.g., rolling over in bed) is insufficient to produce a strong prediction. The anticipator sometimes uses odd but reliable cues. For example, when the inhabitant showers in the morning, he has a habit of listening to a radio in the bathroom. Before walking out of the bathroom, he shuts off the radio. Consequently, a sudden offset of a sustained sound level in the bathroom is a reliable indicator that the bedroom is about to become occupied. On the whole, the anticipator is not entirely dependable, though, primarily because the sparse representation of the environment produced by the sensors does not support perfect predictions.

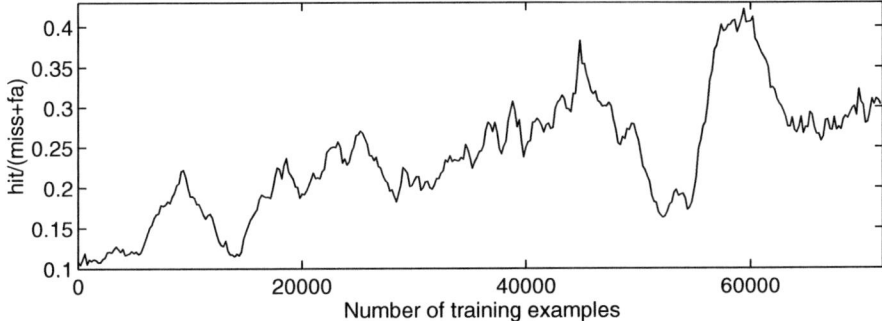

Figure 12.5 Performance of the anticipator network as the number of training examples increases.

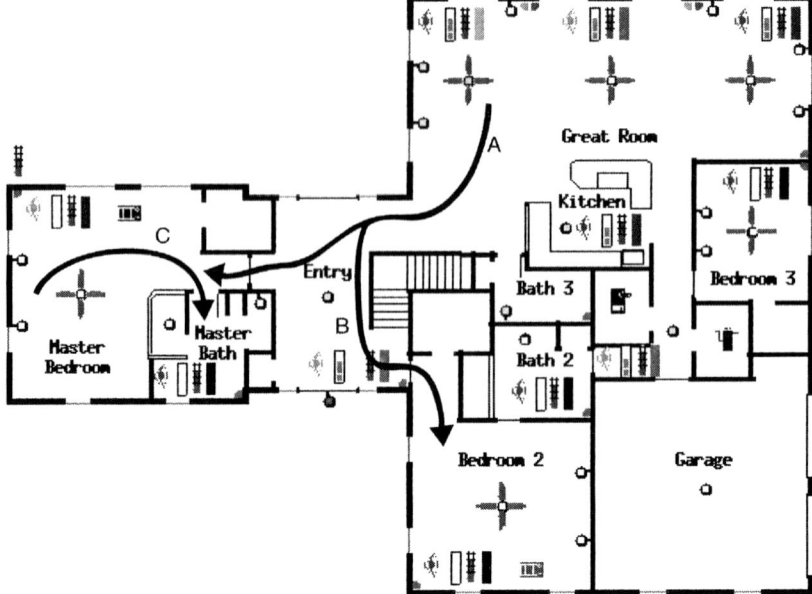

Figure 12.6 A floor plan of the Adaptive House, including locations of sensors and actuators. Three trajectories are indicated by arrows labeled *A*, *B*, and *C*.

12.5.4 ACHE Parameters and Costs

In the current implementation of ACHE, we use an exploration probability, θ, of 0.05, causing the controller to take the action believed to be optimal with probability 0.95, and to try another alternative at the remaining times. Rather than choosing the alternative arbitrarily from the set of actions, as one might do with undirected reinforcement learning, ACHE selected the action with next lower energy cost from the action believed to be optimal. With this choice, ACHE will gradually lower the device setting to minimize energy consumption as long as the inhabitant does not express discomfort.

Determining the appropriate Q table learning rate, α, is tricky. The learning rate must be large enough that ACHE adapts after several experiences, but it must not be so large that a single experience causes ACHE to forget what had been learned in the past. We used a learning rate of 0.3, which provided a reasonable balance between adaptability and stability. The Q learning discount factor, λ, was zero, because event-based segmentation simplified reinforcement learning to a single-step problem with immediate payoff.

Finally, we list the various costs in the lighting control problem. We have already mentioned an energy cost, which was set to $.072 per kilowatt-hour, the actual cost of electricity charged by the local utility company. The discomfort cost was set to $.01 per device whose setting was manually adjusted by the inhabitant. Because this cost could be incurred for *each* device in a zone, and a zone has as many as seven devices, up to $.07 could be charged for inhabitant discomfort each time a zone is entered, which is quite steep relative to energy costs. Two additional costs were incorporated, related to the anticipator. Consider the situation in which the inhabitant exits a zone, the lights in the zone are turned off, and when the inhabitant returns to the zone, the anticipator fails to predict the return. The resulting delay in turning the lights back on will cause inconvenience to the inhabitant, quantified as a cost of $.01 per device that was turned off but should have been set to a nonzero intensity. This cost is incurred only when the anticipator misses the zone entry. The complementary situation is when the anticipator false alarms, i.e., incorrectly predicts a zone entry, and causes lights to be turned on in the zone. (The lights are turned back off after a time-out period if the zone entry does not occur.) A cost should be incurred in this situation to reflect annoyance to the inhabitant, who may notice lights turning on and off in unoccupied zones. We set this cost to $.01 per device that was turned on as a result of an anticipator false alarm.

ACHE's Q table was initialized to the expected energy cost for the corresponding decision, which assumes that the inhabitant has no preference for the device setting. Consequently, devices will not be turned on unless the inhabitant expresses discomfort. Rather than training the anticipator and the controller simultaneously, the anticipator was trained first, over a period of a month, before the controller was turned on.

12.6 RESULTS AND DISCUSSION

Figure 12.7 shows energy and discomfort costs as a function of the number of events experienced by ACHE. The discomfort cost includes the anticipator miss and false alarm costs. The figure reflects 24 days of data collection, and events were logged only during times when it was likely that indoor lighting would be required, from 19:00 to 06:59. To smooth out some of the noise, data points in the figure reflect the mean value in a moving window of 50 events centered on the current event. Although the energy cost decreases fairly steadily, the discomfort costs are quite variable. This is due, at least in part, to a programming error in ACHE that caused the misattribution of some costs. Because time limitations did not allow us to restart ACHE, we corrected the problem near event 1700 and continued ACHE's training. From this point on, ACHE appears to have converged quickly on a low-energy cost, low-discomfort cost solution.

12.6.1 A Training Scenario

ACHE learns quite rapidly, as we illustrate in the following training scenario. To simplify the scenario, assume that the state which serves as input to the Q-learning controller is fixed. The first time that the inhabitant enters a zone (we'll refer to this as a *trial*), ACHE decides, based on the initialization Q values, to leave the light off. If the inhabitant overrides this decision by turning

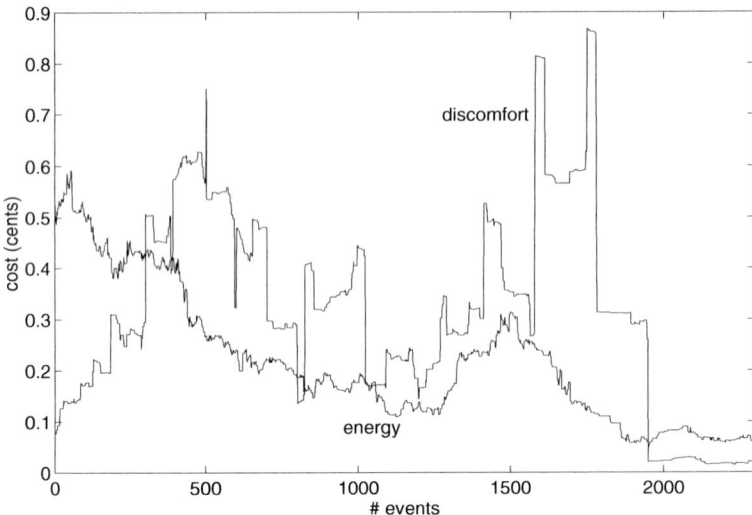

Figure 12.7 Energy and discomfort costs incurred by ACHE as a function of the number of events experienced. The discomfort cost includes anticipator miss and false alarm costs.

on the light, ACHE immediately learns that leaving the light off will incur a higher cost (the discomfort cost) than turning on the light to some intensity (the energy cost). On the next trial, ACHE decides to turn on the light, but has no reason to believe that one intensity setting will be preferred over another. Consequently, the lowest intensity setting is selected. On any trial in which the inhabitant adjusts the light intensity upward, the decision chosen by ACHE will incur a discomfort cost, and on the following trial, a higher intensity will be selected. Training thus requires just three or four trials and explores the space of decisions to find the lowest acceptable intensity. ACHE also attempts to conserve energy by occasionally "testing" the inhabitant, selecting an intensity setting lower than the setting believed to be optimal. If the inhabitant does not complain, the cost of the decision is updated to reflect this fact, and eventually the lower setting will be evaluated as optimal.

This scenario plays out nicely, at least in part, because we assumed that the state serving as input to the Q-learning controller was fixed. In practice, changes in the state lead to complications. For example, one component of the state representation is the number of times the inhabitant has recently moved from one zone to another. As this number increases, the state changes, the Q look-up table switches to a different bin for decision making, and the experience gained in the previous bin is no longer accessible. From the inhabitant's perspective, ACHE appears to forget its recent training. In the long run, this is not a problem, as eventually ACHE acquires sufficient experience in all states. One way of avoiding the inconvenience in the short run is to use a memory-based approach, such as *k*-nearest neighbor, to implement the Q function, rather than a look-up table.

12.6.2 Informal Evaluation

Beyond the performance curve, it is difficult to evaluate ACHE formally. One would really like to know whether ACHE is useful and whether people would want such a system in their homes. Although ACHE appears surprisingly intelligent at times, it can also frustrate. Most of the frustration, however, was due to the implementation using X10 controls, which are painfully slow to respond, especially when ACHE is adjusting multiple banks of lights at once. I also found it disconcerting when ACHE would incorrectly predict my passage into another room and lights would turn on or off in an unoccupied area of the house. This problem can be rectified by increasing the cost of false anticipation errors.

Overall, I found the benefits to outweigh the inconveniences, rapidly becoming accustomed to the automatic control of lighting. Indeed, when ACHE is disabled, the home seems cold and uninviting. Although this may sound implausible to one who hasn't lived in an automated home, reverting to manual control of the lights is annoying and cumbersome. An informal but compelling testament to the value of ACHE is that I left it running long beyond the termination of data collection.

12.7 THE FUTURE

In this final section, I discuss possible extensions of ACHE.

12.7.1 Extensions Not Worth Pursuing

The Adaptive House project has inspired much brainstorming about ways to extend the project further, most of which seem entirely misguided. One idea often mentioned is controlling home entertainment systems—stereos, TVs, radios, etc. The problem with selection of video and audio in the home is that the inhabitants' preferences will depend on their state of mind, and few cues are directly available from the environment—even using machine vision—that correlate with state of mind. The result is likely to be that the system mispredicts often and annoys the inhabitants more than it supports them. The annoyance is magnified by the fact that when inhabitants seek audio or video entertainment, they generally have an explicit intention to do so. This intention contrasts with, say, temperature regulation in a home, where the inhabitants do not consciously consider the temperature unless it becomes uncomfortable. If inhabitants are aware of their goals, achieving the goal is possible with a simple click of a button, and errors—such as blasting the stereo when one is concentrating on a difficult problem—are all but eliminated. The benefit/cost trade-off falls on the side of manual control.

ACHE could always be improved by information provided explicitly by the inhabitants. For example, providing ACHE with the inhabitants' calendar entries in their PDAs would greatly simplify predictions concerning departure and return times; providing ACHE with information about current activities (e.g., hosting a party, preparing dinner, relaxing) would certainly simplify the lighting regulation problems and would eliminate errors the system might make. However, the premise of the project—as I stated at the outset—was to see how intelligent a system could be with a minimal user interface. Any additional information provided to ACHE by the inhabitants would require an additional user interface. It is clear that more information would make for a smarter system, but if a system passes the threshold of usability without requiring this information, it is a strong proof of concept.

12.7.2 Activity Classification

ACHE's control decisions are based on the current state of the environment and predictions concerning future states. For example, the motion and sound cues lead to a prediction of future location, which might lead to a decision to turn on a light. ACHE, however, has no explicit representation of inhabitant activities, e.g., whether the inhabitants are preparing dinner, relaxing, studying, etc. Such an intermediate level of representation could serve a valuable purpose, particularly in integrating sensor information over time and increasing the coherence of control decisions over time. For example, inferring that inhabitants are preparing dinner would allow ACHE to maintain a fixed pattern of lighting even if the moment-to-moment behavior of the inhabitants was difficult to interpret. In a home, the set of activities sufficient to characterize the typical and frequent behaviors of the inhabitants is finite and readily characterized; thus we pose the problem as activity *classification*—choosing one ore more activities from the finite set based on sensor data.

Machine learning researchers have addressed the problem of inferring activities of individuals (Brand & Kettnaker, 2000; Brand, Oliver, & Pentland, 1997; Ivanov & Bobick, 2000; Oliver, Rosario, & Pentland, 2000), although the work has been primarily directed at recognizing actions involving multiple interacting individuals using machine vision and hidden Markov models. In the case of home environments, other sources of sensor data are available, and a primary research challenge is handling interleaved activities (e.g., the inhabitant interrupts dinner preparation to answer the phone or put the clothes in the dryer). Recent work of Girolami and Kaban (2003) does address the problems of multiple activities.

12.7.3 Educating the Inhabitants

In the course of its operation, ACHE constructs models of the inhabitants and the environment. One interesting lesson from the Adaptive House is that as the inhabitant, I also constructed a model of ACHE or, more specifically, a model of ACHE's model of the inhabitant. For instance, if I were at work at 8 p.m., I would realize that under ordinary circumstances, I might have left several hours earlier; consequently, ACHE would be expecting me, and I felt compelled to return home. To some degree, I regularized my schedule in order to accommodate ACHE and its actions. Living with ACHE makes one aware of one's own occupancy and movement patterns. It is not entirely facetious to claim that ACHE trains the inhabitant, just as the inhabitant trains ACHE. Indeed, this interactive training is one of the virtues of living with an Adaptive House. To the extent that the house discovers regularities of the inhabitants' behavior and inhabitants regularize their behavior to accommodate the house, the interaction converges on an ideal situation: inhabitants whose schedules and behavior are predictable, allowing ACHE to both maximize comfort and minimize energy utilization.

Generalizing from this scenario, it seems useful for a smart home to educate its inhabitants concerning their behavior and needs. This principle was fortuitously revealed via a hardware bug in the Adaptive House. The water-flow sensor sometimes malfunctioned and needed to be reset. Rather than checking the sensor daily, we used a heuristic to warn us when a reset was necessary: if the bathroom was occupied for more than 5 min and hot water flow was not detected, a warning message was broadcast throughout the house. This would invariably catch occasions when the inhabitants were showering but the sensor had failed. Additionally, it would also catch occasions when the inhabitants dawdled in the bathroom, e.g., reading on the toilet. Long after the hardware problem was resolved, we left the broadcast message in the system, because it provided useful feedback to the inhabitants about how their time was being spent. Because time is such a precious commodity, a useful function of an intelligent home would be to help inhabitants use their time more efficiently.

Another scenario in which the Adaptive Home could educate its inhabitants concerns energy use. Whenever the inhabitant overrides current setpoints, there are consequences for the expected cost. For example, raising the target temperature from 68 to 70°F will cost more in energy to heat the home. The exact cost depends on the occupancy patterns in the home, the weather, and thermal properties of the home and heating system. Because ACHE models all of these elements, forecasting the additional cost due to a change in setpoint is straightforward. Essentially, ACHE can say, "If you really want the temperature another 2 degrees higher, you should expect to pay another $30 in the coming month."

I described three scenarios in which a smart home could provide feedback to its inhabitants, allowing them to make more informed decisions or better use of their time. Such feedback is not necessarily incompatible with the principle I argued for at the outset of the chapter—the principle that novel user interfaces should be avoided. In the scenarios described here, the feedback provided is expressed in terms individuals can comprehend, and it supports informed decision making. Perhaps the next step in intelligent environments will come from environments that stick their virtual nose in our business.

REFERENCES

Bellman, R. (1957). *Dynamic programming*. Princeton, NJ: Princeton University Press.

Brand, M. & Kettnaker, V. (2000). Discovery and segmentation of activities in video. *IEEE Transactions on Pattern Analysis and Machine Intelligence, 22*, 844–851.

Cohen, M. (2003). The internet chair. *International Journal of Human-Computer Interaction, 15*, 297–311.

Davis, J.W. & Bobick, A. F. (1996). The representation and recognition of action using temporal templates. *IEEE Conference on Computer Vision and Pattern Recognition (CVPR'97)*, San Juan, Puerto Rico.

Girolami, M. & Kaban, A. (2003). Sequential activity profiling: Latent Dirichlet allocation of Markov models. *Neural Information Processing Systems XVII.*

Ivanov, Y.A. & Bobick, A.F. (2000). Recognition of visual activities and interactions by stochastic parsing. *IEEE Transactions on Pattern Analysis and Machine Intelligence, 22*, 852–872.

Markey, K. & Mozer, M.C. (1992). Comparison of reinforcement algorithms on learning discrete functions: Learnability, time complexity, and scaling. *Proceedings of the International Joint Conference on Neural Networks* (Volume I, pp. 853–859). San Diego, CA: IEEE Publishing Services.

Oliver, N.M., Rosario, B., & Pentland, A.P. (2000). A Bayesian computer vision system for modeling human interactions. *IEEE Transactions on Pattern Analysis and Machine Intelligence, 22*, 831–843.

Orr, G.B. & Müller, K.-R. (1998). *Neural networks: Tricks of the trade.* Berlin: Springer.

Sutton, R.S. (1988). Learning to predict by the method of temporal differences. *Machine Learning, 3*, 9–44.

Sutton, R.S. & Barto, A.G. (1998). *Reinforcement learning: An introduction.* Cambridge, MA: MIT Press.

Watkins, C.J.C.H. (1992). Learning from delayed rewards. Unpublished doctoral dissertation. King's College, Cambridge, UK.

Watkins, C.J.C.H. & Dayan, P. (1992). Q learning. *Machine Learning, 8*, 279–292.

CHAPTER 13

Smart Rooms

ALVIN CHEN,[1] RICHARD MUNTZ,[1] and MANI SRIVASTAVA[2]
[1]CS Department and [2]EE Department
University of California at Los Angeles

13.1 INTRODUCTION

The focus and application of computing technology in the past largely involved facilitating and enriching person-to-computer and person-to-person interactions. However, driven by relentlessly shrinking microelectronics, computing technology is undergoing a transformation whereby its primary role is shifting to enabling richer interaction between people and instrumented physical environments. Indeed, in the not too distant future, a single system-on-chip will integrate processor, memory, radio, sensors, and actuators all in a die measuring a few square millimeters, costing little, and consuming only a few milliwatts of power (e.g., the Smart Dust project at Berkeley [Kahn99]). This would allow processing, communication, sensing, and perhaps even actuation capabilities to be unobtrusively embedded in everyday physical objects, leading to systems where these familiar objects act as tetherless peripherals able to react to external stimuli while communicating with each other and with a background computing infrastructure. Such technology promises to bring interaction and intelligence to commonplace inanimate objects in our environment, thus establishing person-to-physical world interaction as the new focus of computing technology. Instrumented physical spaces will monitor environmental conditions, detecting events related to people and objects in the area. They can then act on the sensed information or use it to provide context when responding to queries and commands. This vision was perhaps first advanced in Mark Weiser's seminal article in *Scientific American* [Weiser91], where he advocated using a large number of invisible networked computing systems (i.e., computers hidden everywhere "in the woodwork") to "activate" the world. Weiser envisioned "a physical world that is richly and invisibly interwoven with sensors, actuators, displays, and computational elements, richly and invisibly interwoven, embedded seamlessly in the everyday objects of our lives, and connected through a continuous network."

Smart Environments: Technologies, Protocols, and Applications, edited by D.J. Cook and S.K. Das
ISBN 0-471-54448-5 © 2005 John Wiley & Sons, Inc.

It is only in recent years that technology has reached a stage where the application of computing technology to facilitate unobtrusive person-to-physical world interaction has become feasible. Perhaps the most successful manifestation of this new paradigm has been in the context of indoor spaces, such as rooms, which are instrumented to let the occupants of the physical space interact invisibly with the virtual world of computers as they go about their normal activities. In such smart rooms, various services residing in the underlying networked computing infrastructure continually observe and track what the occupants are doing via multiple sensor modalities, controlling actuators that modify the physical state of the room or provide other feedback to the occupants.

Several research projects have explored smart rooms in recent years. Broadly, the applications of the Smart Room paradigm have been in the context of the workplace, everyday living, entertainment, play, and education. In the context of the workplace, perhaps the earliest project was the Ubiquitous Computing project at Xerox PARC [Weiser91], which explored office and business environments instrumented with devices like active badges for location tracking, as well as active whiteboards and tablets for user interaction. More recently, efforts such as MIT Media Lab's Smart Room [Pentland96], HP's CoolTown [Barton01, Kindberg00] and IBM's BlueSpace [Chou01] have explored workspace applications of smart rooms. In the context of everyday living, Georgia Tech's Aware Home [Kidd99] research initiative is exploring domestic spaces instrumented with distributed sensing and perception technologies with services for localization, activity recognition, capturing of live experiences, etc. In the context of entertainment, research efforts at MIT's Media Lab and UCLA's HyperMedia Studio have explored the use of sensor- and actuator-instrumented spaces for stage shows, film productions, and multimedia exhibits. For example, the HyperMedia Studio's Macbett project [Burke01] used such technology to dynamically adapt lighting and sound to performers' positions and actions. Similarly, UCLA's Augmented Recording project [Su03, Su04] uses smart room technology to augment film and video footage with synchronized data from sensors embedded in the space and put on the performers. Later, in the postproduction phase, the sensor data is used to enhance the editing process and to permit seamless integration of the recorded video footage with computer-generated graphics and video. In a real-time setting, the sensor data can be used to actuate camera movements and follow special effects cues. MIT Media Lab's KidsRoom project [Bobick99] utilizes the smart room paradigm to create an interactive and immersive playspace that responds to children's actions as they are guided through a story set in a child's bedroom. Lastly, several projects have explored the use of smart rooms in the context of learning and education. Georgia Tech's Classroom 2000 project [Abowd99] used an instrumented classroom to capture the traditional university lecture experience. The system automatically generates a rich multimedia transcript and provides access to the recorded lecture by automatically integrating multiple streams of captured information. Lecture notes are projected on a LiveBoard (a huge vertical pen computer in the form of a whiteboard) for the teacher and displayed on pen tablets for the students, while handwritten notes are captured as pen strokes linked to the notes. These are further augmented with audio and video recordings to produce time-stamped, media-enhanced lecture transcripts. UCLA's Smart Kindergarten project [Chen02, Srivastava01], with which the authors are involved, is exploring the use of a sensor-instrumented classroom to target developmental problem-solving environments for early childhood education. It seeks to enhance the education process by providing a childhood learning environment that is customized to each child, adapting to context, coordinating activities for multiple children, and allowing unobtrusive evaluation of the learning process by the teacher. Using a mix of ambient sensors, wearable sensor badges, and sensor-instrumented objects and furniture, the Smart Kindergarten creates a problem-solving environment that is continually sensed in detail. A background computing and data management infrastructure is used for on-line and off-line sensor data processing and mining. This allows the Smart Kindergarten to aid assessment of student learning and group dynamics, mediate adaptive and interactive problem-solving tasks, and provide services such as detailed transcripts of classroom activity that are beneficial to teachers and students.

As the preceding examples demonstrate, a diverse range of smart room applications already exists. In the remainder of this chapter, we explore the goals, technology challenges, and operational constraints that characterize the smart room paradigm. From a technology perspective, we describe the networking, sensing, middleware services, and data management primitives that are essential for realizing a scalable infrastructure for deeply instrumented physical environments. Despite the growing range of applications available, we show that smart rooms face a common set of challenges in providing the intelligent computing environments of the future.

13.2 COMMON GOALS AND TASKS

Although smart rooms are being used for diverse applications in education, entertainment, business, research, and everyday living, there is a commonality of goals underlying these applications. While an office environment may not seem to share many of the characteristics of an interactive stage, the smart room paradigm lends itself to a number of common tools to achieve their divergent goals. This section will describe a number of common themes found in smart room scenarios, giving an overview of how different applications address similar problems in different environments. These common tasks include user presentations, collaboration, environmental interaction, occupant observation, and contextual information enrichment.

13.2.1 Presentation

One of the most common uses of a smart room involves the user-mediated presentation of information to an audience, small or large, local or widely distributed. Whether giving a lecture to students, making a presentation to coworkers, or delivering a monologue to theatergoers, a smart room can facilitate communication while enhancing the experience for the audience. While the end goals may differ, each environment involves the one-to-many delivery of information.

For example, the Smart Classroom [Xie01] is a smart room that facilitates distance learning in which a lecturer presents coursework to students who may be located far away. The Smart Classroom utilizes microphones and speech processing to recognize a limited vocabulary of verbal cues that may trigger the advancement of a slide show, for instance. Camera systems also recognize simple gestures that can serve to invoke commands or disambiguate verbal cues. By amalgamating verbal and visual cues, the Smart Classroom hopes to distinguish between a verbal "next page" command that signals students to turn to the next page in a textbook and one intended to advance a lecture slide show, using the direction in which the lecturer is facing and gestures he might make. In fact, since most smart rooms have an array of different sensors, many projects seek to compose multiple types of data to produce more accurate and useful results.

While delivering information in a very different domain, the Intelligent Studio [Pinhanez95] also utilizes the smart room paradigm to aid in presentation. In this case, the scenario involves an array of pan-tilt-zoom (PTZ) cameras along with a wide-angle camera arranged to cover a television studio. The wide-angle camera provides data for the construction of a world model that identifies and tracks a variety of people and objects on the set of a cooking show. The system uses this world model to direct the PTZ cameras to automatically find and follow important entities while applying various broadcast camera-framing rules (for instance, there must always be extra space in front of a person's face when it is shown in profile). In fact, the system follows a script to aid in the acquisition of new camera angles required to capture future actions. For instance, food preparation may involve an overhead shot of the hands near the cooking area, so the system can set a camera to acquire the appropriate view and focus image segmentation on the likely area of interest based on upcoming script actions. On the other hand, a farewell wave will probably involve a hand moving near the upper third of the chef's body, so the system can adjust its image processing appropriately. Like the Smart Classroom, the Intelligent Studio combines multiple sources of information to produce a more accurate and effective system. In this scenario, the system uses a wide-angle camera's world model and the behavior dictated in a script to automatically position an array of PTZ cameras, as well as focus the efforts of its image processing algorithms.

For a smart room paradigm applied to theater production, Pinhanez's paper on computer theater [Pinhanez97] describes possible scenarios for an instrumented theater that can supplement a theater production, for instance by increasing the actors' freedom of expression. In this form of presentation, the smart room enhances the expressive capabilities of the user, creating a "hyper-actor" who can direct various stage elements, from lighting to music, during a performance. An actor's location on the stage and his gestures can affect the presentation environment, or they can trigger scripted events, advancing the narrative. Similarly in UCLA HyperMedia Studio's Macbett [Burke01] project, lighting and sound are dynamically adapted to performers' positions and movements by using a sensor-instrumented stage.

13.2.2 Collaboration

In addition to enhancing a person's ability to make presentations to others, smart rooms often facilitate collaboration among multiple people. While this most commonly involves people working together in a business setting, educational and entertainment environments involve collaborative efforts as well. For instance, students may work together on a class project, or players may combine their efforts to overcome challenges in an interactive game. Traditional collaborative applications provide interfaces that allow multiple people to access the necessary information and tools, often with a focus on distributed users, but smart environments can blur the boundaries of these interfaces.

IBM's BlueSpace project [Chou01] seeks to address the need for collaboration among a small number of coworkers. Since large meeting rooms may not be available for every spontaneous work group, the project focuses on facilitating collaboration within the confines of a personal office. Since many users find sharing a computer screen to be too confining, the BlueSpace office includes an Everywhere Display (ED) projector, which uses a computer-controlled mirror to direct distortion-corrected images onto nearly any office surface. For easy viewing, the ED projector can display the computer screen on an office wall. Alternatively, when users must gather around a table, the ED projector can move the projection to the table surface. A wireless mouse and keyboard allow flexibility matching that of the projector. The BlueSpace environment can also automatically adjust office lighting for better viewing.

A number of other efforts seek to support collaboration in less technical arenas. For example, a number of projects have dealt with the problem of coordinating musical performances in far-flung locations [Schooler93]. Complex synchronization mechanisms [Escobar94] and auditory systems allow musicians to play together as though they were in the same room. Pinhanez also described scenarios in which computer systems could allow a theater cast to rehearse computer-supported performances or even track intentions well enough to allow for improvisational theater [Pinhanez97].

The Smart Kindergarten [Chen02] project, which provides an instrumented classroom for primary education, includes a variety of "smart toys" usable by children, including the Smart Table [Steurer03]. The Smart Table utilizes a dense array of magnetic or metal contact sensors arranged in a regular grid below or on the surface of a table. When students place objects with magnetic or metal labels on the surface of the Smart Table, it can identify the objects, track their positions, and identify their orientations. Teachers can use the Smart Kindergarten to design interactive puzzles or problem-solving exercises for their students on the Smart Table. For instance, the labeled objects may themselves be small devices capable of showing images or emitting light and sound based on their relative positioning.

Another smart room that facilitates collaboration among children is the MIT Media Lab's KidsRoom [Bobick99], which presents children with an interactive fantasy adventure set in a simulated bedroom. In this case, cameras hidden from view high above the room track the positions of the children as they follow the story. Other concealed cameras track movement and gestures that the children may make. At various points during the narrative, they ensure that the children work together to hide behind objects, "explore" a fantasy world, and direct a "boat" with their rowing motions. A microphone can also detect when the children shout a "magic word" together or remain silent to appease a character in the story. Only through their combined actions can the children advance the narrative. The Kids-Room helps demonstrate the richness of collaborative efforts in the smart room domain, going far beyond traditional computer-supported cooperative work applications.

13.2.3 Interaction

A number of smart room applications provide users with the ability to interact with their environments. Whether this involves accessing computer resources directly through the smart room's interfaces or having the system respond indirectly to the user's actions, smart rooms have opened up new potential for interactive environments. Sensors embedded in the environment and those worn by the user can facilitate a new form of communication, not just between human and computer or computer and computer but between human and environment. Interactivity offers a wealth of new ways to manipulate a room and its computing resources, as well as a flexible method for delivering new forms of artwork and entertainment.

As described earlier, the KidsRoom [Bobick99] offers children an immersive narrative experience in an instrumented area designed to look like a child's bedroom. By concealing its array of sensors and appealing to the storybook nature of its narrative and setting, the KidsRoom encourages participants to interact with the room, each other, and even virtual characters. Cameras can track the children's locations and a microphone detects sound levels, while speakers, lights, and large projection screens allow the room to provide instructions and feedback. For instance, a narrator's voice may tell the children to hide behind a bed to end threatening "monster" sounds, or the children may need to position themselves on special colored rugs to take part in a "monster dance." In fact, gesture recognition algorithms can identify specific dance moves executed by each child, allowing the "monsters" to respond with their own dance moves. By combining a fanciful storyline with embedded devices, the KidsRoom offers a compelling reason for users to interact directly with a smart room, using an immersive interface that relies on unencumbered, natural actions.

While the KidsRoom delivers an entertaining storybook experience for children, it provides a clear realization of the interactive smart room scenarios envisioned by a number of researchers. For instance, the NIST Smart Space Laboratory (http://www.nist.gov/smartspace/) proposes emergency response rooms where one wall consists of a screen and other interfaces. Users of the room can face the screen and see users in a similar room or at other video interfaces. Inserting a document into a slot will fax it to a remote user, who may receive it from a similar slot at the other end, adding to the illusion of a shared physical environment. A number of artists have also embraced the technologies offered by interactive environments.

For instance, researchers have developed the Emergence Engine [Mendelowitz00] to help artists compose virtual worlds that interact with users at a physical display. Pressure pads, cameras, and other sensors can detect a viewer's presence, track his movements, etc., while feeding this data into a series of artificial intelligence behavior algorithms. Virtual creatures might flee from him or attempt to engage him in a "cooperative" activity, like the monster dance of the KidsRoom. The integration of physical data allows the virtual world to react to the viewer, creating an interactive artistic experience.

13.2.4 Observation

While most smart rooms are used to enhance a user's experience, many also provide monitoring and recording capabilities, like those of other research efforts in the sensing domain. Unlike common sensor applications that measure physical characteristics, ecological data, or natural phenomena, smart rooms lend themselves to observations that focus on human behavior. The relatively controlled environment of smart rooms also allows for a good variety of sensors that provide rich context for the recorded data. Computing resources, network connectivity, and energy may be more plentiful in a smart room than a traditional sensor network environment as well.

A number of early efforts at recording events in a smart room involved the annotated recording of presentations. For instance, the Classroom 2000 project [Abowd99] instrumented a classroom to capture lectures in a computationally rich environment. The lecturer used an electronic whiteboard that allowed notes to be written on prepared presentation slides. The electronic whiteboard captured and timestamped the lecturer's pen strokes, which were associated with an audio stream provided by classroom microphones. The project later used commercial speech recognition software to aid in the generation of a text search for jumping to appropriate points in the recorded presentation, though the software was not accurate enough to automatically generate a human-readable text transcript of the lecture.

The MIRA project [Castro00] also extended its videoconference recording to video streams produced during meetings. In addition to its primary video streams, MIRA used Bayesian networks [Pearl88] to combine data from a variety of other sensors, deriving context for the video stream. Since both sensor data and computer-ascribed context involve inherently untrustworthy and noisy data, probabilistic methods allowed MIRA to provide measures of reliability with its predictions while utilizing highly distinct types of data. In fact, the Bayesian networks could be formed into modular *conglomerated services*, which can be recombined to form arbitrarily complex composites utilizing a variety of sensor inputs. Automatic annotations could denote the joining and leaving times of various members, identify speakers, and notice special actions, like writing.

The Smart Kindergarten [Chen02] offers teachers and educational researchers the chance to observe young students as they interact within a typical classroom. By providing a rich array of sensors, including cameras, microphones, and positioning devices, tied together by processing software and reasoning systems, the Smart Kindergarten can help researchers deduce high-level social behaviors from a wealth of contextualized information. For instance, tiny badges equipped with sensor suites [Park02a] provide positioning and orientation information that let the system to derive social grouping patterns. Built-in microphones accompanied by speech processing hardware can track language use among nonnative speakers or record differences in speech patterns when they converse with different social groups. The Smart Kindergarten utilizes data fusion techniques built on belief networks [Pearl88] that can combine information from a wide range of devices to derive high-level context. A database can also record streams of data, whether processed or raw, allowing for context-rich monitoring useful in later assessment or data mining.

A number of efforts using smart rooms for automatically assisted living also monitor occupants and their environment. The Neural Network House [Mozer95] records the environmental settings used by various occupants. Using these observations, it learns the relative desires of its occupants, so it can automatically adjust a room's lighting, heating, and other settings to fit a user's preferences while trying to minimize energy costs across an entire household, even as people move from room to room. The Aware Home [Kidd99] utilizes a Smart Floor that can identify a person solely by his footsteps on force-sensitive load tiles, using profiles for a small user population. This can track a user's movements throughout the household.

13.2.5 Enrichment

Smart rooms can provide a lot of information about their contents, their users, and themselves. Rich arrays of sensors, network connectivity, and computing resources may all reside in a smart room, and many applications will present those capabilities to the user by augmenting the physical world with informational resources. By associating information with the real world, smart rooms can provide a natural interface to a great amount of data, enriching the user's informational experience. The contextual association of information with a physical entity helps the user to process and understand what might otherwise be an overwhelming flood of data produced by the typical smart room.

HP has developed a very information-rich domain with its CoolTown efforts in ubiquitous computing [Barton01, Kindberg00]. Working under the assumption that applications will drive the deployment of ubiquitous computing environments, HP researchers have focused on already popular and open protocols, especially the Hypertext Transfer Protocol (HTTP) of the World Wide Web. Their efforts to enrich the physical world involve giving physical entities, including people, places, and things, a presence on the Web, which can be associated with their physical location. CoolTown environments utilize the passing of Uniform Resource Locators (URLs) from objects and places to personal computing devices and back, in a process they have termed *eSquirting*. Having developed simple Web clients and servers, researchers used infrared beacons to beam URLs to personal digital assistants (PDAs), which could then locate and render the document indicated. For instance, a museum visitor viewing a painting might receive a URL from a nearby beacon. The user can open the URL to find background information, a form for purchasing a print of the painting, and links to related artwork. The user may browse virtual space or continue collecting URLs by moving about the museum. Similarly, the entire museum might be associated with a *PlaceManager*, acting as a Web portal for all of the documents pertaining to the museum's collection. This links virtual information to physical locations while limiting the scope to a physical area of interest. The passing of URLs also adds a layer of indirection that allows lightweight Web browsers on a PDA to display low-fidelity versions of documents, while printers, for instance, can render high-fidelity originals, all without passing more than a short URL.

While CoolTown associates the well-known *Web space* with physical entities, a number of other projects have chosen to display information through nontraditional means, integrated into a smart room and its contents. This work is often a part of research into *augmented reality*. IBM's BlueSpace project [Chou01] uses colored indicator lights to advertise a worker's availability. Different colors lit above his office can politely indicate whether he is in a meeting, busy working, available for interruptions, or out of the office. The Audio Aura project [Mynatt98] tied background auditory cues to physical locations. The project used qualitative methods to provide nonessential information such as seagull cries providing estimates of the number of new e-mails waiting or tones indicating how long ago a person had been in an area. The Digital Family Portrait [Mynatt01] extended this usage of qualitative cues by integrating information with family portraits. For instance, a family could get a sense of an elderly relative's physical health, activity level, and local weather by viewing icons framing a portrait of that relative. By using qualitative feedback, here in the form of image-appropriate icons arranged in bands of varying density, the portrait could convey useful information that helped maintain peace of mind without compromising privacy. These indirect approaches have leveraged the smart room paradigm to provide alternative methods for delivering information that enriches the environment.

13.3 ENABLING TECHNOLOGIES

The infrastructure of a smart room typically consists of three components: (1) a sensing and actuation infrastructure that collects information about the physical space and affects its state, (2) a middleware infrastructure that manages, fuses, mines, and interprets the sensor information and drives the actuation infrastructure, and (3) a networking infrastructure that interconnects the various sensors, actuators, and the middleware infrastructure. As an example, Figure 13.1 shows the architecture of UCLA's Smart Kindergarten [Chen02, Srivastava01]. Its sensing infrastructure consists of cameras, microphones, sensor modules called *iBadges* [Park02a], and sensor-instrumented tables called *Smart Tables* [Steurer03]. Either worn by the students or attached to various objects in the room, the iBadges enable higher-layer services to monitor context in the classroom. The Smart Table keeps track of the

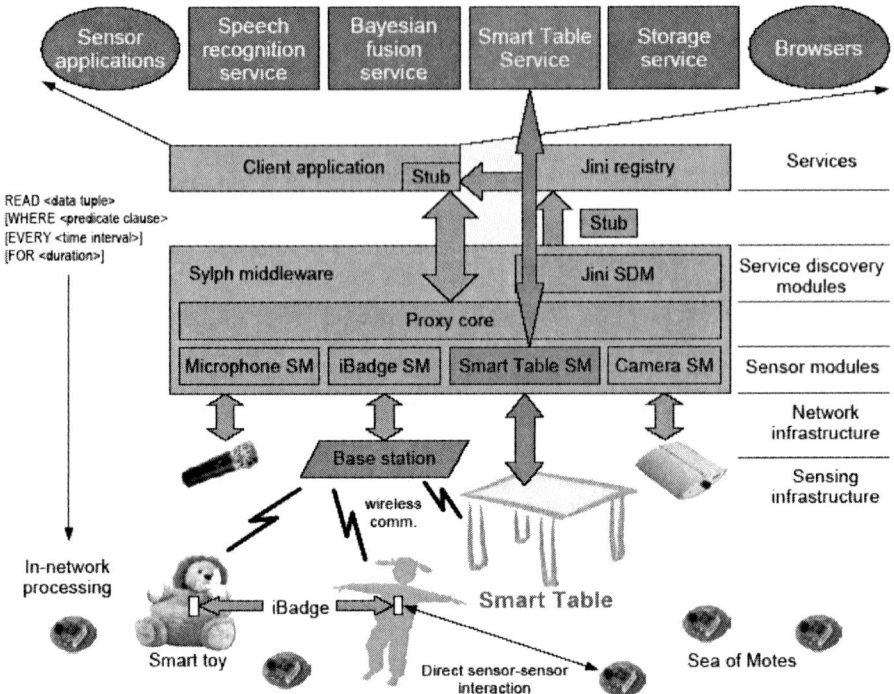

Figure 13.1 System architecture of the Smart Kindergarten.

location and identity of objects places on it, thus providing detailed contextual information about activities such as block manipulations that kids engage in. The middleware infrastructure of the Smart Kindergarten, called *Sylph* [Chen02], provides services that process, store, fuse, manage, and present data collected from the sensor infrastructure. Sylph manages access for high-level applications that perform tasks such as speech recognition, sensor data storage, and data browsing. It also provides a uniform interface to the sensor hardware and advertises services to client applications as new sensor devices register. Clients then use a simple query and execution language to access these sensor services. Smart Kindergarten's network infrastructure uses heterogeneous wireless technologies to tie sensors and actuators to the backend infrastructure, including standard technologies such as Bluetooth as well as proprietary technologies. The heterogeneity is a result of the differing rate and power requirements of different types of sensors.

In the rest of this section we describe the two technology enablers for smart rooms: the sensing and actuation technology, and the system software layer with middleware and runtime services. Other critical technologies are needed as well in a smart room, such as wireless networking. However, we will not describe them there because the solutions to them in smart rooms are fairly similar to those in many other application contexts.

13.3.1 Sensing and Actuation Infrastructure

It is the coupling with the physical world that distinguishes smart room technology from work in fields like multimedia and virtual reality. Sensors and actuators that are deeply embedded in smart room spaces provide the physical coupling, giving the system the ability to measure the state of the physical space and detecting events that indicate changes in that state, while actuators provide feedback to the user and manipulate the state of the environment. Through the sensors, the computing infrastructure maintains a model of the smart room, and the occupants of the room interact with the computing infrastructure via this model, thus treating the entire physical space as the user interface. A variety of sensing and actuation technologies have been explored in the context of a smart room. A brief discussion of some approaches follows.

13.3.1.1 Sensing Technologies for sensing can broadly be classified along two dimensions: what is being sensed and where the sensor is located. In the first dimension, the most commonly sensed pieces of information are (1) information about objects and participants in the space, such as their location, orientation, and identity, and (2) information about commands and actions from participants in the space, such as speech and gestures. In the second dimension, the sensors may be worn by the participants or embedded in objects, such as furniture and appliances that the participants used, or they may be built into the woodwork of the space, such as cameras and microphones attached to the walls and the ceiling. These two dimensions are not always independent, as often sensors are near-field or in-field ones that need to be situated at the location or near the object where the measurement is to be made. Acceleration, tilt, touch, and chemical sensors are examples of this category, and sensors need to be mounted on the object being sensed. On the other hand, far-field sensors can make remote measurements, and thus their location is less constrained if their range is large enough. Sensors such as cameras and microphones belong to this category. An advantage of the latter category of sensors is that they do not require any cooperation from the objects and participants in the space. They are also potentially less intrusive, although emerging technologies utilizing micro-electromechanical systems (MEMS) [Kahn99], thin film sensors, and E-textiles [Marculescu03] will permit the creation of ambient sensors in form factors that are minimally intrusive. We provide a brief overview of sensing technologies being explored beyond well-known devices like cameras and microphones.

Badges and Tags One class of sensor device that has been explored by many researchers are miniature badges and tags with embedded sensors, radios, and processors, which are meant to be worn by people or embedded in objects. Data from the device is sent to the smart room infrastructure via radio communication. A simple example is the commercial RF ID tag technology (http://www.autoidlabs.org/) that provides tags with small amount of memory in which data such as an identity can be stored (usually before being embedded in an object), and subsequently retrieved via remote readers. Another example is the Active Badge [Want92] used in the

Ubiquitous Computing project [Weiser91] at Xerox PARC in the early 1990s, in which an infrared (IR) beacon that permitted IR readers connected to the network infrastructure to keep track of the location of the various badges to the granularity of the coverage area of a reader (typically one room). Indeed, tracking the location of a badge wearer is one of the most important sensing functions that these devices have sought to provide. More recent efforts in developing such devices have had enhancements in two directions. First is the addition of sensors to measure things other than location, such as environmental parameters (e.g., light level, temperature) and information about the wearer (e.g., acceleration). Second is fine-grained location sensing to resolution of a few centimeters as opposed to room-level resolution, as well as sensing of orientation. This is done with assistance from special beacons placed at known locations in the physical world and using range or angle measurements between the badges and the beacons together with signal processing functions such as multilateration and triangulation to calculate the precise location. The SmartBadge [Maguire98] from the Royal Institute of Technology is an example of a badge that does the former, while the Bat system [Ward97] from the now defunct AT&T Research Laboratories in Cambridge is an example of a badge-like device that does the latter. The iBadge [Park02a] from the Smart Kindergarten effort at UCLA, mentioned earlier, is a device that combines both capabilities. Its key subsystems include a localization unit, an environment-sensing unit (temperature, light, humidity, and pressure), an orientation-tilt-acceleration unit (tri-axis magnetometer and accelerometer), a speech-processing unit (with speech I/O, codec, and front-end processing for speech recognition), a wireless communication unit (to talk to Bluetooth access points, and to localization beacons and mote sensors in the immediate vicinity), and a power management unit. Figure 13.2 shows a functional block diagram (a) and a picture of the iBadge (b).

The use of sensor badges worn by a user does have one significant problem: the placement of sensors. Specifically, the optimal positions of different sensors on a body or an object are unlikely to be the same. For example, the microphone should be on the chest near the mouth, a head-tracking unit on the head, a gait-sensing unit on the feet or the torso, and so on. Packaging all of them into a single badge results in suboptimal placement for most of the sensors. An alternative approach would be to distribute the badge functionality among multiple smaller sensing devices that interconnect via short-range body or personal area wireless communication technologies. A hub node can coordinate the devices and also act as a gateway to a surrounding communications infrastructure.

Clothes The emerging technology of E-textiles has encouraged several research groups to explore wearable sensors in the forms of clothes with computation, communication, and sensing capabilities woven into the fabric or incorporated in the buttons attached to the fabric. While less mature than tags and badges, approaches based on E-textiles for wearable sensors have significant usability advantages and can provide better placement of sensors on the body of a wearer. Among the first examples of this approach is the Smart Shirt [Park02b] from Georgia Tech, based on their Wearable Motherboard technology. It is a single-piece undershirt garment woven with a plastic optical fiber integrated into the structure during the fabrication

13.3 ENABLING TECHNOLOGIES

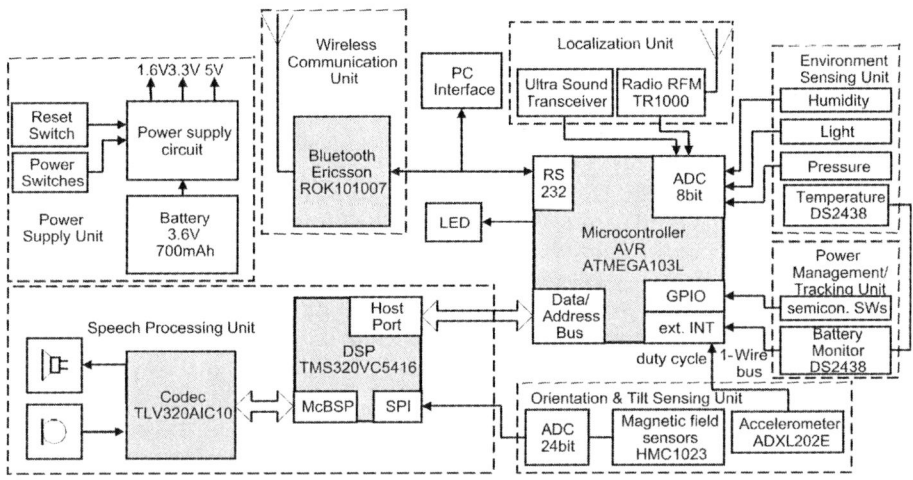

Figure 13.2a Functional block diagram of the iBadge architecture.

process, without any discontinuities at the armhole or the seams. An interconnect technology based on T-connectors (similar to button clips used in clothing) permits the attachment of sensors, such as EKG monitors, microphones, and toxic gas detectors, at any location, as well as local network communication. Moreover, sensing capabilities may be integrated into the fabric itself, such as detection of penetration by projectiles; thin film sensors for temperature, light, and other environ-

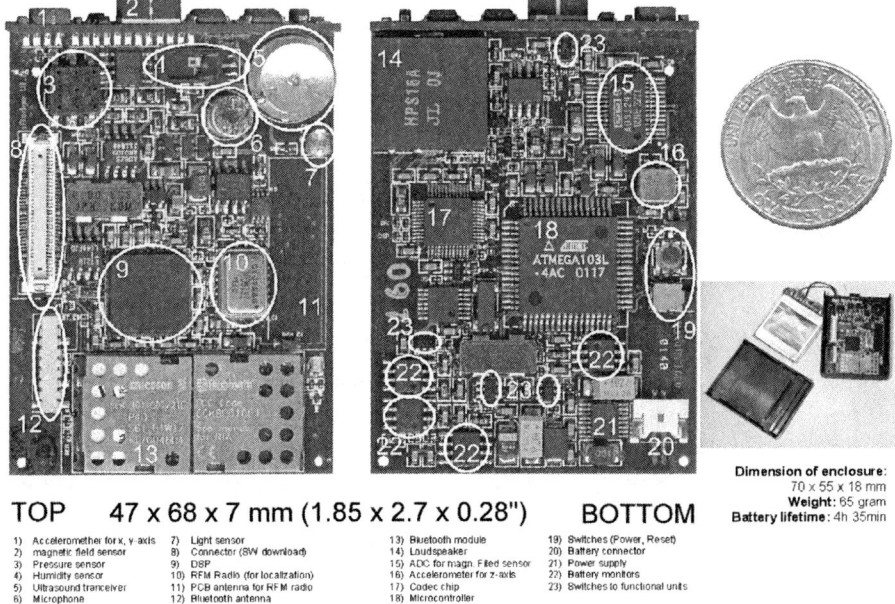

Figure 13.2b Photo of the iBadge wearable sensor badge.

mental components; and regular arrays of integrated sensors such as ultrasound image sensors. Other researchers on this technology include the E-textiles group at Virginia Tech (http://www.ccm.ece.vt.edu/etextiles/), the Coatnet project at CMU (http://www.ece.cmu.edu/~etex/), the Reconfigurable Fabric project at UCLA (http://rfab.cs.ucla.edu/), and the Electronic Textiles research at the Wearable Computing Lab, ETH Zurich (http://www.wearable.ethz.ch/).

Surfaces Another candidate for embedding sensing ability in a smart room is the various surfaces of the room itself—the walls, the floor, and the furniture. Indeed, people and objects come in close contact with the various surfaces of the room. Thus, instrumenting these surfaces with sensors that detect location, identity, or other attributes of the objects in contact can unobtrusively provide detailed context information. Figure 13.3 shows the Smart Table [Steurer03], an example of this approach developed as part of UCLA's Smart Kindergarten project. It can track and identify multiple objects placed on its surface. For example, it may be used to provide detailed monitoring of how a student manipulates blocks as part of a problem-solving task (e.g., sorting blocks into categories or spelling out words). The Smart Table, shown in Figure 13.3, consists of a dense regular grid of magnetic sensors embedded below the table's surface. The objects are instrumented with unique asymmetric magnetic patterns on their underside using embedded magnets or pasted-on magnetic tape, thus inducing a *magnetic image* on to the sensor grid.

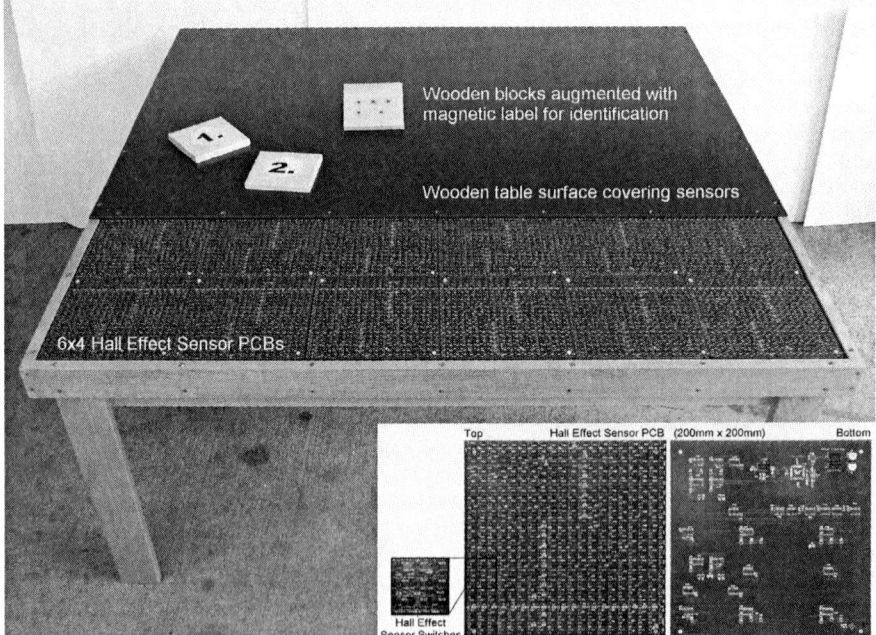

Figure 13.3 The Smart Table sensor-instrumented table.

Signal processing and object recognition techniques are employed to identify, locate, and track these objects.

Another example of sensor-instrumented surfaces is the Sentient Floor (also known as the Active Floor) [Headon01, Headon03], which provides awareness of human body movements such as step, crouch, lift an object, etc. It measures the vertical ground reaction force experienced by the floor's surface using a false floor composed of a regular array of tiles with each corner of every tile resting on a load cell that is shared by four tiles abutting at the corner. Typical primitive movements such as taking a step, jumping, drop landing, sitting down, rising to stand, and crouching are decomposed and recognized in terms of the ground reaction force signal observed by the Active Floor. The movement recognition is done using a Hidden Markov Model that is trained with good signals corresponding to the actions.

13.3.1.2 Actuation
In some smart rooms, the computing infrastructure uses sensor input to derive a physical world model that, in turn, is used to intelligently drive actuators that affect the state of the physical world (e.g., delivering feedback to the occupants of a smart room as a consequence of their actions). Common examples of actuators that provide feedback to occupants include speakers to provide aural feedback and displays to provide visual feedback. In many entertainment applications, actuators may often provide force or tactile feedback as well. Control of the heating, ventilation, and air conditioning systems, light bulbs, fans, window shades, etc., is another common means by which a smart room may respond to a user by changing the state of a physical space.

A far less explored use of actuation is for the smart room to improve and adapt its own sensing capabilities. A key reason for such self-aware actuation is to physically reconfigure the location or perspective of the sensors so as to cope with obstacles. It is extremely hard to have precise up-front knowledge of obstacles in the physical space at the time of sensor deployment, and in any case, the location of obstacles may change over time. In the presence of such uncertainty, providing desired sensor coverage of real-life smart rooms would require a high density of sensors if they were static. This is an issue particularly with sensors that have a narrow field of view (e.g., a zoomed-in camera) or strong directionality (e.g., a directional microphone). In such situations, sensors may be reoriented or repositioned via actuators to provide better readings. A good example is a camera mounted on a pan-tilt platform that may change its perspective somewhat to see around obstacles or to keep an object of interest in its field of view. Other examples include sensors that may move on tracks, wheels, or rails. Recent work at UCLA [Kansal04] has shown that endowing sensors with even limited mobility over small distances can significantly improve their coverage performance, measured as the number of sensors needed to provide the desired coverage. Moreover, with actuators built using MEMS technology, the cost of providing limited actuation will go down substantially, thus providing sensors with self-aware actuation to create more cost-effective smart room deployments with less planning and lower sensor density.

13.3.2 Software Infrastructure

Besides the sensing and actuation system, the other key subsystem in a smart room is the software layer that hosts the applications. This software layer perform two key functions. First, it incorporates various runtime services that are critical for runtime operation of the overall smart room system. Examples include services for location discovery and timing synchronization. Second, its layer provides the middleware through which applications access smart room resources. As an example, in UCLA's Smart Kindergarten, the Sylph middleware [Chen02] provides services that process, store, fuse, manage, and present data collected from the sensing infrastructure. Sylph manages access for high-level applications that perform tasks such as speech recognition, sensor data storage, and data browsing. It also provides a uniform interface to the sensor hardware. The middleware advertises services to client applications as new sensor devices register. Clients then use a simple query and execution language to access these sensor services.

13.3.2.1 Runtime Services The operation of smart rooms needs a variety of primitive services to manage and configure the resources and expose them to applications. The types of services that smart room systems provide go beyond those seen in traditional networked systems, since their functions go beyond mere transport of data. Moreover, the services may either be resident on servers in the back-end computing infrastructure or may be distributed across the sensors and the actuators themselves. The presence of local processing in wireless sensors and actuators is critical to minimize the energy-hungry wireless communications. Developers exploit local processing using in-network computation to realize distributed applications and services.

Two broad new categories of services are needed in smart rooms beyond those needed in traditional networked systems (e.g., data dissemination, security). The first category consists of the self-configuration services that are needed for the smart room to discover its own attributes after an unplanned deployment and to adapt to the environment's dynamics. The second category consists of services needed to sense and control the physical space and the objects in it. Moreover, self-configuration services are critical enablers of the sensing and control services. The sensing services provide crucial information needed by the control services to answer questions such as where an event took place (requires knowledge of sensor locations), when it took place (requires knowledge of clock offsets among sensors), and the value of the event (requires knowledge of transducer calibration settings).

As the preceding discussion suggests, three key self-configuration services are those for discovering location, time, and transducer parameters of various sensors and actuators in a smart room. The knowledge of location, time, and transducer parameters of its own sensors and actuators is crucial for the smart room to develop a meaningful model of the physical world. Much recent work has focused on developing efficient realizations of such self-configuration services, with examples including AhLoS for fine-grained location [Savvides02], TPSN for timing [Ganeriwal03], and Colibration for transducer parameters [Bychkovskiy03].

While these have evolved separately thus far and to different degrees of maturity (the time problem is largely solved, the localization problem remains hard in real-life environments with obstacles and bad geometries, and the transducer parameter problem is largely unsolved without external assistance), there is a significant commonality among these three problems. In fact, they can all be viewed as the problem of calibration where some parameter associated with the sensors and actuators needs to be efficiently estimated while minimizing some error function in the presence of noise and constraints obtained by measurement. For timing synchronization, neighboring nodes measure mutual clock offsets, and the goal is to find an assignment of clock offsets to nodes that is optimal in some sense (e.g., minimum least squares error, maximum likelihood, maximally consistent, etc.). Similarly, in localization, neighboring nodes measure mutual separation and directions, and the goal is to find an assignment of three-dimensional coordinates that is optimal. Lastly, in transducer calibration, the measurements made by nearby sensors in response to the same event are compared to indirectly measure offsets in transducer gains and biases. The goals is to find a globally optimal assignment of these parameters for all the sensors in the smart room. Potentially, a single distributed calibration service may be able to solve these various calibration problems as specific instances of a more general problem.

An important but less explored self-configuration service is self-aware actuation. As discussed earlier, the sensors with actuation abilities may be used to provide improved sensing performance in the presence of obstacles and environmental dynamics. This, in turn, requires two subservices. First, the smart room infrastructure needs to be aware of its own sensor measurement uncertainties. Second, it needs to use this information to actuate its sensors to relocate or reorient them to reduce the uncertainty. This is a complex problem with no adequate solution.

The second category of runtime services, namely, sensing and actuation services, are needed to observe and manipulate the physical space and the objects in it. Services that detect, identify, locate, or track events in the smart room or control actuators (e.g., lights and speakers) are examples of such services. These techniques are closely coupled to the sensing and actuation modalities, and a variety of approaches are used. On the sensing front, examples include computer vision techniques for visual recognition of objects, signal processing estimation techniques for localization of acoustic sources, Bayesian networks for event detection, hidden Markov models for tasks such as speech recognition and movement recognition [Headon01], and physical model–based techniques for light sensing [Wong03]. On the actuation front, which is relatively unexplored, the key challenge is coordinated control of distributed actuators in the presence of the vagaries of wireless communications. Recent work such as [Lemmon03] has only begun to explore these issues.

13.3.2.2 Middleware
The middleware in smart rooms mediates access by the application of the sensing, actuation, computing, storage, and communication resources and the various runtime services by providing appropriate abstractions and Application Programming Interfaces (APIs). In addition, they seek to provide an environment for the developers of the sensors, actuators, and runtime services with a structured set of interfaces to target.

Reflecting the diversity of networked systems in general, a variety of ways have emerged to organize middleware for smart rooms. However, they all share common attributes arising from the observation that smart room requirements differ from those of traditional networked systems. A key requirement is that unlike mobile computing, where the data flow is predominantly downlink (e.g., for Web access), much of the data flow in smart rooms is uplink (sensor information going to back-end services) and peer-to-peer (sensors collaborating to perform their tasks). Also, the scale of these systems in terms of the number of sensors and actuators precludes a traditional address-by-id approach to naming nodes and resources, and node-level approaches to management and tasking. Instead, approaches based on naming resources in a data-centric fashion [Intanagonwiwat00], and programming and managing collectives of sensors and actuators, [Boulis03] have been explored.

Several approaches for organizing the middleware in smart rooms, such as pervasive computing systems, have emerged. One approach is to use Common Object Request Broker (CORBA). For example, the Sentient Computing project at Cambridge [Addlesee01] represents location and resource data in smart rooms via persistent objects implemented using omniORB (http://omniorb.sourceforge.net/), an open source CORBA ORB. Different objects in the physical space are modeled via their own CORBA objects, such as person, phone, computer, etc. Besides the location of the real object, each CORBA object also makes available current properties of the real object and provides an interface to control the real object. For, example, a PZT camera can be made to pan by an application via its corresponding camera software object. The applications see the physical world as the set of these persistent CORBA objects. The objects themselves handle details of transactions, session management, event distribution, etc., thus relieving the applications of these tasks. A key task handled by the middleware is to expose the spatial dimension as a first-class entity to the applications. Spatial monitors are used to transform location data into containment relationships whereby objects in the physical space may have one or more named spaces defined around them. The containment relationships formalize vague spatial relationships. Events corresponding to two or more spaces satisfying some predicate (e.g., two spaces intersecting or one space becoming contained by another) are detected by a quad tree–based indexing method and communicated to applications by a scalable event-handling mechanism.

A second commonly used approach to organizing middleware for a smart room is to view the system as a distributed database with which the applications interact via traditional database queries (e.g., using SQL). In this approach, the sensors nodes are viewed as entities that produce data streams and can also do limited local storage and processing. Based on the queries from the applications, the query handler formulates plans processing of these data streams and storage of the raw or processed data streams by suitable locations within the network. For example, to cope with finite storage and the high cost of wireless communication, summaries of data may be computed and retained or pushed closer to gateway nodes in order to answer queries that need older data or have lower-fidelity requirements, as well to permit a drill-down approach to hunt efficiently for data to respond to a query [Ganesan03].

Many systems, such as TinyDB [Madden03], Cougar [Bonnet00], and Sylph [Chen02], have adopted this database-centric approach to middleware design. In the next subsection we examine one such system, Sylph, in detail.

A third approach is to organize the middleware in terms of data flows between sensors and sensing services. An example is the Smart Flow System from NIST [Rosenthal00], which defines a set of interface objects and a lightweight data flow transport mechanism. A connection broker server mediates establishment of connections between sensor data sources and processing data sinks.

The Smart Kindergarten utilizes a lightweight middleware service known as Sylph [Chen02], which serves as a device manager and extensible proxy service. It consists of a layered architecture with strong abstraction barriers between sensor modules, proxy core, and service discovery modules. The sensor modules manage a variety of sensors and actuators, providing a wide range of software services to the limited devices while exposing a common interface to user applications. The proxy core layers support a number of common features, such as cross-device synchronization, query optimization, and data storage, while mediating access to the sensor modules. They also parse simple text-based user queries into query plans that must be coordinated across the available devices. These query plans are organized as directed graphs of streaming operators, which can combine sensor data, traditional databases, and software processing into conglomerated data services, *fused* through belief networks. Finally, the service discovery modules export access to sensor modules and the virtual *fusion services*, making them available to various directory or discovery mechanisms, like Jini or CORBA. Sylph focuses on modular software components that provide a standardized interface to the myriad computing devices that are becoming available.

Although the Smart Kindergarten currently uses Sylph in a single instrumented classroom, Sylph can be expanded to handle much larger areas of operation. While the Jini discovery service typically spans a single local area network (LAN), it provides simple extensibility through the interlinking of its registrars to reach multiple LANs. However, one can develop a more scalable global view of multiple discovery domains using publish-subscribe mechanisms to organize distributed queries. This distributed view of Sylph will require greater mobility support and query management. Clients can have long-lived queries for objects that move from domain to domain, or they can make high-level queries over a region rather than about specific physical devices. Virtual sensor services using Bayesian networks may be used to fuse data from multiple sensors into generalized information sources. One may also develop procedures to shift query processing to match sensor devices' mobility [Chen03].

The sensor environment's open-ended, dynamic nature also opens up new issues in query management and optimization. For example, multiple clients might wish to access a device simultaneously. In some cases, Sylph's proxy core can easily satisfy multiple requests, tailoring data to clients' constraints (e.g., differing delivery rates). In other cases, Sylph must arbitrate between competing requests. Because some requests might persist for long periods, conflict resolution could require an involved system of priorities and access permissions. Such interactions also interfere with query optimizers, which might need to deal with quality-of-service issues and contested resources. Mobile sensors and processors might even require dynamic task distribution as the environment changes. Clearly, the sensor environment opens up many new challenges to middleware infrastructure.

13.4 OPERATIONAL CONSTRAINTS

13.4.1 Usability

While smart room applications have the potential to revolutionize the use of computing in a wide variety of domains, they must address an array of new usability issues to find actual success. The expansive nature of sensor networks, the uncontrolled and unpredictable environments, the endless streams of available data, and the three-dimensional, embedded interfaces are only a few of the new challenges facing those who seek to use smart rooms. In fact, these usability issues arise for two types of users: those who wish to deploy smart rooms and their applications, and those who need to use such environments once they are available. Researchers need to make smart room technology easily accessible to users who have problems that can be addressed by such applications; otherwise, few will bother to utilize them. Similarly, smart rooms must be easy for people to use once deployed, or there will be little demand for their services. The unique situations arising in smart rooms require new techniques to enhance usability, and researchers are only beginning to address the problems arising from such applications.

Before a smart room can be used to increase workplace productivity or present new forms of entertainment, someone must be able to install and maintain it. Smart rooms inherit many of the deployment problems of sensor networks and mobile computing environments. For instance, Saha and Mukherjee argue that the traditional process of writing applications to handle each type of device will quickly grow unmanageable in a pervasive computing environment, as the number of applications, devices, and users can expand tremendously in a smart environment [Saha03]. In fact, even trying to deploy and configure the many sensors and other devices used by a smart room quickly becomes unreasonably time-consuming, as the devices become smaller and more self-contained, as well as more numerous by orders of magnitude. Sensor network researchers have begun addressing such issues as time synchronization [Elson01, Ganeriwal03], recursive distribution of positioning information [Albowicz01], and self-configuring network topologies [Cerpa02], trying to get distributed but affiliated devices to configure themselves to work effectively with little or no administrative overhead. Similarly, a great deal of effort has gone toward managing the power used by transceivers [Schurgers03] and processors [Rakhmatov03] in embedded devices, as well as developing energy-aware network protocols [Xu01], in order to keep such devices running for extended periods with limited battery reserves. Eventually, long-running smart rooms will require methods for automatically recharging batteries or providing some other means of energy distribution.

A realistic smart environment will likely have to deal with a very heterogeneous array of computing environments. The resources available on each platform may fluctuate widely, as usage may extend from tiny embedded devices to handheld PDAs or even powerful servers, all of which may contribute to a smart room's functionality. Satyanarayanan calls this a need to mask "uneven conditioning" of environments [Satyanarayanan01], since different sectors will deploy pervasive computing technologies at different rates as they become available. Various adaptive technologies seek to compensate for limited or missing functionality, such as network connectivity [Mummert95] or screen resolution [Phan02]. Such "seamless" technologies help bridge the gap between real-world deployment issues and user-level performance.

Given these efforts to increase usability from an administrator's point of view, smart rooms also need approaches that improve usability for the application users. Carnegie Mellon's Project Aura [Garlan02] seeks to produce a distraction-free smart environment where computing resources will not require much user attention. Aura executes proactively, anticipating requests from higher system layers, prefetching files or delegating processing jobs to nearby servers using a variety of platforms. It also seeks to self-tune, adjusting its behavior based on usage patterns and resource availability. Many of Aura's capabilities depend on characterizing user intent and predicting resource levels in the face of user mobility. Aura utilizes a number of components to hide the effects of mobility from the user, allowing him to continue working on a nomadic computing device with a minimal amount of intrusion.

Some smart environments have gone even further, removing the standard interfaces to a computing device. MIT's Intelligent Room Project [Brooks97] seeks to reverse the standard human-computer interaction, which usually attempts to draw the user into the computer's artificial world. Instead, users work as they would without a computer, and the computer works to aid the users where it can. The goal of the Intelligent Room is to keep computation available to the user at all times without having to shift into a "computer mode" of thinking. Users can point at walls, use relative terms like *here* and *nearest*, and request the retrieval of remote information. Unlike a standard system, the computer must now model the user, keeping track of his location and his current actions, much like Aura's predictive models.

While the user still needs to address the Intelligent Room directly, the aforementioned Neural Network House [Mozer95] brings reinforcement learning and other artificial intelligence techniques to bear on a user's behavior, hiding computation from the user completely. While the user goes about his regular daily routine, the system can learn his preferences from observations of occupancy, room temperature, illumination, sound level, and other environmental aspects. Without any explicit instruction, the environment can predict and service the user's needs and also achieve other goals, like the minimization of heating costs or the maintenance of desired hot water temperature. While usability requirements may be met less invisibly in all scenarios, the Neural Network House certainly shows what seamless interaction may look like in the future.

13.4.2 Authoring

Smart room applications face a number of challenges in the realm of usability, but some applications present new challenges in the form of content authoring. Smart rooms offer a new realm of interactive, immersive presentation. While often viewed in a workplace context, smart rooms also offer new venues for entertainment and artwork, whether in the home or at a commercial establishment like a theater or gallery. In scenarios where the user can actually create narratives or modify the environment's behavior, usability concerns must extend to the author as well as his intended audience. Such users will need to control the smart room's behavior much like an administrator, but often without the technical expertise to guide low-level configuration. Artistic demands may also push the boundaries of what smart room technologies may have to offer.

A content author may have difficulty specifying the basic relationships in his envisioned environment, whether a combination of physical and virtual objects or a script including user actions and behaviors. For instance, even the Web's attempt to model a three-dimensional virtual world, the Virtual Reality Modeling Language (VRML), proved to be too technically oriented for the common user. Therefore, researchers developed STEDEL [Lazaridis01], a language that allowed for the specification of spatiotemporal relationships and compositions using natural descriptions of relative position and event sequences rather than absolute coordinates or timed events. Pinhanez [Pinhanez97] saw similar needs for computer theaters, where computer actors should be able to infer users' intentions and relate observations during a performance to generic descriptions in a script. Great challenges remain in helping a computer to understand actions that a user has described in natural terms and then detect those actions among a human cast's many variations.

The implementation of the KidsRoom [Bobick99] demonstrated many of the pitfalls of content authoring in interactive smart environments today. The designers had to keep in mind the physical nature of the room and its components, rather than just the correctness of its execution. For instance, most furniture needed to be nailed down, but the use of a wheeled bed required the placement of cinder blocks to keep children from pushing the bed into the fragile projection screens. The free-ranging nature of physical interaction also required unconventional means for ensuring the continuation of the narrative, such as the use of a narrator and a special *instructional voice* to prod users into performing the actions needed to continue the linear storyline. The system eventually had to ignore unresponsive users, skipping ahead in the narrative even without the proper triggering actions. The authors had to compensate explicitly for the unpredictability of users in a physical environment. They also had to be very accommodating with the allowed inputs, such as accepting gross movements rather than requiring specific gestures or teaching the users the limited interactions the KidsRoom could understand. The current models remain very conservative and require a good deal of planning on the author's part.

As the KidsRoom experience shows, much of the burden of content authoring falls on the shoulders of the author, but artificial intelligence techniques have eased some of these requirements for electronic artists. The Emergence Engine

[Mendelowitz00] provides behavior-based agents to populate the virtual worlds designed for interactive environments. A number of artists have used the engine to design artwork that represents a living world full of artificial entities that pursue various goals, interact with each other and their virtual world, and react to the actions of users who come to experience the artwork. As shown in the case of VRML, many electronic artists find the imperative style of content authoring to be too restrictive and tedious for their creations. The Emergence Engine supplies the artist with agents that exhibit a range of basic behaviors and motivations, allowing the artist to focus on the high-level behaviors he wishes to express in his work. The engine provides simple slider interfaces for the author to adjust the importance of various behaviors, letting him work at an abstract level with the bulk of his creations. The author can then take control of certain aspects of his design by accessing simple scripts that modify agent behaviors. The agents can then be rendered to display devices or otherwise linked to the art display. Generic interfaces to outside data, like readings from pressure plates that detect a viewer's arrival or messages from a joystick used to navigate through the virtual environment, allow the artist to incorporate the physical world into his virtual one. Once again, the system works to model the user as part of its environment, rather than forcing the user to work within the computer's constraints. While the author still maintains artistic control of his narrative or simulation, he can now do so at a higher level without needing to write sophisticated programs. The Emergence Engine does not solve all of the problems that might inhibit the creation of interactive environments by the common user, but it takes steps to make the experience much more accessible without losing the expressiveness available in a smart environment.

13.4.3 Social Implications

Clearly, smart rooms fundamentally change the relationship between users and technology. This change is a complex one, and it is simplistic to say that it is "good" or "bad," as both aspects are present. The same ability to identify and track users via invisible sensors that enriches the interaction between smart room computing infrastructure and their occupants may also be used in Big Brotherly ways that violate privacy and civil rights. Moreover, by extending the reach of the computing infrastructure to the physical world via sensors and actuators, one makes the physical world itself vulnerable to sophisticated security attacks such as denial of service and data tampering. Indeed, for this technology to be socially acceptable at a large scale, the integrity and trustworthiness of the smart room infrastructure must be ensured by coordinated technological and regulatory means. A proper solution will require a broad-based approach spanning technology, social science, public policy, and legal aspects.

Unfortunately, although some initial studies exist, a broad collaborative effort to address these ethical, legal, and social implications (ELSI) of smart room and other pervasive computing technologies is still missing. While the study of ELSI issues is an integral part of fields such as medicine and genetics, where bioethics is a well-established discipline, such is not the case in pervasive computing technology. Indeed, there is not even an agreement on the importance of ELSI issues in technology. There is criticism based on the lack of importance of ELSI and the economic factors [Segelken03]. Deborah Johnson says, "Right now, people are not afraid of it because it is not being built by the government. It's being built by the market and by commercial interests, but once it is all set up in place, it will only take a slight shift in political ideology for it to be used in other ways" [Stone03]. So, before these issues can be properly addressed, their importance in pervasive computing environments must be established, just as it was in medicine and genetics.

The next step will be public dialogue and scientific studies to find solutions. Both technology and government regulations will be a part of that effort, as neither alone will be adequate. Focusing on traditional security and trustworthiness issues from a technology perspective alone will fail to address the degree to which the government and private entities operating smart room infrastructures will have access to personal information. Just as there are laws protecting against unjustified physical searches by police, laws may emerge to prevent unjustified searching and mining of private information from sensor data by the government and corporations. Moreover, traditional methods of security such as passwords work against the unobtrusiveness promised by smart rooms. From a technological perspective, the designers of smart rooms must factor in these concerns in the form of formal metrics at all layers of the system right from the start, as well as considering the unintended consequences of various design choices. Instead of patching security later on, which is always expensive and ineffective, the architecture must provide security hooks that will be used subsequently to enact various operational policies.

Clearly, the understanding of ELSI issues in smart rooms is nascent. Just as it happened in genetics, a broad framework covering privacy, safety, education, and implementation issues needs to emerge. Until then, these issues will remain the "Achilles Heel of Pervasive Computing" [Satyanarayanan03].

13.5 CONCLUSIONS

Smart rooms provide a variety of exciting applications of pervasive computing technology that enrich the interaction between occupants of a physical space and the invisible computing infrastructure. Their highly distributed and deeply physically coupled nature gives rise to challenges that are not faced in traditional networked systems. In this chapter, we examined the available technologies and the unresolved challenges both in the lower layers (the sensors and actuators that enable coupling between the virtual and physical worlds) and in the higher layers (runtime services and middleware) of the computing infrastructure underlying smart rooms. However, the challenge is not merely technological. Operational issues such as usability constraints, authoring environments, and ELSI implications need to be addressed as well. Indeed, even if the technology succeeds, these operational issues, if ignored, will become show stoppers that prevent wide-scale social acceptance of the smart room.

ACKNOWLEDGMENT

This chapter is based on authors' research supported by the National Science Foundation (NSF) under Grant No. ANI-0085773. Any opinions, findings, and conclusions or recommendations expressed are those of the authors and do not necessarily reflect the views of the NSF.

REFERENCES

[Abowd99]   G.D. Abowd, "Classroom 2000: An Experiment with the Instrumentation of a Living Educational Environment," *IBM Systems Journal*, vol. 38, no. 4, 1999, pp. 508–530.

[Addlesee01]   M.D. Addlesee, R. Curwen, S. Hodges, J. Newman, P. Steggles, A. Ward, A. Hopper, "Implementing a Sentient Computing System," *IEEE Computer Magazine*, vol. 34, no. 8, August 2001, pp. 50–56.

[Albowicz 01] J. Albowicz, A. Chen, L. Zhang, L., "Recursive Position Estimation in Sensor Networks," *Proceedings of the 9th International Conference on Network Protocols (ICNP 2001)*, November 2001.

[Barton01]   J. Barton and T. Kindberg, "The Cooltown User Experience," Technical Report 2001–22, HP Laboratories, Palo Alto, CA, February 2001.

[Bobick99]   A.F. Bobick, S.S. Intille, J.W. Davis, F. Baird, C.S. Pinhanez, L.W. Campbell, Y.A. Ivanov, A. Schutte, A. Wilson, "The KidsRoom: A Perceptually-Based Interactive and Immersive Story Environment," *Presence*, vol. 8, no. 4, August 1999, pp. 369–393.

[Bonnet00]   P. Bonnet, J.E. Gehrke, P. Seshadri, "Querying the Physical World," *IEEE Personal Communications*, vol. 7, no. 5, October 2000, pp. 10–15.

[Boulis03]   A. Boulis, C.-C. Han, M.B. Srivastava, "Design and Implementation of a Framework for Efficient and Programmable Sensor Networks," *Proceeding of the First ACM/USENIX International Conference on Mobile Systems, Applications, and Services (MobiSys 2003)*, May 2003.

[Brooks97]   R.A. Brooks, "The Intelligent Room Project," *Proceedings of the 2nd International Cognitive Technology Conference (CT'97)*, August 1997.

[Burke01]   J. Burke, "hypermedia.ucla.edu/projects," June 2001, UCLA Hypermedia Studio. Available at http://hypermedia.ucla.edu/projects/macbett.php

[Bychkovskiy03]   V. Bychkovskiy, S. Megerian, D. Estrin, M. Potkonjak, "Colibration: A Collaborative Approach to In-Place Sensor Calibration," *2nd International Workshop on Information Processing in Sensor Networks (IPSN'03)*, Palo Alto, CA, April 2003.

[Castro00]   P. Castro, M. Mani, S. Mathur, R. Muntz, "Managing Context for Internet Video Conferences: The Multimedia Internet Recorder and Archive," *Proceedings of Multimedia and Computer Networks 2000 (MMCN00)*, January 2000.

[Cerpa02]   A. Cerpa, D. Estrin, "ASCENT: Adaptive Self-Configuring Sensor Networks Topologies," *Proceedings of the 21st International Annual Joint Conference of the IEEE Computer and Communications Societies (INFOCOM 2002)*, June 2002.

[Chen02]   A. Chen, R.R. Muntz, S. Yuen, I. Locher, S.I. Park, M.B. Srivastava, "A Support Infrastructure for the Smart Kindergarten," *Pervasive Computing*, vol. 1, no. 2, April–June 2002, pp. 49–57.

[Chen03]   A. Chen, K.C. Lui, R.R. Muntz, "Query Plans with Roaming Sources: Shifting Streams of Data," *Proceedings of the 8th IEEE International Workshop on Real-time Dependable Systems (WORDS 2003)*, March 2003.

[Chou01] P. Chou, M. Gruteser, J. Lai, A. Levas, S. McFaddin, C. Pinhanez, M. Viveros, D. Wong, S. Yoshihama, "BlueSpace: Creating a Personalized and Context-Aware Workspace," RC22281 (W0112-044), IBM Research Report, December 2001.

[Elson01] J. Elson, D. Estrin, "Time Synchronization for Wireless Sensor Networks," *Proceedings of the 2001 International Parallel and Distributed Processing Symposium (IPDPS 2001)*, April 2001.

[Escobar94] J. Escobar, C. Partridge, D. Deutsch, "Flow Synchronization Protocol," *IEEE/ACM Transactions on Networking*, vol. 2, no. 2, pp. 111–121, April 1994.

[Ganeriwal03] S. Ganeriwal, R. Kumar, M.B. Srivastava, "Timing-Sync Protocol for Sensor Networks," *Proceedings of the ACM SenSys*, November 2003.

[Ganesan03] D. Ganesan, B. Greenstein, D. Perelyubskiy, D. Estrin, J. Heidemann, "An Evaluation of Multi-Resolution Storage for Sensor Networks," *Proceedings of the ACM SenSys*, November 2003.

[Garlan02] D. Garlan, D.P. Siewiorek, A. Smailagic, P. Steenkiste, "Project Aura: Toward Distraction-Free Pervasive Computing," *Pervasive Computing*, vol. 1, no. 2, April–June 2002, pp. 22–31.

[Headon01] R. Headon, R. Curwen, "Recognizing Movements from the Ground Reaction Force," Workshop on Perceptive User Interfaces, November 15–16, 2001.

[Headon03] R. Headon, "Movement Awareness for a Sentient Environment," *Proceedings of the IEEE International Conference on Pervasive Computing and Communications (PerCom 2003)*, March 2003.

[Intanagonwiwat00] C. Intanagonwiwat, R. Govindan, D. Estrin, "Directed Diffusion: A Scalable and Robust Communication Paradigm for Sensor Networks," *Proceedings of the ACM MobiCom*.

[Kahn99] J.M. Kahn, R.H. Katz, K.S.J. Pister, "Mobile Networking for Smart Dust," *ACM/IEEE International Conference on Mobile Computing and Networking (MobiCom 99)*, August 17–19, 1999.

[Kansal04] A. Kansal, E. Yuen, W. Kaiser, G. Pottie, M. Srivastava, "Sensing Uncertainty Reduction Using Low Complexity Actuation," ACM & IEEE Third International Symposium on Information Processing in Sensor Networks (IPSN 2004), April 2004.

[Kidd99] C.D. Kidd, R. Orr, G.D. Abowd, C.G. Atkeson, I.A. Essa, B. MacIntyre, E. Mynatt, T.E. Starner, W. Newstetter, "The Aware Home: A Living Laboratory for Ubiquitous Computing Research," *Proceedings of the 2nd International Conference on Cooperative Buildings (CoBuild'99)*, 1999.

[Kindberg00] T. Kindberg, J. Barton, J. Morgan, G. Becker, D. Caswell, P. Debaty, G. Gopal, M. Frid, V. Krishnan, H. Morris, J. Schettino, B. Serra, M. Spasojevic, "People, Places, Things: Web Presence for the Real World," *Proceedings of the 3rd IEEE Workshop on Mobile Computing Systems and Applications*, December 2000.

[Lazaridis01] I. Lazaridis, M. Vazirgiannis, T. Sellis, "STEDEL: A Language for Interactive Spatio-Temporal Compositions," *Proceedings of the IEEE International Conference on Multimedia (ICME 2001)*, August 2001.

[Lemmon03] M. Lemmon, Q. Ling, Y. Sun, "Overload Management in Sensor-Actuator Networks used for Spatially-Distributed Control Systems," *Proceedings of the ACM SenSys*, November 2003.

[Madden03] S.R. Madden, M.J. Franklin, J.M. Hellerstein, W. Hong, "The Design of an Acquisitional Query Processor for Sensor Networks," *Proceedings of ACM SIGMOD*, June 2003.

[Maguire98] G.Q. Maguire, M. Smith, H.W.P. Beadle, "Smartbadges: A Wearable Computer and Communication System," *6th International Workshop on Hardware/Software Codesign*, 1998.

[Marculescu03] D. Marculescu, R. Marculescu, N.H. Zamora, P. Stanley-Marbell, P.K. Khosla, S. Park, S. Jayaraman, S. Jung, C. Lauterbach, W. Weber, T. Kirstein, D. Cottet, J. Grzyb, G. Troester, "Electronic Textiles: A Platform for Pervasive Computing," *Proceedings of IEEE*, December 2003.

[Mendelowitz00] E. Mendelowitz, "The Emergence Engine: A Behavior Based Agent Development Environment for Artists," *Proceedings of the 12th National Conference on AI (AAAI 2000)*, August 2000.

[Mozer95] M.C. Mozer, R.H. Dodier, M. Anderson, I. Vidmar, R.F. Cruickshank III, D. Miller, "The Neural Network House: An Overview," in *Current Trends in Connectionism*, ed. L. Niklasson, M. Boden. Hillsdale, NJ: Erlbaum, 1995, pp. 371–380.

[Mummert95] L.B. Mummert, M.R. Ebling, M. Satyanarayanan, "Exploiting Weak Connectivity for Mobile File Access," *Proceedings of the 15th ACM Symposium on Operating Systems Principles (SOSP'95)*, December 1995.

[Mynatt98] E.D. Mynatt, M. Back, R. Want, M. Baer, J.B. Ellis, "Designing Audio Aura," *Proceedings of the SIGCHI Conference on Human Factors in Computing Systems (CHI 98)*, April 1998.

[Mynatt01] E.D. Mynatt, J. Rowan, S. Craighill, A. Jacobs, "Digital Family Portraits: Supporting Peace of Mind for Extended Family Members," *Proceedings of the SIGCHI Conference on Human Factors in Computing Systems (CHI 01)*, April 2001.

[Park02a] S. Park, I. Locher, A. Savvides, M.B. Srivastava, A. Chen, R. Muntz, S. Yuen, "Design of a Wearable Sensor Badge for Smart Kindergarten," *Sixth International Symposium on Wearable Computers*, October 7–10, 2002.

[Park02b] S. Park, K. Mackenzie, S. Jayaraman, "The Wearable Motherboard: A Framework for Personalized Mobile Information Processing (PMIP)," *Proceedings of the ACM DAC*, 2002.

[Pearl88] J. Pearl, *Probabilistic Reasoning in Intelligent Systems: Networks of Plausible Inference*, San Mateo, CA: Morgan Kaufmann, 1988.

[Pentland96] A. Pentland, "Smart Rooms," *Scientific American* 274, 1996.

[Phan02] T. Phan, G. Zorpas, R. Bagrodia, "An Extensible and Scalable Content Adaptation Pipeline Architecture to Support Heterogeneous Clients," *Proceedings of the 22nd International Conference on Distributed Computing Systems (ICDCS 2002)*, July 2002.

[Pinhanez95] C.S. Pinhanez, A.F. Bobick, "Intelligent Studios: Using Computer Vision to Control TV Cameras," *Proceedings of the 1995 International Joint Conference on AI Workshop on Entertainment and AI/Alife*, August 1995.

[Pinhanez 97] C.C. Pinhanez, "Computer Theater," *Proceedings of the 8th International Symposium on Electronic Arts (ISEA'97)*, September 1997.

[Rakhmatov 03] D. Rakhmatov, S. Vrudhula, "Energy Management for Battery-Powered Embedded Systems," *ACM Transactions on Embedded Computing Systems (TECS)*, vol. 2, no. 3, August 2003, pp. 277–324.

[Rosenthal00] L. Rosenthal, V. Stanford, "NIST Smart Space: Pervasive Computing Initiative," *IEEE 9th International Workshops on Enabling Technologies: Infrastructure for Collaborative Enterprises (WET ICE'00)*, March 14–16, 2000.

[Saha03] D. Saha, A. Mukherjee, "Pervasive Computing: A Paradigm for the 21st Century," *Computer*, vol. 36, no. 3, March 2003, pp. 25–31.

[Satyanarayanan01] M. Satyanarayanan, "Pervasive Computing: Vision and Challenges," *IEEE Personal Communications*, vol. 8, no. 4, August 2001, pp. 10–17.

[Satyanarayanan03] M. Satyanarayanan, "Privacy: The Achilles Heel of Pervasive Computing?," *IEEE Pervasive Computing*, vol. 2, no. 1, pp. 2–3, January–March 2003.

[Savvides02]   A. Savvides, H. Park, M. Srivastava, "The Bits and Flops of the N-Hop Ultilateration Primitive for Node Localization Problems," *ACM Workshop on Wireless Sensor Networks and Applications* (*WSNA 2002*), September 2002.

[Schooler93]   E. Schooler, "Distributed Music: A Foray into Networked Performance," International Network Music Festival, Electronic Cafe, Santa Monica, CA, September 1993.

[Schurgers03]   C. Schurgers, V. Raghunathan, M.B. Srivastava, "Power Management for Energy-Aware Communication Systems," *ACM Transactions on Embedded Computing Systems* (*TECS*), vol. 2, no. 3, August 2003, pp. 431–447.

[Segelken03]   Roger Segelken and David Brand, "Stephen Hilgartner: ELSI is Under Fire Even as Importance Grows," Cornell Chronicle, February 2003. Available at http://www.news.cornell.edu/Chronicle/03/2.20.03/AAAS.Hilgartner.html.

[Srivastava01]   M. Srivastava, R. Muntz, M. Potkonjak, "Smart Kindergarten: Sensor-Based Wireless Networks for Smart Developmental Problem-solving Environments," *Proceedings of the 7th International Conference on Mobile Computing and Networking* (*MobiCom 2001*). New York: ACM Press, 2001.

[Steurer03]   P. Steurer, M.B. Srivastava, "System Design of Smart Table," *Proceedings of the IEEE International Conference on Pervasive Computing and Communications* (*PerCom 2003*), March 2003.

[Stone03]   A. Stone, "The Dark Side of Pervasive Computing," *IEEE Pervasive Computing*, vol. 2, no. 1, pp. 4–8, January–March 2003.

[Su03]   N.M. Su, "A System for Augmenting Film and Video Footage with Sensor Data," M.S. thesis, UCLA Computer Science Department, September 2003.

[Su04]   N.M. Su, H. Park, E. Bostrom, J. Burke, M.B. Srivastava, D. Estrin, "Augmenting Film and Video Footage with Sensor Data," *Proceedings of the 2004 IEEE International Conference on Pervasive Computing and Communications* (*PerCom 2004*), March 2004.

[Want92]   R. Want, A. Hopper, V. Falco, J. Gibbons, "The Active Badge Location System," *ACM Transactions on Information Systems*, vol. 10, pp. 91–102, January 1992.

[Ward97]   A. Ward, A. Jones, A. Hopper, "A New Location Technique for the Active Office," *IEEE Personal Communications*, vol. 4, no. 5, October 1997, pp. 42–47.

[Weiser91]   M. Weiser. "The Computer for the 21st Century," *Scientific American*, vol. 265, no. 3, September 1991, pp. 66–75.

[Wong03]   J.L. Wong, S. Megerian, M. Potkonjak, "Design Techniques for Sensor Appliances: Foundations and Light Compass Case Study," *40th IEEE/ACM Design Automation Conference* (*DAC 2003*), June 2003.

[Xie01]   W. Xie, Y. Shi, G. Xu, D. Xie, "Smart Classroom—An Intelligent Environment for Tele-education," *Proceedings of the 2nd IEEE International Pacific Rim Conference on Multimedia* (*PCM 2001*), October 2001.

[Xu01]   Y. Xu, J. Heidemann, D. Estrin, "Geography-Informed Energy Conservation for Ad-Hoc Routing," *Proceedings of the 7th Annual ACM/IEEE International Conference on Mobile Computing and Networking* (*MobiCom 2001*), July 2001.

CHAPTER 14

Smart Offices

CHRISTOPHE LE GAL
PRIMA Group, GRAVIR Lab
INRIA

14.1 INTRODUCTION

Offices are places where highly automatizable work is done. Since smart environment researchers often work in offices, not very surprisingly, a natural and popular application of smart environment research is smart offices. In this chapter we consider the office in its more general meaning, i.e., as a place where office work is done. It therefore includes corridors, buildings, meeting rooms, etc. The goal of this chapter is to illustrate the benefits of smart environment technologies in offices and how such technologies could be applied in this subdomain.

Offices have some features that make them more than rooms. Therefore, a smart office is not just another smart environment.

- Office work is usually highly automatizable and computer related. Software is already used for many applications, such as dealing with e-mail, Web interaction, or digital documents. Therefore, we do not want our smart office to simply deal with heaters, display video, or switch lights. We also want it to be useful for what is done every day in offices. For this reason, smart office systems almost always permit binding with existing software and deal with software and hardware heterogeneity.
- Offices play many different roles. They can be workplaces, meeting rooms, discussion rooms, or demonstration rooms. Therefore we want a smart office to be flexible enough to transform itself easily (and sometimes automatically) into a smart workplace, a smart meeting room, and so forth.
- Quite often office users, although not necessarily experts, are not simple end users. Even secretaries are used to dealing with computers and will want to be able to modify the configuration of their smart offices. Moreover, since all

Smart Environments: Technologies, Protocols, and Applications, edited by D.J. Cook and S.K. Das
ISBN 0-471-54448-5 © 2005 John Wiley & Sons, Inc.

users do not have the same programming skills, different abstraction level access to the office configuration would be desirable: an experienced programmer will not want to be limited by a simple menu when trying to specify her or his office behavior; an end user will not want to type code to do so.
- Since offices often support multiple users, smart offices must deal with different people. Some people might prefer oral interaction, while others might possess a personal digital assistant (PDA) and want to use it to interact with office capabilities.

In short, an office is smart if it is able to help its user, that is, its occupant, perform everyday tasks by automating some of them and making the communication between user and machine simpler. Different research domains have contributed to the construction of smart offices, as we will summarize here.

14.1.1 Perceptual User Interfaces

Classical office software uses graphical user interfaces (GUI) for interaction with the user. Despite claims to the contrary, these interfaces are intrusive and not truly user-friendly, because users must engage in explicit dialogue with the computer instead of using more natural methods of interaction. A more advanced class of interfaces, called perceptual user interfaces (PUI), is emerging from the work of human-machine interaction research groups. These interfaces do not use the traditional keyboard-and-mouse couple as an input interface, but instead hear and see the user in his environment, his gesture, and his motions. PUI enable exchanges between man and machine that are no longer based on machine communication methods but on human ones: speech, gesture, interaction with objects, etc.

A significative example of a PUI-based interactive tool is Wellner's MagicDesk [21], and similarly and more recently, Berard's MagicBoard [2] (see Figure 14.1). The MagicBoard is a normal white-board augmented by a video projector and a camera. The MagicBoard is nonintrusive since it can be used like a normal board: the user can write with a normal pen, wipe the board with a normal eraser, and stick documents on it with magnets. Thanks to the camera and the projector, some *augmented* utilization is also possible: the drawing of a *P* triggers the printing of the board content, a finger tap on the board shows a touchable menu, some other gestures allows copying, pasting, and scaling of part of the board, or even solve automatically an equation written on the board.

14.1.2 Interactive Offices

Interactive offices propose to use the benefit of PUI not only for interaction with a single software application but also for communication between the user and all software and hardware resources of an office. The user is not *using* an interactive tool, but rather *living* in an interactive tool. As with the MagicBoard the user can interact with his environment as in a normal office, but can, in addition, use *augmented* features.

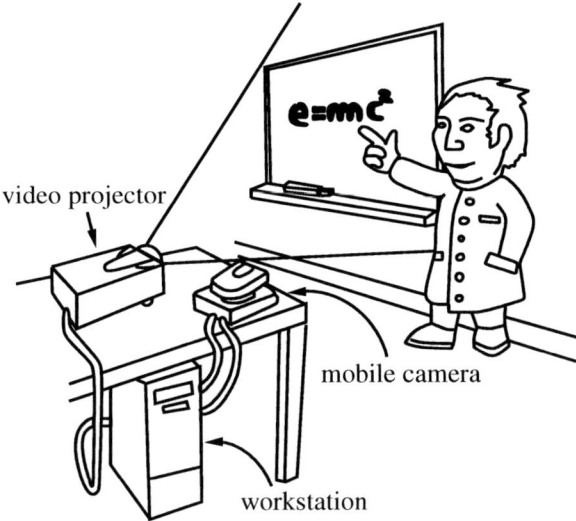

Figure 14.1 Berard's MagicBoard. A video-projector displays digital informations on the physical board. A camera observes the user's gestures and provides to the user interaction capabilities with the digital objects on the board.

The most famous interactive environment is probably the KidsRoom from MIT's Media Lab [1]. The KidsRoom is an immersive environment based on several PUIs. The room contains several video cameras allowing the use of computer vision techniques and detection of the children's activities. Video projectors displays objects and characters. Kids are therefore surrounded by real and virtual objects and can interact with them.

From a technical point of view, the KidsRoom is rather simple. But the experiment is very interesting since it shows how the addition of PUIs in a room can enhance its immersive capability. The idea developed by the KidsRoom therefore inspired many research projects on smart offices. Michael Coen defined in one formula the objective: *Make people interface for computers rather than computer interface for people.*

Coen himself proposed an interactive office named Hal, after the computer imagined by Arthur C. Clarke. Hal comprises a microphone, some video screens, some cameras and a few computer-controlled hardware devices such as a VCR. Thanks to its microphone, Hal is able to recognize predefined orders such as *start the VCR* or questions such as *What is the weather in Boston?* These oral sentences trigger preset reactions from the system. The video cameras are used to recognize pointing gestures and therefore help the interpretation of sentences. For example, Hal is able to react to the sentence *Display the page here* by directing the video projector toward the place indicated by the arm of the speaker.

In addition, Hal contains no intrusive elements: the user wears no specific device (such as an RFID), and the office furniture is normal. The authors wanted the design of the system not to be specific to a given office and easily portable to other offices. Because of these prerequisites, Hal only uses generic sensors such as video cameras and microphones.

14.1.3 Ubiquitous Computing

The aim of the ubiquitous computing field is the same as that of interactive computing: to make interaction with computers more natural. Mark Weiser, a pioneer of ubiquitous computing, stated that computers should be invisible and their usage should require no effort [20]. The proposed methods to obtain such natural interaction differ. For Weiser, computers should be integrated into the human environment as tools. When he suggests that computers should be invisible, he does not mean that they should be hidden, but rather that their usage should be almost unconscious, like the usage of a light switch.

Ubiquitous computing is not computing without learning, but computing that you can use without having to think about it. Because of this principle, Weiser rejects the idea that the communication between man and machine should be done using a human means such as speech. According to Weiser, this is not only unnecessary but would even be an obstacle to the integration of computer tools into the working environment. Giving an explicit oral order is a conscious act that cannot be done as mechanically as switching on the light. For the same reason, Weiser considers a virtual assistant a hindrance to interaction with a computer: when interacting with a virtual assistant, that is, with a computer, the user is conscious of its presence and the computer is not at all invisible.

From a more technical point of view, ubiquitous computing proposes to incorporate electronics in all objects, which can then be context-aware and make decisions: the seat can detect the presence of a user in front of the computer and order a login procedure; the mug, aware that the last drop of coffee has been drunk, can transmit this information to the coffee machine; and so forth.

14.1.4 Context-Aware Offices

A few researchers use the term *context-aware* to describe their work. The term was first used by Schilit and Theimer [17]. They define context as the *location and the identity of all persons and objects present*. According to their definition, a *context-aware application* is an application able to adapt its own behavior to this context.

Dey [7] made this term popular in the smart environment world. He defines context as *any information that can be used to characterize the situation of an entity*, an entity being *a person, a place, or an object considered to be relevant to the interaction between a user and an application, including the user and the application themselves*. This definition is more general than Schilit and Theimer's, which is specific to an application and, furthermore, restricted the context to sensor information. Dey's definition of context also includes information about the state of a software application or the emotional state of users. Using this definition of context, a *context-aware office* is an office that uses context to provide relevant information or services to the user according to the activity of the user.

14.1.5 Intelligent Offices

The terms *intelligent office*, *interactive office*, and *smart office* are often considered equivalent in the literature. Martin [16] defines all of them as *an introduction of computers into the real and physical world*. Coen [5] states that an intelligent room is *a room that listens to you and watches what you do, a room you can speak with, gesture to, and interact with in other complex ways*.

In our opinion, these definitions fit both *context-aware rooms* and *interactive rooms* but not *intelligent rooms*. Many interactive offices do not have a global intelligence but are simply a set of devices controlled by PUI. What make an office *intelligent*, not just *interactive* and *context-aware*, is quite subtle. Even without requiring that it pass the Turing test, we believe that an intelligent office should have a global intelligence. It should know the set of available resources (software, or hardware), track goals, and make decisions about the best way to use the resources in order to achieve the goals. Of course, the border between these concepts is quite fuzzy, and all decisions taken in an office are always the consequence of an explicit or implicit order from the programmer. What makes an office intelligent is the implicitness level of this order. Ordering *set the clock alarm to 6:45* is just an interaction with a device through a PUI. However, to react correctly to the order *I want to wake up at 6:45* the office has to be intelligent; it is given a mission to achieve (having the user awake at 6:45) and must decide how and using which resource will achieve this mission.

14.1.6 Remarks

Smart office is a term that denotes different kinds of computer-enhanced offices:

- Interactive offices are offices where the user can, thanks to PUIs, interact with office applications, using human communication means.
- Context-aware offices adapt their behavior to the context, e.g., the scenario that takes place in the office.
- Ubiquitous computing provides a different way to interact with offices, which makes the computer invisible to the user.
- Intelligent offices are able to decide for themselves how to perform a task, e.g., how to communicate information to the user using the available resources.

Although different, all these smart offices share a common objective: making the communication between user and computer more natural, thus making office work easier. The next section describes examples of smart offices and shows how the different authors deal with the particularities of office environments.

14.2 EXAMPLES OF SMART OFFICES

Although the smart office is a rather young research domain, it became very popular in the end of the 1990s, and today there are dozens of smart office projects all over the world.

14.2.1 Active Badge

The Active Badge [19] application is often, a posteriori, considered to be the first smart office application. Its goal is to automatically forward incoming calls for the user of a building to the closest phone, wherever he is in the building.

Each user must wear a badge that permanently emits a unique ID using infrared waves. Sensors are disseminated all over the building. The localization of the user is considered to be the localization of the last sensor that read his ID, with a confidence factor inversely proportional to the age of this detection of whole set of sensors is regularly polled, and a central database is updated with the new sensed position of each user.

When an incoming call is received, the receptionist uses software that queries the database to know where he or she should forward the call. The interesting point here is that when an application needs to know the position of a user, it does not directly interrogate the sensor itself, but queries a database. This intermediate database frees the applications from concern about how to interact with sensors. Sensors can therefore be replaced or moved without any impact on the application. It is even possible to add new kinds of sensors (e.g., information about which computer the user logged on) without having to change or even restart the application.

This *context server* is what makes Active Badge the first context-aware office application [7], although it, is a very specific application.

14.2.2 The Intelligent Room

The Intelligent Room [18] project started in 1994 at MIT, its objective being to explore the requirements and advantages of human-machine interaction for collaborative work. The Intelligent Room shares with Hal (which is a derivation of the Intelligent Room) the founding principles and the main objective: bringing computers into the physical world to improve the efficiency of the user in everyday tasks. They also share the requirement that the interaction between user and system should be done in the same way as interaction between two humans.

The Intelligent Room has several presentation and perception capabilities. For example, visually it is able to track several people concurrently and to roughly detect the activities of each of these people (is he or she standing? walking? making a pointing gesture?). A speech recognition system permits the use of spoken interrogation. A set of agents browse the Web to get information.

From a software point of view, the Intelligent Room relies on a multiagent system, MetaGlue. One of the main principles of MetaGlue is that central configuration should always be avoided. Instead, MetaGlue provides ways to program agents to automatically discover and use available services in an agent population. To engage in communication, an agent does not need to worry about communication details (machine, port, etc.) but only needs to know the capabilities of the agent to which it wants to "speak."

MetaGlue can be seen both as a dedicated programming language and as an execution platform for the agents. The programming language is an extension of the Java language that provides the programmer easy ways to create agents without the need to consider on which machine each agent will be executed. At runtime the agents might be distributed among available machines.

MetaGlue supports both synchronous and asynchronous communication between agents, and therefore supports architecture that reflects the natural parallelism of the world. MetaGlue allows multimodal interaction, which means that different agents can be used to provide the same information to the system.

One of the key features of MetaGlue is its dynamic nature. It is always possible to introduce an agent into a running system, allowing the system to be very flexible. Combined with the resource discovery capacity, this dynamicity allows, for example, introduction of new media (such as a handheld) in the room and its use as a new output device. Because MetaGlue also provides ways to store the state of an agent, this dynamicity also creates great robustness: if an agent fails, it can be automatically restarted by the system and recover its previously stored state, making the agents "invincible" [10].

14.2.3 Stanford's *Interactive Workspaces*

Standford's *interactive workspaces* project initially aims to investigate the benefit of large displays for collaborative work. A prototype of such an interactive workspace, the iRoom, has been built. The interaction of users with the iRoom is done through large high-resolution, touch-sensitive displays, but also through portable devices such as laptops or PDAs [12]. One feature of the iRoom is that the designers did not focus on how the room should execute actions in reaction to users' wishes, but rather on how the room should simplify the actions.

From a technical point of view, the iRoom relies on the iROS Meta-Operating System. iROS acts as middleware that ties devices together. Exchanges between applications are performed through iROS subsystems:

- The Event Heap stores and forwards messages. Applications select the events in which they are interested using pattern matching over fields and values.
- The Data Heap is used to share data among applications.
- The iCrafter is used to select a service.

One interesting design principle of iROS is decoupling of applications (i.e., modules): applications are designed with low dependence on one another. This independence makes the overall system more robust, since the crash of one application will not cause the crash of others. Moreover, it allows easy replacement of one device by another.

14.2.4 IGD Rostock's Intelligent Environment Laboratory

The Intelligent Environment Laboratory of IGD Rostock proposes a quite different method to create smart environments and smart offices by replacing function-oriented interaction by goal-oriented interaction. Thus, in the laboratory, components do not only provide to other components (or to the system) interfaces to their functions, but also semantic information about the meaning and the effects of these functions [11].

These descriptions take, as in the famous STRIPS system, the form of a set of preconditions that must be fulfilled before an action can be taken and a description of the effects of an action, that is, of the changes it will imply on the state of the environment. Given these descriptions, the intelligent office can use planning to find a strategy to fulfill goals.

Therefore, the interactions in the laboratory are not an exchange of actions to be performed, but of goals to reach. Although quite basic, this matches our definition of an intelligent office.

14.2.5 Remarks

From a technical point of view, smart offices do not differ greatly from more classical robotics systems. They have sensors and actuators and must use information from the context make decisions. Nevertheless, some features make smart offices particular.

- Like many smart environments, they have a large number of independent devices. Most of the intelligent offices we described propose ways to reflect this natural parallelism on their architecture, by using independent agents.
- Compared to other smart environments, the main characteristic of smart offices is that lot of existing software components (libraries or programs) exist and are already being used. Because the users do not want to learn to use specific programs to perform tasks that can be performed with programs he already knows, a smart office often provides ways to reuse or to interface existing software. In some office architectures like Active Badge or iRoom, independence of modules is ensured by intermediates information storage. This decoupling makes it easier to handle heterogeneity of components, and therefore to reuse existing code.
- Many designers also insist on the importance of multimodal capabilities. This is, as we already stated, especially true in office environments. To provide this, some architectures, such as iROS or MetaGlue, provide ways to handle concurrent media. Usage of service discovery, combined with dynamicity, permits use of the best available interface at a given instant.
- IGD Rostock's Intelligent Environment Laboratory provides an alternative to service discovery, by listing not only functions, but also their effects. The best way to perform an action is then chosen by a planning assistant.

The next section describes Monica, our smart office, including its hardware and software components.

14.3 MONICA

We have just seen that smart offices projects are quite numerous. In 1999 we ourselves initiated such a project, called *SmartOffice* or *Monica*.[1]

14.3.1 Hardware Description

Monica is a normal 25 m^2 office with a desktop, some chairs, a whiteboard, and a computer (see the layout in Figure 14.2). In addition, it contains three video projectors. Two of them are used to project information onto the wall and the whiteboard, and the third is used for projection onto the desktop.

Nine cameras are used for computer vision applications. Two cameras are dedicated to the observation of the whiteboard and the desktop, allowing the implementation of a *MagicBoard* and a *MagicDesk*; another camera is used for video conferencing and *MediaSpace* (see below); five mobile cameras and one static wide-angle camera have no specific role and are available for diverse computer vision tasks.

A speaker and some microphones are used for oral interaction. The same microphones might also be used for localization of a speaking user; other microphones are distributed along the board, the walls, and the desktop to detect the position where a finger taps a wall or the desktop. Other actuators and sensors also exist, such as a door-opening detector, a presence detector, and so forth. Altogether, Monica comprises some 50 sensors and actuators.

14.3.2 Software Components

The intelligence of Monica is provided by many software components. Most of them are existing software from our research group.

- **Gesture recognition**: Thanks to Martin's work [16], Monica is able to detect if one of the users of the office performs some prelearned gesture. These gestures are quite simple and localized in time and space, such as movement or pointing gestures. They provide a very simple way to interact with Monica.
- **Three-dimensional (3D) mouse**: Whenever the user must specify a 3D position to a piece software, he can grab any object and use it as a 3D mouse. After an initiating gesture, an object-tracking module will follow the object, and provides the 3D relative position to any module that requests it.

---

[1] Monica is a recursive acronym that stands for Monica is our Office Network with an Intelligent Computer Assistant.

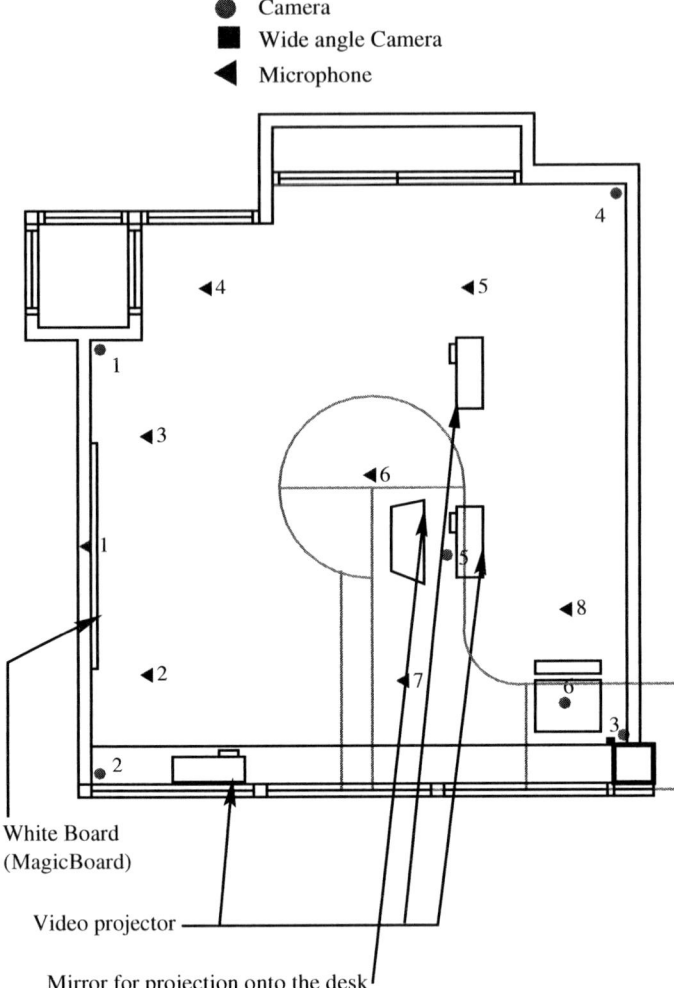

Figure 14.2 Monica is a normal office tooled with sensors and actuators, such as video cameras and video projectors.

- **MagicBoard and MagicDesk**: The two main interfaces of Monica are the MagicBoard and the MagicDesk. They rely on other components, mainly the finger and click detection software.
- **Finger and click detection**: Finger and click detection is used to follow the position of a finger on the desktop or on a wall. The finger can then be used as a mouse for the displayed application. A tap with the finger replaces the mouse click. Finger following is based on computer vision using the Magic-Board and MagicDesk dedicated video camera, as described in [9]. The detection of the click is based on sound localization, using the lag between the arrival

of the tap signal on different microphones, as described in [15]. The combination of a projector with this finger and click detector permits the transformation of any plane surface into a touch-screen. The MagicBoard and the MagicDetector, and more generally the virtual touch screens on which they are displayed, represent the main Perceptual user interface of Monica.

- **Virtual assistant**: In addition to these perceptual interfaces, Monica permits more direct interaction with the system. This direct interaction is done using a speech recognition module (only able to recognize prelearned sentences) and a speech synthesis module. To make this direct interaction more convivial, an animated face, whose expression, eye and mouth opening, orientation, and look direction are controllable and can be displayed on any screen or wall in the room. The virtual assistant is thus able to follow the walking person to whom it is speaking and to emphasize the tone of its answer using different mood appearances.

- **MediaSpace**: The MediaSpace *Comedi*, designed by Coutaz et al. [6], has the goal of allowing several people to work collaboratively as if they were working in the same building. In each office a panel is shown that displays a view of all other offices in the MediaSpace. Information about the *context* (busy, do not disturb, meeting, available, etc.) of the office is also shown. In Monica, the decision to transmit the image of the office to all other clients in the Media-Space uses different criteria, such as the activities in the office, or some explicit or implicit order from the user. Explicit orders can be, for example, given using phycons (described below), whereas implicit orders can come from the scenario detector.

- **Tracker**: This module detect the (x,y) position of each user in the room. It is able to track up to 3 persons simultaneously. Information from the tracker is, for example, used by the virtual assistant to know which direction it should look.

- **Face recognition**: This is used to associate a login id with each user in the room. The face recognition is triggered when the tracker detects that an unidentified user is standing at one of the predefined positions where the face image is easily extractable (two such positions are defined: near the entrance, where the user enters the room and faces one of the cameras, and in front of the computer).

- **Activity detection**: This is one of the major sources of context construction. It is able to detect the class of activity occurring in the room. Detected activities are quite low-level (walking, standing, sitting, falling, etc.) but are used to build higher-level pieces of information in conjunction with an event-based scenario detector [4]. Detected contexts include working, meeting, and speech. The Activity Detector is also used to automatically raise an alarm in case of faintness or as, already seen, to control the MediaSpace.

- **Phycons**: Phycons provide another way to interact with Monica. Phycons are normal physical objects whose presence or position has a special signification for the system. For example, a Rubick's cube on the desktop, with the red face up, means that the user does not want his image to be transmitted on the Media-Space. We believe that this kind of interaction fits very well with the ubiquitous computing standard: because the interface is a very simple interaction with a real object, its usage can be very natural. Although learning is necessary (you have to know that you must use the Rubick's cube to stop the image transmission), such an action can be performed as unconsciously as switching on the light. More details on phycons are given in Hall's thesis [8].

- **Internet agent**: The Internet agent is in charge of any interaction of the office with the Internet. It can run autonomously, for example to detect and announce the arrival of new e-mail for one of the present users or, on the request of a user, to get some information from the Web. Of course, the behavior of this agent must take context into account; for example, it must not announce a new e-mail message during a speech or a meeting.

14.3.3 Remarks

All these software agents are part of a smart office. Indeed, thanks to the PUI, such as MagicBoard or the Gesture Recognition module, the office is interactive. Some of these PUIs, such as the virtual assistant, need a dialog, i.e., an explicit and conscious interaction with the user, using the user's natural means of communication. Some other interaction media, such as phycons, do not use natural communication means, but communication can be performed by the user mechanically, thus making Monica relevant to ubiquitous computing. Using sensors such as trackers, activity detectors or presence detectors, Monica is able to know what is going on in the office and adapt its behavior accordingly. Thus, Monica is also a context-aware office.

However, these components alone are not sufficient to built a smart office. The next section shows how, using a software architecture named Gamma, we can build a smart office out of these components.

14.4 MONICA'S CONTROL ARCHITECTURE

14.4.1 Introduction

To turn this collection of PUIs into a global smart office application, a software architecture is needed. To fit with the specifics of our application, this architecture must meet certain requirements:

- As in other smart office applications, Monica should take into account the natural parallelism of smart environments by allowing parallelism and modularity in the application programming.
- The architecture should also provide easy ways to reuse existing programs or functions. This also implies that the architecture should allow heterogeneity,

since we cannot guarantee that all software has been programmed using the same language.
- We also want to ensure the independence of each module: a module developer should not have knowledge of other modules or of the application. Each module developer should focus only on his own module's capabilities.
- Similarly, the application developer should not worry about the programming details of modules.
- Since Monica should be able to change its behavior according to the context, it must be dynamically reconfigurable. It should therefore be possible to add or replace modules at runtime—for example, to replace the virtual assistant by a simple console or to subsume output of the tracker by a sound-based localization when available. Monica is not a simple application but a set of *behaviors*. Monica itself never starts or stops, but each behavior can be started or stopped at any time.

14.4.2 Software Bus

To build Monica's architecture, we developed a multiagent system named Gamma. Gamma is both a set of programming tools (mainly an API and some meta-programs used to transform a software into a Monica agent) and an execution environment for the agents.

The key component of Gamma's architecture is a software bus. All agents in the system are connected to the bus and only to the bus. The advantage of such a centralized architecture is that it allows easy reconfiguration of the system, making it possible to change any connection independently of the module. Moreover, clients need not care about other clients when trying to connect to the system. They should know only how to connect to the bus.

14.4.3 Communication Scheme

We believe that a bus is necessary to ensure independence of modules, but it is not sufficient. Many systems use a Common Object Request Broker Architecture (CORBA) bus for communication but still request each agent to have knowledge on other modules. In order to avoid this requirement, the communication scheme must extend the abstraction barrier given by the bus to the communication level.

Let P be a client with information, C a client that needs this information, and S the bus. We define two message types:

- In a *push* message, the writing agent initiates the communication and interrupts the recipient agent to give information (usually a fact).
- In a *pull* message, the recipient initiates the communication and receives the data from the writing agent using a nonblocking read.

More detailed descriptions of these messages, including network protocols, can be obtained in [14].

Monica supports three different communication schemes between P and C based on these two message types.

In the *push/push* communication scheme, the client C specifies, at the initialization stage, the information in which it is interested. Each time such information is produced and emitted by P (i.e., is sent by client P to bus S), client C asynchronously (during its execution) receives the message (i.e., S initiates a communication with C and sends the information to it). This mechanism is the classical *publish/subscribe* mechanism.

In the *pull/pull* communication scheme, P specifies at the initialization stage which kind of information it knows, i.e., which kind of question it is able to answer. When C needs a piece of information, it emits a request (i.e., it sends it to S), S forwards the question to P and routes the answer back to C. This mechanism is very similar to the one used in the popular Open Agent Architecture (OAA) multiagent platform [3].

In the *push/pull* mechanism, there is no initialization. When client P produces a piece information, it sends the information to S, which stores it in a central database. When C next requests this information, S sends to it the last stored value given by P. This is the classical mailbox exchange system, and is similar to how Active Badge information is sent from sensors to a query tool.

What we initially called a software bus, S, is found to be a centralized agent that combines more complex roles:

- It acts as OAA's facilitator to transmit requests from C to P.
- It also acts as a publish/subscribe monitor to route produced information from P to C.
- At the same time, it acts as a mailbox and stores information received from P to be able to send them later in response to requests from C, exactly like Active Badge's central database.

14.4.4 Client Programming

Whatever the communication scheme used by a client (it can use all three of them simultaneously), it implies declarative behavior: the client does not connect to other clients to send a message. Nor does it call a remote procedure or a service. Instead, each client emits declarations. These declarations are either a fact proposal, a question, or a wish about what the environment state should be.

The natural way to program a client uses an imperative style. This is especially true when the client is an existing piece of software. Gamma provides a way to easily combine existing imperative code with declarative code to create a client. The programming of a client usually follows four stages:

- **Native code**. The first stage is to program or adapt the *native code*, that is, the actual code of the software, e.g., the source code of Netscape for a browser

14.4 MONICA'S CONTROL ARCHITECTURE

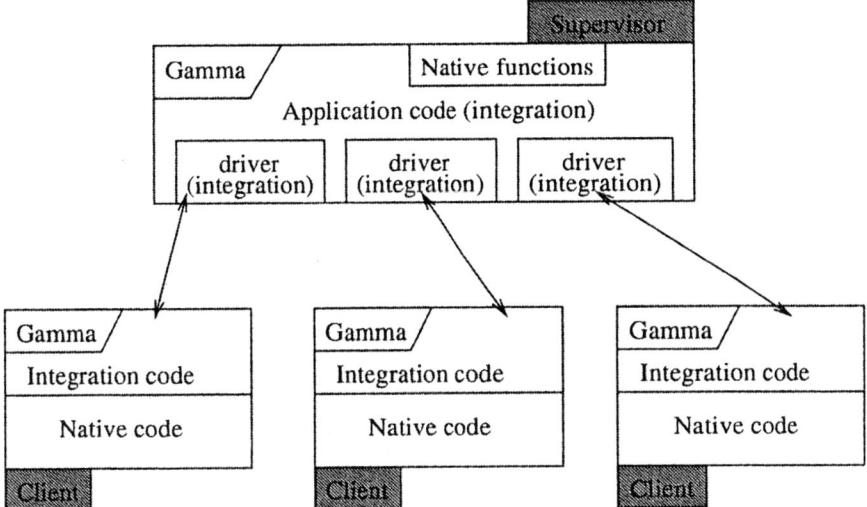

Figure 14.3 The software architecture of Monica is based on a software bus, to which every agent is connected. Each is encapsulated into a Gamma shell that combines native code (usually C++) and code in the integration language to deal with connections to the system. The software bus is implemented by a central agent, called a *supervisor*, also programmed using a combination of integration and native code.

agent. This native code may rely on functions provided by the Gamma API, whose main ones are push and pull. push is used to produce information, whereas pull is used to get information. If the software already exists, the addition of these push instructions in the code is usually the only required modification of the code.

- **Binding with a Gamma shell**. The second stage consists of binding the program to a Gamma shell. This is done automatically using meta-programming tools provided by Gamma. Once this binding is done, the program is enhanced by a command interpreter. The program then performs as usual, but it can be interrupted remotely and requested to execute a shell command, that is, a command in an integration language, as described below. Thanks to an automatically generated interface, the set of shell commands comprises all the internal functions of the native program, as well as accessors and mutators to all its variables.

- **Integration code in the module**. The Gamma shell in which the native code is encapsulated also executes another kind of code called *integration code*. The integration code specifies how the module should interact with the system. More precisely, it specifies how (using which native function) it can reply to a question or how (calling which call-back) it should react to a piece of information. The integration code is written using a dedicated programming language, the integration language, interpreted by the Gamma shell. The integration language is an extension of the Scheme programming language, which

comprises declarative possibilities such as Clips-like forward chaining and Prolog-like backward chaining.
- **Integration code plugged by the module into the supervisor.** The last stage is to write integration code that will be plugged into the supervisor. Although this code is part of the client code, it will be uploaded into the supervisor when the client first connects and then executed by the supervisor. This code is called *driver code* since its role is to specify how the the client integrates with the system and how it can be used by the system. For example, driver code is used to subscribe to a class of information by sending a rule of the form "each time this information is available, please send it to me."

14.4.5 Application Programming

Once a set of agents has been programmed, it is possible to program the application, that is, to program behaviors of the smart office. This is done by sending code to the supervisor to modify its program, called the *application program*. The application program also contains different kinds of code:

- Some native functions can be added to the supervisor Gamma shell and made available to the supervisor integration code.
- Universal knowledge is the part of the supervisor code that is completely independent of the behaviors. Universal knowledge is a set of backward- and forward-chaining rules. An example of such a rule is "if someone is moving in the office, then there must be someone in the office."
- Behavior code specifies how the office should behave. Although different programming styles are permitted by Gamma (imperative, object-oriented, agent-oriented, declarative, etc.), these behavior codes are also usually represented as rules that specify how to *react* to facts or to requests.
- The supervisor can plug into the clients some code that, although part of the supervisor code, will be executed in the client process (and machine when the code is distributed). This is useful, for example, when the supervisor wants to subsume output from a client: such a subsumption could be performed by the supervisor (which then simply ignores information that comes from a client and replaces it by other data). Nevertheless, it is generally better to ask the client itself not to bother the supervisor with this information. This can be done by uploading code into the client to replace its forward rule. This method is used when we want to change the behavior of the office because of a change in the room (e.g., the start of a meeting).

14.4.6 Example

This section illustrates the use of this architecture by presenting an example of an application. This application implements a very simple behavior of the office: the virtual assistant always looks at the user. The components involved in this behavior are the tracker and the virtual assistant.

Creation of the agents

The transformation of these two components into agents, as seen previously, takes four steps.

1. *Modification of native code.* The tracker is a C program whose main loop is

   ```
   for(;;){
      img=grabNewImage();
      updatePositions(personList);
      guiDisplayPositions(personList);
   }
   ```

   In order to produce useful information for the system, the tracker native code must be transformed into:

   ```
   for(;;){
      img=grabNewImage();
      updatePositions(personList);
      guiDisplayPositions(personList);
      // Information production
      for(p=personList; *p; p++)
         push("id,x,y", p->id, p->x, p->0);
   }
   ```

   Since the virtual assistant produces no information (it is a pure actuator), no modification of its native code is needed.

2. The *binding with a Gamma shell* is automatically performed by a meta-program from the header files (.h) of the components before the compilation of the programs.

3. The compiled programs can then be provided an *integration program* to be executed by the Gamma shell to which they are bound. The *integration code* specifies how the program should react to internal or external events. For the tracker the required code is

   ```
   // if (id,x,y) is produced, send it to the supervisor
   (define-forward-rule forwardPositions
      (id x y)
      =>
      (push supervisor person[id].x=x person[id].y=y))
   ```

   This defines a rule, named `forwardPositions`, that reacts to the production of an id, x or y by the native code by forwarding it to the supervisor. This rule might seem useless, since the information could have been pushed to the supervisor directly from the native code. But because the native code cannot be modified dynamically, we prefer this method, which allows, for example, the supervisor to modify the rule to subsume the (*x*,*y*) position.

Similarly, the virtual assistant agent contains integration code to specify how it should react to an event:

```
// if new x,y is received, move eyes accordingly
(define forward-rule move-eye
  (x y)
  =>
  SetEyeAngle(atan((y-my_y)/(x-my_x))))
```

This rule specifies that the virtual assistant should react to an incoming (from the supervisor) (*x*, *y*) position by updating the look direction using the native function `SetEyeAngle`.

4. The latter integration code specifies how to react to an incoming (*x*, *y*) event. In order to receive the event, the virtual assistant agent must inform the supervisor that it wants to receive it. The subscription to the event is also done with integration code, the so-called driver code, plugged into the supervisor by the virtual assistant agent:

```
// If focus point is updated, warn the virtual assistant
(driver-code)
    (define forward-rule assistant-xy-subscription
      (focus)
      =>
      (push assistant x=focus.x y=focus.y)))
```

Behavior programming

In the previous section we created two agents from existing code. Thanks to integration code, these agents are able to provide the (*x*, *y*) position of each person in the room and to look at a given object in the room (the focus). We can now program the wanted behavior. This is done by inserting into the supervisor the rule

```
// If person[0] moved (is updated), update focus point
(define forward-rule follow-person-0
  (person[0])
  =>
  focus=person[0])
```

This example is, of course, very basic (a more complex example, as well as details on the integration language syntax, is presented in [13]), but it illustrates the main principles of a smart office application construction using the Gamma support architecture.

- Developers of modules need no knowledge of other modules in the system. As in the Active Badge project, this is mainly ensured by the presence of an intermediate agent between producers and consumers of informations.
- Similarly, developers of modules have no knowledge of the application in which their modules will participate. Using integration code (mainly rules) plugged into the supervisor, modules only describe their capabilities and prerequisites, using symbolic description, as done in IGD Rostock's Intelligent Environment Laboratory. The actual decision to execute a given action provided by a module is the responsibility of the application developers.
- Each agent encapsulates a shell that can interpret commands written in integration language received at runtime. Since this integration language is an expressive programming language, there is virtually no limit to the possible dynamic modifications of each agent's behavior.

14.5 CONCLUSION

In this chapter we have focused on smart offices, a subdomain of smart environments. *Smart office* is a term by which we refer to an interactive office, ubiquitous-computing enhanced office, context-aware office or intelligent office. Whatever the term used, these smart offices have features that must be taken into account when implementing them: offices are places where existing software is commonly used; where different media can be present, and where various kinds of activities take place. We have described some examples of smart office projects and seen how they address in various ways these specificities.

The smart office Monica, which pretends to be interactive, ubiquitous computing enhanced and context-aware, also addresses these specificities by using a software architecture, Gamma, that embeds each agent in a shell, programmed in an integration language, that is an extension of Scheme.

By this coupling with a shell, Gamma allows easy transformation of existing programs into an agent, which was one of our prerequisites. Thanks to a central agent, which acts similarly to OAA's facilitator, Active Badge's central database and iROS Event Heap, strong independence of Monica's module is ensured. As noted by the iRoom developers, this allows greater reliability in addition to desirable modularity in the development. Furthermore, it permits the building of multimodal interfaces: since the communication between agents is not function-oriented but facts-oriented, an agent does not rely on the presence of a specific medium, and the system can always choose the best available device among the currently available ones. Because each agent can be dynamically replaced, subsumed, or even modified, the system can easily reprogram itself and adapt itself to the context.

The next step is to turn this smart office into an intelligent office. For this inspiration can be found in IGD Rostock's work. We believe that our architecture is generic enough to fit with STRIPS-like planners.

REFERENCES

A. Bobick, J. Davis, and S, Intille. The kidsroom: An example application using a deep perceptual interface. In M. Turk, editor, *Proc. of Workshop on Perceptual User Interfaces (PUI'97)*, pages 1–4, Blanff, Alberta, Canada, October 1997.

F. Brard. *Vision par Ordinateur pour l'interaction homme-machine fortement couple*. PhD thesis, Université Joseph Fourier, Grenoble, January 2000.

A. Cheyer and D. Martin. The open agent architecture. *Journal of Autonomous Agents and Multi-Agent Systems*, 4(1):143–148, March 2001.

O. Chomat. *Caractrisation d'lments d'Activits par la Statistique Conjointe de Champs Rceptifs*. PhD thesis, Institut National Polytechnique de Grenoble, Grenoble, September 2000.

M.H. Coen. Building brains for rooms: Designing distributed software agents. In *Proc. of Ninth Conference on Innovative Applications of Artificial Intelligence*, pages 971–977, Providence, Rhode Island, 1997.

J. Coutaz, F. Brard, E. Carraux, and J.-L. Crowley. Early experience with the mediaspace comedi. In *Proc. of IFIP Conference on Engineering for Human-Computer Interaction (EHC198)*, Heraklion, Crete, Greece, September 1998.

A.K. Dey. *Providing Architectural Support for Building Context-Aware Applications*. PhD thesis, Georgia Institute of Technology, November 2000.

D. Hall, *Viewpoint independant recognition of objects from local appearances*. PhD thesis, Institut National Polytechnique de Grenoble, Grenoble, 2001.

D. Hall, C. Le Gal, J. Martin, O. Chomat, T. Kapuscinski, and J.L. Crowley. Magicboard: A contribution to an intelligent office environment. In *Proc. of the International Symposium on Intelligent Robotic Systems*, 1999.

T. Hammond, K. Gajos, R. Davis, and H. Shrobe. An agent-based system for capturing and indexing software design meetings. In *In Proc. of the International Workshop on Agents in Design (WAID'02)*, Cambridge, MA, August 2002.

T. Heider and T. Kirste. Intelligent environment lab. *Computer Graphics Topics*, 15(2):8–9, 2002.

B. Johanson, A. Fox, and T. Winograd. The interactive workspaces project: Experiences with ubiquitous computing rooms. *IEEE Pervasive Computing Magazine*, 1(2), April–June 2002.

C. Le Gal. *Intergration and control of vision-based processus for intelligent environments*. PhD thesis, Institut National Polytechnique de Grenoble, Grenoble, France, 2003.

C. Le Gal, J. Martin, A. Lux, and J.L. Crowley. Smartoffice: Design of an intelligent environment. *IEEE Intelligent Systems*, 16(4), July–August 2001.

C. Le Gal, A.E. Özcan, K. Schwerdt, and J.L. Crowley. A sound magicboard. *In Proc. of Third International Conference on Multimodal Interfaces*, Beijing, 2000.

J. Martin. *Reconnaissance de gestes en vision par ordinateur*. PhD thesis, Institut National Polytechnique de Grenoble, Grenoble, France, July 2000.

B.N. Schilit and M.M. Theimer. Disseminating map information to mobile hosts. *IEEE Network*, 8(5):22–32, September–October 1994.

M. Torrance. Advances in human–computer interaction: The intelligent room. In *Proceedings of CHI*, Denver, Colorado, May 1995.

R. Want, A. Hopper, V. Falcao, and J. Gibbons. The active badge location system *ACM Transactions on Information Systems*, 10(1):91–102, January 1992.

M. Weiser. The world is not a desktop. *Interactions*, 1(1):7–8, January 1994.

P. Wellner. The digital desk calculator: Tactile manipulation on a desktop. In *ACM Symposium on User Interface Software and Technology*, pages 27–33, November 1991.

CHAPTER 15

Perceptual Environments

ALEX PENTLAND

The Media Laboratory
Massachusetts Institute of Technology

15.1 INTRODUCTION

Inanimate things are coming to life. However, these stirrings are not those of Shelley's Frankenstein or the humanoid robots dreamed of in artificial intelligence laboratories. This new awakening is more like that of Walt Disney: the simple objects that surround us are gaining sensors, computational powers, and actuators. As a result, desks and doors, TVs and telephones, cars and trains, eyeglasses and shoes, and even the shirts on our backs are all changing from static, inanimate objects into adaptive, reactive systems that are more useful and efficient.

Imagine a house that always knows where your kids are and tells you when they might be getting into trouble. Or an office that knows when you are in the middle of an important conversation and shields you from interruptions. Or a car that knows when you are sleepy and should stop for coffee. Or glasses that can recognize the person you are talking to and whisper her name in your ear. All of these are examples of demonstrations we have built in my laboratory, and several have already become the basis of commercial products.

To change inanimate objects like offices, houses, cars, or glasses into smart, active helpmates, we must give them what I call *perceptual intelligence.* They need to begin paying attention to people and the surrounding situation just as another person would. That way, they can begin to adapt their behavior to us rather than the other way around. If you can imagine raising a child in a closed, dark, soundproof box with only a telegraph connection to the outside world, you can understand how difficult it is for computers to become intelligent and helpful. They exist in a world that is almost completely disconnected from ours, so how can they understand our desires?

In the language of cognitive science, perceptual intelligence is the ability to solve the frame problem. It involves being able to classify the current situation so that you

---

Smart Environments: Technologies, Protocols, and Applications, edited by D.J. Cook and S.K. Das
ISBN 0-471-54448-5 © 2005 John Wiley & Sons, Inc.

know what variables are important and thus can take appropriate action. Once a computer has the perceptual intelligence to know who, what, when, where, and why, simple statistical learning methods are probably sufficient for the computer to determine what aspects of the situation are significant and to answer a wide variety of useful questions.

15.2 PERCEPTUAL INTELLIGENCE, NOT UBIQUITOUS COMPUTING

My goal is to make machines that are aware of their environment, and in particular are sensitive to the people who interact with them. They should know who we are, see our expressions and gestures, and hear the tone and emphasis of our voice. People often equate perceptual intelligence with ubiquitous computing (or artificial intelligence), but I believe that my approach is very different.

For instance, I do not care that there are computers everywhere, or that they have artificial intelligence, because I believe that most tasks do not require complex reasoning. Instead, they require appropriate perceptual abilities and simple learned responses (i.e., perceptual intelligence). Consequently, the fact that it is often convenient to have a general-purpose computer in the system is largely beside the point.

Moreover, I am against the idea of having everything tightly and continuously networked together. Such ubiquitous networking and its attendant capacity to concentrate information has too close a resemblance to George Orwell's dark vision of a government that controls your every move. Instead, I propose that *local* intelligences—mainly perceptual intelligence—combined with relatively sparse, user-initiated networking can provide most of the benefits of ubiquitous networking, while at the same time making it more difficult for outsiders to track and analyze the user's behavior.

15.3 ADAPTIVE INTERFACES

A key idea of perceptual interfaces is that they must be adaptive both to the overall situation and to the individual user. As a consequence, much of our research focus is on learning the user's behaviors and how they vary as a function of the situation. For instance, we have built systems that learn the user's driving behavior, thus allowing the automobile to anticipate the driver's actions (Pentland and Liu 1999) and systems that learns typical pedestrian behaviors, allowing them to detect unusual events (Oliver et al., 1998).

Most recently, we have built audiovisual systems that learn word meanings from natural audio and visual input (Roy and Pentland 1997, 1998). This automatically acquired vocabulary can then be used to understand and generate spoken language. Although simple in its current form, this effort is a first step toward a more fully grounded model of language acquisition. The current system can be applied to human-computer interfaces that use spoken input. A significant problem in designing effective interfaces is the difficulty of anticipating a person's word choice and associated intent. Our system addresses this problem by learning the vocabulary of each user together with its visual grounding. We are investigating several practical applications, including adaptive human-machine interfaces for browsing, assistive technologies, education, and entertainment.

15.4 EXPERIMENTAL TESTBEDS

To realize my vision of helpful, perceptually intelligent environments, I have created a series of experimental testbeds at the Media Laboratory. These testbeds can be divided into two main types: *smart rooms* and *smart clothes*. The idea of a smart room is a little like that of a butler, i.e., a passive observer who usually stands quietly in the corner but who is constantly looking for opportunities to help. Smart clothes, on the other hand, are more like a personal assistant. They are like a person who travels with you, seeing and hearing everything that you do and trying to anticipate your needs and generally smooth your way.

Both smart rooms and smart clothes are instrumented with sensors (currently, mainly cameras and microphones, but also sensors for physical quantities like pressure and distance and biosensors for heart rate and muscle action), which allow the computer to see, hear, and interpret users' actions. People in a smart room can control programs, browse multimedia information, and experience shared virtual environments without keyboards, special sensors, or special goggles. Smart clothes can provide personalized information about the surrounding environment, such as the names of people you meet or directions to your next meeting, and can replace most computer and consumer electronics. The key idea is that because the room or the clothing knows something about what is going on, it can react intelligently.

The first smart room was developed in 1991; now there are smart rooms in Japan, England, and several places in the United States. They can be linked together by ISDN telephone lines to allow shared virtual environments and cooperative work experiments. Our smart clothes project was started in 1992 and now includes many separate research efforts.

15.5 SMART ROOMS

In this section I will describe some of the perceptual capabilities available to our smart rooms and provide a few illustrations of how these capabilities can be combined into interesting applications. This list of capabilities is far from exhaustive; mainly it is a catalog of the most recent research in each area.

15.5.1 Real-Time Person Tracking Using a Dynamic 3-D Model

To act intelligently in a day-to-day environment, the first question you need to answer is: where are the people? The human body is a complex dynamic system whose visual features are time-varying, noisy signals. Accurately tracking of the state of such a system requires the use of a recursive estimation framework. The elements of the framework are the observation model relating noisy low-level features to the higher-level skeletal model, and vice versa, and the dynamic skeletal model itself.

This extended Kalman filter framework reconciles the two-dimensional (2-D) tracking process with high-level three-dimensional (3-D) models, thus stabilizing the 2-D tracking by directly coupling an articulated dynamic model with raw pixel measurements. Some of the demonstrated benefits of this added stability include increased 3-D tracking accuracy, insensitivity to temporary occlusion, and the ability to handle multiple people.

The dynamic skeleton model currently includes the upper body and arms. The model interpolates those portions of the body state that are not measured directly, such as the upper body and elbow orientation, by use of the model's intrinsic dynamics and the behavior (control) model. The model also rejects noise that is inconsistent with the dynamic model (see Figure 15.1).

The system runs on two SGI machines at 20–30 Hz and has performed reliably on hundreds of people in many different physical locations, including exhibitions, conferences, and offices in several research labs. The *jitter* or noise observed experimentally is 0.9 cm for 3-D translation and 0.6 degrees for 3-D rotation when the system is operating in a desk-sized environment.

One of the main advantages is feedback from a 3-D dynamic model to the low-level vision system. Without feedback, the 2-D tracker fails if there is even partial self-occlusion from a single camera's perspective. With feedback, information from the dynamic model can be used to resolve ambiguity during 2-D tracking. For additional information see Wren and Pentland (1997).

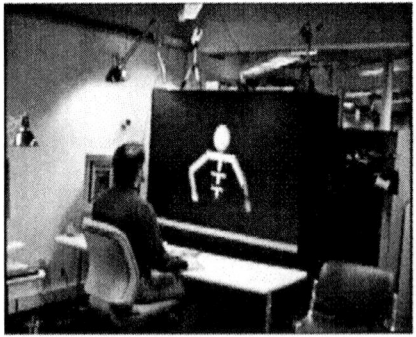

Figure 15.1 The system uses 2-D observations to drive a 3-D dynamic model of the skeleton. This dynamic model uses a control law that chooses typical behaviors when it is necessary to choose from among multiple possible legal trajectories. Predictive feedback from the dynamic model is provided by setting priors for the 2-D observations process. It is real-time and self-calibrating and has been successfully integrated into applications ranging from physical rehabilitation to a computer-enhanced dance space.

15.5.2 Self-Calibration

By collecting a set of three blob correspondences (face, left hand, right hand) over a number of frames (50–100 total correspondences) and computing the stereo calibration using a Levenburg-Marquart estimator on the batch of correspondences. The mean residual RMS error from this self-calibration process is typically about 2.25 cm. The relative error of reconstruction of hand position over this trajectory is therefore about 1.8%. The sources of error include not only noise and modeling error, but also hand movement error, since the trajectory followed by the person is not exact and the hand shape changes. Thus, only a fraction of this relative error should be counted as computational error. For additional information see Azerbayejani and Pentland (1996).

15.5.3 Recognizing Hand Gestures

We have used the recovered 3-D body geometry for several different gesture recognition tasks, including a real-time American Sign Language reader (Starner, Weaver, and Pentland 1998) and a system that recognizes t'ai chi gestures and trains the user to perform them correctly (see Figure 15.2) (Becker and Pentland 1996). Typically, these systems have a gesture vocabularies of 25 to 65 gestures and recognition accuracy above 95%.

Although we have used standard hidden Markov models (HMMs) to recognize such gestures with near-perfect accuracy, we have found the training of such models to be labor-intensive and difficult. This is because use of HMMs to describe multipart signals (such as two-handed gestures) requires a large amount of training, and even so, the HMM parameter estimation process is typically unstable.

To improve on this situation, we have developed a new method of training a more general class of HMM called the *Coupled HMM*. Coupled HMMs allow each hand to be described by a separate state model and the interactions between the hands to be modeled explicitly and economically. The consequence is that much less training data is required, and the HMM parameter estimation process is much better conditioned. For additional detail see Brand, Oliver, and Pentland (1997).

Figure 15.2 Left: accurate, real-time recognition of a 40-word American Sign Language vocabulary; right: recognizing and teaching t'ai chi gestures using the Coupled HMM method.

15.5.4 Driver's Intention

The interior of an automobile is a special type of room, one of considerable importance. In many areas, the average worker spends 14 hours a week in an automobile. Perhaps more importantly, over 40,000 people die in automobile accidents each year, and the majority of accidents are attributable to driver error.

Together with Dr. Andy Liu at the Nissan Cambridge Basic Research facility, we decided to try to build a smart room version of an automobile interior. Our goal was to develop safer cars by having the automobile "observe" the driver, continuously estimate the driver's internal state (what action the driver is taking), and respond appropriately. To accomplish this, we observed the driver's hand and leg motions while driving in the simulator. We used this data to build HMM models of each type of driver action (e.g., passing, turning, stopping, car following, lane change, speeding up).

Finally, we used these models to classify the driver's action as quickly as possible. We did this by again observing the driver's actions and comparing the observed pattern of action to each of our HMM models. We found that the system was able to identify accurately what action the driver was beginning to execute.

Surprisingly, we were able to determine what the driver was doing almost as soon as the action started. Our accuracy in classifying the driver's action was 97% within 0.5 s of the beginning an action, rising to over 99% accuracy within 2 s. This sort of accuracy in determining the driver's intention should allow us to adapt the car's performance more accurately and quickly to suit the situation and to warn the driver about possible dangers.

15.5.5 Head Tracking and Shape Recovery

Because of their importance to communication and fine detail, the human head and face require more detailed analysis than the rest of the body. We have therefore developed a system that estimates the 3-D head pose, 3-D facial structure, and skin texture at 20 Hz using a single SGI O2 computer. Like the body tracking system discussed above, this system uses feedback from its 3-D structure to guide interpretation of the 2-D features.

The system initializes itself by finding the face using a coarse model of head shape and skin-like color. A 3-D face model is then aligned with the eyes, nose, and mouth, and eigenface measurements confirm and optimize the detection of the face. The system then tracks the facial features using eight normalized correlation 2-D patch trackers. While the 2-D trackers follow the face, the system continuously estimates the rigid structure that could correspond to the face using an Extended Kalman Filter (EKF). Thus, the individual 2-D trackers function as a single 3-D object.

Having recovered the 3-D pose using an EKF, we can normalize the face image by warping it in 3-D into a frontal mug shot and analyze it using a statistical model that has been trained by a 3-D head scanner to learn to predict a full 3-D facial structure from a frontal mug shot of any individual (Figure 15.3). Thus, we can recover in real time estimates of the facial pose (in 3-D), as well as its texture and a full 3-D

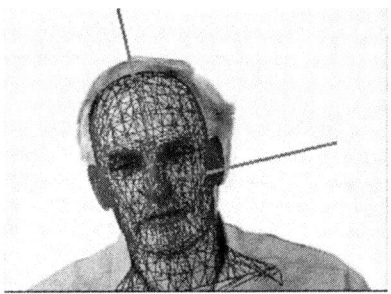
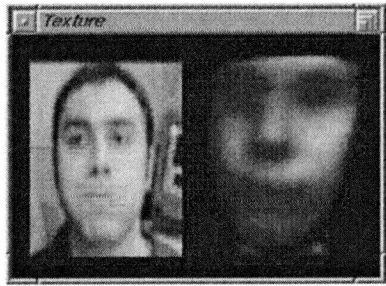

Figure 15.3 Real-time tracking of the head pose using an EKF (left) allows us to "undo" projective effects and make a statistical estimate of the 3-D head structure directly from the intensity image data (image and estimated structure shown at the right).

structural model. These form a very compact, complete 3-D description of the face (100 bytes of data) that is recovered from live video images at over 20 Hz. For additional information see Jebara and Pentland (1998).

15.5.6 Audio Interpretation

Audio interpretation of people is as important as visual interpretation. Although much work has been done on speech understanding, virtually all of this work assumes a closely placed microphone for input and a fixed listening position. Speech recognition applications, for instance, typically require near-field (<1.5 ms) microphone placement for acceptable performance. Beyond this distance, the signal-to-noise ratio of the incoming speech affects the performance significantly; most commercial speech recognition packages typically break down over a 4 to 6 dB range.

The constraint of near-field microphone placement makes audio interpretation very difficult in an unconstrained environment, so it is necessary to find a solution that allows the user to move around with minimal degradation of performance. Our solution to this problem is to use our vision-based head-tracking capability to "steer" a microphone so that it focuses on the user's head. This is accomplished by the technique of beam forming with an array of microphones. For additional information see Basu, Casey, Gardner, Azarbayjani, and Pentland (1996).

15.5.7 Learning in the Interface

Traditional HCI interfaces have hard-wired assumptions about how a person will communicate. In a typical speech recognition application the system has some preset vocabulary and (possibly statistical) grammar. For proper operation, the user must limit what she says to the words and vocabulary built into the system. However, studies have shown that in practice it is difficult to predict how different users will use available input modalities to express their intents. For example, Furnas and colleagues did a series of experiments to see how people assigned keywords for operations in a mock interface. They concluded that "There is no one good access term for most objects. The idea of an 'obvious,' 'self-evident,' or 'natural' term is a myth! ... Even the best possible name is not very useful .... Any keyword system capable of providing a high hit rate for unfamiliar users must let them use words of their won choice for objects." Our conclusion is that effective interfaces require adaptive mechanisms that can learn how individuals use modalities to communicate.

We have therefore built a trainable interface that lets the user teach it the words and gestures to be used and what they mean. Our current work focuses on a system that learns words from natural interactions; users teach the system words by simply pointing to objects and naming them. Currently, training time is approximately linear in the number of terms to be learned, with only a few teaching examples required per learned term. This work demonstrates an interface that learns words and their domain-limited semantics through natural multimodal interactions with people. The interface, embodied as an animated character named Toco the Toucan, can learn acoustic words and their meanings by continuously updating association weight vectors that estimate the mutual information between acoustic words and attribute vectors that represent perceptually salient aspects of virtual objects in Toco's world. Toco is able to learn semantic associations (between words and attribute vectors) using gestural input from the user. Gestural input enables the user to specify naturally which object to attend to during word learning (Figure 15.4). For additional information see Roy and Pentland (1997, 1998).

15.5.8 Recognizing Face and Voice

Once the person has been found, and visual and auditory attention has been focused on him, the next question to ask is: who is it? The question of identity is central to smart behavior, because who is giving a command is often as important as what the command is. Perhaps the best way to answer the "who is it?" question is to

Figure 15.4 Toco the Toucan in both his robotic and computer graphics form. This computer graphics demonstration of word and gesture learning for human-machine interactions was called "the best demo" at SIGGRAPH "96" by the *Los Angeles Times*.

recognize the person by facial appearance and by speech. Our speech-based speaker identification system is now in daily use to annotate the U.S. Congressional Record; for additional information see Roy and Malmud (1996).

For face recognition we have developed a new Bayesian [maximum a posteriori (MAP)] method that may be viewed as a generalized nonlinear extension of Linear Discriminant Analysis (LDA) or "FisherFace" techniques for face recognition (Figures 15.5 and 15.6). The performance advantage of this probabilistic matching technique over standard Euclidean nearest-neighbor eigenspace matching is demonstrated using results from DARPA's 1996 FERET face recognition competition, in which this algorithm was found to be the top performer. Moreover, our nonlinear generalization has distinct computational/storage advantages over these linear methods for large databases. For additional information see Moghaddam, Wassudin, and Pentland (1997).

15.5.9 Expression Recognition

Facial expression is almost as important as identity. For instance, a car should know if the driver is sleepy, and a teaching program should know if the student looks bored. So, just as we can recognize a person once we have accurately located her face, we can analyze the person's facial motion to determine her expression. The lips are of particular importance in interpreting facial expression, so we have recently focused on tracking and classification of lip shape.

The first step in processing is to detect and characterize the shape of the lip region. For this task we developed the LAFTER system, first reported in Oliver, Bernard, Coutaz, and Pentland (1997) (Figure 15.7). This system uses a on-line EM algorithm to make MAP estimates of 2-D head pose and lip shape, runs at 30 Hz on a personal computer (PC) and has been used successfully on hundreds of users in many different locations and laboratories. Using lip shape features derived from LAFTER, we can train HMMs for various mouth configurations. Recognition accuracy for eight different users making over 2000 expressions averaged 96.5%.

Such a 2-D approach is not appropriate for applications that require 3-D models of the user or where head pose can vary widely. We have therefore developed a

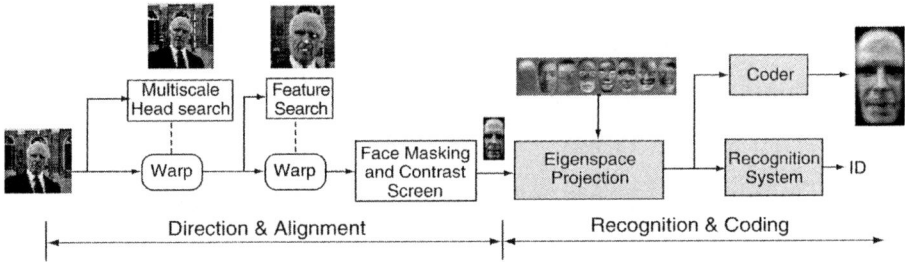

Figure 15.5 Organization of our Bayesian face recognition and image coding system.

354 PERCEPTUAL ENVIRONMENTS

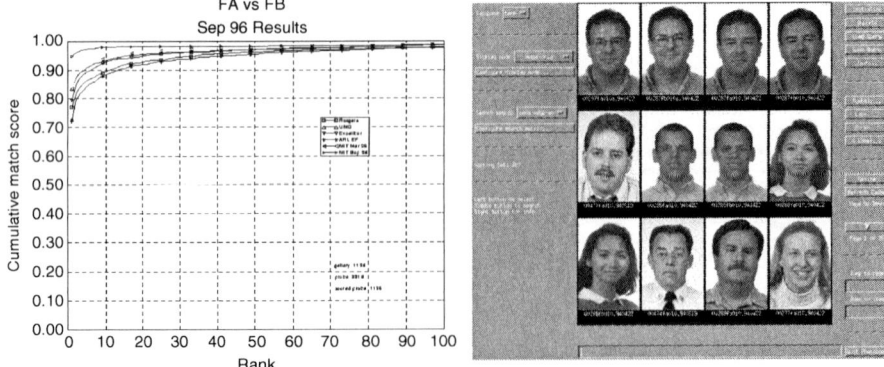

Figure 15.6 The graph on the left shows cumulative recognition rates for frontal FA/FB views for the competing algorithms in the FERET 1996 test. The top curve (labeled "MIT Sep 96") corresponds to our Bayesian matching technique. Note that second placed is standard eigenface matching (labeled "MIT Mar 95"). The curve labeled "UMD" is the LDA or Fisherface algorithm. On the right is the typical FERET image database search result using our algorithm; the top four images are all of the same person.

method of estimating 3-D lip shape by using a FEM (Finite Element Mesh) model that has been trained with 3-D data so that its motions must conform to the subspace of typical human lip motions (Figure 15.8). The 3-D model is fit to video data using a refinement of the LAFTER system's color and shape segmentation output, allowing us to make a local MAP estimate of 3-D lip shape despite variations in head pose. This method allows us to estimate the correct lip shape robustly by matching the distributions of the observations and those implied by the learned model. For additional information see Basu, Oliver and Pentland (1997).

15.5.10 Haptic Input

Almost every room has a chair, and body posture information is important for assessing user alertness and comfort. Our smart chair therefore senses the pressure

 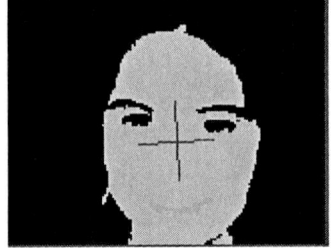

Figure 15.7 The LAFTER system finds and tracks face and facial features at 30 Hz, feeding facial feature geometry for HMM expression recognition.

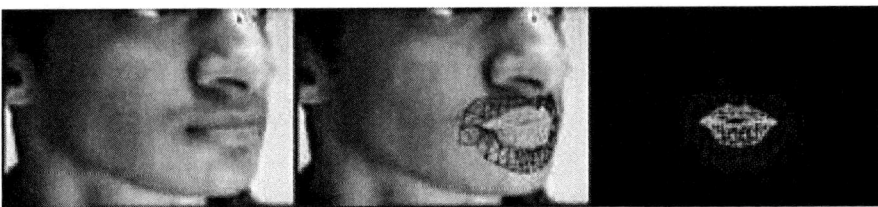

Figure 15.8 Fitting a 3-D FEM to facial data, allowing us to extract pose-invariant 3-D lip shape.

distribution patterns in the chair and classifies the seating postures of its user. Two Tekscan sensor sheets (each consisting of a 42-by-48 array of force-sensitive resistor units) are mounted to the seatpan and the backrest of the chair and output 8-bit pressure distribution data. These data are collected, and the posture is classified using image modeling and classification algorithms.

The current version of the real-time seating posture classification system uses the appearance-based method developed by Pentland, Moghaddam, and Starner for face recognition. For each new pressure distribution map to be classified, the distance-from-feature-space (DFFS) for each of the M postures is calculated and compared to a threshold. The posture class that corresponds to the smallest DFFS is used to label the current pressure map, except when all DFFS values exceed the threshold, in which case the current posture is declared unknown. The algorithm runs in real time on a Pentium PC, with a classification accuracy of approximately 95% for 21 different postures (seated upright, leaning forward, right/left leg crossed, etc.).

15.6 SMART CLOTHES

So far, I have presented matters mostly from the smart room perspective, where the cameras and microphones are passively watching people move around. However, when we build the computers, cameras, microphones, and other sensors into a person's clothes, the computer's view changes from a passive third person to an active first-person vantage point. This means that smart clothes can be more intimately and actively involved in the user's activities, making them potentially an intelligent Personal (Digital) Assistant, (Mann 1997, Pentland 1998, Starner 1997).

For instance, if you build a camera into your eyeglasses, then the face recognition software can help you remember the name of the person you are looking at by whispering her name in your ear. Or if you build a phased-array microphones into your jacket, then our word-spotting software can remind you of relevant facts (Figure 15.9). For example, if someone mentions the "Megadeal contract," the word-spotting software can project Megadeal's finances onto the display built into your glasses. If you build a Global Position Sensor (GPS) into your shoes, then navigation software can help you find your way around by whispering directions in your ear or showing a map on the display built into your glasses.

356 PERCEPTUAL ENVIRONMENTS

Figure 15.9 The author wearing a variety of new technologies. The glasses (built by Microoptical of Boston) contain a computer display that is nearly invisible to others. The jacket has a keyboard that is literally embroidered into the cloth. The lapel has a "context sensor" that can classify the user's surroundings and, of course, there is a computer that is not visible in this photograph. Photo by Sam Ogden.

15.6.1 Mobile Perceptual Intelligence

The mobility and physical closeness of a wearable computer make it an attractive platform for perceptual computing. A camera mounted in a baseball cap can observe the user's hands and feet. This allows observation of gestures and body motion in natural, everyday contexts. In addition, the camera acts as an interface for the computer. For example, the user's fingertip becomes the system's mouse pointer by tracking the color of the user's hand. Similarly, hand tracking can be used for recognizing American Sign Language. Our current implementation recognizes sentence-level American Sign Language in real time with over 97% word accuracy on a 40-word vocabulary. See Starner, Weaver, and Pentland (1998).

By pointing the camera in the direction of the user's gaze, a sense of world context may be obtained. For example, the computer may assist the user by suggesting possible shots in a game of billiards or may provide names for the faces of persons at a cocktail party. Figure 15.10, for instance, illustrates an Augmented Reality system that helps the user play billiards. A camera mounted on the user's head tracks the table and balls, estimates the 3-D configuration of the table, balls, and user, and then creates a graphics overlay (using a see-though HMD) showing the user the best shot. For additional information see Jebara, Eyster, Weaver, Starner, and Pentland (1997).

In controlled environments, object identification is possible. For instance, if objects of interest have bar tags on visible surfaces, then a wearable camera system can recognize the bar code tags in the environment and overlays 3-D graphics, text, or video on the physical world. The computer scans the user's visual field, identifies

Figure 15.10 Stochasticks wearable billiards advisor. Left: the user; right: what the user sees.

potential tags, and then applies self-consistency checks to eliminate false hits. The codes in the tags are recognized, and the appropriate information is then visually linked to the object.

When 3-D alignment of graphics is needed, the corners of a 2-D tag are located and the camera's position is estimated. Multiple tags can be used in the same environment, and users can add their own annotations to the tags through wireless contact with a annotation database. In this way, the hypertext environment of the World Wide Web is brought to physical reality. Such a system may be used to assist in the repair of annotated machines such as photocopiers or provide context-sensitive information for museum exhibits. Current work addresses the recognition and tracking of untagged objects in the office and outside environments to allow easy, socially motivated annotation of everyday things. For additional information see Starner et al. (1997).

15.7 CONCLUSION

It is now possible to track people's motion, identify them by facial appearance, and recognize their actions in real time using only modest computational resources. Using this perceptual information, we have built smart rooms and smart clothes that have the potential to recognize people, understand their speech, allow them to control computer displays without wires or keyboards, communicate by sign language, and warn the user that he is about to make a mistake.

We are now beginning to apply such perceptual intelligence to a much wider variety of situations. For instance, we are now working on prototypes of displays that know if you are watching, credit cards that recognize their owners, chairs that adjust to keep you awake and comfortable, and shoes that know where they are. We imagine building a world where the distinction between inanimate and animate objects begins to blur and the objects that surround us become more like helpful assistants or playful pets than insensible tools.

ACKNOWLEDGMENTS

This research was supported by ARPA, ONR, ARL, BT and the Things That Think industrial consortium. Portions of this chapter have appeared in *Scientific American*, in April 1996 and December 1998. Many of the examples and figures are drawn from IEEE, ACM, and ICASSP conference proceedings.

REFERENCES

Papers and technical reports are available at our website: http://www.media.mit.edu/vismod

Azerbayejani, A., and Pentland, A. (1996) "Real-Time Self-Calibrating Stereo Person Tracking Using 3-D Shape Estimation from Blob Features," *ICPR '96*, Vienna, Austria.

Basu, S., Casey, M., Gardner, W., Azarbayjani, A., and Pentland, A. (1996) "Vision-Steered Audio for Interactive Environments," *Proceedings of IMAGE'COM 96*, Bordeaux, France, May.

Basu, S., Oliver, N., and Pentland, A. (1998) "3D Modeling and Tracking of Human Lip Motions," *Proceedings of ICCV'98*, Bombay, India, January 4–7.

Becker, D., and Pentland, A. (1996) "Using a Virtual Environment to Teach Cancer Patients T'ai Chi, Relaxation and Self-Imagery," Perceptual Computing Technical Report No. 390, MIT Media Laboratory.

Brand, M., Oliver, N., and Pentland, A. (1997) "Coupled HMMs for Complex Action Recognition," *IEEE CVPR '97*, San Juan, Puerto Rico, June 1997.

Jebara, T., Eyster, C., Weaver, J., Starner, T., and Pentland, A. (1997) "Stochasticks: Augmenting the Billiards Experience with Probabilistic Vision and Wearable Computers," *IEEE Intl. Symposium on Wearable Computers*, Cambridge, MA, October 23–24.

Jebara, T., Russell, K., and Pentland, A. (1998) "Mixtures of Eigenfeatures for Real-Time Structure from Texture," *Proceedings of ICCV'98*, Bombay, India, January 4–7.

Mann, S. (1997) "Smart Clothing: The Wearable Computer and WearCam," *Personal Technologies*, Vol. 1, No. 1, March 1997.

Moghaddam, B., Nastar, C., and Pentland, A. (1997) "Beyond Eigenfaces: Probabilistic Matching for Face Recognition," Perceptual Computing Technical Report No. 443, MIT Media Laboratory.

Oliver, N., Bernard, F., Coutaz, J., and Pentland, A. (1997) "LAFTER: Lips and Face Tracker," *IEEE CVPR '97*, San Juan, Puerto Rico, June 1997.

Oliver, N., Rosario, B., and Pentland, A. (1998) "Statistical Modeling of Human Interactions," *IEEE Conference on Computer Vision and Pattern Recognition (CVPR98), Workshop on the Interpretation of Visual Motion*, Santa Barbara, CA, June 21–27.

Pentland, A. (1996) "Smart Rooms, Smart Clothes," *Scientific American*, Vol. 274, No. 4, pp. 68–76.

Pentland, A. (1998) "Wearable Intelligence," *Scientific American Presents*, Special Issue on Intelligence, Vol. 9, No. 4.

Pentland, A., and Liu, A. (1999) "Modeling and Prediction of Human Behavior," *Neural Computation*, Vol. 11, pp. 229–242.

Roy, D., and Malamud, C. (1996) "Speaker Identification Based Text to Audio Alignment for an Audio Retreival System," Perceptual Computing Technical Report No. 395, MIT Media Laboratory.

Roy, D., and Pentland, A. (1997) "Word Learning in a Multimodal Environment," *ICASSP '98*, Seattle, November 1998.

Roy, D., and Pentland, A., (1998) "An Adaptive Interface: Learning Worlds and their Audiovisual Grounding," *International Conference on Speech and Language*, Sydney, Austrialia, December.

Starner, T., Mann, S., Rhodes, B., Levine, J., Healey, J., Kirsch, D., Picard, R., and Pentland, A. (1996) "Visual Augmented Reality Through Wearable Computing," *Presence, Teleoperators and Virtual Environments*, Vol. 5, No. 2, pp. 163–172.

Starner, T., Weaver, J., and Pentland, A. (1998) "Real-Time American Sign Language Recognition from Video Using Hidden Markov Models," *IEEE Transactions on Pattern Analysis and Machine Vision*, June 1996.

Wren, C., and Pentland, A. (1998) "Dynamic Modeling of Human Motion," Perceptual Computing Technical Report No. 415, MIT Media Laboratory.

CHAPTER 16

Assistive Environments for Individuals with Special Needs

ABDELSALAM HELAL and CHOONHWA LEE

Computer and Information Science and Engineering Department
University of Florida

WILLIAM C. MANN

Department of Occupational Therapy
University of Florida

16.1 INTRODUCTION

As we age, we experience normal declines in vision, hearing, cognition, and movement. We also develop chronic conditions such as arthritis, heart and circulatory disorders, glaucoma, and tinnitus. The cost of home health services for older persons with disabilities is increasing with the rapidly growing elder population. For example, 1 in 10 elders in the United States suffer from Alzheimer's disease (AD). It is estimated that one in five elders will have AD by 2050. In 2002, AD resulted in health-related expenditures of more than $61B [Koppel 2002]. Quality of life and independence are impacted by disabilities, and our health and caregiver systems will be increasingly stressed as the number of elders increases. Hence, there is a significant need for cost-effective ways to help elders maintain their independence and, at the same time, reduce the caregiver burden. The impressive wireless and portable technologies we have today and the emerging mobile computing paradigm offer a unique opportunity to develop pervasive applications and environments designed to support the elderly. Such environments will enable cost-effective self-care and will maintain a higher quality of life and independence for our oldest population.

In this chapter, we define assistive environments for the elderly and use a scenario-based approach to illustrate the benefits of these environments. We then present a specific assistive environment, which we call *Matilda Smart House*, and which we prototyped inside the Pervasive Computing Laboratory at the Computer

---

Smart Environments: Technologies, Protocols, and Applications, edited by D.J. Cook and S.K. Das
ISBN 0-471-54448-5   © 2005 John Wiley & Sons, Inc.

Science Department, University of Florida. We present our reference middleware architecture and several applications that we built in that experimental house. Finally, we review research on smart environments for elders with disabilities, as well as elder health care applications and practices.

16.2 SMART ENVIRONMENTS FOR THE ELDERLY

While age-related declines and chronic conditions can severely impact our ability to do everyday tasks, it is possible to design our environment, and add tools—assistive devices—that facilitate independence. Many assistive devices are common mechanical tools such as wheelchairs, walkers, bath seats, and magnifiers. Electronic assistive devices, many of which use computer-based technology, further extend the potential for helping a person remain independent. These include voice output devices for people who are blind, assistive listening devices for people with hearing impairment, reminder devices for people with cognitive impairment, and power-assisted wheelchairs for people with mobility impairment. Assistive devices such as these are effective in decreasing the impact of declines in functional status and in reducing health-related costs [Mann et al. 1999].

However, each of the assistive devices mentioned above has limitations and is typically used by a smaller subgroup of elders with disabilities in limited situations. These devices also require direct interactions with the owners. Ubiquitous computing opens up new possibilities for enhancing the independence and quality of life for older people. Ubiquitous computing technology centered on smart environments can serve elders' needs by enabling communication among devices and the environment. To emphasize the application domain, we refer to smart environments for elder care as *assistive environments*.

16.2.1 Assistive Environments

Envisioned by Mark Weiser in the early 1990s, ubiquitous computing means that *computation embedded in the environment is available everywhere to assist users in accomplishing their daily tasks* [Weiser 1991]. In the ubiquitous computing world, computation is embedded in physical objects such as clothing, coffee cups, tabletops, walls, floors, doorknobs, roadways, and so forth. For example, while reading a morning newspaper, our coffee placed on a tabletop is kept warm at our favorite temperature. A door opens automatically by sensing current running on our hand or, more intelligently, by detecting our fingerprints or sensing our approach. The computation is seamlessly and invisibly integrated into physical artifacts within the environments, and is always ready to serve us without distracting us from our daily practices.

This vision mandates a holistic approach emphasizing interaction and cooperation among computational devices rather than the individual devices themselves. The limited ability of a single device to sense and control environments needs to be complemented and enhanced through cooperation. The intelligence to infer a person's intention and situation within the environment is referred to as *context awareness*. The environment must be aware of relevant context in order to provide appropriate services to the person in an unobtrusive way. Minimizing human attention, the most precious resource in the pervasive computing environment [Satyanarayanan 2001], is the ultimate goal of ubiquitous computing.

From this view of general ubiquitous computing, we now turn to smart home environments designed for the needs of frail elders. Beyond existing home automation systems, a smart house for older persons must simplify and assist in the completion of everyday tasks. More specifically, future smart houses will become *assistive environments* and will represent an evolution from a single assistive device to a space of integrated elements that collectively assist elders. Based on monitored context and on interpretation of events, the smart house will proactively assist the occupant in performing daily activities. It will keep the person informed and aware, and will also assist with tasks. For instance, the smart house may assist in opening or locking the front door remotely (e.g., from the master bedroom). It may remind the elder to take medications on time. Such assistance is made possible by the intelligence of the house, which monitors both the house and its occupants. Since the elder's benefit by the assistive environment is effectively determined by the house's sensing capability, we need to look at what can be monitored. Some of these features are currently available, while others are being developed.

- *Monitor the house:* Today's home monitoring systems (e.g., security and air temperature control systems) can be enriched to (1) monitor appliances, e.g., turn the stove off if the pot has become too hot; (2) monitor lighting inside and outside the home to ensure that there is appropriate lighting for the time of day, weather conditions, and activity in the room; (3) monitor moisture, that is, detect leaks or water on the floor and provide appropriate alerts; and (4) monitor the mailbox and provide an alert when mail has been delivered.
- *Monitor the elder's health:* The house collects physiological data (e.g., blood pressure, body temperature, and blood glucose level) on the resident, and detects sudden changes and trends over time. An important aspect of health for many elders relates to taking the appropriate medications, at the appropriate times of day, following directions such as taking them with liquids or food. The smart house will alert the person when it is time to take the medication or, alternatively, alert the person not to take medication if it has already been taken. This same system will alert the pharmacy when a medication is getting low so that the pharmacist can contact the person to arrange delivery. The medication containers will have an (RFID) tag that the system will use to tell the person which medication he is holding, and to share additional information, such as "Be sure to take it with food" or "If you are experiencing dizziness from this medicine, contact your doctor right away."
- *Monitor the elder's independence or self-care-related needs:* Monitoring self-care and implementing strategies with distance technology significantly expands the use of telemedicine from a focus on body signs and compliance with medical regimens to include a functional (self-care) perspective. The

smart house is able to (1) monitor daily self-care needs, (2) identify the need for a home health care visit, (3) support self-administered interventions, and (4) provide information and training to enhance daily functional performance.

- *Monitor the elder's activities, movement, and behavior in the house:* The house can determine if someone has fallen and alert a family member or formal care provider. It will determine if someone has not arisen from bed, has tossed and turned all night, has had too many or too few trips to the bathroom, or has not been drinking enough liquids or eating enough food. In each case, an appropriate person is alerted to a potential need for assistance.

In conclusion, we define an assistive environment as a smart environment specifically designed to serve individuals with special needs, including older people and people with disabilities. Elements of the environment such as sensors, devices, and systems act together in a self-organized fashion to deliver the most suitable support in response to the occupant's needs and context.

Below is an account of an imaginary day in the life of one elder to illustrate how the assistive smart house can help a person with disabilities. The scenario reflects the vision of our Smart House, and stresses the importance and effectiveness of technology fusion with the house and with the elder's everyday life.

16.2.2 A Day in the Assistive Smart House

Mrs. Smith is 87 years old, widowed, and lives alone. She no longer drives because her vision is moderately impaired, and arthritis makes it difficult for her to grasp the steering wheel and turn. She is also a bit forgetful but still plays cards regularly with a group in her community. Her daughter, Sally, who lives 12 miles away, assists with trips to the grocery store and doctor, while Mrs. Smith's friends and neighbors help by driving her to church and the community center where she plays cards. Mrs. Smith had a fall 2 years ago that resulted in a hip fracture, but she recovered well and walks slowly with a cane. Mrs. Smith's son, Tommy, lives 800 miles away, but has kept in close touch by phone and visits at least every 3 months. Sally and Tommy recently helped Mrs. Smith to move from her large two-story home into a smaller ranch-style home set up as a smart house.

16.2.2.1 Bathroom and Bedroom   When Mrs. Smith gets up in the morning, the time is tracked. If it is significantly earlier or later, the smart house notes this. She goes to the toilet—a smart toilet that can determine a person's blood pressure, temperature, and blood sugar level. This information can be analyzed by the smart house to determine if there is a need to alert Sally or Tommy or her family physician, Dr. Jones.

Mrs. Smith completes her other basic activities of daily living—taking a shower, combing her hair, and getting dressed. While her forgetfulness is not severe, the smart house is ready to help prompt her through these activities should Mrs. Smith need help in the future. Monitors and speakers in the bathroom and bedroom provide auditory and visual prompts for brushing teeth, combing hair, bathing, and dressing. The smart house remembers if these activities have been completed.

16.2.2.2 Hall and Kitchen After completing these basic morning ADLs (activities of daily living),[1] Mrs. Smith goes to the kitchen to prepare her breakfast. On the way from the bedroom, her movement is tracked by a number of sensors. Should she stop and stand in one place or fall, the smart house will ask her if she requires assistance. She can respond that she has stopped to look at some pictures, and the house will know she is safe. The movement tracking system is also able to ascertain if she has fallen, and will ask her if she needs to have a call placed for emergency assistance. She could respond that she fell but did not hurt herself, is able to get up, and there is no need for a call. Alternatively, she could instruct the smart house to place the call. If she does not respond at all, the smart house places calls in this order: first, to Sally; second, if she does not answer, to a personal emergency response (PER) operator for emergency assistance. Mrs. Smith does not fall today, but she feels much more secure knowing that if this happens, the smart house will find her help.

On the way to the kitchen, the smart house tells Mrs. Smith that the morning paper has been delivered to her mailbox.

16.2.2.3 Kitchen The smart house offers a number of features for Mrs. Smith in the kitchen. She can call on the smart house for suggestions for breakfast—providing a menu based on the diet recommended by a nutritionist who works with Dr. Jones. Today she decides she is going to make instant oatmeal, using her smart microwave oven. The smart microwave oven recognizes what Mrs. Smith is preparing from an electronic tag on the package and automatically sets up the appropriate time and power. This microwave oven is also able to determine if the food or object is not safe—if it contains a substance that could cause an allergic reaction. The smart house tracks the food that she is eating for breakfast.

Mrs. Smith uses four medications, one of which she takes in the morning and evening and the other three in the morning after breakfast. Today, a half hour after eating breakfast, she is still enjoying the morning paper and has not yet taken her morning medication. The smart house reminds Mrs. Smith that it is time to take her morning medication. She has a medication caddy designed to dispense the appropriate medications, at the appropriate time, into a small dish. After she takes her morning medication, the smart medication caddy recognizes that Mrs. Smith's Vioxx is down to a 4-day supply, so a message is sent to the pharmacy regarding the need for a refill. Mrs. Smith receives a call later in the morning from the pharmacist asking her if she would like the refill, and if so, whether it would be convenient to have it delivered by Joe, the delivery man, in about 1 hour. When Joe arrives, the doorbell rings through the speakers in the kitchen, where Mrs. Smith is still reading the paper. She looks up at the monitor and recognizes Joe. She instructs the smart house to open the front door. Joe comes in, greets Mrs. Smith, and places the Vioxx in her medication caddy. When Joe leaves, the smart house locks the door behind him.

---

[1] ADLs are "activities related to personal care and include bathing or showering, dressing, getting in or out of bed or a chair, using the toilet, and eating" [National Center for Health Statistics].

16.2.2.4 Beyond the House: Getting Out
At noon, Mrs. Smith's next door neighbor stops by to give her a ride to the community center, where she plays cards for the afternoon, followed by dinner out with her bridge partner. Mrs. Smith always carries her smart phone (i.e., an Internet-enabled phone with an on-board computing platform) with her when she leaves the house. While she is traveling, the smart phone tracks her location and can provide assistance if she requires it, as well as make traditional voice calls. When she returns home, information about her trip will automatically be sent to the house. Before Mrs. Smith stopped driving 3 years ago, her smart phone interfaced with her car, and through sensors in her car, it was able to alert her if she was driving too slowly or swaying from lane to lane. Based upon feedback from this smart phone/car system, she decided it would be best to stop driving.

16.2.2.5 Back Home for the Evening
Arriving home after dinner, Mrs. Smith is reminded by the smart house to take her evening medications. She then watches the news for an hour and completes her nighttime ADLs. Before she retires to bed at about 9 p.m., Mrs. Smith asks, "Are all of the doors and windows locked?" The smart house quickly checks and gives her an accurate security report. Mrs. Smith's bed includes biosensors that track her body temperature, heart rate, breathing rate, and movement while sleeping. The smart house notes these measurements.

16.2.2.6 Data Analysis and Reports
An important aspect of the smart house is its ability to interpret data—including movement patterns. If Mrs. Smith tosses and turns every night, then this is not unusual behavior and probably is not a reason, at least by itself, to send an alert to Sally or Tommy. On the other hand, if Mrs. Smith typically sleeps calmly, but on one night is tossing and turning and is up from bed several times during the night, Sally will receive a call.

Sally can get a daily, weekly, or monthly report of her mother's health and behavior. She checked the report of this "day in the smart house" and learned that her mother had slept well, was up at her normal time, had two good meals at home, was out in the afternoon and for dinner (which she knew was appropriate because she plays cards on this day), had taken her medications, and had had a medication delivery. Since her mother moved into the smart house, Sally has felt much less stress and worry—much of the burden of caregiving had been lifted. Sally still calls her mother each day, but she no longer feels she is being intrusive by asking many questions. She knows how her mother is doing before she places the call.

When Mrs. Smith visits Dr. Jones, he has available, through the Internet, a summary of her vital signs and her sleeping, eating, and activity patterns. He receives a one-page summary with clearly marked alerts for any potential health problems. Should Dr. Jones need more information, he can request more detailed reports. He has had several patients with this smart house technology, and has been able to identify early symptoms of depression and dementia and provide appropriate treatment.

16.3 MATILDA SMART HOUSE

The Matilda Smart House project is a multidisciplinary effort to innovate pervasive applications and environments to support elder independence. The project is funded by the National Institute on Disability and Rehabilitation Research through the Rehabilitation Engineering Research Center (RERC) program (see http://www.rerc.ufl.edu) and hosted at the University of Florida Pervasive Computing Laboratory. Matilda Smart House explores the use of emerging smart phones and other wireless technologies to create assistive environments and "magic wands" that enable older persons with disabilities to interact with, monitor, and control their surroundings. By integrating the smart phone with assistive environments, elders are able to handle a large number of tasks such as turning appliances on and off, checking and changing the status of locks on doors and windows, and ordering groceries. The project also tests smart phones that can remind users to take medications or call in prescription drug refills automatically.

16.3.1 The Smart House Instrumentation

Matilda Smart House (an in-laboratory mockup house as depicted in Figure 16.1) occupies about 500 ft^2 in the University of Florida's Pervasive Computing Laboratory. It consists of a bedroom, a bathroom, a living room, and a kitchen, and is accessible from the Web through four live web cams (http://www.icta.ufl.edu/labcam.html). Figure 16.2 also shows several snapshots of the Smart House. This house serves as a development platform and an in-laboratory testbed of our prototype system and applications. We are building a full-scale house, called the Gator-Tech Smart House, in the Oak-Hammock Continuous Care Retirement Community in Gainesville, Florida, to evaluate experimentally and clinically the effectiveness of assistive environments.

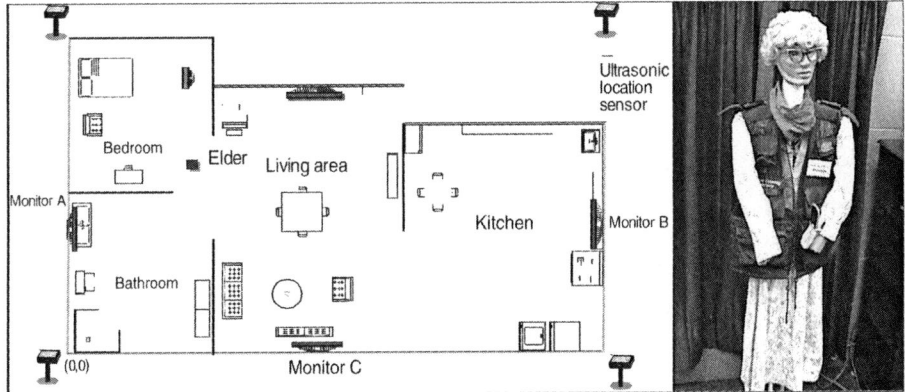

Figure 16.1 Matilda Smart House.

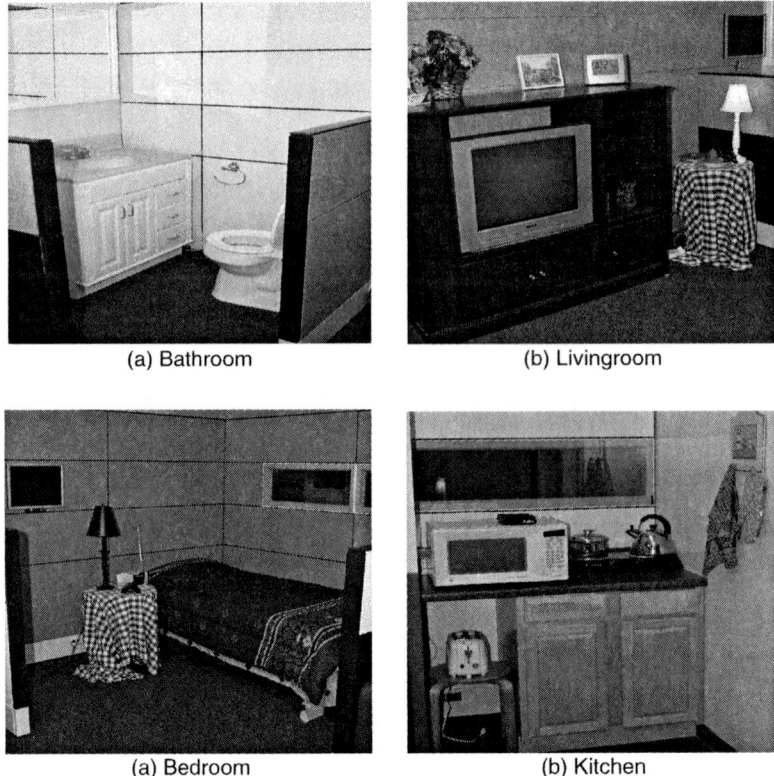

Figure 16.2 Snapshots of Matilda Smart House.

As indicated in Figure 16.1, four ultrasonic receivers are placed in the ceiling above each corner of the house perimeter. Also, four flat panel monitors are mounted on each wall to deliver visual messages to the occupant. The mockup house is instrumented with other sensors and devices, including J2ME smart phones as user devices, floor sensors, water leak sensors, RFID tags, X-10-controlled devices (door, mailbox, curtain, lamp, and radio), and networked devices (microwave, refrigerator, and cameras). Some of them are shown in Figure 16.3.

A robot that simulates elder movement (Matilda) is integrated into this space as a research instrument for experiments in location-based systems. Two location beacon emitters are placed on Matilda's shoulders. The emitter signals, picked up by ultrasonic receivers on the ceiling, track her position. Currently, Matilda is mounted on a remote control (RC) car that supports limited movements (Figure 16.1). The RC car will soon be replaced with a professional robotic platform controlled by an embedded PDA via a wireless connection to the house (Figure 16.3c). Furthermore, Matilda's movements can be preprogrammed, and her response to environmental changes and events can be monitored and recorded. The Matilda frame will be replaced with a new frame that has pneumatic joints to

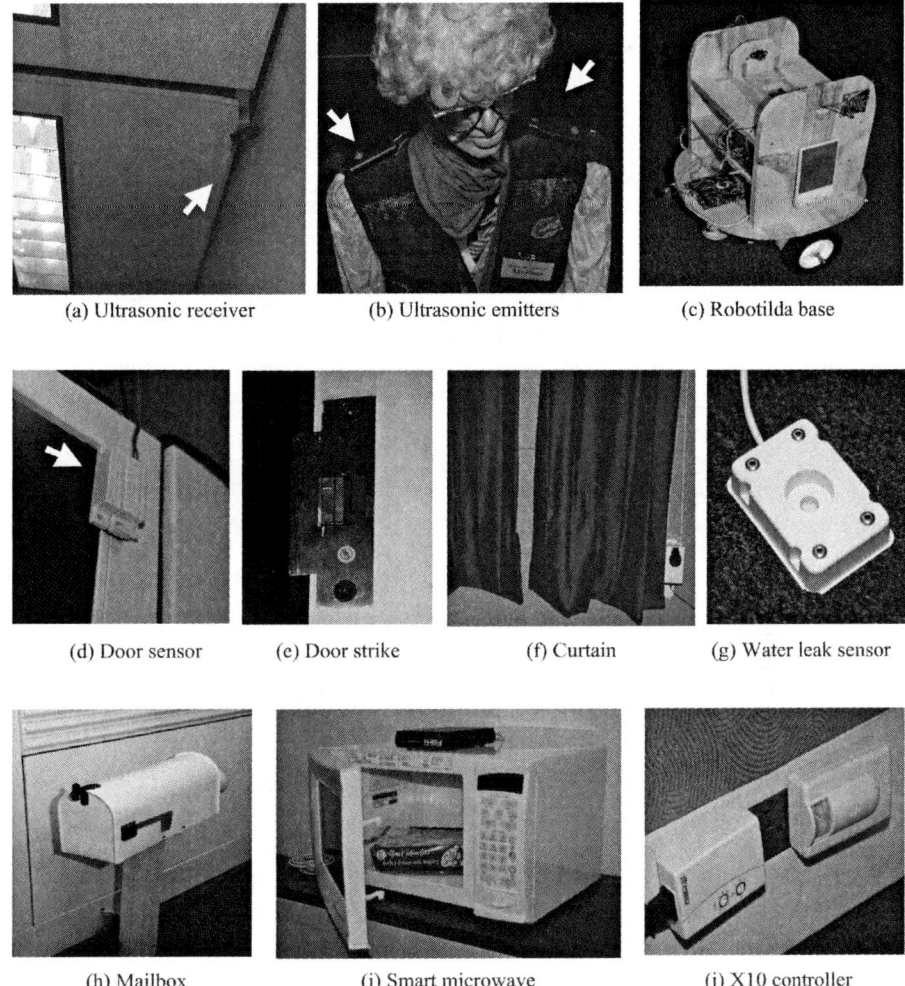

Figure 16.3 Sample sensors in Matilda Smart House.

allow her to sit, stand, and lay in bed. This will provide a simulation instrument that can run for weeks following a pregenerated program of daily activities and behaviors. With this robotic system, we will test our pervasive computing applications and devices.

The heart of the smart house is the ultrasonic location system. Location information is essential for context awareness, and will be supplemented and refined by other sensed information. We will briefly review heavily investigated location sensor technologies [Hightower and Borriello 2001] (for further details, readers are referred to corresponding chapters in this book) and describe our ultrasonic indoor location system.

16.3.1.1 Location Systems Tracking and positioning systems are not the same. With positioning systems, users receive location information from the environment and calculate their own position. This provides privacy in possibly hostile environments for the users. A tracking system is a location system that allows a central computer or controller to continuously keep track of the user's locations. Since privacy in nonhostile home environments is not a primary issue, a tracking system is more appropriate. We give a brief overview of the technologies and existing systems that may be used to create a tracking system.

Low-Frequency RF Sensor Low-frequency sensors in location systems tend to work in the 418, 433, or 900 MHz spectrum. RF transceivers are inexpensive, and there has been research on their implementation. Low-frequency tracking systems use Time Difference of Arrival (TDOA) or strength-of-signal measurements to triangulate position. An example is the SpotOn system at the University of Washington [Hightower et al. 2000], which relies on strength-of-signal measurements to provide locations within 3 m. Unfortunately, this is insufficient accuracy for a smart home environment.

Infrared System An Infrared tracking system works by a mobile device emitting infrared waves at predefined time intervals. These waves are received and Time of Arrival (TOA) algorithms are then used to calculate position. An example of this type of system is AT&T's Active Badge system [Want et al. 1992]. Its disadvantages are undue interference caused by sunlight and accuracy.

Ultrasonic Sensors Ultrasonic sensors work in the 40 to 130 kHz range and use TOA to acquire distance information. This distance information is then applied to trilateration formulas. Ultrasonic receivers calculate the distance to a transmitter by using a predefined frequency. Multiple receivers make it possible to calculate the varied distances from each receiver and thereby obtain an accurate location. Ultrasonic sensors are subject to loss of signal due to obstruction, false signals by reflections, and interference from high-frequency sounds. However, most of these limitations can be reduced through careful planning, which results in a highly accurate system. The most famous example is AT&T's BAT System [Addlesee et al. 2001], which achieved an accuracy of within 3 cm for 95% of the readings through a ceiling-mounted ultrasonic receiver grid.

16.3.1.2 Ultrasonic Location System Based on the analysis of available positioning/tracking technologies, and based on the requirements of the smart house, we are experimenting with ultrasonic technology. Presently we are using Hexamite's Low Cost Positioning System (HLCPS), which allows the receivers and transmitters to communicate within a distance of up to 16 m [Hexamite].

The ultrasonic location system is made up of three different devices: HE900M pilots (Figure 16.3a), HE900T beacons (Figure 16.3b), and a HE485 RS485/RS232 converter. The stationary pilots act as receivers, and the mobile beacons are transmitters. The Hexamite system uses a high-speed RS485 serial connection to relay location information. Each beacon is lightweight and small, roughly the size of a cellular phone battery (i.e., $\frac{1}{4} \times 2\frac{1}{2}$ inches). The beacons have a lithium battery, which lasts for 24 hours in active mode and 300 hours in deep sleep mode. They can be programmed by the pilots to enter a deep sleep mode. By placing two HE900Ts on Matilda's shoulders, the system is able to acquire both her position and her orientation. The HE900M reception angle is 130° at 6 m and 85° at 8 m. By placing one HE900M in every corner of an area, it is possible to achieve 360° coverage of the mobile beacons. The pilots are set up so that each one can synchronize with the beacons. Initially, all pilots simultaneously broadcast a synchronization signal to the beacons. At the receipt of the first signal, the beacon responds. The TOA from the beacon response is sensed by the pilots to generate the pilot-to-beacon distance measurement. All of these measurements are then sent to the home computer. This system is highly accurate and currently obtains positions within 22 cm without reflective corrections. This accuracy can be further increased to within 3 cm through reflective correction. Further details on our location system appear in an earlier paper [Helal et al. 2003].

16.3.2 Reference Middleware Architecture for Assistive Environments

Several pervasive spaces have been deployed as pilot projects or components of a larger project. Most have focused on specific technologies to build the smart spaces, overlooking a long-term, systematic plan for space evolution and interoperation. A wide variety of devices and services from different manufacturers and developers will constitute the future pervasive computing environment, where platform and vendor independence will inevitably be an issue.

System evolution and interoperability can be enabled through the concepts of services (i.e., application components) and context awareness. Services from different sources can interact via a standardized service interface, even though they are unknown to each other. Context information and events will provide an anchor for the service interaction, as well as for the intelligence of the smart environments. As illustrated in Figure 16.4, our middleware architecture for assistive environments centers on context-aware service discovery issues, including (1) context information sensing, abstraction, and use, (2) service-oriented infrastructure architecture and applications, and (3) service repository and context-aware resource discovery.

16.3.2.1 Context-Aware Resource Discovery At the base of our reference architecture is a vocabulary of primitive context information directly for physical sensors in the house. It can be further extended by application components (i.e., services) for their own needs, and such additions are shared among other services.

The pieces of raw, individual context can be aggregated by a Context Information Manager (CIM) to represent high-level, abstracted context. The CIM maintains a context database made up of instances of the primitive and derived context information in order to fulfill context information requests by the Generic Services and the Service Repository. If the request is of a new context type, its definition and

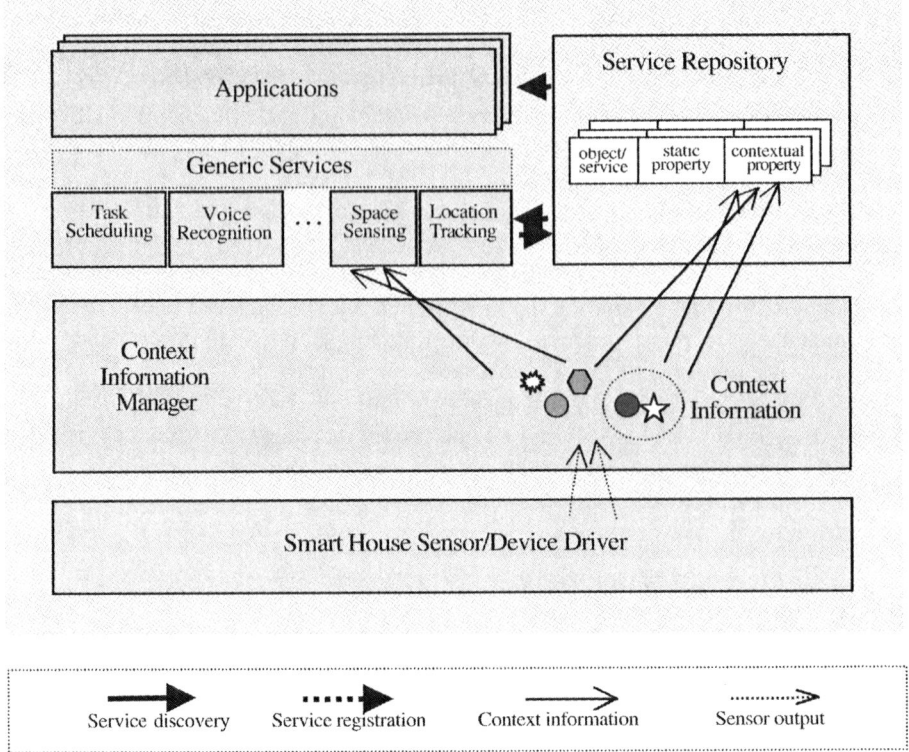

Figure 16.4 Reference middleware architecture for assistive environments.

handling logic are added to the CIM. It is the requester's responsibility to provide the context derivation definition, a context abstraction module, and a filtering and callback mechanism. The new definition is added to the vocabulary, and the abstraction module contains logic to extract the higher-level context from low-level context information. As an example, an abstraction module can determine Matilda's current room for her location coordinate. A reference to a callback routine may also be provided when the requester wants to be notified of context changes. The filter can screen minor changes to keep the requester from being unnecessarily interrupted. We note that, in most cases, the context extension is done by the Generic Services that we discuss later; such additions benefit other services and applications.

An entry in the Service Repository represents a service in the infrastructure. Alternatively, it may indicate an object in the house, which can be a fixed object (e.g., a window, a room, or the house itself) or a movable object such as Matilda or a vacuum cleaner. The objects are initially populated by one of our core services, the Space Sensing Service, briefly described below. This way, the infrastructure provides a unified view of the environment regardless of whether a query is about a service or an object. The entry consists of an object/service name, descriptive attributes (i.e., static property in Figure 16.4), and possibly variable context information (i.e., contextual property). Some context information may play a crucial role in enabling efficient resource discovery. For example, Matilda's location information may be able to reduce objects of potential interest to a smaller set sorted according to the distance to her. Context information relevant to the resource discovery is to be attached as contextual property to corresponding entries to facilitate the discovery process. Also, the contextual property is updated dynamically as the corresponding context changes. In summary, context-aware resource discovery enables efficient interactions with services and objects in the environment by helping to produce a high-quality query result.

16.3.2.2 Generic Services and Applications To support rapid application development and facilitate service composition, our middleware provides a set of generic services. As indicated in Figure 16.4, they are discovered and used by other core services or applications. The following is our current list of generic services.

- *Automated/scheduled task service* performs scheduled or triggered tasks (e.g., reminders, alerts) if their condition is met. For example, if the house discovers that Matilda may be becoming dehydrated, through monitoring of her activities such as drinking water and going to the bathroom, it automatically launches a reminder service suggesting that she should drink a glass of water. Our mobile Patient Care-Giving Assistant and General Reminder System applications discussed in Section 16.3.3 use this task service. A simple rule language is employed to describe the schedule/conditions and corresponding actions.
- *Voice recognition service* provides voice-to-text translation service to other services and applications.
- *Camera vision service* tracks object movements in the camera's view.
- *Event broker service* delivers an application-specific event to subscribed clients when a certain condition specified in terms of context information exists.
- *Location service* provides the location information (e.g., x and y coordinate) of Matilda or objects being tracked.
- *Space sensing service* monitors the placement and movement of objects in the house and is able to present the information with regard to the house floor plan. This service may be useful for a map application, or it can be used to locate a certain object in the house.
- *Persistent storage service* stores streaming sensor data that may be used for trend analysis, historical context extraction, and statistics later on.
- *Web service service* is a proxy to access Web services on the Internet. For instance, a grocery shopping application makes use of this service to order some food from online Web service shops.

The above generic services are combined to build real applications. We are presently upgrading our current smart phone-based home control application to be capable of INCITS/V2 (Alternative Interface Access Protocol) to support universal access to the application from any device [INCITS V2 Technical Committee].

16.3.2.3 OSGi-Based Prototype To achieve the service-oriented reference architecture we are envisioning, we have based our assistive environment infrastructure on the Open Services Gateway Initiative (OSGi) [Marples and Kriens 2001], which provides a managed, extensible framework to connect various devices and services. By defining a standard execution environment and service interface, and by promoting dynamic discovery and collaboration of devices and services from possibly different sources, the goals of openness and extensibility of the smart house are attainable. In this sense, the OSGi framework is an ideal match for our need for an extensible software infrastructure that can adapt to changes (such as declining health conditions over time and the introduction of new devices, sensors, and services). Moreover, we have found the framework's connectivity support to the outside world to be another noteworthy feature, which supports remote control and diagnosis applications by family members and caregivers.

An OSGi environment (to be exact, an OSGi Service Platform) is made up of a Java virtual machine, an OSGi Framework, and a set of bundles. The Framework provides general-purpose, secure support for deploying extensible and downloadable Java-based service applications known as *bundles* [OSGi Alliance]. Running on top of a Java virtual machine, it provides a shared execution environment where bundles are installed, updated, and uninstalled without requiring the system to be restarted. The Framework also manages dependencies among bundles and services to facilitate their interaction. A bundle may register zero or more services with the Framework's service registry, which are discovered through the registry by others. The service registry provides a simple service discovery functionality based on a service interface name and a collection of key/value pair properties. The basic functionality is being extended to support the contextual property and context-aware service discovery feature of our reference architecture. The registry's need for context information handling and update is backed by the underlying CIM. The smart house device/sensor drivers in Figure 16.4 are implemented as OSGi device bundles, and all other components, including the Applications, the Generic Services, and the CIM, are mapped to a separate service bundle.

The assistive space built on the OSGi framework provided a solid infrastructure so that our application development team could focus on integrating the smart phone (and, by extension, the resident) with the smart environments and various pervasive computing applications.

16.3.3 Sample Applications

Several elder-care applications have been developed to demonstrate the effectiveness of the assistive environment and modular application design based on the OSGi service concept. They include the Remote Monitoring Application, the mobile Patient Care-giving Assistant, the General Reminder System, the Augmented Awareness System, and the SmartWave Application. Many devices and sensors (e.g., appliances, lights, door latches, mailbox sensors, water leak sensors, and window/door lock sensors) are attached to X-10 device drivers in the OSGi framework. In most cases, the front end of the applications has been implemented as a J2ME MIDlet running on Matilda's smart phone.

16.3.3.1 Remote Monitoring Applications We have implemented a simple remote monitoring application using our OSGi-based Ultrasonic location bundle and Event broker bundle. The application simply subscribes to the location events to be notified of any change of Matilda's location and orientation. The smart house services requests submitted by remote monitoring users (family members) by shipping an applet that connects back to the house to bring location updates. Figure 16.5 shows the applet displaying the floor plan of the Matilda Smart House as well as Matilda's live position.

16.3.3.2 Mobile Patient Care-Giving Assistant We have developed an attention capture application, the mobile Patient Care-Giving Assistant (mPCA) [Giraldo et al. 2002]. The application is activated when a particular task needs to be done by the elder at a given time. It first attempts to capture the elder's attention. Once the system achieves this, it delivers the task to be done by the elder (e.g., the elder needs to drink water). The task is delivered in video clip form that is played on

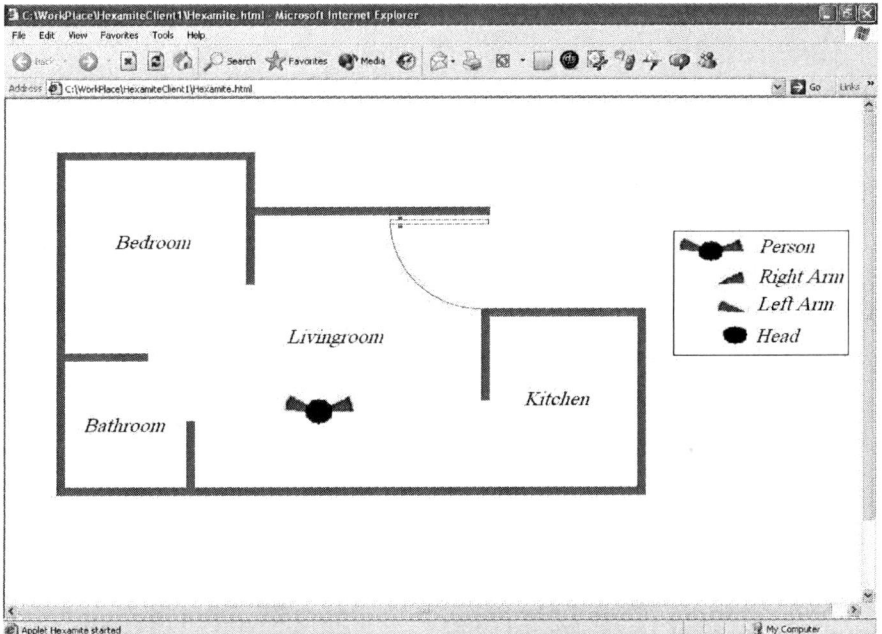

Figure 16.5 An Applet showing Matilda Smart House and Matilda's location and orientation on a Web browser.

one of the four flat panel monitors, as seen in Figure 16.1. With the help of the ultrasonic location service, the application determines the appropriate monitor to be activated (the one that the elder is facing). The attention capture in mPCA attempts to use alternative mechanisms in an increasing order of intervention and interactivity. This ranges from simply calling the elder's name (this message is played in the smart phone) and requesting the elder to respond in a certain way (e.g., say "yes"). If attention is not secured, richer audio signaling is attempted by playing special songs and sounds, followed by calling the elder's name and making a confirmation request. If this fails, the vibrator on the phone is actuated and the person's name is called by familiar voices (prerecorded family members). The protocol progresses to using visual cues by playing a video clip on the video monitor facing the elder.

16.3.3.3 General Reminder System The General Reminder System (GRS) reminds the elder to perform everyday tasks such as taking medications and keeping doctors' appointments. For example, auditory/vocal reminder messages can be sent to the elder's smart phone (especially when she is out of the smart house). Alternatively, the LCD display that she is facing may provide a medication reminder according to her medication schedule. The house issues a voice warning if she picks up the wrong medicine bottle, which is detected by a barcode scanner attached to her phone. This scanning activity is tracked by the home computer so that the house can order a refill when the quantity of medication goes below a certain level.

16.3.3.4 Augmented Awareness System The goal of the Augmented Awareness System (AAS) is to enhance the occupant's awareness by sending notices when certain events happen (e.g., mail delivery, someone at the door, water leak). The system also automates many tasks (e.g., controlling appliances, lighting, curtains, and windows/doors). Voice interface is supported to minimize distractions and the effort required to control the environment.

16.3.3.5 The Smartwave: Intelligent Cooking System As people get older, even something as simple as cooking a microwavable meal can become overwhelming due to the small buttons and the complex cooking instructions written in small print on the cooking package. SmartWave is an intelligent cooking system that allows people to enjoy a hot meal with ease. The system uses a customized microwave along with an RFID reader to allow the microwave to be programmed automatically to cook the requested food package. The elder simply removes the package from the freezer, waves it over the RFID reader, places the food in the microwave oven, and closes the door. Then the cooking begins automatically, using information stored in the RFID tag on the food package (i.e., the correct time and power level on the microwave are automatically set).

Our SmartWave prototype consists of a microwave, an RFID reader, and a controller, as depicted in Figure 16.6. The prototype uses a customized microwave oven allowing full control via a standard serial port. A microcontroller (i.e., Microchip's PIC16F628) is used in conjunction with electronic switches to simulate pressing of the keypad. This interface method was chosen to allow the microwave oven to retain

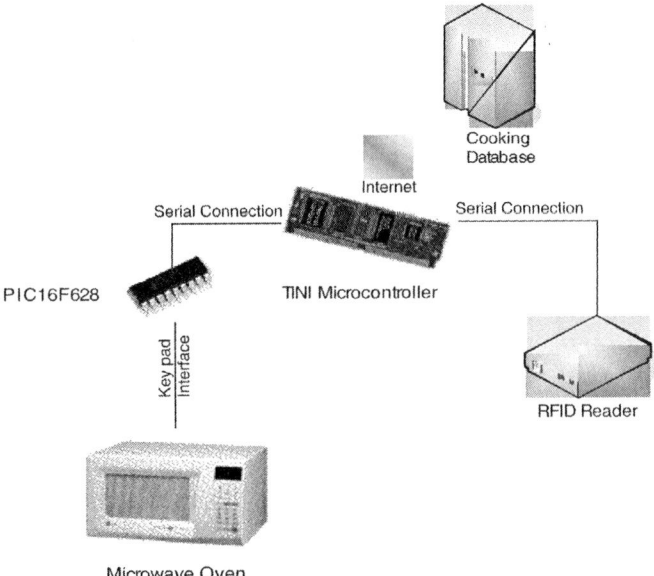

Figure 16.6 The SmartWave intelligent cooking system.

all of its safety features; the microcontroller simply replaces the user's finger electronically. An RFID reader is used to determine which food packet is being cooked. The cooking instructions can be embedded in the RFID tag or stored in a remote database pointed to by the RFID tag. The Dallas Semiconductor TINI board is the heart of the system. It performs the tasks of reading data from the RFID reader, interpreting the cooking instructions, and translating them into a sequence of key presses that are sent to the microwave oven.

16.4 RELATED ELDER-CARE SYSTEMS AND ENVIRONMENTS

There have been many efforts to utilize computer technology to enhance the quality of life, resulting in numerous experimental trials and real-life deployments of the systems and applications. They include smart offices, smart homes, and smart shopping malls. Some of them target specific demographic groups, such as elders. Their primary concerns are the elders' health, comfort, safety, and support for independent living at home.

Tele-health applications promote the autonomy and well-being of the elderly through technology. Remote health care includes "remote diagnostics and monitoring, and delivery of therapy and rehabilitation" [Rauhala-Hayes et al. 1998]. Remote diagnostics can be accomplished via simple phone conversation or videophone teleconsultation, while remote monitoring involves transmission of data measured by vital sign sensors such as body temperature and blood pressure. Video-telephony plays an important role in remote monitoring and therapy delivery.

Smart home technology has been recognized as an efficient and effective means of ensuring the safety, well-being, comfort, and security for people with disabilities who want to live independently in their homes. In Tönsberg, Norway, eight smart care flats were built to support independent living for older people with dementia [Rauhala-Hayes et al. 1998]. The Tönsberg flat equipment includes fire alarm, automatic door and lighting control, stove heat sensor, PCs, and pagers, which look much like today's standard home automation. Fall detectors and weight-detecting beds are also used. If a smoke detector is triggered, a fire alarm goes off, alerting the service center staff members, either by opening a video connection to their computer or by paging them. The lights are automatically turned on, and all doors and emergency exits are unlocked. In addition, the house can alert the staff or family members if the elder gets up during the night (which is sensed by the weight sensors in the bed) and does not return to bed within a certain time period. There might be a need to check whether the elder has fallen or wandered inside or outside the house. The adopted technologies reflect the technology that was available when the project began (i.e., the mid-1990s), which is considered common home automation technology today. Elite Care's Oatfield Estates, discussed below, can be viewed as an advanced version of the trial, featuring more ubiquitous computing technologies.

There have been numerous experimental rollouts of pervasive computing systems from the laboratory into real life that study impacts on our daily lives. Elite Care's Oatfield Estates [Stanford 2002] is among the few projects to have built pervasive computing environments specifically designed to assist the elderly in living independently. Their "Extended Family Residences" are an assisted living complex that fosters family-style interactions among the residents and the caregiving staff. The elder can still maintain independence and participate in social activities, with assistance being offered when needed by the staff, who live in the same complex. Pervasive sensors and technologies are built into the environments to monitor the seniors' vital signs and movements. The elders carry an infrared/radio frequency (IR/RF) tag as a replacement for their apartment key by which the environment can track their movement. Weight sensors built into their beds allow unobtrusive measurements of their sleep and weight. Sudden weight changes can be determined without intrusive daily measurements. Vital signs and activity logging enable early detection and treatment of health problems. Computers and Web connections within the complex allow residents to communicate with family members and neighbors. The assistive living complex features a mix of technologies and human beings. The assistive environment provided by pervasive computing technology is complemented and humanized by personal care delivery.

The Digital Family Portraits [Mynatt et al. 2001] and Family Intercom [Nagel et al. 2001], which are part of Georgia Tech's Aware Home Research Initiatives, address the issues of independent living and communication among extended family members living across wide geographic distances. A family member living at a distance receives health information about an elder—typically a parent. The digital portrait frame is annotated with several icons indicating the elder's health, social activity, and physical activity over time, as well as local weather conditions. For example, butterfly icons surrounding the elder's picture in her son's house convey information about her days that can be read at a glance (i.e., allowing him to see how she is doing in a moment), and the butterfly size indicates the level of her physical activity for the day. Touching a butterfly will display more specific information, including her movements and activities throughout the day, indoor and outdoor temperatures, and so on. A digital family portrait is a qualitative visualization of his mother's activity that has been seamlessly integrated into the everyday artifact, i.e., a picture on the wall.

In the Aware Home projects, context awareness is focused on the recognition of low-level context information from the sensors. For example, an RFID-based positioning system can provide room-level location information (which is refined by camera vision), and an elder's health can be monitored by vital sensors. High-level context information that Aware Home assumed to be available has been a main issue in other projects [Haigh et al. 2002; Intille et al. 2002; Kautz et al. 2002; Mozer 1998; Pollack et al. 2002] where researchers have been exploring the use of artificial intelligence (AI) technologies to achieve the desired level of context abstraction.

The I.L.S.A. (Independent LifeStyle Assistant) at Honeywell Laboratories is a multiagent-based caregiver system that integrates various sensors and actuators in an elder's home, including motion detectors, pressure pads, door contact sensors, toilet flush sensors, a medication caddy, and a panic button [Guralnik and Haigh 2002; Haigh et al. 2002]. The multiagent system supports functionalities similar to those of our Matilda Smart House: monitoring of the elder and the environment; cognitive assistance such as reminders, alarm and alerts to caregivers and family members; offline report generation; and remote access to information about the elder and the home. The system exploits machine learning techniques to adapt itself as its environment changes over time in order to recognize the occupant's behavior patterns. This learned behavior model is used to assess the situation in order to infer the elder's intent and needs, as well as to plan and execute appropriate actions or responses. The design principles of the I.L.S.A. architecture are also similar to ours: modularity to enable a customized system configuration for different home layouts and sensing capabilities, interaction among components, and adaptability to environmental evolution. However, the architecture is based on the JADE agent framework, while our reference architecture is based on the OSGi framework. A task is assigned to an I.L.S.A. agent, which may be a device-monitoring agent, reminder agent, behavior recognizer agent, or planner agent. The agent is analogous to a service bundle in the OSGi framework. Since the bundle allows flexible system composition and changes, the agent can also support customized system configuration and evolution. To enable component integration and communication, the I.L.S.A. architecture defines a public ontology for interagent communication that may be viewed as an equivalent to the context vocabulary in our architecture. The IHome project [Lesser et al. 1999] is another multiagent system used to manage an intelligent home. Another example of a home that can learn and adapt to the lifestyle of the occupants can be found in [Mozer 1998].

The Assisted Cognition project [Kautz et al. 2002] also explores the synthesized use of ubiquitous computing and AI technologies for older people with limited cognitive capabilities. The Assisted Cognition systems, such as the Activity Compass and the Adaptive Prompter, are based on a layered architecture which comprises sensor, data fusion, behavior recognition, plan and intention recognition, and intervention layers. The architecture employs machine learning technologies from noisy sensor data to track elder activities, to learn and interpret their everyday behavior patterns, and to understand their needs. From this understanding, the systems can determine when they should intervene to offer help to the elder. The Activity Compass tracks user activities to guide the elder to her desired destination (in either an indoor or outdoor environment) by displaying an arrow on her handheld device when she becomes disoriented. The Adaptive Prompter guides the elder through a series of individual steps of an ADL, e.g., visual/audio prompts for her to pick up the toothbrush in the bathroom in the morning. The Nursebot project [Pollack et al. 2002] has similar goals of promoting independence and a good quality of life for cognitively impaired elders. The project has developed a robotic assistant to help the elderly by providing cognitive reminders of everyday activities. The robot also functions as a navigation system to guide the elders through their environments.

Even if a piece of context information is small, its effectiveness in the use of a preventive health care system has been demonstrated in [Intille et al. 2002]. The system continuously monitors the patient's health in the home environment. Along with monitoring vital signs, it uses simple multiple-choice health-related questions (to be asked one at a time), that can detect a broader range of health problems earlier than the vital sign readings alone. The system selects the most appropriate question from its current question set, which is updated according to the potential evidence of health problems learned via a Bayesian network. The system makes use of context information (e.g., location information) to determine the right place and time to ask the questions. For example, the best time for a sleeping problem question would be when the elder is next to the bed in the early morning.

The CUSTODIAN suite [Dewsbury et al. 2001] is a set of tools used to design and validate smart homes for people with special needs. The tool user first selects a sample from the Standard Smart Home library, which serves as a starting point of the design process to communicate required functionalities for clients. From this base standard smart home, the tool can add or remove devices/functionality in accordance with the individuals' specific needs. It can also be used to validate the smart home's design or demonstrate the design to the clients. An advantage of this approach is an easy calculation of the house's cost from the baseline cost. Most importantly, the template-based approach ensures that untrained people with no technical knowledge can design safe smart homes, minimizing the chance of omission and defects in the design.

16.5 CONCLUSION

We have been exploring the emerging fields of pervasive computing and smart phone technology to innovate what we call *assistive environments*, places especially designed to promote independence and a good quality of life for older people.

We have developed a reference architecture for assistive environments and have used it to build a smart house prototype and sample applications. Through our explorations to date, we have learned that flexible and intuitive interactions with the environment are required to achieve the main goals. This gives rise to new design requirements, including multiple modalities, implicit context-aware input, and coordination of multiple input/output streams.

ACKNOWLEDGMENTS

This research has been supported by a research center grant from the National Institute on Disability and Rehabilitation Research (NIDRR) and two donations from the College of Engineering at the University of Florida and Microsoft Corporation.

REFERENCES

Addlesee, M., Curwen, R., Hodges, S., Newman, J., Steggles, P., Ward, A., and Hopper, A. 2001. "Implementing a Sentient Computing System," *IEEE Computer Magazine*, vol. 34, no. 8 (Aug.), pp. 50–56.

Dewsbury, G., Taylor, B., and Edge, M. 2001. "Designing Safe Smart Home Systems for Vulnerable People," in *Proceedings of the First Dependability and Healthcare Informatics Workshop*, Edinburgh, Scotland, pp. 65–70.

Giraldo, C., Helal, A., and Mann, W.C. 2002. "mPCA—A Mobile Patient Care-Giving Assistant for Alzheimer Patients," in *Proceedings of the First International Workshop on Ubiquitous Computing for Cognitive Aids (UbiCog'02)*, Gothenberg, Sweden.

Guralnik, V. and Haigh, K.Z. 2002. "Learning Models of Human Behaviour with Sequential Patterns," in *Proceedings of the AAAI 2002 Workshop on Automation as Caregiver: The Role of Intelligent Technology in Elder Care*, Edmonton, Alberta, Canada, pp. 24–30.

Haigh, K.Z., Phelps, J., and Geib, C.W. 2002. "An Open Agent Architecture for Assisting Elder Independence," in *Proceedings of the First International Joint Conference on Autonomous Agents and Multi-Agent Systems*, Bologna, Italy, pp. 578–586.

Helal, A., Winkler, B., Lee, C., Kaddoura, Y., Ran, L., Giraldo, C., Kuchibhotla, S., and Mann, W.C. 2003. "Enabling Location-Aware Pervasive Computing Applications for the Elderly," in *Proceedings of the first IEEE International Conference Pervasive Computing and Communications (PerCom 2003)*, Dallas-Fort Worth, Texas, pp. 531–538.

Hexamite, "Local Positioning System" [online]. Available at http://www.hexamite.com

Hightower, J. and Borriello, G. 2001. "Location Systems for Ubiquitous Computing," *IEEE Computer Magazine*, vol. 34, no. 8 (Aug.), pp. 57–66.

Hightower, J. Want, R., and Borriello, G. 2000. "SpotOn: An Indoor 3D Location Sensing Technology Based on RF Signal Strength," *University of Washington Technical Reports: CSE 2000-02-02*.

INCITS V2 Technical Committee—Information Technology Access Interfaces [online]. Available at http://www.v2access.org/index.html

Intille, S.S., Larson, K., and Kukla, C. 2002. "Just-in-Time Context-Sensitive Questioning for Preventative Health Care," in *Proceedings of the AAAI 2002 Workshop on Automation as Caregiver: The Role of Intelligent Technology in Elder Care*, Edmonton, Alberta, Canada, pp. 54–59.

Kautz, H., Fox, D., Etzioni, O., Borriello, G., and Arnstein, L. 2002. "An Overview of the Assisted Cognition Project," in *Proceedings of the AAAI 2002 Workshop on Automation as Caregiver: The Role of Intelligent Technology in Elder Care*, Edmonton, Alberta, Canada, pp. 60–65.

Koppel, R. 2002. "Alzheimer Disease: The Cost to U.S. Businesses in 2002" [online]. Available at http://www.alz.org/Media/newsreleases/archived/2002/062602ADCosts.pdf

Lesser, V., Atighetchi, M., Benyo, B., Horling, B., Raja, A., Vincent, R., Wagner, T., Xuan, P., and Zhang, S.X. 1999. "A Multi-Agent System for Intelligent Environment Control," in *Proceedings of the Third International Conference on Autonomous Agents*, Seattle, Washington, pp. 291–298.

Mann, W.C., Ottenbacher, K.J., Fraas, L., Tomita, M., and Granger, C.V. 1999. "Effectiveness of Assistive Technology and Environmental Interventions in Maintaining Independence and Reducing Home Care Costs for the Frail Elderly: A Randomized Trial," *Archives of Family Medicine*, vol. 8, no. 3 (May–June), pp. 210–217.

Marples, D. and Kriens, P. 2001. "The Open Services Gateway Initiative: An Introductory Review," *IEEE Communications Magazine*, vol. 39, no. 12 (Dec.), pp. 110–114.

Mozer, M.C. 1998. "The Neural Network House: An Environment that Adapts to its Inhabitants," in *Proceedings of the American Association for Artificial Intelligence Spring Symposium on Intelligent Environments*, Menlo Park, California, pp. 110–114.

Mynatt, E.D., Rowan, J., Craighill, S., and Jacobs, A. 2001. "Digital Family Portraits: Supporting Peace of Mind for Extended Family Members," in *Proceedings of the SIGCHI Conference on Human Factors in Computing Systems 2001*, Seattle, Washington, pp. 333–340.

Nagel, K., Kidd, C., O'Connell, T., Dey, A., and Abowd, G. 2001. "The Family Intercom: Developing a Context-Aware Audio Communication System," in *Proceedings of the Third International Conference on Ubiquitous Computing 2001 (Ubicomp'01)*, Atlanta, Georgia, pp. 176–183.

National Center for Health Statistics, *NCHS Definitions* [online]. Available at http://www.cdc.gov/nchs/datawh/nchsdefs/ADL.htm

OSGi Alliance, "OSGi Service Platform" [online]. Available at http://www.osgi.org/resources/spec_download.asp

Pollack, M.E., Brown, L., Colbry, D., Orosz, C., Peintner, B., Ramakrishnan, S., Engberg, S., Matthews, J.T., Dunbar-Jacobs, J., McCarthy, C.E., Thrun, S., Montemerlo, M., Pineau, J., and Roy, N. 2002. "Pearl: A Mobile Robotic Assistant to the Elderly," in *Proceedings of the AAAI 2002 Workshop on Automation as Caregiver: The Role of Intelligent Technology in Elder Care*, Edmonton, Alberta, Canada, pp. 85–92.

Rauhala-Hayes, M., Dolphin, C., Clarkin, N., and Cullen, K. 1998. *Good Practice in Using the Information Society for the Benefit of Older People and Disabled People*, Jyväskylä, Finland: Gummerrus Printing.

Satyanarayanan, M. 2001. "Pervasive Computing: Vision and Challenges," *IEEE Personal Communications Magazine*, vol. 8, no. 4 (Aug.), pp. 10–17.

Stanford, V. 2002. "Using Pervasive Computing to Deliver Elder Care," *IEEE Pervasive Computing Magazine*, vol. 1, no. 1 (Jan.–Mar.), pp. 10–13.

Want, R., Hopper, A., Falcao, V., and Gibbons, J. 1992. "The Active Badge Location System," *ACM Transaction on Information Systems*, vol. 10, no. 1 (Jan.), pp. 91–102.

Weiser, M. 1991. "The Computer for the 21st Century," *Scientific American*, vol. 256, no. 3 (Sept.), pp. 94–104.

PART 5
CONCLUSIONS

CHAPTER 17

Ongoing Challenges and Future Directions

SAJAL K. DAS and DIANE J. COOK
Department of Computer Science and Engineering
The University of Texas at Arlington

17.1 SYNOPSIS OF THE BOOK

This section summarizes the contributions of the chapters in this book. Chapter 1 sets the stage by defining smart environments and identifying their salient features.

Sensor networks are the key to gathering information needed by smart environments, whether in buildings, utilities, industrial facilities, homes, on shipboard, in transportation system automation, or elsewhere. Chapter 2 provides a comprehensive review of technology, architectures, communication protocols, signal processing, self-organization and decision-making capabilities of wireless sensor networks and smart sensors.

Chapter 3 discusses the key attributes of powerline communication (PLC) as an emerging technology for internetworking smart environments and the use of PLC to establish a robust in-building Ethernet class network infrastructure, as well as a high-speed networking protocol to support high-quality audio and video services in smart appliances and entertainment systems.

A state-of-the-art survey of wireless communications technology, discussing the evolution of this field with respect to the requirements of pervasive computing environments, is presented in Chapter 4. The chapter also introduces existing and emerging technologies for body, personal, and local wireless networks and their standards as they apply to developing pervasive and/or smart infrastructures.

Chapter 5 discusses the characteristics and design issues of middleware services and platforms that facilitate rapid development, ease of integration, transparency, scalability, improved reliability, and interoperability of systems that make smart environments possible.

Smart Environments: Technologies, Protocols, and Applications, edited by D.J. Cook and S.K. Das
ISBN 0-471-54448-5   © 2005 John Wiley & Sons, Inc.

A networked appliance (often referred to as an *Internet appliance*) is a dedicated-function consumer device containing a networked processor. Chapter 6 deals with home networking and the emergence of networked appliances, technology issues and challenges, and characteristics of deployment environments.

Chapter 7 targets the design and evaluation of interfaces for humans in smart environments. Enhanced environments require implicit means of communication with inhabitants, and central to a successful design of such interfaces is an understanding of human cognition and the meaning of routine human activities in these environments.

Chapter 8 addresses how smart environments embody the trend toward an increasingly connected and automated society by linking devices to everyday tasks and settings. Such environments adapt to changing conditions and communicate with humans in an intelligent way to reach certain goals. Their design and implementation require multidisciplinary knowledge of machine learning, human-machine interfaces, decision making, databases, wireless mobile and sensor networking, multimedia, and pervasive computing.

The theme of Chapter 9 is protocols, algorithms, and technologies for effective location prediction in smart environments. Location determination involves not only the use of a customized wireless link layer, but also statistical estimation algorithms for processing the raw data streams (e.g., radio signal strength) to extract location parameters with an acceptable confidence level. The location determination and prediction techniques are presented in this chapter under a unifying *estimation theory* framework.

Designing smart environments necessitates complex decision-making technologies that can adapt to the inhabitants in a scalable manner. Chapter 10 provides an overview of various automated, intelligent techniques for this purpose with application to the MavHome smart home project. It also discusses issues related to ensuring safety in the presence of automated actions.

Interacting and exchanging information with smart environments must be secured, private, and trustworthy. Chapter 11 first considers the characteristics that make smart environments unique in their requirement for security, privacy, and trust and then surveys related work on these issues.

Chapter 12 discusses the lessons learned from a real smart home, the Adaptive House. Built on the premise that there should be no user interface beyond the sorts of controls one would ordinarily use, this house monitors various aspects of the environment (indoor and outdoor) for intelligence building. The chapter also describes the control system architecture of this house and the challenges involved in implementing it.

Chapter 13 explores the goals, challenges, and operational constraints that characterize the smart room paradigm, in which the application of computing technology facilitates unobtrusive person-to-physical world interaction. The issues include networking, sensing, middleware services, and data management primitives essential for achieving a scalable infrastructure for deeply instrumented physical environments.

The focus of Chapter 14 is smart offices, a subdomain of smart environments. In addition to reviewing various smart office–related projects, this chapter discusses in detail the features, software, and control architectures of Monica, an interactive, ubiquitous computing enhanced, and context-aware office environment.

Perceptual intelligence is used to change inanimate objects like offices, houses, cars, or glasses into smart, active helpmates; it provides the ability to classify the current situation, identify significant variables, and take appropriate actions. Chapter 15 investigates how perceptual information helps build smart rooms and smart clothes that have the potential to recognize people, understand their speech, communicate by sign language, and warn them they are about to make a mistake.

Chapter 16 deals with assistive technology for the elderly using a scenario-based approach. It presents a prototype of an assistive environment, the reference middleware architecture, and several applications built on it. The chapter concludes with research reviews of smart environments for elders with disabilities, and elder healthcare applications and practices.

17.2 ONGOING CHALLENGES FOR SMART ENVIRONMENTS

Research on smart environments has made great strides in recent years, but a number of challenges remain. We look at some of the issues here and outline directions for future work.

17.2.1 Database Support for Smart Environments

A critical technology area for smart environments is database design and creation. Database support for this application presents special challenges. First, a large amount of sensor data is constantly collected and must be assimilated in real time to support prediction, decision making, and related algorithms. In addition, much of the data captured from the environment and fed to the environment will represent multimedia information and will require special handling for this purpose. Recent work on active databases supports the design of database rules that trigger events when a condition is detected. Active databases can therefore be used to respond quickly to environmental conditions and reduce the burden on the decision maker. Similarly, research on streaming databases can be used for efficient processing of multimedia information acquisition and dissemination by sensors.

17.2.2 Complex Prediction Tasks

Prediction of the location and activities of inhabitants has been addressed fairly successfully by existing algorithms such as the ones described in this book. However, simplifying assumptions are made for these algorithms that will need to be relaxed to address more realistic situations. In particular, inhabitants' activity patterns are not likely to remain stagnant, but to change over time. This will occur either abruptly, as when a new inhabitant enters the setting, or gradually; the smart environment must recognize and adapt to these changes. The efficiency of such predictive platforms lies in intelligent learning of these patterns in an efficient way. While in-building sensors are designated for acquisition of necessary information, the role of the algorithms is to process the captured data and subsequently trigger the respective actuators in precise time. Optimality of such information processing is achieved only if the scheme reduces the uncertainty associated with the dynamism of inhabitants' movement and activity patterns.

Prediction algorithms will also be improved if activities can not only be anticipated but also identified by type, perhaps as part of a more abstract whole. For example, a smart office can benefit from recognizing that its inhabitant is entering the room simply to pick up a briefcase and leave for the day, not to stay and initiate a new project. As a result, the predictions will thus be context aware, where the context is not only location but also may encompass intent or desire.

Finally, these algorithms must be able to perform in the presence of multiple inhabitants, who may be engaging in complex interactions. These inhabitants may have unique patterns that overlap in time or space, and may also have patterns that occur only when combinations of inhabitants occupy the space at the same time. The environment must either be able to recognize the various inhabitants and respond to each one appropriately or be able to respond to the group as a whole. The activities of individual inhabitants may often be in conflict with each other, which increases the complexity of such algorithm design issues.

17.2.3 Robotic Assistants

Many of the current projects view a smart environment as a stationary entity that responds to the actions of mobile inhabitants. However, a broader definition can encompass mobile robotic agents that are also designed to assist the environment's inhabitants. These robots can perform household duties such as cleaning laundry and washing dishes; accomplishing physical tasks not possible for some inhabitants, such as replacing a light bulb in a tall ceiling fixture; and even representing the inhabitants' interface with the outside world.

17.2.4 Networking Support for Smart Environments

In smart environments, large amounts of data will be exchanged between devices forming a network to make the environment ready for the inhabitant's next move or action. The data can represent information acquired from the surroundings or multimedia data requested by the inhabitants. Thus, network connectivity needs to be maintained continuously. Moreover, networked mobile devices such as robotic agents, mobile sensors, and inhabitants' personal gadgets should be able to interact autonomously with other devices to increase local low-level decisions, maintain seamless communication paths, and discover available services. Recent progress in indoor-networking technologies (like DSL, cable modem, IEEE 802.11, etc.) and the rapid proliferation of smart handheld devices (like palmtops and personal digital assistants) has already set the stage for the required networking support. However, the essence of any smart environment can only be achieved with seamless connectivity between heterogeneous networking components and energy-efficient, secured routing in resource-poor wireless mobile networks, including smart sensors.

17.2.5 Increasing the Scope of Smart Environments

Although we tend to view a smart environment as a single rather confined space, many of the technologies can be generalized to encompass larger realms such as smart communities, shopping centers, hospitals, highways, airports, amusement parks, and cities. If individual smart homes and businesses can cooperate on decisions such as the time and amount of energy usage, for example, brownouts and blackouts can be avoided. If smart environments can combine their technologies, they will not only learn from the experience of one family or group, but also improve their performance based on the experience of many environments and inhabitants in order to continuously expand and improve the expected benefits of smart environments over the years.

17.3 SMART ENVIRONMENT PROJECTS

- Adaptive House
  http://www.cs.colorado.edu/ ~ mozer/nnh
- Agent-based Intelligent Reactive Environments (AIRE)
  http://www.ai.mit.edu/projects/aire
- Ambiente roomware
  http://www.ipsi.fgh.de/ambiente
- AVIARY
  http://cvrr.ucsd.edu/aviary
- Aware Home
  http://www.cc.gatech.edu/fce/ahri
- Changing Places/House_n
  http://architecture.mit.edu//house_n
- Cisco Internet Home
  http://www.cisco.com/warp/public/3/uk/ihome
- Edinvar Assisted Interactive Dwelling HOUSE
  http://www.stakes.fi/tidecong/732bonne.html
- Ericsson IT Apartments
  http://www.e2-home.com
- Essex Intelligent Inhabited Environments Group (IIEG)
  http://cswww.essex.ac.uk/intelligent-buildings
- Gloucester Smart House
  http://www.dementua-voice.org.uk/Projects_GloucesterProject.htm
- IBM wired home
  http://www-3.ibm.com/software/pervasive

- Icepick Technologies
  http://www.icepick.com
- Intel Proactive Health
  http://www.intel.com/research/prohealth
- Intelligent Building Group (EIBG)
  http://www.ibgroup.org.uk
- Intelligent Home Project
  http://mas.cs.umass.edu/research/IHome
- Intelligent Space Project
  http://dfs.iis.u-tokyo.ac.jp/~leejooho/ispace
- Internet Home Alliance
  http://www.internethomealliance.com
- MavHome
  http://mavhome.uta.edu
- Microsoft Easy Living
  http://research.microsoft.com/easyliving
- Philips smart home
  http://www.smarthomeforum.com/start/show_news.asp?NID = 178
- PRIMA
  http://www-prima.imag.fr/Prima
- Smart Homes Foundation
  http://www.smart-homes.nl/engels/index.html
- Stanford Interactive Workspaces
  http://iwork.stanford.edu
- Sun Dot Com Home
  http://www.sun.com/smi/Press/sunflash/2000-01/sunflash.20000106.1.html

Index

Absolute geographical positioning, wireless sensor networks, 39
Access:
    addressing and, network appliances (NA) problems, 139–143
    capture and, human experience applications, 161–162
ACHE (Adaptive Control of Home Environments) architecture, home automation, 283–289. *See also* Home automation; Smart rooms
Acoustic sensors, physical transduction principles, 33–34
Acoustic wave sensors, physical transduction principles, 34
Active Badge:
    location estimation techniques, 205–206
    smart office example, 328
Active Bat, location estimation techniques, 206–208
Active power control, power management, 21
Active RFID tags, LANDMARC, location estimation techniques, 209–210
Actuation infrastructure, smart rooms, 309
Adaptive Control of Home Environments (ACHE) architecture, home automation, 283–289. *See also* Home automation; Smart rooms
Adaptive home. *See* Home automation
Adaptive interfaces, perceptual environments, 346–347
Adaptive routing, communication networks protocols and routing, 18–19
Addressing, access and, network appliance (NA) problems, 139–143
Agent-based Intelligent Reactive Environments (AIRE, MIT), middleware, 120

Agent-oriented middleware, 113
ALOHA scheme, multiple access protocols, 17
Ambient intelligence, pervasive computing technology, 64
Amplitude shift keying, power line infrastructure, 49
Anticipator, home automation, 285–288
Appliances. *See* Network appliances (NA)
Architecture:
    ACHE, home automation, 283–289
    middleware, 106–107
    Monica project, 334–341
    pervasive computing technology, IEEE 802.11 standards, 71
Artificial intelligence, middleware, 102–106
Assistive environments, 361–383
    applications, 374–377
    daily activities, 364–366
    instrumentation, 367–371
    middleware, 371–374
    overview, 361–362
    related systems, 377–380
    ubiquitous computing, 362–364
Asynchronous connection-less (ACL) link, bluetooth based WPAN, IEEE 802.15 standards, pervasive computing technology, 87
Attenuation, power line channel characteristics, 51
Audio interpretation, perceptual environments, 351
Authoring, of content, smart rooms constraints, 316–317
Automated decision making. *See* Decision making

394   INDEX

Automatic repeat request (ARQ), bluetooth based WPAN, IEEE 802.15 standards, pervasive computing technology, 87
Automotive domain:
 driver's intention, perceptual environments, 350
 network appliances (NA), 131–132, 138–139
Aware Home Research Initiative (AHRI, Georgia Institute of Technology), middleware, 120–121

Badges, sensing infrastructure, smart rooms, 305–306
Bathroom, assistive environments, 364
Beacon-enabled networks, IEEE 802.15 standards, low-rate WPAN, 93–94
Bedroom, assistive environments, 364
Biological transducers, physical transduction principles, 31
Biosensors, physical transduction principles, 32
Bluetooth, wireless local area network (WLAN), history and standards, 26
Bluetooth based WPAN, IEEE 802.15 standards, pervasive computing technology, 85–88
Bolometers, physical transduction principles, 31
Broadband Internet access, power line communication technology, 58–60
Building automation, wireless sensor networks, 43–44. *See also* Home automation; Smart rooms; specific automation applications
Bus topology, wireless sensor networks, communication networks, 16

Capacitive sensors, physical transduction principles, 29
Capture, access and, human experience applications, 161–162
Carrier frequency system (CFS), power line infrastructure, 49
Carrier sensed multiple access (DSMA) technique, power line communication protocols, 55
CEBus protocol, power line communication technology, 55
Channel characteristics (power line communication technology), 50–53
 attenuation, 51

 electromagnetic compatibility, 52–53
 noise, 51–52
Chemical transducers, physical transduction principles, 31
Chemiresistors, physical transduction principles, 31–32
Classroom, human experience laboratory, 167. *See also* Smart rooms
Client-server architecture, middleware, 106–107
Client-server networks, Gigabit Ethernet, history and standards, 25
Clothing, sensing infrastructure, smart rooms, 306–308
Code Division Multiple Access (CDMA), multiple access protocols, communication networks protocols and routing, 17
Collaboration, smart rooms, 299–300
Collaborative operation, network appliances (NA), 137–138
Collision avoidance, power line communication protocols, 57
Common Object Request Broker Architecture (CORBA), middleware standards, 115, 312
Communication:
 device, smart environment features, 4–6
 middleware, 106
Communication networks:
 hierarchy, wireless sensor networks, 21–24
  described, 22–24
  distributed routing, decision making, and digital signal processing, 24
 history and standards, 25–26
 power management, wireless sensor networks, 20–21
 protocols and routing, wireless sensor networks, 16–19
  deadlock and livelock, 19
  flow control, 19
  headers, 16–17
  multiple access protocols, 17
  open systems interconnection reference model (OSI/RM), 17–18
  routing, 18–19
  switching, 17
 wireless sensor networks, 14–26
Compatibility, electromagnetic, power line channel characteristics, 52–53
Complexity, network appliances (NA), 136–137

Component Object Model/Distributed Component Object Model (COM/DCOM), middleware standards, 115
Computer vision technology, location estimation techniques, 211
Conditioning, signal processing, wireless sensor networks, 39–41
Connected environments, device communication, 4–6
Content authoring, smart rooms constraints, 316–317
Contention-window inter-frame spacing, power line communication protocols, 58
Context-aware computing, human experience applications, 160–161
Context-aware offices, smart offices, 326–327
Context-aware resource discovery, assistive environments, 371–373
Continuous interaction, human experience applications, 162
Cooking. *See* Kitchen
Costs:
   home automation, 288–289
   network appliances (NA), 136
Counter intelligence (MIT), middleware, 121
Cricket Location Support System, 199–202

Databases, middleware, 111, 117
Deadlock, communication networks protocols and routing, 19
Dead reckoning, location estimation techniques, 217–219
Decision making, 229–247
   approaches to, 230–235
      learning algorithms, 234–235
      planning algorithms, 233–234
      reactive and rule-based systems, 231–233
   case study (MavHome), 236–241
      experiments, 238–241
      reinforcement learning, 236–237
   distributed and hierarchical agents, 242–245
   hierarchical networks, wireless sensor networks, 24
   improvements in, MavHome case study, 188
   overview, 229–230
   predictive models, 235–236
   safety concerns, 241–242
   smart environment features, 7
   wireless sensor networks, 42–43

Device communication, smart environment features, 4–6
Digital signal processing (DSP):
   hierarchical networks, wireless sensor networks, 24
   wireless sensor networks, 41–42
Distance-based strategies, location estimation techniques, 216–217
Distributed Computing Environment (DCE), middleware standards, 115–116
Distributed coordination function (DCF), MAC layer specification, IEEE 802.11 standards, pervasive computing technology, 72–74. *See also* Enhanced distributed coordination function (EDCF)
Distributed inter frame space (DIFS), MAC layer specification, IEEE 802.11 standards, pervasive computing technology, 73
Distributed output, human experience, 156–158
Distributed routing, hierarchical networks, wireless sensor networks, 24
Distributed system services, middleware, 113–114
Driver's intention, perceptual environments, 350
DSSS PHY layer specification, pervasive computing technology, IEEE 802.11 standards, 72

Easy Living project (Microsoft), middleware, 122–123
Elderly, human experience laboratory, 169. *See also* Assistive environments
Electrochemical transducers, physical transduction principles, 32
Electromagnetic compatibility, power line channel characteristics, 52–53
Electromagnetic sensors:
   location estimation techniques, 211
   physical transduction principles, 29
Electromagnetic spectrum, physical transduction principles, 33
Emergent operation, network appliances (NA), 137–138
Enhanced distributed coordination function (EDCF), quality of service, IEEE 802.11 standards, pervasive computing technology, 82–83. *See also* Distributed coordination function (DCF)
Enrichment, smart rooms, 302–303

396 INDEX

Ethernet, history and standards, 25
Experimental testbeds, perceptual environments, 347
Expression recognition, perceptual environments, 353–354
Exteroceptors, wireless sensor networks, 13

Face recognition, perceptual environments, 352–353
Family, human experience laboratory, 169–170
Feature interaction, network appliances (NA), 138, 143–147
Ferrets, headers, communication networks protocols and routing, 16
Field effect transistor (FET), physical transduction principles, 31–34
File-sharing architecture, middleware, 106
Fixed routing, communication networks protocols and routing, 18
Flits, switching, communication networks protocols and routing, 17
Flow control, communication networks protocols and routing, 19
Flow control units, switching, communication networks protocols and routing, 17
Frameworks, middleware, 113
Frequency Division Multiple Access (FDMA), multiple access protocols, communication networks protocols and routing, 17
Fully connected networks, wireless sensor networks, communication networks, 15

Geographical positioning, absolute, wireless sensor networks, 39
Geometric representation schemas, location estimation techniques, 212–213
Gigabit Ethernet, history and standards, 25
Global Positioning System (GPS), location estimation techniques, 197–198

Hall effect, physical transduction principles, 29
Hand gesture recognition, perceptual environments, 349
Handshaking protocols, headers, communication networks protocols and routing, 16–17
Haptic input, perceptual environments, 354–355

Headers, communication networks protocols and routing, 16–17
Head tracking, perceptual environments, 350–351
Hierarchical networks:
 distributed routing, decision making, and digital signal processing, 24
 wireless sensor networks, 21–24
High-rate WPAN, IEEE 802.15 standards, pervasive computing technology, 88–91
High-speed WLANs, IEEE 802.11a and 11g standards, pervasive computing technology, 81
High-voltage lines, power line infrastructure, 48–49
Home automation, 273–277, 273–294. *See also* Assistive environments; Network appliances (NA); Smart offices; Smart rooms
 ACHE architecture, 283–289
  anticipator, 285–288
  generally, 283–284
  occupancy model, 285
  parameters and costs, 288–289
  Q-learning controller, 284–285
 decision making:
  distributed and hierarchical agents, 242–245
  safety concerns, 241–242
 evaluation, 291
 future prospects, 291–293
 human experience laboratory, 168–170
 lighting, 277–278, 281–283
 MavHome case study, 181–191
  components of, 188–191
  decision making, 188, 236–241
  inhabitant actions, 185–188
  repetition recognition, 182–185
 network appliances (NA) domain, 132–134
 optimal control, 279–280
 training scenario, 289–290
 wireless sensor networks, 43–44
HomePlug 1.0 protocol, power line communication technology, 55–58
HomePlug AV protocol, power line communication technology, 58
Home RF, wireless local area network (WLAN), history and standards, 26
Human experience, 153–174
 applications, 159–162
  capture and access, 161–162
  context-aware computing, 160–161

continuous interaction, 162
  assessment, 165–166
  design, 163–165
    interaction models, 163–164
    settings, 164–165
  living laboratories, 166–170
    classroom, 167
    home, 168–170
    office, 168
  overview, 153–154
  physical interaction, 154–159
    implicit input, 155–156
    multiscale and distributed output, 156–158
    physical/virtual integration, 158–159
Hybrid coordination function, quality of service, IEEE 802.11 standards, 83–84

IBM Pervasive Computing Lab, middleware, 121
Implicit input, human experience, 155–156
Information acquisition/dissemination, from intelligent sensor networks, smart environment features, 6
Infrared sensor, assistive environments, 370
Infrastructure, network appliances (NA), 136
Infrastructure-based networks, pervasive computing technology, 68
Infrastructure for Capture and Access (INCA), middleware, AHRI, 120–121
Infrastructure-less networks, pervasive computing technology, 68–69
Inhabitant actions, MavHome case study, 185–188
Input, implicit, human experience, 155–156
Institute of Electrical and Electronics Engineers (IEEE):
  communication networks history and standards, 25–26
  802.11 standards, pervasive computing technology, 69–84
    architecture, 71
    DSSS PHY layer specification, 72
    generally, 69–70
    high-speed WLANs, 81
    IEEE 802.11b specification, 77–81
    MAC layer specification, 72–74
    power saving specification, 74–77
    quality of service, 81–84
  802.11b standards, pervasive computing technology, 77–81
  802.11e standards, pervasive computing technology, quality of service, 81–84
  802.15 standards:
    low-rate WPAN, pervasive computing technology, 91–94
    pervasive computing technology, 84–94
      Bluetooth based WPAN, 85–88
      high-rate WPAN, 88–91
  smart sensors, 26–28
Integration, physical/virtual, human experience, 158–159
Intelligent Environment Laboratory (IGD Rostock), smart office example, 330
Intelligent offices, smart offices, 327. See also Smart offices
Intelligent Room, smart office example, 328–329. See also Smart rooms
Interaction models, human experience design, 163–164
Interactions, smart rooms, 300–301
Interactive LANDscape (I-LAND, AMBIENTE), middleware, 121–122
Interactive offices, smart offices, 324–326
Interactive workspaces, smart environments, middleware, 122
Interactive workspaces project (Stanford), smart office example, 329
Interdigitated-gate electrode field effect transistor (IGEFET):
  physical transduction principles, 31–34
  wireless sensor networks, signal processing, 40
International Standards Organization (ISO), open systems interconnection reference model (OSI/RM), 17
Internet:
  broadband Internet access, power line communication technology, 58–60
  connection statistics on, 47
Isarithmic schemes, flow control, communication networks protocols and routing, 19

Java language, middleware standards, 116
Junction-based photosensors, physical transduction principles, 30

Kalman Filter, digital signal processing, wireless sensor networks, 41–42

Kanban schemes, flow control, communication networks protocols and routing, 19
Kitchen, assistive environments, 365, 376–377

LANDMARC, location estimation techniques, 209–210
Learning, perceptual environments, 351–352
Learning algorithms, decision making, 234–235
LeZi-Update algorithm, location estimation techniques, 221–223
Lighting, home automation, 277–278, 281–283
Livelock, communication networks protocols and routing, wireless sensor networks, 19
Localization:
    assistive environments, 370–371
    wireless sensor networks, 37–39
Location estimation techniques, 193–228
    current location, 196–212
        device-oriented, 197–204
            Cricket System, 199–202
            Global Positioning System (GPS), 197–198
            RADAR technology, 202–204
            wireless cellular networks, 198–199
        network-centric technology, 204–210
            Active Badge, 205–206
            Active Bat, 206–208
            LANDMARC, 209–210
            3D-iD system, 208–209
            wireless cellular networks, 210
        nonradio technologies, 211–212
    future location, 216–224
        dead reckoning, 217–219
        distance-based strategies, 216–217
        issues in, 223–224
        LeZi-Update algorithm, 221–223
        profile-based algorithms, 219–220
    overview, 193–196
    representation schemas, 212–216
        geometric, 212–213
        symbolic, 213–216
LonWorks protocol, power line communication technology, 55
Low-frequency sensor, assistive environments, 370

Low-pass filtering, wireless sensor networks, signal processing, 40–41
Low-rate WPAN, IEEE 802.15 standards, pervasive computing technology, 91–94
Low-voltage lines, power line infrastructure, 48–49

Machine learning, prediction algorithms, 181
MAC layer:
    IEEE 802.11 standards, pervasive computing technology, 72–74
    IEEE 802.15 standards, low-rate WPAN, 93–94
Magnetic field sensors, physical transduction principles, 29
Magnetic sensors, physical transduction principles, 29
Maintenance, network appliances (NA), 136–137
Markov Decision Process (MDP), prediction algorithms, 179–180
Matilda Smart House. *See* Assistive environments
MavHome (University of Texas at Arlington), 181–191
    decision making, 188, 236–241
    experiments, 238–241
    reinforcement learning, 236–237
    inhabitant actions, 185–188
    middleware, 122
    repetition recognition, 182–185
Medium-voltage lines, power line infrastructure, 48–49
Meetings, smart rooms, 299–300
Memory, human experience laboratory, 169
Mesh networks, wireless sensor networks, communication networks, 15
Message-oriented middleware, 107–110
Metal-oxide gas sensors, physical transduction principles, 32
Microelectromechanical systems (MEMS):
    power management, wireless sensor networks, 20–21
    wireless sensor networks, signal processing, 40
Middleware, 101–127
    architectural basics, 106–107
    assistive environments, 371–374
    defined, 101–102
    design, 117–119
    forms of, 107–113
        agent-oriented, 113

database connectivity, 111
  message-oriented, 107–110
  object-oriented, 110–111
  remote procedure call, 111–112
  transaction processing, 107
  web services, 112–113
frameworks, 113
needs, wants, and desires, 102–106
overview, 101–103
services, 113–114
smart environments, 119–124
  AHRI (Georgia Institute of Technology), 120–121
  AIRE (MIT), 120
  counter intelligence (MIT), 121
  Easy Living project (Microsoft), 122–123
  IBM Pervasive Computing Lab, 121
  I-LAND (AMBIENTE), 121–122
  interactive workspaces, 122
  MavHome (University of Texas at Arlington), 122
  sentient computing (Cambridge University), 123
  Smart Space Laboratory (NIST), 123–124
smart rooms, 311–314
standards, 114–117
  COM/DCOM, 115
  CORBA, 115
  databases, 117
  DCE, 115–116
  Java language, 116
  protocols, 117
  web services, 116
ubiquitous computing, 114
Monica project, 331–341
  control architecture, 334–341
    application programming, 338
    client programming, 336–338
    communication scheme, 335–336
    example, 338–341
    generally, 334–335
    software bus, 335
  hardware, 331
  software, 331–334
Moore's law, xiii
Motivation:
  definition, 256–257
  privacy, 255–256
  security, 252
  smart environments, 257–259
Multiagent systems:
  decision making, 243–244

middleware, 113
Multiple access protocols, communication networks protocols and routing, 17
Multiscale output, human experience, 156–158

Network appliances (NA), 129–149. *See also* Assistive environments; Home automation; Smart offices; Smart rooms
  current deployment, 138–139
  defined, 129
  domains of, 131–136
    automotive, 131–132
    home environment, 132–134
    Personal Area Network (PAN), 132
    possibilities of, 134–136
  emergence of, 130–131
  future prospects, 147–148
  issues in, 136–138
  problems in, 139–147
    addressing and access, 139–143
    feature interaction, 143–147
Networking standards and regulations, smart environment features, 8–9
Network topology, wireless sensor networks, communication networks, 14–16
Noise, power line channel characteristics, 51–52
Non-beacon-enabled networks, IEEE 802.15 standards, low-rate WPAN, 93
Nonradio technologies, location estimation techniques, 211–212

Object-oriented middleware, 110–111
Observation, smart rooms, 301–302
Occupancy model, home automation, 285
OFDM modulation, power line communication technology, 53–54
Offices, human experience laboratory, 168. *See also* Smart offices
Open Services Gateway Initiative (OSGi), assistive environments, 374
Open systems interconnection reference model (OSI/RM), communication networks protocols and routing, 17–18
Optical fiber technology, physical transduction principles, 31
Optical transducers, physical transduction principles, 30
Output, multiscale and distributed, human experience, 156–158

Packet routing networks, headers, communication networks protocols and routing, 16
Peer-to-peer networks:
　Gigabit Ethernet, history and standards, 25
　wireless sensor networks, communication networks, 15
Perceive-reason-act design, middleware, 102–106, 119
Perceptual environments, 345–359. *See also* Assistive environments; Home automation; Smart environments; Smart offices; Smart rooms; Wireless sensor networks
　adaptive interfaces, 346–347
　experimental testbeds, 347
　overview, 345–346
　smart clothing, 355–357
　smart rooms, 347–355
　　audio interpretation, 351
　　driver's intention, 350
　　expression recognition, 353–354
　　face and voice recognition, 352–353
　　hand gesture recognition, 349
　　haptic input, 354–355
　　head tracking and shape recovery, 350–351
　　learning, 351–352
　　real-time person tracking, 347–348
　　self-calibration, 349
　ubiquitous computing contrasted, 346
Perceptual user interfaces, smart offices, 324
Personal Area Network (PAN), network appliances (NA), 132
Pervasive computing technology, 63–99. *See also* Ubiquitous computing
　IEEE 802.11 standards, 69–84
　　architecture, 71
　　DSSS PHY layer specification, 72
　　generally, 69–70
　　high-speed WLANs, 81
　　IEEE 802.11b specification, 77–81
　　MAC layer specification, 72–74
　　power saving specification, 74–77
　　quality of service, 81–84
　IEEE 802.15 standards, 84–94
　　Bluetooth based WPAN, 85–88
　　high-rate WPAN, 88–91
　overview, 63–64
　smart spaces, 64–67
　technologies, 67–69
Photoconductive sensors, physical transduction principles, 30

Photoelectric effect, physical transduction principles, 30
Photovoltaic effect, physical transduction principles, 30
Physical carrier sensing range, IEEE 802.11b specification, 79–81
Physical interaction (human experience), 154–159
　implicit input, 155–156
　multiscale and distributed output, 156–158
　physical/virtual integration, 158–159
Physical layer, IEEE 802.15 standards, low-rate WPAN, 93
Physical transduction principles, wireless sensor networks, 28–34
Physical/virtual integration, human experience, 158–159
Piconet, bluetooth based WPAN, IEEE 802.15 standards, 86–88
Piezoelectric effect, physical transduction principles, 28–29
Piezoresistive effect, physical transduction principles, 28
Planning algorithms, decision making, 233–234
Plan recognition, prediction algorithms, 180
Power line communication technology, 47–62
　broadband Internet access, 58–60
　channel characteristics, 50–53
　　attenuation, 51
　　electromagnetic compatibility, 52–53
　　noise, 51–52
　infrastructure, 48–49
　OFDM modulation, 53–54
　overview, 47–48
　protocols, 54–58
　　CEBus protocol, 55
　　HomePlug 1.0 protocol, 55–58
　　HomePlug AV protocol, 58
　　LonWorks protocol, 55
　　X-10 protocol, 54–55
　regulatory constraints, 49–50
　security, 60–61
Power management, communication networks, 20–21
Power saving specification, IEEE 802.11 standards, 74–77
Prediction algorithms, 175–192
　approaches of, 177–181
　　machine learning, 181
　　Markov Decision Process (MDP), 179–180

plan recognition, 180
  sequential matching, 178–179
case study (MavHome), 181–191
  components of, 188–191
  decision making improvements, 188
  inhabitant actions, 185–188
  repetition recognition, 182–185
decision making, 235–236
overview, 175–176
role of, 176–177
Predictive capabilities, smart environment features, 7
Presentations, smart rooms, 297–298
Pressure sensors, location estimation techniques, 212
Privacy, 255–259. *See also* Security; Trust
  motivation, 255–256
  overview, 249–251
Profile-based algorithms, location estimation techniques, 219–220
Proprioceptors, wireless sensor networks, 13
Protocol(s):
  middleware standards, 117
  power line communication technology, 54–58
    CEBus protocol, 55
    HomePlug 1.0 protocol, 55–58
    HomePlug AV protocol, 58
    LonWorks protocol, 55
    X-10 protocol, 54–55
Protocol multiplexing, bluetooth based WPAN, IEEE 802.15 standards, 86

Q-learning controller, home automation, 284–285, 290
Quality of service, IEEE 802.11 standards, pervasive computing technology, 81–84

RADAR technology, location estimation techniques, 202–204
Reactive-based decision making systems, 231–233
Real-time person tracking, perceptual environments, 347–348
Regulatory constraints, power line communication technology, 49–50
Reinforcement learning:
  decision making, 234–235
  hierarchical, 244–245
  MavHome case study, 236–237
  home automation, 279–280
Relative layout positioning, wireless sensor networks, 37–38

Remote control devices, smart environment features, 3–4
Remote procedure call, middleware, 111–112
Remote sensors, physical transduction principles, 33
Repetition recognition, MavHome case study, 182–185
Representation schemas (location estimation techniques), 212–216
  geometric, 212–213
  symbolic, 213–216
Resonant temperature sensors, physical transduction principles, 30
RF-identification, power management, wireless sensor networks, 20
Riccati equation, digital signal processing, wireless sensor networks, 42
Ring topology, wireless sensor networks, communication networks, 15–16
Ripple carrier signaling, power line infrastructure, 49
Robot kinematic transformations, relative layout positioning, wireless sensor networks, 37–38
Routing, communication networks protocols and routing, 18–19
Rule-based decision making systems, 231–233

Safety concerns, decision making, 241–242
Security, 252–255. *See also* Privacy; Trust
  definition, 252–253
  motivation, 252
  network appliances (NA), 137, 140–143
  overview, 249–251
  power line communication technology, 60–61
  smart environments, 253–255
Seebeck effect, physical transduction principles, 30
Segmentation-reassembly, bluetooth based WPAN, IEEE 802.15 standards, 86
Self-calibration, perceptual environments, 349
Self-organization, wireless sensor networks, 37–39
Sensing infrastructure:
  assistive environments, 367–371
  smart rooms, 305–309
Sensor(s). *See also* Wireless sensor networks
  acoustic sensors, physical transduction principles, 33–34

Sensor(s). (*Continued*)
  acoustic wave sensors, physical transduction principles, 34
  IEEE, 26–28
  information acquisition/dissemination from, smart environment features, 6
Sensor fusion, digital signal processing, wireless sensor networks, 41–42
Sentient computing, middleware, 123
Sequential matching, prediction algorithms, 178–179
Services, middleware, 113–114
Session Initiation Protocol (SIP), network appliances (NA), 140–143
Shape recovery, perceptual environments, 350–351
Signal processing (wireless sensor networks), 39–42
  conditioning, 39–41
  digital processing, 41–42
Smart clothing:
  perceptual environments, 355–357
  sensing infrastructure, smart rooms, 306–308
Smart environments. *See also* Assistive environments; Home automation; Perceptual environments; Smart offices; Smart rooms; Wireless sensor networks
  agenda of challenges, xiii–xv
  challenges of, 389–391
  features, 3–9
    device communication, 4–6
    enhanced services by smart devices, 6–7
    intelligent sensor networks, information acquisition/dissemination from, 6
    networking standards and regulations, 8–9
    predictive and decision-making capabilities, 7
    remote control devices, 3–4
  future prospects, 389–391
  middleware, 119–124
    AHRI (Georgia Institute of Technology), 120–121
    AIRE (MIT), 120
    counter intelligence (MIT), 121
    Easy Living project (Microsoft), 122–123
    IBM Pervasive Computing Lab, 121

I-LAND (AMBIENTE), 121–122
interactive workspaces, 122
MavHome (University of Texas at Arlington), 122
sentient computing (Cambridge University), 123
Smart Space Laboratory (NIST), 123–124
research in, xiii, 9
revolution in, xi–xii
schematic view of, 4
wireless sensor networks, 13–46
Smart home, wireless sensor networks, 43–44. *See also* Home automation
Smart offices, 323–343
  context aware offices, 326–327
  examples, 328–331
    Active Badge, 328
    discussed, 330–331
    Intelligent Environment Laboratory (IGD Rostock), 330
    Intelligent Room, 328–329
    interactive workspaces project (Stanford), 329
  intelligent offices, 327
  interactive offices, 324–326
  Monica project, 331–341
    control architecture, 334–341
    application programming, 338
    client programming, 336–338
    communication scheme, 335–336
    example, 338–341
    generally, 334–335
    software bus, 335
    hardware, 331
    software, 331–334
  overview, 323–324
  perceptual user interfaces, 324
  term of, 327
  ubiquitous computing, 326
Smart rooms, 295–322. *See also* Assistive environments; Home automation; Smart offices
  constraints, 314–318
    content authoring, 316–317
    social implications, 317–318
    usability, 314–315
  functions, 297–303
    collaboration, 299–300
    enrichment, 302–303
    interactions, 300–301
    observation, 301–302
    presentations, 297–298
  overview, 295–297

perceptual environments, 347–355
  audio interpretation, 351
  driver's intention, 350
  expression recognition, 353–354
  face and voice recognition, 352–353
  hand gesture recognition, 349
  haptic input, 354–355
  head tracking and shape recovery, 350–351
  learning, 351–352
  real-time person tracking, 347–348
  self-calibration, 349
  technologies, 303–314
    actuation infrastructure, 309
    generally, 303–304
    sensing infrastructure, 305–309
    software, 310–314
Smart sensors. *See* Sensor(s)
Smart Space Laboratory (NIST), middleware, 123–124
Smart spaces, pervasive computing technology, 64–67. *See also* specific applications
Social implications, smart rooms constraints, 317–318
Solar cells, physical transduction principles, 31
Special frames, headers, communication networks protocols and routing, 16
Standards (middleware), 114–117. *See also* Institute of Electrical and Electronics Engineers (IEEE)
  COM/DCOM, 115
  CORBA, 115
  databases, 117
  DCE, 115–116
  Java language, 116
  protocols, 117
  web services, 116
Star topology, wireless sensor networks, communication networks, 15–16
Store-and-forward switching, communication networks protocols and routing, 17
Surfaces, sensing infrastructure, smart rooms, 308–309
Switching, communication networks protocols and routing, 17
Symbolic representation schemas, location estimation techniques, 213–216
Synchronous connection-oriented (SCO) link, bluetooth based WPAN, IEEE 802.15 standards, 87

Tags, sensing infrastructure, smart rooms, 305–306
Temperature compensation, wireless sensor networks, signal processing, 40
Thermal sensors, physical transduction principles, 29
Thermocouples, physical transduction principles, 30
Thermomechanical transduction, physical transduction principles, 30
Thermopiles, physical transduction principles, 30
Thermoresistive effects, physical transduction principles, 30
3D-iD system, location estimation techniques, 208–209
3D tracking, perceptual environments, 347–348
Three-tier client-server architecture, middleware, 107
Time division duplex (TDD), bluetooth based WPAN, IEEE 802.15 standards, 87
Time Division Multiple Access (TDMA):
  multiple access protocols, 17, 18
  power management, 20
Token ring network, history and standards, 25
Transaction processing, middleware, 107
Transducers, wireless sensor networks, 28–34
Transmission Control Protocol (TCP) schemes, flow control, 19
Transmission range, IEEE 802.11b specification, 78–79
Trust, 259–266. *See also* Privacy; Security
  definition, 260–261
  generally, 259–260
  new approach to, 263–266
  overview, 249–251
  smart environments, 261–263
Tunneling sensing, physical transduction principles, 29
Two-tier client-server architecture, middleware, 106–107

Ubiquitous computing, 153. *See also* Pervasive computing technology
  assistive environments, 362–364
  middleware, 114
  perceptual environments contrasted, 346
  smart offices, 326
  term of, 153

Ultrasonic sensor, assistive environments, 370–371
Ultra wideband (UWB) radio:
    high-rate WPAN, IEEE 802.15 standards, 90–91
    wireless sensor networks, 39
Usability, smart rooms constraints, 314–315
User interface, decision making and, wireless sensor networks, 42–43

Virtual-cut-through switching, communication networks protocols and routing, 17
Virtual/physical integration, human experience, 158–159
Virtual sensors, IEEE, 28
Vision technology, location estimation techniques, 211
Voice recognition, perceptual environments, 352–353

Web services, middleware, 112–113, 116
Window schemes, flow control, communication networks protocols and routing, 19
Wireless body area network (WBAN):
    IEEE 802.15 standards, 84–94
    smart spaces, 66–67
    technologies, 67–69
Wireless cellular networks, location estimation techniques, 198–199, 210
Wireless local area nework (WLAN):
    high-speed, pervasive computing technology, IEEE 802.11a and 11g standards, 81
    history and standards, 25–26
    pervasive computing technology:
        IEEE 802.11 power specifications, 75–77
        smart spaces, 66–67
        technologies, 67–69
Wireless personal area nework (WPAN):
    IEEE 802.15 standards, 84–94
    smart spaces, 66–67
    technologies, 67–69
Wireless sensor networks, 13–46
    building and home automation, 43–44
    commercially available sensors, 34–37
    communication networks hierarchy, 21–24
        described, 22–24
        distributed routing, decision making, and digital signal processing, 24
    communication networks history and standards, 25–26
    communication networks power management, 20–21
    communication networks protocols and routing, 16–19
        deadlock and livelock, 19
        flow control, 19
        headers, 16–17
        multiple access protocols, 17
        open systems interconnection reference model (OSI/RM), 17–18
        routing, 18–19
        switching, 17
    communication networks topology, 14–16
    decision making, 42–43
    IEEE, 26–28
    measurements for, summary table, 35
    overview, 13–14
    self-organization and localization, 37–39
    signal processing, 39–42
        conditioning, 39–41
        digital processing, 41–42
    transducers and physical transduction principles, 28–34
World Wide Web. *See* Web services
Wormhold switching technique, communication networks protocols and routing, 17

X-10 protocol, power line communication technology, 54–55